Reconstructing Power and Hegemony in Public International Law

Mark Klamberg · Katinka Svanberg ·
Love Rönnelid
Editors

Reconstructing Power and Hegemony in Public International Law

Liber Amicorum Pål Wrange

ASSER PRESS

Springer

Editors
Mark Klamberg
Faculty of Law/Department of Law
Stockholm University
Stockholm, Sweden

Katinka Svanberg
Faculty of Law/Department of Law
Stockholm University
Stockholm, Sweden

Love Rönnelid
Faculty of Law/Department of Law
Stockholm University
Stockholm, Sweden

ISBN 978-94-6265-742-7 ISBN 978-94-6265-743-4 (eBook)
https://doi.org/10.1007/978-94-6265-743-4

This work was supported by Stiftelsen Juridisk Fakultetslitteratur, Stiftelsen för Rättsvetenskaplig Forskning, Justitierådet Edvard Cassels Stiftelse.

This T.M.C. ASSER PRESS imprint is published by the registered company Springer-Verlag GmbH, DE, part of Springer Nature.
The registered company address is: Heidelberger Platz 3, 14197 Berlin, Germany

Photo by Charlotte Carlberg Bärg

Academic Writings of Pål Wrange

This list of Pål Wrange's academic writings gives an idea of his areas of interest.

1. Wrange P (2026 forthcoming) Sovereignty and Cyberspace. In: Max-Planck Encyclopedia of International Law, Oxford University Press
2. Wrange P (2026 forthcoming) Digital Sovereignty. In: Max-Planck Encyclopedia of International Law. Oxford University Press
3. Wrange P (forthcoming) Securitizing climate change, but gently: Sweden and the establishment of "climate-related security risks" in the Security Council's mandate. In: Review of Sweden's membership of the Security Council 2017–2018, commissioned by the Foreign Relations Committee of the Swedish Parliament. Submitted
4. Wrange P (2026 forthcoming) Collective Security. In: Mallinder L (ed) Encyclopedia of Law and Peace. Edward Elgar, Cheltenham
5. Wrange P, Engdahl O (2025) Security and the Formation and Application of International Law. Nordic Journal of International Law 94(1):1–5
6. Wrange P (2024) The Obligation to Settle Cyber Disputes Peacefully: Arbitration, Conciliation, Fact-Finding and Other Mechanisms. In: Tsagourias N et al (eds) The Peaceful Settlement of Cyber Disputes. Hart Publishing, Oxford, pp. 237–266
7. Wrange P, Pedersen AK (2023) International Law in the Nordic Countries. In: van Aaken A et al (eds) The Oxford Handbook of International Law in Europe. Oxford University Oxford, pp. 677–696
8. Wrange P (2023) Handledaren – orakel, korrekturläsare eller extramamma? [The supervisor – oracle, proofreader or surrogate mother?]. In: Leviner P et al (eds) Kreativitet, strategi och etik i rättsvetenskap. Stiftelsen Juridisk Fakultetslitteratur, pp. 227–254

9. Wrange P, Kassoti E (2022) On the Importance of Framing: How the European Commission Successfully Argued for an Illegal Trade Agreement with Morocco. In: Symmons C et al (eds) Justice on Trial: Law, Politics and Western Sahara. IPJET, Leiden, pp. 253–280
10. Wrange P (2022) The 16th Annual Conference of the European Society of International Law: Welcome Remarks. European Journal of International Law 32(4):1335–1340
11. Wrange P (2022) SDG 16, Promote peaceful and inclusive societies for sustainable development, provide access to justice for all and build effective, accountable and inclusive institutions at all levels. In: Ebbesson J, Hey E (eds) The Cambridge Handbook on the United Nations Sustainable Development Goals and International Law. Cambridge University Press, Cambridge, pp. 399–421
12. Wrange P (2020) Western Sahara, the European Commission and the politics of international legal argument, In: Duval A, Kassoti E (eds) The Legality of Economic Activities in Occupied Territories: International, EU Law and Business and Human Rights Perspectives. Routledge, London, pp. 163–198
13. Wrange P (2020) Sovereignty, Belligerency and the New Normal in Cyberspace. In: Bishai LS (ed) Law, Security and the State of Perpetual Emergency. Palgrave Macmillan, Cham, pp. 67–105
14. Wrange P (2019) Self-Determination, Occupation and the Authority to Exploit Natural Resources: Trajectories from Four European Judgments on Western Sahara. Israel Law Review 52(1):3–29
15. Wrange P (2019) Protecting which peace for whom against what? A conceptual analysis of collective security. In: Bailliet CM (ed) Research Handbook on International Law and Peace. Edward Elgar, Cheltenham, pp. 107–126
16. Wrange P (2018) Authority, legitimacy and military violence: de facto combatant privilege of non-state armed groups through amnesty. In: Deland M et al (eds) International Humanitarian Law and Justice: Historical and Sociological Perspectives. Routledge, London, pp. 60–75
17. Wrange P (2017) Does who matter? The various forms of authority to use military force. Ethics & International Affairs 31(2):191–212
18. Wrange P (2017) International Humanitarian Law Without the State? Scandinavian Studies in Law 62:145–162
19. Wrange P (2017) The Crime of Aggression, Domestic Prosecutions and Complementarity. In: Kress C, Barriga S (eds) The Crime of Aggression: A Commentary, part III. Cambridge University Press, Cambridge, 704–751
20. Reisinger A, Wrange P (2017) The Specificity of the Crime of Aggression. In: Kress C, Barriga S (eds) The Crime of Aggression: A Commentary. Cambridge University Press, Cambridge, pp. 307–350

21. Wrange P (2014) Intervention in National and Private Cyberspace and International Law. In: Ebbesson J et al (eds) International Law and Changing Perceptions of Security: Liber Amicorum Said Mahmoudi. Brill Nijhoff, Leiden and Boston, pp. 307–326
22. Wrange P (2014) Protecting which peace for whom against what? A conceptual analysis of collective security. In: Bailliet CM, Mujezinović Larsen K (eds) Promoting Peace Through International Law. Oxford University Press, Oxford, pp. 86–108
23. Wrange P (2012) Sedelmayer v. Russian Federation. American Journal of International Law 106(2):347–353
24. Wrange P (2011/12) Svenskt genombrott – statsimmuniteten i två HD-avgöranden [Swedish breakthrough – state immunity in two Supreme Court decisions]. Juridisk Tidskrift 4:800–824
25. Wrange P (2011) Aggressionsbrottet och Internationella brottmålsdomstolen [The crime of aggression and the International Criminal Court]. Totalförsvarets folkrättsråd, Försvarsdepartementet, Stockholm
26. Wrange P (2010) The crime of aggression and complementarity. In: Bellelli R (ed), International Criminal Justice: Law and Practice from the Rome Statute to Its Review. Routledge, London, pp. 591–607
27. Wrange P (2009) The EU Guidelines on Promoting Compliance with International Humanitarian Law. Nordic Journal of International Law 78(4):541–552
28. Wrange P (2008) Neutrality, Impartiality and Our Responsibility to Uphold International Law. In: Engdahl O, Wrange P (eds), Law at War: The Law as it Was and the Law as it Should Be: Liber Amicorum Ove Bring. Martinus Nijhoff Publishers, Leiden / Boston, pp. 285–304
29. Wrange P (2005) Folkmord, andra internationella brott och den internationella straffrätten [Genocide, other international crimes and international criminal law]. In: Gunner G, Namli E (eds), Allas värde och lika rätt: Perspektiv på mänskliga rättigheter [The dignity of all and equal rights: perspectives on human rights]. Studentlitteratur, Lund, pp. 309–326
30. Wrange P (2003) Of Power and Justice. German Law Journal 4(9):935–962
31. Wrange P (2000) The American and British Bombings of Iraq and International Law. Scandinavian Studies in Law 39:491–514
32. Wrange P (1999) Downtown, Midtown, Uptown - Review of Louis Henkin, International Law: Politics and Values (Martinus Nijhoff Publishers, Dordrecht, 1995) and Thomas M. Franck, Fairness in International Law and Institutions (Oxford University Press, 1995). Nordic Journal of Human Rights 68(1):53–83
33. Wrange P (1998) Terrorism och folkrätt [Terrorism and international law], Internationella Studier 3:8-19
34. Wrange P (1996) War, freedom, knowledge and the naming of sovereigns. Paletten No 2/3:105–111

35. Wrange P (1994) The Concept of Sovereignty - Alive and Kickin'. Juridisk Tidskrift 2:350–366
36. Wrange P (1998/99) De brittiska och amerikanska bombningarna av Irak [The British and American bombings of Iraq]. Juridisk Tidskrift 3:620–638
37. Wrange P (1996) An Open Letter to My Students-Theory, Practice and Life in International Law. Nordic Journal of International Law 65(3–4):569–595
38. Wrange O (1995) Kollektiv säkerhet? [Collective Security]. In: Ahlin, P (ed) Tandlös eller tiger: sju uppsatser om FN [Toothless or tiger: seven essays on the UN]. Juristförlaget, Stockholm, pp. 147–189
39. Wrange P (1994) Från domstolsession till jamsession eller Martti Koskenniemi och juridikens slut [From court session to jam session or Martti Koskenniemi and the end of law]. Retfaerd 17(64):3–23
40. Wrange P (1993/94) Om vetenskaplig autism och akademisk inskränkthet [On scholarly autism and academic narrowness]. Juridisk Tidskrift 2:661–664
41. Wrange P (1991/92) Reflections on law, schizophrenia and the Gulf Crisis. Juridisk Tidskrift 2:378–381
42. Wrange P En diskussion utan innehåll? Critical legal studies och folkrätten [A discussion without content? Critical legal studies and international law]. Juridisk Tidskrift 2:256–270

Monographs, edited books and volumes

43. Bring O, Klamberg M, Mahmoudi S and Wrange P (2020) Sverige och folkrätten [Sweden and International Law], 6th edn. Norstedts Juridik, Stockholm
44. Deland M, Klamberg M and Wrange P (eds) (2018) International Humanitarian Law and Justice: Historical and Sociological Perspectives. Routledge, London
45. Wrange P, Zamboni M and Wahlgren P (2016) Law without the State? Scandinavian Studies in Law 62
46. Bring O, Mahmoudi S and Wrange P (2014) Sverige och folkrätten [Sweden and International Law], 5th edn. Norstedts Juridik, Stockholm
47. Ebbesson J, Jacobsson M, Klamberg M, Langlet D and Wrange P (2014) (eds) International Law and Changing Perceptions of Security: Liber Amicorum Said Mahmoudi. Nijhoff, Leiden, pp. 307–326
48. Bring O, Mahmoudi S and Wrange P (2011) Sverige och folkrätten [Sweden and International Law], 4th edn. Norstedts Juridik, Stockholm
49. Engdahl O, Wrange P (2008) (eds), Law at War: The Law as it Was and the Law as it Should Be: Liber Amicorum Ove Bring. Martinus Nijhoff Publishers, Leiden / Boston
50. Wrange P (2007) Impartial or Uninvolved? The Anatomy of 20th Century Doctrine on the Law of Neutrality. Stockholm University Law Department, Stockholm / Elanders, Visby, Dissertation (1,106 pp.)

Tabula Gratulatoria to Pål Wrange

André Andersson, Stockholm
Simon Andersson, Stockholm
Jens Bartelson, Lund
Mats Bergsmeden, Stockholm
Morten Bergsmo, Florence
Ulf Bjereld and Marie Demker, Göteborg
Erik and Christine Björk, Brooklyn
Niels M. Blokker, Leiden

Mia Carlsson, Stockholm
Kelly Chen, Stockholm
Lianne Colonna, Stockholm
Julia Dahlqvist, Stockholm
Petter Danckwart, Örebro/Stockholm
Pierre d'Argent, Brussels
Martin Davidowicz, Uppsala
Joanna Drewert, Stockholm
Ulf Edström, Knivsta
Simone Ek, Stockholm
Marika Ericson, Knivsta

Mariana Fakih, Stockholm
Rolf Einar Fife, Oslo
Agata Fijalkowski, Leeds
David Fisher, Sundbyberg
Olga Glukovska Schaefer, Stockholm
Adam Green, Stockholm
Aeyal Gross, Tel Aviv
Stellan Gärde, Stockholm
Nikola Hajdin, Stanford

Mia Hallén, Stockholm
Henrik Hammargren, Värmdö
Petra Herzfeld Olsson, Stockholm
Ellen Hey, Rotterdam
Luis Hinojosa Martinez, Granada
Kaj Hober, Uppsala
Fredrik A. Holst, Stockholm
Olle Jens, Stockholm
Valentin Jeutner, Lund

Märta Johansson Radwan, Örebro
Niklas Kebbon, Stockholm
David Kennedy, Boston
Jann Kleffner, Stockholm
Andreas Knutsson, Stockholm
Anastasiya Kotova, Malmö
Niels Krabbe, Brännö
Anders Kruse, Helsingfors

Göran Lambertz, Uppsala
Carl Lebeck, Stockholm
Ylva Lennartson Hartmann, Stockholm
Gustaf Lind, Solna
Stefan Lindgren, Skarpnäck
Sally Longworth, Stockholm
Per Lundberg, Lidingö
Peter Lundberg, Båstad
Björn Lundqvist, Bromma
Branka Marušić, Stockholm

Göran Millqvist, Stockholm
Jérôme Monsenego, Stockholm
Olle Mårsäter, Uppsala
Caroline Nordklint, Stockholm
Jan Paju, Stockholm
Photini Pazartzis, Athen
Roger Persson-Österman, Stockholm
Jens Petersson, Stockholm
Anne Ramberg, Stockholm

Jane Reichel, Stockholm
Michaela Ribbing, Stockholm
Kristina Riegert, Södertörn

Rolf Ring, Lund
Andrew Robertson, Melbourne
Åsa Romson, Stockholm
Johan Schelin, Stockholm
Per Sevastik, Solna
Seyad Sideek, Stockholm

David Silverlid, Örebro
Teresa Simon Almendal, Djursholm
Erik Sinander, Stockholm
Gustaf Sjöberg, Stockholm
John Stauffer, Stockholm
Fredrik Stenhammar, Stockholm
Fredrik Svensson, Stockholm
Cecilia Tengroth, Stockholm
Per Erik Thomas, New York
Rebecca Thorburn Stern, Stockholm

Torbjörn Tännsjö, Stockholm
William Underwood, Stockholm
Jessika Van Der Sluijs Björkman, Stockholm
Peter Wahlgren, Stockholm
Erik Wennerström, Strasbourg
Rhodri Williams, Åland
Åsa Wikforss, Stockholm
Ola Wiklund, Norra Lagnö
Pontus Winter, Uppsala

Anna Wrange, Gustavsberg
Gertrud Wrange, Fårösund
Mildred Wrange, Bandhagen
Måns Wrange, Stockholm
Mauro Zamboni, Stockholm
Åsa Örnberg, Stockholm
Unnamed friend

Contents

Abbreviations

ADB	Asian Development Bank
AIIB	Asian Infrastructure Investment Bank
ASEAN	Association of Southeast Asian Nations
AU	African Union
BBNJ Agreement	Agreement under the United Nations Convention on the Law of the Sea on the Conservation and Sustainable Use of Marine Biological Diversity of Areas Beyond National Jurisdiction
BRICS	Brazil, Russia, India, China, and South Africa
CA3	Common Article 3 of the 1949 Geneva Conventions
CAVV	Advisory Committee on Public International Law
CERD	Convention on the Elimination of All Forms of Racial Discrimination
CFSP	Common Foreign and Security Policy
CIL	Customary International Law
CLCS	Commission on the Limits of the Continental Shelf
CLS	Critical Legal Studies
COI	Commission of Inquiry
COP27	2022 United Nations Climate Change Conference or Conference of the Parties of the UNFCCC (United Nations Framework Convention on Climate Change)
COP	Conference of the Parties
CRA	Credit Rating Agency
CRC	Convention on the Rights of the Child
CRC	Country Risk Classification
CRC	Chemical Review Committee
CSCE	Conference on Security and Co-operation in Europe
CSDP	Common Security and Defence Policy
DRC	Democratic Republic of the Congo
DSSI	Debt Service Suspension Initiative

DSU	Understanding on Rules and Procedures Governing the Settlement of Disputes
EAEU	Eurasian Economic Union
ECtHR	European Court of Human Rights
ECTS	European Credit Transfer and Accumulation System
EDA	European Defence Agency
EEC	European Economic Community
EEZ	Exclusive Economic Zone
EFTA	European Free Trade Association
ENMOD Convention	Convention on the Prohibition of Military or Any Other Hostile Use of Environmental Modification Techniques
EPC	European Political Cooperation
ESCR	International Covenant on Economic, Social and Cultural Rights
ESDP	European Security and Defence Policy
ESM	Environmentally Sound Management
EU	European Union
EVS	European Values Survey
FARC	Fuerzas Armadas Revolucionarias de Colombia (Revolutionary Armed Forces of Colombia)
FCIC	Financial Crisis Inquiry Commission
FRD	Friendly Relations Declaration
FRY	Federal Republic of Yugoslavia
FYROM	Former Yugoslavian Republic of Macedonia
G20	Group of Twenty
G77	Group of 77
GATT	General Agreement on Tariffs and Trade
HRJ	Human Rights Justification
IAC	International Armed Conflict
ICC	International Criminal Court
ICCPR	International Covenant on Civil and Political Rights
ICJ	International Court of Justice
ICL	International Criminal Law
ICPA	International Centre for the Prosecution of the Crime of Aggression in Ukraine
ICRC	International Committee of the Red Cross
ICSID	International Centre for Settlement of Investment Disputes
ICTR	International Criminal Tribunal for Rwanda
ICTY	International Criminal Tribunal for the former Yugoslavia
IGO	Intergovernmental Organization
IHL	International Humanitarian Law
IHRL	International Human Rights Law
ILC	International Law Commission
IMF	International Monetary Fund
INC	International Negotiating Committee

IPC	International Petroleum Corporation
IPCC	Intergovernmental Panel on Climate Change
IRA	Irish Revolution Army
ISA	International Sea-Bed Authority
ISDA	International Swaps and Derivatives Association
JEP	Colombia's Jurisdicción Especial para la Paz
KFOR	Kosovo Force
KLA	Kosovo Liberation Army
LOAC	Law of Armed Conflict
LOS Convention	Law of the Sea Convention, also referred to as UNCLOS
LRA	Lord's Resistance Army
MERCOSUR	Common Market of the South
MINURSO	UN Mission for a Referendum in Western Sahara
NATO	North Atlantic Treaty Organization
NC	Nordic Council
NDB	New Development Bank
NDC	Nationally Determined Contributions
NGO	Non-Governmental Organization
NIAC	Non-International Armed Conflict
NORDEFCO	Nordic Defence Cooperation
NRSRO	Nationally Recognised Statistical Rating Organisation
NSGT	Non-Self-Governing Territory
OAU Charter	Charter of the Organisation of African Unity
OECD	Organisation for Economic Co-operation and Development
OPCW	Organisation for the Prohibition of Chemical Weapons
OSCE	Organization for Security and Co-operation in Europe
OTP	Office of the Prosecutor
PCA	Permanent Court of Arbitration
PCIJ	Permanent Court of International Justice
PESCO	Permanent Structured Cooperation
PfP	Partnership for Peace
PIC	Prior Informed Consent
PIF	Pacific Island Forum
PMOI	People's Mojahedin Organization of Iran
POW	Prisoners of War
PRC	People's Republic of China
R2P	Responsibility to Protect doctrine
RST	Riksföreningen Sverige-Tyskland
SCO	Shanghai Cooperation Organization
SCSL	Special Court for Sierra Leone
SDGs	Sustainable Development Goals
SIDS	Small Island Developing States
SPS Agreement	Agreement on the Application of Sanitary and Phytosanitary Measures
TEU	Treaty on European Union

UDHR	Universal Declaration on Human Rights
UN	United Nations
UNCLOS	United Nations Law of the Sea Convention
UNCTAD	United Nations Conference on Trade and Development
UNEP GC	UNEP Governing Council
UNEP	United Nations Environment Program
UNESCO	United Nations Scientific and Cultural Organization
UNFCCC	United Nations Framework Convention on Climate Change
UNGA	UN General Assembly
UNHRC	United Nations Human Rights Council
UNSC	UN Security Council
UNSCOP	UN Special Committee on Palestine
USSR	The Soviet Union
VCLT	Vienna Convention on the Law of Treaties
WB	World Bank
WEU	West European Union
WHO	World Health Organization
WTO	World Trade Organization
WVS	World Values Survey

Chapter 1
Introduction—The World Order at a Crossroads

Mark Klamberg, Katinka Svanberg, and Love Rönnelid

Contents

Abstract This book intends to bring together international scholars for a dialogue on the role of international law from a critical perspective. It is about devotion, compassion, and love for international law. It is written in the dark times of the 2020s, to invigorate thinking about global justice and human dignity. It is a tribute to Pål Wrange, Professor of International Law at the Stockholm University Faculty of Law, for his pioneering work in critical scholarship and interest in legal philosophy. This tripartite introduction will reflect on the current state of the international world order, elucidate how Pål Wrange's work may assist us in understanding where we are heading, and touch upon this book's individual contributions and chapters.

Keywords Hegemony · Imperialism · Multipolarity · Pax Americana · Critical Doctrinalism · Identities · Historicising International Law · Lawfare

1.1 The World Order at a Crossroads

International law as part of the world order is under contestation—some would say under an existential threat. Among the various ways of understanding where we risk heading, three themes may be identified: the division of the world into spheres of

M. Klamberg (✉) · K. Svanberg · L. Rönnelid
Faculty of Law/Department of Law, Stockholm University, Stockholm, Sweden
e-mail: mark.klamberg@juridicum.su.se

K. Svanberg
e-mail: lilykatinka.svanberg@gmail.com

L. Rönnelid
e-mail: love.ronnelid@juridicum.su.se

M. Klamberg et al. (eds.), *Reconstructing Power and Hegemony in Public International Law*, https://doi.org/10.1007/978-94-6265-743-4_1

influence, the rule of law being replaced by authoritarianism, and the rise and fall of Pax Americana.

With respect to the first theme, the division of the world into spheres of influence, concepts of power and hegemony are often associated with describing the governance of the world in terms of empires. It is conceivable that several empires may coexist at the same point in time. After World War II, we had two empires: the West, led by the United States, competing with the socialist empire dominated by the Soviet Union. The world was divided into spheres of influence, where the borders between empires could be found in central Europe, the Korean peninsula, proxy conflicts in South East Asia, the Middle East, Africa, and Latin America. With the dissolution of the Soviet Union and the decline of communist ideology, the United States appeared as the perpetual world hegemon. From a European perspective, the division of the world into spheres of influence appeared a distant memory, as many of the former communist bloc Eastern European States became members of the EU and NATO. The Western liberal world order was established, with liberal democracy and the rule of law as benchmarks in a unipolar world, where the US was the only superpower. Critics of that power configuration call the US-dominated system hegemonic, with the US enforcing an imperial world order supported by international legal institutions and NATO. They would criticise that the gap between the Global South and the Global North was maintained, and any addition to the Western-dominated United Nations Security Council Permanent Members seemed impossible. We may be at a point in time when the previous world order appears to be partly falling apart—the question is if the replacement of one hegemon (perhaps with a troika) will deliver economic prosperity to the Global South or otherwise lead to effects envisaged by previous critics. We may be at a point in time when global pessimism and fatigue have befallen the current international world order with distrust in the normative framework established by the UN Charter after WWII. We are at a crossroads: the question is if a multipolar world order will lead to worse outcomes or even could meet some of the hopes embodied in previous critiques.

As our colleagues in international relations have reminded us since the 1990s, there will always be revisionist powers that seek to regain or establish their sphere of influence—it may be Russia, Iran, or the People's Republic of China. Until now, the United States with its allies, has potentially supressed such revisionism for a while. Under President Trump, US policy has changed, with US claims of control over the Panama Canal, Canada, and Greenland. Some describe it as a return to the traditional US strategy as pronounced in the Monroe Doctrine (1823), namely the initial goal that the Western hemisphere should be free of European interference. The later and somewhat more implicit assumption: domination by the US of the Western hemisphere is paired with a US retreat from the rest of the world. Such a mindset would fit well with the ambitions of Russia and China. Some might question whether the Trump administration will fully retreat from the world scene, as illustrated by its significant role in the Middle East, but for the sake of argument let us assume that the world will be divided into three major centres of power: The Western hemisphere or the Americas, dominated by the US, Euro-Asia, where Europe and Russia struggle against each other, and Asia, dominated by China. African States will try to keep their independence, constantly challenged by the interests of the three major powers. How will international law operate in such an environment? Some technical and discrete fields such as diplomatic and consular, and telecommunications law, may be able to function as today. For other, more contentious fields relating to human rights law, international criminal justice, environment, and trade, there will be less 'international law' in a global sense; there may be regional legal regimes but little more. Conflict between States over territory may become a more prevalent phenomenon. Some areas that we may have perceived as fairly stable, universal, and uncontested could also fall apart, such as the law of the sea and space law. The idea of collective security will probably revert in part to how it was designed in Yalta 1945—emphasising that the world should be divided in spheres of influence, historian Professor Niall Ferguson tells us that Cold War II has already begun.[1] To the extent such a geopolitical arrangement proves stable, the use of force may be restrained or prevented.

The second theme relates to the rule of law, the ideal that all individuals and institutions within a state should be accountable to the same laws and that citizens should have equal access to justice and public institutions. The rule of law is arguably intertwined with and demands respect for key human rights, such as the right to life and safety, non-discrimination, redress for rights violations, the presumption of innocence, access to justice, the right to a fair trial before an independent and impartial court, and freedom of expression, and the right to information. The concept of the rule of law has been developed at the national level, with attributes that belong in a Western Liberal Democracy. Some have also argued in favour of a rule of law among nations.[2] Transposed to the international level, the rule of law would require legal equality among nations, compulsory jurisdiction for international courts to provide access to justice, that these courts are independent and impartial, and the enforcement of international law beyond self-help only. The two levels of the rule of law are arguably connected.[3] Somewhat distressingly, the 2024 edition of the World Justice Project (WJP) Rule of Law Index reveals that a majority of countries are experiencing continuing backsliding when it comes to the rule of law, marked by executive overreach, diminished human rights, and justice systems that are failing to meet people's needs.[4] More countries are dominated by leaders adhering to the ideal of a 'strong man', with examples including Trump, Putin, Erdogan, Netanyahu, Orban, Xi Jinping, etc.

At the international level, the idea of spheres of influence is an appeal to the same authoritarian ideals at the expense of many of the rule-of-law ideals. We can call it a democratic backlash evident in Europe and beyond, keeping in mind that liberal democracy as a system is relatively young, whereas autocracy and dictatorship have long traditions.

---

[1] Hoover Institution 2023.

[2] Corell 2008.

[3] Janse 2012, pp. 28–32.

[4] *See* The World Justice Project Rule of Law Index 2024, available at https://worldjusticeproject.org/rule-of-law-index/downloads/WJPIndex2024.pdf. Accessed 22 April 2024.

Moving on to the final theme, the global order of Pax Americana might be at its end. As this is an allusion to the Roman peace, we may want to consider the fall of the Roman Empire when the Germanic king Odoacer deposed the child emperor in Rome, Romulus Augustulus (476 A.D.). Before its fall, Rome suffered from increasing political, economic, and military ineffectiveness. Thus, with President Trump's dismantling of the US federal state institutions, the world trade system, and NATO, it is tempting to say that we are witnessing similar patterns of imperial collapse. Rome can be said to have provided the foundation for a regional order of the time (perceived as international for a large part of the human population). Are we now witnessing the fall of the most recent international hegemon and the international legal system associated with it? Even though the US has certainly challenged international institutions on occasions, even before the current president, it was still the key power behind creating and upholding the modern international institutions: collective security through the UN, the monetary order of the Bretton Woods system, and trade liberalisation anchored in the World Trade Organization. Are we entering into the dark ages—millennia of lawlessness where crude power is the only real currency? With the risk of inviting comments drawing on a contemporary online debate about male fascination with the Roman Empire, please bear with us as we continue the comparison.

It is often forgotten that the Roman Empire did not entirely disappear in 476 A.D., it was only the Western Roman Empire that fell. The Eastern Roman Empire continued to exist for another thousand years (until the fall of Constantinople in 1453). The common narrative has it that it was intersected by the glossators—scholars in Western Europe who in the 11th and 12th centuries studied and resurrected Roman law. The post-glossators brought ideas and legal concepts from ancient Rome to merchant Italian cities and other European countries, paralleling the Renaissance and its rediscovery of classical philosophy, literature, and art. Where is Eastern Rome today, and if it falls—like Constantinople—who will be the glossators? How can we prevent and shorten the Dark Ages? European legal scholars are likely to invoke the European Union and international law scholars. However, modern "Rome" is arguably broader and more robust than that. The modern and progressive values relating to world order are shared by countries around the globe, including in the Americas, Africa, Asia, and Oceania. Also, international lawyers do not hold a monopoly on knowledge about or appreciation and pursuit of international justice and the rule of law. Not only States and elites, but the general public arguably also share these values. Then, despite the lack of enthusiasm and support for the international world order from some of today's major powers, let us not despair in pessimism and defeatism. If some international institutions currently appear weak or seem poised to be abandoned by major powers, like-minded States and populations should stand firm, preserving order and justice where possible, while awaiting the renaissance of a more robust, inclusive, and just international world order.

In the same vein, as Anne Orford argues later in this book, international lawyers need not automatically position themselves in opposition to various processes of change. Some aspects of the international system may actually require change. Orford encourages us to think strategically, positively, and pragmatically during this time of transformation—what may be is what we make it be.

1.2 A Tribute to Professor Pål Wrange

This book is dedicated to Professor Pål Wrange, celebrating his contributions as a diplomat, teacher, scholar, and public intellectual. Professor Wrange was one of the first people to introduce critical legal studies (CLS) in legal scholarship in Sweden and beyond in the 1990s. Throughout his career, Wrange has been passionate about different forms of critical analysis of law, for which reason his network of significant scholars, both within and outside the critical legal traditions, has contributed texts on the theme of *Reconstructing Power and Hegemony in Public International Law*. Most scholars endeavour to have a critical approach to their object of study. However, what do we mean by 'critical'? This has been a theme throughout the career of Professor Wrange, present already in his publications from the early 1990s[5] and his doctoral thesis *Impartial or Uninvolved: the Anatomy of 20th Century Doctrine on the Law of Neutrality* in 2007, to the series of retreats he has organized with doctoral candidates in Gimo (2016–2018, 2021-virtual, 2022, and 2024), Oxford (2019), Fort Vuren (2023), and Florence (2025).

Beyond his contributions to international legal theory and neutrality,[6] Wrange has covered diverse issues such as international lawmaking,[7] foundational issues of the international legal order,[8] self-determination,[9] collective security and use of force,[10] international criminal law,[11] international humanitarian law,[12] non-State actors,[13] immunities,[14] and cyberspace law,[15] and international economic law.[16]

Professor Wrange has always advocated for scholars to be open-minded and willing to engage with other disciplines.[17] As a former international law adviser

[5] Wrange 1990/91; Wrange 1994a.

[6] Wrange 2007; Wrange 2008.

[7] Wrange 2021.

[8] Wrange, 1994/95; Wrange 1994b; Wrange 1996; Wrange 2003; Bring et al. 2020.

[9] Schöldtz and Wrange 2006; Wrange and Helaoui 2015; Wrange 2019b; Wrange 2020b; Wrange 2022.

[10] Wrange 1995; Wrange 1991; Wrange 1998/99; Wrange 1999; Wrange 2000; Wrange 2019a.

[11] Wrange 2005; Wrange 2010; Wrange 2011; Coracini and Wrange 2017; Wrange 2017a.

[12] Wrange 2009; Wrange 2017b.

[13] Wrange 2017b.

[14] Wrange 2011/12; Wrange 2012.

[15] Wrange 2014; Wrange 2020a; Wrange 2024.

[16] Bring et al. 2020, chapter 17.

[17] Wrange 1993; Wrange and Engdahl 2025.

at the Swedish Ministry of Foreign Affairs, he appears to have had the relationship between theory and practice close to his heart throughout his career.[18]

1.3 Critical Perspectives on International Law

Introducing this book, Part I asks what it is to be critical. Is it a core feature of any academic work or does the word signify a more specific approach? Is it possible to be both critical and doctrinal at the same time and, if so, what would critical doctrinalism be like? What is the aim of critical legal research: to unveil the 'true' meaning of the law, to expose power and hierarchy, to find arguments for policy change, or perhaps all or any of these and even more? Are critical insights merely useful to clarify and explain the law, or are they foundational to the project of international law and/or the project of research in international law? Love Rönnelid introduces the section on critical doctrinalism by investigating what happens when a scholar rejects a the commonly accepted dichotomies between internal and external approaches, practical and theoretical contributions, and between descriptive and normative research. He suggests three strategies for doing critical doctrinal research. Ulf Linderfalk argues that even discretionary application of the law has boundaries; these can be described as 'constraining criteria'. Far from constituting any homogenous set of norms founded on law, constraining criteria reflect, each in their own way, different conceptions of an international legal system. Astrid Kjeldgaard-Pederson explores—through the lens of her version of 'critical doctrinalism'—the apparent disagreement between the ICJ and the ICC concerning the head of state immunity, which is currently actualized by the ICC arrest warrants against Vladimir Putin, Benjamin Netanyahu, and Min Aung Hlaing. Lastly, based on a discussion of the international legal regime for critical infrastructure, Martin R. Leopardi exposes how the law of the sea includes several inherently political concepts and principles.

Part II deals with the construction and redefinition of identities. One way of understanding these phenomena is to portray identities as a result of past or ongoing historical, political, pragmatic, philosophical, and/or socially constructed stories.[19] This is how identities are constructed. The modern nation-state assumes unambiguous distinctions between inside/outside and self/other.[20] A postmodern approach to identity would involve 'moving beyond the hard boundaries and centralised sovereignty characteristic of the Westphalian, or "modern" state, and towards permeable boundaries and layered sovereignty'.[21] Nicholas Tsagourias and Agnes Rydberg seek to re-define Statehood in the face of rising sea levels and aim to explore how we might move forward into a new era of Statehood in light of climate change-induced sea level rise and small island developing States' loss of habitable land. It considers several

[18] Wrange 1993; Wrange and Engdahl 2025.

[19] Michael 1996, p. 2.

[20] Rumelili 2004, pp. 27–28.

[21] Buzan and Diez 1999, p. 42, footnote 3.

different legal options, including ex-situ nations ('de-territorialized' Statehood), the creation of new artificial territory, purchasing territory, and 'floating' States. Jonas Ebbesson continues by describing how the two tracks of international law, on climate change and human rights, have developed and how they now converge. In the context of the dispute over Western Sahara, Sia Spiliopoulou Åkermark examines how the counterproposals to the UN made by Morocco and Polisario in 2007 affect the understandings and regulations of self-determination and decolonization. Moreover, she asks how the idea of compromise should be understood. The subsequent chapters all deal with the impact that Russia's invasion of Ukraine has had on long-term self-identification, neutrality, and alliances. Per Ahlin discusses whether membership in a military alliance, such as NATO, will change the role of international law in Swedish security policy, whereas Per Cramér examines the same matter through the lens of European Law. Phoebe Okowa attempts to make sense of African responses to the war in Ukraine against the backdrop of the norms on the use of force contained in the UN Charter. More specifically, she asks whether the African States' response to Russia's invasion of Ukraine should be described in terms of neutrality or equivocation.

Part III asks what the role of scholars is—are they merely conduits of transferring objective knowledge and neutral commentators?[22] Some argue that scholars can have a more active role in unmasking underlying, somewhat hidden assumptions or maybe even take an activist approach, whereas others would see scholars as vehicles of socialization, reproduction, and domination of existing power structures.[23] What is the relation between practice and theory, and what does being critical have to do with it? Anne Orford argues that international lawyers should not automatically position themselves in opposition to the current processes of change. International lawyers should not necessarily defend all existing laws and institutions. Instead, they should think in strategic, positive, or at least pragmatic terms about the roles that international lawyers might play in a time of transformation. In the next chapter Iain Cameron offers his reflections about why it is worthwhile teaching and researching international law. Mats Deland describes the political and theoretical choices made by the Swedish law professor Karl Olivecrona, who in 1940 chose to take the side of Nazi Germany. He was not the only Swedish scholar who during the interwar years held a critique of the world order created after the Versailles peace treaty, yet he is the most well-known legal scholar who also succumbed to the lure of Nazi Germany. Lastly, David Schneiderman analyses investment law from a 'Weberian' perspective.

Part IV revolves around the politics of historicizing international law. The turn to history in international law may be described as an expansion of the research scope beyond only describing the content of prescriptive norms by including international legal history and its theory. There is arguably always a political agenda underlying the process of writing the history of international law.[24] With an overt approach to historicizing international law, the politics of its history becomes obvious.[25] Jens Bartelson

[22] Barnhizer 1988, p. 128; Posner 1981.

[23] Golsorkhi et al. 2009, pp. 781–782.

[24] de la Rasilla 2021, pp. 13, 15.

[25] Ibid., p. 14.

examines the debate on whether contextualization and historicization threaten the critical purchase and autonomy of international law. Ove Bring writes about how Carl von Clausewitz downgraded the importance of international law and peace policy, and how his position provoked an antithesis of Hegelian nature that was in tune with the liberal societal attitudes at the time. This in turn, led to a kind of synthesis through later humanitarian regulation of armed conflict. Klamberg discusses two phenomena in the field of international criminal justice that both relate to time: the politics of historical truth-seeking and intertemporal law. Lastly, Martti Koskenniemi, in his contribution on State sovereignty, examines the writings of four German-speaking academics from the late 19th and early 20th centuries and their thinking about the modern 'sovereign State'. Moreover, he suggests that the view of 'State sovereignty' that became an important part of the conceptual arsenal in this context, gave international law a formalist orientation that not only compelled it to refrain from substantive engagement with the injustices of the world, but also allowed it to become an instrument to perpetuate them.

Part V examines to what extent and how international law is an instrument and part of warfare. The law can be viewed as the penultimate technique of power and social control and as a substitute for overt force.[26] 'Lawfare' signifies how States, the military, and influential non-profit organizations use international law to legitimize and critique the use of military force.[27] It is a 'strategy of using—or misusing—law as a substitute for traditional military means to achieve an operational objective'.[28] A more negative connotation would be that it entails the 'abuse of the law and legal systems for strategic political or military ends'.[29] Ola Engdahl describes the critical role of international law in contemporary conflicts. Said Mahmoudi takes on a modern challenge, namely 'hybrid' naval warfare, and its intended legal implications. Although the concepts of 'warfare' or 'naval warfare' are fairly clear, the increasing use by commentators and actors of the qualifier 'hybrid' may create ambiguity. Mahmoudi warns of the risk of States taking the increased occurrence of hybrid warfare as an excuse to expand the legal possibility of more use of force in international relations. Sarah M. H. Nouwen explains that the fragile balance between reconciliation and reparation, on the one hand, and retribution, on the other, was partly disrupted in Uganda and diverged from the course envisioned during the Juba Peace Talks. In the context of the Russia-Ukraine war, Marie Jacobsson takes on the increasing attention on responsibility for environmental (war) crimes. This is a topical question brought to light by the Russian invasion of Ukraine and the alleged crimes against the environment taking place, such as the destruction of the Kakhovka Dam, placing nuclear plants at risk, etc. Katinka Svanberg suggests that the quest for self-determination by ethnic minorities has been the main cause of conflict in Europe in the last 100 years. She does a case study of military conflicts in Europe from the

[26] Barnhizer 1988, p. 161.

[27] Werner 2010, p. 61.

[28] Dunlap Jr 2008, p. 146.

[29] *See* The Lawfare Project. https://www.thelawfareproject.org/whatwedo. Accessed 22 March 2024.

1920s and up to today's war in Ukraine, to trace whether ethnic minorities can ever claim a right to remedial secession and under what circumstances. Sally Longworth explores the underlying philosophies of international human rights law and international humanitarian law to critically consider the limits to the reconciliation of the two fields. Lastly, Joachim Åhman makes a critical appraisal of the somewhat vague possibility in treaties to invoke national security exceptions in the context of international economic law.

The authors in Part VI reconsider the concepts and phenomena of hegemony/imperialism/colonialism. Some academics defined global society at the start of this millennium as shifting from a system of sovereign equality under universal legal norms to the imperial supremacy of the US.[30] The US has been referred to by Habermas as a self-appointed hegemon.[31] But imperialism and colonialism are not the same thing. Imperialism refers to the method by which the metropolis maintains an empire over other States, whereas colonization refers to the activity of 'settling territories' and 'annexation'. Imperialism can also be regarded as a way for the metropolis to create a hierarchy of power that limits the ability of other States to make sovereign decisions. It need not imply economic or territorial domination.[32] However, it is arguably wrong to assume an uninterrupted continuity of the international legal order and that the empires are eternal.[33] Conversely, in a state of empire, some States are likely to press for a revision of that order. Russia would be the prime example; it has increasingly engaged in coercive diplomacy to restore a 'neo-empire' in the former Soviet space, behaving unilaterally as an aspiring hegemon in a 'Russia First' approach,[34] which has included the use of force, as shown in Ukraine. Matilda Arvidsson and Gregor Noll seek in their chapter to answer the question of if—and if so: how—the Russian and Chinese receptions of the *Großraum* concept developed by Carl Schmitt in 1939/41 intersect and reinforce each other at critical junctures. Next, David Langlet explores how current legal regimes balance sovereign decision-making, economic interests, and environmental and health protection in the context of 'toxic dumping' of hazardous substances from the Global North in developing countries. Inger Österdahl observes that although the UN Security Council has long been unrepresentative of the international society of States, the geopolitical balance of power is nearing a tipping point, in favour of the hereto less well-represented. The Russian invasion of Ukraine may be the triggering factor, accentuated, possibly, by the recent Israel-Hamas war. Hans Corell outlines the potential lessons learned from the Russian aggression against Ukraine for a future world order. Kangle Zhang examines private authority in international finance as illustrated by the case of credit rating agencies. One of his conclusions is that this infrastructure is made and constantly shaped by political and economic powers through legal means. Maria Grahn-Farley

[30] Zemanek 2005, p. 3.

[31] Habermas 2003, p. 706.

[32] Doyle 1986, pp. 31–37; Cowell 2017, pp. 670–671.

[33] Grewe 2000, p. 9.

[34] Sagramoso 2020, p. 354.

applies the legal theory of human rights justifications for the Russian full-scale invasion of Ukraine, whereby she demonstrates how Russia uses such justifications. Lastly, Jonas Tallberg discusses contestation and legitimacy in global governance. One of his conclusions is that contestation may be seen as a natural component of a dynamic political system of global governance, albeit open to criticism and debate.

We would like to thank T.M.C. Asser Press and Frank Bakker for their great interest in this book. We would like to express our appreciation for the advice from the advisory editorial committee consisting of Said Mahmoudi, Marie Jacobsson, and Martin Ratcovich Leopardi. The editors have benefited greatly from the swift editorial assistance of Anas A. Qazi and proofreading by Linnéa Holmén. Stiftelsen Juridisk Fakultetslitteratur (The Foundation of Jurisprudential Literature), Stiftelsen för Rättsvetenskaplig Forskning (The Foundation for Jurisprudential Research) and Justitierådet Edvard Cassels Stiftelse (Justice Edward Cassel's Foundation) have given generous grants for costs relating to editorial assistance, proofreading, publishing open access, stipends for editorial work, and launch-related activities, for which we are sincerely thankful.

References

Barnhizer DR (1988) Prophets, Priests, and Power Blockers: Three Fundamental Roles of Judges and Legal Scholars in America. University of Pittsburgh Law Review 50(1)

Bring O et al (2020) Sverige och folkrätten [Sweden and public international law], 6th edn. Norstedts Juridik AB, Stockholm

Buzan B, Diez T (1999) The European Union and Turkey. Survival 41(1):41–57

Coracini AR, Wrange P (2017) The Specificity of the Crime of Aggression. In: Kreß C, Barriga S (eds) The Crime of Aggression: A Commentary, part II. Cambridge University Press, Cambridge, pp. 307–350

Corell H (2008) The right climate for the rule of law. International Bar News, pp. 20–22. https://www.havc.se/res/SelectedMaterial/20080421corellrightclimateforrol1.pdf. Accessed 20 April 2025

Cowell F (2017) Inherent Imperialism: Understanding the Legal Roots of Anti-Imperialist Criticism of the International Criminal Court. Journal of International Criminal Justice 15(4):667

De la Rasilla I (2021) International Law and History: Modern Interfaces. Cambridge University Press, Cambridge

Doyle MW (1986) Empires. Cornell University Press, Ithaca and London

Dunlap Jr CJ (2008) Lawfare Today: A Perspective Commentary. Yale Journal of International Affairs 3(1):146–154

Golsorkhi D et al (2009) Analysing, Accounting for and Unmasking Domination: On Our Role as Scholars of Practice, Practitioners of Social Science and Public Intellectuals. Organization 16(6):779–797

Grewe WG (2000) The Epochs of International Law. (Translated and revised by Michael Byers) De Gruyter, Berlin

Habermas J (2003) Interpreting the Fall of a Monument. German Law Journal 4:701–708

Hoover Institution (2023) Cold War II: Niall Ferguson On The Emerging Conflict With China. https://www.hoover.org/research/cold-war-ii-niall-ferguson-emerging-conflict-china. Accessed 20 April 2025

Janse R (2012) Rule of Law: A guide for politicians. The Raoul Wallenberg Institute of Human Rights and Humanitarian Law / The Hague Institute for the Internationalisation of Law, Lund and The Hague
Michael M (1996) Constructing Identities. Sage Publications, London, Thousand Oaks, New Delhi
Posner EA (1981) The Present Situation in Legal Scholarship. Yale Law Journal 90(5):1113–1130
Rumelili B (2004) Constructing identity and relating to difference: understanding the EU's mode of differentiation. Review of International Studies 30(1):27–47
Sagramoso D (2020) Russian Imperialism Revisited: From Disengagement to Hegemony. Routledge, London
Schöldtz M, Wrange P (2006) Swedish Foreign Policy on the Western Sahara conflict. In: Olsson C (ed) The Western Sahara Conflict: The Role of Natural Resources in Decolonization. Nordiska Afrikainstitutet, Uppsala, pp. 22–24
Werner WG (2010) The Curious Career of Lawfare. Case Western Reserve Journal of International Law 43:61–72
Wrange P (1990/91) En diskussion utan innehåll? Critical legal studies och folkrätten [A discussion without content? Critical legal studies and international law] Juridisk Tidskrift 2:256–270
Wrange P (1991) Reflections on law, schizophrenia and the Gulf Crisis. Juridisk Tidskrift 2:378–381
Wrange P (1993) Om vetenskaplig autism och akademisk inskränkthet [On scholarly autism and academic narrowness]. Juridisk Tidskrift 3:661–664
Wrange P (1994a) Från domstolsession till jamsession eller Martti Koskenniemi och juridikens slut [From court session to jam session or Martti Koskenniemi and the end of law]. Retfaerd 17(64):3–23
Wrange P (1994b) 'The Concept of Sovereignty—Alive and Kickin'. Juridisk Tidskrift 6(2)
Wrange P (1995) 'Kollektiv säkerhet? [Collective Security?] In: Ahlin P (ed) Tandlös eller tiger: sju uppsatser om FN [Toothless or tiger: Seven essays on the UN], vol 189. Juristförlaget, Stockholm, pp. 147–189
Wrange P (1996) An Open Letter to My Students-Theory, Practice and Life in International Law. Nordic Journal of International Law 65(3–4):569–595
Wrange P (1998/99) 'De brittiska och amerikanska bombningarna av Irak. [The British and American bombings of Iraq]. Juridisk Tidskrift 3:620–638
Wrange P (1999) "Downtown, Midtown, Uptown", Review of Louis Henkin, International Law: Politics and Values (Martinus Nijhoff Publishers, Dordrecht, 1995) and Thomas M. Franck, Fairness in International Law and Institutions (Oxford University Press, 1995). Nordic Journal of Human Rights 68(1):53–83
Wrange P (2000) The American and British Bombings of Iraq and International Law. Scandinavian Studies in Law, 39:491–514
Wrange P (2003) Of Power and Justice. German Law Journal 4(9):935–962
Wrange P (2005) Folkmord, andra internationella brott och den internationella straffrätten [Genocide, other international crimes, and international criminal law]. In: Gunner G, Namli E (eds) Allas värde och lika rätt: Perspektiv på mänskliga rättigheter [The equal value and rights of all: Perspectives on human rights]. Lund, pp. 309–326
Wrange P (2007) Impartial or Uninvolved? The Anatomy of 20th Century Doctrine on the Law of Neutrality. Dissertation, Elanders, Visby
Wrange P (2008) Neutrality, Impartiality and Our Responsibility to Uphold International Law. In: Engdahl O, Wrange P (eds) Law at War: The Law as it Was and the Law as it Should Be: Liber Amicorum Ove Bring. Martinus Nijhoff Publishers, Leiden and Boston, pp. 285–304
Wrange P (2009) The EU Guidelines on Promoting Compliance with International Humanitarian Law. Nordic Journal of International Law 78(4):541–552
Wrange P (2010) The crime of aggression and complementarity. In: Bellelli R (ed) International Criminal Justice: Law and Practice from the Rome Statute to Its Review. Routledge, pp. 591–607
Wrange P (2011) Aggressionsbrottet och Internationella brottmålsdomstolen [The crime of aggression and the International Criminal Court]. Totalförsvarets folkrättsråd, Försvarsdepartementet, Stockholm

Wrange P (2011/12) Svenskt genombrott—statsimmuniteten i två HD-avgöranden [Swedish breakthrough—state immunity in two Supreme Court decision]. Juridisk Tidskrift 4:800–824
Wrange P (2012) Sedelmayer v. Russian Federation (Case Note). American Journal of International Law 106(2):347–353
Wrange P (2014) Intervention in National and Private Cyberspace and International Law. In: Ebbesson J et al (eds) International Law and Changing Perceptions of Security. Brill Nijhoff, Leiden and Boston, pp. 307–326
Wrange P (2017a) The Crime of Aggression, Domestic Prosecutions and Complementarity. In: Kreß C, Barriga S (eds) The Crime of Aggression: A Commentary, part III. Cambridge University Press, Cambridge, pp. 704–751
Wrange P (2017b) International Humanitarian Law Without the State? Scandinavian Studies in Law 62:145–162
Wrange P (2019a) Protecting which peace for whom against what? A conceptual analysis of collective security. In: Bailliet CM (ed), Research Handbook on International Law and Peace. Edward Elgar, Cheltenham, pp. 107–126
Wrange P (2019b) Self-determination, occupation and the authority to exploit natural resources: Trajectories from four European judgments on Western Sahara. Israel Law Review 52(1), pp. 3–29
Wrange P (2020a) Sovereignty, belligerency and the new normal in cyberspace. In: Bishai LS (ed) Law, Security and the State of Perpetual Emergency. Palgrave Macmillan, pp. 67–105
Wrange P (2020b) Western Sahara, the European Commission and the politics of international legal argument. In: Duval A, Kassoti E (eds), The Legality of Economic Activities in Occupied Territories: International, EU Law and Business and Human Rights Perspectives. Routledge, London, pp. 163–198
Wrange P (2021) The 16th Annual Conference of the European Society of International Law: Welcome Remarks. European Journal of International Law 32(4):1335–1340
Wrange P (2022) On the importance of framing: how the European Commission successfully argued for an illegal trade agreement with Morocco. In: Thomas K et al (eds) Justice on Trial: Law, Politics and Western Sahara. International Platform of Jurists for East Timor, Leiden, pp. 253–280
Wrange P (2024) 'The Obligation to Settle Cyber Disputes Peacefully: Arbitration, Conciliation, Fact-Finding and Other Mechanisms. In: Tsagourias N et al (eds) The Peaceful Settlement of Inter-State Cyber Disputes. Hart Publishing, Oxford, pp. 237–265
Wrange P, Engdahl O (2025). Security and the Formation and Application of International Law. Nordic Journal of International Law 94(1):1–5
Wrange P, Helaoui S (2015) Occupation/annexation of a territory: Respect for international humanitarian law and human rights and consistent EU policy. European Parliament. https://www.europarl.europa.eu/RegData/etudes/STUD/2015/534995/EXPO_STU(2015)534995_EN.pdf. Accessed 20 April 2025
Zemanek K (2005) Is the Nature of the International Legal System Changing? Austrian Review of International and European Law 8(1):3–10

Mark Klamberg is Professor in Public International Law at Stockholm University and Deputy Director at the Stockholm Center for International Law and Justice (SCILJ). He has the following affiliations and appointments: research fellow with the Centre for International Law Research and Policy (CILRAP), fellow with the American University Washington College of Law, Washington D.C., nonresident Senior Fellow with the Atlantic Council, Washington D.C., expert to the Consultative Council at the National School of Judges of Ukraine, expert for OSCE ad hoc missions as part of its human dimensions mechanism (also known as the Moscow mechanism), and board member for the Raoul Wallenberg Institute of Human Rights and Humanitarian Law, Lund. He did his post doc at the University of Oxford, Institute for European and Comparative

Law, and has been a scholar-in-residence at the School of International Service (SIS), American University, Washington D.C., and Senior Fellow at the Carter School of Peace and Conflict Resolution, George Mason University, Arlington

Lily Katinka Svanberg holds LL.D. and LL.M. degrees from Stockholm University Law Faculty, as well as an LL.M. from New York University. She is an Australian Government of Education Laureate Fellow at Melbourne University. She has served as an international postdoctoral researcher at the University of Miami and as a visiting lecturer at West Virginia University and Senior University Lecturer at Stockholm University. Her research interests include international peace and security, the right to self-determination, treaty law, and maritime security.

Love Rönnelid is a Senior Associate Lecturer in International Law at Stockholm University specializing in international economic law and the political economy of international law. His research and teaching interests concern matters such as the political economy of international investment law, the effects of global economic governance on the economies of developing states, and the history of international economic law. Before joining Stockholm University, he held research positions at Harvard University and Stockholm University. He presented his dissertation, which concerns the genealogy of international investment law, at Uppsala University in 2018.

Part I
Critical Doctrinalism

Chapter 2
Critical Doctrinalism

Love Rönnelid

Contents

Abstract This contribution investigates the tension between critical approaches to legal scholarship and doctrinalism, arguing that there is a risk of weak capacity for power analysis where a rejection of doctrinalism implies a rejection of doctrinal sources of law as a field of study. It highlights how some commonplace dichotomies shaping discussions around doctrinalism shroud the power of doctrinalism. These are a dichotomy between internal and external analysis, between practice and theory, and between description and normativity. The contribution argues for rejecting these dichotomies as a way towards better performing power analysis of doctrinal sources. It discusses three strategies to perform power analysis of the law: finding the problematization in law, historicization, and analysis of outcomes at the group level. They each operate to create breaks with some of the typical assumptions in doctrinal analysis. The strategies may all be combined to create diverse ways of analyzing the power wielded through doctrinalism.

Keywords Doctrinalism · Critical approaches to law · Problematization · Power analysis · Legal history · Distributive analysis · Public international law

---

L. Rönnelid (✉)
Stockholm University, Stockholm, Sweden
e-mail: love.ronnelid@juridicum.su.se

M. Klamberg et al. (eds.), *Reconstructing Power and Hegemony in Public International Law*, https://doi.org/10.1007/978-94-6265-743-4_2

2.1 Surveying the Relationship Between Critical Thinking and Doctrinalism

The standard form of scholarship in many law schools is often called doctrinalism, the doctrinal method, or the like.[1] It is not uncommon to imagine critical approaches to legal scholarship, typically focused on scrutinizing power, as standing in contradiction with doctrinalism. The present text explores the tension between doctrinalism and critical thinking. The idea is to indicate what might be lost when critical approaches to law reject the study of doctrinal sources, as well as to outline a few strategies for doing critical research with those very materials—here called critical doctrinalism.[2] Doctrinalism builds on a number of theoretical ideas or assumptions, which are seldom clearly spelled out and, to the extent they are, may often be contested. This text aims to clarify some of the assumptions implicit in discussions about doctrinalism. It does so by showing that doctrinalism is oftentimes defined in contradiction to other forms of legal analysis through three dichotomies. After rejecting these dichotomies, it becomes easier to study the same materials as doctrinal scholars, but from the point of view of power analysis.

The very meaning of doctrinal scholarship is open to interpretation and contested. Consider the following quote by an observer sympathetic to doctrinalism: "The doctrinal method has been widely criticised, largely because it has never been explicated sufficiently for non-lawyers—or for lawyers themselves!"[3] The doctrinal method is often linked to the similarly contested theory of legal positivism, itself declared to be so unclear as to be "positively unhelpful".[4] This, however, does not appear to be a hinderance for it remaining the dominant mode of writing in legal scholarship. At any rate, the lack of clarity on the concept does not prevent discernment of overarching themes in scholarship regarded as doctrinal or in discussions about doctrinalism. Consider the following two representative quotes from scholarship explaining doctrinalism:

> It explains, makes coherent or justifies a segment of the law as part of a larger system of law.[5]

---

[1] In countries inspired by the German tradition, it seems more common to call this "legal dogmatics". For a discussion on terminology in different countries, *see, e.g.*, Smits 2017, p. 210, in particular footnote 15 (discussing diverging meanings in Germany and France). The meaning of the concept of "doctrine" also comes with other connotations in Anglophone countries; for an excellent overview and approach to creative restructuring of doctrine in such a setting, *see* Schlag and Griffin 2020.

[2] This text is intended to be in the spirit of and in conversation with the thinking of Professor Pål Wrange, who has in many important ways made space for thinking that engages critically with traditional legal materials.

[3] Hutchinson 2015, p. 131. *See also* Smits 2017, p. 208: "It has been observed time and again that despite the persistence of this type of research, we are insufficiently aware of its exact nature."

[4] Kammerhofer 2010, para 1: "It has become a well-worn cliché to declare that the term 'legal positivism' is now so unclear as to be positively unhelpful." For an excellent exposé over how positivism became the dominant school of thought in international law, *see* García-Salmones Rovira 2013.

[5] Duncan and Hutchinson 2012, p. 84.

> In sum, the primary characteristic of the doctrinal method is the search for coherence and clarity in all the legal materials that may have a bearing on the legal principle or dilemma under investigation.[6]

Several core ideas in the doctrinal tradition, broadly resurfacing in writings about the tradition, can be discerned here. Some common traits of doctrinalism are the idea of (re)constructing a system, a commitment to creating clarity or coherence, the idea of ascertaining the law neutrally (free from morals or politics), and a commitment to the task of justifying the law. Thus, though there is no point in describing the doctrinal tradition as something overly determined, these are typical claims about it from writers who subscribe to it.

These ideas and commitments held by doctrinal scholars tend to lead to a way of reasoning which is overall subservient to the existing power configuration in an area of law. This is explicitly apparent when it is stated that doctrinalism includes the task of justifying the law, or where such justification is nevertheless a part of the relevant form of scholarship.[7] Although this is not always explicitly apparent in work on doctrinalism, the overall uncritical adoption of the present power configuration by doctrinal scholars appears central to the commonplace resistance to doctrinalism by other strains of scholarship. Diverse strands of critical legal thinking—which typically aim to highlight and scrutinize power—are likely to resist this deference to, and underplaying of, power inherent in law and legal ideas. Seen from this angle, it should come as no surprise that critically inclined scholars are skeptical of the doctrinal tradition.

Perhaps for this reason, it is common for critical voices to reject doctrinalism in a broad sense. Consider for example this quote by Günter Frankenberg in his entry on critical theory in legal scholarship in the Max Planck Encyclopaedia of International Law: "Hence, methodologically speaking, new Critical Theory is programmatically anti-doctrinalist but otherwise eclectic."[8] Elsewhere, he similarly summarizes that critical legal thinkers are "self-consciously refraining from doctrinal analysis".[9] Of course, being anti-doctrinalist can mean many different things—in particular when considering the ambiguities of doctrinalism in the first place. Nevertheless, it seems the quotes above capture an sensibility among many critical scholars. It is my experience that such an attitude also at times includes a rejection of studying the same materials as doctrinal scholars.

This article claims that to the extent that such a rejection of doctrinalism includes a rejection of the study of doctrinal materials, it comes with certain risks for approaches aiming to render visible the way in which power is exercised in society.[10] In particular,

---

[6] Egan 2018, p. 27.

[7] Smits 2017, p. 219 *et seq.*, argues that it is a role of doctrinalism to justify he law.

[8] Frankenberg 2010, para 29.

[9] Frankenberg 2010, para 34. I of course do not mean to imply that Frankenberg would espouse a view that doctrinal materials would not be worthy to study critical. I do however think the quote captures that this idea is fairly common in some types of scholarship branded as critical.

[10] It makes sense to read the present critique of that position as related to Marks 2009, who discusses on p. 2 the worry that critical thought in emphasizing that the world could be different might

it seems that rejecting doctrinalism might risk focusing attention away from places where power operates.[11] It seems that doctrinalism, whatever it might mean in detail, in some ways is central to the ways in which law, legal ideas, and lawyers exercise power. Consequently, it seems central for those interested in scrutinizing power to engage with it.

Showing how power is exercised often constitutes a way of demanding responsibility. Who else but legal scholars, one might ask, are likely to be able to scrutinize in depth how law, legal ideas and lawyers wield power? The argument not to reject the importance of doctrinal thinking is strengthened by the fact that the language of law has enjoyed a steep increase in importance, at least for a while. Friedrich Kratochwil wrote in 2014 that "law now provides in large part the vocabulary for contemporary politics".[12] At that point in time, certainly, the move towards judicialization appeared all but unstoppable. Now, writing more than twenty years later, the situation perhaps comes across somewhat differently.[13] Still, to the extent that scholars think that law and lawyers exercise significant power worthy of scrutiny, there are strong reasons to engage critically with doctrinalism where it constitutes the dominant mode of wielding such power. This, of course, does not imply that critically minded thinkers should engage with doctrinal materials in the same way as in the doctrinal tradition. Later in this text, we will return to some possible strategies for engaging with doctrinal materials without the aforementioned assumptions.

Before we turn our attention to some possible strategies for critical doctrinalism, it is helpful to paint a picture of how discussions on approaches to legal scholarship oftentimes play out. Three dichotomies are helpful for bringing some order to the debates about legal methodologies. These dichotomies are prevalent in discussions on legal scholarship. Making the dichotomies explicit is intended to clarify how critical doctrinalism can engage with similar materials as doctrinal scholars, but with other assumptions. Each dichotomy clarifies aspects of how the dominant forms of doctrinal scholarship are commonly discerned from other approaches to legal scholarship. I will argue that each of the dichotomies shrouds the way in which power operates and that accepting them makes it harder to carry out legal power analysis. By contrast, rejecting them makes it easier to perform power analysis of doctrinal materials.

---

underemphasize the systemic constraints and pressures that made a phenomenon turn out the way it did.

[11] For the influential view that critique is about uncovering the techniques of rule in order to allow ways to resist it, *see* Foucault 1990.

[12] Kratochwil 2014, p. 1.

[13] Of course, the way and extent to which law is politicized and politics is judicialized remain themselves important areas of study.

2.2 Dichotomies Shaping Discussions on Doctrinalism

2.2.1 The Dichotomy Between Internal and External

It is commonplace to view the doctrinal method as "internal", as opposed to "external" perspectives.[14] Although this metaphor is seldom discussed in depth, it is common to hold that doctrinalism is "internal".[15] This view was popularized by Herbert Hart, who employed it to draw a distinction between the disposition towards rules as either a "member of the group which accepts and uses them as guides to conduct" or one who acts "merely as an observer who does not himself accept them".[16] This distinction makes it is clear that there is a normative commitment to a group identity implicit in the internal perspective, as Hart claims that the internal perspective is held by someone as a member of a group. Moreover, there is something of a skepticism towards the external perspective in Hart's description, in that those adopting it are deemed to be "merely" observers (who do not accept the rules).

This negative view of those not being part of the group is interesting. In other contexts of knowledge production, being a disinterested observer instead typically comes with a positive connotation. Take journalism for example. For a journalist, the disinterested position vis-à-vis those they interview or observe is generally seen as positive for the value of the information they produce. In the doctrinal tradition, however, being a participant who shares the normative commitment of a group is instead generally viewed positively (rather than being "merely" an observer, as Hart has it). As will be discussed in relation to the last dichotomy below, this commitment to the normative positions of the group is often seen not only as compatible with, but typically as enhancing the claims to neutrality and objectivity of doctrinal scholars.

It is often claimed that there is some space for critique within a traditional doctrinal position. Consider the following quote:

> [B]ecause [legal doctrine] *works to sustain a specific vision of social order*, it must in some way stifle others. Put simply, doctrinal legal scholarship cannot be critical in the same sense as external critique, or present a more *fundamental challenge* to the legal system, without ceasing to be doctrine, for to do so would be to abandon its sense of 'being'. However, doctrinal scholarship can be critical in the sense of immanent critique because it works with law's internal contradictions and contrasts its rules to a teleology that is found within the law itself.[17]

---

[14] Smits 2017, p. 210 holds that "it is an essential feature of the doctrinal approach that it adopts an internal perspective".

[15] For a discussion on how the internal/external metaphor is constructed, *see* Schlag 1991, p. 916 *et seq.*

[16] Hart 1961, p. 89: "When a social group has certain rules of conduct [...] it is possible to be concerned with the rules, either merely as an observer who does not himself accept them, or as a member of the group which accepts and uses them as guides to conduct. We may call these respectively the 'external' and the 'internal' points of view."

[17] Byrne and Olsen 2024, p. 23 (emphases added).

In line with this quote, the internal perspective is usually not perceived as compatible with more far-reaching forms of critique.[18] However, there is no need to perceive critique that takes the dominant normative preferences of the current configuration of the law seriously as necessarily being less expansive. Rather, obtaining a deep sense for the normative commitments of the relevant law users appears central to many forms of far-reaching critique. (I employ the term law users to include the various actors who use the law to argue about and justify behavior, in order to highlight that this might be all sorts of people and entities.) By way of contrast, forms of critique that do not correctly appreciate which understanding of the world it took to read the law in a particular way risk missing the mark or misconstruing the strategic terrain of action.

The more shared the normative position is among law users, the more the law appears to them as a system. This system is then premised on a commitment to justify this particular reading of a field of law. As mentioned above, participation in the doctrinal project requires a commitment to creating a collective vision of social order within the relevant group of law users: "The legal knowledge of doctrinal legal scholarship is a form of collectively shared knowledge."[19] Seen from this perspective, the doctrinalist's claim to construct coherence presupposes this common collective knowledge and constitutes a commitment to work towards a more broadly shared worldview. Participation in sustaining this worldview consequently requires sensitivity to how other participants signal their ideas about social order and how the boundaries of legality are policed or challenged. This becomes clear when lawyers discuss the prevalent or dominant view of some legal issue.[20] A central question for critical doctrinalism, then, becomes finding out which ideas make up this collective form of justification. Typically, the collective nature of doctrinal thinking is not explicitly discussed in doctrinal discourse. Yet, to anyone who has been in places where power operates through legal discourse, it seems clear that legal actors operate to sense and adjust to the position of each other in various ways. Being a skilled lawyer in a field in part includes acquiring a sensitivity to the signaling in that field, what the sensitive issues are, and which ideas are seen as beyond the bounds of current collective knowledge.

The internal-external dichotomy appears to shroud the fact that the internal perspective largely concerns a normative commitment to a shared sense of worldview—a normative commitment to ideals within a group. In reality, the boundaries of inside and outside need not be viewed so sharply. Some actors are squarely in the mainstream, whereas others are working within the tenor of the collectively shared language to subvert it.[21] A person with deep knowledge of the collective worldview

[18] Litowitz 1998, p. 129: "In contrast, external theorists provide radical critiques that shake the foundations of the legal edifice or attempt to destabilize an area of law."

[19] Byrne and Olsen 2024, p. 24.

[20] The dominant or ruling view, or the "*herrschenden Meinung*".

[21] This might resemble what Esquirol (2021), p. 1112 calls strategic essentialism.

might well be equally effective when engaging with the doctrinal discourse—if they are ready to put on the mask and perform that role.[22]

2.2.2 The Practice-Theory Dichotomy

Another dichotomy is one where the dominant doctrinal perspective is perceived as practical and where other approaches are more likely to be perceived as theoretical.[23] Perhaps this dichotomy is linked to the idea of doctrinalism as internal to the current legal imaginary and that consequently such scholarship often is seen as practical. This in turn is related to the shared dominant view of problems within the collective of law users.[24] This practicality of doctrinalism is thus linked to its use of, and proximity to, legal authority and sources. The expression "black letter law" is often invoked as a way of lending weight to legal practice which is perceived as close to legal sources. Often, the argument about legality is connected to a view of legal sources as creating a system.[25] Within this system, the job of the doctrinalist is seen as descriptive. It appears that this systemic nature of law is most believable for those who are close to the collective preferences of the currently dominant view of the relevant group of interpreters or law users. Getting a sense for how this group constructs a sense of a system is central to the type of critical doctrinalism discussed below.

As doctrinal scholars typically share the same normative commitments as the lawyers they are studying, they are able to speak with authority about the contents of this legal system, as their interpretation of the law is aligned with legal outcomes. This in turn grants authority to doctrinal scholars and helps shore up the political weight of doctrinalism by associating it with power.[26] Sometimes, the justificatory work performed by doctrinal scholars is seen as both justificatory and apolitical simultaneously, as when it is held that: "[Doctrinal work] allows to justify law through the system, turning law into an apolitical entity."[27] This idea of the work justifying law as apolitical is comprehensible when one considers that the doctrinal tradition

[22] As I am aware of Pål's appreciation of classical music, I did do my best to find fitting commentary to "Vesti la Giubba" to add here. The most interesting, I found was Kate Gonzales, "What Makes it Great? Refiguring 'Vesti la giubba' and crossing genres as subversion" (self-published online), which discusses how European classical music comes across in the US and how such expectations relate to race and class.

[23] In writings about doctrinalism, it is often said that doctrinalism is "close to practice" or the like. *See, for example*, the discussion in Duncan and Hutchinson 2012, p. 107 *et seq.*

[24] Smits 2017, p. 217 discusses the "search for practical solutions".

[25] Like the quotes in the beginning of the text, many scholars writing about doctrinalism emphasize the idea of a system. *See, e.g.*, Smits 2017, p. 213, holding that the "first aim of legal doctrine is to describe the existing law". *See also* Lieblich 2021, p. 44, also viewing these types of questions as descriptive.

[26] Somewhat similarly, Kennedy 2016, p. 10: "Legal ideas structure and legitimate forms of authority, and those authorities enforce and deepen law's own claim to predict and state the conditions under which coercion will back up assertions of entitlement."

[27] Smits 2017, p. 220.

assumes a similar normative commitment to the values within the relevant group of law users, as discussed above. Seen from a point of view where the worldview and normative commitments are shared, it makes certain sense to perceive normative justification as apolitical. This very sense of the doctrinal work being apolitical is central as a force for reproduction of power relations in the law.

The affiliation of doctrinalism with legal practice and power also contributes to giving the approach a commonsensical quality. The practical quality of doctrinalism might help explain why the theoretical assumptions underpinning doctrinal scholarship are often poorly spelled out.[28] Attempts to shore up the academic potential of legal scholarship, not infrequently in the context of research funding, often tries to legitimize doctrinalism as a scholarly endeavor.[29] Moreover, the practical quality of doctrinalism within the dichotomy contributes to portraying non-doctrinal approaches as theoretical, also in the sense of being esoteric.

The practical quality of doctrinal legal scholarship also appears related to a commonplace focus on individual cases and decisions. This focus on individual legal cases contributes to a tradition not much interested in seeing broader trends or studying the overarching effects of the law.[30] Some of the strategies for doing critical doctrinalism discussed below actively break this narrow focus, by aggregating legal outcomes over time or at the group level. Moreover, doctrinal scholarship's proximity to practice contributes to a shared sense of purpose with those using law outside of legal academia. As mentioned above, the sensitivity to the values in the practical legal field help doctrinal lawyers foresee the outcomes of practitioners. By legitimizing the practice (sometimes with scholarly credibility), they in turn add to the power of those using the law elsewhere by contributing to the symbolic power of knowledge generation springing from universities (or other institutions that wield power in areas of knowledge generation). Furthermore, the capacity to predict legal outcomes lends credibility to the idea of doctrinalism as descriptive, which in turn helps enforce the idea that this form of research is more objective. This will be further discussed in relation to the next dichotomy below.

Charting a course where the practical-theoretical dichotomy is avoided seems central to performing effective power analysis of the law. There is ample theory underpinning the worldview of legal doctrinalism (though it is usually not clearly spelled out).[31] Conversely, a considerable amount of scholarship sometimes characterized as theoretical operates close to practical matters, in particular when it aims to scrutinize power. The central matter here appears to be finding ways to operate close to where power is exercised, but in a way which is not caught up in the particular way those wielding doctrinal legal power see the world (or in their implicit theory about

[28] See the sources in n. 4 above, on the claim that doctrinalism not being well explained.

[29] *See, for example,* Duncan and Hutchinson 2012, p. 86.

[30] In some contexts, it is part of the disciplinary policing of doctrinalism to describe such approaches as constituting "sociology of law" or the like.

[31] For example, Duncan and Hutchinson 2012, p. 99: "Unfortunately the doctrinal method is often so implicit and so tacit that many working within the legal paradigm consider that it is unnecessary to verbalize the process."

things, if you will). Figuring out this dominant worldview constitutes a first move, opening up numerous avenues for investigating the power of law, lawyers, and legal ideas.

2.2.3 *The Dichotomy Between Description and Normativity*

A third dichotomy guiding discussions on doctrinalism is the one between description and normativity. In this dichotomy, doctrinalism is often portrayed as a standard descriptive first step, to which other perspectives can later be added.[32] It is not uncommon for scholars to portray doctrinalism as the standard form of legal research which first has to be ascertained, before other, more complex tasks can be added: the law must first be ascertained (descriptively) only to later be illuminated by other (normative) perspectives. Within this worldview, the doctrinal reading of the law is objective, but can be illuminated by various normative perspectives. When the dichotomy between description and normativity is construed in this way, the normative perspectives in effect operate to reify the neutrality of doctrinalism and lend it an additional air of objectivity.[33]

The idea of doctrinalism being descriptive is often discussed in terms of a particular relationship to legal texts, as mentioned above. The underlying idea appears to be that what renders doctrinalism more descriptive is the fact that it remains close to legal sources as interpreted by doctrinal lawyers close to legal practice. The dichotomy between description and normativity is often captured in the split between *lege lata* and *lege ferenda*. In this dichotomous way of thinking, critical approaches are usually constructed as normative and subjective. As we know, branding a form of knowledge as subjective is generally not considered a positive. Critique is thus viewed as an external type of normative argumentation which can be set apart from the internal descriptive and objective form. Invoked in this way, the dichotomy serves the dual purpose of contesting the significance of critique and reinforcing doctrinalism as neutral and objective.

The view of doctrinalism as descriptive is linked to particular aims of the description. Recall the quote at the beginning of this text about a "search for coherence and clarity" in "all legal materials".[34] Such a perspective appears to indicate that further enquiry will create more clarity and coherence. The emphasis on *all* legal materials similarly seems to imagine that looking at more materials will allow for further clarity. These assumptions are of course far from obvious. One can also imagine the opposite, that introducing further sources or creating further argumentation will

[32] *See generally,* Hutchinson 2015. Such a viewpoint also comes out in Lieblich 2021, pp. 44–45 (describing traditional doctrinal analysis as descriptive) and p. 49 (writing about descriptive components in critical research). *See also,* Duncan and Hutchinson 2012, p. 101.

[33] For claims about neutrality of doctrinalism, *see, e.g.,* Smits 2017, p. 213; Egan 2018, p. 29; Duncan and Hutchinson 2012, p. 116.

[34] See the full quote above in connection with n. 7.

allow for more contradiction and uncertainty.[35] However, if the factor allowing for relative predictability of outcomes is the worldview of the relevant law users, one can easily imagine that people in the field might reason to a point where they perceive the law to be clear and coherent for those that broadly share this worldview.

Someone who does not share this viewpoint can still work to find out the normative commitment underpinning a particular perception of clarity and coherence, even without sharing that worldview.[36] A helpful strategy in so doing is to describe materials where one can understand the ideas that sustain a particular vision of social order through law. This can be done by highlighting how one or another actor must have viewed the world in order to interpret the law in *that* particular way. That is, describing materials that help make clearer the normative commitments implicit in exercises of power through law.[37] In so doing, one can paint a picture of the dominant worldview in a field—a description of the normative positions of legal actors with power.

As in many other fields of knowledge, there are strong reasons to reject the dichotomy between description and normativity in law.[38] It is simply not the case that concerns about what the law "should be" are separate from discussions about what the law "is". Both these forms of legal argumentation concern giving reasons for preferred outcomes.[39] Clearly normative positions are accepted or implicit in dogmatic argumentation. The focus then becomes one of asking other types of questions when approaching the legal materials: *which* normative concerns are accepted as neutral and objective in such legal argumentation, *which* are not (perhaps because they are perceived as moral, political, or otherwise normative), *why* that appears to happen, *how* that process is justified, *what* effects such a selection of normative concerns has, and *who* it benefits.

2.3 Strategies for Critical Doctrinalism

2.3.1 Finding the Power in the Problematization

As discussed above, doctrinalism seems central to how legal power operates and is justified. If accepting that legal doctrine broadly understood appears to be a place where important power is exercised, it makes sense for scholars interested in power

[35] The debate around legal indeterminacy, largely concerned questions such as these.

[36] This is acknowledged also within the positivist tradition. *See, for example,* Raz 2009, pp. 156–157 (famous example of rule following and acceptance).

[37] It is in this way I have read the famous intervention about description by Orford 2012.

[38] Putnam 2002, p. VII, discusses how the fact-value dichotomy misconstrues the discipline of economics and also "that very similar issues arise in the law". *See also* Lieblich 2021, p. 44, describing critical research questions as not fitting into the descriptive/normative dichotomy.

[39] Both doctrinal and non-doctrinal methods give *reasons* for different normative positions. Regarding reasons as the essence of the study of norms, *see* Kratochwil 1989.

to focus their attention there. If accepting that doctrinal sources can be helpful for figuring out how power is exercised, the next questions become how those materials embody, shroud, justify, or enable some exercise of power.

An important step is to move beyond the problem-solving mindset characteristic of doctrinalism into a mindset which instead observes how law users construct what they perceive to be the problem or how they imagine solving it. The move discussed here is a transition from being a participant in the interpretative construction of the law to taking on a mindset where one attempts to understand the worldview of those exercising power.[40] Instead of asking what the purpose of the law *is*, one should start asking what the purpose has *become*, who *made* it that way, and what that might *lead to* in the world.[41] What does the dominant way of constructing coherence in the law reveal about the positions of those in power to shape and use it?[42] Every legal interpretative question then becomes a place where the politics of the interpreter is interrogated and revealed. The work of figuring out what is taken for granted is aided by questions that help the researcher's imagination:[43] What must one believe about the world to choose a narrow reading over a broad one? Which object and purpose must one envision in order to read a treaty in a particular way?[44] How is the idea of state consent used by lawyers in some particular context (rather than looking for what the state consented to)?[45] How does a particular reading of the preamble of a treaty reflect a taken-for-granted understanding of what the legal problem to be solved is? Which is the overall implicit teleology that allows law users to perceive the law as coherent?

A helpful way of spelling out such a shift in mindset comes from Robert Cox. He discerns between "problem solving theory" and "critical theory".[46] Problem solving theory takes a certain way of viewing the world for granted and operates in accordance therewith. Critical theory instead investigates how that way of viewing the problem

---

[40] I first really understood this move from Dreyfus and Kelly 2011, for example on pp. 14 *et seq.*, where they discuss what a particular "way of life" entails. For a legal take of this kind of thinking, *see* Koskenniemi 2016, suggesting on p. 730 that researchers should "answer the question 'what does it take to *believe* that this rule or this policy is the better one'".

[41] This approach thus broadly coincides with ideas from traditions called poststructural or structuralist. For similar thinking but different terminology, *see* Bacchi 2015 and Koskenniemi 2016.

[42] Such an implicit way of viewing the world has been called different things in the literature. In one US tradition, the underlying thinking often seems to be described as "making the background visible" or the like, *see* Kennedy 2016, p. 116 *et seq.* Koskenniemi 2005, p. 606 *et seq.*, describes something similar as the "structural bias" in the field.

[43] Kennedy 2016, p. 90: "Ideas that become common sense are rarely formulated directly. Spelling them out requires a kind of imaginative and empathetic reconstruction." *See also* Pahuja 2021, who discusses the qualities of different kinds of research questions. As mentioned previously, questions such as those following this sense in the main text are inspired by Bacchi 2013, but adapted to a legal context. I want to thank Pål Wrange for arranging the CRIL workshops during which several excellent participants have helped me think more clearly about these ideas.

[44] For an exposé on the role of teleology in legal thinking, *see* Koskenniemi 2012.

[45] For an inspiring analysis along these lines, *see* Craven 2018.

[46] Cox 1981, p. 128 *et seq.*

is constructed. The approach suggested here takes the way law constructs and solves problems as a point of departure, but strives to retain critical distance from it in order to understand what this way of representing the problem says about the power of law, lawyers, or legal ideas.[47] The relevant question is no longer how to solve a problem in the prevalent framing, but rather finding out how the problem is represented in these materials and how the relevant law users envision solving it.[48] The same "doctrinal" materials are then studied, but with another point of departure—a form of critical doctrinalism, if you will.

Although doctrinal materials often appear to be a place where power is in some sense exercised, the stakes of law differ quite a bit between different situations. At times, it is clear that law holds stakes of importance. At other times, it might appear that legal-technical debates come across as fairly insignificant. For scholars who are interested in how law, legal ideas, and lawyers wield power, a preliminary question could be to discern the types of legal technicalities that hold a relevant political stake from those that do not. There is a broad tradition trying to figure out the stakes in questions where technocracy makes it hard to discern the motives behind legal positions.[49] Another central question becomes to what extent a particular doctrinal question holds a distributive stake at all. Does the interpretation of the particular question at hand directly affect the outcome in some politically meaningful way? In some situations, it is clear that debates around a doctrinal concept or rule significantly affect the world in some way. A question of, say, compensation to a corporation for changes to the regulation in the minerals sector clearly contains such stakes. So does a debate on whether or not "gig workers" should be included in the legal definition of an employee (thereby enjoying certain types of protection).

In other instances, such stakes may simply not be there. Take for example the conventional debates between different "theories" in the law, such as between reliance and interest in contract or treaty law or perhaps between the declaratory and constitutive theories of recognition of states. Though these debates might in some sense affect the overall reading of an area of law, there are instances where they appear not to reflect tangible interests. In the latter situation, taking note of the debate is not meaningless. In these instances, the doctrinal debate might rather constitute a form of technical discourse that leads attention away from questions of significance. A central matter for critical doctrinal scholarship becomes how to discern legal questions that hold a significant stake from those that do not. It is worthwhile to remember that the latter questions are not without importance. When a doctrinal field of law focuses strongly on seemingly insignificant issues, that might be precisely how power shrouds itself. By focusing attention on a debate around technical issues of little import, the legal discussion in effect diverts attention from the real stakes.

[47] In asking these questions throughout this text, I have found helpful the simple rigor of the questions suggested by Bacchi 2013.

[48] For a discussion on framing in a legal context, *see* Schlag and Griffin 2020, chapter 2.

[49] For an inspiring discussion, *see* Kennedy 2001, focusing largely on figuring out the motives behind or stakes contained in various positions in private law argumentation.

2.3.2 Rendering Power Visible Through Historicization

It is clear that power is exercised through law in an individual legal case or proceeding. Already first-year law students are taught that one can choose to interpret text in a wide variety of ways. A part of being a proficient lawyer is to learn to develop plausible interpretations of the law that defend different interests. Nevertheless, the aggregate power that naturally comes with the capacity to favor different interests is commonly underplayed in the doctrinal tradition. As the legal outcomes are viewed as natural for those belonging to an accepted collective of interpreters, little power is visible to them. For those interested in how law, legal ideas, and lawyers exercise power, a core question becomes how to make this power visible so that it can be evaluated.[50]

As power comes across clearly in individual instances, one strategy to render power more visible is to highlight the impact of accumulated legal choices or underlying ideas about the law over time. Such historicization might both help show trends in how legal power is exercised and help highlight the degree to which the worldview of interpreters with power is unified (or under challenge). What is changing might be either the practical effects of the law or changes hiding under legal-linguistic stability. Perhaps some group of lawyers keeps talking about the rule of law, but actually means very different things over time?[51] Or sometimes, changes in terminology might allow underlying structures to remain stable. If rules on extraterritorial property protection were upheld by gunboats and the idea of "civilisation" during 19th century imperialism but later justified as forms of "good governance" or "rule of law", this says something about how justifications for similar rules have changed.[52] In other situations, technical language may obscure distinct legal changes. Are significant shifts in state aid or public procurement rules hidden in legal technicalities justified by stable economic ideas? If so, the distributive effect of the law could change even as the overarching discussion remains broadly the same.

One influential way of thinking about how legal power is exercised is through the idea of imagining legal power as being exercised by "people with projects".[53] This is a helpful way into the shift towards surveying the worldview and politics of legal actors that invites historicization. As soon as one starts imagining every legal situation as an opportunity for pushing a project, every instance of legal framing or interpretation can be understood as one instance in a trajectory of events through which legal power is exercised.[54] One risk with thinking of legal power as a matter of people with projects might be that one portrays legal power as overly agent-oriented. Perhaps a particular scholar might appear to embody the current worldview of the

---

[50] An effect of ascribing power to some actor is to demand responsibility for that exercise of power from them. *See* Guzzini 2005.

[51] An excellent analysis of different types of rule of law can be found in Santos 2006.

[52] I have discussed this matter in Rönnelid 2018, in particular in chapters 2–4 and 10.

[53] *See, for example,* Lang and Marks 2013. *See also* Heathcote 2016.

[54] For an argument that highlights some risks with historical scholarship in international law, *see* Arvidsson and McKenna 2020.

field, but this need not mean that this individual remade the law in their image. They might simply be a particularly clear reflection of the zeitgeist at one moment when their worldview is losing influence. However, as long as one looks at people with projects as instantiations of legal power that also operates through broadly shared, even taken-for-granted, ideas about legal governance, the image appears to remain beneficial.

Historicization can render legal power more visible, as it constitutes one way of bringing out how the projects, worldviews, teleologies, or interpretative choices of legal actors add up.[55] It is an antidote to the unwillingness to localize power among law users, commonplace in doctrinalism. It can help correctly identify agency of people, groups, and ideas. Historically informed narratives of how the legal techniques for wielding power operate also help inform readers about the strategic possibilities of certain fields of law as a tool for societal change.[56]

2.3.3 Highlighting Broader Interests Through Group Analysis

Another way of making clear the stakes of law is to look at its effects. Here again, accumulating the impact of decisions can serve to render legal power more visible. In this instance, however, we are not aggregating over time, but rather aggregating the *impact* of individual cases and trying to figure out how they add up at the group level. Although the outcome of how one chooses to interpret, say, the Sanitary and Phytosanitary Measures Agreement of the World Trade Organization might matter in a discrete instance, a broader worldview on how it is deemed correct to interpret the agreement might affect numerous situations.[57] This becomes particularly powerful when the settled reading can be shown to advantage or disadvantage one or another group, for example a certain type of state or a particular class of individuals. Thinking about how a collectively shared idea about the law takes effect at the group level constitutes another type of aggregation to render legal power clearer. The relevant questions then depend on the types of groups that one considers worthwhile highlighting: Does a particular set of legal interpretations favor consumers over producers, employers over employees, developed or developing countries, or corporation over states?

Perhaps some sets of actors are able to make use of the law not only to win individual cases but also to affect the long-term interpretation of the law so as to

---

[55] For an important discussion on the role of history in international legal scholarship, *see* Orford 2021.

[56] I have promised myself to stop quoting in full my favorite passage by Friedrich Kratochwil on the role of historicity for understanding agency. The interested reader can find this passage in Kratochwil 2006, pp. 20–21. This also seems related to the important discussion in Marks 2009.

[57] An interesting example of how international trade law can be analyzed by way of different problematization and their effects can be found in Kennedy 2006, p. 140.

favor their collective interest?[58] How does the law construct who belongs to one or another group or the rights and obligations accruing to them as members of that legal category? Is the way in which the discussion about law operates rendering the interests of one or another group visible or invisible?[59] What is it in the particular dominant framing that highlights one interest over another? The effect of this analysis might be most striking where the result of lawyering has reached a point which comes across as surprising to outsiders: What does it say about current human rights law that it is deemed natural for human rights to be afforded to corporations, but not for humans to invoke these rights against corporations?[60] In instances where people outside the field react with surprise at the current consensus, there is critical potential in highlighting this. In other instances, the work of legal ideas might be so successful as to naturalize some phenomenon also for outsiders. Perhaps international law operates to direct attention with respect to issues of global warming towards states in a way that misconstrues or underplays corporate power?[61] Alternatively, the operation of international law renders it more natural to identify developing country governments as culprits for their countries' economic situations?

One important source of inspiration for carrying out this type of analysis can be derived from the tradition of distributive analysis. This tradition provides tools for thinking about how law allows different capabilities to different groups, for example by highlighting who is able to act according to the law, what the default position is when a group does not act, and tools for analyzing how value flowing from legal interactions is distributed among groups making use of the law.[62] As doctrinal lawyers are typically not used to thinking about how their interpretations favor different groups, there is plenty of work to be done in this respect. Two additional approaches also deserve to be highlighted in brief.[63] First, we have the approach to identify the hidden other side of legal phenomena, through an analysis of how rights for someone always create obligations for someone else, or the like.[64] This can help illuminate the impact of law. A second approach is to notice how sovereignty and property are operating in tandem in much of the law to allow different types of rule.[65] This

---

[58] This is, I think, the most helpful way of making use of Galanter 1974. I have previously applied this framework to third-party funding with respect to international investment law claims in Rönnelid 2021.

[59] A good example of this kind of research can be found in Perrone 2022.

[60] I have discussed these questions, among other things, in Rönnelid 2024.

[61] I have discussed issues such as these in Rönnelid 2023.

[62] A classic text in distributive analysis is Hale 1923. An excellent overview of Hale's rich thinking can be found in Samuels 1972. The broader tradition of distributive analysis was largely resuscitated through Kennedy 1991. For a global take on this tradition, *see* Kennedy 2016, chapter 6.

[63] It seems noteworthy that all of the suggested approaches highlighted here have their seeds in American Legal Realism.

[64] For a very influential approach, *see* Hohfeld 1917. For an updated (perhaps more user-friendly) version, *see* Schlag 2015.

[65] Famously identified in Cohen 1927. Koskenniemi 2021 surveys how ideas of property and sovereignty have operated in the exercise of global power.

is particularly impactful in highlighting costs to the public where private rights are extended or in illuminating the public power it takes to uphold private interests.

2.4 Final Reflections

The meaning of doctrinalism is not possible to pin down with certainty. However, some ways in which the debate around it operate can be illuminated through the above-discussed commonly accepted dichotomies. Where accepted, these three dichotomies operate to portray doctrinalism as internal, practical, descriptive, and objective. Conversely, the dichotomies operate so as to construe other ways of studying law as external, theoretical, normative, and subjective. The dichotomies also operate to grant power to doctrinal scholars by portraying such scholarship as a more certain form of knowledge. This might on the one hand help explain why critical scholars are rejecting doctrinalism. On the other hand, this power is itself a worthy field of study. At least for those interested in scrutinizing power, doctrinal materials and their construction appear to make up an important area of analysis. Of course, these materials cannot be approached with the same assumptions as those used by participants in doctrinal discussions. Instead, doctrinal materials should be studied as attempts to wield power. As discussed above, the effect of ascribing power to those that wield it is often to demand justification for how that power is exercised.[66]

The classifications in the three dichotomies do not operate neatly together. For example, it is striking how the original Hartian explicit normative commitment to a system is viewed as coexisting with the idea of doctrinalism as a neutral endeavor. This might be a reason for rejecting doctrinalism as a helpful general theory about the law. However, it need not be a reason for rejecting the study of the same sources as doctrinal scholars, but with a view to figure out how ideas in the legal field become viewed as neutral and help structure and justify legal power. Instead of joining the endeavour to create systemic coherence and clarity, a critical examination of doctrinal scholarship investigates how coherence was created, which clarity was achieved, and who benefits from it. For example, research in this vein might include asking questions about *which* balance of interests was considered proportionate by some actor with authority, *how* the telos of a field of law was constructed, or *who* benefits from the settled interpretation of some area of law.

I hope this text has indicated some ways in which one can deviate from the typical assumptions of the doctrinal scholars in order to critically study the same types of sources. The strategies of scrutinizing the worldview, finding stakes, historicizing, and aggregating effects at the group level can be combined in numerous ways. Critical work in the sense of work scrutinizing power is often best executed close to a field where power is exercised, as is oftentimes the case in legal doctrine. Thus, a rejection

---

[66] Guzzini 2005 claims that ascribing power to some entity entails "moving actions into the scrutiny of a public realm where justifications are needed".

of doctrinal sources of law might risk lessening the capacity of scholars to scrutinize power.

References

Arvidsson M, Bak McKenna M (2020) The turn to history in international law and the sources doctrine: Critical approaches and methodological imaginaries. Leiden Journal of International Law 33(1):37
Bacchi C (2013) Introducing the 'What's the Problem Represented to be?' approach. In: Bletsas A, Beasley C (eds) Engaging with Carol Bacchi—Strategic Interventions and Exchanges. Adelaide University Press
Bacchi C (2015) The Turn to Problematization: Political Implications of Contrasting Interpretive and Poststructural Adaptations. Open Journal of Political Science 5(1):1
Cohen M (1927) Property and Sovereignty. Cornell Law Review 13:8
Cox RW (1981) Social Forces, States and World Orders: Beyond International Relations Theory. Millennium: Journal of International Studies 10(2):126
Craven M (2018) Ends of Consent. In: Bowman MJ, Kritsiotis D (eds) Conceptual and Contextual Perspectives on the Modern Law of Treaties. Cambridge University Press
Dreyfus H, Kelly SD (2011) All Things Shining—Reading the Western Classics to Find Meaning in a Secular Age. Simon & Schuster
Duncan N, Hutchinson T (2012) Defining and Describing What We Do: Doctrinal Legal Research. Deakin Law Review 17(1):83
Egan S (2018) The doctrinal approach in international human rights law scholarship. In: McConnell L, Smith R (eds) Research Methods in Human Rights. Routledge
Esquirol J (2021) Making the Critical Moves: A Top Ten in Progressive Legal Scholarship 92:1179
Frankenberg G (2010) Critical Theory. In: The Max Planck Encyclopedia of International Law (online version). Oxford University Press
Foucault M (1990) What is Critique?. Originally given as a lecturer before the French Society of Philosophy on 27 May 1978, published in written as Foucault M (1990) Qu'est-ce que la critique? Critique et Aufklärung. Bulletin de la Société française de la philosophie 84(2):35
Galanter M (1974) Why the "Haves" Come Out Ahead: Speculations on the Limits of Legal Change. Law & Society Review 9(1):95
García-Salmones Rovira M (2013) The Project of Positivism in International Law. Oxford University Press
Guzzini S (2005) The Concept of Power: a Constructivist Analysis. Millennium: Journal of International Studies 33(3):495–521
Hale R (1923) Coercion and distribution in a supposedly non-coercive state. Political Science Quarterly 38(3):470
Byrne WH, Olsen HP (2024) Doctrinal Legal Science: A Science of Its Own? Canadian Journal of Law & Jurisprudence 37(2):1
Hart HLA (1961) The Concept of Law. Oxford University Press
Heathcote G (2016) From 'people with projects' to 'encountering expertise': a feminist reading of Kennedy's A World of Struggle. London Review of International Law 4(3):467–476
Hohfeld WN (1917) Fundamental Legal Concepts as Applied in Judicial Reasoning. Yale Law Journal 26(8):710–770
Hutchinson T (2015) The Doctrinal Method: Incorporating Interdisciplinary Methods in Reforming the Law. Erasmus Law Review 8(3):130
Kammerhofer J (2010) Legal Positivism. In: The Max Planck Encyclopedia of International Law (online version). Oxford University Press
Kennedy (1991) The Stakes of Law, or Hale and Foucault. Legal Studies Forum 15:327

Kennedy D (2001) The Political Stakes in "Merely Technical" Issues of Contract Law. European Review of Private Law 1:7–28
Kennedy D (2006) The "Rule of Law," Political Choices, and Development Common Sense. In: Trubeck D, Santos A (eds) The New Law and Economic Development: A Critical Appraisal. Cambridge University Press
Kennedy D (2016) A World of Struggle — How Power, Law, and Expertise Shape Global Political Economy. Princeton University Press
Koskenniemi M (2005) From Apology to Utopia: The Structure of International Legal Argument 2nd edn. Cambridge University Press
Koskenniemi M (2012) Law, Teleology and International Relations: An Essay in Counterdisciplinarity. International Relations 26(1):3
Koskenniemi M (2016) What is Critical Research in International Law? Celebrating Structuralism. Leiden Journal of International Law 29(3):727
Koskenniemi M (2021) To the Uttermost Parts of the Earth: Legal Imagination and International Power 1300–1870. Cambridge University Press
Kratochwil F (1989) Rules, Norms, and Decisions—On the Conditions of Practical and Legal Reasoning in International Relations and Domestic Affairs. Cambridge University Press
Kratochwil F (2006) History, Action and Identity: Revisiting the 'Second' Great Debate and Assessing its Importance for Social Theory. European Journal of International Relations 12(1):5–29
Kratochwil G (2014) The Status of Law in World Society: Meditations on the Role and Rule of Law. Cambridge University Press
Lang L, Marks S (2013) People with Projects: Writing the Lives of International Lawyers. Temple International & Comparative Law Journal 27:437
Lieblich E (2021) How to Do Research in International Law? A Basic Guide for Beginners. Harvard International Law Journal Online 62
Litowitz DE (1998) Internal versus External Perspectives on Law: Toward Mediation. Florida State University Law Review 26(1):127
Marks S (2009) False Contingency. Current Legal Problems 62(1):1
Orford A (2012) In Praise of Description. Leiden Journal of International Law 25(3):609
Orford A (2021) International Law and the Politics of History. Cambridge University Press
Pahuja S (2021) Practical Methodology: Writing about How We Do Research. In: Deplano R, Tsagourias N (eds) Research Methods in International Law—A Handbook. Edward Elgar Publishing
Perrone NM (2022) Local Communities, Extractivism, and International Investment Law: the Case of Five Colombian Communities. Globalizations 19(6):837–853
Putnam H (2002) The Collapse of the Fact-Value Dichotomy and Other Essays. Harvard University Press
Raz J (2009) The Authority of Law. Oxford University Press
Rönnelid L (2018) The emergence of routine enforcement of international investment law—effects on investment protection and development. Uppsala University
Rönnelid L (2021) The Distributive Impact of Third-Party Funding in Investment Arbitration. juridikum—zeitschrift für kritik, recht, gesellschaft 1:125
Rönnelid L (2023) What legal research in sustainable development could become. In: Dahlberg M et al (eds) De Lege 2022: Hållbarhet ur ett rättsligt perspektiv [Sustainability from a legal perspective]. Iustus Förlag
Rönnelid L (2024) Rights critique and rights of nature—a guide for developing strategic awareness when attempting to protect nature through legal rights. Nordic Environmental Law Journal 2:61
Santos A (2006) The World Bank's Uses of the 'Rule of Law' Promise in Economic Development. In: Trubeck D, Santos A (eds) The New Law and Economic Development: A Critical Appraisal. Cambridge University Press
Samuels WJ (1972) The Economy as a System of Power and Its Legal Bases: The Legal Economics of Robert Lee Hale. University of Miami Law Review 27(3):261

Schlag P (1991) Normativity and the Politics of Form. University of Pennsylvania Law Review 139(4):801
Schlag P (2015) How to Do Things with Hohfeld. Law and Contemporary Problems 78:185
Schlag P, Griffin A (2020) How to Do Things with Legal Doctrine. University of Chicago Press
Smits JM (2017) What Is Legal Doctrine? — On The Aims and Methods of Legal-Dogmatic Research. In: Van Gestel R et al (eds) Rethinking Legal Scholarship. Cambridge University Press

Love Rönnelid is a Senior Associate Lecturer in International Law at Stockholm University specializing in international economic law and the political economy of international law. His research and teaching interests concern matters such as the political economy of international investment law, the effects of global economic governance on the economies of developing states, and the history of international economic law. Before joining Stockholm University, he held research positions at Harvard University and Stockholm University. He presented his dissertation, which concerns the genealogy of international investment law, at Uppsala University in 2018.

Chapter 3
The Exercise of Discretion in International Law—The Different Functions of Constraining Criteria

Ulf Linderfalk

Contents

Abstract In international law, the exercise of discretion is subject to pre-established constraining criteria. These are typically not explicit in the norms that confer the discretion. This explains the importance of the scholarly study of constraining criteria as well as some of its methodological difficulties. Study is further complicated by the different functions that constraining criteria serve. As this chapter argues, constraining criteria reflect, each in its own way, two fundamentally different conceptions of an international legal system. In the one case, the international legal system is seen as a series of norms that serve the common purposes of the states and international organizations that create them. In the other, it is conceived as a system with certain inherent moral or technical features, which are partly beyond any lawmaker's control. The chapter directs attention to a few judicial decisions that help to illustrate precisely this point.

Keywords International legal decision-making · Discretion · Constraining criteria · Function of constraining criteria

U. Linderfalk (✉)
Faculty of Law, Lund University, Lund, Sweden
e-mail: ulf.linderfalk@jur.lu.se

Faculty of Law, University of A Coruña, A Coruña, Spain

M. Klamberg et al. (eds.), *Reconstructing Power and Hegemony in Public International Law*, https://doi.org/10.1007/978-94-6265-743-4_3

3.1 Constraining Criteria and the Legitimacy of Legal Decisions

This article addresses a fundamental element of international legal decision-making: the exercise of discretion. A "legal decision", bluntly put, is a decision about the way to apply a law in concrete cases. "Discretion" is a power conferred by a lawmaker on a legal decision-maker. It enables the legal decision-maker to make decisions in conformity with a legal rule, while at the same time giving this person or institution the possibility to choose between different courses of action.[1] A legal decision-maker exercises discretion when it avails itself of a decision-making power thus framed. Below are a few real-world examples that can serve to illustrate the phenomenon:

- As provided by Article 5 of the Interim Accord concluded in 1995 between the governments of Greece and the Former Yugoslavian Republic of Macedonia (FYROM), the two governments shall "continue negotiations" with a view to settle outstanding differences over the name of the latter country.[2] Yet, they have the discretion to decide how, precisely, negotiations are to be conducted and when.[3]
- As provided by a rule of customary international law, a treaty concluded between two states shall be interpreted in accordance with the ordinary meaning of the treaty terms.[4] Yet, these states have the discretion to decide whether the ordinary meaning is to be determined based on the language in use at the time of conclusion of the treaty, or the language in use at the time of interpretation.[5]
- As provided by Article 15 of the Statute of the International Criminal Tribunal for the Former Yugoslavia, the judges of the Tribunal shall adopt rules of procedure and evidence for a series of matters such as the protection of victims and witnesses.[6] Yet, it leaves to the judges to decide precisely how victims and witnesses are to be protected and when.[7]

In international law, discretion is increasingly common.[8] In a world where international law is expanding rapidly to meet new challenges and desires of a steadily growing international society, the conferral of discretion has become the preeminent

---

[1] *See, e.g.*, Galligan 1990, p. 4. As American philosopher Ronald Dworkin has pointed out, "discretion" can be used in several different senses. This is what Dworkin refers to as "discretion in the strong sense". *See* Dworkin 1977, p. 32.

[2] 1891 UNTS 7.

[3] ICJ, *Application of the Interim Accord of 13 September 1995 (The Former Republic of Macedonia v. Greece)*, Judgment of 5 December 2011, ICJ Reports 2011, p. 644, paras 127–138.

[4] *See, e.g.*, *Dispute regarding Navigational and Related Rights (Costa Rica v. Nicaragua)*, ICJ Reports 2009, p. 213, para 47.

[5] *See, e.g.*, Linderfalk and Hilling 2015, pp. 34–59.

[6] The Statute was established by the adoption of UN Security Council Resolution 827. It was amended by later resolutions.

[7] *See, e.g.*, Zahar and Sluiter 2008, pp. 20–21.

[8] *See, e.g.*, Ginsburg 2004, p. 1.

strategy to make the international legal systems efficient.[9] This practice raises questions of legitimacy: Does the exercise of discretionary powers produce an outcome that is acceptable to the relevant constituencies?

To answer this question, once again, you need to consider the law. As lawyers readily recognize, there is no such thing as an absolute legal discretion in the sense of a power to act at will.[10] In all cases, international law makes the exercise of discretion subject to pre-established "constraining criteria". To be able to make well-founded assessments of the legitimacy of international legal decisions, you need knowledge of these criteria. This is so whether you conceive of a legal decision as legitimate because it is consistent with the law, or because it conforms to certain presupposed moral or political principles.[11]Without knowledge of constraining criteria, in the former case, there is a risk that you will understand a decision as legitimate, although it is actually not. In the latter case, there is a risk that you will understand a decision as illegitimate, although the problem is not the decision, but the law itself.

Research on constraining criteria is underdeveloped.[12] It is not that constraining criteria have gone unnoticed in legal scholarship, but research has been consistently "piecemeal". To the best of my knowledge, in no case have scholars examined more than a single branch of international law (e.g., WTO law), a single treaty (e.g., the European Convention on Human Rights), or a single treaty provision (e.g., Article 36 of the Statute of the International Court of Justice). They have engaged only with a very limited selection of single principles and general precepts, such as: the doctrine of abuse of rights;[13] the importance of the purposes of an international organization;[14] good faith;[15] proportionality;[16] the principle of state sovereignty;[17] the principle of legality;[18] and the principle of human dignity.[19] I have earlier referred to this as the "piecemeal approach".[20] This approach misses some of the essential features of discretion. Most importantly, it overlooks the different functions of constraining criteria.

Discretion being a power conferred by a lawmaker, it is far too easy to think that in international law, constraining criteria must be motivated by a desire to respect

---

[9] This seems to be due to several factors, such as the increased pace of changes of real-world conditions and the need for technical detail in legal decisions. Both trends prompt the kind of flexibility that discretion offers. There is also the growth of the international community, which comes with the need to accommodate a plurality of political opinions and moral values. Discretion is good at enabling this, too.

[10] *See, e.g.*, Galligan 1990, pp. 4–7.

[11] *See, e.g.*, Gill-Pedro 2022, pp. 203–216.

[12] *See* Linderfalk 2026.

[13] *See, e.g.*, De Brabandere 2012, p. 609.

[14] *See, e.g.*, De Brabandere 2009, pp. 55–76.

[15] *See, e.g.*, Linderfalk 2020a, pp. 259–273.

[16] *See, e.g.*, Linderfalk 2020b, pp. 422–437.

[17] *See, e.g.*, Zarbiyev 2012, p. 1.

[18] *See, e.g.*, Gallant 2009.

[19] *See, e.g.*, Le Moli 2022, pp. 105–111.

[20] See Linderfalk 2019, pp. 407–430.

lawmakers' intentions. As preliminary studies indicate, this is certainly not the case with all of the criteria. Far from constituting any homogenous set of norms founded on a single theory of law, constraining criteria reflect, each in its own way, two fundamentally different conceptions of an international legal system: in the one case, a series of norms that serve the common purposes of the states and international organizations that create them; in the other, a system with certain inherent moral or technical features, which are partly beyond any lawmakers' control.[21] Depending on whether a criterion responds to the former or the latter of these two conceptions, I will refer to it as "endemic" or "systemic", respectively.

A good knowledge of the different functions of constraining criteria is key to a well-founded assessment of the legitimacy of legal decision-making. Without knowledge of the different functions of constraining criteria, people will wrongly conceive of legal decisions as incoherent and incomprehensible. Such misunderstandings will politicize the discussions that the exercise of discretion tends to cause among the public and make these discussions largely unproductive. They will raise exaggerated doubts about the legitimacy of particular forms of legal decision-making (e.g., international investment arbitration), of particular decision-makers (e.g., the International Criminal Court), and of international law itself. A fuller knowledge of the different functions of constraining criteria would help to give discussions a more constructive direction.

It is the objective of this chapter to increase the attention of international lawyers and scholars to these different functions of constraining criteria and to provide illustration of how they play out in legal decision-making. The method that I will be using is rational reconstruction in the sense of German philosopher and sociologist Jürgen Habermas.[22] If you conceive of legal norms as reasons for action, as I do, constraining criteria cannot be observed as such. What can be observed are the ways in which constraining criteria manifest themselves in legal decisions and the utterances of legal decision-makers. To be able to infer anything from these utterances about the existence of constraining criteria, you need to make certain assumptions. You need to assume that decision-makers are committed to certain standards of communication and argumentation. Most importantly, as Habermas emphasizes, you need to assume that decision-makers act as they themselves consider socially appropriate.[23] Inductive reasoning, together with this seemingly simple assumption, will help to make explicit the inescapable logical conditions of legal decisions, including constraining criteria, and the particular conception of an international legal system that each one presupposes.

[21] Ibid., pp. 425–428.

[22] *See* Linderfalk 2022.

[23] *See* Habermas 1984, p. 307.

3.2 Endemic Criteria

3.2.1 The Principle of Good Faith

When a discretion is conferred by way of a treaty, it is exercised subject to the principle of good faith.[24] Consider, for example, the judgment of the International Court of Justice in the case concerning the *Application of the Interim Accord of 13 September 1995*.[25] In its application to the Court, the Government of Greece contended that the Applicant had breached the obligation imposed by the Interim Accord of 13 September 1995 between the FYROM and Greece. As provided by Article 5, para 1 of the Accord:

> [t]he Parties agree to continue negotiations under the auspices of the Secretary-General of the United Nations pursuant to Security Council resolution 845 (1993) with a view to reaching agreement on the difference described in that resolution and in Security Council resolution 817 (1993).

This provision imposed on the two parties the obligation to "continue negotiations". At the same time, it conferred on them the discretion to decide, more precisely, how negotiations were to be conducted and when.

In response to the claim of a breach of Article 5, para 1, the Court stressed that it is a requirement following implicitly from this provision that the parties must negotiate in good faith.[26] As the Court noted, the parties to the Accord have an obligation "not only to enter into negotiations, but also to pursue them as far as possible, with a view to concluding agreements".[27] So understood, Article 5, para 1 did not impose on the parties the obligation to reach an agreement; nor did it require that lengthy negotiations be pursued of necessity. As the Court seemed keen to convey, the provision entailed an obligation of conduct. In exercising the discretion conferred under Article 5, para 1, the parties would have to conduct themselves so as not to frustrate the object and purpose of the provision—the creation of conditions favorable to reaching an agreement. As the Court explained:

> States must conduct themselves so that the "negotiations are meaningful". This requirement is not satisfied, for example, where either of the parties "insists upon its own position without contemplating any modification of it" or where they obstruct negotiations, for example, by interrupting communications or causing delays in an unjustified manner or disregarding the procedures agreed upon. Negotiations with a view to reaching an agreement also imply that the parties should pay reasonable regard to the interests of the other.[28]

---

24 *See* Linderfalk 2020a, pp. 1–32.

25 *Application of the Interim Accord of 13 September 1995*, above n. 3.

26 Ibid., para 131.

27 Ibid., para 132. Quotes are from the PCIJ in *Railway Traffic between Lithuania and Poland*.

28 Ibid., para 132. References to earlier case law have been omitted.

The principle of good faith, in the sense in which the International Court applied it in this case, suggests a deference to the intention of treaty parties. In the terminology of the Court, the "object and purpose" of Article 5, para 1, was shorthand for the state of affairs that the Governments of Greece and the FYROM sought to obtain by including this provision in the Interim Accord. Good faith, in this case at least, served as an endemic constraining criterion.

3.2.2 *The Abuse of Rights Doctrine*

The abuse of rights doctrine is a criterion that serves to constrain the exercise of discretion in many branches of international law. One of them is European human rights law. This is for obvious reasons, as Article 17 of the European Convention explicitly establishes a "Prohibition of abuse of rights":

> Nothing in this Convention may be interpreted as implying for any State, group or person any right to engage in any activity or perform any act aimed at the destruction of any of the rights and freedoms set forth herein or at their limitation to a greater extent than is provided for in the Convention.

As the abuse of rights doctrine is often described, a right must not be exercised so as to render its purpose ineffective.[29] Although the reference in Article 17 to the "destruction" of rights and freedoms does not itself reveal the purpose to be protected by the application of the provision, that purpose is clear from Strasbourg case law. The European Convention secures to everyone who finds him- or herself within the jurisdiction of a state party the enjoyment of a number of rights—the rights laid down in the Convention and its additional protocols. The enjoyment by individuals of these rights is not an end in itself. As stated by the Court in *United Communist Party of Turkey and Others v. Turkey*, "the Convention was designed to maintain and promote the ideals and values of a democratic society".[30] Admittedly, the way the relationship between human rights and political democracy is described in the European Convention, instrumentality works both ways. In the preamble to the Convention, effective political democracy is described as a means to ensure the maintenance and further realization of human rights and fundamental freedoms. At the same time, in the case law of the Strasbourg Court, securing to everyone within the jurisdiction of a state party the enjoyment of the rights and freedoms laid down in the Convention is seen as a means for the protection of the ideals and values of a democratic society. This idea about the relationship between human rights and democracy poses a limit to the discretion that state parties exercise when implementing rights. As the Court phrased it in *Refah Partisi*, "no one must be

---

[29] *See, e.g.*, De Brabandere 2012.

[30] ECtHR, *United Communist Party of Turkey and Others v. Turkey*, Judgment, 30 January 1998, Application Nos 133/1996/752/951, para 45.

authorized to rely on the Convention's provisions in order to weaken or destroy the ideals and values of democratic society".[31]

The European Court and Commission have many times applied Article 17 to declare applications wholly or partly incompatible *ratione materiae* with the provisions of the Convention.[32] In *Kasymakhunov and Saybatalov*,[33] Russian courts had convicted the two applicants for their membership in a prohibited extremist Islamic organization called Hizb ut-Tahrir al-Islami. They both complained that this conviction violated the rights that they were to enjoy according to Articles 9, 10, and 11 of the European Convention. The Court stressed the relevance of Article 17 in this case. As a point of general clarification, it remarked that in pleading the rights laid down in any of Articles 9–11, a political party or other association might attempt to derive therefrom the right to conduct activities intended to destroy the rights or freedoms set forth in the Convention and thus bring about the destruction of democracy. Article 17 sought to prevent this: it serves to guarantee that the Convention is not applied for purposes contrary to the ideals and values of a democratic society.[34]

In addressing the particular facts of the *Kasymakhunov and Saybatalov* case, the Court noted that the applicants were engaged in spreading the ideology and distributing the literature of Hizb ut-Tahrir, the aims of which were "clearly contrary to the values of the Convention".[35] Among other things, the organization urged members to fight the unfaithful with weapons and to kill any citizens of "enemy States".[36] It proposed to introduce capital punishment for apostasy from Islam and to ban all political parties not based on this religion. It intended to set up a regime based on *sharia*, which, in the words of the Court, could "hardly be regarded as complying with the democratic ideal that underlies the whole of the Convention". This was so particularly with regard to the legal status of women and the way in which *sharia* would intervene in all spheres of private and public life. Furthermore, according to Hizb ut-Tahrir's Draft Constitution, only Muslims would have the right to vote and be

---

[31] ECtHR, *Refah Partisi (The Welfare Party) and Others v. Turkey*, Judgment, 13 February 2003, Application Nos 41340/98, 41342/98, 41343/98 and 41344/98, para 99.

[32] *See, e.g.*, European Commission of Human Rights, *German Communist Party v. Germany*, Decision, 20 July 1957, Application No 250/57; European Commission of Human Rights, *Glimmerveen and Hagenbeek v. the Netherlands*, Decision, 11 October 1979, Application Nos 8348/78 and 8406/78; European Commission of Human Rights, *Marais v. France*, Decision, 24 June 1996, Application No 31159/96; ECtHR, *Schimanek v. Austria*, Decision, 1 February 2000, Application No 32307/96; ECtHR, *Norwood v. the United Kingdom*, Decision, 16 November 2004, Application No 23131/03; ECtHR, *WP and Others v. Poland*, Decision, 2 September 2004, Application No 42264/98 ECHR 2004-VII; ECtHR, *Pavel Ivanov v. Russia*, Decision, 20 February 2007, Application No 35222/04; ECtHR, *Paksas v. Lithuania*, Judgment, 6 January 2011, Application No 34932/04; ECtHR, *Hizb ut-Tahrir and Others v. Germany*, Decision, 12 June 2012, Application No 31098/08; ECtHR, *Kasymakhunov and Saybatalov v. Russia*, Judgment, 14 June 2013, Application Nos 26261/05, 26377/06.

[33] *Kasymakhunov and Saybatalov v. Russia* (n. 32).

[34] Ibid., paras 104–105.

[35] Ibid., para 106.

[36] Ibid., para 107.

elected, to become State officials, or to acquire membership of political parties.[37] The Court concluded that the dissemination of the political ideas of Hizb ut-Tahrir by the two applicants clearly constituted an activity falling within the scope of application of Article 17.[38] Article 17, in this case, serves to constrain the discretion that contracting parties are exercising in implementing Convention rights domestically. It serves as an endemic criterion, following as it does from an explicit provision of the Convention and its preamble.

3.2.3 The Intention of Treaty Parties

According to Article 31, para 1 of the 1969 Vienna Convention on the Law of Treaties (VCLT), "[a] treaty shall be interpreted in good faith in accordance with the ordinary meaning to be given to the terms of the treaty in their context and in the light of its object and purpose". This provision, while requiring consideration of the ordinary meaning of the treaty, confers a discretion on the parties. It leaves to them to determine whether consideration shall be had to the meaning ascribed to the terms of the treaty at the time of its conclusion or the meaning ascribed at the time of interpretation. This discretion is not absolute. To illustrate, consider the *Dispute Regarding Navigational and Related Rights.*[39]

The application of Costa Rica, together with the arguments put forth by the two parties, prompted the International Court to clarify the meaning of the Treaty of Territorial Limits concluded in 1858. The Treaty established Nicaragua's dominion and sovereign jurisdiction over the waters of the San José River. At the same time, it affirmed Costa Rica's right to navigate the lower course of the River for purposes of commerce (Sp. "con objetos de comercio"). Nicaragua argued that the ordinary meaning of "commerce" excluded all services, such as passenger transport, "because in 1858 the word 'commerce' necessarily meant trade in goods and did not extend to services, the inclusion of services being a very recent development".[40]

In addressing this argument, the ICJ affirmed that, as a matter of principle:

> [T]he terms used in a treaty must be interpreted in light of what is determined to have been the parties' common intention, which is, by definition, contemporaneous with the treaty's conclusion.[41]

As it immediately added, it did not necessarily follow that no account should ever be taken of the meaning of a treaty at the time of interpretation:

> [T]here are situations in which the parties' intent upon conclusion of the treaty was, or may be presumed to have been, to give the terms used – or some of them – a meaning or content

[37] Ibid., paras 107–111.

[38] Ibid., para 113.

[39] *Dispute regarding Navigational and Related Rights*, above n. 4.

[40] Ibid., para 58.

[41] Ibid., para 63.

> capable of evolving, not one fixed once and for all, so as to make allowance for, among other things, developments in international law. In such instances it is indeed in order to respect the parties' common intention at the time the treaty was concluded, not to depart from it, that account should be taken of the meaning acquired by the terms in question upon each occasion on which the treaty is to be applied.[42]

The Court decided that in the application of Article 31, para 1 of the VCLT, it would have to ascribe to the terms of the treaty the meaning that they have at the time of interpretation. Anxious to justify this conclusion, the Court emphasized that, in 1858, it was the intention of the parties to the Treaty of Territorial Limits that it would remain in force for a very long time:

> [W]here the parties have used generic terms in a treaty, the parties necessarily having been aware that the meaning of the terms was likely to evolve over time, and where the treaty has been entered into for a very long period or is "of continuing duration", the parties must be presumed, as a general rule, to have intended those terms to have an evolving meaning.[43]

The Court, obviously, did not conceive of the discretion conferred under the rule of ordinary meaning as tantamount to a power to act at will. The discretion was to be exercised subject to the constraint imposed by the purpose of this rule, which—like other parts of Articles 31–33 of the VCLT—is to establish what the parties to a treaty intended it to communicate. This purpose serves to explain the many details of the provisions laid down in Articles 31–33, but, as confirmed by the Court, it serves also as a constraining criterion in cases where these provisions leave to the discretion of the parties to determine an issue, such as the basis of the ordinary meaning.

3.3 Systemic Criteria

3.3.1 The Principle Jura Novit Curia

Other constraining criteria are founded on other motivating reasons. Take for instance the principle *jura novit curia*, as applied by the European Court of Human Rights. According to Article 32 of the European Convention, "[t]he jurisdiction of the Court shall extend to all matters concerning the interpretation and application of the Convention and the Protocols thereto which are referred to it as provided in Articles 33, 34, 46 and 47".[44] This provision confers on the Court a discretion to settle a number of procedural issues that may arise in the course of its exercise of jurisdiction. Examples include the admissibility of complaints raised by an applicant in communication with the Grand Chamber in cases where those complaints do not correspond to claims raised earlier before a Chamber. That is to say: Article 32 leaves it to the Grand Chamber to decide whether to accept such complaints or reject them.

---

[42] Ibid., para 64.

[43] Ibid., para 66.

[44] ETS No 5.

In making such decisions, the Court has often referred to the *jura novit curia* principle. As it has typically remarked, it is not bound by the legal characterization of facts given by an applicant or a government but is free to make this characterization itself.[45] It is certainly not impossible to explain the relevance of the *jura novit curia* principle to the application of the European Convention by reference to the intentions of its parties. The *jura novit curia* principle is often described as a general principle of law, in the sense of Article 38, para 1(c) of the Statute of International Court of Justice.[46] It could be argued that the parties to the European Convention intended to incorporate into the Convention all relevant general principles of law, so that every time that a provision of the Convention is applied, each of those principles will have to be considered. This suggestion raises questions of legal justification: How can this intention of the contracting parties be established? It also raises the intertemporal question common to all situations of understanding a treaty over time: Did the contracting parties intend to incorporate into the European Convention and Protocols the general principles of law that were applicable at the time of conclusion of each document, or the general principles as they evolve over time? To avoid all of these questions, the better way of understanding the practice of the European Court would be to consider it to be constrained by criteria that flow from an idea of judicial proceedings which is common to all systems of law and which exists apart from any lawmakers' intention.

3.3.2 The Principle of Sustainable Development

Consider the judgment of the International Court in the *Pulp Mills on the River of Uruguay* case.[47] To cut the story short, Uruguay had authorized the construction of a pulp mill in the River Uruguay. This had prompted the Government of Argentina to bring before the International Court a number of claims of violations of provisions of the 1975 Statute of the River Uruguay, among them Article 27:

> The rights of each Party to use the waters of the river, within its jurisdiction, for domestic, sanitary, industrial and agricultural purposes shall be exercised without prejudice to the application of the procedure laid down in articles 7 to 12 when the use is liable to affect the régime of the river or the quality of its waters.[48]

Article 27 recognizes the power of the parties to authorize activities such as the construction and operation of a pulp mill. As the Court noted, this power is not unlimited: due regard must be paid to the interests of the other riparian state in the

---

[45] *See, e.g.*, ECtHR, *Case of Radomilja and Others v. Croatia*, Grand Chamber, Judgment, 20 March 2018, Application Nos 37685/10 and 22768/12, para 126. For earlier examples, *see* ibid., para 115.

[46] *See, e.g.*, Shelton 2013, pp. 189–211.

[47] ICJ, *Case Concerning Pulp Mills on the River Uruguay (Argentina v. Uruguay)*, ICJ Reports 2010, p. 14, at para 177.

[48] 1295 UNTS 339.

shared resource and to its environmental protection.[49] Article 27, the Court explained, embodies the idea of sustainable development and the balance between economic development and environmental protection that is its essence.[50] Reader should recall the short history of the principle of sustainable development. It did not appear in a legally binding international instrument until the conclusion of the 1992 Climate Change Convention.[51] This being the case, it is indeed very difficult to explain this finding of the Court in terms of any intention of the parties to the 1975 Statute. The finding would seem to flow instead from a more recent idea of the function of international environmental law, which now transcends the understanding of this entire sphere of regulation.

3.3.3 The Public Interest Criterion and NGO Interventions in International Investment Arbitration

Recent decades have seen an increased involvement of non-governmental organizations (NGOs) in international investment arbitration proceedings.[52] Typically, NGOs cannot be claimants in such proceedings. Instead, they try to gain access to the relevant fora by intervening as *amici curiae*. Whether unsolicited submissions by NGOs (*amicus curia* briefs) shall be accepted is an issue that regulatory frameworks often leave to the discretion of arbitration tribunals to decide. Article 44 of the 1965 ICSID Convention serves as a good example:

> Any arbitration proceeding shall be conducted in accordance with the provisions of this Section and, except as the parties otherwise agree, in accordance with the Arbitration Rules in effect on the date on which the parties consented to arbitration. If any question of procedure arises which is not covered by this Section or the Arbitration Rules or any rules agreed by the parties, the Tribunal shall decide the question.[53]

In the case of *Suez/Vivendi v. Argentina*,[54] this provision came into focus when an ICSID Tribunal received a request from five Argentinian NGOs to present legal arguments as *amici curiae*. The Claimant asked the Tribunal to refuse the request, whereas the Respondent expressed its approval. The Tribunal noted that neither the ICSID Convention nor the Arbitration Rules specifically authorized or specifically permitted the submission of non-parties of *amicus curia* briefs. Article 44 of the ICSID Convention in fact left this issue to the discretion of the Tribunal itself. As the Tribunal immediately added, it exercised this power subject to certain conditions,

---

[49] *Case Concerning Pulp Mills on the River Uruguay*, above n. 47, para 177.

[50] Ibid.

[51] *See, e.g.*, Beyerlin and Marauhn 2011, p. 74.

[52] On this phenomenon, *see* De Brabandere 2011, pp. 85–114.

[53] 575 UNTS 159.

[54] *Aguas Argentinas, S.A., Suez, Sociedad General de Aguas de Barcelona, S.A. and Vivendi Universal, S.A. v. The Argentine Republic*, ICSID Case No. ARB/03/19, Order in Response to a Petition for Transparency and Participation as Amicus Curiae, 15 May 2005.

one of which was "the appropriateness of the subject matter of the case".[55] It noted, in this context, the necessity of a public interest:

> Courts have traditionally accepted the intervention of amicus curiae in ostensibly private litigation because those cases have involved issues of public interest and because decisions in those cases have the potential, directly or indirectly, to affect persons beyond those immediately involved as parties in the case.[56]

In examining whether such an interest existed, the Tribunal stressed that the focus should not be on the law that it involved. As the responsibility of a state is always at stake in ICSID arbitration—as opposed to the liability of a corporation arising because of private law—a public interest is in some sense always present when a dispute is brought before an ICSID Tribunal. The focus should be rather on the subject matter of the dispute, which in this case was certainly of public interest, as it centered around the water distribution and sewage systems of the city of Buenos Aires and surrounding municipalities. As the Tribunal noted:

> [t]hose systems provide basic public services to millions of people and as a result may raise a variety of complex public and international law questions, including human rights considerations. Any decision rendered in this case, whether in favor of the Claimants or the Respondent, has the potential to affect the operation of those systems and thereby the public they serve.[57]

As is evident, the public interest criterion served to constrain the Tribunal when it decided whether to allow the five NGOs to intervene in the case as *amici curiae*. This criterion would seem to have little to do with the purpose of the ICSID Convention, but would seem to flow instead from an idea of the function of arbitration in investment and other economic matters generally, much like the principle of sustainable development in the *Pulp Mills* case. The Tribunal touches upon this issue in a subsequent paragraph, stating that:

> The acceptance of *amicus* submissions would have the additional desirable consequence of increasing the transparency of investor-state arbitration. Public acceptance of the legitimacy of international arbitral processes, particularly when they involve states and matters of public interest, is strengthened by increased openness and increased knowledge as to how these processes function. It is this imperative that has led to increased transparency in the arbitral processes of the World Trade Organization and the North American Free Trade Agreement. Through the participation of appropriate representatives of civil society in appropriate cases, the public will gain increased understanding of ICSID processes.[58]

---

[55] Ibid., para 17.

[56] Ibid., para 19.

[57] Ibid.

[58] Ibid., para 22.

3.4 Concluding Observations

In international law, the exercise of discretion is subject to pre-established constraining criteria. These have different functions. As this chapter illustrates, constraining criteria reflect, each in its own way, two fundamentally different conceptions of an international legal system: in the one case, a series of norms that serve the common purposes of the states and international organizations that create them; in the other, a system with certain inherent moral or technical features, which are partly beyond any lawmakers' control. Depending on whether a criterion responds to the former or the latter of these two conceptions, I referred to them as "endemic" or "systemic", respectively.

Interestingly, endemic and systemic criteria seem to be unequally present in the practice of different parts of international law. Systemic criteria are more notably present in the practice of the special regimes so-called. It is possible to understand this observation to reflect the fact that in those parts of international law, lawyers often have a very clear common idea of what desirable state or states of affairs they are pursuing.[59] Endemic criteria are more notably present in the practice of general international law. It is possible to understand this to reflect the fact that in this part of international law, lawyers typically have no common idea of what desirable state or states of affairs they are pursuing, but merely defer to the intention of international lawmakers.[60] The application by the European Court of the abuse of rights doctrine should not distract us. Nothing prevents international law specialists from seeing "their" portion of the international legal system as, at the same time, a set of norms that serve the common purposes of those who created them, and a system with certain inherent moral or technical features—although, obviously, this suggestion does not apply the other way around. For those of us who are interested in understanding the construction of the increasingly specialized international legal system, this observation is certainly worthy of further, more systematic, investigation.

References

Beyerlin U, Marauhn T (2011) International Environmental Law. Hart Publishing

De Brabandere E (2009) Post-Conflict Administrations in International Law: International Territorial Administration, Transitional Authority and Foreign Occupation in Theory and Practice. Brill, Leiden

De Brabandere E (2011) NGOs and the "Public Interest": The Legality and Rationale of Amicus Curiae Interventions in International Economic and Investment Disputes. Chicago Journal of International Law 12(1):85–114

De Brabandere E (2012) 'Good Faith', 'Abuse of Process' and the Initiation of Investment Treaty Claims. Journal of International Dispute Settlement 3(3):609–636

Dworkin R (1977) Taking Rights Seriously. Harvard University Press

[59] *See* Linderfalk and De Brabandere 2024.

[60] Ibid.

Gallant KS (2009) The Principle of Legality in International and Comparative Criminal Law. Cambridge University Press
Galligan J (1990) Discretionary Powers: A Legal Study of Official Discretion. Oxford University Press
Gill-Pedro E (2022) Legality and Legitimacy in International Law. In: Linderfalk U (ed) The International Legal System as a System of Knowledge. Edward Elgar Publishing
Ginsburg T (2004) Bounded Discretion in International Judicial Lawmaking. Virginia Journal of International Law 45:1–42
Habermas J (1984). The Theory of Communicative Action, Vol I: Reason and the Rationalization of Society (translated into English by T McCarthy). Beacon Press, Boston
Le Moli G (2022) AI vs Human Dignity: When Human Underperformance is Legally Required. Révue européenne du droit 3:105–111
Linderfalk U (2019) The Exercise of Discretion In International Law: Why Constraining Criteria Have a Proper Place In the Analysis of Legal Decision-Making. German Yearbook of International Law 62:407–430
Linderfalk U (2020a) Good Faith and the Exercise of Treaty-Based Discretionary Powers. In Bartels L, Paddeu F (eds) Exceptions in International Law. Oxford University Press
Linderfalk U (2020b) Proportionality and International Legal Pragmatics. Nordic Journal of International Law 89:422–437
Linderfalk U (2022) Rational Reconstruction and International Legal Reasoning. Hague Yearbook of International Law. https://ssrn.com/abstract=4300851. Accessed 1 April 2025. (forthcoming, on file with author)
Linderfalk U (2026) Legal Research: The State of the Art and the Way Forward. In: Linderfalk U (ed) The Exercise of Discretion in International Law. Edward Elgar Publishing (forthcoming, on file with author)
Linderfalk U, De Brabandere E (2024) International Law and the Significance of Disciplinary Boundaries: Special Regimes as Communities of Practice. Cambridge University Press
Linderfalk U, Hilling M (2015) The Use of OECD Commentaries as Interpretative Aids: The Static/Ambulatory-Approaches Debate Considered from the Perspective of International Law. Nordic Tax Journal 1:34–59
Shelton D (2013) Jura Novit Curia in International Human Rights Tribunals. In: Boschiero N et al (eds), International Courts and the Development of International Law: Essays in Honour of Tullio Treves. T.M.C. Asser Press, The Hague
Zahar A, Sluiter G (2008) International Criminal Law. Oxford University Press
Zarbiyev F (2012) Judicial Activism in International Law: A Conceptual Framework for Analysis. Journal of International Dispute Settlement 3:247–278

Ulf Linderfalk is Professor of International Law at the Faculty of Law, Lund University, Lund, Sweden, and a Distinguished Researcher at the Faculty of Law, University of A Coruña, A Coruña, Spain.

Chapter 4
Personal Immunity Before the International Criminal Court

Astrid Kjeldgaard-Pedersen

Contents

Abstract This chapter explores the apparent disagreement between the International Court of Justice (ICJ) and the International Criminal Court (ICC) concerning personal immunity, which was recently actualized by the ICC's arrest warrants against Vladimir Putin, Benjamin Netanyahu, and Min Aung Hlaing as well as by the establishment of The Special Tribunal for the Crime of Aggression against Ukraine. The ICC's leading judgment from 2019 in the case concerning (now former) President Bashir of Sudan is, on crucial points, at odds with the leading ICJ judgment on personal immunity in *Arrest Warrant* from 2002. This situation poses a significant legal and political dilemma for governments of ICC member states, who are forced to make a choice between complying with the ICC's interpretation of their obligations under the ICC Statute and the ICJ's findings concerning their obligations under customary international law. Identifying the "true" meaning of the law is also a genuine challenge for doctrinal legal scholars and as such a good case study for

---

A. Kjeldgaard-Pedersen (✉)
CERES - Centre for Law and Security, Faculty of Law, University of Copenhagen, Copenhagen, Denmark
e-mail: astrid.kjeldgaard-pedersen@jur.ku.dk

M. Klamberg et al. (eds.), *Reconstructing Power and Hegemony in Public International Law*, https://doi.org/10.1007/978-94-6265-743-4_4

what it might mean to engage in "critical doctrinalism" in the field of international law.

Keywords Critical doctrinalism · ICJ · ICC · Personal immunity · International crimes

4.1 Introduction

One of the overarching questions posed in this *liber amicorum*, in celebration of Pål Wrange's pioneering work in Critical Legal Studies and his interest in legal philosophy, is whether it is possible for an international legal scholar to be critical and doctrinal at the same time. The answer of course depends on the meaning attributed to "doctrinal" and "critical", respectively—neither of which is a fixed term in international legal scholarship. In this chapter, I will attempt to illustrate—through the example of the intricate question of personal immunity before the International Criminal Court (ICC)—what one version of "critical doctrinalism" might look like. The chapter by no means purports to provide—in the limited space available—a comprehensive analysis of the concepts "doctrinal" and "critical" in the context of international law. For the present purposes, "doctrinalism" is simply defined as a quest to determine the "true" meaning of the law by interpreting—using the recognized principles of interpretation (with all their inherent uncertainties)—the sources of international law (with all of their inherent uncertainties).[1] Doctrinal analysis may lead to exposure of power and hierarchy and may very well provide a basis for arguments regarding policy change.[2] But that is not its primary aim. If we were to point out a normative underpinning for "doctrinalism", it could be that for the international legal system to be an instrument of good—even in dark times like the 2020s[3]—we need to ensure that we can all, at least, agree on the methodological fundamentals. When doctrinal legal analysis proves a frustrating endeavor, in the sense that it leads to a result that the scholar in question finds morally problematic, he or she may find comfort in the fact that the stability and reliability of the international legal system as such is "a greater good" not to be compromised.[4] The topic of the present chapter—personal immunity before the ICC—provides an excellent example of the dilemma in which doctrinal scholars may find themselves. As then-international law professor Dire Tladi (now a judge at the International Court of Justice (ICJ)) stated at the end of a 2020 blog post: "PS: for the record, and I have said so before, I do not support immunity, but I believe if it is [to] be eroded, it should happen in an orderly fashion, following the methodology of international law."[5] The question of

[1] See Chapter 2 for Love Rönnelid's detailed analysis of 'critical doctrinalism'.

[2] Klamberg et al. 2026.

[3] Ibid.

[4] See also Chapter 2, p. XX.

[5] Tladi 2020.

course immediately arises: What is an orderly fashion? And this is where "critical" may be said to enter the equation, as further developed in Section 4.5. Before we can meaningfully embark on this analysis, however, we need to look closer at the example of personal immunity before the ICC.

The chapter proceeds as follows. Section 4.2 briefly introduces the international legal rules on personal immunity and the way in which these rules have been impacted by the development of international criminal law since World War II. Section 4.3 outlines the current ICC cases regarding Putin, Netanyahu, and Hlaing, including the rules on ICC member states' duty to cooperate with the Court. Section 4.4 presents the leading precedents on personal immunity from the ICJ and the ICC. Section 4.5 conducts a "critical doctrinalist" appraisal of the ICC's approach to personal immunity by way of three recent examples: First, Section 4.5.1. studies the negotiations for The Special Tribunal for the Crime of Aggression against Ukraine. Second, Section 4.5.2 examines Pre-Trial Chamber II's decision of 24 October 2024 regarding Putin's recent visit to Mongolia. Third, Section 4.5.3 explores the reactions of ICC member states to the arrest warrant issued against Netanyahu on 21 November 2024. Finally, Section 4.6. sums up the conclusions of the chapter.

4.2 Personal Immunity in International Law and the Development of International Criminal Law

The rules on immunities are among the oldest in international law. The basic idea behind granting personal immunity to high-ranking state officials is that the individuals who are the state's most important agents in international relations should be afforded extraordinary protection. This is not for their own benefit, but because they must be able to perform their duties, including engaging in international cooperation, without undue impediments. While in office, the head of state, the head of government, and the foreign minister of a state—also known as the "troika"[6]—enjoy immunity not only for actions performed on behalf of the state but also for private acts.

Since the Nuremberg and Tokyo trials, which definitively established the principle of individual criminal responsibility under international law, the focus when assigning responsibility for international crimes has increasingly shifted towards individuals rather than states.[7] Important milestones in this development include the

---

[6] So far, the ILC has concluded in its ongoing work on *Immunity of State officials from foreign criminal jurisdiction* that only the troika—and no other ministers—enjoy personal immunity. *See* International Law Commission 2022, Chapter VI, Section C(1), article 3 (p. 190). The Nordics have expressed agreement with "...the assessments and conclusions of the ILC as set out in paras 11–15 of the commentaries that the customary rules on immunity ratione personae as they presently stand cover the Head of State, Head of Government and Minister for foreign affairs". *See* Permanent Mission of Norway 2022, p. 4.

[7] This can, for example, be illustrated by the fact that the Geneva Conventions' provisions on state liability for violations of humanitarian law are only applied to a limited extent, whereas the

UN Security Council's use of its powers under Chapter VII of the UN Charter to establish the International Criminal Tribunal for the former Yugoslavia (ICTY) in 1993 and the International Criminal Tribunal for Rwanda (ICTR) in 1994. However, the most groundbreaking event was undoubtedly the adoption of the Rome Statute of the International Criminal Court (ICC Statute) in 1998, which in 2025 has been ratified by 125 countries.

The development of international criminal law has, unsurprisingly, given rise to a number of questions concerning the immunity of state officials.[8] A state is, in principle, responsible for the actions of its representatives, which is why all state officials enjoy (functional) immunity when acting on behalf of the state. However, at the same time, the state representative is an independent subject of responsibility in international criminal law. Do the rules on immunity still apply to state officials accused of international crimes in foreign courts—or even in an international criminal court? And what does it mean for the assessment that the state's top leaders, who are often the most responsible for international crimes, are also the ones who enjoy the most extensive (i.e., personal) immunity?

As the current ICC cases involving Russia's president, Vladimir Putin, Israel's prime minister, Benjamin Netanyahu, and general and acting state leader of Myanmar, Min Aung Hlaing, make readily apparent, these are not just interesting theoretical questions. Knowing the extent of the personal immunity of state leaders before the ICC is of very real practical importance for all ICC member states, which—as outlined below—are under an obligation to cooperate with the ICC.[9] It is also crucial for the ad hoc international criminal tribunal established to prosecute those responsible for Russia's aggression against Ukraine since 24 February 2022.[10]

4.3 The ICC Cases Concerning Putin, Netanyahu, and Hlaing

As a treaty-based court, the ICC primarily has jurisdiction over crimes committed on the territory of or by nationals of a member state. In addition, however, the ICC can exercise jurisdiction if the UN Security Council refers a case to the Court, pursuant to Article 13(b) of the ICC Statute, or if a non-member state accepts the ICC's jurisdiction with respect to a particular case under Article 12(3). Given that neither Russia, Israel nor Myanmar has ratified the ICC Statute, the three cases concerning Putin, Netanyahu, and Hlaing are based on the acceptance of Ukraine, Palestine, and

---

international legal rules on the criminal prosecution of individuals have had significant practical relevance.

[8] *See also* Kjeldgaard-Pedersen 2005, pp. 19–20.

[9] As discussed further in Section 4.5.1, the issue was recently highlighted when Putin visited Mongolia in September 2024.

[10] As the focus of the chapter is on the ICC, the Special Tribunal for the Crime of Aggression against Ukraine is discussed only briefly in Section 4.5.1.

Bangladesh of the Court's jurisdiction over crimes committed on their respective territories.

On 17 March 2023, the ICC issued an arrest warrant for Russia's president, Vladimir Putin, and the Russian Commissioner for Children's Rights, Maria Lvova-Belova.[11] At the time, neither Ukraine nor Russia had acceded to the ICC Statute, but Ukraine made declarations in 2014 and 2015 granting the ICC jurisdiction to prosecute international crimes committed on Ukrainian territory since 2014.[12] On this basis, the ICC Prosecutor opened an investigation into the situation in Ukraine on 2 March 2022. The investigation covers war crimes, crimes against humanity, and genocide, but not the invasion itself—the crime of aggression. This is because the ICC only has jurisdiction over the crime of aggression if the aggressor state has ratified the ICC Statute.[13] The charges against Putin in the arrest warrant concern the war crime of unlawful deportation and unlawful transfer of population (children) from occupied areas of Ukraine to Russia.

Palestine acceded to the ICC Statute on 2 January 2015. On 21 November 2024, Pre-Trial Chamber I issued arrest warrants for three individuals: Hamas leader Mohammed Diab Ibrahim Al-Masri ("Deif"), Israel's prime minister, Benjamin Netanyahu, and Israel's former defense minister, Yoav Gallant.[14] Deif is accused of being responsible for the terrorist attack on 7 October 2023 and the serious crimes committed in connection with it, including hostage-taking and rape and other sexual assaults against hostages. Netanyahu and Gallant are broadly accused of using—between 8 October 2023 and at least 20 May 2024—starvation of civilians as a method of warfare, as well as a number of other specific war crimes (intentionally causing great suffering or serious injury to body or health, or cruel treatment, willful killing, and intentional attacks on the civilian population) and crimes against humanity (murder, extermination, persecution, and other inhumane acts) committed in that connection.

On 27 November 2024, the ICC prosecutor filed an application for an arrest warrant before Pre-Trial Chamber I regarding the "Situation in Bangladesh/Myanmar", which has been under investigation since 2019, on the basis of Bangladesh's accession to the ICC Statute in 2010.[15] According to the prosecutor, there are reasonable grounds to believe that the general and chairman of the State

---

[11] https://www.icc-cpi.int/news/situation-ukraine-icc-judges-issue-arrest-warrants-against-vladimir-vladimirovich-putin-and. Accessed 20 May 2025. Since then, arrest warrants have been issued against Sergei Ivanovich Kobylash, Viktor Nikolayevich Sokolov, Sergei Kuzhugetovich Shoigu, and Valery Vasilyevich Gerasimov. *See* https://www.icc-cpi.int/situations/ukraine. Accessed 20 May 2025.

[12] The ICC Statute entered into force for Ukraine on 1 January 2025.

[13] ICC Statute, Article 15*bis* (5) reads: "In respect of a State that is not a party to this Statute, the Court shall not exercise its jurisdiction over the crime of aggression when committed by that State's nationals or on its territory."

[14] https://www.icc-cpi.int/news/situation-state-palestine-icc-pre-trial-chamber-I-issues-warrant-arrest-mohammed-diab-ibrahim. Accessed 20 May 2025.

[15] ICC, *Situation in the People's Republic of Bangladesh/Republic of the Union of Myanmar*, PT. Ch. III, Decision Pursuant to Article 15 of the Rome Statute on the Authorisation of an Investigation into the Situation in the People's Republic of Bangladesh/Republic of the Union of Myanmar, 14

Administration Council, Min Aung Hlaing, "…bears criminal responsibility for the crimes against humanity of deportation and persecution of the Rohingya, committed in Myanmar, and in part in Bangladesh…" in 2017.[16]

4.3.1 *Member States' Obligation to Cooperate with the ICC*

Article 86 of the ICC Statute imposes a general obligation on member states to cooperate with the ICC "…in its investigation and prosecution of crimes within the jurisdiction of the Court". In addition, the ICC can make specific requests for member states to cooperate with the Court in accordance with Article 87. Article 87(7) includes a provision on the consequences of a breach of the obligation to collaborate with the ICC:

> Where a State Party fails to comply with a request to cooperate by the Court contrary to the provisions of this Statute, thereby preventing the Court from exercising its functions and powers under this Statute, the Court may make a finding to that effect and refer the matter to the Assembly of States Parties or, where the Security Council referred the matter to the Court, to the Security Council.

Article 89(1) specifically regulates requests for the arrest and surrender of a person to a state on the territory of which the person is located:

> The Court may transmit a request for the arrest and surrender of a person, together with the material supporting the request outlined in article 91, to any State on the territory of which that person may be found and shall request the cooperation of that State in the arrest and surrender of such a person. States Parties shall, in accordance with the provisions of this Part and the procedure under their national law, comply with requests for arrest and surrender.

According to Article 98(1), the scope of requests from the ICC is limited by the rules on immunity under certain circumstances:

> The Court may not proceed with a request for surrender or assistance which would require the requested State to act inconsistently with its obligations under international law with respect to the State or diplomatic immunity of a person or property of a third State, unless the Court can first obtain the cooperation of that third State for the waiver of the immunity.

The ICC Statute's provisions on cooperation have, unsurprisingly, raised the question of whether the ICC can compel member states to surrender a sitting member of the troika from a non-member state. As illustrated in the following, the ICJ and ICC appear to disagree on the answer to this question.

November 2019, ICC-01/19-27. https://www.icc-cpi.int/sites/default/files/CourtRecords/CR2019_06955.PDF. Accessed 20 May 2025.

[16] https://www.icc-cpi.int/news/statement-icc-prosecutor-karim-aa-khan-kc-application-arrest-warrant-situation-bangladesh. Accessed 20 May 2025.

4.4 The Leading Precedents Concerning Personal Immunity from the ICJ and the ICC

The question of personal immunity for high-ranking state officials was brought before the ICJ in the early 2000s. At the time, some commentators were surprised that the ICJ did not readily interpret the development of international criminal law, including individual responsibility for international crimes and universal jurisdiction, as a basis for establishing that an exception regarding personal immunity for the troika had been formed in parallel, in relation to national courts and especially before international courts.[17]

4.4.1 The ICJ's 2002 Judgment in the Arrest Warrant *case*

Arrest Warrant[18] concerned then-foreign minister of the DRC, Abdoulaye Yerodia Ndombasi, and was issued by a Belgian judge on 11 April 2000. The charges against Yerodia included serious violations of the Geneva Conventions and crimes against humanity. According to the arrest warrant, before assuming the role of foreign minister, Yerodia had incited racial violence in a series of public speeches, which led to massacres of Tutsis in Kinshasa. On 17 October 2000, the DRC requested that the ICJ annul the Belgian arrest warrant, which, according to the DRC, constituted a violation of the inviolability and immunity afforded to foreign ministers in criminal matters.[19]

In para 61 of *Arrest Warrant*, the majority of 13 ICJ judges listed the four situations where the rules on immunity do not prevent a criminal case against a member of the troika. These are prosecution 1) in the state representative's own state, 2) in the courts of a foreign state with the consent of the home state, 3) in the courts of a foreign state, provided the necessary jurisdictional competence exists, and provided the individual no longer holds the troika position, and the actions in question were committed before the term of office or are private actions committed during the term of office, and 4) in an international criminal court that possesses the necessary jurisdictional competence.

As the fourth situation is particularly relevant in the present context, para 61(4) is worth quoting in its entirety:

> [A]n incumbent or former Minister for Foreign Affairs may be subject to criminal proceedings before *certain* international criminal courts, *where they have jurisdiction.* Examples include the International Criminal Tribunal for the former Yugoslavia, and the International Criminal Tribunal for Rwanda, established pursuant to Security Council resolutions under Chapter VII of the United Nations Charter, and the future International Criminal Court

[17] *See* Kjeldgaard-Pedersen 2005, p. 214.

[18] ICJ, *Arrest Warrant of 11 April 2000 (Democratic Republic of the Congo v. Belgium)*, Judgment, I.C.J. Reports 2002, p. 3 ("*Arrest Warrant*").

[19] Ibid., para 17.

> created by the 1998 Rome Convention. The latter's Statute expressly provides, in Article 27, para 2, that "[i]mmunities or special procedural rules which may attach to the official capacity of a person, whether under national or international law, shall not bar the Court from exercising its jurisdiction over such a person". (emphasis added)

The words "certain" and "where they have jurisdiction" suggest that the majority did not believe that the rules on personal immunity were *per se* inapplicable in an "international criminal court". Rather, para 61 lists examples of international legal instruments that have set aside the customary rules on immunities in connection with the establishment of specific international criminal courts. As regards the ICTY and the ICTR, immunities are set aside due to the binding nature of Security Council resolutions adopted under Chapter VII of the UN Charter. Concerning the ICC, Article 27(2) of the ICC Statute states that "[i]mmunities or special procedural rules which may attach to the official capacity of a person, whether under national or international law, shall not bar the Court from exercising its jurisdiction over such a person". The ICJ did not address the significance of Article 27(2) vis-à-vis representatives of third states who are subject to the ICC's jurisdiction, for example because they are accused of committing international crimes on the territory of an ICC member state. Remarkably, para 61(4) has nonetheless been interpreted—including by the ICC, as discussed below—to mean that immunities are by definition set aside before an "international criminal court".[20] This reading was invoked for example by the Special Court for Sierra Leone (SCSL) on 31 May 2004, in a decision concerning the immunity of the president of Liberia, Charles Taylor.[21]

4.4.2 The ICC Appeals Chamber's 2019 Ruling in the Bashir *case*

On 4 March 2009, the ICC issued an arrest warrant for Sudan's then-president Omar al-Bashir. The ICC's jurisdiction in the case was based on a referral of the "situation in Darfur" to the ICC in Security Council Resolution 1593(2005). This led to a series of cases involving ICC member states that allowed Bashir to visit their territory without arresting and surrendering him to the ICC. The ICC's Pre-Trial Chamber found in all instances that the customary rules on personal immunity did not relieve ICC member states of their obligation to arrest and surrender Bashir to the ICC. The issue was first addressed in detail by Pre-Trial Chamber I in 2011 in a case concerning Malawi.[22] The Pre-Trial Chamber concluded, among other things, that:

---

[20] *See, for example,* Coracini and Trahan 2022.

[21] SCSL, *Prosecutor v. Taylor*, A. Ch., Decision on Immunity from Jurisdiction, 31 May 2004, SCSL-2003-01-1, para 50. As regards its own status, the SCSL found in para 39: "The Agreement between the United Nations and Sierra Leone is thus an agreement between all members of the United Nations and Sierra Leone. This fact makes the Agreement an expression of the will of the international community. The Special Court established in such circumstances is truly international."

[22] ICC, *Prosecutor v. Omar Hassan Ahmad Al Bashir*, PT. Ch. I, Decision Pursuant to Article 87(7) of the Rome Statute on the Failure by the Republic of Malawi to Comply with the Cooperation

> ...all the States referenced above have ratified this Statute and/or entrusted this Court with exercising "its jurisdiction over persons for the most serious crimes of international concern". It is facially inconsistent for Malawi to entrust the Court with this mandate and then refuse to surrender a Head of State prosecuted for orchestrating genocide, war crimes and crimes against humanity. To interpret article 98(1) in such a way so as to justify not surrendering Omar Al Bashir on immunity grounds would disable the Court and international criminal justice in ways completely contrary to the purpose of the Statute Malawi has ratified.[23]

Furthermore, the Pre-Trial Chamber concluded that:

> (...) the international community's commitment to rejecting immunity in circumstances where international courts seek arrest for international crimes has reached a critical mass. If it ever was appropriate to say so, it is certainly no longer appropriate to say that customary international law immunity applies in the present context.[24]

The *Malawi Decision* was severely criticized by several international law scholars, who questioned the soundness of the Pre-Trial Chamber's legal analysis.[25] In 2014, Pre-Trial Chamber II had another opportunity to address the issue—this time in relation to the Democratic Republic of the Congo (DRC).[26] In the *DRC Decision*, the ICC judges (one of whom had also participated in the *Malawi Decision*) based their reasoning on UN Security Council Resolution 1593(2005) arguing that the "[g]overnment of Sudan ... shall cooperate fully with and provide any necessary assistance to the Court and the Prosecutor pursuant to this resolution".[27] A few years later, in the 2017 *South Africa Decision*, Pre-Trial Chamber II again referred to Resolution 1593(2005)—although not in exactly the same way. This time the Chamber, by majority, found that "for the limited purpose of the situation in Darfur, Sudan has rights and duties analogous to those of states parties to the Statute".[28] According to the *South Africa Decision*, the resolution should be interpreted to mean that Sudan is equated with an ICC member state for the purpose of immunities, cf. Article 27(2). Commentators generally received the *DRC Decision* and the *South Africa Decision* more favorably than the *Malawi Decision*.[29] It was therefore surprising that the Appeals Chamber on 6 May 2019—when presented with the question in a case concerning Jordan—reverted to the reasoning of the *Malawi Decision*, albeit

---

Requests Issued by the Court with Respect to the Arrest and Surrender of Omar Hassan Ahmad Al Bashir, 12 December 2011, ICC-02/05-01/09-139 ("*Malawi Decision*").

23 Ibid., para 41.

24 Ibid., para 42.

25 *See* Akande 2011; Nouwen and Albanese 2009; Jacobs 2011.

26 ICC, *Prosecutor v. Omar Hassan Ahmad Al Bashir*, PT. Ch. II, Decision on the Cooperation of the Democratic Republic of the Congo Regarding Omar Al Bashir's Arrest and Surrender to the Court, 9 April 2014, ICC-02/05-01/09-195 ("*DRC Decision*").

27 *See* UNSC 2005, para 2. *See also* ibid., para 29.

28 ICC, *Prosecutor v. Omar Hassan Ahmad Al Bashir*, PT. Ch. II, Decision under article 87(7) of the Rome Statute on the non-compliance by South Africa with the request by the Court for the arrest and surrender of Omar Al-Bashir, 6 July 2017, ICC-02/05-01/09-302 ("*South Africa Decision*"), para 88. *See further* Knottnerus 2017.

29 *See further* Akande 2009; Papillon 2010.

with one significant modification.[30] In para 113 of the *Jordan Decision*, the Appeals Chamber essentially flipped the burden of proof for the existence of a customary international law on its head:

> … there is neither State practice nor *opinio juris* that would support the existence of Head of State immunity under customary international law vis-à-vis an international court. To the contrary, as shown in more detail in the Joint Concurring Opinion of Judges Eboe-Osuji, Morrison, Hofmański and Bossa, such immunity has never been recognised in international law as a bar to the jurisdiction of an international court.

In para 115, the Appeals Chamber further explained that "…international courts act on behalf of the international community as a whole. Accordingly, the principle of *par in parem non habet imperium*, which is based on the sovereign equality of States, finds no application in relation to an international court such as the International Criminal Court."[31]

In summary, the Appeals Chamber—instead of arguing that an exception to personal immunity had developed—asserted that there is generally no immunity before an "international court", as there is no state practice and *opinio juris* to support such a rule:

> The Appeals Chamber notes further that, given the fundamentally different nature of an international court as opposed to a domestic court exercising jurisdiction over a Head of State, it would be wrong to assume that an exception to the customary international law rule on Head of State immunity applicable in the relationship between States has to be established; rather, the *onus* is on those who claim that there is such immunity in relation to international courts to establish sufficient State practice and *opinio juris*. As further explained in the Joint Concurring Opinion of Judges Eboe-Osuji, Morrison, Hofmański and Bossa, there is no such practice or *opinio juris*.[32]

The reasoning is attractive, as it gets around the problem of documenting the existence of sufficient state practice and *opinio juris* to establish a new customary norm—or in this case, a new exception to an existing customary norm. Nevertheless, it raises several doctrinal questions.

[30] *See further* Akande 2019, including Dov Jacobs' and Göran Sluiter's comments. *See also* Anderson 2019.

[31] ICC, *The Prosecutor v. Omar Hassan Ahmad Al-Bashir*, A. Ch., Judgment in the Jordan Referral re Al-Bashir Appeal, 6 May 2019, ICC-02/05-01/09-397-Corr ("*Jordan Decision*"), para 115. *See also* ICC, *The Prosecutor v. Omar Hassan Ahmad Al-Bashir*, Joint Concurring Opinion of Judges Eboe-Osuji, Morrison, Hofmański and Bossa, 17 May 2019, ICC-02/05-01/09-397-Anx1-Corr ("*Al-Bashir Joint Concurring Opinion*"), paras 56–60.

[32] *Jordan Decision*, para 116. In para 103 the Appeals Chamber concludes that "Article 27 of the Rome Statute...reflects the status of customary international law". *See also Al-Bashir Joint Concurring Opinion*, para 446.

4.5 A "Critical Doctrinalist" Appraisal of the ICC's Approach to Personal Immunity

As it was rendered more the 17 years after *Arrest Warrant* (and is, arguably, not directly at odds therewith), the *Jordan Decision* is currently widely accepted—even by doctrinal legal scholars—as the leading precedent on personal immunity before international courts.[33] Tom Dannenbaum, for example, claims: "To be sure, this theory is controversial…However, the very fact of its repeated assertion by international authorities gives it weight." In contrast, some commentators continuously criticize the ICC Appeals Chamber's reasoning[34] and some even call for an ICJ Advisory Opinion on the matter.[35] The latter group—which we for present purposes might label "the critical doctrinalists"—take issue with, in particular, two interconnected aspects of the *Jordan Decision* which they find difficult to reconcile with the "true" meaning of the law. For one, the Appeals Chamber does not adequately explain how a group of states can do collectively what they cannot do individually.[36] What is the legal basis for deviating from the fundamental principle that treaties bind only the parties, not third states without their consent?[37] Second, even if we were to accept that personal immunity does not apply before "an international court acting on behalf of the international community", para 115 of the *Jordan Decision* fails to define this key notion in a satisfactory—clear and operational—manner.[38] As illustrated in the following, these legal challenges have played a key role in relation to three recent significant developments: 1) the negotiations for The Special Tribunal for the Crime of Aggression against Ukraine, 2) the ICC's reaction to Putin's visit to Mongolia in September 2024, and 3) states' reactions to the ICC arrest warrant issued against Netanyahu in November 2024.

---

[33] Dannenbaum 2022. *See also, for example*, Wanigasuriya 2024; McDougall 2023, pp. 220–223.

[34] Kjeldgaard-Pedersen 2021, including further references.

[35] Tladi 2020; Nouwen 2019. *See also* Akande 2016. Notably, Kenya did propose on behalf of the African member states that the UN General Assembly request an advisory opinion of the ICJ on "the consequences of legal obligations of States under different sources of international law with respect to immunities of Heads of State and Government and other senior officials". *See,* in this regard, Permanent Representative of Kenya 2018. This idea was abandoned, however, when Bashir was ousted as president of Sudan in April 2019. *See also* Haque 2020.

[36] *See further* Kjeldgaard-Pedersen 2021.

[37] Vienna Convention on the Law of Treaties, opened for signature 23 May 1969, 1155 UNTS 331 (entered into force 27 January 1980) (VCLT), article 34: "A treaty does not create either obligations or rights for a third State without its consent."

[38] *See further* Nuridzhanian 2024. *See also* Kjeldgaard-Pedersen 2015. Notably, para 56 of *Al-Bashir Joint Concurring Opinion,* above n. 30, defines an "international court" as "…an adjudicatory body that exercises jurisdiction at the behest of two or more states" (emphasis added).

4.5.1 *Personal Immunity before The Special Tribunal for the Crime of Aggression against Ukraine*

Soon after Russia began its full-scale invasion of Ukraine on 24 February 2022, Ukraine and allies began to discuss how Putin and other Russian leaders could be held accountable for the crime of aggression, which as mentioned in Section 4.3 is not covered by the ICC's jurisdiction. During an on-the-record meeting hosted by Chatham House on 6 March 2022, the Foreign Minister of Ukraine, Dmytro Kuleba, along with, among others, prominent international legal experts launched a declaration seeking to create a special criminal tribunal for aggression in Ukraine.[39]

Some scholars, e.g. Carrie McDougall, have argued based on the *Jordan Decision* that Putin would not be immune if such a tribunal was "international enough":

> "The broader the treaty's state membership (or endorsement) is, the stronger the argument will be that the Tribunal is also sufficiently international in nature to exclude the applicability of immunities."[40]

In contrast, the CAVV,[41] an independent committee consisting of ten international law scholars, who advise the government and parliament in the Netherlands on international legal issues contended as follows in a September 2022 report on "Challenges in prosecuting the crime of aggression: jurisdiction and immunities":

> Since the ICJ held in the Arrest Warrant case that heads of state, heads of government and ministers of foreign affairs can claim personal immunity before the national courts of other states – even if they are suspected of committing international crimes – it would seem that an international tribunal which has not been established by the suspect's home state, and which lacks a Chapter VII basis must also respect this personal immunity.[42]

Arguably positioned somewhere in the middle, Tom Dannenbaum's scholarship is noteworthy in this context because he explicates the relevance of normative coherence in relation to the question of personal immunity before international criminal courts.[43] Specifically, Dannenbaum emphasizes—following *Arrest Warrant*—that

---

[39] https://www.chathamhouse.org/events/all/research-event/criminal-tribunal-aggression-ukraine. Accessed 20 May 2025.

[40] McDougall 2023, pp. 220–223. *See also* Heller 2023.

[41] Advisory Committee on Public International Law (CAVV). *See* https://www.advisorycommitteeinternationallaw.nl/. Accessed 20 May 2025.

[42] CAVV 2022, p. 14. The Committee further notes: "If the Netherlands nonetheless wishes to support a legal development in keeping with the view of the Special Court for Sierra Leone and the International Criminal Court, it should in any event advocate a distinctive and restrictive definition of the term 'international tribunal'. It should be noted, incidentally, that in the event of such a development, high-ranking Dutch officials, in particular the prime minister and minister of foreign affairs, would also not be entitled to personal immunity before an international tribunal." *See also* CAVV 2024. Kevin Jon Heller has expressed a similar view, *see* Heller 2022.

[43] The account of Dannenbaum's argument relies in part on his oral presentation entitled PIL Discussion Group: Immunities and the Crime of Aggression - A Search for Normative Coherence given at All Souls College, Oxford University (and online) on 30

state leaders are granted personal immunity, because of the critical function they fulfill in the interest of the entire legal system. Due to the risk of abuse—in the shape of false accusations that prevent state leaders from fulfilling their crucial functions—neither the number of states involved in the establishment of a tribunal nor whether it is based on a treaty can, according to Dannenbaum, be decisive for the immunity question. Rather, the crux of the matter is the extent to which the tribunal may be said to—impartially—represent the international community. Dannenbaum appears to reason that the personal immunity of a particular state leader can be set aside if the systemic risk of abuse is genuinely dismantled. He claims in relation to the crime of aggression against Ukraine that "although a tribunal created with General Assembly approval would be well positioned to avoid status immunities, the conditions under which this could be true of tribunals without that global endorsement are less clear".[44] Whereas a critical doctrinalist approach would applaud Dannenbaum's emphasis on ensuring normative coherence, a problem remains in the lack of support for his argument in the formal sources of international law. As also implied by the CAVV, the General Assembly does not have the formal authority in the UN Charter to override the customary rules on personal immunity—which the Security Council does. In essence, the challenges to the ICC's reasoning would thus remain even if the special tribunal were endorsed by the General Assembly. In any event, a different model was ultimately adopted.

On 4 February 2025, the European Commission, the European External Action Service, the Council of Europe, Ukraine, and 37 states presented the key elements in the documents that will provide the legal foundation for The Special Tribunal for the Crime of Aggression against Ukraine.[45] The documents—specifically 'the draft bilateral agreement between Ukraine and the Council of Europe on the establishment of the Special Tribunal', 'the Special Tribunal's draft statute'[46] and 'the draft enlarged partial agreement on the management of the Special Tribunal'—became publicly available on 24 June 2025. It is readily apparent that the question of personal immunity was among the sticking points during the negotiations.[47] The adopted model largeby upholds the personal immunity of the troika before The Special Tribunal. Article 23(5) provides:

> "Where the indictment concerns a Head of State, Head of Government or Minister of Foreign Affairs, the Pre-Trial Judge shall not confirm the indictment and shall order the proceedings

January 2025. *See* https://www.law.ox.ac.uk/content/event/pil-discussion-group-immunities-and-crime-aggression-search-normative-coherence. Accessed 20 May 2025. *See further* references, above n. 32.

[44] Dannenbaum 2022, p. 873.

[45] https://www.eeas.europa.eu/delegations/council-europe/major-step-towards-holding-russia-accountable-its-war-aggression-against-ukraine_en.

[46] Hereinafter *Special Tribunal Statute.*

[47] *See also* Article 24 on "Duties and powers of the Prosecutor with respect to investigations". Article 24(4) reads: "In the conduct of an investigation concerning persons holding office as Head of State, Head of Government or Minister of Foreign Affairs during their term in office or while an appropriate waiver has not been presented to the Special Tribunal, the measures in para 3 may be taken only insofar as they do not amount to measures of constraint.". *See further* Ellis 2025.

> be suspended until that person no longer holds that office or an appropriate waiver has been presented to the Special Tribunal. During the suspension, the Pre-Trial Judge shall not otherwise act upon the indictment."[48]

Given that they deviate significantly from the *Jordan Decision*, it is pertinent to ask whether provisions on personal immunity in the Special Tribunal Statute should be read as a challenge to the ICC's approach. Article 1 of the Special Tribunal Statute, however, provides that the Tribunals' jurisdiction is "...based on the territorial jurisdiction of Ukraine". This provision could be seen as an indication that the parties do not want to categorize The Special Tribunal as "an international criminal court" so as to avoid challenging the ICC on the personal immunity issue. In the *Jordan Decision*, four out of five ICC judges found that "[a]n 'international court' ... is an adjudicatory body that exercises jurisdiction at the behest of two or more states."[49] The four judges elaborate in para 58, that "[t]he source of the jurisdiction that the court is meant to exercise is the ultimate element of its character as an international court...", and para 61 speaks of "... the advantages of an international criminal court as a court that exercises no national jurisdiction...". Thus, by explicitly and exclusively basing the jurisdiction of The Special Tribunal on the territorial jurisdiction of Ukraine, the question of whether there is universal jurisdiction for the crime of aggression becomes a non-issue, and so does the question of whether there is sufficient support from 'the international community' to override personal immunity following the *Jordan Decision.* In other words, the fact that the parties to The Special Tribunal decided to uphold personal immunity for the troika is not a direct challenge to ICC's definition of "an international court" and ensuing legal consequences as regards the rules on personal immunity.[50] In a broader perspective, The Special Tribunal Statute does, nonetheless, convey a signal that personal immunity for state leaders is still a strong norm of customary international law.[51]

That the ICC remains committed to the legal reasoning set forth in the *Jordan Decision* was confirmed when Pre-Trial Chamber II of the ICC had an opportunity to revisit "the personal immunity problem" following Putin's visit to Mongolia on 10 September 2024.

---

[48] *See also* Article 25(2). The tribunal may under certain circumstances, cf. Article 29, conduct proceedings in the absence of the accused. However, under Article 23(5), *in absentia* prosecution is not possible *vis-à-vis* the troika, because the indictment cannot be confirmed before the state leader in question has left office.

[49] *Al-Bashir Joint Concurring Opinion*, para 58.

[50] In Kjeldgaard-Pedersen 2015, I argue that the deciding factor for the legal status of a court is whether it is based on a source of national respectively international law. By this standard The Special Tribunal would be an international court.

[51] The savings clause in Article 5 of the Statute does not alter this reading, but it does testity to disagreement among the parties.

4.5.2 Pre-Trial Chamber II's Decision of 24 October 2024 in the **Putin** *case*

On 24 October 2024, ICC Pre-Trial Chamber II found under Article 87(7) that Mongolia—by failing to arrest Putin and surrender him to the Court when he visited Mongolia on 10 September 2024—had violated its obligation to comply with a request from the ICC and referred the non-compliance to the Assembly of States Parties.[52] Those seeking more guidance from the ICC on what it takes for a court to be "international enough" to disregard the customary rules on personal immunity were—once again—disappointed by the ICC's reasoning.

In its submissions to the Court of 10 October 2024, Mongolia explains at length why it disagrees with the *Jordan Decision*—essentially repeating the arguments invoked by "critical doctrinalist" scholars in response to the ICC's findings. Mongolia argues *inter alia* that there is neither evidence of general practice that Article 27(2) of the ICC Statute reflects customary international law[53] nor *opinio juris.*[54] Furthermore, Mongolia observes that the *Jordan Decision*'s reasoning relating to the concept of "the international community" does not constitute a valid legal argument, as it rests on a misinterpretation of *Arrest Warrant*, para 61(4).[55] However, even if this were not the case, Mongolia contends that the ICC "[w]ith only 124 member states…lacks universal acceptance, raising serious doubts as to whether it can genuinely be regarded as exercising '*jus puniendi* on behalf international community as a whole.'"[56] Also, Mongolia finds that "…if individual states cannot unilaterally exercise jurisdiction over a foreign Head of State, they cannot collectively delegate such authority to an international court unless the relevant third State has explicitly waived its immunity".[57]

Seemingly determined to assert the "true" meaning of the law, Pre-Trial Chamber II begins, in para 21, by recalling the rule on functional or teleological interpretation of a treaty enshrined in Article 31 of the Vienna Convention on the Law of Treaties. Having then reiterated the relevant provisions in the ICC Statute, the Pre-Trial Chamber states that Article 27 of the ICC Statute removes all international law immunities, including personal immunity, and is binding on all member states as well as states that have accepted the Court's jurisdiction, like Ukraine. The Pre-Trial

[52] ICC, *Situation in Ukraine*, PT. Ch. II, Finding under article 87(7) of the Rome Statute on the non-compliance by Mongolia with the request by the Court to cooperate in the arrest and surrender of Vladimir Vladimirovich Putin and referral to the Assembly of States Parties, 24 October 2024, ICC-01/22-90 ("*Mongolia Decision*"), para 40.

[53] ICC, *Situation in Ukraine*, ICC-01/22-89-Anx ("*Mongolia's Submissions*"), paras 19–35.

[54] Ibid., paras 46–57.

[55] Ibid., para 64: "[t]he persuasiveness of this *obiter dictum* from the ICJ is undermined by the lack of any supporting legal reasoning. It did not present any evidence for the existence of such a rule in customary international law, nor did it provide the necessary legal definitions. This lack of clarity undermines the authority of the *obiter* as a definitive legal position on the matter."

[56] Ibid., para 85.

[57] Ibid., para 86.

Chamber explains that "[w]hether these persons are nationals of States Parties or nationals of non-States Parties is irrelevant"[58] and then argues:

> 28. Therefore, any arguable bilateral obligation that Mongolia may owe to the Russian Federation to respect any applicable immunity that international law may allow to Heads of State is not capable of displacing the obligation that Mongolia owes to the Court, which is tasked with exercising its jurisdiction on grave crimes of international concern that threaten the peace and the security of the States Parties to the Statute, and even of the international community as a whole. Given its nature and purpose, such a multilateral obligation cannot be altered or superseded by any bilateral commitments that may conflict with the Rome Statute's objectives.

paras 29–30 reiterate the ICC's previous reading of *Arrest Warrant*, para 61(4), cf. above, whereas paras 31–32 explain why the ICC fulfils the criteria for an international criminal court acting on behalf of the international community as a whole. Remarkably, para 33 of the *Mongolia Decision* then returns to the arguments put forward in paras 27–28 and elaborates on what may be characterized as a dualistic hierarchy with the ICC Statute taking precedence over Mongolia's customary law obligations vis-à-vis the Russian Federation.

> When the Court, as part of its mandate to investigate, prosecute, and adjudicate 'the most serious crimes of concern to the international community as a whole', including as in the present situation alleged violations of the Geneva Conventions of 1949, which are universally ratified, requests the cooperation for arrest of an individual who is suspected of having committed such crimes, the duties a State Party has, both towards the Court and other States Parties, pursuant to the Statute supersede its horizontal relation with the State of the nationality of the sought person, regardless of whether that State is or not a State Party. This creates a system of variable legal obligations. While at the interstate horizontal level personal immunity operates according to the *par in parem non habet jurisdictionem* principle, it does not operate in the vertical relation between the Court and States Parties. The vertical nature of the obligations towards the Court supersedes traditional interstate immunity principles, meaning that States Parties must act in accordance with their obligations under the Statute, even if it conflicts with horizontal relations with non-States Parties.

Even if we did buy into the argument that Mongolia is obliged—irrespective of Article 98[59]—to arrest and surrender Putin to the ICC under the ICC Statute, it remains unexplained by the Chamber on what legal basis the 125 ICC member states—by adopting Article 27 of the ICC Statute—can do together what they cannot do individually:

> The principle under article 27 of the Statute means that a State Party would not be acting "inconsistently with its obligations under international law" by arresting and surrendering State officials, including Heads of State, irrespective of their nationality, where the Court finds to have jurisdiction. To the contrary, in the present circumstances should a State Party

58 *Mongolia Decision*, above n. 43, para 27.

59 As regards Article 98, the Pre-Trial Chamber finds *inter alia* finds in *Mongolia Decision*, above n. 43, para 35: "The latter is a purely procedural provision according to which the Court may take into account certain State's pre-existing obligations in the context of requests for cooperation. The wording and the context of article 98(1) suggests that it refers only to acts of government activities which are typically conducted abroad and are protected by the safeguards on diplomatic immunity for certain officials and buildings."

> grant personal immunity to the President of the Russian Federation for the purposes of the implementation of the Request for Cooperation, it would be acting inconsistently with its international obligations under the Statute, which may, under specific conditions, amount to a violation of international law.[60]

The ICC's insistence on the prevalence of member states' obligations under the ICC Statute over the obligations owed to third states under customary international law may be said to run counter to the systemic coherence of international law. From a critical doctrinalist perspective, it is regrettable that the Pre-Trial Chamber, on 29 November 2024[61], rejected Mongolia's request for leave to appeal the Article 87(7) Finding (including a request for an oral hearing and *amici curiae* submissions) in relation to inter alia "the interplay between Article 27 and 98, the role of customary international obligation and bilateral agreements, and the compatibility of these obligations with broader principles of international law".[62] As Mongolia stressed, "[t]hese are issues of systemic importance not only for Mongolia but for the functioning of the ICC and its relationship with States Parties and non-States Parties alike".[63] The reactions to the 21 November 2024 arrest warrant against Netanyahu provide significant support for Mongolia's point.

4.5.3 *Reactions to the Arrest Warrant of 21 November 2024 against Benjamin Netanyahu*

Immediately after the arrest warrant was announced on 21 November 2024, some ICC member states publicly declared their willingness to arrest and surrender Netanyahu should he appear on their territories. The Dutch defense minister Caspar Veldkamp, for example, stated that "the Netherlands implements the Rome Statute 100 percent" and vowed to cut off non-essential diplomatic contact with the accused.[64] EU High Representative for Foreign Affairs and Security Policy, Josep Borell, declared at a joint news conference with Jordanian foreign minister Ayman Safadi on 21 November 2024 that the ICC's decision to issue an arrest warrant against Netanyahu "is a binding decision on all states, all state parties of the court, which include all members of the European Union" and "must be respected and implemented".[65]

---

[60] Ibid., para 36.

[61] ICC, *Situation in Ukraine*, PT. Ch. II, Decision on Mongolia's requests for leave to appeal, temporary stay of the proceedings and related matters, 29 November 2024, ICC-01/22-111.

[62] ICC, *Situation in Ukraine*, Annex to the Registry Transmission of a "Request for Oral Hearing in Lieu of Written Reply" Received from Mongolia, 26 November 2024, ICC-01/22-108-Anx, para 9.

[63] Ibid.

[64] https://nltimes.nl/2024/11/21/icc-issues-arrest-warrants-israeli-hamas-leaders-netherlands-arrest-netanyahu. Accessed 20 May 2025.

[65] https://www.youtube.com/watch?v=vwSqPbgyb_Q. Accessed 20 May 2025.

Some ICC member states—including consistent and vocal supporters of the ICC—expressed themselves in rather vague terms. Norway's foreign minister, Espen Barth Eide, said that "[i]t is important that the ICC carries out its mandate in a judicious manner. I have confidence that the Court will proceed with the case based on the highest fair trial standards." Similarly, Sweden's foreign minister, Maria Malmer Stenergard, stated that Sweden and the EU "support the court's important work and protect its independence and integrity".

Given that Denmark was about to take up a non-permanent seat on the UN Security Council on 1 January 2025, it was perhaps particularly important for foreign minister Lars Løkke Rasmussen to express on 22 November 2024 that "Denmark obviously complies with its international law obligations".[66] With seemingly deliberate ambiguity, however, this statement does not specify whether the prevalent international legal obligations in question are the customary rules on personal immunity or the obligation to collaborate with the ICC. During subsequent parliamentary debates concerning the arrest warrant against Netanyahu, the Danish government has explained that personal immunities may pose an obstacle, but that the final decision on the matter is up to "Danish law enforcement authorities".[67]

Although a number of states—like Denmark—have alluded to the immunity issue without openly taking a final stance, a few states have explicitly challenged the legal merit of the ICC's approach and, on that basis, denied to arrest and surrender Netanyahu.[68] The French government—which immediately after the arrest warrant against Netanyahu called the matter "*juridiquement complexe*"[69]—subsequently expressed the following view:

> France will respect its international obligations, on the understanding that the Rome Statute requires full cooperation with the International Criminal Court (ICC) and also provides that a State cannot be required to act in a manner inconsistent with its obligations under international law with respect to the immunities of States not party to the ICC. Such immunities apply to Prime Minister Netanyahu and other relevant ministers and will need to be taken into consideration should the ICC request their arrest and surrender.[70]

It is also relevant to note that the Netherlands added a significant caveat about a week after the issuing of the arrest order. On 29 November 2024, Dutch prime minister Dick Schoof stated that if Netanyahu were to travel to the Hague to participate in meetings of the Organisation for the Prohibition of Chemical Weapons (OPCW), he

---

[66] https://www.dr.dk/nyheder/udland/loekke-reagerer-paa-arrestordre-danmark-bakker-op-om-den-internationale. Accessed 20 May 2025.

[67] Danish Foreign Policy Committee, https://www.ft.dk/samling/20241/almdel/UPN/bilag/62/2961474/index.htm. Accessed 20 May 2025.

[68] Ingber 2024.

[69] https://www.lemonde.fr/international/article/2024/11/26/mandat-D-arret-de-la-cpi-contre-netanyahou-en-france-un-malaise-au-sommet-de-L-etat-et-une-incertitude-juridique_6414735_3210.html. Accessed 20 May 2025.

[70] https://www.diplomatie.gouv.fr/fr/dossiers-pays/israel-territoires-palestiniens/article/israel-cour-penale-internationale-27-11-24. Accessed 20 May 2025. *See also* reports of a similar statement from Italy: https://www.quotidiano.net/esteri/tajani-rassicura-netanyahu-immunita-da-56c6d3b9. Accessed 20 May 2025.

would not be arrested, because the 1946 Convention on Privileges and Immunities of the United Nations[71] specifically grants immunity to representatives from UN member states when participating in meetings of UN bodies.[72]

As there this no difference from a legal point of view between the obligations of member states towards the ICC in the cases against Putin, Netanyahu, and Hlaing, it is remarkable that the immunity question received relatively limited public attention in relation to both Hlaing and Putin—even after the Pre-Trial Chamber's *Mongolia Decision.* The apparent politicization in the Netanyahu case of an issue which is essentially legal is in itself problematic from a critical doctrinalist perspective. Yet, it remains difficult to blame the governments of ICC member states for their ambiguity regarding the arrest warrant against Netanyahu when both the quality and the consistency of the guidance they receive from the ICC leave much to be desired.

4.6 Conclusion

This chapter has attempted to show—through the example of the question of personal immunity before the ICC—what it might mean to engage in "critical doctrinalism" in the field of international law. Against the background of the current cases concerning incumbent state leaders—in particular the ICC's 24 October 2024 decision regarding Putin's visit to Mongolia and member states' reactions to the arrest warrant of 21 November 2024 against Netanyahu—it is suggested that "critical doctrinalism" is not merely concerned with determining the "true" meaning of the law. Insisting on consistent and coherent legal reasoning across the board is ultimately about ensuring the long-term resilience of international law and its core institutions. As both the Mongolia case and member states' reactions to the arrest warrant against Netanyahu show, the ICC puts a strain on its relationship with even its adamant supporters when it stretches its legal mandate under the ICC Statute beyond the breaking point. In that sense, "critical doctrinalist" analysis can be seen as an approach to bringing back "beliefs in the rule of law", which the introduction of this *liber amirocum* calls for.[73] This may, of course, seem paradoxical, given that personal immunity is an obvious obstacle to accountability for the most serious crimes under international law, which is exactly what the ICC was created to ensure. Still, to exempt "international criminal courts"—without a precise definition of that notion and without attempting to document that a new customary norm has emerged—from the well-established rules on the personal immunity is hardly "an orderly fashion, following the methodology of international law".[74]

[71] Convention on the Privileges and Immunities of the United Nations, opened for signature 13 February 1946, 1 UNTS 15 (entered into force 16 September 1946).

[72] https://www.reuters.com/world/dutch-see-options-netanyahu-visit-despite-icc-arrest-warrant-2024-11-29/. Accessed 20 May 2025.

[73] Klamberg et al. 2026.

[74] Tladi 2020.

References

Akande D (2009) The Legal Nature of Security Council Referrals to the ICC and its Impact on Bashir's Immunities. Journal of International Criminal Justice 7(2):333–352

Akande D (2011) ICC Issues Detailed Decision on Bashir's Immunity (. . . At long Last . . .) But Gets the Law Wrong. EJIL:Talk! https://www.ejiltalk.org/icc-issues-detailed-decision-on-bashir%E2%80%99s-immunity-at-long-last-but-gets-the-law-wrong/. Accessed 20 May 2025

Akande D (2016) An International Court of Justice Advisory Opinion on the ICC Head of State Immunity Issue. EJIL:Talk! https://www.ejiltalk.org/an-international-court-of-justice-advisory-opinion-on-the-icc-head-of-state-immunity-issue/. Accessed 20 May 2025

Akande D (2019) ICC Appeals Chamber Holds that Heads of State Have No Immunity Under Customary International Law Before International Tribunals. EJIL:Talk! https://www.ejiltalk.org/icc-appeals-chamber-holds-that-heads-of-state-have-no-immunity-under-customary-international-law-before-international-tribunals/. Accessed 20 May 2025

Anderson K (2019) ICC Appeals Chamber resurrects controversial customary international law argument to find Al-Bashir has no immunity before international courts. ILA Reporter. https://www.ejiltalk.org/icc-appeals-chamber-holds-that-heads-of-state-have-no-immunity-under-customary-international-law-before-international-tribunals/. Accessed 20 May 2025

CAVV (2022) Challenges in prosecuting the crime of aggression: jurisdiction and immunities. https://www.advisorycommitteeinternationallaw.nl/publications/advisory-reports/2022/09/12/challenges-in-prosecuting-the-crime-of-aggression-jurisdiction-and-immunities. Accessed 20 May 2025

CAVV (2024) The long-term consequences of establishing an alternative tribunal for the crime of aggression and other options for prosecuting Russia's President Putin. https://www.advisorycommitteeinternationallaw.nl/publications/advisory-reports/2024/1/24/consequences-of-establishing-a-tribunal-for-the-crime-of-aggression. Accessed 20 May 2025

Coracini AR, Trahan J (2022) The Case for Creating a Special Tribunal to Prosecute the Crime of Aggression Committed Against Ukraine (Part VI): On the Non-Applicability of Personal Immunities. Opinio Juris. https://www.justsecurity.org/84017/the-case-for-creating-a-special-tribunal-to-prosecute-the-crime-of-aggression-committed-against-ukraine-part-vi-on-the-non-applicability-of-personal-immunities/?utm_source=feedly&utm_medium=rss&utm_campaign=the-case-for-creating-a-special-tribunal-to-prosecute-the-crime-of-aggression-committed-against-ukraine-part-vi-on-the-non-applicability-of-personal-immunities. Accessed 20 May 2025

Dannenbaum T (2022) Mechanisms for Criminal Prosecution of Russia's Aggression Against Ukraine. Just Security. https://www.justsecurity.org/80626/mechanisms-for-criminal-prosecution-of-russias-aggression-against-ukraine/. Accessed 20 May 2025

Ellis M (2025) International Law at the Precipice: Holding Leaders Accountable for the Crime of Aggression in Russia's War Against Ukraine https://www.justsecurity.org/110851/holding-leaders-accountable-crime-aggression/. *Just Security*. Accessed 20 May 2025

Haque AA (2020) Head of State Immunity is Too Important for the International Court of Justice. Just Security. https://www.justsecurity.org/68801/head-of-state-immunity-is-too-important-for-the-international-court-of-justice/. Accessed 20 May 2025

Heller KJ (2022) Creating a Special Tribunal for Aggression Against Ukraine Is a Bad Idea. Opinio Juris. https://opiniojuris.org/2022/03/07/creating-a-special-tribunal-for-aggression-against-ukraine-is-a-bad-idea/. Accessed 20 May 2025

Heller KJ (2023) The Jordan Appeal Supports a Hybrid Tribunal Denying Personal Immunity. Opinio Juris. https://opiniojuris.org/2023/02/06/the-jordan-appeal-judgment-supports-a-hybrid-tribunal-denying-personal-immunity/ Accessed 20 May 2025

Ingber R (2024) Mapping State Reactions to the ICC Arrest Warrants for Netanyahu and Gallant. Just Security. https://www.justsecurity.org/105064/arrest-warrants-state-reactions-icc/. Accessed 20 May 2025

International Law Commission (2022) Report of the International Law Commission, Seventy-third session, UN Doc A/77/10. https://docs.un.org/en/A/77/10. Accessed 20 May 2025

Jacobs D (2011) A Sad Hommage to Antonio Cassese: The ICC's confused pronouncements on State Compliance and Head of State Immunity. Spreading the Jam. https://dovjacobs.com/2011/12/15/a-sad-hommage-to-antonio-cassese-the-iccs-confused-pronouncements-on-state-compliance-and-head-of-state-immunity/. Accessed 20 May 2025

Kjeldgaard-Pedersen A (2005) Statsrepræsentanters immunitet [Immunity of State representatives], Thomson, Copenhagen

Kjeldgaard-Pedersen A (2015) What Defines an International Criminal Court?: A Critical Assessment of 'the Involvement of the International Community' as a Deciding Factor. Leiden Journal of International Law 28(1):113–131

Kjeldgaard-Pedersen A (2021) Is the Quality of the ICC's Legal Reasoning an Obstacle to Its Ability to Deter International Crimes? Journal of International Criminal Justice 19(4):939–957

Klamberg M, Svanberg K, Rönnelid L (2026). Introduction - The World Order at a Crossroads between Spheres of Influence and Rule of Law. In Klamberg M et al. (eds) Reconstructing Power and Hegemony in Public International Law, Asser, The Hague.

Knottnerus A (2017) The Immunity of al-Bashir: The Latest Turn in the Jurisprudence of the ICC. EJIL:Talk! https://www.ejiltalk.org/the-immunity-of-al-bashir-the-latest-turn-in-the-jurisprudence-of-the-icc/. Accessed 20 May 2025

McDougall C (2023) The Imperative of Prosecuting Crimes of Aggression Committed against Ukraine. Journal of Conflict & Security Law 28:203–230

Nuridzhanian G (2024) International Enough? A Council of Europe Special Tribunal for the Crime of Aggression. Just Security. https://www.justsecurity.org/96320/council-of-europe-ukraine-tribunal/. Accessed 20 May 2025

Nouwen S (2019) Return to Sender: Let the International Court of Justice Justify or Qualify International-Criminal-Court Exceptionalism Regarding Personal Immunities. Cambridge Law Journal 78(3):596–611

Nouwen S, Albanese M (2009) Arresting Bashir: How the ICC has Violated its own Statute, African Arguments. https://africanarguments.org/2009/03/arresting-bashir-how-the-icc-has-violated-its-own-statute/. Accessed 20 May 2025

Papillon S (2010) Has the United Nations Security Council Implicitly Removed Bashir's Immunity. International Criminal Law Review 10:275–288

Permanent Mission of Norway to the UN (2022) Joint Nordic comments on the International Law Commission's Draft articles on Immunity of State officials from foreign criminal jurisdiction. https://legal.un.org/ilc/sessions/75/pdfs/english/iso_nordic.pdf. Accessed 20 May 2025

Permanent Representative of Kenya (2018) Letter dated 9 July 2018 from the Permanent Representative of Kenya to the United Nations addressed to the Secretary-General, UN Doc. A/73/144. https://documents.un.org/doc/undoc/gen/n18/229/36/pdf/n1822936.pdf. Accessed 20 May 2025

Tladi D (2020). Sudan Agrees to Send Al Bashir to the ICC: What Now for the Law? Opinio Juris. https://opiniojuris.org/2020/02/12/sudan-agrees-to-send-al-bashir-to-the-icc-what-now-for-the-law/. Accessed 20 May 2025

UN Security Council (2005) Resolution 1593, UN Doc. S/RES/1593. https://documents.un.org/doc/undoc/gen/n05/292/73/pdf/n0529273.pdf. Accessed 20 May 2025

Wanigasuriya A (2024) Putin Travels to Mongolia: What Prevents His Arrest? Opinio Juris. https://opiniojuris.org/2024/09/04/putin-travels-to-mongolia-what-prevents-his-arrest/. Accessed 20 May 2025

Astrid Kjeldgaard-Pedersen is Professor of International Law at the Faculty of Law, University of Copenhagen, Copenhagen, Denmark. Her research interests revolve around the role of the individual in the international system, international law and military operations, and Nordic approaches to international law. She is the editor-in-chief of the *Nordic Journal of International Law*.

Chapter 5
Critical Perspectives in the Law of the Sea—The Regulation of Underwater Infrastructure as an Example of Facilitation and Limitation in Parallel

Martin Ratcovich Leopardi

Contents

Abstract Like international law in general, the law of the sea is prone to critique. Its contents are the result of political processes. Moreover, it includes at its core several inherently political concepts and principles. State references to the law of the sea often take place in political contexts. Nevertheless, critical perspectives are noticeably rare in law of the sea scholarship. The chapter suggests that critical perspectives may be beneficial for deeper understanding of the law of the sea. By attaching significance not only to the black letters of the law, but also to other factors that shape the impact of law, critical perspectives may aid understanding of how the law operates and is used for policy reasons. This does not mean that doctrinal analysis is meaningless or that traditional legal methods used to establish the content of the law should be altered to cover non-legal sources. Rather, critical perspectives can serve as a complement to aid understanding of political interests underlying existing rules and principles. The chapter discusses the example of the international legal regime for critical underwater infrastructure. Several recent events have resulted in calls for increased attention to this, including to the regulation under international law. Against the background of a discussion of how the existing legal framework is an example of facilitation and limitation in parallel, the chapter calls for more critical perspectives in law of the

M. Ratcovich Leopardi (✉)
Ministry for Foreign Affairs of Sweden, Stockholm, Sweden
e-mail: martin.ratcovich.leopardi@gov.se

Stockholm Centre for International Law and Justice (SCILJ), Stockholm, Sweden

M. Klamberg et al. (eds.), *Reconstructing Power and Hegemony in Public International Law*, https://doi.org/10.1007/978-94-6265-743-4_5

sea scholarship generally and a more nuanced understanding of the international law framework for critical underwater infrastructure.

Keywords Critical legal studies · Law of the sea · Critical underwater infrastructure · Submarine cables and pipelines · Maritime operations · Critical doctrinalism

5.1 Introduction

Several dichotomies are at the centre of the law of the sea—a clash of opposing interests: freedom and sovereignty, international and national, independence and subjugation, autonomy and authority, public and private, *et cetera.* States have long sought to be able to use and thrive from the seas and oceans across the globe, free from the interference of others, while at the same time maintaining the power to control marine areas around their coasts. By way of illustration, fisheries can be lucrative even when conducted far off shore as enabled by the freedom of the high seas.[1] However, the risk of naval intrusions into sovereign territory is always there, particularly when foreign ships are entitled to navigate right up to shore.[2]

The law of the sea strikes a balance between such competing interests—a balance that permeates basically all aspects of the 'legal framework within which all activities in the oceans and seas must be carried out'.[3] On the one hand, every State has the right to sail ships flying their flag across the globe.[4] On the other hand, the sovereignty of the State extends to the territorial sea,[5] far beyond what can be seen from the shore.[6] Moreover, all States have the right to overfly international waters,[7] but the airspace above the territorial sea is within the control of the coastal State.[8]

The international legal regime governing underwater infrastructure is no exception to this balance of interests. For example, the laying of submarine cables and pipelines is part of the freedoms of the high seas, but all States may establish conditions for cables and pipelines entering their territories or territorial seas. Moreover, there is limited room for protective measures amounting to enforcement jurisdiction relating

[1] The freedoms of the high seas comprise the freedom of fishing: *see, e.g.*, United Nations Convention on the Law of the Sea, opened for signature 10 December 1982, 1833 UNTS 3, entered into force 16 November 1994 (LOSC), art 87(1)(e).

[2] Ships of all States, including warships, enjoy the right of innocent passage through the territorial sea; *see, e.g.*, ibid., arts 17, 29–32.

[3] United Nations General Assembly 2024, para 6.

[4] *See, e.g.*, LOSC, above n. 1, art 91.

[5] *See, e.g.*, ibid., art 2.

[6] The maximum breadth of the territorial sea is 12 nautical miles: ibid., art 3. The distance to the horizon seen from the perspective of a person of average height standing at the edge of the beach (170 cm above sea level) is about two nautical miles.

[7] The freedoms of the high seas comprise the freedom of overflight: ibid., art 87(1)(b).

[8] Aircraft do not enjoy the right to innocent passage through the territorial sea: *cf.*, ibid., art 17.

to foreign ships. Although this limitation is sometimes conceived of as an obstacle to basic protection of underwater infrastructure, it also serves to further the use and enjoyment of such infrastructure. Similar dichotomies exist elsewhere in the international legal framework for critical underwater infrastructure, to be further discussed below.[9]

Despite the interest-driven character of the law of the sea, critical perspectives are noticeably rare in law of the sea scholarship. Although the balance of interests depicted above is standard in textbook introductions to the law of the sea, thorough research into the competing interests of States is rare.

This chapter suggests that critical perspectives may foster deeper insights into the law of the sea. There are different views on the meaning of critical perspectives and it is noted, first, that all such perspectives are relatively unusual in law of the sea scholarship. Second, it is claimed that such perspectives could help enhance the understanding of this body of law. The regulation of critical underwater infrastructure is discussed as an example.[10] Although the parameters of the chapter do not allow a full-fledged inquiry of either the general assertion—that critical perspectives may be beneficial to scholarly research in the law of the sea—or the concrete example—the international law framework for underwater infrastructure—the chapter calls for critical approaches in law of the sea scholarship and a nuanced understanding of the international legal regime governing underwater infrastructure.

5.2 Law of the Sea Scholarship is Predominantly Doctrinal

Much like other branches of international law, scholarship in the law of the sea, including international maritime law, has usually been dominated by a traditional positivist approach.[11] The law is normally taken to be neutral and underlying power relations and differences are largely ignored, to the extent they are not reflected in the generally accepted sources of law.[12] Generally speaking, the bulk of scholarship on the law of the sea deals with substantive matters of contemporary significance, such as the extent and implication of sovereignty to marine areas, the allocation of States' rights and duties in respect of the seas and oceans, and the rights of States in maritime activities and the duties owed to others when engaging in such activities,

[9] *See below* Sect. 5.4 The International Legal Framework for Critical Underwater Infrastructure—Facilitation and Limitation in Parallel.

[10] No pun intended—*critical* is a term of many meanings.

[11] At least since the nineteenth century—for an account of older times, *see* Papanicolopulu 2024, pp. 157–178.

[12] Not much has been written about law of the sea scholarship. However, The International Journal of Marine and Coastal Law has recently published a set of reflective articles on the nature of law of the sea scholarship, the origins of which are an agora hosted by the Interest Group on the Law of the Sea of the European Society of International Law at the Society's 16th Conference held in Stockholm in 2021—*see, e.g.*, Barnes 2023; Ridings 2023; Papanicolopulu 2024; Kastner 2023, pp. 793–808.

including related to the marine environment and the common heritage of mankind. By contrast, more comprehensive approaches—where the interests and power relations underlying existing rules and regulations are included as data for the purpose of answering research questions—are scarce.[13]

5.3 The Law of the Sea is Prone to Critique

In sharp contrast, critical scholarship demonstrates that the assumption of neutrality underlying traditional positivist approaches is artificial. By presupposing that the law is neutral and ignoring political factors, such approaches risk overlooking relevant information—distancing legal scholarship from reality and making its findings less relevant for solving real problems.[14]

It is easy to think that the law of the sea is distinct in some way, so that critical perspectives would be less relevant than what is generally the case in international law scholarship. However, this is not very likely—for several reasons.

First, like law in general, the law of the sea is continuously evolving and subject to development through political processes and consideration.[15] Already at its first session in 1949, the United Nations International Law Commission (ILC) decided to give priority to a key law of the sea matter, the regime of the high seas, as a topic for codification. The telling response of the United Nations General Assembly was to add another law of the sea matter to the ILC agenda, namely the regime of territorial waters.[16] The negotiations that followed, with the adoption of the Geneva Conventions in 1958—the Convention on the Territorial Sea and the Contiguous Zone, the Convention on the High Seas, the Convention on Fishing and Conservation of the Living Resources of the High Seas, and the Convention on the Continental Shelf—were packed with political interest, including developments of customary law in parallel with the treaty negotiations.[17] The processes leading to the entry into force

[13] However, there are examples of innovative perspectives. *See, e.g.*, Papanicolopulu 2019; Rayfuse 2015. *See also* Miéville 2005, pp. 197–224.

[14] For more thorough discussions of critical scholarship, *see* the contributions of Rönnelid 2026 and Kjeldgaard-Pedersen 2026.

[15] *See, e.g.*, Wrange 2003, p. 40: 'The saying that international law is "dynamic" can be used to justify anything. But, it is a relevant truism that international law is not only a system of valid law (which has to be frozen every time the question "what is valid law" is to be answered). It is also a developing system, and the lawyers as actors take part in that development.'

[16] United Nations General Assembly 1949.

[17] Convention on the Territorial Sea and the Contiguous Zone, opened for signature 29 April 1958, 516 UNTS 205 (entered into force 10 September 1964); Convention on the High Seas, opened for signature 29 April 1958, 450 UNTS 11 (entered into force 30 September 1962); Convention on Fishing and Conservation of the Living Resources of the High Seas, opened for signature 29 April 1958, 559 UNTS 285 (entered into force 20 March 1966); Convention on the Continental Shelf, opened for signature 29 April 1958, 499 UNTS 311 (entered into force 10 June 1964).

of the LOSC were no different in this regard.[18] The presence of political interests in the development of the modern law of the sea was not a novelty; there had been clear State interests in this field of law in the past as well. The Dutchman Hugo Grotius' foundational work, *Mare Liberum*, was to a large extent a defence of the Dutch East Indian Company, and the main opponent, the Englishman John Selden, in his work *Mare Clausum*, defended far-reaching British claims.[19] Contemporary developments are no different. Major political forces and interests are present and at play in the processes concerning the Agreement under the United Nations Convention on the Law of the Sea on the Conservation and Sustainable Use of Marine Biological Diversity of Areas Beyond National Jurisdiction (BBNJ Agreement),[20] the negotiations within the International Sea-Bed Authority (ISA)[21] and the work of the Commission on the Limits of the Continental Shelf (CLCS).[22] Another example is the so-called omnibus resolution on oceans and the law of the sea, which has become one of the bulkiest resolutions adopted on an annual basis by the General Assembly.[23] Given the presence of political interests throughout the development of the law of the sea, it may seem a little odd that academic endeavours in this field tend to turn a blind eye to political factors.

Second, the law of the sea includes at its core several inherently political concepts and principles. The principle of sovereignty, the principle of freedom and the principle of the common heritage of mankind, as well as more specific principles, such as the

---

[18] For general accounts of the codification of the law of the sea, *see, e.g.*, Rothwell and Stephens 2010, pp. 6–14; Tanaka 2019, pp. 26–37.

[19] *See, e.g.*, Treves 2015, p. 4; Churchill and Lowe 1999, p. 4; Wendel 2007, p. 8.

[20] Agreement under the United Nations Convention on the Law of the Sea on the Conservation and Sustainable Use of Marine Biological Diversity of Areas Beyond National Jurisdiction, opened for signature 20 September 2023, not yet in force, BBNJ Agreement. See below n. 24 and accompanying text.

[21] For example, at the 29th session of the ISA Assembly, held in June–August 2024, some thirty member States called for a precautionary pause or moratorium on deep seabed mining: *see generally* https://deep-sea-conservation.org/solutions/no-deep-sea-mining/momentum-for-a-moratorium/governments-and-parliamentarians/. Accessed 10 October 2024. The background was a request by Nauru pursuant to the so-called two-year rule contained in the Agreement relating to the Implementation of Part XI of the United Nations Convention on the Law of the Sea of 10 December 1982, opened for signature 28 July 1994, 1836 UNTS 3 (entered into force 16 November 1994), Annex, Section 1(15)(b), by which the ISA was to complete the adoption of exploitation regulations within a prescribed time of two years. Pursuant to Section 1(15)(c) of the same Agreement, if the ISA did not manage to finalise the exploitation regulations by July 2023, mining operators could nevertheless submit applications for the approval of a plan of work for exploitation, which the Council of the ISA would have to consider despite the absence of the regulations.

[22] For example, in July 2024 China submitted a letter to the CLCS claiming it has 'indisputable sovereignty' over certain features and marine areas involved in a preceding submission by Vietnam and requested the CLCS not to consider the claim by Vietnam as this 'seriously infringes on China's sovereignty, sovereign rights and jurisdiction in the South China Sea.' Soon thereafter, Vietnam submitted a letter by which it 'resolutely rejects … China's [letter]'. *See* Permanent Mission of the People's Republic of China to the United Nations 2024; Permanent Mission of the Socialist Republic of Viet Nam to the United Nations 2024.

[23] *See, e.g.*, United Nations General Assembly 2023.

precautionary principle and the principle of equity and the fair and equitable sharing of benefits, are all filled with political interests and controversies. This was very clear in the processes leading up to the BBNJ Agreement, where the provision setting forth general principles and approaches for the achievement of the objectives of the Agreement remained contentious until the very end of the negotiations.[24]

Third, State references to the law of the sea often take place in very political contexts. Examples include Türkiye's recurring statements regarding the status of the LOSC,[25] China's references to historical circumstances[26] and maritime powers' traditional emphasis on navigational rights and freedoms. These can all be examined from the perspective of contemporary disputes and contestations.[27]

Like in other areas of law, critical perspectives may help to reveal political interests underlying existing rules and principles of the law of the sea. By being attentive not only to the black letters of the law and what is covered by the accepted sources of law, but also to other factors that shape and influence the impact of law, critical perspectives may aid an understanding of how the law operates and is used for policy reasons. A more nuanced appreciation of the meaning and function of existing law may, for natural reasons, be beneficial also for normative considerations in respect of future law. It may help 'reveal some of the law's inherent biases, hegemonic tendencies and power relations'.[28]

Although a more comprehensive and inclusive research agenda may increase knowledge about the law of the sea, this does not mean that conventional scholarship is necessarily obsolete or pointless. For example, legal doctrinal analysis may still serve vital purposes for critical research endeavours. Depending on context, it may also be more useful for specific purposes; for example, doctrinal arguments often have a prominent place in international courts and tribunals. The argument put forward here is not that traditional legal methods used to establish the content of law must be altered and expanded to cover also non-legal sources. Rather, the argument is that such findings can be complemented by attention to political interests, for example how the law reflects and promotes certain interests over others. The principal purpose remains to better understand the law—what it means and how it works. For reasons of

[24] BBNJ Agreement, above n. 20, art 7. For an account of the final stages of the negotiations, *see* Kantai et al. 2023.

[25] For example, Türkiye has repeatedly called for a vote and voted against the adoption of the omnibus resolution on oceans and the law of the sea. By way of explanation, it has been stated that Türkiye is not a party to the LOSC, above n. 1, and that Türkiye does not agree with references in the resolution to the LOSC having a 'universal and unified character' and that the LOSC 'sets out the legal framework within which all activities in the oceans and seas must be carried out'. *See, e.g.*, Permanent Mission of Türkiye to the United Nations 2023.

[26] *See, e.g.*, Ministry of Foreign Affairs of the People's Republic of China 2015. *See also* the *South China Sea Arbitration*, in which the Arbitral Tribunal declared *inter alia* that 'China's claims to historic rights … are contrary to the [LOSC] and without lawful effect'. Arbitral Tribunal Constituted Under Annex VII to the 1982 United Nations Convention on the Law of the Sea, *South China Sea Arbitration*, Award, 12 July 2016, PCA Case N° 2013–19, p. 473.

[27] *See generally* Jia 2017; Mahmoudi 1989, p. 157.

[28] Kastner 2023.

illustration, the following section discusses the international legal regime governing critical underwater infrastructure.

5.4 The International Legal Framework for Critical Underwater Infrastructure—Facilitation and Limitation in Parallel

Despite increasing use of the term 'critical underwater infrastructure', it has no uniform legal definition. The law of the sea contains detailed rules on submarine cables and pipelines, on the one hand, and artificial islands, installations and structures, on the other. These are distinct concepts but arguably encompass what in colloquial usage is generally meant by 'critical underwater infrastructure'. Importantly, the notion of 'critical' is largely irrelevant to the relevant legal framework—the law of the sea makes no significant difference between infrastructure serving critical purposes and infrastructure that does not.

Underwater infrastructure within the territorial sea is generally subject to the sovereignty of the coastal State over the territorial sea.[29] Although ships of all States enjoy the right of innocent passage through the territorial sea, the passage of a ship that engages in 'any act aimed at interfering with any systems of communication or any other facilities or installations of the coastal State' is prejudicial to the peace, good order or security of the coastal State, which renders the passage non-innocent.[30] The coastal State may take the necessary steps in its territorial sea to prevent passage that is not innocent.[31] Moreover, the coastal State is expressly permitted to adopt laws and regulations relating to innocent passage through the territorial sea in respect of the protection of cables and pipelines.[32] Although this is not an exhaustive description of all issues regarding underwater infrastructure in the territorial sea, it suffices for the assertion that the legal regulation of underwater infrastructure in the territorial sea is fairly straightforward from a law of the sea perspective. The situation in international waters is a different story.

To start with, the freedom of the high seas comprises the freedom to lay submarine cables and pipelines.[33] Although the 1884 Convention for the Protection of Submarine Telegraph Cables did not contain a clear provision to this end,[34] there are good reasons to believe that a right for all States to lay submarine cables in the high

[29] *Cf.* LOSC, above n. 1, art 2.1, recognizing that the sovereignty of the coastal State extends to the territorial sea.

[30] Ibid., article 19(2)(k).

[31] Ibid., article 25.1.

[32] Ibid., article 21(1)(c).

[33] Ibid., article 87.1.

[34] Convention for the Protection of Submarine Telegraph Cables, opened for signature 14 March 1884, 163 CTS 241 (entered into force 1 May 1888).

seas existed even prior to the adoption of the 1958 Convention on the High Seas,[35] which expressly included among the freedoms of the high seas the laying of not only submarine cables but also pipelines.[36] Furthermore, all States have the right to lay submarine cables and pipelines also on the continental shelf,[37] though the course of pipelines is subject to the consent of the coastal State.[38] Naturally, none of the laying rights and freedoms stands unlimited, but all are subject to various obligations to pay due regard. Such obligations may relate to, inter alia, the interests of other States in their exercise of the freedoms of the high seas,[39] to activities in the area[40] or to cables or pipelines already in position.[41]

'Artificial islands, installations and structures' make up a different concept, subject to other regulation. Although their erection is among the freedoms of the high seas,[42] only the coastal State has jurisdiction over them in the exclusive economic zone.[43] This puts artificial islands, installations and structures in a distinctly different legal position than submarine cables and pipelines, with the latter generally involving more complex issues concerning State jurisdiction. For example, according to the International Law Association Committee on Submarine Cables and Pipelines under International Law (ILA Committee), the extent to which the State laying the cable or pipeline, or the State of nationality of the private owner or operator of the cable or pipeline, as the case may be, has jurisdiction over a cable or pipeline is not clear. Furthermore, according to the ILA Committee, it is unclear what powers, if any, the coastal State has over cables and pipelines that simply pass its continental shelf, as opposed to ones that enter its territory or territorial sea or that connect artificial islands, installations and structures under its jurisdiction. In addition to the various legal intricacies arising from the multi-faceted involvement of non-state actors in the laying and operation of submarine cables and pipelines, the uncertainty regarding jurisdiction over such cables and pipelines is one of the main issues identified as meriting further consideration by the ILA Committee.[44]

Although there are clearly many legal intricacies related to other aspects of underwater infrastructure, security issues have come at the forefront of political concern.

---

[35] For example, in 1927, the Institut de Droit International recognized that freedom of the high seas includes the freedom to lay submarine cables: *see* International Law Association Committee on Submarine Cables and Pipelines under International Law 2020, paras 32, 57 and further references there.

[36] Convention on the High Seas, above n. 17, article 2. *See also* LOSC, above n. 1, articles 87 and 112.

[37] Ibid., article 79.1.

[38] Ibid., article 79.3.

[39] Ibid., article 87.2.

[40] Ibid.

[41] Ibid., article 79.5.

[42] Ibid., article 87.2.

[43] Ibid., article 60.1.

[44] *See, e.g.*, International Law Association Committee on Submarine Cables and Pipelines under International Law 2020, paras 28–29, 75. *See also* International Law Association Committee on Submarine Cables and Pipelines under International Law 2024, paras 10, 182–186.

Several recent events, such as the explosions on the Nord Stream pipelines in 2022 and multiple cuts to cables and pipelines in the Baltic Sea thereafter, have drawn attention to the vulnerability of critical underwater infrastructure.[45] Consequently, the international community has called for improved protection of 'offshore installations, submarine cables and pipelines and other critical infrastructure'.[46] The call of the General Assembly encompasses more than legal matters but the international law framework has attracted more interest than before. The ILA Committee is a case in point. Established in 2018, the Committee has thus far produced three interim reports, providing a general survey of the law as well as analyses of the differences between marine scientific research and surveys for laying cables and pipelines, and the measures that States can take in response to intentional acts of damage.[47] Although the Committee is still active, it is already clear from the work it has concluded that there are many complex legal issues regarding underwater infrastructure. Another clear example is the plea of the Baltic Sea NATO Allies in 2025 to 'identify further measures in accordance with international law of the sea, including the freedom of navigation, to prevent and effectively respond to wilful damaging of critical undersea infrastructure or irresponsible behaviour'.[48]

A characteristic feature of critical underwater infrastructure is the comparatively low level of public authority and control. Most of the infrastructure is owned by private entities, which often have the main expertise and technical capacities, triggering questions about whether individuals can acquire rights directly under international law.[49] Going back to the negotiations preceding the introduction of these rules, a central interest was to facilitate the use of submarine cables and pipelines.[50] However, a competing interest was the ability of coastal States to protect themselves against threats associated with cables and pipelines. This was clear in the negotiations that would result in the compromise reflected in Article 79.3 LOSC, pursuant

[45] Examples include the Finland-Estonia Baltic Connector gas pipeline, the Sweden-Lithuania BCS East West Interlink data cable, the Finland-Germany C-Lion1 data cable and the Finland-Estonia Estlink 2 power cable. *See also* ibid., para 5.

[46] United Nations General Assembly 2023, para 118. *See also* NATO 2023: 'any deliberate attack against Allies' critical infrastructure … including critical undersea infrastructure, will be met with a united and determined response'; Council of the European Union 2023, p. 29: 'Protecting critical infrastructure in the maritime domain is a key priority'; Baltic Sea NATO Allies 2025: 'We are deeply concerned by actions, be they negligent or malicious, which cause damage to or threaten the functioning of critical undersea infrastructure … Any attack against our infrastructure will be met with a robust and determined response'.

[47] *See generally* https://www.ila-hq.org/en_GB/committees/submarine-cables-and-pipelines-under-international-law. Accessed 9 September 2024.

[48] Baltic Sea NATO Allies 2025.

[49] The main view among the members of the ILA Committee is that individuals do not acquire such rights under international law: *see* International Law Association Committee on Submarine Cables and Pipelines under International Law 2020, para 19.

[50] *Cf.* Convention for the Protection of Submarine Telegraph Cables, above n. 34, preamble: 'being desirous to secure the preservation of telegraphic communications made by means of submarine cable'.

to which the delineation of the course for the laying of pipelines on the continental shelf is subject to the consent of the coastal State.[51]

Recognising the presence of such competing interests in the legal framework, it should be no surprise that the room for enforcement action is carefully limited. Succinctly, the ILC noted in its commentary to the 1958 Convention on the High Seas that 'the law of the high seas contains certain rules ... which are designed, not to limit or restrict the freedom of the high seas, but to safeguard its exercise in the interest of the entire international community'.[52] It is for precisely this reason that the law of the sea not only provides for unlimited powers to lay and operate submarine cables and pipelines, but also sets firm parameters for the measures that States can take on an individual basis to protect such infrastructure.

It is in this way that what first may appear to be a contradiction—facilitation and limitation in parallel—effectively promotes a joint overarching interest: to further the possibilities to lay and operate submarine cables and pipelines. For this reason, any calls for new standards and norms providing greater opportunities for the exercise of State jurisdiction to protect critical underwater infrastructure must be careful not to undermine the very community interest that such protection measures would ultimately seek to uphold: the use and enjoyment of underwater infrastructure.[53] The relevant question remains what more can be done *in accordance with the LOSC* to enhance the security of underwater infrastructure.

5.5 Appraisal

The purpose of critical perspectives in legal scholarship need not be to remove the distinction between legal doctrinal analysis and other perspectives. Rather, it is a way for the international lawyer to include considerations of how the law works—how it operates, evolves and shapes reality; the power dynamics behind the law. To call for more critical perspectives is thus not to advocate a new content of the law. Rather, it is an argument for deeper insights into the significance of the law. Or in Pål's own words: 'The liberation suggested by critical legal scholars, such as Martti [and admittedly—Pål himself], offers no new dogmas, no regime for the liberated law, only a way to liberate.'[54]

---

[51] Englender 2017, p. 622.

[52] United Nations International Law Commission 1956, p. 278.

[53] *See, e.g.*, Davenport 2012, pp. 219–220; Beckman 2014, pp. 290–294.

[54] Wrange 2003, p. 37.

References

Baltic Sea NATO Allies (2025) Joint Statement of the Baltic Sea NATO Allies Summit 14 January 2025. https://www.presidentti.fi/joint-statement-of-the-baltic-sea-nato-allies-summit/. Accessed 20 April 2025.

Barnes R (2023) Reflections on the Waters: Law of the Sea Scholarship and Practice. International Journal of Marine and Coastal Law 38:1–10

Beckman R (2014) Protecting Submarine Cables from Intentional Damage: The Security Gap. In Burnett D R et al. (eds) Submarine Cables: The Handbook of Law and Policy. Brill, Leiden, pp. 290–294

Council of the European Union (2023) Council Conclusions on the Revised EU Maritime Security Strategy (EUMSS) and its Action Plan. https://www.consilium.europa.eu/media/67499/st14280-en23.pdf. Accessed 21 October 2024

Churchill RR, Lowe AV (1999) The Law of the Sea, 3rd edn. Manchester University Press, Manchester

Davenport T (2012) Submarine Communications Cables and Law of the Sea: Problems in Law and Practice. Ocean Development and International Law 43:201–242

Englender D J (2017) Article 79. In Proelss A (ed) United Nations Convention on the Law of the Sea—A Commentary. Beck, München, pp. 618–627

International Law Association Committee on Submarine Cables and Pipelines under International Law (2020) Interim Report 2020. https://www.ila-hq.org/en_GB/documents/interim-report-of-the-ila-committee-on-submarine-cables-and-pipelines-15-sept-final. Accessed 20 October 2024

International Law Association Committee on Submarine Cables and Pipelines under International Law (2024) [Third] Interim Report 2024. https://www.ila-hq.org/en_GB/documents/ilathi-1-1. Accessed 20 October 2024

Jia BB (2017) Part III: Straits Used for International Navigation. In Proelss A (ed) United Nations Convention on the Law of the Sea: A Commentary. Beck, München, pp. 272–333

Kantai T et al. (2023) Summary of the Resumed Fifth Session of the Intergovernmental Conference on an International Legally Binding Instrument under the UN Convention on the Law of the Sea on the Conservation and Sustainable Use of Marine Biodiversity of Areas Beyond National Jurisdiction: 20 February–4 March 2023. Earth Negotiations Bulletin 25(250):1–19. https://enb.iisd.org/marine-biodiversity-beyond-national-jurisdiction-bbnj-igc5-resumed-summary. Accessed 11 October 2024

Kastner P (2023) Teaching Law of the Sea from a Critical Perspective. International Journal of Marine and Coastal Law 38:793–808

Kjeldgaard-Pedersen (2026) Personal Immunity before the International Criminal Court. In Klamberg M et al. (eds), Reconstructing Power and Hegemony in Public International Law. Liber Amicorum Pål Wrange. T.M.C. Asser Press, The Hague

Mahmoudi S (1989) Customary International Law and Transit Passage. Ocean Development and International Law 20:157–174

Miéville C (2005) Between Equal Rights. Brill, Leiden

Ministry of Foreign Affairs of the People's Republic of China (2015) Statement . . . on the Award on Jurisdiction and Admissibility of the South China Sea Arbitration by the Arbitral Tribunal Established at the Request of the Republic of the Philippines. https://www.mfa.gov.cn/eng/zy/gb/202405/t20240531_11367307.html. Accessed 16 August 2024

NATO (2023) Vilnius Summit Communiqué. https://www.nato.int/cps/en/natohq/official_texts_217320.htm. Accessed 21 October 2024

Papanicolopulu I (ed) (2019) Gender and the Law of the Sea. Brill, Leiden

Papanicolopulu I (2024) The Law of the Sea in Past Scholarship. International Journal of Marine and Coastal Law 39:157–178

Permanent Mission of the People's Republic of China to the United Nations (2024) Communication dated 29 July 2024. https://www.un.org/depts/los/clcs_new/submissions_files/vnm95_24/20240729ChnNvUn001E.pdf. Accessed 18 September 2024

Permanent Mission of the Socialist Republic of Viet Nam to the United Nations (2024) Communication dated 18 September 2024. https://www.un.org/depts/los/clcs_new/submissions_files/vnm95_24/20240918VietNamNVSGCLCSEN.pdf. Accessed 18 September 2024
Permanent Mission of Türkiye to the United Nations (2023) Explanation of Position and Vote by Türkiye at the 78th General Assembly on 'Sustainable Fisheries' and 'Oceans and the law of the sea'. https://estatements.unmeetings.org/estatements/10.0010/20231205150000000/wkdJHGrGyFSb/a6W0MfC6dzsJ_en.pdf. Accessed 16 August 2024
Rayfuse R (2015) Some Reflections on What's Wrong with the Law of the Sea. In Ryngaert C et al. (eds), What's Wrong with International Law? Liber Amicorum A.H.A. Soons. Brill, Leiden, pp. 13–29
Ridings PJ (2023) The Influence of Scholarship on the Shaping and Making of the Law of the Sea. International Journal of Marine and Coastal Law 38:11–38
Rothwell DR and Stephens T (2010) The International Law of the Sea. Hart, Oxford
Rönnelid L (2026) Critical doctrinalism. In Klamberg M et al. (eds), Reconstructing Power and Hegemony in Public International Law. Liber Amicorum Pål Wrange. T.M.C. Asser Press, The Hague
Tanaka Y (2019) The International Law of the Sea, 3rd edn. Cambridge University Press, Cambridge
Treves T (2015) Historical Development of the Law of the Sea. In Rothwell D R et al. (eds), The Oxford Handbook of the Law of the Sea. Oxford University Press, Oxford, pp. 1–23
United Nations General Assembly (1949) Recommendation to the International Law Commission to Include the Regime of Territorial Waters in its List of Topics to be Given Priority, UN Doc. A/RES/374(IV)
United Nations General Assembly (2024) Oceans and the Law of the Sea, UN Doc. A/RES/ 79/144
United Nations International Law Commission (1956) Articles Concerning the Law of the Sea with Commentaries, UN Doc. Yearbook of the International Law Commission, 1956, vol. II, pp. 265–301
Wendel P (2007) State Responsibility for Interferences with the Freedom of Navigation in Public International Law. Springer, Berlin
Wrange P (2003) The Prince and the Discourse—Commenting and Advising on International Law. In Petman J and Klabbers J (eds.), Nordic Cosmopolitanism—Essays in International Law for Martti Koskenniemi. Brill, Leiden, pp. 33–47

Martin Ratcovich Leopardi LL.D., LL.M., is Senior Legal Adviser on International Law, Ministry for Foreign Affairs of Sweden, and Fellow of the Stockholm Centre for International Law and Justice. The views presented in the chapter are, of course, solely those of the author and not attributable to the Government of Sweden or the Ministry for Foreign Affairs of Sweden.

Part II
Constructing and Redefining Identities

Chapter 6
Re-Defining Statehood in the Face of Rising Sea Levels

Nicholas Tsagourias and Agnes Rydberg

Contents

Abstract Climate projections indicate that, within the next century, nine Small Island Developing States (SIDS) can be expected to disappear due to rising sea levels. Under traditional understandings of Statehood, a State cannot exist without defined territory. Rising sea levels therefore pose an existential threat to the SIDS set to disappear by 2100. This chapter considers the role and place of territory in the construction of Statehood, its relation to sovereignty, State continuity and State identity. It explores how we might move forward into a new era of Statehood in light of climate change-induced sea level rise by considering four different legal options: *ex-situ* nations, the creation of new artificial territory, purchasing territory and 'floating' States. The main takeaway is that international law's construction of Statehood has always responded to factual changes and the needs of the international society and, therefore, in the era of climate change, it should equally exhibit flexibility and adaptability.

Keywords Sea level rise · Statehood · Climate change · De-territorialised States · Self-determination · Territorial integrity

N. Tsagourias (✉) · A. Rydberg
University of Sheffield, Sheffield, UK
e-mail: nicholas.tsagourias@sheffield.ac.uk

A. Rydberg
e-mail: a.v.rydberg@sheffield.ac.uk

M. Klamberg et al. (eds.), *Reconstructing Power and Hegemony in Public International Law*, https://doi.org/10.1007/978-94-6265-743-4_6

6.1 Introduction

Against the backdrop of climate change, States worldwide are working to reduce its impact and explore ways to mitigate or adapt to its adverse effects. Although these efforts remain welcome, they may reasonably be seen as insufficient and delayed: many countries, notably Small Island Developing States (SIDS), are already experiencing adverse effects of climate change, including sea level rise and an increased frequency of extreme weather events. For several SIDS – which lie at or are just a few metres above sea level—rising sea levels can lead to the vanishing of their land, and—ultimately—their extinction. In fact, climate projections foresee the disappearance of 48 islands, including nine island States, by 2100 due to rising sea levels.[1]

Under the Montevideo Convention on the Rights and Duties of States,[2] 'defined' territory is considered to be a constituent element of Statehood.[3] However, what happens when the territory of a State becomes partially or entirely submerged? Does such a State lose its Statehood? If so, what happens to its sovereignty, identity and the citizenship of its people?

This chapter explores the question of how Statehood should be constructed in light of climate change-induced sea level rise and SIDS' eventual loss of habitable land. It considers the role and place of territory in the construction of Statehood, its relation to sovereignty, State continuity and State identity and then discusses four options of 'alternative' legal Statehood: *ex-situ* nations, the creation of new artificial territory, purchasing territory, and the idea of 'floating' States. The main takeaway is that international law's construction of Statehood has always responded to factual changes and the needs of the international society and, therefore, in the era of climate change it should equally exhibit flexibility and adaptability. Our discussion may also have broader implications for the understanding of Statehood in view of the emergence of de-territorialised States.

6.2 The Theory and Practice of Statehood

Article 1 of the Montevideo Convention on the Rights and Duties of States lays down four criteria for an entity to be qualified as a State under international law: (i) a permanent population; (ii) a clearly defined territory; (iii) government; and

[1] UNGA 2017. Oppenheimer et al. 2019, pp. 321–445; Camprubí 2016; Wong 2013. As Tuvalu's former PM Apisai Ielemia stated 'the climate change impact is an unprecedented threat to our nationhood. It is an infringement of our fundamental rights to nationality and statehood'. https://www.un.org/en/chronicle/article/threat-our-human-rights-tuvalus-perspective-climate-change. Accessed 4 May 2025.

[2] Convention on Rights and Duties of States, opened for signature 26 December 1933, 165 LNTS 19 (entered into force 26 December 1934) (Montevideo Convention).

[3] Ibid., Article 1.

(iv) capacity to enter into relations with other States.[4] These criteria have acquired customary law status.[5] Although these criteria describe what a State should look like, a State is more than the aforementioned factors. A State is a political, legal, economic, social, cultural and historical construct comprising of individuals and communities pursuing a shared destiny.[6] It is therefore important to take a more comprehensive look at the components of the State. We will do so in relation to territory, which is the focus of this chapter.

Territory primarily represents the physical and geographical component of a State and includes its land, territorial sea and airspace. Territory is linked to another component on the Montevideo list—that of effective government. This is because the emergence of the State as a political and legal institution relied first on the ability of a given power to control a distinct portion of territory in the physical and geographical sense, acquiring title to that territory and, subsequently, having the ability to effectuate full authority and power over that territory and its people.[7] An effective government thus denotes the entitlement of a certain authority to exercise power over certain territory, coupled with the effectivity of its exercise.

Territory is also closely linked to sovereignty, a primary attribute of States. Sovereignty denotes supreme, plenary and exclusive power.[8] Territory represents the primary domain over which sovereignty can be exercised. This means that territory is not only a physical and geographical concept but also a political and legal concept[9] denoting the scope, nature and practice of sovereign authority exemplified in the concept of territorial sovereignty. However, sovereignty as authority and power is not necessarily confined by physical, geographical boundaries.[10] The exercise of sovereignty may extend beyond a State's physical and geographical territory, as in the case of extraterritorial jurisdiction, or extend to de-territorialised spaces, as in the case of cyberspace. In these spaces, a State can exercise sovereign authority and power equivalent to that exercised over its physical and geographical territory and, consequently, re-territorialise these spaces normatively, if not physically.[11]

Be that as it may, a question that can be asked is what happens if physical territory is lost. Does this mean that the entity loses its status as a State? The Montevideo Convention does not provide any answer, but some would argue that the loss of territory would mean that a State loses its Statehood. It has been said for example that '[a] state's existence may be said to continue as such so long as an identified

---

[4] Ibid.

[5] Germano-Polish Mixed Arbitral Tribunal, *Deutsche Continental Gas-Gesellshaft v Polish State*, 1 August 1929, 5 ILR 11, pp. 14–15; Institut de Droit International 1936, pp. 185–187; Arbitration Commission of the Peace Conference on Yugoslavia, Opinion No. 1, reprinted in Pellet 1992, p. 182.

[6] Loughlin 2010, Chapter 7; Krasner 1984, p. 223.

[7] PCA, *Island of Palmas Case (or Miangas) (United States v Netherlands)* (Award) (1928) II RIAA 829, p. 840; League of Nations 1920, pp. 8–9.

[8] On sovereignty, *see* Wrange 1994, p. 350.

[9] Buchanan 2003, pp. 232–233.

[10] Krasner 1993, p. 235; Krasner 1999; Osiander 2001, p. 252.

[11] Tsagourias 2018, p. 523.

polity exists with respect to a significant part of a given territory…'.[12] Oppenheim has even stated that 'a State without a territory is not possible'.[13]

Others argue that there is a distinction to be made between the acquisition of Statehood and the maintenance of this status, such that the requirements of the Montevideo Convention only apply when determining the emergence of a State but not when determining a State's continued existence.[14] In international law, there is a strong presumption in favour of the continuity of States, even if territory or effective control are lost,[15] unless a State dissolves itself through peaceful or violent means. Said slightly differently, the international law mantra is 'once a State, always a State'—unless the State dissolves. This is because the institution of the State plays a constitutive, ontological and functional role in international law and relations[16] and because the continuity of States underpins international peace and stability.[17] Otherwise, international law and relations will become too unpredictable and uncertain. Of course, the reaction of other States and international organisations—in particular their continuous recognition—can compensate for loss of territory or effective government.[18]

There is a nexus between the continuity of States and their identities.[19] State identity can have a formal meaning but also a substantive one. It can refer to the identity of a State as a State but also to its particular State identity. The first is the set of attributes that make up a State according to international law, for example the Montevideo requirements. This identity is uniform in that all States share the same identity as States. The latter is the particular political, legal, social, cultural, historical and economic attributes that define a particular State. States, as argued above, are constructs comprising of human communities that come together to realise their individual and collective destiny. This aspect of State identity may differ between States and is an expression of a State's self-determination.[20] Although the attributes that form the identity of a State are subject to change, the question is whether a State can exhibit more or less the same formal and substantive attributes even after certain

---

[12] Crawford 2007, p. 671.

[13] Oppenheim 1955, p. 548. *See also* König 2022, pp. 33–35.

[14] International Law Commission 2024a, paras 24–25, 75. Examples of States that have lost their territory are the Holy See, which lost its territory between 1870 and 1929 when Italy annexed its lands, the Order of St. John, which lost its territory in 1798 after Napoleon expelled them from Malta, and in the case of governments in exile when their territories were occupied. *See* International Law Commission 2022, paras 112–154; Wong 2013, p. 7.

[15] Pacific Islands Forum (2023) 2023 Declaration on the Continuity of Statehood and the Protection of Persons in the Face of Climate Change-Related Sea-Level Rise, para 8. https://forumsec.org/publications/2023-declaration-continuity-statehood-and-protection-persons-face-climate-change. Accessed 4 May 2025; International Law Commission 2024a, paras 26–28; Crawford 2007, pp. 37, 55–59, 89, 667–669; Marek 1954, pp. 15–24.

[16] Tsagourias and Buchan 2021, p. 9.

[17] Green 2024, p. 144; Green 2014. *See also* International Law Commission 2024b, para 28.

[18] Crawford 2007, pp. 55–58; Grant 1999, p. 435; Stoutenburg 2013, pp. 72–76.

[19] Marek 1954, pp. 1–6.

[20] International Law Commission 2022, para 88.

disruptive events. To put it differently, the question for State identity and continuity is whether a State can still act as a State and still be that particular State after a disruptive event; for example, after its territory has gone under water.[21]

The above are important observations when it comes to SIDS because they reveal the degree of flexibility that informs current approaches to Statehood. This flexibility extends above and beyond the Montevideo criteria, with certain additional caveats in the case of SIDS. First, whereas existing approaches to Statehood respond to disruptive events which are mainly political or military—such as governmental failure or wars—the SIDS' lack of territory as the result of climate change is due to a geophysical event of global dimensions, whose cause and effects cannot be confined or attributed to the affected States. Second, the loss of territory in the case of SIDS will be total and permanent, in contrast to other instances where loss is temporary or partial.

6.3 A New Era of Statehood in Light of Rising Sea Levels

Faced with high sea level rise, several SIDS have adopted innovative strategies, such as coastal defences or polders, to ensure their own survival. However, these are short-term preventive and conservationist measures which are inadequate to stop the partial or complete submergence of their territory. The most important question is how their Statehood can be preserved even if their territory becomes partially or completely submerged. The remainder of this section considers four options intended to address this issue. They are the possibility of nations *ex situ*, the creation of new artificial territory, purchasing and leasing territory and the idea of 'floating' States. All these options are informed by the principle of State continuity endorsed by the SIDS themselves as well as the International Law Commission.[22]

6.4 Nations *Ex Situ*

Nations *ex situ* refers to a status in which a State is 'de-territorialised' or lacks land-based territory but continues its existence as a sovereign State with the associated rights and benefits. In early September 2023, Tuvalu—which is expected to be one of the first countries in the world to be completely lost due to climate change—enacted constitutional amendments including a new definition of Statehood. The Constitution

[21] For example, Art 2(1) of Tuvalu's Constitution says: 'The State of Tuvalu within its historical, cultural and legal framework shall remain in perpetuity in the future, notwithstanding the impacts of climate change or other causes resulting in loss to the physical territory of Tuvalu'.

[22] International Law Commission 2022, para 194. Most recently, the Pacific Islands Forum released a Declaration on 9 November 2023 stating: 'international law supports a presumption of continuity of statehood and does not contemplate its demise in the context of climate change-related sea-level rise'. *See* Pacific Islands Forum 2023, above n. 15, paras 12–13.

of Tuvalu Bill 2022 stipulates that '[t]he State of Tuvalu within its historical, cultural and legal framework shall remain in perpetuity in the future, notwithstanding the impacts of climate change or other causes resulting in loss to the physical territory of Tuvalu'.[23]

The Tuvaluan Foreign Minister Simon Kofe announced during COP27 that Tuvalu will become the First Digital Nation, as a solution to secure its survival. Accordingly, Tuvalu will digitally recreate its land, archive its history and culture, and move all governmental functions into a digital space. The creation of a digital nation would allow Tuvalu to retain its identity and to continue to function as a State even if it goes under water entirely.[24]

Furthermore, a permanent digital replica of Tuvalu would function as a substitute to the requirement of a 'defined territory' under the Montevideo Convention, to allow for the lawful preservation of Tuvalu's Statehood. In fact, Foreign Minister Kofe has called on all countries forming relations with Tuvalu to recognise the Statehood of the nation as permanent, even if Tuvalu loses all its land territory due to sea level rise.[25] Tuvalu's proactive stance in this regard can perhaps be explained by a statement made in 2015 by Tuvalu's Permanent Representative to the UN, Aunese Simati, saying that Tuvalu does not 'want to give the signal that we are giving up on our country. We can't be called Tuvaluans if we live in another country. We still want the world to know that we have our country in Tuvalu'.[26] Some States, including Venezuela, the Bahamas, Saint Kitts, St Lucia, Vanuatu, Niue, Palau, Gabon, and Taiwan have recognised Tuvalu's Statehood as permanent.

Tuvalu's call on other States to recognise its Statehood as permanent regardless of physical territory no doubt underscores the urgency of recognising *ex-situ* nations. Tuvalu's stance also exhibits a deep commitment to its national identity by emphasising that Tuvaluans wish to remain connected to their homeland regardless of geographical or physical displacement. This form of Statehood reflects what was said earlier: that territory is a political concept and effective government implies the ability to exercise sovereign authority and power even beyond a State's physical and geographical territory. There is also a strong focus on the continuity and identity of Statehood, with Tuvalu functioning in the same manner and exhibiting the same attributes even after losing its physical territory. Such an approach to Statehood may however be criticised by purists as being too flexible and undermining the long-standing criteria of Statehood.

---

[23] Constitution of Tuvalu, Article 2(1). https://perma.cc/PDV3-YVSB. Accessed 4 May 2025.

[24] *See* https://www.gfmd.org/pfp/ppd/19211#:~:text=Summary%3A,functions%20into%20a%20digital%20space. Accessed 25 July 2024.

[25] Friends of the Earth Australia 2022.

[26] Komai 2015.

6.5 Creation of Artificial Territory

In 2004, the Maldives started engaging in a complex form of geo-engineering by pumping sand from the seabed in order to build a new artificial island within its territorial sea. The island, called Hulhumalé, saw part of the island of Malé's population being relocated there. A new city, dubbed the 'City of Hope', was built on Hulhumalé in order to help relieve the overcrowding that currently blights Malé. The construction of man-made islands, which remain above water at high tide and which are permanently fixed to the bottom of the sea, is possible today thanks to the technological advancements of the 21st century. The problem with such artificially constructed islands is that international law does not recognise them as a 'State' or as physical, natural territory, which, for instance, would be capable of generating maritime zones.[27]

That said, the question has been raised whether a different assessment could be made regarding artificial islands built from low-tide elevation, which is a naturally formed area of land surrounded by and above water at low tide but submerged at high tide.[28] In that case, one may say that there is 'territory', albeit occasionally submerged.[29] However, the International Court of Justice (ICJ) has pointed out that international treaty law is silent on the question of whether low-tide elevations can be considered to be 'territory'.[30] Furthermore, according to the Court, there is no uniform and widespread State practice which could have given rise to a customary rule unequivocally permitting or excluding appropriation of low-tide elevations.[31]

Therefore, current law does not support a general assumption that low-tide elevations are territory in the same sense as islands, although nothing prevents future developments in this field.[32] Moreover, in the *South China Sea Arbitration*, the Arbitral Tribunal stated that 'notwithstanding the use of the term "land" in the physical description of a low-tide elevation, such low-tide elevations do not form part of the

[27] Crawford 1989, p. 279; Caligiuri 2022, pp. 27–28. Caligiuri discusses two cases: Consiglio di Stato, *Soc. Spic e Rosa c Ministero della Marina Mercantile e Capitaneria di Porto di Rimini* (1969) and *Re Duchy of Sealand* (Administrative Court of Cologne) (1978), where the Court held that an abandoned British Second World War platform attached to the seabed off the coast of the United Kingdom was not a state due to it lacking the requirement of territory which must 'consist in a natural segment of the earth's surface' and 'come into existence in a natural way'. Naturally formed islands would be capable of generating maritime zones as provided for by Article 121 UNCLOS, stipulating that an island 'is a naturally formed area of land, surrounded by water, which is above water at high tide', not including rocks which cannot sustain human habitation. However, Article 60 UNCLOS provides that '[a]rtificial islands, installations and structures do not possess the status of islands. They have no territorial sea of their own, and their presence does not affect the delimitation of the territorial sea, the exclusive economic zone or the continental shelf'.

[28] UNCLOS, Article 13.

[29] Caligiuri 2022, pp. 27–28.

[30] ICJ, *Maritime Delimitation and Territorial Questions between Qatar and Bahrain (Qatar v Bahrain)*, Judgment, 16 March 2001, 2001 ICJ Reports 40, para 205.

[31] Ibid.

[32] Ibid.

land territory of a State in the legal sense'.[33] Artificial islands on low-tide elevations are also inherently unstable, as their existence depends on fluctuating tide levels and environmental conditions.

6.6 Purchasing Territory

If a State threatened by rising sea levels purchases territory from another State, a critical question is whether the purchasing State can retain its Statehood. In the late 2000s, the Maldives was the first State to consider the idea of buying land in India or Sri Lanka as an insurance policy against climate change induced rising sea levels.[34] Furthermore, in 2014, Kiribati made a final payment on a 2,210 hectare area of land on Vanua Levu, Fiji's second largest island, in a bid to enhance its economic and social resilience to the effects of climate change.[35] The purchase was part of the Government's development plans to address economic and food security issues resulting from climate change.[36] In most cases, however, the seller State maintains formal sovereignty over the territory. For example, Kiribati's purchase of Fiji territory does not confer sovereignty over the land—instead Kiribati becomes a mere private owner of the land. In this capacity, Kiribati has the right to occupy the land subject to the purchase, extract its natural resources and construct buildings, but the territorial State—Fiji—retains sovereignty over the land.[37]

Only if the seller State renounces its sovereignty over the transferred territory, and effects this through the conclusion of a treaty, will sovereignty pass to the purchasing State. It seems then that purchasing territory is an unlikely solution to territorial extinction, as that practice is quite rare in contemporary international relations and, more critically, it does not involve the transfer of sovereignty over the leased or purchased territory.[38] It may also undermine the right to self-determination of the local population.

Another option would be for a State to retain its sovereignty over the transferred territory but allow for the self-governance of that territory by the State threatened with rising sea levels. In this case, the territory would be under the effective control of the latter State but remain formally under the sovereignty of the seller State. If territory and sovereignty do not need to coincide, as was noted above, this may be

[33] Permanent Court of Arbitration, *South China Sea Arbitration (Philippines v China)*, Award of 12 July 2016, para 309.

[34] Sri Lanka and India were targets because they had cultures, cuisines and climates similar to that of the Maldives. *See* https://www.theguardian.com/environment/2008/nov/10/maldives-climate-change. Accessed 27 July 2024.

[35] Press Release, RNZ, 'Kiribati completes Fiji land purchase' (28 May 2014) available at <https://www.rnz.co.nz/international/pacific-news/245690/kiribati-completes-fiji-land-purchase>.

[36] Ibid.

[37] As noted by Crawford, to accept that a State could sell a portion of its territory to another state would undermine the principle of self-determination, *see* Crawford 2007, p. 717.

[38] Stewart 2023, p. 143.

a viable answer to the loss of territory. Joint sovereignty over a transferred territory may also be established, at the same time securing the internal self-determination of the territory's people. However, these models may require painstaking negotiations and may not prevent eventual conflicts or cessation.

6.7 Floating States

The last proposal to preserve the Statehood of sinking States is the construction of 'floating States', which can be 'anchored, towed or moved by ocean currents or winds', to replace the submerged land territory.[39] As noted elsewhere, the legal status of floating islands is very unclear.[40] One approach, alluded to by Judge Alvarez in his separate opinion in the *Corfu Channel* case, is that floating islands would be subject to the sovereignty of the coastal State.[41] They could potentially also be classified as ships and vessels, insofar as the floating islands would have certain navigational equipment 'or are fixed to the bottom of the sea when under operation but otherwise movable'.[42] Their mobility and potential to travel across different jurisdictions complicate their status, although there may be provisions for regulating their sovereign rights when moving, as in the case of warships. For critics, such fluidity will undermine the certainty and stability that territory offers to States.

6.8 Conclusion: Towards Redefining Statehood

How to approach Statehood in light of sea level rise is one of the many complex challenges facing contemporary international law. To say that States cease to exist because their territory has been submerged, even if they can still exhibit the other attributes of Statehood, would be unfair, in particular because they are not responsible for such loss and because neither their government nor their people have expressed a wish to terminate their Statehood. If their Statehood is to continue, new legal solutions need to be found.

In this chapter, we have discussed certain options: *ex-situ* nations, the creation of new artificial territory, purchasing territory and 'floating' States. These options offer potential long-term solutions, although legal and/or political challenges remain. In

---

[39] Caligiuri 2022, pp. 30–31.

[40] Ibid.

[41] ICJ, *Corfu Channel (United Kingdom v. Albania)*, Individual Opinion by Judge Alvarez, 9 April 1949, 1949 ICJ Reports 39.

[42] Caligiuri 2022, p. 30. The author discusses a Dutch Supreme Court case, which held that the fact that a houseboat was connected to mooring posts by steel shackles and could not move at all, except for rising and falling with the water level for about half a metre, did not alter its qualification as a 'vessel' and it was therefore 'movable property', *see* Dutch Supreme Court, Case No. 07/13305, Judgement of 15 January 2010, ECLI:NL:HR:2010:BK9136.

legal terms, it can also be argued that to the extent that the submerged territory once formed part of a State and there are no competing claims to such territory by any other State, it should continue to be treated as State territory. In the *Western Sahara Advisory Opinion,* the ICJ recognised title to territory by pre-colonial inhabitants who exhibited social and political organisation,[43] whereas in *Eastern Greenland,* the Permanent Court of International Justice (PCIJ) held that the standard of proof of effective control over territory is low when a claim to territory is uncontested.[44] One can also employ a legal fiction and argue that such a State still has a defined territory because partially or entirely submerged or uninhabitable territory does not cease to exist in reality.

All these options are interesting and require serious consideration but one needs to address the underlying fundamental question of how Statehood can be formally redefined to include de-territorialised States which perform State functions and exhibit State identity. This chapter has shown that international law and relations have already shown some flexibility in their approach to Statehood at the point of its creation and more critically in relation to its continuation, while still paying lip service to the traditional criteria of Statehood.

Adapting the definition of Statehood to render it future-proof to climate change challenges is the only way forward that can ensure the stability inherent to such a firmly established institution. A new definition may be criticised by purists for bringing about a fundamental paradigm shift in international law or for creating a two-tiered system of Statehood.[45] However, such criticism is unfair not only because the theory and practice of State creation and continuation—as already mentioned—have always exhibited flexibility and adaptability, but also because the threat to statehood posed by rising sea levels is serious and real. It should also be pointed out that the criteria of Statehood as formulated in the Montevideo Convention are historically and politically conjectural, reflecting the state of affairs created by the Peace of Westphalia. They project a certain conception of the State which indeed became the dominant one, but this does not mean that the criteria are immutable or that a different conception which reflects a different conjecture is not possible, in particular if that conjecture (climate change) will affect almost all States, not only the SIDS, and will define Statehood in the years to come. To put it differently, the question is whether past choices should still dictate future possibilities.

In our opinion, what is needed—if Statehood is to retain its import in international law and relations—is to reimagine Statehood in an era of unprecedented environmental change and to do so before a destructive event occurs.

---

[43] ICJ, *Western Sahara,* Advisory Opinion, 16 October 1975, 1975 ICJ Reports 12, paras 80–81.

[44] Permanent Court of International Justice, *Legal Status of Eastern Greenland, Denmark v Norway,* Judgment, 5 April 1933, PCIJ Series A/B No 53, p. 46.

[45] Stewart 2023, p. 146.

References

Buchanan L (2003) The Making and Unmaking of Boundaries: What Liberalism Has to Say. In: Buchanan A, Moore M (eds) States, Nations, and Borders: The Ethics of Making Boundaries. CUP, Cambridge

Caligiuri A (2022) Sinking States: The statehood dilemma in the face of sea-level rise. Questions of International Law Zoom-out 91:23–37

Camprubí AT (2016) Statehood Under Water: Challenges of Sea-level Rise to the Continuity of Pacific Island States. Brill, Leiden

Crawford J (1989) Islands as Sovereign Nations. International and Comparative Law Quarterly 38:277–298

Crawford J (2007) The Creation of States in International Law. OUP, Oxford

Friends of the Earth Australia (2022) Protecting Tuvalu's Statehood. http://www.foe.org.au/protecting_tuvalus_statehood. Accessed 4 May 2025

Green A (2014) Three Reconstructions of 'Effectiveness': Some Implications for State Continuity and Sea-level Rise. Oxford Journal of Legal Studies 44:201–229

Green A (2024) Statehood as Political Community: International Law and the Emergence of New States. CUP, Cambridge

Grant TD (1999) Defining Statehood: The Montevideo Convention and Its Discontents. Columbia Journal of Transnational Law 37(2):403–457

Institut de Droit International (1936) Resolutions Concerning the Recognition of New States and New Governments. American Journal of International Law 30(4):185–187

International Law Commission (2022) Sea-level rise in relation to international law. Second issues paper by Patrícia Galvão Teles and Juan José Ruda Santolaria. UN Doc. A/CN.4/752

International Law Commission (2024a) Sea-level rise in relation to international law Additional paper to the second issues paper (2022) by Patrícia Galvão Teles and Juan José Ruda Santolaria. UN Doc. A/CN.4/774

International Law Commission (2024b) Seventy-fifth session, Study Group on sea-level rise in relation to international law: Report. UN Doc. A/CN.4/L.1002

Komai M (2015) Tuvalu and Kiribati have different policies on relocation. https://reliefweb.int/report/tuvalu/tuvalu-and-kiribati-have-different-policies-relocation. Accessed 22 July 2024

König C (2022) Small Island States and International Law: The Challenge of Rising Seas. Routledge, Abingdon

Krasner SD (1984) Approaches to the State: Alternative Conceptions and Historical Dynamics. Comparative Politics 16:223–246

Krasner SD (1993) Westphalia and All That. In: Goldstein J, Keohane R (eds) Ideas and Foreign Policy: Beliefs, Institutions, and Political Change. Cornell University Press, Ithaca, NY

Krasner SD (1999) Sovereignty: Organized Hypocrisy. Princeton University Press, Princeton

League of Nations (1920) Report of the International Committee of Jurists entrusted by the Council of the League of Nations with the task of giving an advisory opinion upon the legal aspects of the Aaland Islands question. League of Nations Official Journal, Special Supplement 4

Loughlin M (2010) Foundations of Public Law. OUP, Oxford

Marek K (1954) Identity and Continuity of States in Public International Law. Librairie E Droz

Oppenheim L (1955) International Law: A Treatise. Longmans, Green & Co, London

Oppenheimer M et al (2019) Sea Level Rise and Implications for Low-Lying Islands, Coasts and Communities. In: Pörtner H-O et al (eds) IPCC Special Report on the Ocean and Cryosphere in a Changing Climate. Cambridge University Press, Cambridge, UK and New York, NY, USA

Osiander A (2001) Sovereignty, International Relations, and the Westphalian Myth. International Organization 55(2):251–287

Pellet A (1992) The Opinions of the Badinter Arbitration Committee A Second Breath for the Self-Determination of Peoples. European Journal of International Law 3(1):178–185

Stewart M (2023) Cascading Consequences of Sinking States. Stanford Journal of International Law 59:131–186

Stoutenburg JG (2013) When do States disappear? Thresholds of effective statehood and the continued recognition of 'deterritorialized' island States. In: Gerrard MB, Wannier GE (eds) Threatened Island Nations: Legal Implications of Rising Seas and a Changing Climate. CUP, Cambridge

Tsagourias N (2018) Law, Borders and the Territorialisation of Cyberspace. Indonesian Journal of International Law 15:523–548

Tsagourias N, Buchan R (2021) Research Handbook on International law and Cyberspace. Edward Elgar, Cheltenham

UN General Assembly (2017) Follow-up to and implementation of the SIDS Accelerated Modalities of Action (SAMOA) Pathway and the Mauritius Strategy for the Further Implementation of the Programme of Action for the Sustainable Development of Small Island Developing States, UN Doc. A/RES/72/217

Wong D (2013) Sovereignty Sunk? The Position of 'Sinking States' at International Law. Melbourne Journal of International Law 14:346–391

Wrange P (1994) The Concept of Sovereignty—Alive and Kickin'. Juridisk Tidskrift 6(2):350–372

Nicholas Tsagourias is Professor of International Law at the University of Sheffield. He is also Visiting Professor at the Paris School of International Affairs, Sciences Po, and Senior Fellow at the West Point Military Academy. His research interests are in the fields of international law and the use of force, international humanitarian law, international criminal law, and cybersecurity and he has published widely across these fields. Professor Tsagourias is Co-Editor In Chief of the Journal of Conflict and Security Law (OUP) and General Editor of the Elgar Series on New Technologies and International Law.

Agnes Rydberg is Lecturer in International Law at the University of Sheffield. Her research interests are in the fields of the law of treaties, international environmental law, maritime dispute settlement, climate change law and climate change litigation. She has published extensively on these areas. Agnes is the Deputy Director of the Sheffield Centre for International and European Law. She holds a PhD in Public International Law from Queen Mary University of London, where she also completed an LLM. She also has a BSc in International Law from Orebro University in Sweden. Dr Rydberg is a General Editor of the Elgar Series on Principles of International Environmental Law.

Chapter 7
International Law from Below—The Case of *Klimaseniorinnen*, Climate Change, and Human Rights

Jonas Ebbesson

Contents

Abstract This article explores the nexus of international law on climate change and human rights, and argues that the numerous climate lawsuits around the world transform the application, implementation, and enforcement of international law on climate change. It describes how the two tracks of international law, on climate change and human rights, have developed and how they now converge, as revealed by the 2024 judgment of the European Court of Human Rights in the case *Klimaseniorinnen Schweiz and Others v Switzerland*. This ruling, as well as the numerous national climate lawsuits, show the dynamic and complexity of international law on climate change. They also show how international law is applied on several levels and at different scales simultaneously—not only in global contexts, but also in national cases, and not only top-down, but also from below. Thus, *Klimaseniorinnen* illustrates how different fields of international law—on climate change, human rights, and participatory rights in environmental matters—can be integrated, rather than fragmented.

J. Ebbesson (✉)
Department of Law, Stockholm University, Stockholm, Sweden
e-mail: jonas.ebbesson@juridicum.su.se

M. Klamberg et al. (eds.), *Reconstructing Power and Hegemony in Public International Law*, https://doi.org/10.1007/978-94-6265-743-4_7

Keywords International law · Climate change · Human rights · Environment protection · Klimaseniorinnen Schweiz · European Convention on Human Rights · Aarhus Convention · Integration of law

7.1 International Law, Climate Change, and Human Rights

The impact of climate change on human rights is old news. This connection has been discussed since the 1990s—and the two fields of climate change and human rights have since then become more and more intertwined in international law and policy. Yet it was not until 2024 and the ruling of the European Court of Human Rights (ECtHR) in *Klimaseniorinnen Schweiz and Others v Switzerland* (*Klimaseniorinnen*)[1] that the climate change and human rights nexus was confirmed by an international human rights court, and a state was found to violate human rights by not taking sufficient measures to prevent climate change.

In this article, I briefly sketch how international law on climate change and human rights, respectively, developed before *Klimaseniorinnen.* I then use the ruling to show how the two tracks merge and how international law operates from above *and* below.

Both the international concerns for climate change and the international acknowledgement of a human right in relation to climate change can be traced back to the 1972 UN Conference on the Human Environment in Stockholm in 1972 (Stockholm Conference).[2]

It has been somewhat ignored that the 1972 Stockholm Action Plan on the Human Environment—adopted 20 years before the global treaty regime on climate change would be agreed—recommends governments to be mindful of activities in which there is an appreciable risk of *effects on climate.* To that end, they are asked to "[c]arefully evaluate the likelihood and magnitude of climatic effects and disseminate their findings to the maximum extent feasible before embarking on such activities" and to "[c]onsult fully other interested States when activities carrying a risk are being contemplated or implemented".[3] This Recommendation did not engender much international activity, and it would take another decade and a half before climate change was really on the international policy agenda.

The human rights outcome of the Stockholm Conference has been much more noticed and discussed. Through the Stockholm Declaration on the Human Environment, it was agreed for the first time, at the global scale, that:

> Man has the fundamental right to freedom, equality and adequate conditions of life, in an environment of a quality that permits a life of dignity and well-being.[4]

---

[1] ECtHR, *Verein Klimaseniorinnen Schweiz and Others v. Switzerland*, Judgment, 9 April 2004, Application No 53600/20 (*Klimaseniorinnen Schweiz and Others v. Switzerland*).

[2] United Nations Conference on the Human Environment 1972.

[3] Ibid., Action Plan for the Human Environment, p. 20, Recommendation 70.

[4] Ibid., Stockholm Declaration on the Human Environment, p. 4, Principle 1.

This bold and radical message did not really reflect international law at the time, nor did it result in much activity or policy right away. Yet, in hindsight, it is clear that the Stockholm Declaration has had a significant impact on the development of international law on human rights and the environment—and for the climate change and human rights nexus as well. That said, the road from Stockholm to Strasbourg has been quite bumpy, and it involves both regional tracks and global routes, not least via Rio de Janeiro.[5]

7.2 The Climate Change Track

Despite the Recommendation on "climatic effects" in the 1972 Action Plan, it was not until the second half of the 1980s that things started to change. In 1988, the UN General Assembly (UNGA) recognized climate change as a common concern for mankind and initiated several activities in the UN organization.[6] At that time, the Intergovernmental Panel on Climate Change (IPCC) was established as the world's leading framework for governments, scientists, and others to provide authoritative scientific assessments on climate change. The IPCC reports have been important for climate lawsuits, also with respect to human rights.

As indicated by its title, the UN Framework Convention on Climate Change (UNFCCC),[7] adopted at the UN Conference on Environment and Development in Rio de Janeiro 1992, was to become *the global framework* for negotiations, decision-making, and law-making on climate change. The UNFCCC provides the procedural and institutional basis for long-term cooperation and sets out important principles and concepts to that end. It is also from the UNFCCC that more detailed obligations and regulations have been developed through new treaties—the 1997 Kyoto Protocol[8] and the 2015 Paris Agreement[9]—and decisions by the Conference of the Parties (COP). Today, the Paris Agreement is the key treaty for defining states' legal obligations to respond to climate change. Still, it does not oblige the parties to reduce their emissions of greenhouse gases by a certain rate or to take specific measures to mitigate or adapt to climate change.

Instead, they are obliged to undertake "ambitious efforts" through nationally determined contributions (NDC), with a view of achieving the purpose of the Agreement.[10]

[5] Ebbesson 2022.

[6] UNGA 1988.

[7] United Nations Framework Convention on Climate Change, opened for signature 9 May 1992, 1771 UNTS 107 (entered into force 21 March 1994).

[8] Kyoto Protocol to the United Nations Framework Convention on Climate Change, opened for signature 11 December 1997, 2303 UNTS 162 (entered into force 16 February 2005).

[9] Paris Agreement, opened for signature 12 December 2015, 3156 UNTS 79 (entered into force 4 November 2016).

[10] Ibid., Article 3.

Lacking a clear obligation on the degree or speed of greenhouse gas emission reductions, the overall aim set out in the Paris Agreement, i.e., of "[h]olding the increase in the global average temperature to well below 2°C above pre-industrial levels and pursuing efforts to limit the temperature increase to 1.5°C above pre-industrial levels",[11] has become all the more important as a benchmark and point of reference for the parties' action when determining and reviewing their NDCs—and their responsibilities in climate lawsuits.

There is not a word about human rights in the UNFCCC, and it was only at the climate summit in Cancún 2010 (COP 16) that the Conference of the Parties, for the first time, cautiously noted the adverse effects of climate change on the enjoyment of human rights.[12] In the Paris Agreement, human rights are mentioned discreetly, only in the preamble, to the effect that the parties acknowledge that they should "respect, promote and consider their respective obligations on human rights" when taking action to address climate change.[13]

In terms of a normative "flowchart"—metaphorically—the general obligations to prevent climate change and the mandate to adopt further specific protocols and agreements are set out, on top, in the UNFCCC. The obligations are then specified by the Paris Agreement and COP decisions, and the obligations flowing from these global treaties trickle down, through the NDCs, to be implemented at the regional (EU), national (state), and sub-national levels, by laws and other means, so as to reach and apply to members of the public and corporations. In this way, international law on climate change applies and is implemented *from above.*

The crux of the matter is that, despite the Paris Agreement's ambitious objective and despite recurring events at the annual COPs, climate research shows that this transition is too slow. The measures taken by states and corporations are neither adequate nor sufficient. In many countries, the development is going in the wrong direction, with increased rather than reduced emissions.

7.3 The Human Rights Track

None of the international human rights instruments adopted before 1972 makes any reference to the environment, let alone to climate change. This is not surprising, given that the notion of the environment as we think of it today did not exist until the 1960s, and it was only included in global policy documents at and after the Stockholm Conference.[14]

[11] Ibid., Article 2(1).

[12] Conference of the Parties to the United Nations Framework Convention on Climate Change 2010.

[13] Paris Agreement, preamble, recital 11.

[14] Ebbesson 2022, p. 80. *See* Warde et al. 2018, pp. 7–15, arguing, at p. 159, that at the 1972 Stockholm Conference the concept had reached "the highest pinnacles of global diplomacy and prestige".

Steps were taken in the 1970s and 1980s to highlight the human rights-environment connection, for instance in the 1981 African Charter on Human and Peoples' Rights,[15] but it was not until the early 1990s that this connection would flourish.

The 1992 Rio Declaration on Environment and Development did little, compared with the Stockholm Declaration, to strengthen the notion of a human right in relation to the environment.[16] Yet, it would have a significant impact on the development of international law on participatory rights in environmental matters by asserting that each individual shall have access to environmental information, the opportunity to participate in decision-making, and effective access to judicial and administrative proceedings, including redress and remedy.[17]

Soon after the Rio Conference, the UN Economic Commission for Europe started negotiations on what would become the 1998 Aarhus Convention on Access to Information, Public Participation in Decision-Making and Access to Justice in Environmental Matter (Aarhus Convention).[18] Among the issues addressed in the Aarhus Convention, it obliges the parties to recognize and support associations, organizations, and groups promoting environmental protection, and to ensure that their national legal systems also do so.[19] This means, for instance, that such associations shall have standing in judicial or administrative procedures to challenge acts and omissions by public authorities and private actors which may contravene national laws relating to the environment.[20]

In parallel, in the early 1990s, the ECtHR started developing its jurisprudence on the application of the European Convention on Human Rights (European Convention)[21] in environmental cases. Again, without any reference to environment in the European Convention, the Court construed the right to respect for private and family life and the right to life as providing rights for individuals—and positive and regulatory duties for the state parties—in environmental contexts. Early cases confirmed that the right to respect for private and family life sets limits, in the balance of interest,

---

[15] *Cf.* African Charter on Human and Peoples' Rights, opened for signature 27 June 1981, 1520 UNTS 217 (entered into force 21 October 1986), Article 24: "All peoples shall have the right to a general satisfactory environment favorable to their development."

[16] The Rio Declaration on Environment and Development, principle 1, sets out that "Human beings are at the centre of concerns for sustainable development. They are entitled to a healthy and productive life in harmony with nature". *See* United Nations Conference on Environment and Development 1992 (Rio Declaration).

[17] Ibid., principle 10.

[18] Aarhus Convention on Access to Information, Public Participation in Decision-Making and Access to Justice in Environmental Matters, opened for signature 25 June 1998, 2161 UNTS 447 (entered into force 30 October 2001) (Aarhus Convention).

[19] Ibid., Article 3(4).

[20] Ibid., Article 9.

[21] Convention for the Protection of Human Rights and Fundamental Freedoms, opened for signature 4 November 1950, 213 UNTS 221 (entered into force 3 September 1953).

on what an individual must cope with in terms of nuisance,[22] and also implies the right to know which risks you are exposed to.[23]

The Court's jurisprudence would develop through numerous cases, and clarify both the substantive and procedural dimensions of these rights and the implied positive and regulatory obligations of the convention parties. The Court would also set out what the right to a fair trial requires, for instance as regards the scope of review, in environmental cases.[24] Importantly, in its reasoning and motivation, the ECtHR refers to other relevant international acts, such as the Rio Declaration and the Aarhus Convention.[25]

Despite its comprehensive case law on environmental matters, the ECtHR had not, prior to 2024, ruled in any case on states' responsibility to take sufficient measures to prevent climate change.

7.4 The Tracks Converge

7.4.1 International Law from Below

Frustrated by the slowness of governments to tackle climate change, associations, interest groups, and individuals around the world have turned to national courts and sued states for their lack of climate responsibility, in several cases with success. In these claims, the plaintiffs refer to applicable national laws and sometimes to constitutional provisions, including on fundamental human rights. We see this for instance in cases against the states of Pakistan, Colombia, the Netherlands, Belgium, and Germany.[26] Importantly, *international law*, not least the UNFCCC with the Paris Agreement, and international human rights treaties are also central to many climate lawsuits.

Thus enters international law *from below*,[27] when non-state actors use and invoke international law, and push for the enforcement of international law in cases *against*

---

[22] ECtHR, *López Ostra v. Spain*, Judgment, 9 December 1994, Application No 16798/90.

[23] ECtHR, *Guerra and others v. Italy*, Judgment, 19 February 1998, Application No 116/1996/735/932.

[24] ECtHR, *Karin Andersson and Others v. Sweden*, Judgment, 25 September 2014, Application No 29878/09.

[25] For a concise overview of the case law of the ECtHR in environmental cases, *see* European Court of Human Rights 2024.

[26] Annual updates on the numerous climate lawsuits around the world are provided by the Grantham Research Institute on Climate Change and the Environment; *see* Setzer and Higham 2024.

[27] Although the reference to international law from below draws on Rajagopal 2003, as regards international law and social movements, international institutions and human rights, he provides a thorough theoretical basis, and takes the perspective of the Third World social movement, which I am not doing here. Niehaus 2023 furthers the notion of international law from below by examining climate litigation in national courts as a means for developing and shaping "global climate constitutionalism".

states in *national courts*. Here, the two tracks of international climate change and human rights law converge. This happened also in the ECtHR when Klimaseniorinnen, an association for older women acting against climate change, referred to the goals of the Paris Agreement and contended that the omission of Switzerland to take sufficient climate measures violated their members' right to life and right to private and family life under the European Convention. It also claimed that Switzerland infringed their right to a fair trial and right to effective remedy.

Unlike the Swiss judiciary, the ECtHR opened its door and ruled in their favor.

7.4.2 Construing Human Rights on Access to Justice in Light of Other International Law

To have the claims tried on the merits in court, Klimaseniorinnen had to pass two tests. First, they needed standing before the domestic courts of Switzerland, which they—wrongly—did not get; second, they needed standing before the ECtHR, which they got.

The right to a fair trial applies in cases where there is a dispute concerning a civil right. The original action by Klimaseniorinnen included several requests to have Switzerland reduce its greenhouse gases emissions and align with the 2 °C target. The ECtHR noted that the applicants' action largely concerned requests for legislative and regulatory action, thus falling outside the scope of the right to a fair trial. Somewhat surprisingly, but in line with the Court's reasoning on the right to respect for private and family life, the Court found the claims by the four individual applicants in the case inadmissible, because it did not think that the dispute they had brought was or could have been directly decisive for their specific rights.[28]

Yet, the Court was satisfied that some of the interests brought by the association Klimaseniorinnen were such as to trigger a dispute with a direct and sufficient link to the rights of members of the association, "bearing in mind the specific role of associations in the climate-change context".[29] Moreover, the Court found that the association had demonstrated that it sought to defend specific civil rights of its members in relation to the adverse effects of climate change. Therefore, the association was considered to have victim status regarding its lack of access to justice. And because it could not have its case tried in a Swiss court, the ECtHR concluded that Switzerland violated Klimaseniorinnen's right to a fair trial.[30]

When examining standing before itself, the Court first considered whether individuals can have standing in the context of climate change. Based on its concern to provide effective protection of the Convention rights and its concern not to "slip into *de facto* admission of *actio popularis*", the Court proceeded to set criteria for

---

[28] *Klimaseniorinnen Schweiz and Others v. Switzerland*, above n. 1, paras 624–625.

[29] Ibid., para 618.

[30] Ibid., paras 638–640.

the standing of individuals, which the Court itself found "especially high".[31] In this respect too, it concluded that the application was inadmissible, as none of the four individuals who brought the case against Switzerland with Klimaseniorinnen fulfilled the victim status criteria.[32]

Instead, the Court took recourse to standing for associations. Here, the case law of the ECtHR has been quite clear. In principle, associations have *not* been in a position to rely on health considerations to allege a violation of the right to private and family life.[33] Only in very exceptional cases have associations been granted standing before the ECtHR as representatives of a victim even without specific authority,[34] and these previous cases did not relate to the environment. Given that the four applicants who applied to the ECtHR next to the Klimaseniorinnen were denied standing, how should the Court consider the position of the association Klimasenorinnen itself? After reasoning back and forth,

> [t]he Court considers it appropriate in this specific context to acknowledge the importance of making allowance for *recourse to legal action by associations* for the purpose of seeking the protection of the human rights of those affected, as well as those at risk of being affected, by the adverse effects of climate change, *instead of* exclusively relying on proceedings brought by *each individual* on his or her own behalf.[35]

This is where the Court turned to the Aarhus Convention.

> In this connection, when devising the test for the standing of associations in climate-change litigation under the Convention, the Court finds it pertinent to have regard to the Aarhus Convention, the importance of which has already been noted in its case-law.[36]

Although the Court wrongly stated that climate change litigation is not covered by the Aarhus Convention[37]—which it is[38]—it correctly noted that the Aarhus Convention highlights the need for non-governmental organizations to have access to justice in environmental matters. In doing so, it referred to how, in the Aarhus Convention, non-governmental organizations promoting environmental protection and meeting any requirements under national law are deemed to have an interest giving them access to justice.

---

[31] Ibid., paras 484–488 (quotes in paras 484 and 488).

[32] Ibid., para 535.

[33] Ibid., para 473.

[34] The Court refers in *Klimaseniorinnen Schweiz and Others v. Switzerland*, above n. 1, paras 476 and 477, to its ruling in *Centre for Legal Resources on behalf of Valentin Câmpeanu v. Romania*, Judgment, 17 July 2014, Application No 47848/08, where this is further set out.

[35] *Klimaseniorinnen Schweiz and Others v. Switzerland*, above n. 1, para 499 (emphasis added).

[36] Ibid., para 501.

[37] Ibid., para 494.

[38] According to Article 9(3) of the Aarhus Convention, members of the public—including non-governmental organizations—meeting "the criteria, if any" in national law shall have access to administrative or judicial procedures to challenge acts and omissions by public authorities—including the government—which contravene provisions of its national law relating to the environment. The state's obligations to protect against climate change may be set out in provisions in specific climate laws but can also stem from provisions on human rights; all these provisions then relate to the environment.

The Court was mindful of the different natures and purposes of the two legal frameworks, and again of not accepting an *actio popularis* (which the Aarhus Convention does not require). After having set the criteria for associations—including that any association must be "able to demonstrate that it can be regarded as genuinely qualified and representative to act on behalf of members or other affected individuals within the jurisdiction who are subject to specific threats or adverse effects of climate change on their lives, health or well-being as protected under the Convention"[39]—the Court swiftly concluded that the association Klimaseniorinnen met these criteria and had the necessary *locus standi* in these proceedings.[40]

Thus, the door was open to examine the climate change complaints on the merits. But the keys were given only to the association Klimaseniorinnen, not to the four individuals.

7.4.3 Construing Human Rights on Climate Change in Light of Other International Law

When examining the right to respect for private and family life, the Court paid significant attention to the facts and scientific findings on climate change,[41] as well as to the relevant legal frameworks and practice. Importantly, the Court in its ruling not only considered the European Convention, but also relevant parts of the UNFCCC, the Kyoto Protocol, the Paris Agreement, COP decisions, the Aarhus Convention, resolutions and other material by the UNGA, the UN Human Rights Council (including the special procedures under other human rights treaties of global scope), the Council of Europe, European Union law, and other regional human rights mechanisms.[42] The Court also considered some comparative findings and an overview of domestic case law concerning climate change.

This is where the Court opened the door for international law on climate change to enter from below. It did so, but not by directly applying the legal frameworks referred to in the previous paragraph. Rather, the Court accurately construed the obligations of the parties under the European Convention to address climate change *in the light of these other international legal frameworks.*

> The Court cannot ignore the above-noted developments and considerations. On the contrary, it should be recalled that the Convention is a living instrument which must be *interpreted in the light of present-day conditions, and in accordance with developments in international law,* so as to *reflect the increasingly high standard being required in the area of the protection of human rights,* thus necessitating greater firmness in assessing breaches of the fundamental values of democratic societies.[43]

---

[39] *Klimaseniorinnen Schweiz and Others v. Switzerland*, above n. 1, para 502.

[40] Ibid., para 526.

[41] Ibid., paras 64–120.

[42] Ibid., paras 133–231.

[43] Ibid., para 434 (emphasis added).

This was also where the Court clarified how scientific evidence matters for its considerations, thus explaining and justifying how the Court construed the right to private and family life, taking into account risks, uncertainties, and the complex issue of causality. It continued:

> Indeed, an appropriate and tailored approach as regards the various Convention issues which may arise in the context of climate change, required for the reasons set out ... above, *needs to take into account the existing and constantly developing scientific evidence* on the necessity of combating climate change and the urgency of addressing its adverse effects, including the grave risk of their inevitability and their irreversibility, as well as the scientific, political and judicial recognition of a link between the adverse effects of climate change and the enjoyment of (various aspects of) human rights.[44]

The Court's ruling on the substance is not surprising, yet an important confirmation of each state's climate responsibility, fully in line with the Court's previous jurisprudence, and also in line with the international legal development on climate responsibility.[45] The ECtHR, just like the national courts dealing with climate change lawsuits, trusted the science on climate change and took climate change seriously. There was no denial or skepticism whatsoever.

> The Court notes that there is cogent scientific evidence demonstrating that climate change has already contributed to an increase in morbidity and mortality, especially among certain more vulnerable groups, that it actually creates such effects and that, in the absence of resolute action by States, it risks progressing to the point of being irreversible and disastrous.[46]

Climate change, the Court asserted, affects older women's opportunities to enjoy the right to respect for private and family life (the Court decided to limit its examination to the right to respect to private and family life, but did not rule out that the right to life can also be infringed by climate change).[47] Our basic human rights cannot be protected unless our living environment and the climate allow a life of dignity and well-being.

Although its earlier jurisprudence in environmental cases is relevant when applying the European Convention to climate change,[48] the Court sought to develop a more "tailored approach" as regards the issues that may arise in the context of climate change, such as causation, proof, the effects of climate change on the enjoyment of human rights, positive obligations, and the proportion of state responsibility.[49] The Court also reflected on the global dimensions of climate change, and wisely emphasized that each state must do its reasonable share to reduce greenhouse gas emissions and their harmful effects.[50]

---

[44] Ibid. (emphasis added).

[45] *See, for instance,* the International Tribunal on the Law of the Sea, *Advisory Opinion at the Request of the Commission of Small Island States on Climate Change and International Law*, 21 May 2024, Case No. 31.

[46] *Klimaseniorinnen Schweiz and Others v. Switzerland*, above n. 1, para 478.

[47] Ibid., paras 356–358.

[48] Ibid., paras 414–421.

[49] Ibid., paras 422–444.

[50] Ibid.

Based on the reasoning above and without setting out in detail what the national legislation should look like, the Court declared that effective protection of private and family life required that each state "undertake measures for the substantial and progressive reduction of their respective [greenhouse gas] emission levels, with a view of reaching net neutrality within, in principle, the *next three decades*". In order not to shift the burdens to future generations, this must be done immediately, with intermediate targets leading to net neutrality and with legally binding regulation ensuring phase-out. According to the Court, each state has a wide margin of appreciation as regards the means for climate transition, but less leeway in setting the timeline to reach the goal of net neutrality.[51]

Switzerland was found to be in breach of the European Convention for not having an effective regulatory framework in place prescribing quantified reductions of the country's greenhouse gas emissions. This was possible because international law *on climate change* could enter into the courtroom from below through human rights law—and because Klimaseniorinnen used the keys to Strasbourg.

7.5 International Law, Climate Change, and the Flapping of Butterflies' Wings

Klimaseniorinnen and the numerous climate lawsuits in national courts transform the application, implementation, and enforcement—even our *perception*—of international law on climate change. Possibly, they also lead to better compliance with international law and more effective climate transition. Although it is not a new phenomenon that national courts refer to international treaties in environmental cases, we have never before seen such a focused approach in so many jurisdictions as in the climate lawsuits. *Klimaseniorinnen* confirms the approach taken by national courts.

The *Klimaseniorinnen* ruling had more than 100 references to the Paris Agreement and about 50 references to the Aarhus Convention (as well as references to other international law and policy instruments), and both treaties were significant for the Court's reasoning and the outcome. As pointed out, this is not because the Court decided the case on the basis of these legal frameworks, but because it accurately construed the obligations under the European Convention to address climate change in the light of other international legal frameworks.

Thus, *Klimaseniorinnen* and the national climate lawsuits show how dynamic and complex international law on climate change is. It develops and is applied on several levels and at different scales simultaneously: not only in global contexts, but also in national cases, and not only top-down, but also from below. In addition, *Klimaseniorinnen* illustrates how different fields of international law—on climate change, human rights, and participatory rights in environmental matters—can be integrated, rather than fragmented.

[51] *Klimaseniorinnen Schweiz and Others v. Switzerland*, above n. 1, paras 548–553 (quote in para 548; emphasis added).

Obviously, the climate lawsuits will not by themselves resolve the climate crisis—and it is not for the courts to step into the shoes of the legislators. Still, the judiciary is an essential part of the climate transition. Climate lawsuits highlight and examine states' responsibilities, and they increase the pressure on states to live up to their legal obligations. Importantly, they also show that climate transition can take place within the framework of democracy and the rule of law.

Klimaseniorinnen will influence legal developments and the discourse on rights, responsibilities, and climate change around the world. Not only the flapping of butterflies' wings can cause hurricanes on the other side of the world. The dedication and energy of older women can achieve that as well.

7.6 Postscript

On 25 July 2025, after this article was completed, in its Advisory Opinion on *Obligations of States in Respect of Climate Change* the International Court of Justice (ICJ) confirmed that states' obligations to protect from climate change stem not only from the UNFCCC and Paris Agreement, but also from the UN Charter, UNCLOS, other multilateral environmental agreements, customary international law—and from *international human rights law*. According the ICJ, in order to guarantee the effective enjoyment of human rights, states must take measures to protect the climate system and other parts of the environment, including mitigating and adaptive measures "with due account given to the protection of human rights, the adoption of standards and legislation, and the regulation of the activities of private actors." Without engaging in the question of standing and while remaining at a general level, the Advisory Opinion accords well with the ruling in *Klimaseniorinnen*, both in illustrating how different fields of international law are integrated, and in confirming the human rights-climate change nexus.

References

Conference of the Parties to the United Nations Framework Convention on Climate Change (2010) Report of the Conference of the Parties on its Sixteenth Session, Cancún, 29 November to 10 December 2010, Decision 1/CP.16. FCCC/CP/2010/7/Add.1

Ebbesson J (2022) Getting it Right: Advances of Human Rights and the Environment from Stockholm 1972 to Stockholm 2022. Environmental Policy and Law 52:79–92

European Court of Human Rights (2024) Environment and the European Convention on Human Rights (Factsheet—Environment and ECHR). European Court of Human Rights, Strasbourg

Niehaus M (2023) Global Climate Constitutionalism "from Below": The Role of Climate Change Litigation for International Climate Lawmaking. Springer, Wiesbaden

Rajagopal B (2003) International Law from Below: Development, Social Movements and Third World Resistance. Cambridge University Press, Cambridge

Setzer J, Higham C (2024) Global Trends in Climate Change Litigation: 2024 Snapshot. Grantham Research Institute on Climate Change and the Environment, London School of Economics and Political Science, London

United Nations Conference on the Human Environment (1972) Report of the United Nations Conference on the Human Environment, Stockholm, 5–16 June 1972, UN Doc. A/CONF.48/14/Rev.1

United Nations Conference on Environment and Development (1992) Report of the United Nations Conference on Environment and Development, Rio de Janeiro, 3–14 June 1992, UN Doc. A/CONF.151/26 (Vol. I)

UN General Assembly (1988) Resolution 43/53 Protection of global climate for present and future generations of mankind (6 December 1988), UN Doc. A/RES/43/53

Warde P et al (2018) The Environment: A History of the Idea. Johns Hopkins University Press, Baltimore

Jonas Ebbesson is Professor of Environmental Law, former Dean of the Faculty of Law (2012–2017), and Director of the Stockholm Environmental Law and Policy Centre at Stockholm University in Sweden. He is former Chair (2011–2021) and Member (2005–2021) of the Compliance Committee to the UNECE Convention on Access to Information, Public Participation in Decision-making and Access to Justice in Environmental Matters (Aarhus Convention). He is a member of the Swedish Academy of Letters, History and Antiquities. His research essentially focuses on transboundary dimensions of environmental law, including international law on participatory rights and human rights in environmental matters; transboundary corporate responsibility; and climate change litigations.

Chapter 8
An Obligation to Compromise? Between Statehood and Autonomy in the Case of Western Sahara after 2007

Sia Spiliopoulou Åkermark

Contents

Abstract In 2007, after years of stalemate, Morocco and Frente Polisario both presented proposals for the future of Western Sahara to the United Nations. Matters such as the quest for a referendum, the management of Western Sahara's natural resources and territorial autonomy as a possible option formed part of those proposals. Since then, perceptions of the need for a 'compromise' have been expressed regularly, especially in diplomatic circles, and violence has reappeared on the ground. Such violence and weak political support have made the operation of the UN Mission for a Referendum in Western Sahara (MINURSO) increasingly problematic. The proposal put forward by Morocco revolves around the notion of territorial autonomy. However, territorial autonomy remains an open concept in international law while it has important connotations in comparative constitutional theory. Where do we stand today as regards the 2007 proposals? How are understandings and regulations of self-determination and decolonisation as core elements of law and international relations affected? How is the concept of compromise to be understood?

Keywords Western Sahara · Colonialism · Territorial autonomy · Compromise · Self-determination · Dispute resolution

---

S. Spiliopoulou Åkermark (✉)
Åbo Akademi University, Åbo/Turku, Finland
e-mail: sia.spiliopoulouakermark@abo.fi

M. Klamberg et al. (eds.), *Reconstructing Power and Hegemony in Public International Law*, https://doi.org/10.1007/978-94-6265-743-4_8

8.1 Introduction

Much like the history of any place on earth, the history of Western Sahara is complex and entangled in the broader legal and political circumstances of the region and the world; there is no easy way to tell its complex story.[1] Still, law must make things simple enough to be manageable. In the present text, I focus on the proposals presented by Morocco and Frente Polisario (Western Sahara's liberation movement, hereinafter Polisario), respectively, in 2007 to solve the dispute over Western Sahara. As we are now noting the 50th anniversary of the 1975 Advisory Opinion on Western Sahara by the International Court of Justice (ICJ) and the dispute remains unresolved, there is reason to review current trends and prospects.[2]

Western Sahara, a former Spanish colony, was in 1963 put on the United Nations' list of Non-Self-Governing Territories (NSGTs), in accordance with Article 73 UN Charter and following the adoption by the General Assembly (1960) of the *Declaration on the Granting of Independence to Colonial Countries and Peoples* (Resolution 1514).[3] In its 1975 Advisory Opinion on Western Sahara, the ICJ did not find Western Sahara to be a *terra nullius*, as it had been inhabited, albeit sparsely, by socially and politically organised tribes in constant movement across borders. The Court rather found that there were no ties between Western Sahara and Morocco or Mauritania which could detract from the relevance of Resolution 1514, requiring the decolonisation of Western Sahara through the expression of the 'free and genuine will' of the peoples of the 'Territory'. The Court also referred to Resolution 1514, which required that '[i]mmediate steps shall be taken, in Trust and Non-Self-Governing Territories or all other territories which have not yet attained independence, to *transfer all powers to the peoples* of those territories, without any conditions or reservations, in accordance with their *freely expressed will and desire*' (emphasis added).

During 1988–1991, following armed struggles and violence, a settlement plan was negotiated and endorsed by the parties.[4] The plan provided for the preparation of a referendum on independence for Western Sahara and paved the way for the establishment by the Security Council of the UN Mission for a Referendum in Western Sahara (MINURSO). There is neither need nor space for expanding here on the many stages of the political, legal and military situation of Western Sahara. The goal is not to tell the 'full' story of the case of Western Sahara, but rather to contextualise and

[1] Wrange 2019; Allen and Trinidad 2024.

[2] ICJ, *Western Sahara*, Advisory Opinion, 1975 ICJ Reports 12.

[3] UNGA 1960a.

[4] UNSC 1988; UNSC 1990a; UNSC 1991. Most authors conclude that the non-implementation of the plan is due mainly to lack of cooperation by Morocco. Both sides (Morocco and Polisario) had given their agreement in principle to the settlement plan brokered by the UN in cooperation with the Organisation of African Unity. The plan is found in the Report of the UN Secretary General on the Situation concerning Western Sahara, *see* UNSC 1990b.

analyse the 2007 proposals by the two main actors, namely the Kingdom of Morocco and Polisario.[5]

The 2007 proposal by Morocco aiming at some form of autonomy for Western Sahara has in recent years received some political and diplomatic support, although the nature and legal effect of this support remain unclear.[6] It is rather unusual that the international community shows enthusiasm in favour of territorial autonomy as a form of governance.[7] Recent studies have found more than 230 territorial autonomy arrangements introduced internationally in the period 1990–2019, but have also highlighted that many of them failed within a few years, especially when violence occurred.[8] There is therefore reason to deepen our understanding of the conditions necessary for viable solutions, including territorial autonomy, as well as of any arguments against the introduction of such solutions.

The diplomatic language of compromise in the case of Western Sahara has been in use for some time now, including in recent resolutions adopted by the UN Security Council (SC). For instance in Resolution 2703 (2023), the SC lamented the renewed breakout of hostilities and encouraged 'the parties to demonstrate further political will towards a solution including by expanding upon their discussion of each other's proposals and recommitting to UN efforts *in a spirit of realism and compromise*, further encouraging neighbouring countries to make contributions to the political process; and stressing the importance of all concerned expanding on their positions in order to advance a solution'.[9] In this resolution, the term 'compromise' is repeated no less than five times, first by emphasising the commitment of the SC and its members 'to assist the parties to achieve *a just, lasting, and mutually acceptable political solution, based on compromise, which will provide for the self-determination of the people of Western Sahara* in the context of arrangements consistent with the principles and purposes of the Charter of the United Nations, and noting the role and responsibilities of the parties in this respect'.[10] As noted by the EU Advocate General in a recent Opinion, '[s]cholarship suggests that, since 2018, support for the 2007 autonomy plan by the Kingdom of Morocco appears to be growing. Likewise, the rhetoric in the UN SC resolutions appears to have changed. Thus, starting in 2018, the text of such resolutions often stresses the need to "achieve a realistic, practicable, enduring and mutually acceptable political solution to the Western Sahara question

[5] For a discussion on the identity and history of the Sahrawis, *see* Castellino and Domínguez-Redondo 2013.

[6] Allen and Trinidad 2024.

[7] Spiliopoulou Åkermark 2011; Spiliopoulou Åkermark and Stephan 2013.

[8] Schulte and Carolan 2023, with references.

[9] UNSC 2023 [on extension of the mandate of MINURSO until 31 Oct. 2024], emphasis added.

[10] Ibid. The language of compromise is found in the draft resolution put forward by the United States (S/2023/802). By contrast, the first brief resolution on the extension of the mandate of MINURSO, UN SC Resolution 1228(1999) did not refer to compromise but aimed at MINURSO working towards the implementation calendar and voter identification. Compromise has thus been finding its way to what Wrange describes as the 'standard language' of the SC, *see* Wrange, footnote 18, p. 6.

based on compromise".'[11] In the following sentence, Advocate General Ćapeta adds that '[a]t the same time, the resolutions reiterate that any political solution must provide "for the self-determination of the people of Western Sahara in the context of arrangements consistent with the principles and purposes of the [UN] Charter"'. One should therefore enquire what is required of a compromise for it to be *just, lasting and mutually acceptable*, while at the same time providing for the self-determination of the people of Western Sahara. There is a gap created by the fact that the General Assembly (GA) and the ICJ have approached the issue of Western Sahara mainly as a matter of self-determination in the context of decolonisation, whereas the SC has rather emphasised peace and security.[12] The positions of Morocco and Polisario, as well as the actions of other States, international organisations and judicial organs, thus influence the (re-)conceptualisation of the nature of the dispute, of the identities of the actors involved, and even of international law itself.

After this brief background, I shall now turn to the proposals made by the parties in 2007.

8.2 The Proposals of 2007

8.2.1 The 2007 Proposal by Morocco

By Letter (11 April 2007) from the Permanent Representative of Morocco to the United Nations, via the President of the SC, Morocco presented its proposal for 'an autonomy statute for the Sahara region'.[13] The idea that autonomous arrangements could be devised for Western Sahara was an *interim feature* of the rejected Baker Peace Plan in the early 2000s, but Morocco's proposal now envisaged the granting of autonomy as a permanent solution.[14]

---

[11] CJEU, *European Commission and Council of the European Union v Front Polisario*, Opinion of Advocate General Ćapeta, 21 March 2024, Joined Cases C-779/21 P and C-799/21 P, ECLI:EU:2024:260, paras 27–28. The European Court of Justice (ECJ) delivered its Judgment on 4 October 2024 (alongside judgment in two other adjacent cases), *see* CJEU, *European Commission and Council of the European Union v Front Polisario*, Judgment, 4 October, Joined Cases C-779/21 P and C-799/21 P, ECLI:EU:C:2024:835. The Grand Chamber of the ECJ upheld the *locus standi* of Polisario and rejected the appeals of the European Commission and the Council of the European Union seeking the setting aside of the judgment of the General Court of the European Union of 29 September 2021, *Front Polisario* v *Council* (T-279/19) by which that court had annulled Council Decision (EU) 2019/217 on the conclusion of the agreement between the European Union and the Kingdom of Morocco establishing an association between the European Communities and their Member States, on the one part, and the Kingdom of Morocco, on the other part. The Grand Chamber upheld international law and did not pursue the debate on compromise, for which reason this latest judgment is not discussed further here.

[12] Corell 2020.

[13] UNSC 2007a.

[14] Allen and Trinidad 2024, p. 17.

According to the proposal, 'the Kingdom of Morocco guarantees to all Sahrawis, inside as well as outside the territory, that they will hold a privileged position and play a leading role in the bodies and institutions of the region, without discrimination or exclusion'. Furthermore, 'the Sahara populations will themselves run their affairs democratically, through legislative, executive and judicial bodies enjoying exclusive powers. They will have the financial resources needed for the region's development in all fields, and will take an active part in the nation's economic, social and cultural life.' The State will keep its powers 'in the royal domains, especially with respect to defence, external relations and the constitutional and religious prerogatives of His Majesty the King'. The autonomy statute was to be the outcome of negotiations. It is unclear who the parties to these negotiations would be. Such an autonomy statute 'shall be submitted to the populations concerned in a free referendum'. The proposal did not refer to Western Sahara, the people of Western Sahara or to Polisario as representative of that people.

As regards the envisaged scope of the autonomy, the proposal by Morocco used ample human rights and rule of law references; however, it presented the issue as a matter of internal affairs. It described the powers of the 'Sahara autonomous Region' in keeping with 'democratic principles and procedures, and acting through *legislative*, executive and *judicial bodies*, the populations of the Sahara autonomous Region shall exercise powers, within the Region's territorial boundaries' (emphasis added) and with a non-exclusive list of subject matters, including the 'region's local administration, local police force and jurisdictions; economic development, regional planning, promotion of investment, trade, industry, tourism and agriculture; the region's budget and taxation; infrastructure: water, hydraulic facilities, electricity, public works and transportation; housing, education, health, employment, sports, social welfare and social security; cultural affairs, including promotion of the Saharan Hassani cultural heritage; and environment'. For such purposes, the 'Sahara autonomous Region will have the financial resources required for its development in all areas', although such resources were to be collected and allocated by the State. The proposal mentioned legislative, executive and judicial bodies, but it was left open who should be represented in these bodies and how they were to be elected. A legislative function was mentioned, but the wording rather suggested an executive nature for the envisaged bodies. The juridical order was understood as falling under the King's prerogative. The proposal defined (also in a non-exclusive manner) the exclusive powers of the central State, namely, the attributes of sovereignty, especially the flag, the national anthem and the currency; the attributes stemming from the constitutional and religious prerogatives of the King, as Commander of the Faithful and Guarantor of freedom of worship and *of individual and collective freedoms*; national security, external defence and defence of territorial integrity; external relations; the Kingdom's *juridical order* (emphasis added).[15] What was characteristic of the proposal was that autonomy was understood primarily as a domestic process. The proposal conceptualised the Western Sahara case as an internal dispute that could be dealt with within the framework of a domestic legislative initiative.

[15] UNSC 2007a.

The proposal was sent to the UN SC shortly after the completion of the process of Morocco's Equity and Reconciliation Commission (*Instance Equité et Réconciliation*), which examined disappearances, torture and other crimes that took place during the period of the reign of King Hassan II (1961–1999).[16] The process was initiated by the newly installed king, Mohammed VI, through royal decree, without a role for parliament and with emphasis on the accounts of victims and on monetary compensation. The commission worked in 2004–2006, but accountability and sanctions were not part of its mandate.[17] Observers have directed criticism at the absence of accountability and sanctions, and at deficits as regards the situation in Western Sahara. According to Vairel, of the twelve public hearings scheduled, only eight took place. The Laayoune session was postponed, then cancelled, because of the May 2005 riots. Vairel summarises: 'At the end of May 2005, demonstrations began in Western Sahara [...] against the transfer of a Sahrawi detainee. Protests turned into riots and struggles against security forces that used excessive force, according to many observers. 21 people were arrested and sentenced to prison for up to 20 years.' Such exclusion resulted in Sahrawis representing 'only 2 per cent of the sampling whereas Western Sahara was the first region, and one of the worst, affected by enforced disappearance', and nearly a quarter of claims originated in Western Sahara areas.[18] Vairel concludes that 'by focusing on victims but not naming torturers, the authorities found a way to accommodate international and national pressure for truth and reconciliation without threatening the regime', i.e., the continuity of the royal family. The scope of more structural recommendations by the Commission, such as the independence of the judiciary, remained limited.[19]

8.2.2 The 2007 Proposal by Polisario

A few days after the communication of the Moroccan initiative, on 16 April 2007, the permanent representative of South Africa to the United Nations transmitted to the president of the SC a proposal by Polisario 'for a mutually acceptable political solution that provides for the self-determination of the people of Western Sahara'.[20] In its introduction, Polisario described the Western Sahara matter as a *decolonisation issue* and pointed out that 'on 29 January 2002, at the request by the Security Council, the UN Legal Counsel clearly established that Morocco was not the administering power of the territory, that the Madrid Agreement of 1975 dividing the territory between Morocco and Mauritania did not transfer any sovereignty to its signatories

---

[16] Hazan 2008; Vairel 2008.

[17] For s summary of the 2006 report and its several volumes see https://archive.cndh.ma/an/rubriques/documentation/publications/report-equity-and-reconciliation-commission-ier. Accessed 14 May 2025.

[18] Vairel 2008, p. 238; Hazan 2008; Fombad 2022.

[19] Hazan 2008.

[20] UNSC 2007b.

and, finally, that the status of Western Sahara, as Non-Self-Governing Territory, had not been affected by this agreement'. Indeed, the work by the Legal Counsel allowed for the adoption of the so-called Baker Plan endorsed in SC Resolution 1495(2003).[21]

A free and fair referendum on self-determination was, according to Polisario, a precondition for the settlement of the dispute. This would entail 'holding of a genuine referendum on self-determination in Western Sahara in strict conformity with the spirit and letter of the UN GA resolution 1514 (XV) and within the format envisaged in the Baker Plan, namely the choice between independence, integration into the Kingdom of Morocco, and self-governance'.[22] The language of the three possibilities for the exercise of self-determination had its origin in UN GA Resolution 1541(XV), passed the day after Resolution 1514. Resolution 1541 defines the principles for this process and announces that an NSGT can be said to have reached a full measure of self-government through (alternatively):

- Emergence as a sovereign independent State;
- Free association with an independent State;
- Integration with an independent State.[23]

According to Polisario's proposals, guarantees could be negotiated and granted for the Moroccan population residing in Western Sahara for ten years, as well as to the Kingdom of Morocco in the political, economic and security domains 'in the event that the referendum on self-determination would lead to independence'. Such guarantees could include a) the mutual recognition of and respect for the sovereignty, independence, and territorial integrity of the two countries, in accordance with the principle of the intangibility of the borders inherited from the independence period; b) the granting of guarantees concerning the status and the rights and obligations of the Moroccan population in Western Sahara, including its participation in the political, economic and social life of the territory of Western Sahara. In this respect, the Saharawi State could grant the Saharawi nationality to any Moroccan citizen legally established in the territory who applied for it; c) the agreement on equitable and mutually advantageous arrangements permitting the development and joint exploitation of the existing natural resources or those that could be discovered during a determined period of time; d) the setting up of formulas of partnership and economic cooperation in different economic, commercial and financial sectors; e) the renunciation by the two parties, on a reciprocal basis, of any compensation for the material destructions that had taken place since the beginning of the conflict in Western Sahara; f) the conclusion of security arrangements with the Kingdom of Morocco as well as with the countries of the region that might be interested; g) the commitment of the Saharawi State to work closely with the Kingdom of Morocco as well as with the

[21] For the text of the Baker Plan as well as of the views of the parties to this plan, *see* Report of the Secretary-General on the situation concerning Western Sahara, *see* UNSC 2003.

[22] Allen and Trinidad 2024, n. 83.

[23] *See* UNGA 1960b, Principles VI–VII. Although Principle VI highlights the three modes, Principle VII emphasises the centrality of the need for the expression of the free and voluntary voice of the peoples, including the freedom to 'determine' the constitutional status of the NSGT.

other countries of the region with a view to bringing to conclusion the integration process of the Maghreb; and h) cooperation for maintenance of peace, stability and security of the whole region in the face of different threats that target it.

8.2.3 Some Comments on the Two Proposals

Until now, the Moroccan autonomy proposal has been assessed in scholarship mainly from the perspective of internal democracy.[24] It has also been argued that the main advantage of the proposal was that it reignited negotiations, increased international interest and infused constitutional processes in Morocco with some energy after a new constitution was put into place in 2011, with regionalisation very much seen as a promising executive tool.[25] Although this may be true, my argument is more fundamental. The autonomy proposal, as it now stands, alters the way we think about the role and reach of international law and about the interrelationship of different branches of law. The two proposals stand for different understandings of not only the possible outcomes of the dispute, but also its very nature and thereby the body of law that should be used to regulate it. For Morocco, Western Sahara is a matter of internal security and diversity. This is in line with what Morocco has argued since at least the 1970s, i.e., that it holds sovereignty over the territories and has acted accordingly, e.g., through the 'Green March', the Berm (a fortified sand wall separating Western Sahara from Morocco from north to south), the economic agreements with the EU,[26] the Morocco-Israel agreement, followed by recognition by Israel of Moroccan sovereignty over Western Sahara, after such recognition by the United States under president Trump in 2020, and recent facilitation of consulates by various countries in Western Sahara. Still, it has consistently referred to the Southern or Sahara regions (rather than to Western Sahara, the Sahrawi people, or Polisario). The emphasis here is on the territorial integrity of the State. Executive regional autonomy is the available option, according to Morocco. The body of law to be used is, in this understanding, that of domestic law, providing for a form of autonomy of an executive nature, as opposed to territorial autonomy as the exclusive legislative power or an internationalised regime, as emphasised by scholars.[27] The referendum to be presented to the region's populations would only provide for the option of autonomy, according to the proposal. In effect, it presents one body of law (autonomy, minority and human rights through domestic means) to limit the effects of another body of law (self-determination, decolonisation and international law more broadly).

By contrast, the proposal by Polisario understands the issue of Western Sahara as a process of decolonisation and self-determination, to be solved through multiparty international negotiations and a referendum offering at least the three options

[24] Khakee 2011; Allen and Trinidad 2024.

[25] Khakee 2011.

[26] Wrange 2019; Corell 2020; Allen and Trinidad 2024.

[27] *See, e.g.*, Suksi 2011; Hannum 1996.

identified in UN SC Resolution 1541 (1960), i.e., independence, association or integration. The details of the Polisario proposal are shaped under the assumption that independence would be a likely outcome, even though other options could be made available to voters in a referendum. *Both proposals seem to agree that a referendum is needed.* As this has been an issue under contestation, one may argue that this is a step forward, although neither side has explained how such a referendum would be implemented. The hundreds of thousands of Sahrawi refugees in Algeria, the construction of the Berm, the status of Moroccan settlers after the Green March, and the use of mining and development projects in the territory controlled by Morocco have affected the population profile of the territory and this needs to be considered in whatever way is chosen to establish the expression of the will of those concerned. Is it possible to genuinely establish 'the interests and wishes of the people of Western Sahara' unless a referendum is held, asks Corell.[28] Formally, this has been and is the task of MINURSO. Under the current circumstances, this task could not be fulfilled by either side in the dispute.

8.3 Potential Implications of Western Sahara for International Law and the Global Order

The Western Sahara case puts to the test the decolonisation and self-determination concepts as they have been developed in the UN Charter, in resolutions by the UN GA and SC, including the Friendly Relations Declaration (1970),[29] countless peace agreements, the two UN Covenants on Human Rights with common Article 1 on self-determination, and case law of the ICJ and the African Court of Human Rights.[30] The status of NSGTs, the duties of other States towards them, including the integrity of any NSGT and of its people, the right of people to define their future political status with its connotations of democratic principles, emancipatory strivings and

---

[28] Corell 2020, p. 431.

[29] The Friendly Relations Declaration (UN GA Resolution 2625 (XXV) 1970) asserts that 'subjection of peoples to alien subjugation, domination and exploitation constitutes a violation of the principle [of self-determination], as well as a denial of fundamental human rights and is contrary to the Charter' constituting 'a major obstacle to the promotion of international peace and security'. On external and internal self-determination, *see* Alfredsson 2019.

[30] ICJ, *Legal Consequences for States of the Continued Presence of South Africa in Namibia (South West Africa) notwithstanding Security Council Resolution 276 (1970)*, Advisory Opinion, 21 June 1971, 1971 ICJ Reports 16; ICJ, *East Timor (Portugal v. Australia)*, Judgment, 30 June 1995, 1995 ICJ Reports 90; ICJ, *Legal Consequences of the Construction of a Wall in the Occupied Palestinian Territory*, Advisory Opinion, 9 July 2004, 2004 ICJ Reports 136; ICJ, *Legal Consequences of the Separation of the Chagos Archipelago from Mauritius in 1965*, Advisory Opinion, 2019 ICJ Reports 95; ICJ, *Legal Consequences arising from the Policies and Practices of Israel in the Occupied Palestinian Territory, including East Jerusalem*, Advisory Opinion, 19 July 2004. The African Court of Human Rights pronounced on Western Sahara in *Bernard A. Mornah v. Republic of Benin et al.*, Judgment, Application No 028/2018, 22 September 2022.

rights to natural resources,[31] as well as the concept of territorial autonomy in the strict sense—all are at stake in the case of Western Sahara.

Although the Western Sahara case is not high on the agenda of international affairs, or—as Bourdieu would say—seems to carry limited symbolic power, 'it has the potential to shake the legal and political architecture of the UN order to its foundations'.[32] There are many other open cases that are likely to be affected, including the future of Palestine, New Caledonia,[33] West Papua,[34] Tibet,[35] indigenous emancipation processes throughout the world, and—more broadly—efforts to address ongoing consequences of colonialism and oppression.[36]

The case of Western Sahara affects our thinking about law and the open question of the continued relevance of the international rule of law.[37] As we have seen, the SC, guided by the United States, has increasingly used the language of 'the necessary compromise' with support given to the idea of an executive autonomy as the only viable option.[38] There is a growing body of literature on compromise. Some of the questions discussed are: What is the difference between consensus and compromise? What are the elements of compromise? Might compromise with the goal of peace sacrifice justice? What makes a compromise just (or fair)? Are there limits to a compromise? Limitations of space do not allow me to go into this matter in depth. In brief, compromise is not a concept found in international law. Rather, the UN Charter includes an obligation to refrain from threat and use of armed force, a duty of peaceful solution of disputes and respect of the peoples of NSGTs. *There is no legal obligation to compromise.* Of relevance are rather the moral and philosophical elements of a compromise.[39] First, a compromise recognises the (at least partial) legitimacy of claims made by the other side. As the Kingdom of Morocco does not recognise the Sahrawi people, a compromise seems not only empirically non-attainable, but also logically impossible. A compromise between the rulers and the current population in the territories controlled by Morocco may be possible, but it would not be a compromise between the parties to the dispute that has been before the UN and international society since 1963. A compromise must combine *end-state fairness* with *process fairness*, say scholars, pulling us, once more, into the issue of a referendum and the mandate of MINURSO, and into the criteria of legality

[31] EU vessels fishing in Western Sahara waters have been documented, i.a., by the Western Sahara Resource Watch. *See, e.g.*, https://wsrw.org/en/archive/4222. Accessed 14 April 2025.

[32] Allen and Trinidad 2024, p. 86.

[33] New Caledonia is among the remaining NSGTs. *See* https://www.un.org/dppa/decolonization/en/nsgt. Accessed 14 April 2025. *See* David and Tirard 2022.

[34] McCorquodale et al. 2020.

[35] Seymour and Changching 1998.

[36] Castellino 2024. For the concept of double colonisation and on Swedish recognition policies regarding Western Sahara, *see* Badarin 2021.

[37] Corell 2020 has referred to UN SC Presidential Statement of 21 February 2014 on the importance of the rule of law at national and international levels, *see* UNSC 2014.

[38] Such support has also been given by EU countries, including France and Spain, two States facing challenges regarding autonomy and decolonisation.

[39] Spang 2023; several contributions in Knight 2018; Jones and O'Flynn 2013; Nachi 2004.

and legitimacy. Indeed, there is acceptable compromise and there is, according to Margalit, also 'rotten compromise', meaning compromise resulting in an inhuman political order characterised by persistent systematic cruelty. Sometimes the party suffering such dehumanisation is not even a party to the compromise agreement.[40] Such rotten compromises should be rejected, argues Margalit.

We are in no better position today than when John Morley asked in his work 'On Compromise' (1886): How should the balance between principles and expediency be achieved? His reflections resonate still today:

> A principle, if it be sound, represents one of the larger expediencies. [...] It is better to bear the burden of impracticableness, than to stifle conviction and to pare away principle until it becomes more hollowness and triviality. What is the sense, and what is the morality, of postponing the wider utility to the narrower?

The principles of self-determination and decolonisation have played an important role in increasing the global diversity of voices and alleviating some of the injustices of previous centuries. The independence of Morocco is one such result. As argued by Morley, timing and particular circumstances need to be thoroughly assessed and openly discussed before the appropriate balance between principles and expediency can be found. Should considerations of justice and the rule of law be overruled by the expediency of security or economic gain? As things now stand, the case of Western Sahara carries considerably more symbolic power than originally anticipated and has the potential to reshape international law.

References

Alfredsson G (2019) The Right to Self-Determination in International Law. In: Akbulut O, Aktoprak E (eds) Minority Self-Government in Europe and the Middle East: From Theory to Practice. Brill Nijhoff, Leiden, pp. 3–31

Allen S, Trinidad J (2024) The Western Sahara Question and International Law: Recognition Doctrine and Self-Determination. Taylor & Francis

Badarin E (2021) Recognition of states and colonialism in the twenty-first century: Western Sahara and Palestine in Sweden's recognition practice. Third World Quarterly 42(6):1276–1294

Castellino J (2024), Calibrating Colonial Crime: Reparations and the Crime of Unjust Enrichment. Bristol University Press

Castellino J, Domínguez-Redondo E (2013) The Identity Question: Who Are the Sahrawis and What Is Their 'Home'? In: Boukhars A, Roussellier J (eds), Perspectives on Western Sahara: Myths, Nationalisms, and Geopolitics. Rowman & Littlefield Publishers, pp. 29–54

Corell H (2020) Keynote address on Western Sahara at the 2019 Annual Conference of the Belgian Society of International Law. Revue Belge de Droit International / Belgian Review of International Law 53(2):423–433

David C, Tirard M (2022) La Nouvelle-Calédonie Après Le Troisième Référendum D'autodétermination du 12 Décembre 2021: 40 Ans Pour Rien? [New Caledonia After The Third Self-Determination Referendum On 12 December 2021: 40 Years For Nothing?] La Revue Des Droits De L'Homme. https://doi.org/10.4000/revdh.14593. Accessed 14 April 2025

[40] Margalit 2009, p. 54.

Fombad CM (2022) Transitional Justice in Africa—The Experience with Truth Commissions. GlobaLex, New York University. https://www.nyulawglobal.org/globalex/africa_truth_commissions.html. Accessed 14 April 2025

Hannum H (1996) Autonomy, Sovereignty, and Self-determination: The Accommodation of Conflicting Rights, Revised Edition. University of Philadelphia Press, Philadelphia

Hazan P (2008) The Nature of Sanctions: The Case of Morocco's Equity and Reconciliation Commission. International Review of the Red Cross 90(870): 399–407. https://doi.org/10.1017/S1816383108000313. Accessed 14 April 2025

Jones P, O'Flynn I (2013) Can a Compromise Be Fair? Politics, Philosophy & Economics 12(2):115-135. https://doi.org/10.1177/1470594X12447773. Accessed 14 April 2025

Khakee A (2011) The Western Sahara Autonomy Proposal and Political Reform in Morocco. Norwegian Peacebuilding Resource Centre. https://www.um.edu.mt/library/oar//handle/123456789/16044. Accessed 14 April 2025

Knight J (ed) (2018) Compromise. NOMOS LIX, New York University Press. https://doi.org/10.18574/9781479857425. Accessed 14 April 2025

Margalit A (2009) On Compromise and Rotten Compromises. Princeton University Press. https://doi.org/10.1515/9781400831210. Accessed 14 April 2025

McCorquodale R et al (2020) Territorial Integrity and Consent in the Chagos Advisory Opinion. International and Comparative Law Quarterly 69(1):221–238

Nachi M (2004) The Morality In/of Compromise: Some Theoretical Reflections. Social Science Information 43(2):291-305. https://doi.org/10.1177/0539018404042583. Accessed 14 April 2025

Schulte F, Carolan G (2023) What's Law Got to Do with It? How the Degree of Legalization Affects the Durability of Post-Conflict Autonomy Agreements. Ethnopolitics 23(4):409–434. https://doi.org/10.1080/17449057.2023.2207876. Accessed 14 April 2025

Seymour JD, Changching C (eds) (1998) Tibet Through Dissident Chinese Eyes: Essays on Self-Determination. Routledge, New York

Spang F (2023) Compromise in Political Theory. Political Studies Review 21(3):594–607. https://doi.org/10.1177/14789299221131268. Accessed 14 April 2025

Spiliopoulou Åkermark S (ed) (2011) The Åland Example and Its Components: Relevance for International Conflict Resolution. The Åland Islands Peace Institute

Spiliopoulou Åkermark S, Stephan S (2013) Rethinking Territorial Arrangements in Conflict Resolution - Introduction to the Special Issue of the International Journal on Minority and Group Rights. International Journal on Minority and Group Rights 20(1):1–3. https://doi.org/10.1163/15718115-02001001. Accessed 14 April 2025

Suksi M (2011) Sub-State Governance Through Territorial Autonomy: A Comparative Study in Constitutional Law of Powers, Procedures and Institutions. Springer Berlin, Heidelberg

UN General Assembly (1960a) Declaration on the granting of independence to colonial countries and peoples, UN Doc. A/RES/1514 (XV). https://docs.un.org/en/A/res/1514(xv). Accessed 14 April 2025

UN General Assembly (1960b) Principles which should guide Members in determining whether or not an obligation exists to transmit the information called for under Article 73 e of the Charter, UN Doc. A/RES/1541 (XV). https://docs.un.org/en/A/RES/1541(XV). Accessed 14 April 2025

UN Security Council (1988) Resolution 621 (1988) of 20 September 1988, UN Doc. S/RES/621. https://digitallibrary.un.org/record/46339?v=pdf. Accessed 14 April 2025

UN Security Council (1990a) Resolution 658 (1990) of 27 June 1990, UN Doc. S/RES/658. https://digitallibrary.un.org/record/92969?ln=en&v=pdf. Accessed 14 April 2025

UN Security Council (1990b) The Situation Concerning Western Sahara, Report of the Secretary-General, UN Doc. S/21360. https://docs.un.org/en/S/21360. Accessed 14 April 2025

UN Security Council (1991) Resolution 690 (1991) of 29 April 1991, UN Doc. S/RES/690. https://docs.un.org/en/S/RES/690(1991). Accessed 14 April 2025

UN Security Council (2003) Report of the Secretary-General on the situation concerning Western Sahara, UN Doc. S/2003/565. https://docs.un.org/en/S/2003/565. Accessed 14 April 2025

UN Security Council (2007a) Letter dated 11 April 2007 from the Permanent Representative of Morocco to the United Nations addressed to the President of the Security Council, UN Doc. S/2007/206. https://docs.un.org/en/S/2007/206. Accessed 14 April 2025

UN Security Council (2007b) Letter dated 16 April 2007 from the Permanent Representative of South Africa to the United Nations addressed to the President of the Security Council, UN Doc. S/2007/210. https://digitallibrary.un.org/record/597426?ln=en&v=pdf. Accessed 14 April 2025

UN Security Council (2014) Statement by the President of the Security Council, UN Doc. S/PRST/2014/5. https://docs.un.org/en/S/PRST/2014/5. Accessed 14 April 2025

UN Security Council (2023) Resolution 2703, UN Doc. S/RES/2703. https://docs.un.org/en/s/res/2703%20(2023). Accessed 14 April 2025

Vairel F (2008) Morocco: From Mobilizations to Reconciliation? Mediterranean Politics (Frank Cass & Co.) 13(2):229-241. https://doi.org/10.1080/13629390802127547. Accessed 14 April 2025

Wrange P (2019) Self-Determination, Occupation and the Authority to Exploit Natural Resources: Trajectories from Four European Judgments on Western Sahara. Israel Law Review 52(1):3-29. https://doi.org/10.1017/S0021223718000274. Accessed 14 April 2025

Sia Spiliopoulou Åkermark is Professor of Law at Åbo Akademi University (Finland), Jur. Dr./LLD, Docent at Uppsala University and senior fellow at SCILJ. Previously, she worked as Director of the Åland Islands Peace Institute. Sia has worked in academia, non-governmental organisations and research institutions around the world. Her work focuses on diversity, constitutional pluralism, minorities, territorial autonomies, peaceful resolution of conflicts and legal restraints on the use of force. She has been an expert member and president of the Advisory Committee on the Framework Convention on National Minorities of the Council of Europe and a member on the Truth Commission on Tornedalen (Sweden).

Chapter 9
Sweden as a Member of NATO—How Might the Role of International Law in Swedish Foreign Policy Change?

Per Ahlin

Contents

Abstract Sweden has a long history of neutrality and military non-alignment, but in March 2024 the country became a member of NATO. It was a big step for a nation that had had neutrality, or at least military non-alignment, as part of its identity for more than 200 years. It was a policy that led to the perception that Sweden had a unique voice and a unique role to play. On the other hand, we had already witnessed a gradual process where Sweden step by step instead sought security through cooperation with other states. In this regard, Swedish EU membership marked a significant change in the non-alignment stance. Ultimately, non-membership in NATO was all that remained of the old policy. This article discusses whether membership in a military alliance will change the role of international law in Swedish security policy in any substantial way or if Sweden's position is consistent regardless of whether the country pursues a policy of neutrality or acts as a member of the EU and now a member of NATO.

Keywords Sweden · NATO · International law · World order · Human rights · Conflict prevention · UN Charter · Security Council

P. Ahlin (✉)
Stockholm University, Stockholm, Sweden
e-mail: per.ahlin@juridicum.su.se

M. Klamberg et al. (eds.), *Reconstructing Power and Hegemony in Public International Law*, https://doi.org/10.1007/978-94-6265-743-4_9

9.1 Introduction

In earlier studies of the role of international law in Swedish security policy,[1] I have come to the conclusion that Sweden in its defense of international law and of functioning international organizations acts like a typical small or medium-sized state. The same holds true regarding the need for stability and predictability in the international system. In this respect, the Swedish stance has been consistent over time. It could also be argued that there was a constant thesis: for a small state, it is necessary to ensnare other states with agreements and memberships in a range of organizations in order to raise the cost of violations of international law. It is clear that Sweden has never really been an advocate of a literal interpretation of the UN Charter—Sweden has been more secure when the spirit of the UN Charter has taken precedence over its letter.[2]

Sweden differed from most other small or medium-sized countries in that it had an identity as a neutral state. For one thing, this kept Sweden out of alliances. It also led to the perception that Sweden had a unique voice and a unique role to play. This has gradually changed—starting with EU membership and ending with membership in NATO. However, as we will see later in this text, the perception of uniqueness remains among Swedish opponents to NATO membership.

With this text, my purpose—apart from honoring my old friend Pål—is to see if Sweden's use of and attitude toward international law will change with membership in NATO. However, as my earlier studies covered the time up to 2017, I will start by asking if anything changed between 2018 and the Swedish application for membership in May 2022. The short answer is no.

9.2 Swedish Positions 2018–May 2022

Leading policymakers in Sweden often talk about the importance of upholding international law and respecting the international rules of the game, as this creates security for a small state. To take just one example: In the Security Council, Sweden has spoken about the need for a "rule-based international order".[3] In Sweden's view, respect for the UN Charter is not a matter of political will, but a legal obligation.[4] The UN is emphasized as a guarantor for the global security order and is therefore considered to be of crucial importance for Sweden.[5] In the 2021 statement on foreign policy, Foreign Minister Ann Linde emphasized that the government was

[1] Ahlin 1993; Ahlin 2017.

[2] Ahlin 2017, p. 194.

[3] UNSC 2017a; UNSC 2017b.

[4] UNSC 2018a. The Committee on Foreign Affairs (Utrikesutskottet) has stated that the principles of intergovernmental cooperation set out in the UN Charter form the basis of the global collective security system and that it is important to protect this basis. 2020/21:UU8, p. 7.

[5] Committee on Foreign Affairs 2018/19:UU12, p. 11.

striving for a world order based on international law, where rules and agreements would take precedence over the rights of the strong, and where the UN would remain a cornerstone of Swedish foreign policy.[6]

Sweden protects international law, works for legal regulations of international problems, protects legal certainty when international sanctions are introduced, and takes a positive stance for court solutions, sometimes even in relation to issues of great political importance.

The view of the legal value of norms also remains. Sweden prefers binding legal regulation but can also argue based on non-binding documents when this is considered justified. When it comes to human rights, the Swedish view seems to be that the important thing is not the legal value of the norm, but whether or not it is actually respected. Even within the Organization for Security and Co-operation in Europe (OSCE), Sweden has worked with non-binding standards. This attitude persists. For example, the Swedish Committee on Foreign Affairs in March 2022 stated that, through its actions, Russia had "violated the set of rules and principles, binding under international law as well as politically binding, which make up the European security order".[7]

One of the changes noted during the period 1993–2017, as compared with the preceding period, was that state sovereignty went from something that Sweden protected to something that, according to the Swedish view, must not be an obstacle to efforts against states that violate human rights.[8] This view grew even stronger during the time now studied, which became clear during Sweden's two years in the UN Security Council in 2017–2018. The government states, in its communication about the years in the Council, that there was a "trend of increased demands for respect for non-interference, territorial integrity, and sovereignty".[9] This was a trend that Sweden did not appreciate and which was clearly felt in three areas that have been given more space in Swedish politics since the end of the Cold War: human rights, conflict prevention, and individual accountability for crimes.

Human rights are a central part of Swedish foreign policy and are intended to permeate all policy areas. In a government communication (*regeringsskrivelse*) from the beginning of the 2000s, it is stated that increased respect for human rights is a key Swedish concern and that gross violations of fundamental freedoms and rights are no longer the internal affairs of individual states. In Sweden's view, state sovereignty should not be a legitimate protection behind which massive violations of human rights could be allowed to continue.[10] This view remains. In March 2022, the Swedish

---

[6] https://regeringen.se/tal/2021/02/utrikesdeklarationen. Accessed 5 May 2025.

[7] Committee on Foreign Affairs 2021/22:UU11, p. 18 (translation by the author).

[8] In other circumstances, the Swedish position is still that "States (...) have an obligation to respect the sovereignty of other States, and a breach of this obligation would amount to a wrongful act and give rise to State responsibility". Government Offices of Sweden 2022, p. 2.

[9] Government Communication 2018/19:104, p. 18 (translation by the author).

[10] Government Communication 2000/01:2.

Committee on Foreign Affairs emphasized that the protection of human rights is a cornerstone of Sweden's overall foreign policy.[11]

Conflict prevention has also been part of the Swedish profile. Already in 1999, the government presented a Swedish action program for preventive diplomacy.[12] Sweden wanted to see a culture of conflict prevention, where it would be considered natural and possible to react to early warning signals, to seek knowledge about the causes of conflict, and to develop appropriate instruments to deal with threatening situations.

Demanding individual accountability for crimes has also been important to Sweden. During the period studied in my book *Efter neutralitetspolitiken*, temporary criminal tribunals were established for the former Yugoslavia[13] and for Rwanda.[14] In 1998, the Rome Statute of the International Criminal Court (ICC) was adopted; it entered into force on 1 July 2002. Sweden was optimistic and believed that this type of court could reduce the risk of international use of force. Court solutions can also contribute to reconciliation, which in turn reduces the risks of renewed armed conflict.[15] In a similar vein, Sweden has emphasized the importance of fighting impunity. This view remains in the more recent period. In May 2021, the government emphasized that, through the provisions of the Rome Statute and the operation of the court, "important steps were taken to counter the impunity that previously largely existed for these crimes when they were not prosecuted at the national level".[16] In March 2022, the Committee on Foreign Affairs emphasized the importance of the ICC being able to fight impunity.[17]

As stated above, these three issues, central to the Swedish profile, were apparent during Sweden's two years in the Security Council, not least because they came into conflict with mainly Russia's and China's strong adherence to state sovereignty.[18] It became clear that Sweden wanted a more active Security Council and therefore had a generous interpretation of what constituted a threat to international peace and security under Article 39 UN Charter, but a narrow interpretation of the non-intervention principle in Article 2:7 UN Charter. In the Swedish view, the scope for what constitutes "matters which are essentially within the domestic jurisdiction", as expressed in the article, is limited—and should remain so. Sweden wants to see activity on the part of the UN.

During its membership, Sweden tried to involve the Council more deeply in work on conflict prevention. That did not turn out well. The government notes in its report that preventive diplomacy can sometimes be controversial, "as some member states,

---

[11] Committee on Foreign Affairs 2021/22:UU7, p. 9.

[12] Swedish Ministry of Foreign Affairs 1999.

[13] UNSC 1993a; UNSC 1993b.

[14] UNSC 1994.

[15] Government Communication 2000/01:2, p. 18.

[16] Government Bill 2020/21:204, p. 59 (translation by the author). *See also, for example*, UNGA 2014.

[17] Committee on Foreign Affairs 2021/22:UU7, p. 12.

[18] *See* Ahlin 2020/21.

including some of the permanent members, consider risk situations to constitute internal affairs and thus that they do not fit within the category of threats to international peace and security".[19] It was also clear that Sweden rarely neglected an opportunity to emphasize the need for individual accountability in the event of crime.[20] This is within the scope of the broad security concept that Sweden applies. As emphasized above, the Swedish view is that impunity can generate conflict and that demanding accountability can contribute to reconciliation and thus to more sustainable peace processes.

Sweden believes that any violation of human rights can constitute a threat to international peace and security and consequently is an issue that belongs on the Security Council's agenda. According to Sweden, promoting respect for human rights is a central task for the Security Council.[21] The view that there is a clear connection between human rights and international peace and security was put forward by Sweden several times in the Council.[22] At home, the Committee on Foreign Affairs has emphasized that human rights form a central part of international law and are a prerequisite for maintaining peace and security.[23] Prevention, accountability for crimes, and respect for human rights are thus constants of international law in Swedish security policy.

With respect to human rights, mainly Russia and China resist. For example, in a meeting of the Security Council, the Russian delegate emphasized that violations of human rights cannot "be considered as an issue related to the primary responsibility of the Security Council for maintaining international peace and security".[24] The government describes the difficulty of even discussing human rights in the Security Council as a "significantly worrying trend that intensified during the membership period".[25] In June 2022, the government wrote about the increasing global headwinds for human rights,[26] and the Committee on Foreign Affairs, for its part, has emphasized that the "rules-based world order" is increasingly being challenged and that more countries are questioning the "universality and validity" of human rights.[27]

During Sweden's time in the Security Council, it became evident that the country has a broad interpretation of what constitutes a threat to international peace and security. Sweden stated, among other things, that scarce natural resources can cause conflicts,[28] that corruption can lead to the destabilization of weak states and thus to

---

[19] Government Communication 2018/19:104, p. 23 (translation by the author).

[20] UNSC 2017d; UNSC 2017e; UNSC 2017f; UNSC 2017h; UNSC 2018e; UNSC 2018f; UNSC 2018j.

[21] UNSC 2017g.

[22] UNSC 2017i; UNSC 2017j; UNSC 2017k.

[23] Committee on Foreign Affairs 2021/22:UU7, p. 9.

[24] UNSC 2017g.

[25] Government Communication 2018/19:104, p. 138 (translation by the author).

[26] Government Communication 2021/22:236, p. 35.

[27] Committee on Foreign Affairs 2019/20:UU15, p. 8.

[28] UNSC 2018i.

conflict,[29] that the use of chemical weapons is a threat to international peace and security,[30] that climate change can pose a security threat,[31] and that "food insecurity can trigger conflict".[32]

Another change that could be identified in my previous study related to the view on the veto right in the UN Security Council. During the days of the neutrality policy, the veto was seen as a safety valve because it meant that Sweden could not be forced to take a position in a conflict between great powers. After the end of the Cold War, the veto has been seen as a brake pad, as it may prevent the Security Council from acting on occasions when this is desired by Sweden. That view remains. Sweden wants to limit the use of the veto and completely abolish it in situations of mass abuse.[33] In the Security Council, Sweden has emphasized that the use of the veto to protect "narrow national interests in situations of mass atrocities is totally unacceptable".[34] It is obvious that the objective—from the Swedish side—is a more powerful Security Council; the aforementioned view of the veto is completely in line with Sweden's interpretation of state sovereignty. A world where the Security Council has a narrow interpretation of what constitutes an internal matter, where the use of the veto is limited, and where the purpose of the UN Charter is allowed to rule at the expense of the letter of the Charter, is a world where the Council is more effective and where Sweden is considered to be more secure.

With this point of view, it is natural that Sweden will not protect a state's sovereignty when it prevents actions that are desired by Sweden. It is clear that Sweden wants to see a strict interpretation of the non-intervention principle or, to put it more concretely, of what constitutes an internal matter. With the same starting point, it is reasonable that Sweden has a broad concept of security and a generous interpretation of what constitutes a "threat" to peace under Article 39 UN Charter—just as human rights are a matter for the Security Council. Given this point of view, it is also completely understandable that Sweden strives to limit the use of the veto.

Another change that can be noted is that climate change has climbed closer to the top of Sweden's foreign policy agenda. Climate and security were priority issues during Sweden's time in the Security Council[35] and are considered to influence Sweden's security policy. In October 2020, the government stated that climate change means that more people in vulnerable areas may be forced to migrate to neighboring countries, which may in turn cause unrest and eventually lead to violent riots or armed conflict.[36] In the statement of foreign policy in June 2022, the Foreign Minister emphasized that climate change contributes to increased tensions and conflicts, and

[29] UNSC 2018h.

[30] UNSC 2018d.

[31] UNSC 2018g.

[32] UNSC 2018b.

[33] Government Communication 2018/19:104, p. 138.

[34] UNSC 2018a.

[35] UNSC 2019.

[36] Government Bill 2020/21:30, p. 67. *See also* Committee on Foreign Affairs 2021/22:UU6, p. 10.

that we must take climate-related security threats very seriously.[37] The need for prevention, not least in the form of early warnings, has been emphasized by Sweden.[38] The Security Council has emphasized that climate change can negatively affect the stability of an area.[39]

The global situation has deteriorated in recent years, quite apart from the Russian invasion of Ukraine, not least in the sense that there are more countries moving in an authoritarian direction than in a democratic one.[40] The government stated in 2020 that the European security order was fundamentally challenged, as were the norms, collaborations and institutions that form the basis of European security. "The broad concept of security, the multilateral rules-based world order, including international law, and the joint commitments regarding human rights, democracy, and the principles of the rule of law are increasingly being questioned."[41] It is, the government continues, of great importance for Sweden that the European security order is maintained and respected. Continued undermining of the respect for these principles would, according to the government, have consequences for Sweden's security.[42]

9.3 Application for Membership

Russia's invasion of Ukraine in February 2022 worsened Sweden's security situation and Sweden applied for membership in NATO in May 2022. More or less overnight, 200 years of non-alignment were thrown overboard. The government that took office after the 2022 election declared that it wanted to "primarily pursue a Swedish and European foreign policy".[43] Membership in NATO was a central part of this foreign policy.

Article 5 of the NATO Charter is central to all discussions regarding membership. It states that Member States must take "such action as it deems necessary, including the use of force", to assist a Member State that has been subjected to armed attack. However, it is up to each individual Member State to decide what "action" it "deems necessary". In the bill on Swedish NATO membership, the government stated that there is no legally binding obligation on members to deploy armed forces; what is required is that a party takes the measures "it deems necessary".[44] However, even if there is no obligation to take military action in the NATO Charter, the expectation

[37] Regeringen.se/tal/2022/06/utrikesdeklarationen-2022. Accessed 4 May 2025.

[38] UNSC 2018g; UNSC 2019.

[39] UNSC 2017c; UNSC 2018c.

[40] *See, for example*, https://freedomhouse.org/report/freedom-world/2022/global-expansion-authoritarian-rule. Accessed 18 April 2025.

[41] Government bill 2020/21:30, p. 32 (translation by the author).

[42] Ibid., p. 69.

[43] Regeringen.se/tal/2023/022/utrikesdeklarationen-2023. Accessed 4 May 2025.

[44] Government Bill 2022/23:74, p. 35.

of military help from a defense alliance is naturally high, just as it is as a result of Article 42:7 of the Treaty of Lisbon. Article 5 is central to NATO.

9.4 Sweden as a Member

Sweden became a member of the alliance in March 2024 and the question is how membership will affect foreign policy. Will Sweden have to radically change its policy? The Green Party (*Miljöpartiet*) and the Left Party (*Vänsterpartiet*), which voted against the government's proposal for a Swedish membership, think so. They have offered arguments that resemble those heard during the long period of neutrality and non-alignment. Membership would increase the risk of Sweden being drawn into wars and conflicts that we do not choose ourselves. Sweden's work for disarmament would be weakened and Swedish freedom of action would be limited.[45] The Green Party was also clear that the very core of foreign policy was at risk. Jacob Risberg of the Green Party emphasized that "The Green Party wants Sweden to be a strong foreign policy voice for maintaining democracy and peace in accordance with international law" when the parliament (*riksdagen*) debated the government's bill. "Our ability to do that will be altered but also limited by NATO membership", he continued.[46]

However, the government and the majority in parliament were of a different opinion. Cramér writes that the Swedish ambitions to be a clear, active actor that contributes to long-term security policy stability beyond the primacy of the balance of power seem to remain even after membership in NATO.[47] In the statement of foreign policy in June 2022, Foreign Minister Ann Linde declared that Sweden, as a NATO member, would not lose its global voice. Sweden would continue to stand up for international law, solidarity, disarmament, democracy, equality, human rights, and a rules-based world order. Even with membership, foreign policy would be "global, multilateral, and based on international law".[48] The government at the time prioritized its closest neighbors but there was no indication that the role of international law in foreign policy would diminish in case of a change of government. "The rules-based international system, respect for the UN Charter, and the protection of human rights remain fundamental to foreign policy", underscored Prime Minister Ulf Kristersson in the statement of government policy in October 2022.[49] This rules-based world order continues to be challenged by Russia and China, in particular. Maintaining that order and ensuring respect for international law "constitute central and long-term security policy interests for Sweden", according to the Defense Committee

---

[45] Minutes of the Parliament 2022/23:79 (translation by the author).

[46] Ibid.

[47] Cramér 2022, p. 496.

[48] Regeringen.se/tal/2022/06/utrikesdeklarationen-2022. Accessed 4 May 2025.

[49] Regeringen.se/tal/2022/10/regeringsförklaringen-den-18-oktober-2022. Accessed 4 May 2025.

(*Försvarsberedningen*).[50] The alternative was considered to be a world ruled by great powers, where the sovereignty and territorial integrity of smaller states would not be respected.

In the statement of foreign policy of 2023, Foreign Minister Tobias Billström said that Russia had shown boundless contempt for international law and the most fundamental rules of the UN Charter. He talked about the importance of accountability for crimes, about the need for disarmament, about violence not being allowed to take precedence over justice, and that the Swedish policy would have an important global dimension.[51] In the bill on Swedish NATO membership, the government emphasized that Sweden, even as a member, could promote fundamental values in foreign and security policy and that Sweden must continue to be a strong voice for international law, human rights, democracy, and the principle of the rule of law, as well as equality.[52] Thus, the official rhetoric is essentially the same, even after the application for membership and change of government.

The Committee on Foreign Affairs also noted that there was strong support in parliament for Sweden to continue to "pursue a value-based foreign policy and be a strong voice for democracy and human rights". NATO membership, the Committee continued, would not pose "any obstacles" to continuing to pursue such issues.[53] The investigation into the consequences for Sweden of the deteriorating security policy situation emphasized that membership in NATO would not affect Sweden's opportunities to promote basic values in foreign and security policy—membership would constitute a complement to Sweden's involvement in the EU, the UN, and the OSCE.[54] It is possible that a shift in the view of the UN can be discerned in Committee statements. The UN has traditionally been considered a "cornerstone" of Swedish foreign policy, but in March 2023 the Committee on Foreign Affairs spoke of the UN as an "important arena" for foreign policy.[55] The Committee on Defense highlighted the UN as "one of" the main administrators of a rules-based world order.[56]

An investigation performed as early as 2016 found little evidence that Sweden's role as a mediator and international conflict resolver would diminish with NATO membership.[57] A Finnish Committee investigating the consequences of membership also reasoned along the same lines. A report by the latter Committee held that: "Experience shows that membership (or non-membership) in NATO does not seem to have any significance for a small country's ability to take diplomatic initiatives in global forums."[58]

---

[50] Swedish Defence Committee 2023, p. 165.

[51] Regeringen.se/tal/2023/022/utrikesdeklarationen-2023. Accessed 4 May 2025.

[52] Government Bill 2022/23:74, p. 44.

[53] Committee on Foreign Affairs 2021/22:UU20, p. 9.

[54] Utrikesdepartementet 2022, p. 39.

[55] Committee on Foreign Affairs 2022/23:UU7, p. 19.

[56] Swedish Defence Committee 2023, p. 16.

[57] Swedish Government Official Reports (SOU) 2016:57, p. 145.

[58] Finska Utrikesministeriet 2016, p. 45 (translation by the author).

Nor would disarmament efforts necessarily need to be slowed down. In the foreign policy declaration of 2022, it was highlighted that Sweden would continue to be a strong voice for disarmament, non-proliferation, and arms control, and that the goal was a world free of nuclear weapons.[59] In the same month and year—June 2022—the Committee on Foreign Affairs assessed that Sweden's continued involvement in matters of disarmament, non-proliferation, and arms control would not be affected by NATO membership.[60]

In my book *Efter neutralitetspolitiken*, it was established that Sweden has consistently acted on the basis of the notion that, with the help of law, states can be entangled in commitments and dependencies that make the cost of a breach of the norms as high as possible. This creates stability and predictability that is favorable for a small or medium-sized state. This view has not changed, and the official speeches echo the same sentiments on this matter even after the membership application and the change of government in autumn 2022.

Ever since the end of the Cold War, and not least since Sweden's entry into the EU, it has been clear that Sweden has moved from the policy of neutrality and non-alignment and rather seeks security through cooperation with others, which is natural for a state of Sweden's size.[61] Membership in an international organization gives a small or medium-sized state an influence far greater than its size would normally warrant. In the words of the Committee on Foreign Affairs, it gives "an opportunity for Swedish positions to have an impact".[62] Sweden has therefore worked for the UN to be as effective as possible, has been a committed member of the OSCE, and has put the EU at the center of its foreign policy. From that perspective, it can be said that NATO appeared to constitute an outlier, as it was a multilateral organization that Sweden could have joined but did not want to join. This applies not least in view of the fact that everything that has been said about influence, compliance with norms, and other aspects that are central to Sweden when it comes to the UN and the EU to a large extent also applies to NATO. The defense alliance had also been praised by the government even before the question of Swedish membership was discussed. It was seen as a "central actor" for European security and integration as well as for international crisis management. NATO was said to uphold the collective security guarantees within the alliance and be "the clearest manifestation of the transatlantic link". The organization, the government stated, also constitutes "the most important forum for a broad security policy dialogue between North America and Europe".[63]

After the Russian invasion of Ukraine, however, what was previously said about the UN and the EU has also been considered to apply to NATO. Now, the government speaks about its work for a more peaceful and safer world being conducted in, and in close cooperation with, organizations such as the EU, NATO, the UN,

---

[59] Regeringen.se/tal/2022/06/utrikesdeklarationen. Accessed 4 May 2025.

[60] Committee on Foreign Affairs 2021/22:UU20, p. 10.

[61] Keohane and Martin 1995; Goetschel 1998; Thorhallsson and Wivel 2006.

[62] Committee on Foreign Affairs 2022/23:UU7, p. 18 (translation by the author).

[63] Government Communication 2020/21:56, p. 18 (translation by the author).

and the OSCE.[64] The aforementioned investigation states that Sweden as a NATO member would "participate fully" in the security policy discussion and decision-making and "be able to assert Swedish interests and values". It is also said that, as a member, "Sweden would have greater influence on security and defense policy issues in Europe".[65] One could therefore see the Swedish application for membership in the defense alliance as a step consistent with previous efforts to expand the nation's influence through international organizations. As early as 2016, an official report highlighted that the most obvious consequence of NATO membership would be that Sweden gained access to a multilateral transatlantic platform where it could further Swedish security policy interests.[66]

Thus, there is nothing to suggest that the role of international law in Swedish security policy will change in any decisive sense through membership in NATO. Sweden uses international law as an instrument to achieve security, not least by defending and promoting a rules-based order, and will continue to do so.

9.5 In One Aspect, More Consistent

The big changes compared with in the past concern the view of NATO, the view of the defense alliance's importance for Sweden's security, and the view of Sweden's opportunities for influence. The government says that NATO membership provides increased opportunities to assert Swedish interests and values and at the same time emphasizes that Russia's invasion of Ukraine has made it clear that Russia does not consider itself bound by the rules-based world order on which Sweden bases its security.[67] Thus, although international law and non-alignment have served as protection, they are no longer enough. The protection that international law can provide is threatened by Russia's lack of respect for the rules-based world order. Non-alignment is no longer thought to give Sweden security—on the contrary, it is thought to create insecurity. In the investigation into the consequences of the deteriorating security policy situation, it was stated that all Nordic and Baltic countries would be subject to collective defense obligations if Sweden and Finland became members of NATO. "The uncertainty that currently prevails about how a joint approach would be designed in a security policy crisis or in the event of an armed attack would decrease", the investigation emphasizes. It also holds (with words similar to those previously used about non-alignment) that Sweden through NATO membership would not only

[64] Government Bill 2022/23:1, Utgiftsområde 5, p. 27.

[65] Utrikesdepartementet 2022, p. 39 (translation by the author).

[66] Swedish Government 2016, p. 155.

[67] Government Bill 2021/22:246, p. 1.

strengthen its own security, "but also contribute to the security of like-minded neighboring countries".[68] In a marked change, what was previously said about influence in other organizations now also applies to NATO. In that respect, the attitude towards Swedish engagement in international organizations can be said to have become more consistent.

References

Ahlin P (1993) Folkrätten i svensk säkerhetspolitik [Public international law in Swedish security policy]. Juristförlaget
Ahlin P (2017) Efter neutralitetspolitiken [After the neutrality policy]. Jure
Ahlin P (2020/21) Kampen om non-interventionsprincipen—Sverige i FN:s säkerhetsråd 2017–2018 [The struggle over the non-intervention policy—Sweden in the UN Security Council 2017–2018]. Juridisk Tidskrift 4: 892–912
Cramér P (2022) Ett svenskt Natomedlemskap i ett europeiskt sammanhang [A Swedish NATO membership in a European context]. Europarättslig Tidskrift 4: 485–497
Finska Utrikesministeriet (2016), 3/2016. Konsekvenserna av ett eventuellt finskt Natomedlemskap. En bedömning [The consequences of a potential Finnish NATO membership. An assessment]
Goetschel L (1998) The Foreign and Security Policy Interests of Small States in Today's Europe. In: Goetschel (ed) Small States Inside and Outside the European Union. Springer Science + Business Media
Government Offices of Sweden (2022) Position Paper on the Application of International Law in Cyberspace
Keohane RO, Martin LL (1995) The Promise of Institutionalist Theory. International Security 20(1): 39–51
Swedish Defense Committee (2023) Ds 2023:19, Allvarstid. Försvarsberedningens säkerhetspolitiska rapport 2023 [A time of urgency. The Swedish Defense Committee's report of security policy 2024]
Swedish Government (2016) Swedish Government Official Reports (SOU) 2016:57, p. 155
Swedish Ministry of Foreign Affairs (1999) Ds 1999:24, Preventing Violent Conflict - A Swedish action plan
Thorhallsson B and Wivel A (2006) Small States in the European Union: What Do We Know and What Would We Like to Know? Cambridge Review of International Affairs 19(4): 651–668
UN General Assembly (2014) 34th plenary meeting, 30 October 2014, UN Doc. A/69/PV.34
UN Security Council (1993a) Resolution 808, UN Doc. S/RES/808
UN Security Council (1993b) Resolution 827, UN Doc. S/RES/827
UN Security Council (1994) Resolution 955, UN Doc. S/RES/955
UN Security Council (2017a) 7876th meeting, 2 February 2017, UN Doc. S/PV.7876
UN Security Council (2017b) 7886th meeting, 21 February 2017, UN Doc. S/PV.7886
UN Security Council (2017c) Resolution 2349, UN Doc. S/RES/2349
UN Security Council (2017d) 7915th meeting, 5 April 2017, UN Doc. S/PV.7915
UN Security Council (2017e) 7919th meeting, 7 April 2017, UN Doc. S/PV.7919
UN Security Council (2017f) 7925th meeting, 13 April 2017, UN Doc. S/PV.7925
UN Security Council (2017g) 7926th meeting, 18 April 2017, UN Doc. S/PV.7926
UN Security Council (2017h) 7934th meeting, 8 May 2017, UN Doc. S/PV.7934
UN Security Council (2017i) 7947th meeting, 23 May 2017, UN Doc. S/PV.7947
UN Security Council (2017j) 8047th meeting, 13 September 2017, UN Doc. S/PV.8047

[68] Ministry Publications Series (Ds) 2022:7, p. 43 (translation by the author).

UN Security Council (2017k) 8144th meeting, 20 December 2017, UN Doc. S/PV.8144
UN Security Council (2018a) 8185th meeting, 21 February 2018, UN Doc. S/PV.8185
UN Security Council (2018b) 8213th meeting, 23 March 2018, UN Doc. S/PV.8213
UN Security Council (2018c) Resolution 2408, UN Doc. S/RES/2408
UN Security Council (2018d) 8225th meeting, 9 April 2018, UN Doc. S/PV.8225
UN Security Council (2018e) 8228th meeting, 10 April 2018, UN Doc. S/PV.8228
UN Security Council (2018f) 8293rd meeting, 25 June 2018, UN Doc. S/PV.8293
UN Security Council (2018g) 8307th meeting, 11 July 2018, UN Doc. S/PV.8307
UN Security Council (2018h) 8346th meeting, 10 September 2018, UN Doc. S/PV.8346
UN Security Council (2018i) 8372nd meeting, 16 October 2018, UN Doc. S/PV.8372
UN Security Council (2018j) 8381st meeting, 24 October 2018, UN Doc. S/PV.8381
UN Security Council (2019) 8451st meeting, 25 January 2019, UN Doc. S/PV.8451
Utrikesdepartementet (2022) Ds 2022:7 Ett försämrat säkerhetspolitiskt läge—konsekvenser för Sverige [Deterioration of the security environment—implications for Sweden]

Per Ahlin is associate professor in international law at Stockholm University. His research interests lie in international law and constitutional law, especially the role that international law can play in foreign policy and the relationship between international law and constitutional law.

Chapter 10
Sweden, NATO and European Integration

Per Cramér

Contents

Abstract On March 7 2024, Sweden acceded to the Washington Treaty to become a member of the North Atlantic Treaty Organization. In so doing, Sweden abandoned its position as a militarily non-aligned state with the ambition to stay neutral in relation to the belligerents in armed conflicts, a position that had been maintained with relative consistency since 1814. Thus, the normative role of the law of neutrality for the formulation of Swedish foreign and security policy was brought to an end.

The chapter has been written within the framework of the research project *The legal framework for civil protection and preparedness* that is financed by the Swedish Civil Contingencies Agency (MSB).

P. Cramér (✉)
School of Business Economics and Law, University of Gothenburg, Gothenburg, Sweden
e-mail: per.cramer@law.gu.se

M. Klamberg et al. (eds.), *Reconstructing Power and Hegemony in Public International Law*, https://doi.org/10.1007/978-94-6265-743-4_10

In this chapter, it is argued that this change in the Northern European security policy landscape should be seen in a larger context of a successive shift, where the Swedish relationship to the integration processes of the European Union, in combination with cooperation within the frameworks of the Partnership for Peace and the Organization for Security and Co-operation in Europe, has played a central role for a reformulation of the policy of non-alliance. Thereby, the relationship between the policy and the law of neutrality was weakened step by step.

The objective of this contribution is to reflect on, and contribute to a deeper understanding of, these legal/political processes, with a specific focus on the Swedish experience. It is my ambition to give input to the much-needed discussions on formulating a forward-reaching Swedish policy of alliance.

Keywords Non-Alliance · Collective Self-Defence · NATO · EU · OSCE · Charter of Paris · Helsinki Final Act

10.1 Introduction

On May 17 2022, the Swedish Minister of Foreign Affairs signed an application for membership in the North Atlantic Treaty Organization (NATO). This important act was preceded by a *prima facie* rapid and radical reorientation of the Swedish security and defence policy. The immediate motive for this reorientation can be found in Russia's illegal military aggression against the territorial integrity of Ukraine, which underlined a deteriorating security situation in Europe in general, and in the Nordic-Baltic region in particular.[1] Defence and security policy considerations against the backdrop of rapidly changing threat perceptions led to the conclusion that it was in the national interest to be a part of the reciprocal obligations on collective defence expressed in Article 5 of the Washington Treaty.[2] Thus, Sweden abandoned its position as a militarily non-aligned state with the ambition to stay neutral in relation to the belligerents in armed conflicts, a position that had been maintained with relative consistency since 1814.

Following a parallel reorientation of its national security and defence policy, Finland also decided to apply for membership in NATO, thereby leaving its position

[1] The most elaborate official analysis on which the decision to apply for membership in NATO was based can be found in the conclusions by the special parliamentary group that was established on March 16 2022, as a reaction to the Russian aggression against Ukraine. *See* Utrikesdepartementet 2022a. An official translation to English is found in Swedish Ministry of Foreign Affairs 2022.

[2] The North Atlantic Treaty, opened for signature 4 April 1949, 34 UNTS 243 (entered into force 24 August 1949).

of military non-alliance, a position that was originally established through the Soviet-Finnish Agreement of Friendship, Cooperation and Mutual Assistance concluded in 1948.[3]

These changes in the Northern European security policy landscape might seem drastic, or even revolutionary. However, they should be seen in a larger context of a successive shift, where the Swedish and Finnish relationships to the integration processes taking place within the European Union (EU) have played, and play, a central role. In a reciprocal way, the changing positions of two EU Member States, from military non-alliance to being included in NATO, have an effect on the internal dynamics of the EU.

The objective of this brief chapter is to reflect on, and contribute to a deeper understanding of, these legal/political processes, with a specific focus on the Swedish experience. Thereby, it is my ambition to give input to the much-needed discussions on formulating a forward-reaching Swedish policy of alliance.

10.2 Background

To further the understanding of the Swedish decision to become a member of NATO, it must be placed in a politico-historical context. Accordingly, it is relevant to start with a reflection on the concepts of neutrality, permanent neutrality and non-alliance as well as the development of the Swedish policy positions relating to these concepts.

10.2.1 Neutrality, Permanent Neutrality and Non-Alignment

The law of neutrality is a part of public international law that regulates the relations between neutral and belligerent states during armed conflict.[4] In brief, the law of neutrality establishes a balance of rights and duties: The neutral state is obliged to maintain military impartiality in its relations to the belligerents and secure that neutral territory is not used by them for military operations, whereas the belligerents have a duty to leave the neutral state outside the military operations and respect its territorial integrity.[5] Typically, neutrality has been perceived as an instrument for smaller states to avoid being involved in great-power conflicts.

---

[3] Treaty of Friendship, Cooperation and Mutual Assistance, Moscow 6 April 1948, 48 UNTS 149. Regarding the role of the treaty for formulating Finnish security policy during the Cold War, *see* Korhonen 1973.

[4] For an in-depth study of the concept of neutrality in international law, *see* Wrange 2007.

[5] The central regulation of the relations between belligerent and neutral states is found in two of the conventions adopted at the Peace Conference in the Hague 1907: Convention (V) Respecting the Rights and Duties of Neutral Powers and Persons in Case of War on Land, and Convention (XIII) Concerning the Rights and Duties of Neutral Powers in Naval War.

Neutrality in its legal sense presupposes the existence of an armed conflict. Permanent neutrality means that a state, through a commitment under international law, has undertaken to be neutral in relation to belligerents in all current and future armed conflicts. Accordingly, permanent neutrality includes peacetime obligations: The sovereignty of a permanent neutral state is limited in that it cannot enter any international obligations that could limit its ability to fulfil the obligations of impartiality under the law of neutrality in its relations to the belligerents in an armed conflict. The most evident peacetime obligations of a permanently neutral state are that it is prohibited from entering a military alliance or allowing foreign military installations on its territory. Beyond these legally based limitations to its sovereignty, a permanently neutral state is free to formulate its foreign and security policy. Nevertheless, to sustain necessary international trust in its ambition and ability to fulfil the legal duties of neutrality in its relations to belligerent states, its peacetime foreign and security policy must be consistent and based on an objective application of transparently communicated norms and principles.

A state that has unilaterally declared that it will follow a peacetime policy of non-alignment, with the objective of maintaining neutrality in relation to the belligerents in armed conflicts, is not a permanently neutral state in the legal sense. This is because it is not duty-bound to fulfil the obligations under the law of neutrality in its relations to belligerent states and such a self-chosen foreign and security policy position may be unilaterally abandoned at any time. However, in order to maintain the necessary international legitimacy for its special position, such a state has to maintain the same limitations in the peacetime exercise of its sovereignty as a *de jure* permanent neutral state is legally bound to do. As long as this policy is maintained, it may therefore be categorised as a *de facto* permanent neutral state.

10.2.2 The Development of a Swedish Foreign and Security Policy of Non-Alignment Related to Neutrality

The Swedish policy of neutrality constituted an independently chosen self-proclaimed position that was developed in phases from the Vienna Conference in 1815 and onwards. Its development should be seen as an adaption of the foreign and security policy of a small state geographically located between great powers displaying mutual hostility. By the beginning of the 20th century, this position had been established as a fundamental principle of Swedish policy. It was however made clear at an early stage that Sweden had no intention to enter into an obligation of permanent neutrality under international law. Such a move was perceived as an undesirable and unacceptable limitation of national sovereignty.[6] In the same vein,

[6] A motion to initiate international negotiations for a treaty-based recognition of, and guarantees for, a Swedish commitment to permanent neutrality was turned down by the parliament in 1883. The main arguments were that such a treaty-based commitment would give foreign powers an undesired influence over Swedish policy development. *See* Andra Kammarens Tredje Tillfälliga Utskotts

proposals to establish permanent neutrality as a principle of national constitutional law never obtained the political support necessary to be realised.

Nevertheless, in relation to the Russo-Japanese war that broke out in 1904, the Swedish government declared 'a confirmation of our *steady intention to always* abide to the strictest and most impartial neutrality during warlike entanglements between foreign powers'.[7] In concordance with this position, Sweden actively contributed to the codification of the law of neutrality that took place during the Peace Conference in the Hague in 1907.[8]

Thus, already in the beginning of the 20th century, the Swedish position was characterised by a duality which was maintained thereafter: The steadiness of the intention to stay neutral in relation to belligerent states was consistently underlined, with strong emphasis. Simultaneously, it was made clear that this position was not a Swedish obligation, but constituted a sovereign choice which did not limit Swedish formal sovereignty. This separated Sweden from Switzerland, and later Austria, which both have the position of *de jure* permanent neutral states recognised under international law, a position which is also reconfirmed in national constitutional law.[9]

Nevertheless, as long as Swedish political decision-makers did not abandon the political aim to be able to fulfil the state's obligations under the law of neutrality in times of war, Sweden had to abide by the same limitations of its sovereignty as *de jure* permanent neutral states. From this follows that Sweden could be characterised as a *de facto* permanent neutral state, but with a status that could be changed unilaterally through a political decision.

During the two world wars of the 20th century, Sweden declared its neutrality in relation to the belligerent great powers and their allies. The fundamental obligation of a neutral state's military impartiality, in exchange for a belligerent's respect of its territorial integrity, constituted the backbone of Swedish policy during both these massively destructive armed conflicts. However, it should be noted that the law of neutrality was imperfectly fulfilled. Rather, it became a normative baseline for continuous negotiations between Sweden and the belligerents, where both belligerent sides

---

Utlåtande 1883, pp. 7–8. A number of similar motions, of which some proposed negotiations for regional Nordic permanent neutrality, were turned down by the Swedish parliament in the subsequent years. *See* Lindberg 1958, pp. 145–154.

[7] SFS 1904 (emphasis added, translation by the author).

[8] *See* Bring 2008, pp. 155–159. The Hague Conventions I, III–VII, IX, XI and XIII were ratified by Sweden on 27 November 1909, *see* SFS 1910.

[9] Federal Constitution of the Swiss Confederation, Article 173, according to which the Federal Assembly has the duty to take measures to safeguard external security and the independence and neutrality of Switzerland. The official translation to English is available at https://www.fedlex.admin.ch/eli/cc/1999/404/en, accessed 28 October 2024. Regarding the recent official formulation on Swiss neutrality policy, *see* Swiss Federal Council 2022.

Austrian permanent neutrality is based on a unilateral declaration of the Austrian Parliament. The declaration was made in the course of the withdrawal of occupying Allied Forces and constituted a condition for regaining Austrian national sovereignty under the Austrian State Treaty 1955. The declaration was subsequently enacted as a constitutional act of parliament as an integral part of the Austrian constitution. *See* Bundesverfaßungsgesetz vom 26 Okt 1955 über die Neutralität Österreichs, BGBI 211/1955.

demanded respect for the balance of power at the time of negotiation. In order to attain the overriding objective of preserving its territorial integrity, Sweden made a number of concessions, deviating from its duties under the law of neutrality in favour of the belligerent that was in a position of relative strength at a given time.[10] In addition, one important explicit exception from the principled policy of neutrality should be noted: After the Soviet aggression against Finland 1939, Sweden explicitly declared a non-neutral position. Throughout the subsequent Finno-Soviet war, Sweden took the position of being a non-belligerent participant actively supporting the Finnish war efforts through the supply of war materials and providing Swedish volunteers with weaponry and other equipment. In this case, Nordic solidarity was given primacy over the policy principle of neutrality in relation to belligerent states.[11]

The fact that Sweden managed to maintain its territorial integrity during the two world wars nevertheless strengthened the general national legitimacy of the idea of peacetime non-alliance and wartime neutrality in the relations to surrounding great powers displaying mutual hostility.

10.2.3 Swedish Positioning During the Cold War: Tension Between Ideological and Economic Affinity with the West and Military Non-Alliance

In brief, the Swedish foreign and security policy that emerged after the end of the Second World War was based on three interrelated objectives. First, to support the vision of a peaceful world order, based on international law, through the development of multilateral structures for international collaboration, most importantly the United Nations (UN) and the system for collective security established through the UN Charter. Second, to promote deeper Nordic cooperation and, third, not to get directly involved in either of the mutually hostile military blocs that were rapidly developing around the two ascending superpowers.

Accordingly, the obligations under the UN Charter were given priority over the objective of staying neutral and, in connection with its accession to the Charter, Sweden declared its unconditional commitment to fulfil the country's obligations, including the execution of Security Council decisions on sanctions against belligerent

---

[10] This balancing act between preserving Sweden's territorial integrity and the full exercise of its national sovereignty in accordance with the law of neutrality has been described and analysed in a number of scholarly publications. *See* Cramér 1998, pp. 182–188, 214–229.

It can be noted that Switzerland, during the two world wars, experienced a similar situation of continuous negotiations with the belligerents where the law of neutrality constituted a baseline from which deviations were made in favour of the belligerent party that at the time was in a position of relative strength. Regarding Switzerland, *see further* in Bonjour 1978.

[11] Regarding the Swedish policy in relation to Finland during the Winter War 1939–1940, *see* Wahlbäck 1964, pp. 205–227.

states. Neutrality was perceived as a fall-back position that would be relevant if the system of collective security under Chapter VII of the UN Charter failed.[12]

In the Nordic context, Sweden took initiatives for deeper military collaboration, including the establishment of a Nordic alliance for collective self-defence based on non-alliance in relation to the great powers.[13] Largely because of the differences in experiences during the Second World War, this initiative failed to gain support outside Sweden. Denmark and Norway instead decided to join NATO in 1949.

During the Cold War, the Swedish peacetime policy of neutrality became explicitly related to the bi-polar balance of power between East and West which deadlocked the UN collective security system. Accordingly, Sweden explicitly ruled out entering any international commitment that would limit its ability to abide by the law of neutrality in case of war between the two blocs. Most importantly, Sweden decided it would not enter any kind of commitment regarding collective self-defence or allow access to Swedish territory by foreign powers.[14] This was encapsulated in the official formula for the Swedish position as a *de facto* permanent neutral state that was developed by the early 1950s, reading 'non-alliance in times of peace aiming for neutrality in case of war'.[15] In its public pronouncements regarding the meaning of this oft-repeated position, the Swedish government underlined that Sweden as a *de facto* permanent neutral state had to abide by the same limitations on its sovereignty as the *de jure* permanent neutrals Switzerland and Austria.[16] Thus, the law of neutrality was given the role of a normative framework for the Swedish peacetime foreign and security policy.[17]

However, Sweden explicitly declared that it shared an ideological and economic affinity with the Western democracies, a position that was reaffirmed through entering international agreements. In 1950, Sweden acceded to the General Agreement on Tariffs and Trade.[18] The following year, Sweden entered as a party to the International Monetary Fund and the World Bank.[19] The country's adherence to liberal democratic values was reconfirmed through its participation in establishing the Council

---

[12] Statement by Prime Minister Hansson to the Parliament's First Chamber October 22 1945, Riksdagens protokoll Första kammaren 1945:32, pp. 4–5.

[13] *See* statement by Prime Minister Erlander to the Parliament's First Chamber February 9 1949, Riksdagens protokoll Första kammaren 1949:5, pp. 12–20.

[14] Ibid., p. 19.

[15] This formula was used by the Swedish government with a very high degree of consistency from the early 1950s until 1992.

[16] *See* speech by Prime Minister Erlander at the Congress of the Metalworkers' Union, August 22 1961. https://www.svenskatal.se/tal/tage-erlander. Accessed 13 October 2024. A translation into English is found in Andrén 1975, pp. 51–64.

[17] *See* n. 13 above, p. 19.

[18] The Annecy Protocol of Terms of Accession to the General Agreement on Tariffs and Trade, Annecy 10 October 1949, 62 UNTS 122, SÖ 1950:113.

[19] Articles of Agreement of the International Monetary Fund, Washington DC 27 December 1945, 2 UNTS 39, SÖ 1953:74. Articles of Agreement of the International Bank for Reconstruction and Development, Washington DC 27 December 1945, 2 UNTS 134, SÖ 1953:75.

of Europe in 1949[20] and the Nordic preference was manifested by active contributions to the creation of the inter-parliamentary Nordic Council in 1952.[21] It should be noted that all these structures for international collaboration were of intergovernmental character, meaning that Sweden could not, through its participation, be bound by additional duties contradicting its national political priorities. This was seen in contrast to the economic integration in Western Europe that started with the establishment of the Coal and Steel Community in 1952 and expanded through the European Economic Community (EEC) and the European Atomic Energy Community in 1958. The process of economic and political integration that was foreseen in the framework of the three Communities clearly had supranational characteristics that, from a Swedish perspective, were considered incompatible with a credible peacetime policy of non-alliance aiming for neutrality in times of war.[22] However, this did not prohibit Sweden from actively participating in the establishment of the intergovernmental European Free Trade Association (EFTA) in 1960[23] or from entering a Free Trade Agreement with the EEC in 1972.[24]

With all this taken together, there was an underlying tension within the Swedish position with regard to the escalating bi-polar balance of power between East and West, combining military impartiality with economic and ideological affinity with the West. Against this backdrop, Sweden initiated a military reinsurance policy with the objective of securing military support from the West in case the country's policy of neutrality failed and was not respected by the East. However, this reinsurance policy did not include any binding commitments, which would have formally infringed upon the country's ability to maintain neutrality in any armed confrontation between the two great-power blocs.[25]

---

[20] Statute of the Council of Europe, London 5 May 1949, 87 UNTS 103, SÖ 1949:38. It should be noted that the Swedish accession to the Council of Europe was made conditional on that military issues were not brought up on the agenda of the Council. The Swedish Government also underlined that the organisation had an intergovernmental character, and that Sweden thereby could avoid being bound by new obligations against its national political will. *See* Af Malmborg 1994, pp. 268–284.

[21] Kungl. Maj.ts proposition till riksdagen angående inrättande av ett nordiskt råd, Prop. 1952:206 [Royal Bill to the Parliament on Instatement of a Nordic Council, Government Bill 1952:206].

[22] *See* n. 16 above.

[23] Konventionen angående upprättandet av Europeiska frihandelssammanslutningen [Convention on the establishment of the European Free Trade Association], Stockholm January 4, 1960. Entered into force 3 May 1960. SÖ 1960:1. This regional free trade area, operating in parallel to the Communities, included at its establishment Austria, Denmark, Norway, Portugal, Sweden, Switzerland and the United Kingdom.

[24] Agreement Between the Kingdom of Sweden and the European Economic Community, Brussels 22 July 1972, EUR-Lex Document 21972A0722(02).

[25] The Swedish reinsurance policy during the Cold War was not publicly accounted for before 1994. *See* Sverige Neutralitetspolitikkommissionen 1994. Available in an unofficial translation into English, *see* Commission on Neutrality Policy 1994.

10.3 An Active Peacetime Policy of Neutrality

As a consequence of an escalating arms race between East and West, including ever larger nuclear arsenals, the concept of permanent neutrality gained a somewhat new, independent meaning from the mid-1950s and onwards. This meaning could be seen as a logical consequence of the Cold War doctrine of mutual assured destruction: When the alternatives for the future to an increasing extent were not perceived to be peaceful coexistence or victory for one side, but peaceful co-existence or the total and immediate destruction of everything, the idea of being neutral during a major armed confrontation between the two dominating powers no longer was perceived as a realistic option. Thus, the status of permanent neutrality, *de jure* or *de facto*, became a question of actively seeking to further continued peaceful co-existence rather than passively avoiding belligerency. Sweden, Switzerland and Austria all developed policies, with somewhat different characteristics, along this line. To remain, at least formally, free from international commitments that would risk limiting their ability to abide by the rules of neutrality in times of war constituted a fundamental legitimising factor for these policies of neutrality. In concrete terms, this included actions with the objective of defusing tensions between the two dominating superpowers, such as willingness to act as mediators, contribute to UN peacekeeping missions, hosting conferences on disarmament and international confidence-building, as well as taking up protective power assignments. In the case of Sweden, a globalist approach became a distinct feature of its foreign policy, including strong support of the UN system and the process of decolonisation.

The European neutrals were given an increased margin of manoeuvre during the détente period of the 1970s. The clearest example is the contribution by the neutral and non-aligned states within the framework of the Conference on Security and Co-operation in Europe (CSCE), an ambulating diplomatic conference that included both East and West, which led up to the Final Act of the Helsinki Conference in 1975.[26] Albeit in the format of a political agreement, the Final Act constituted a substitute for a non-existing Peace Treaty after the Second World War, reconfirming the sovereign equality of all participating states, their territorial integrity and the fulfilment in good faith of obligations under international law.[27]

---

[26] Conference on Security and Co-operation in Europe, Final Act, Helsinki August 1, 1975, 14 ILM 1272 (1975). The Final Act of the Helsinki Conference became the start of a process of consecutive negotiations that included all European states, the USA and Canada. Such negotiations took place in Belgrade 1977–1978, Madrid 1980–1983 and Vienna 19861989. Interesting analytical accounts of the roles played by the neutral and non-aligned bloc in the CSCE process are found in the anthology Neuhold 1984. For an analysis with a specific focus on the negotiations during the Helsinki Conference, *see* Fisher 2009.

[27] The decalogue of the Final Act for peaceful co-existence between the participating states reads as follows:

I. Sovereign equality, respect for the rights inherent in sovereignty.
II. Refraining from the threat or use of force.
III. Inviolability of frontiers.
IV. Territorial integrity of States.

Because of this development, the popular legitimacy of permanent neutrality gained strength in Sweden as well as in Switzerland and Austria. Moreover, the value of permanent neutral states as catalysts for de-escalation within the framework of bi-polar balance of power gained international recognition. This was considered achieved primarily through their ability to act as brokers in negotiations and messengers of initiatives that could not have been put forward directly by any of the mutually hostile great powers due to the risk of weakening their negotiation positions in the bi-polar setting.

10.4 The End of the Cold War and Hopes for an All-European Peace Order

At the end of the Cold War, in concordance with the logic of an active peacetime policy of neutrality, Sweden gave its full support to the development of a stable all-European peace order in accordance with the principles laid down in the Helsinki Final Act which were reconfirmed in the Paris Charter for a New Europe 1990. Through this Charter, developed within the framework of the CSCE, the Heads of State or Government of 34 states jointly declared that the Cold War was over:

> *We, the Heads of State or Government of the States participating in the Conference on Security and Co-operation in Europe, have assembled in Paris at a time of profound change and historic expectations. The era of confrontation and division of Europe has ended.*
>
> *We declare that henceforth our, relations will be founded on respect and co-operation.*
>
> *Europe is liberating itself from the legacy of the past. The courage of men and women, the strength of the will of the peoples and the power of the ideas of the Helsinki Final Act have opened a new era of democracy, peace and unity in Europe.*[28]

In this hopeful security policy environment, the special roles played by the European permanently neutral states as intermediaries between mutually hostile great powers decreased in importance. In the absence of a threat of an armed confrontation between the great powers, the question of Swedish wartime neutrality seemed increasingly irrelevant or obsolete. Instead, the primary Swedish foreign and security policy objective became to contribute to that no new demarcation lines would develop in Europe and that a sustainable peace order beyond the logic of balance

---

V. Peaceful settlement of disputes.
VI. Non-intervention in internal affairs.
VII. Respect for human rights and fundamental freedoms, including the freedom of thought, conscience, religion or belief.
VIII. Equal rights and self-determination of peoples.
IX. Cooperation among States.
X. Fulfilment in good faith of obligations under international law.

[28] Charter of Paris for a New Europe, 21 November 1990, 30 ILM 190 (1991).

of power be established.[29] This included strong support for strengthening the CSCE process, which was transformed from an ambulating diplomatic conference into the Organization for Security and Co-operation in Europe (OSCE) in 1995.[30]

Simultaneously, the perceived threat of territorial aggression was widely replaced by a much more diffuse and complex set of threat perceptions that included terrorism, proliferation of weapons of mass destruction, state failure, regional conflicts, international organised crime and the disruption of the flow of vital resources.

During the early 1990s, such partial decoupling between national defence and national territory became a general trend that soon was internalised in the strategic thinking of NATO and the West European Union (WEU).[31] Both these organisations, created for collective defence, declared themselves ready to take on new responsibilities relating to international crisis management. Of particular importance from a European perspective was the Petersberg Declaration of the WEU 1992, in which the Member States of this alliance stated its readiness to conduct humanitarian and rescue tasks, peacekeeping tasks and tasks of combat forces in crisis management, including peace-making.[32]

This development had a strong influence on the continued shift in Swedish security and defence policy priorities. During the following years, Swedish security and defence policy became based on the perception that there was no immediate threat against the country's territorial integrity. The country's defence capacity was radically reduced. The idea of national defence capacity related to the geographically defined national territory was successively substituted by an ambition to contribute to peacekeeping, peace-shaping missions and humanitarian or other crisis management operations beyond the national borders, in accordance with the UN Charter.[33] This shift in policy focus was well in tune with Sweden's traditional strong support for multilateral cooperation based on the UN system.

---

[29] Riksdagens protokoll [Minutes of Parliament] 1995/96:55, p. 6.

[30] In 1993, the CSCE was given the status of a regional arrangement by the United Nations, under Chapter VIII of the UN Charter. The OSCE established its headquarters in Vienna. Regarding this transformative process, *see* McGoldrick 1993.

[31] Concerning NATO, *see* The Alliance's New Strategic Concept, Rome, 7–8 November 1991, paras 7–14. https://www.nato.int/cps/en/natolive/official_texts_23847.htm?selectedLocale=en. Accessed 5 May 2025.Concerning the WEU, *see* WEU Contribution to the European Union Intergovernmental Conference of 1996, Madrid, 14 November 1995, paras 31–64, 92–110. https://www.cvce.eu/content/publication/2002/1/29/38375bab-4a1c-4d94-a713-03c9b5fe8c95/publishable_en.pdf. Accessed 5 May 2025.

[32] Petersberg Declaration made by the WEU Council of Ministers, Bonn, 19 June 1992.

[33] Regeringens proposition [Government Bill] 1996/97:4, Totalförsvar i förnyelse—etapp 2 [Total defense in renewal—stage 2].

10.4.1 *Reassessment of the Policy of Neutrality in Light of Expansion and Deepening of the European Integration Process*

The changes in the geopolitical situation made it possible for Sweden, unhampered by neutrality considerations, to reassess the country's position regarding participation in the European integration process. On 1 July 1991, the Swedish government filed an application for membership in the European Communities, without any demands on derogations regarding the ability to abide by the law of neutrality in case of war. In the preparatory report preceding the decision to apply for membership, the government concluded that the rapid development in Europe in recent years had profoundly changed the preconditions for Sweden to participate in deeper regional cooperation with supranational elements.

This said, the government underlined that certain issues relating to common actions on economic sanctions and trade in armaments could lead to problems regarding the credibility of the policy of neutrality. However, the Swedish government was convinced that the decision-making system in the Communities, even considering foreseen new forms of co-operation, would allow individual Member States to safeguard their national security policy interests.[34]

These new forms of co-operation were clearly foreseeable through the Maastricht negotiations on the Treaty on European Union (TEU), which were finalised in February 1992.[35] A central element of this adaptation of the European integration process to the post-Cold War political landscape was the adoption of treaty provisions on the formulation of a Common Foreign and Security Policy (CFSP), far more ambitious than the established highly informal European Political Cooperation (EPC).[36]

The Swedish application for membership was therefore analysed in light of the draft TEU that was yet to be ratified by the Member States, rather than the existing Community Treaties.

The TEU entered into force in November 1993. It included provisions on the formulation of a CFSP that should encompass all questions related to the security of the Union, 'including the eventual framing of a common defence policy, which might in time lead to a common defence'.[37] This development within the EU was partly reflected in the policy statement of the Swedish Government in October 1991, that 'the formulation of Swedish foreign and security policy will change in a

[34] Riksdagens protokoll [Minutes of Parliament] 1990/91:132, pp. 4–8.

[35] Treaty on European Union, Maastricht 7 February 1992. Entered into force November 1, 1993. EUR-Lex Document 11992M/TXT (TEU 1993). The EU became an umbrella structure for the European Communities and two additional pillars of cooperation: The Common Foreign and Security Policy (CFSP) and Justice and Home Affairs.

[36] Single European Act, EUR-Lex Document 11986U/TXT, Article 30.

[37] TEU 1993, Article J.4(1).

changing Europe'.[38] This was a prelude to a subsequent reformulation of the country's fundamental security and defence policy formula. In April 1992, the Foreign Affairs Committee declared that 'Sweden's military non-alliance aiming for neutrality in case of war in our nearby area remains'.[39] This wording introduced a geographic limitation to the ambition to stand neutral in case of war, inserting an element of uncertainty and ambiguity, and thus decreasing the foreseeability of Swedish wartime policy. The new wording was introduced during the process of negotiations on the Swedish Accession Treaty and had been adopted when Sweden joined the Union in 1995.

In the accession process, the Swedish application was analysed together with applications for membership in the Communities filed by Austria in 1989, Finland in 1992 and Switzerland in 1992.[40] The Commission concluded that '[t]he accession of the EFTA countries who have applied for membership—Austria, Sweden, Finland and Switzerland—should not pose insuperable problems of an economic nature, and indeed would strengthen the Community in a number of ways. The question of neutrality, and its compatibility with the common foreign and security policy, is however of particular concern.'[41]

In its final report regarding the membership applications from Sweden, the Commission concluded that:

> *There is a strong consensus in Sweden favouring a full and active role for Sweden within the European Union. There remain reservations, however, regarding the eventual framing of a common defence policy and these reservations are even more marked as regards the possible*

---

[38] Regeringsförklaring [Statement of Government Policy] 4 October 1991, Riksdagens protokoll [Minutes of Parliament] 1991/92:6, §4.

[39] Utrikesutskottets yttrande [Report of the parliamentary Foreign Affairs Committee], 1991/92:UU2Y, Säkerhetspolitiska överväganden m.m. inför beslut om totalförsvarets utveckling [Security policy considerations, etc., ahead of a decision on the development of the total defense], p. 4.

[40] It should be noted that Austria in its application referred to the Federal Constitutional Law of 26 October 1956 establishing the country's *de jure* permanent neutrality as a constitutional principle, *see* https://www.cvce.eu/content/publication/2005/11/4/8ede7e56-6922-46c2-99db-dc5da0eb0c22/publishable_en.pdf. Accessed 5 May 2025.

Switzerland's application for accession to the European Communities did not include a similar reference to neutrality as a constitutional principle, *see* Switzerland's application for accession to the EEC, 20 May 1992. The proposal for a Swiss ratification of the European Economic Area agreement, and thereby also the proposal to commence negotiations for accession to the European Communities, was defeated in a referendum 6 December 1992. Since then, Switzerland has developed its relations with the EU through bilateral agreements in order to safeguard its economic integration with the EU, *see* https://www.fdfa.admin.ch/europa/en/home/bilateraler-weg/ueberblick.html. Accessed 5 May 2025.

Finland's application for accession to the European Communities referred to the specific historic context of the country's policy of non-alliance as an instrument to further Nordic security policy stability which had benefitted Europe as a whole. The application did not include a demand for an explicit derogation relating to the maintenance of national non-alliance, *see* https://www.cvce.eu/en/obj/finland_s_application_for_accession_to_the_european_community_from_the_revue_du_marche_commun_et_de_l_union_europeenne_june_1992-en-e80ab57c-2372-4b22-8735-1ed15339c16a.html. Accessed 5 May 2025.

[41] European Commission 1992a, p. 18.

establishment, in time, of a common defence. The Community would need, in the context of the accession negotiations, to ascertain further the full nature of the present Swedish policy in order to be satisfied that this would not hamper the possible evolution in time of a common European defence.[42]

The reformulation of the Swedish foreign and security policy doctrine must be seen in the context of the Commission's assessment. The remaining potential legal-political tension between the reformulated Swedish doctrine and the obligations under the chapter of the TEU on the development of a Common Foreign and Security Policy was defused through references to the intergovernmental character of the decision-making process for formulating the CFSP and a reservation of more general character regarding the development of the CFSP:

The policy of the Union in accordance with this article shall not prejudice the specific character of the security and defence policy of certain Member States and shall respect the obligations of certain Member States under the North Atlantic Treaty and be compatible with the common security and defence policy established within that framework.[43]

The wording of the first element of this provision, relating to the specific character of the security policy of certain Member States, had been developed by the Irish government during the negotiations on the Maastricht Treaty with the objective of safeguarding the Irish position as a military non-aligned Member State of the EU. In the context of the Swedish accession to the Union, this reservation was perceived to be a guarantee that EU Membership was compatible with national military non-alliance.

It should also be noted that, by explicitly recognising *both* the military non-alliance of certain Member States and the alliance within NATO of other Member States, the TEU excluded questions relating to territorial defence from the CFSP agenda. Accordingly, the subsequent development of the CFSP primarily became focused on international crisis management and the furthering of military capacity building.

10.4.2 The Integration of the Petersberg Tasks into the TEU and Further Swedish Downplaying of the Relation to the Concept of Neutrality

The CFSP chapter of the TEU was considerably expanded through the entry into force of the Amsterdam Treaty in 1999,[44] when the so-called Petersberg Tasks that had been adopted by the WEU in 1992[45] were transferred to the EU, thereby establishing

[42] European Commission 1992b, p. 14.

[43] TEU (1993), Article J.4(4).

[44] Treaty of Amsterdam amending the Treaty on European Union, the Treaties establishing the European Communities and certain related acts, Amsterdam 2 October 1997. Entered into force 1 May 1999. EUR-Lex Document 11997D/TXT.

[45] *See* n. 32 above.

a European Security and Defence Policy (ESDP) as a part of the CFSP.[46] However, the ESDP did not establish a common defence. Such a development was declared to be a long-term non-binding goal without any set timeline.[47] It should be noted that the incorporation of the Petersberg tasks into the TEU was largely the result of a Swedish-Finnish initiative tabled during the negotiations. The motive behind this path of action by these two non-aligned EU Member States was to effectively bar the introduction of obligations relating to common territorial defence into the TEU, a development which would have been in open contradiction with the policy of military non-alliance.[48] In the Swedish Government's Foreign Policy Declaration 1999, the importance of upholding a clear dividing line between crisis management and territorial defence was underlined.[49] By focusing on ambitious crisis management operations based on UN mandates, it was the Swedish ambition to continue to keep the issue of territorial defence outside the EU agenda. This was in full harmony with that Sweden in 1994 entered into a collaboration with NATO under the Partnership for Peace (PfP) framework. The objective of the partnership was to enhance security policy stability through concrete military and confidence-building cooperation in Europe, including to contribute to international military crisis management operations mandated by the UN Security Council or the OSCE.[50]

Sweden soon demonstrated active loyalty to the implementation of the ESDP and the development of the PfP. The country contributed with military and civilian resources to most of the crisis management and capacity-building operations decided upon within these frameworks.[51]

Against the backdrop of the developing European peace order, the objective of abiding by the law of neutrality in case of war was perceived as becoming increasingly irrelevant. The Swedish security policy doctrine was reformulated in 2002 and given the character of a policy of non-alignment with a geographically limited option to be neutral in case of war: 'Sweden is military non-aligned. This line of security policy with a *possibility* for neutrality in conflicts in our neighbourhood has served us well.'[52] Thus, Sweden remained non-aligned. However, in the eyes of other states, the objective of the non-alignment was moot and the trust in a Swedish intention to be neutral in case of war became weak or non-existent.

---

[46] TEU 1999, Article J.7(2).

[47] TEU 1999, Article J.7(1).

[48] Rieker 2006, pp. 72–75. Lee-Ohlsson 2009, p. 127.

[49] Riksdagens protokoll [Minutes of Parliament] 1998/99:53, p. 5.

[50] Partnership for Peace: Framework Document issued by the Heads of State and Government participating in the Meeting of the North Atlantic Council. Brussels 11 January 1994.

[51] *See* Government of Sweden 2007.

[52] Regeringens deklaration vid 2002 års utrikespolitiska debatt i Riksdagen [The Government's declaration at the 2002 foreign policy debate in Parliament], 13 February 2002, p. 6 (emphasis added, translation by the author).

10.5 The Recoupling of National Territory and National Defence and the Entering of Collective Defence into the Framework of the TEU

During the first decade of the 21st century, the geopolitical tensions in Europe increased and the linkage between national territory and defence gradually returned in the strategic thinking of both NATO and the EU.[53] This was reflected in initiatives for developing the ESDP through integrating the collective defence provisions of the WEU into the TEU. Such ideas were brought up during the intergovernmental negotiations on the Constitutional Treaty that commenced in 2002 and were finalised in the following year.[54] After the rejection of the draft constitutional treaty in the Dutch and French processes for ratification, a renewed process of intergovernmental negotiations led to the Lisbon Treaty, which was signed in December 2007 and entered into force in 2009.[55]

Through the Lisbon amendment to the TEU, the ESDP was transformed into a more ambitious Common Security and Defence Policy (CSDP) that included a reciprocal provision on aid and assistance if a Member State was the victim of an armed aggression, displaying similarities to Article 5 of the Washington Treaty:

> *If a Member State is the victim of armed aggression on its territory, the other Member States shall have towards it an obligation of aid and assistance by all the means in their power, in accordance with Article 51 of the United Nations Charter. This shall not prejudice the specific character of the security and defence policy of certain Member States.*
>
> *Commitments and cooperation in this area shall be consistent with commitments under the North Atlantic Treaty Organisation, which, for those States which are members of it, remains the foundation of their collective defence and the forum for its implementation.*[56]

It should be noted that this provision, in its second sentence, includes a reservation with reference to the *special character of the security and defence policy of certain Member States*. Thus, the obligation of alliance established in the first sentence would not be in conflict with the policy of military non-alliance pronounced by a number of Member States. Moreover, it should be underlined that the alliance provision of the TEU according to the second paragraph was explicitly made subordinate to the commitments following from membership in NATO.

It should in this context be underlined that Sweden explicitly stated that it did not view the accession to the Lisbon Treaty as an acceptance of the obligations that

[53] *See* Council of the EU 2009. The European Security Strategy was initially adopted on 12 December 2003. Regarding the development of the strategic thinking of NATO, *see* the official account at https://www.nato.int/cps/en/natohq/topics_56626.htm Accessed 28 October 2024.

[54] *See* the Draft Treaty Establishing a Constitution for Europe, adopted by the European Convention 10 July 2003. EUR-Lex Document C:2004:310:TOC.

[55] Treaty of Lisbon amending the Treaty on European Union and the Treaty establishing the European Community, Lisbon 13 December 2007. Entered into force 1 December 2009. EUR-Lex Document 12007L/TXT.

[56] TEU, Article 42(7).

follow from entering a reciprocal system for collective self-defence. In the proposal to the Parliament on ratification of the Lisbon Treaty, the Swedish government made the assessment, with reference to the second sentence of Article 42(7), that nothing in the CSDP should hinder those Member States that wished to conduct a policy of non-alliance from doing so. Accordingly, the Swedish government stated that Article 42(7) did not establish any obligations regarding territorial defence for non-aligned EU Member States, like Sweden.[57] This view was confirmed in the official report by the parliamentary working group on the changed security environment following Russia's aggression against Ukraine, laying the ground for the application for NATO membership. Here, the legal argument was elaborated by an additional reference to TEU Article 4.2, stating that '[i]n particular national security remains the sole responsibility of each Member State'. It was also stated that the conditions for a shift towards collective defence within the EU were lacking.[58] The conclusions presented in the report were referred to in the government's proposition for the Swedish accession to the Washington Treaty.[59]

10.5.1 Sweden at the Crossroads

By 2008, the increasing geopolitical tensions in Europe had led to a common understanding that the vision for a stable all-European peace order was becoming increasingly distant. Sweden chose not to return to a more traditional policy of neutrality, which would have been legally possible under TEU Article 42(7). Rather, Sweden underlined its loyalty to the process of integration within the framework of the Union in the context of a developing confrontative balance of power in Europe. This shift in Swedish security policy thinking also had a clear Nordic focus, which was given a concrete expression in 2009 when the Parliament adopted a unilateral solidarity declaration. On the one hand, the declaration confirmed that Sweden stayed out of military alliances. However, it was underlined that Sweden was fully sovereign to define the closer meaning of the policy of military non-alliance.[60] Somewhat puzzlingly, the declaration continued with a statement expressing a strategy according to the logic of alliance: 'Threats to peace and our security can best be averted collectively and in cooperation with other countries. It is impossible to imagine military conflicts in our region that would affect only one country. Sweden will not remain passive if another EU Member State or Nordic country suffers a disaster or an attack. We expect these countries to take similar action if Sweden is affected. Sweden should therefore be in a position to both give and receive military support.'[61]

---

[57] Regeringens proposition [Government Bill] 2007/08:168, p. 252.

[58] Utrikesdepartementet 2022, above n. 1, p. 28.

[59] Regeringens proposition [Government Bill] 2022/23:74, pp. 9–11.

[60] Ibid., p. 20. For an insightful commentary on the solidarity declaration, *see* Wieslander 2022, pp. 40–42.

[61] Swedish Ministry of Defence 2007, p. 11; Försvarsutskottet 2009, pp. 16–17, 20.

Most importantly, through this declaration, the objective of staying neutral in case of war had been erased from the Swedish security and defence policy doctrine and the relations to the law of neutrality as a normative baseline for the Swedish policy were abandoned. Thus, the motive behind, and objective of, continued non-alliance became unclear both to the outside world and in the domestic political setting. However, this unilateral declaration did not mean that Sweden entered into a military alliance based on reciprocal agreement. The central, and somewhat ambiguous, importance of the declaration was that Sweden, while maintaining formal non-alliance, confirmed a commitment to the provision on collective self-defence in TEU, Article 42(7), and included Nordic states not members of the EU in this commitment. The Nordic dimension of Swedish defence and security policy was thereafter increasingly strengthened, foremost through the establishment of a formalised Nordic Defence Cooperation (NORDEFCO) in 2009.[62]

The reformulated Swedish policy may be described as continued formal peacetime non-alignment decoupled from neutrality. From the perspective of other states, it meant that the expectation of Swedish neutrality in case of war was substituted by an expectation of active support to EU Member States and Nordic non-members if they became victims of armed aggression. However, this expression of solidarity was framed as a unilateral declaration, not a formal commitment under international law.

An illustrative example of how the outside world perceived the Swedish change of direction is found in the official Swiss statement 'Clarity and guidelines on neutrality policy', where it is concluded that Sweden finally abandoned neutrality in 2009 when it decided to join the new NORDEFCO structure.[63]

Following the entry into force of the Lisbon Treaty, Sweden became a loyal contributor to the CSDP, also beyond crisis management. The country intensified its engagement within the framework of the CSDP on issues relating to territorial defence. Sweden became an active member of the European Defence Agency (EDA) which has as its objective to support the Council and the Member States in their effort to improve the Union's defence capabilities[64] and the Permanent Structured Cooperation (PESCO) with the objective of deepening defence cooperation between the EU Member States.[65] Sweden has also contributed to the establishment of the European Defence Fund with the objective of supporting a competitive European

---

[62] The objective of NORDEFCO is to strengthen the participants' national defence, explore common synergies and facilitate efficient common solutions. *See further* https://www.nordefco.org/the-basics-about-nordefco. Accessed 13 October 2024. For an analysis of the initial development and impact of the cooperation within the framework of NORDEFCO, *see* Forsberg 2013.

[63] Swiss Federal Council 2022.

[64] *See* Council Decision (CFSP) 2015/1835 of 12 October 2015 defining the statute, seat and operational rules of the European Defence Agency (recast). EUR-Lex Document 32015D1835. The EDA was set up in 2004 with Sweden as a participating state from the start. At present, all EU Member States are members of the EDA. *See further* https://eda.europa.eu. Accessed 13 October 2024.

[65] *See* Council Decision (CFSP) 2017/2315 of 11 December 2017 establishing permanent structured cooperation (PESCO) and determining the list of participating Member States. EUR-Lex Document 32017D2315. PESCO was established in 2017 with Swedish participation. At present, all EU Member States, except Denmark and Malta, participate in PESCO. *See further* https://www.pesco.europa.eu. Accessed 13 October 2024.

defence industry, thereby decreasing reliance on non-European suppliers of armaments.[66] Regarding strategic development, Sweden has actively contributed to the Union Strategic Compass with the objective of making the EU a stronger and more capable security provider.[67]

10.6 Reaching a Tipping Point Following Escalating Russian Aggression

Following the increasing number of conflicts within the post-Soviet territory, most importantly the illegal Russian annexation of Crimea in 2014, Sweden's defence policy was adapted to changing perceptions of threat to its territorial integrity. The budget allocations for national defence were increased[68] and the country entered into a more ambitious cooperation with NATO as an Enhanced Opportunity Partner, primarily focusing on political dialogue, joint exercises and sharing information.[69] In 2016, this collaboration was further deepened when Sweden entered into a Host Nation Support Agreement with NATO, with the objective of better enabling Sweden to efficiently provide and receive military support from NATO in the event of crisis or war. Moreover, the agreement explicitly stated the objective of enabling foreign military forces to operate and carry out assignments on Swedish territory. Even if the agreement did not establish any obligation for Sweden to allow the presence of foreign troops on its territory, the spirit of the agreement clearly contradicted the obligations of a neutral state in relation to belligerent states. Thus, the Host Nation Support Agreement confirmed that the Swedish continued policy of non-alliance was decoupled from an ambition to fulfil the duties under the law of neutrality in case of war.[70]

Nevertheless, the policy of formal non-alignment continued to have the status of a fundamental principle for Swedish security and defence policy. In the Government's declaration on foreign policy 2021, following a reconfirmation of the solidarity declaration, it was clearly stated that:

---

66 *See further* https://defence-industry-space.ec.europa.eu/eu-defence-industry/european-defence-fund-edf-official-webpage-european-commission_en. Accessed 13 October 2024. *See also* the web page of the Commission Directorate-General for Defence Industry and Space: https://defence-industry-space.ec.europa.eu/index_en. Accessed 13 October 2024.

67 Council of the EU 2022.

68 Regeringens proposition [Government Bill] 2014/15:109 Försvarspolitisk inriktning—Sveriges försvar 2016-2020 [Defense policy direction—Sweden's defense 2016–2020].

69 https://www.nato.int/cps/en/natohq/topics_132726.htm. Accessed 13 October 2024.

70 Regarding the Swedish motives for entering the Host Nation Support Agreement with NATO, *see* Regeringens proposition [Government Bill] 2015/16:152 Samförståndsavtal om värdlandsstöd [Host Nation Support Agreement]. For insightful comments on the Host Nation Support Agreement, *see* Ahlin 2018, pp. 32–36.

> *Our non-participation in military alliances serves us well and contributes to stability and security in northern Europe. It requires an active broad and responsible foreign and security policy combined with enhanced defence cooperation...and credible national defence capabilities.*[71]

As a direct reaction to the full-scale Russian armed aggression against Ukraine on 24 February 2022, the EU, with strong Swedish support, immediately condemned the flagrant Russian violation of its obligations under international law.[72] As a member of the EU, Sweden has since then firmly stood behind decisions on increasingly comprehensive sanctions against Russia and Belarus and support to the Ukrainian war efforts and civil society.[73] On a unilateral level, Sweden has, for the first time since the Soviet aggression against Finland 1939, supported a belligerent state with weapons and other war materials: not declaring itself neutral, but rather taking the position as a non-belligerent participant.[74]

The armed aggression against Ukraine led to a perception of increasing threats of future Russian aggression in the Nordic-Baltic region. It also constituted a definite end to the hopes of establishing a European Peace Order in accordance with the Paris Declaration on a New Europe. These hopes rather became a dream for the distant future.

Against this backdrop, the Swedish decision to apply for membership in NATO was a non-dramatic development of a policy development that had started in the early 2000s. The timing of the application was synchronised with Finland and it is clear that the Finnish decision to seek membership in the Western military defence alliance had an impact on Swedish political decision-makers.

10.7 NATO Membership and Sweden's Relations to EU Law

As a consequence of Sweden's and Finland's accession to the Washington Treaty, the security and defence policy identities of these two EU Member States had to been redefined, in order to be in harmony with the strategic principles that have been developed within NATO.[75] In addition to the reciprocal commitment on collective self-defence, in accordance with Article 51 of the UN Charter, membership requires

---

[71] Government of Sweden 2021.

[72] *See* European Council 2022.

[73] *See further* the account of EU sanctions against Russia given by the European Council at https://www.consilium.europa.eu/en/policies/sanctions-against-russia/. Accessed 13 October 2024.

[74] *See further* the Swedish government's account for military support to Ukraine at https://www.government.se/government-policy/swedens-support-to-ukraine/military-support-to-ukraine/. Accessed 13 October 2024.

[75] NATO 2022.

integration into the common military command structure and common defence planning of NATO. The relations of Sweden and Finland to EU law were thereby transformed in certain areas, primarily in relation to Part 2 of the TEU on the development of the CSDP as a part of the CFSP.

At a general level, the rules laid down in TEU Part 2 establish a framework for the successive development of the CSDP, including the progressive framing of a common Union defence policy. And that '... this will lead to a common defence, when the European Council, acting unanimously, so decides. It shall in that case recommend to the Member States the adoption of such a decision in accordance with their respective constitutional requirements.'[76]

Thus, the development of a common defence within the framework of the EU is, according to the TEU, an option which could be used by the Member States, acting unanimously and in accordance with their respective national constitutional requirements. It should also be noted that the provisions on the CSDP include the general double-edged reservation that was integrated as an element of the CFSP already through the Maastricht Treaty, that: '...[t]he policy of the Union in accordance with this Section shall not prejudice the specific character of the security and defence policy of certain Member States and shall respect the obligations of certain Member States, which see their common defence realised in the North Atlantic Treaty Organization (NATO), under the North Atlantic Treaty and be compatible with the common security and defence policy established within that framework.'[77]

It may accordingly be concluded that the CSDP, as it stands today, does not include the establishment of a common territorial defence. Rather, the CSDP is a dynamic concept that shall primarily provide the Union with operational capacity for the deployment of peacekeeping missions outside the Union, conflict prevention and strengthened international security, in accordance with the principles of the UN Charter.[78] These are the Petersberg Tasks that were transferred from the WEU to the EU through the Amsterdam Treaty. In addition, the Member States undertake to progressively improve their military capabilities, which will strengthen their capacity for territorial defence.[79]

Although the CSDP does not establish a common defence, the TEU, as accounted for above, includes a reciprocal provision on collective self-defence. This provision also includes the reservation that it 'shall not prejudice the specific character of the security and defence policy of certain Member States' and that 'commitments and cooperation in this area shall be consistent with commitments under the North Atlantic Treaty Organisation, which, for those States which are members of it, remains the foundation of their collective defence and the forum for its implementation.'[80]

---

[76] TEU, Article 42(2).

[77] Ibid.

[78] TEU, Article 42(1).

[79] TEU, Article 42(3). This undertaking is primarily executed through the collaboration between the Member States within the framework of the EDA.

[80] TEU, Article 42(7).

Thus, the rules on contributing to the Union's operative capacity for crisis management operations outside Union territory, as well as the obligation to assist a Member State that has been victim of armed aggression on its territory, refer to the same two-sided reservation related to a Member State's policy of non-alliance or its obligations as a member of NATO. As concluded above, the consequence of this reservation is that issues directly related to territorial defence are currently excluded from the agenda of the CSDP. From this follows that the TEU provision on collective self-defence in Article 42(7) primarily has the character of a fall-back position. This would gain in relevance in case a Member State's non-alliance or, most importantly, alliance within NATO would not constitute an effective instrument for strengthening the defence of the national territory. In that case, the TEU also opens for the establishment of a common European defence when the Member States, unanimously, so decide.[81]

Against this backdrop, the Swedish accession to the Washington Treaty only bears with it limited effects on the country's position under EU law. This essentially in the sense that Sweden is no longer covered by the reservation provisions related to the specific character of the security and defence policy of certain Member States but instead belongs to the group of Member States that are members of NATO and for which that alliance is *the foundation of their collective defence and the forum for its implementation.* From this follows that the provision on collective defence in TEU 42(7), as long as NATO is perceived as functioning, will have a limited bearing on Sweden and that the adjacent Swedish unilateral solidarity declaration of 2009 has largely lost its relevance with regard to territorial defence.

With this said, TEU Article 42(7) may be invoked in situations of crisis that do not amount to an armed attack against the territorial integrity of an EU Member State. So far, this has happened once, when France relied on it in the aftermath of the terrorist attacks in Paris 2015. It should here be noted that the provision has an intergovernmental character and does not create competences for the EU. When it is invoked, Member States have to agree bilaterally on the forms of assistance that will be provided.[82]

---

[81] This interpretation of TEU, Article 42(7) is challenged by some contributors to the doctrine: From an Irish perspective, Karen Devine argues that the reservation clause relating to the specific character of the security and defence policy of certain Member States in TEU Article 42 lacks normative content and should be assessed only as a *...rhetorical device for elites to use in their referendum campaign arguments to persuade the Irish electorate that neutrality is preserved. See* Devine 2011, p. 355. Accordingly, TEU Article 42(7) must be construed as an obligation of alliance.

In a contribution to an investigation by the Ministry of Defence, Ove Bring argues that Sweden, through its unilateral declaration of solidarity, accepted to be bound by the alliance commitment in TEU Article 42(7) under public international law. Consequently, according to Bring, the reservation clause in TEU Article 42 has no validity with regard to Sweden.

The interpretation put forward in this chapter finds support among several other European and international law scholars. *See, as examples*, Koutrakos 2011, pp. 238–239; Österdahl 2021.

[82] In this case, the French invocation of Article 42(7) was discussed in the Council of the EU: *Ministers expressed their unanimous and full support for France and their readiness to provide all the necessary aid and assistance. In the coming days France will have bilateral discussions with other member states... The High Representative underlined that this is not a CSDP operation, but an activation of bilateral aid and assistance. See* Council of the EU 2015, p. 6.

This type of application of Article 42(7) could be developed in the future, resulting in a more elaborate demarcation of responsibilities between the EU and NATO.

Lastly, it should be underlined that the provisions on crisis management and capacity building in TEU Article 42 will continue to have high direct relevance for Sweden.

10.7.1 Possible Effects on the Internal Dynamics of the EU

Sweden's and Finland's entry as members of NATO leaves only four non-aligned Member States of the EU: Austria, Cyprus, Ireland and Malta. This may be described as an increase in the homogeneity of the Union's identity with respect to security and defence policy. Thereby, the demarcation lines between EU and NATO competencies will gain in clarity and questions related to territorial defence will be more firmly excluded from the CSDP agenda and be brought up under the framework of NATO.

Moreover, the Swedish and Finnish memberships in NATO contribute to an increased harmonisation among Union Member States regarding armament standards and military operative structures. This will most likely mean that specific national Swedish and Finnish interests to a lesser extent have to be brought up, and handled, within the CSDP. The increased homogeneity within the sphere of security and defence policy will also further the community of interests and thereby facilitate deeper integration within areas covered by the CSDP. A partial shift of internal EU dynamics is likely, at least on the margin, to contribute to a further deepening of the military capacity building within the framework of PESCO, a continued elaboration of the EU Strategic Compass, and decreased obstacles to collaboration between European armaments producers and procurers of armaments. These are all areas where Sweden has demonstrated active engagement.

These changes in the internal dynamics of the Union are furthered by that the EU has to adapt itself to the geopolitical reality that constituted a tipping point for Sweden and Finland to apply for NATO membership. This political reality includes new threat perceptions dominated by risks of continued Russian aggression threatening the territorial integrity of EU Member States, as well as the consequences of terrorist actions and cyberattacks to both vital infrastructures and the stability of democratic systems. It is a reality where the solidarity among EU Member States is put to the test and in which the coordination between the Union and NATO gains in importance. The NATO membership of Sweden and Finland will most likely contribute positively to such co-ordination. It could here be noted that Sweden has declared its intention to work for a close collaboration between the EU and NATO.[83]

[83] Government of Sweden 2024a, p. 6.

10.8 Final Reflections on a Nascent Swedish Policy of Alliance

The Swedish accession to the Washington Treaty, entering as a member of NATO,[84] must be seen as a final step in a successive process of change which started with the end of the divisive bi-polar balance of power that dominated the world during the Cold War.

The Swedish decision to apply for membership in an alliance for collective military self-defence should also be viewed as an exercise of the fundamental principle that was formulated during the early 1900s; that the policy of non-alliance was a unilateral expression of national sovereignty which ultimately remained unhampered by said policy.

The initial phase of the re-orientation of Sweden's security and defence policy during the 1990s and the early 2000s constituted an adaptation to a new security policy landscape in which the hopes of the establishment of a stable all-European peace order in concordance with the principles of UN Charter, the Helsinki Final Act and the Charter of Paris were nurtured. These hopes were well-aligned with the objectives of the active peacetime policy of neutrality that Sweden had developed during the Cold War. However, in such a peace order, there would be no instrumental need for *de jure* or *de facto* permanent neutral states as intermediaries between mutually hostile great powers or as catalysts for peaceful coexistence. Thus, the *raison d'être* for Sweden's active peacetime policy of neutrality was eroded when the final goal of this policy seemed attainable.

This opened for deeper active participation in the European integration process through EU membership and deeper cooperation with NATO, supplemented by a continued strong Swedish engagement within collaborative structures of an all-European character such as the OSCE and the Council of Europe.

The Swedish adaptation meant that the aim to abide by the law of neutrality in case of war was successively substituted by expressions of regional solidarity within the Nordic region, and the EU. The established Swedish engagement in UN peacekeeping operations was translated into active participation in international crisis management operations in concordance with the UN Charter, under the aegis of the CSDP or the PfP. This also meant that the issue of defence was largely decoupled from national territorial borders and the territorial defence capabilities were radically reduced.

As a result of increasing geopolitical tensions, the question of territorial defence regained its importance. Sweden from 2008 and onwards involved itself in increasingly ambitious international collaborations on military defence at the bilateral and regional levels. However, the policy of non-alignment was maintained, albeit with an increasingly dim relation to the aim for neutrality in case of war. Accordingly, the law of neutrality successively lost its normative meaning for the formulation of Sweden's foreign and security policy.

---

[84] Sweden acceded to the Washington Treaty, 7 March 2024, SÖ 2024:1.

The return of an accelerating confrontative division in Europe, manifested in the outbreak of an illegal military aggression against the territorial integrity of a sovereign European state, effectively killed the hopes to realise the vision of a stable all-European peace order for the foreseeable future. This forced Sweden to choose between the return to a strict policy of non-alliance, aiming for neutrality in case of war, or to engage in an alliance for collective defence. Given the circumstances—that Sweden had already engaged in far-reaching military collaboration and explicitly expressed its solidarity with the fellow EU Member States and Nordic non-members in case of any of them being a victim of military aggression—the first was not perceived as a realistic or morally defensible choice. It was also clear that neighbouring Finland, with an 830-mile territorial border to Russia, would apply for membership in NATO, which created a strong incentive for Sweden to follow suit.

Today, Sweden must meet the challenges of redefining its national security and defence policy as an EU Member State that sees its common defence realised in NATO in accordance with the Washington Treaty. This involves full integration into an established military infrastructure as well as political participation within the framework of an intergovernmental organisation.

In its foreign policy declaration of 10 June 2022, less than a month after the Swedish application for NATO membership, the Swedish government declared its intention to commit fully to obligations under the Washington Treaty, but also that Sweden, as a NATO member, would not lose its global voice and that the country's foreign policy would continue to be multilateral and based on international law. It was underlined that Sweden wanted to see an EU that could assume greater responsibility for its own security. Moreover, the declaration included central elements that are similar to the active peacetime policy of neutrality developed in the context of the Cold War bi-polar balance of power: Most notably, it was stated that Sweden will remain a strong diplomatic voice for disarmament, non-proliferation and arms control. The declaration also expressed somewhat utopian hopes for a return of the OSCE's role as a platform for dialogue and accountability when circumstances allow.[85]

These themes were developed in the Statement of Government Policy following Sweden's accession to NATO on 20 March 2024.[86] This statement made it explicit that Sweden's membership of NATO was perceived as a direct result of the Russian full-scale invasion of Ukraine. It was furthermore made clear that Sweden, as a loyal member of NATO and the EU, will pursue an *alliance policy* based on solidarity, aiming to enhance security and stability in neighbouring countries and throughout the Euro-Atlantic area. This alliance-based foreign and security policy was to be built on cohesion in the EU and NATO and cooperation in the Nordic and Baltic Sea regions, and in frameworks of the UN, the OSCE and the Council of Europe.[87] In addition, the fundamental importance of the transatlantic link, as manifested through NATO was

[85] Government of Sweden 2022.

[86] Government of Sweden 2024b.

[87] Ibid., pp. 4–5.

underlined, *but must never be taken for granted*.[88] Lastly, the Swedish government seemed to aim for creating a balance between the logic of a defensive alliance and a number of central policy elements that were developed in the earlier peacetime policy of neutrality. It was reconfirmed that Sweden, as a member of NATO, will work to ensure that the Helsinki Final Act and the Charter of Paris are upheld.[89] Moreover, while expressing support for NATO's strategic deterrence, Sweden declared that it would remain a strong voice for arms control, disarmament and non-proliferation.[90]

The concrete outcome of the nascent Swedish policy of alliance will be elaborated over the years to come and it is clear that the process that lies ahead will include a number of challenging conflicts of interest that require prioritisation. Further, it should be discussed in which ways the unique Swedish experiences of non-alliance during more than 200 years can be utilised for formulating a policy of alliance that enhance long-term security, stability and prosperity in Europe and beyond.

References

Af Malmborg, M (1994) Den ståndaktiga nationalstaten—Sverige och den västeuropeiska integrationen 1945–1959 [The steadfast nation-state—Sweden and Western European integration 1945–1959]. Lund University Press, Lund

Ahlin P (2018) Efter neutralitetspolitiken. Folkrätten i svensk säkerhetspolitik 1993-2017 [Post-neutrality policy. International law in Swedish security policy 1993–2017]. JURE, Stockholm

Andrén N (1975) Sweden and Europe. Cooperation and Conflict 1975, pp. 51–64

Bonjour E (1978) Swiss Neutrality During Two World Wars. In: Luck JM et al (eds) Modern Switzerland. Sposs, Palo Alto

Bring O (2008) Neutralitetens uppgång och fall eller den gemensamma säkerhetens historia [The rise and fall of neutrality or the history of common security], Atlantis, Stockholm

Bring O (2013) En folkrättslig tolkning av solidaritetsklausulerna: Säkerhetspolitiskt och försvarspolitiskt samarbete som en internationell förpliktelse [An international law understanding of the solidarity clauses: Security and defence cooperation as an international obligation], Bilaga 2 [Annex 2], Försvarsdepartementet. Rapport från Utredningen om Sveriges internationella försvarspolitiska samarbete Fö 2013:B. Försvarspolitiskt samarbete—effektivitet, solidaritet, suveränitet [Report from the Inquiry on Sweden's international defence policy sovereignity Fö 2013:B. Defence political collaboration—efficiency, solidarity, sovereignity], pp. 81–89

Commission on Neutrality Policy (1994) Had there been a war - preparations for the reception of military assistance 1949–1969. https://lagen.nu/sou/1994:11. Accessed 13 October 2024

Council of the EU (2009) European Security Strategy: A Secure Europe in a Better World. https://www.consilium.europa.eu/media/30823/qc7809568enc.pdf. Accessed 13 October 2024

[88] Ibid., p. 8. It should be noted that the bilateral transatlantic link between Sweden and the United States regarding military defence has been formalised through the Agreement on Defence Cooperation between the government of the Kingdom of Sweden and the Government of the United States of America, Stockholm 5 December 2023. Entered into force 15 August 2024. Regeringens proposition [Government Bill] 2023/24:141 Avtal om försvarssamarbete med Amerikas förenta stater [Agreement on defense cooperation with the United States of America].

[89] Ibid., p. 5.

[90] Ibid., p. 6. *See also* Regeringens proposition [Government Bill] 2022/23:74 Sveriges medlemskap i Nato [Sweden's membership in NATO], p. 25. Utrikesdepartementet 2022b, p. 59. Government of Sweden 2024a, pp. 4–5.

Council of the EU (2015) 14120/15, Outcome of the Council Meeting, 3426th Council Meeting, Foreign Affairs. https://data.consilium.europa.eu/doc/document/ST-14120-2015-INIT/en/pdf. Accessed 5 May 2025

Council of the EU (2022) A Strategic Compass for Security and Defence, Doc No. 7371/22. https://data.consilium.europa.eu/doc/document/ST-7371-2022-INIT/en/pdf. Accessed 13 October 2024

Cramér P (1998) Neutralitet och europeisk integration [Neutrality and European integration]. Norstedts, Stockholm

Devine K (2011) Neutrality and the development of the European Union's common security and defence policy: Compatible or competing? Cooperation and Conflict 46(3):334–369

European Commission (1992a) Europe and the Challenge of Enlargement. Bulletin of the European Communities Supplement 3/92. http://aei.pitt.edu/1573/1/challenge_of_enlargement_June_92.pdf. Accessed 28 October 2024

European Commission (1992b) The challenge of enlargement—Commission opinion on Sweden's application for membership (31 July 1992). Bulletin of the European Communities Supplement 5/1992. https://www.cvce.eu/en/obj/commission_opinion_on_sweden_s_application_for_membership_31_july_1992-en-78f85c30-b61e-47d1-9da6-acfab7451ed2.html. Accessed 13 October 2024

European Council (2022) European Council conclusions on Russia's unprovoked and unjustified military aggression against Ukraine, EUCO 18/22. https://www.consilium.europa.eu/media/54495/st00018-en22.pdf. Accessed 13 October 2024

Fisher T (2009) Neutral Power in the CSCE: the N+N States and the making of the Helsinki Accords 1975. Nomos Verlag, Vienna

Forsberg T (2013) The rise of Nordic defence cooperation: a return to regionalism? International Affairs 89(5): 1161–1181

Försvarsutskottet (2009) Betänkande 2008/09:FöU10. Försvarets inriktning [The focus of our defence]

Government of Sweden (2007) Government's Communication 2007/08:51, National strategy for Swedish participation in international peace-support and security-building operations, 13 March 2008. https://www.government.se/contentassets/f1eeedbd51784b4db60c2a2d3fea4738/national-strategy-for-swedish-participation-in-international-peace-support-and-security-building-operations. Accessed 13 October 2024

Government of Sweden (2021) Statement of Government Policy in the Parliamentary Debate on Foreign Affairs, 24 February 2021. https://www.government.se/contentassets/d338be2ed4564ceabfed57540ce47221/statement-of-government-policy.pdf. Accessed 13 October 2024

Government of Sweden (2022) Statement of Government Policy in the Parliamentary Debate on Foreign Affairs, 10 June 2022. https://www.government.se/contentassets/9e7ed2449dc54caa99f326f876a43322/statement-of-foreign-policy-june-2022.pdf. Accessed 13 October 2024

Government of Sweden (2024a) Statement of Government Policy following Sweden's accession to NATO in the Parliamentary Debate on Foreign Affairs, 20 March 2024. https://www.government.se/contentassets/ae441755aa5141e7af64f44c22db1be7/statement-of-government-policy-following-swedens-accession-to-nato.pdf. Accessed 13 October 2024

Government of Sweden (2024b) Statement of Government Policy in the Parliamentary Debate on Foreign Affairs, 14 February 2024. https://www.government.se/contentassets/6b1f96a253034f7d917d3aaf773efe41/statement-of-foreign-policy-2024.pdf. Accessed 13 October 2024

Korhonen K (1973) Treaty of Friendship, Cooperation and Mutual Assistance between the Soviet Union and Finland: Some Aspects of International Politics. Cooperation and Conflict 8(3–4):183–188

Koutrakos P (2011) The role of law in Common Security and Defence Policy: functions, limitations and perceptions. In: Koutrakos P (ed). European Foreign Policy: Legal and Political Perspectives. Edward Elgar, Cheltenham

Lee-Ohlsson F (2009) Sweden and Development of the European Security and Defence Policy: A Bi-Directional Process of Europeanization. Cooperation and Conflict 44(2):123–142

Lindberg F (1958) Den svenska utrikespolitikens historia [The history of Swedish foreign policy], volume III:4. P.A. Norstedt & söners förlag, Stockholm

McGoldrick D (1993) The Development of the Conference on Security and Cooperation in Europe—From Process to Institution. In: Jackson BS, McGoldrick D (eds) Legal Visions of the New Europe. Graham & Trotman/Martinus Nijhoff, London/Dordrecht/Boston

NATO (2022) Strategic Concept, Adopted by Heads of State and Government at the NATO Summit in Madrid 29 June 2022. https://www.act.nato.int/wp-content/uploads/2023/05/290622-strategic-concept.pdf. Accessed 6 February 2024

Neuhold H (ed) (1984) CSCE N+N Perspectives. The Process of the Conference on Security and Co-operation in Europe from the Viewpoint of the Neutral and Non-Aligned Participating States. Wilhelm Braumüller, Vienna

Österdahl I (2021) Sweden's Collective Defence Obligations or this is Not a Collective Defence Pact (or Is It?): Considerations of International and Constitutional Law. Nordic Journal of International Law 90(2):127–160

Rieker P (2006) Europeanization of National Security Identity: the EU and the Changing Security Identities of the Nordic States. Routledge, London

SFS (1904) 1904:12 Kungl Maj:ts nådiga kungörelse med vissa bestämmelser i afseende å Sveriges neutralitet under krig mellan främmande makter [Royal Proclamation with certain provisions regarding Sweden's neutrality during wars between foreign powers]

SFS (1910) 1910:153 Internationella överenskommelser afslutade vid den andra fredskonferensen i Haag [International agreements concluded at the Second Hague Peace Conference]

Sverige Neutralitetspolitikkommissionen (1994) Om kriget kommit- förberedelser för mottagandet av militärt bistånd 1949-1969 [Had there been a war—preparations for the reception of military assistance 1949–1969]. SOU 1994:11

Swedish Ministry of Defence (2007) Ds 2007:46. Säkerhet i samverkan, Försvarsberedningens omvärldsanalys [Security in collaboration, the Committee on Defence Policy's intelligence study]

Swedish Ministry of Foreign Affairs (2022) Ds 2022:8 Deterioration of the security environment—implications for Sweden

Swiss Federal Council (2022) Clarity and guidance on neutrality policy - Federal Council report in response to Postulate 22.3385 put forward by the Council of States Foreign Affairs Committee (FAC-S), 11.04.2022.

Utrikesdepartementet (2022a) Ds 2022:7 Ett försämrat säkerhetspolitiskt läge—konsekvenser för Sverige [Deterioration of the security environment—implications for Sweden]

Utrikesdepartementet (2022b) Ds 2022:24 Sveriges medlemskap i Nato [Sweden's membership in NATO]

Wahlbäck K (1964) Finlandsfrågan i svensk politik 1937-1940 [The matter of Finland in Swedish politics 1937–1940]. Stockholm University, Stockholm

Wieslander A (2022) "The Hultqvist doctrine"—Swedish security and defence policy after the Russian annexation of Crimea. Defence Studies 22(1):35–59

Wrange P (2007) Impartial or uninvolved? The anatomy of 20th Century doctrine on the Law of neutrality. Stockholm University Press, Stockholm

Per Cramér is full Professor of International Law and holds the Jean Monnet Chair in European Integration Law at the School of Business Economics and Law at the University of Gothenburg. During the period 2010–2024, he held the position of Dean for the School of Business, Economics and Law. His main areas of research concern the external identity of the European Union with a special focus on the relationship between the Common Foreign and Security Policy and the Common Commercial Policy of the EU. At present, he is engaged as leader and participating researcher in the project The legal framework for civil protection and preparedness, financed by the Swedish Civil Contingencies Agency (MSB).

Chapter 11
Neutrality or Equivocation: The Response of African States to the Ukraine Conflict

Phoebe Okowa

Contents

Abstract The Ukraine conflict has caught the public imagination not only because of its proximity to the West but also because of its wider ramifications for the world at large. This article attempts to make sense of the response by African States to the Ukraine conflict, as expressed in their voting patterns in recent United Nations resolutions, and the extent to which they are consistent with the international law of neutrality. Although the abstentions by African States are not explicitly driven by the international law of neutrality, they are consistent with it. Additionally, the motivations across the African States have varied, which is reflected in their mixed voting records. One explanation for their pattern of voting may be an act of protest against an international system which takes insufficient account of African perspectives. If so, this would also provide additional impetus for reform of the United Nations Security Council to increase its membership from Africa, so as to ensure the maintenance of international peace and security.

Keywords Ukraine · Armed conflict · Neutrality · UN Charter · Use of force

P. Okowa (✉)
Queen Mary University, London, United Kingdom
e-mail: p.n.okowa@qmul.ac.uk

M. Klamberg et al. (eds.), *Reconstructing Power and Hegemony in Public International Law*, https://doi.org/10.1007/978-94-6265-743-4_11

11.1 Introduction

The Ukraine conflict has caught the public imagination not only because of its proximity to the West, but also because it is one of the few inter-State conflicts since 1945 that has directly involved a super-power, with potential ramifications beyond the two States at war. It is also only the second time since 1945 that one State has annexed the territory of another with the declared aim of extinguishing its existence as a separate and independent State.[1] More immediately, the conflict entails a potential threat to former Soviet satellite States, especially the Baltic States and Poland. Given that these States are also members of the North Atlantic Treaty Organization (NATO) (with Russian neighbours Finland and Sweden acceding to the NATO treaty in 2023 and 2024, respectively),[2] there is concern that escalation could bring Russia into a confrontation with NATO. If so, it is not far-fetched to contemplate the situation spiralling into a broader global conflict.

This chapter attempts to make sense of African responses to the war in Ukraine against the backdrop of the norms on the use of force contained in the Charter of the United Nations (UN Charter). Specifically, it examines whether the abstentions or non-participation of African States in the recent United Nations (UN) General Assembly resolutions concerning Russia's invasion of Ukraine engage with, and are consistent with, the law of neutrality as an optional act or, alternatively, if they fall within the margin of discretion left to States under the doctrine of neutrality. More broadly, the UN resolutions to be discussed provide a lens through which to consider wider African concerns about the legal framework of collective security and to explore the tensions between presumed double standards in the application of the rules concerning use of force as well as the continuing marginalization of the perspectives of African States.

To be clear, these concerns of African States have always been present but have, until recently, received insufficient consideration in mainstream discourses in public international law. The law on neutrality has been Professor Wrange's life's work and it is particularly fitting to combine the law of neutrality and Global South perspectives in a *Festschrift* to mark his retirement, especially given his pioneering contributions to the field of critical legal studies.

This chapter will advance three broad arguments. First, the abstentions by African States are not explicitly driven by neutrality in the legal sense, as provided for in the Hague Convention of 1907 (Hague Convention).[3] Nevertheless, they are consistent with the basic tenets of neutrality as impartiality and non-participation, especially

---

[1] The only other situation being Iraq's invasion of Kuwait in 1991, *see* Weller 2010.

[2] North Atlantic Treaty, opened for signature 4 April 1949, 34 UNTS 243 (entered into force 24 August 1949); Protocol to the North Atlantic Treaty on the Accession of the Kingdom of Sweden, opened for signature 5 July 2022 (entered into force 7 March 2024); Protocol to the North Atlantic Treaty on the Accession of the Republic of Finland, opened for signature 5 July 2022 (entered into force 4 April 2023).

[3] Convention (V) respecting the Rights and Duties of Neutral Powers and Persons in Case of War on Land, opened for signature 18 October 1907, UKTS 6 (1971) (entered into force 26 January 1910) (Fifth Hague Convention 1907).

as the UN Security Council had been unable to adopt any binding resolutions that would stand in tension with law on neutrality. Second, African responses to the Ukraine conflict may be seen as an act of protest and an expression of autonomy against an international system that consistently undermines African perspectives.[4] In particular, the world's focus on Ukraine has thrown into sharp relief the UN's perceived indifference to other serious conflicts presently taking place in Africa, including in Ethiopia (the Tigray War from 2020 to 2022), Sudan (whose civil war resumed in 2023), and the Democratic Republic of the Congo (with its ongoing conflict with M23 flaring up in 2022). Acknowledgement of this reality provides force to the argument that a substantial re-orientation of the UN Security Council is necessary for it to properly fulfil its mandate of maintaining international peace and security. This may include a rethinking of its composition to reflect excluded key constituencies and to interact more meaningfully with African States whose concerns have dominated the Security Council's agenda. Third, however mistaken, the abstentions by African States may be seen as driven by solidarity with an ally that—for all its flaws—has historically supported anti-colonial and anti-imperialist struggles in Africa.

11.2 Mapping the Terrain of African Responses to the Ukraine Conflict

The war in Ukraine is a notable example of African States taking a decisive stand by not directly supporting either party to a conflict. However, far from being disinterested, continued engagement by African States indicates a renewed and complex African autonomy in global decision-making.[5] From this perspective, the Ukraine conflict is of interest because it has brought to the fore a long-standing complaint of African States, namely, the asymmetrical enforcement of the international law on the use of force when great-power interests are at stake.[6]

The maxim is familiar to even a casual observer of international affairs: the strong do what they can and the weak suffer what they must.[7] Powerful States, and those they support, can effectively ignore the rules of international law on use of force without attracting serious legal consequences. Recent examples include Russia's invasion of Ukraine in 2022, the United States' invasion of Iraq in 2003, and the ongoing support given to Israel in the face of some of the most egregious violations of rules

---

[4] The African Union, for instance, strongly opposed NATO's disastrous intervention in Libya in 2011. Libya, to this day, remains in a state of instability. *See* Roberts 2011.

[5] *See, generally,* Staeger 2023.

[6] This was explicitly mentioned by Ghana's Permanent Representative to the United Nations, Mr Harold Agyeman, during the 11th Emergency Session's third plenary meeting ('Indeed, there is plenty of blame to go around in this Hall and throughout our Organization's history. Powerful States have thrown the Charter out of the window when it suited them and unilateral actions have been taken without due regard.'). *See* UNGA 2022a, p. 6.

[7] Thucydides 1914, Book V, Chapter XVII.

of international law in the occupied Palestinian territories. At the same time, there is a prevailing sentiment among African States that their region's own serious conflicts, such as the Tigray War or the ongoing Sudanese civil war, attract very limited interest from the rest of the world. Seen in this light, the abstentions by African States on the Ukraine conflict may be nothing more than acts of protest against an international rule-based order that does not apply its rules equally and evenly.

At the outset, it is worth reiterating the obvious, yet often overlooked fact that African States are not a homogeneous group and so their perspectives on the Ukraine conflict vary enormously. This is particularly noticeable in the voting patterns of African States for UN resolutions concerning the Ukraine conflict. The UN General Assembly convened its 11th emergency special session on 28 February 2022 (11th Emergency Session); ironically, Russia's Security Council veto (and the Security Council's corresponding inability to maintain international peace and security) is precisely what made such a procedure necessary.[8] The 11th Session, which at present remains adjourned, has so far seen six resolutions regarding the Ukraine conflict. They are ES-11/1 (calling for the withdrawal of Russian troops),[9] ES-11/2 (calling for the protection of civilians and other humanitarian consequences),[10] ES-11/3 (calling to suspend Russia from the UN Human Rights Council),[11] ES-11/4 (declaring that Russia's staged referenda in four Ukrainian territories are invalid under international law),[12] ES-11/5 (calling for reparations for Ukraine),[13] and ES-11/6 (principles of the UN Charter underlying peace in Ukraine).[14,15]

With the exception of Resolution ES-11/3 (suspension of Russia from the Human Rights Council) and Resolution ES-11/5 (reparations for Ukraine), the voting of African States is split roughly evenly between what may be broadly termed 'pro-Russia' and 'pro-Ukraine' positions. Although it may be expected that resolutions

---

[8] Charter of the United Nations, opened for signature 26 June 1945, 1 UNTS XVI (entered into force 24 October 1945) (UN Charter), Chapter V; UNGA 1950; UN 2022, rules 8–10.

[9] Votes by African States: 'Yes' 28 (52%); 'No' 1 (2%); 'Abstain' 17 (31%); 'Non-voting' 8 (15%). Votes by all UN Member States (including African States): 'Yes' 141 (73%); 'No' 5 (3%); 'Abstain' 35 (18%); 'Non-voting' 12 (6%). Percentage figures are rounded up to total 100%.

[10] Votes by African States: 'Yes' 27 (50%); 'No' 1 (2%); 'Abstain' 20 (37%); 'Non-voting' 6 (11%). Votes by all UN Member States (including African States): 'Yes' 140 (72%); 'No' 5 (3%); 'Abstain' 38 (20%); 'Non-voting' 10 (5%). Percentage figures are rounded up to total 100%.

[11] Votes by African States: 'Yes' 10 (19%); 'No' 6 (11%); 'Abstain' 24 (44%); 'Non-voting' 14 (26%). Votes by all UN Member States (including African States): 'Yes' 93 (49%); 'No' 24 (13%); 'Abstain' 58 (31%); 'Non-voting' 18 (7%). Percentage figures are rounded up to total 100%.

[12] Votes by African States: 'Yes' 30 (56%); 'No' 0 (0%); 'Abstain' 19 (35%); 'Non-voting' 5 (9%). Votes by all UN Member States (including African States): 'Yes' 43 (74%); 'No' 5 (3%); 'Abstain' 35 (18%); 'Non-voting' 10 (5%). Percentage figures are rounded up to total 100%.

[13] Votes by African States: 'Yes' 15 (28%); 'No' 5 (9%); 'Abstain' 27 (50%); 'Non-voting' 7 (13%). Votes by all UN Member States (including African States): 'Yes' 94 (49%); 'No' 14 (7%); 'Abstain' 73 (38%); 'Non-voting' 12 (6%). Percentage figures are rounded up to total 100%.

[14] Votes by African States: 'Yes' 30 (55%); 'No' 2 (4%); 'Abstain' 15 (28%); 'Non-voting' 7 (13%). Votes by all UN Member States (including African States): 'Yes' 141 (73%); 'No' 7 (4%); 'Abstain' 32 (16%); 'Non-voting' 13 (7%). Percentage figures are rounded up to total 100%.

[15] UNGA 2022f; UNGA 2022g; UNGA 2022h; UNGA 2022i; UNGA 2022j; UNGA 2023.

affirming core international law principles (such as ES-11/1, ES-11/2, ES-11/4, and ES-11/6) would receive broad support, voting patterns were motivated by a range of both principled and less principled considerations.

A significant number of African States, the majority of UN Member States, condemned the invasion by, *inter alia*, calling for the withdrawal of Russian troops (Resolution ES-11/1) or rejecting the legality of Russia's referenda in Donetsk, Luhansk, Kherson, and Zaporizhzhia (Resolution ES-11/4). This likely was in no small part due to Russia's imperialist ambitions, which are premised on the spurious claim that an autonomous Ukrainian national identity is a historical fiction.[16] Leaving these claims unchallenged would naturally pose a threat to the territorial integrity of States that had emerged from the disintegration of colonial empires—particularly in Africa, where the ethnic composition of populations transcends national boundaries. For many of these States, especially those without powerful militaries, the UN Charter's core principles play an existential role in guaranteeing security.[17] Territorial integrity, sovereignty, and the self-determination of peoples have not only been bedrock principles of the UN Charter but also of the African Union, as embodied in its founding instruments. The 1955 Bandung Conference, for instance, was the springboard for the influential Non-Aligned Movement, and re-affirmed the commitment of African and Asian States to the core principles of self-determination, mutual respect for sovereignty, equality of States, non-aggression, and non-interference in international affairs.[18] The preambular provisions of the Charter of the Organisation of African Unity (OAU Charter) proclaim a determination to 'safeguard and consolidate the hard-won independence as well as the sovereignty and territorial integrity of states and to fight neo-colonialism in all its forms'.[19] The OAU Charter also gives these principles concrete form in Articles II and III. The OAU Charter further clarifies the African Union's (AU's) purpose as including the defence of members' 'sovereignty, territorial integrity, and independence' and reaffirms the 'inalienable right to independent existence' of its members.[20] Yet, against this background, the large number of recorded abstentions by African States during the 11th Emergency Session appears to be in direct conflict with the AU's founding ideals to which all its members are committed.

The disconnect between the aspirations in the UN's and AU's founding documents and the support for the ethno-nationalist rhetoric that underpinned the invasion of Ukraine informed a number of the interventions that were critical of Russia's actions.

---

[16] The subject of Ukrainian national identity is not a recent invention and has been the focus of increasing scholarly attention since the fall of the Soviet Union, *see* Himka 2006. Even current realpolitik critiques of NATO enlargement as provoking Russian aggression still downplay the possibility of a genuine desire among the Ukrainian people to determine their own national direction, *see, e.g.*, Mearsheimer 2014.

[17] Mauritius, for instance, possesses no standing army, which makes the principles in the UN Charter all the more important. UNGA 2022b, p. 21.

[18] Final Communiqué of the Asian-African conference of Bandung (24 April 1955).

[19] Charter of the Organisation of African Unity, 479 UNTS 39 (entered into force 25 May 1963) (OAU Charter), Preamble.

[20] Ibid., Articles II, III.

As Kenya's Permanent Representative to the United Nations Dr Martin Kimani observed, a commitment to the principles of sovereignty and territorial integrity, however imperfect, is the foundational basis for the security of all States. In a widely praised speech that is worth quoting in full, he noted that:[21]

> Kenya and almost every African Country was birthed by the ending of empire … We believe that all States formed from empires that have collapsed or retreated have many peoples in them yearning for integration with peoples in neighbouring States. This is normal and understandable. After all, who does not want to be joined to their brethren and to make common purpose with them? However, Kenya rejects such a yearning from being pursued by force. We must complete our recovery from the embers of dead empires in a way that does not plunge us back into new forms of domination and oppression. …
>
> Kenya registers its strong concern and opposition to the recognition of Donetsk and Luhansk as independent States. We further strongly condemn the trend in the last few decades of powerful states, including members of the Security Council, breaching international law with little regard. … Let me conclude by reaffirming Kenya's respect for the territorial integrity of Ukraine within its internationally recognized borders.

It is true that the record of African votes in the General Assembly is complex. There were very few outright 'no' votes on any of the 11th Emergency Session resolutions; the most received (six 'no' votes from the Central African Republic, Republic of the Congo, Eritrea, Ethiopia, Gabon and Mali) were for Resolution ES-11/3, to suspend Russia from the Human Rights Council, a resolution that was particularly criticized for being overly politicized.[22] As for the six 'no' votes, although the voting parties did not explain their votes during the 11th Emergency Session, it may be observed that Russia, as well as its paramilitary operations headed by the Wagner Group, has significant operations in the Central African Republic and Mali (which both either abstained or voted no on every 11th Emergency Session Resolution).[23] Notably, Resolution ES-11/4 (unlawful referenda in Ukraine), arguably the one most expressive of the norms of territorial integrity and self-determination, did not attract any 'no' votes from African States.

Although a majority of African States boldly proclaimed fidelity to the principles of multilateralism and the foundational ideals of the Charter, an equally significant number of African States either abstained or failed to register a vote either way.[24] Angola, for instance, insisted on support for the principles of the OAU Charter in voting 'yes' for Resolution ES-11/4,[25] yet abstained from all other votes in the 11th Emergency Session. Uganda and South Africa gave reasons for their abstentions, citing their membership of the Non-Aligned Movement and a commitment to

---

[21] UNSC 2022, p. 8.

[22] Egypt, for example, stated that the resolution was not related to the unlawful use of force and was 'related to politicizing United Nations organs and specialized agencies … [which] … undermines its credibility and that of international multilateralism'. UNGA 2022d, p. 9.

[23] Doboš and Purton 2024.

[24] *See* voting records compiled from Staeger 2023 in n. 9–14 above.

[25] UNGA 2022e, p. 12.

neutrality as the best way to advance the objectives of peace.[26] South Africa was particularly committed to neutrality and has abstained from every single 11th Emergency Session resolution. In the case of Uganda, it argued that a vote either way would be particularly problematic for it as the incoming chair of the Group of 77 and the Non-Aligned Movement.[27] Moreover, it is difficult to discern from the contexts in which these statements were made whether neutrality was to be understood in the ordinary sense as simply meaning impartiality or in the strict legal sense: as a norm of international law pursuant to the Hague Convention of 1907,[28] which demands absolute impartiality and non-participation in the support of either party to a conflict.

11.3 Abstention as an Expression of Neutrality

In their statements explaining its abstention from the 11th Emergency Session resolutions, South Africa argued that maintaining a neutral stance was crucial if it was to play a mediating role in the resolution of the conflict.[29] Its view was that one-sided resolutions are largely unhelpful and could potentially be a major stumbling block to meaningful dialogue. It is noteworthy that the resolutions that adopted a particularly punitive stand towards Russia, such as Resolution ES-11/5 (reparations for Ukraine) or Resolution ES-11/3 (expulsion of Russia from the UN Human Rights Council), received the least support among African States, but also among UN Member States in general.[30]

The international law of neutrality seeks to regulate the legal relationship between States engaged in an armed conflict with each other as well as with those States not involved in said armed conflict. Many agree that neutrality should be a principled option available to States, especially those that on account of their influence on one or more of the parties may be called upon to play a mediating role in the conflict. Moreover, neutrality as an institution has many acknowledged virtues. It has the distinct advantage of localizing conflict by limiting much of war and its effects to the belligerent parties and broadly lessening the impact of war on peacetime activities, including commerce. The principal right of a neutral State is that of inviolability; its principal duties are those of abstention, non-participation, and impartiality.[31] More importantly, the neutral State must refrain from assisting one party to the conflict, to ensure equal treatment of belligerent States.

[26] *See* the address by Mr. Macky Sall, President of the Republic of Senegal in UNGA 2022k; Kazibwe 2023; UNGA 2022c, pp. 20–21.

[27] In a tweet explaining Uganda's abstention, the Permanent Representative to the UN, Ambassador Adonia Ayebare explained that: 'As incoming Chair of the Non-aligned movement (NAM) NEUTRALITY is key. Uganda will continue to play a constructive role in the maintenance of peace and security both regionally and globally' cited in Kiiza 2022.

[28] Greenwood 1987.

[29] *See* UNGA 2022c, pp. 20–21.

[30] *See* n. 9–14 above.

[31] Palchetti 2015, p. 1224.

Yet questions have been raised whether this pre-existing law of neutrality has survived the very radical changes in the legal regime on the use of force that were ushered in by the UN Charter.[32] The doubts have been exacerbated by the fact that, until the recent outbreak of war in Ukraine, there was hardly any contemporary State practice in support of, or against, neutrality as understood in international law prior to the UN Charter. As is well known, the UN Charter imposes an obligation to settle international disputes by peaceful means and to refrain from the threat or use of force in international relations.[33] In the event of an act of aggression, a threat to, or a breach of international peace, the UN Security Council is empowered to take enforcement action on behalf of all Member States—including the use of force—in order to maintain or restore international peace and security.[34] Moreover, the obligation not to use force in inter-State relations is owed *erga omnes* and, as a result, all States have an interest in ensuring compliance with this obligation.[35] Not only that, States may be placed under a positive duty to react to an unlawful use of force, and not to recognize any situations arising from violations of those duties on account of the *jus cogens* character of the norms prohibiting the use of force. It has therefore been argued that these new obligations under the UN Charter are incompatible with the prior law on neutrality, in that the UN Charter *prima facie* obligates Member States to take an active stand against violations of the prohibition on use of force even in the absence of institutional machinery for distinguishing between aggressor and victim States.[36] There are those who go as far as proclaiming that the institution of neutrality is no longer relevant, because it has either fallen into desuetude or continues to exist but is qualified so as to permit support to a victim fighting an unjust war or a war of aggression.[37] If these putative limitations to the law of neutrality (as it exists post-1945) are correct, then it follows that the claims of neutrality that accompanied the 11th Emergency Session resolutions have no purchase.

As a matter of strict law, the presumption of desuetude is not to be lightly invoked and the International Court of Justice (ICJ), when called upon to interpret treaties, has consistently upheld their validity in the absence of the clearest evidence that the parties had agreed to abandon their continued application.[38] Accordingly, the codified law on neutrality in the Hague Convention of 1907 remains good law *qua* treaty, but also customary law.[39] The ICJ in the *Nuclear Weapons Advisory Opinion* confirmed the continuing relevance of the law on neutrality, although it accepted

---

[32] On the impact of collective security on neutrality, *see* Lauterpacht 2004.

[33] UN Charter, above n. 8, Article 2.

[34] UN Charter, above n. 8, Article 42.

[35] ILC Articles on the Responsibility of States for Internationally Wrongful Acts, Article 48, reproduced in International Law Commission 2001.

[36] Lauterpacht 1952, p. 221; Greenwood 1987, p. 50.

[37] Schmitt 2023.

[38] Thirlway, p. 404; *see* International Law Commission 1966, p. 237, for the Report of the ILC on the Law of Treaties.

[39] Fifth Hague Convention 1907, above n. 3;Convention (XIII) Concerning the Rights and Duties of Neutral Powers in Naval Warfare, opened for signature 18 October 1907 (entered into force 26 January 1910).

that its content must now be evaluated in light of the rules in the UN Charter.[40] The nuances in the current law of neutrality cannot be explored in full here, but it seems clear that neutrality remains an option in the absence of binding UN Security Council action against an aggressor State. It could also be argued that, even in the absence of a UN Security Council resolution, States are under an obligation not to remain neutral in situations where the use of force is a flagrant violation of the UN Charter; such an obligation may include obligations on States not to recognize the violation or give assistance to the aggressor State.

There is the additional consideration that the UN Charter framework institutionalizes individual and collective self-defence, with the result that a victim of aggression, like Ukraine, may be legally entitled to invoke customary international law duties on use of force and invite other States to come to its assistance (although Ukraine does not appear to have done so). There are also related obligations under Article 25 of the UN Charter, enjoining all States to offer every assistance to the UN in the discharge of its obligations under Chapter VII of the UN Charter and to refrain from giving assistance to any State against which the UN is taking action.[41]

As alluded to above, Russia's use of its veto power has effectively prevented the UN Security Council from adopting binding resolutions on the Ukraine conflict. There are therefore no binding Security Council resolutions which qualify or abrogate the application of the law on neutrality with respect to the war in Ukraine. At the same time, the *jus cogens* character of the norm prohibiting the use of force operates to prevent recognition of, or the rendering of assistance in support of, Russia's unlawful use of force and its *de facto* annexation of Ukraine's territory (the latter of which was the subject of Resolution ES-11/4, which saw the strongest support from both African and UN Member States among all the 11th Emergency Session resolutions). Beyond the operation of these two principles, neutrality remains an option. Thus, the claims of neutrality made by African States when abstaining from voting in the 11th Emergency Session, it is submitted, are entirely consistent with the applicable legal framework. To recap, the law on neutrality requires neutral States to be impartial; specifically, they must not participate in hostilities through acts such as the sharing of intelligence information or providing funding or war-related assistance to belligerent States.[42] Abstaining or refusing to vote in favour of the 11th Emergency Session resolutions is entirely consistent with the current law on neutrality, even considering the changes in law introduced by the UN Charter.

What then is to be made of the allegation that shortly after abstaining from the resolutions on Ukraine, South Africa was engaged in joint military operations with Russia and China?[43] South Africa argued that it remained neutral and that the joint military operations were routine and had been planned for some time to boost South Africa's own defence capabilities. In its defence, South Africa argued that it had,

---

[40] ICJ, *Legality of the Threat or Use of Nuclear Weapons*, Advisory Opinion, 8 July 1996, 1996 ICJ Reports 226, p. 261, para 89.

[41] UN Charter, above n. 8, Article 25.

[42] Schmitt 2023.

[43] BBC News 2023.

since 2011, held joint military exercises with the United States, as well as France and Germany, and that these operations were not necessarily in aid of any party to a conflict. This explanation is broadly correct, as the law on neutrality has traditionally required some nexus between the impugned act and the conduct of the belligerents in the battlefield, to amount to a tangible contribution to the war effort. Abstaining from a resolution or conducting military exercises may be politically suspect but strictly speaking does not fall foul of the law on neutrality and is broadly in line with the neutrality asserted by other BRIC countries, such as India, in relation to the conflict in Ukraine.[44]

11.4 Abstention as an Act of Protest Against Double Standards

It is possible to view the African responses to the Ukraine conflict in the UN General Assembly as an implied corrective to the double standards by Western governments and institutions (including academia) with respect to their own illegal uses of force and tolerance, if not outright support, for pro-Western dictatorships. Indeed, this point was explicitly raised by several African States during the 11th Emergency Session.[45] The abstentions or non-votes, it may be argued, are not rejections of UN Charter norms on the use of force and self-determination of peoples (even staunch Russian allies pledge support for said norms),[46] but rather an opportunity for a recalibration of UN institutions, like the Security Council, that would ensure equal and even-handed treatment of all global conflicts.

The norms underpinning such an approach do not appear to be in question, even among detractors of the current UN system. The complaint by African States relates to the modalities of their application, and the perpetuation of double standards in favour of powerful States. It is a cardinal principle of the rule of law that like cases should be treated alike; in international affairs, this is firmly grounded in the sovereign equality of States. As Lord Bingham eloquently observed: 'The moment that a State treats the rules of international law as binding on others but not on itself, the compact on which the law rests is broken.'[47] This is of course true of individual States as well as when they act collectively through UN institutions. It is true that the decision-making in both the Security Council and the General Assembly has largely been driven by political considerations. It is the interest of great powers rather than the demands of the equal application of the law or the gravity of the transgression that has been the main driver of Security Council action. In response, African States are insisting on their autonomous agency in how the rules on international law are interpreted; and their support can no longer be taken for granted.

[44] Atlantic Council 2023.

[45] See above.

[46] Even Russian allies in Africa did not vote 'no' on ES-11/4.

[47] Bingham 2010, p. 124.

11.5 Negative Votes as a Primer for Security Council Reform

It is no secret that African States have long been disillusioned with the composition and decision-making process in the UN Security Council. Despite African issues dominating the agenda of the Security Council, there is still no permanent African representation, and case for reform has been on the agenda without much progress for at least the last 40 years.[48] In particular, there has been understandable criticism by African States over the use of the veto, which has also caused complications in the UN's response to the Ukraine conflict. The Security Council is now mainly seen as a stumbling block to meaningful action and as essentially protecting the geo-political interests of the permanent members and their allies. In particular, the Council has failed to be an honest broker when the geo-political interests of the permanent members clash with those of other UN members. The failure of the Security Council to provide a comprehensive and meaningful response to global armed conflicts is generally viewed by many as posing an existential threat to the world order. Furthermore, the indifference to African conflicts (such as in Ethiopia, Sudan, and Yemen) occurring at the same time as the Ukraine conflict supports this view. The abstentions and non-participation could be viewed more positively as essentially as an attempt to force the issue of reform back on the agenda. The African abstentions and votes against the invasion could be viewed as an act of protest against a system that is widely seen as both compromised and not consistently effective, and a plea for an even-handed approach to all conflicts.

11.6 Conclusions

It is of course possible that the votes in the 11th Emergency Session were driven by pragmatic considerations of self-interest. The war in Ukraine had resulted in a colossal increase in commodity prices, especially fossil fuels and grains that African states are particularly dependent on.[49] Many arguably felt patronized by the expectation that they should show solidarity when Russia posed an existential threat to European interests and not elsewhere.

For States such as South Africa, Mozambique, or Angola, abstention in the UN was an act of solidarity with those States that had proved dependable allies in their national liberation movements. South Africa for instance has never forgotten the role that the Soviet Union played in its struggle for independence. However, it may be asked whether solidarity with an ally should trump fidelity to the UN Charter norms and principles, including respect for territorial integrity and self-determination of peoples. One way out of the conundrum is to see it not as a tension between competing

[48] African Union Executive Council 2005.

[49] Okou et al. 2022.

values but rather as two distinct processes that are not in conflict. An abstention on a crucial resolution with the distinct objective of promoting peace is not necessarily in and of itself an abandonment of the core principles of territorial integrity and self-determination of peoples. Many of the States that abstained also confirmed their continuing commitment to the UN Charter's principles.

References

African Union Executive Council (2005) The common African position on the proposed reform of the United Nations. 7th Extraordinary Session, Doc No. Ext/EX.CL/2 (VII)

Atlantic Council (2023) What we learned from the Russia-China-South Africa Military Drills. https://www.atlanticcouncil.org/blogs/new-atlanticist/what-we-learned-from-the-russia-china-south-africa-military-drills/. Accessed on 15 January 2025

BBC News (2023) Why is South Africa's navy joining exercises with Russia and China? https://www.bbc.com/news/world-64380572. Accessed on 15 January 2025

Bingham T (2010) The Rule of Law. Penguin, London

Doboš B, Purton A (2024) Proxy Neo-Colonialism? The Case of the Wagner Group in the Central African Republic. Insight on Africa 16(1):7–21

Greenwood C (1987) The Concept of War in Modern International Law. International and Comparative Law Quarterly 36(2):283–306

Himka JP (2006) The Basic Historical Identity Formations in Ukraine: A Typology. Harvard Ukrainian Studies 28:483–500

International Law Commission (1966) Yearbook of the International Law Commission 1966, Volume II. A/CN.4/SER.A/1966/Add.1. https://legal.un.org/ilc/publications/yearbooks/english/ilc_1966_v2.pdf. Accessed 6 May 2025

International Law Commission (2001) Yearbook of the International Law Commission 2001, Volume II Part Two. A/CN.4/SER.A/2001/Add.1 (Part 2). https://legal.un.org/ilc/publications/yearbooks/english/ilc_2001_v2_p2.pdf. Accessed 1 March 2025

Kazibwe K (2023) Uganda again abstains from vote on Russia's invasion of Ukraine even after Zelensky call to Museveni. https://nilepost.co.ug/news/154460/uganda-again-abstains-from-vote-on-russias-invasion-of-ukraine. Accessed 15 January 2025

Kiiza C (2022) Ukraine War: Why Uganda abstained from Voting Against Russia at UN. https://chimpreports.com/ukraine-war-why-uganda-abstained-from-voting-against-russia-at-un/. Accessed 6 May 2025

Lauterpacht H (1952) Oppenheim's International Law, Volume II, 7th edn. Longmans, Green & Co, London

Lauterpacht H (2004) International Law: Being the Collected Papers of Hersch Lauterpacht Volume 5, Disputes, War, and Neutrality, Parts IX-XIV. Cambridge University Press, Cambridge

Mearsheimer J (2014) Why the Ukraine Crisis is the West's Fault: The Liberal Delusions That Provoked Putin. Foreign Affairs 93(5):77–89

Okou C et al (2022) Africa Food Prices Are Soaring Amid High Import Reliance. https://www.imf.org/en/Blogs/Articles/2022/09/26/africa-food-prices-are-soaring-amid-high-import-reliance. Accessed on 15 January 2025

Palchetti P (2015) Consequences for Third States As a Result of an Unlawful Use of Force. In: Weller M (ed) The Oxford Handbook of the Use of Force in International Law. Oxford University Press, Oxford, pp. 1224–1239

Roberts H (2011) Who said Gaddaffi Had to Go? London Review of Books 33(22)

Schmitt M (2023) "Strict" Versus "Qualified" Neutrality. https://lieber.westpoint.edu/strict-versus-qualified-neutrality/. Accessed 15 January 2025

Staeger U (2023) The war in Ukraine, the African Union, and African Agency. African Affairs 122(489):559–586
Thirlway H (2013) The Law and Procedure of the International Court of Justice: Fifty Years of Jurisprudence Volume II. Oxford University Press, Oxford
Thucydides (1914) History of the Peloponnesian War. Translated by Richard Crawley. London Dent, London
United Nations (2022) Rules of Procedure of the General Assembly, UN Doc. A/520/Rev.20
UN General Assembly (1950) Uniting for Peace, Resolution 377(V), UN Doc. A/RES/377(V)
UN General Assembly (2022a) Eleventh Emergency Special session, 3rd plenary meeting, 1 March 2022, UN Doc. A/ES-11/PV.3
UN General Assembly (2022b) Eleventh Emergency Special session, 4th plenary meeting, 1 March 2022, UN Doc. A/ES-11/PV.4
UN General Assembly (2022c) Eleventh Emergency Special session, 5th plenary meeting, 2 March 2022, UN Doc. A/ES-11/PV.5
UN General Assembly (2022d) Eleventh Emergency Special session, 10th plenary meeting, 7 April 2022, UN Doc. A/ES-11/PV.10
UN General Assembly (2022e) Eleventh Emergency Special session, 14th plenary meeting, 12 October 2022, UN Doc. A/ES-11/PV.14
UN General Assembly (2022f) Aggression against Ukraine, Resolution ES-11/1, UN Doc. A/RES/ES-11/1
UN General Assembly (2022g) Humanitarian consequences of the aggression against Ukraine, Resolution ES-11/2, UN Doc. A/RES/ES-11/2
UN General Assembly (2022h) Suspension of the rights of membership of the Russian Federation in the Human Rights Council, Resolution ES-11/3, UN Doc. A/RES/ES-11/3
UN General Assembly (2022i) Territorial integrity of Ukraine: defending the principles of the Charter of the United Nations, Resolution ES-11/4, UN Doc. A/RES/ES-11/4
UN General Assembly (2022j) Furtherance of remedy and reparation for aggression against Ukraine, Resolution ES-11/5, UN Doc. A/RES/ES-11/5
UN General Assembly (2022k) Seventy-seventh session, 4th plenary meeting, 20 September 2022, UN Doc. A/77/PV.4, pp. 11–13
UN General Assembly (2023) Principles of the Charter of the United Nations underlying a comprehensive, just and lasting peace in Ukraine, Resolution ES-11/6, UN Doc. A/RES/ES-11/6
UN Security Council (2022) 8970th meeting, 21 February 2022, UN Doc. S/PV.8970
Weller M (2010) Iraq and the Use of Force in International Law. Oxford University Press

Phoebe Okowa is a Judge at the International Court of Justice, The Hague, the Netherlands and an Associate Member of the Institut de droit international. Until her election to the Court, she was Professor of Public International Law at Queen Mary University London, and a Member of the UN International Law Commission. She is the author of a wide range of publications on various topics in international law, including on international environmental law. She has undertaken extensive advisory work for Governments and has appeared as counsel and advocate before the International Court of Justice and the International Tribunal for the Law of the Sea.

Part III
The Role of Scholars: Neutral Commentators or Activists?

Chapter 12
The Role of International Lawyers in a Changing (Physical and Political) Climate

Anne Orford

Contents

Abstract International law is undergoing a period of transformation in the context of a rapidly changing climate and the new geopolitical situation to which it is giving rise. Many international lawyers view the current era of exit from or challenge to existing international laws and institutions as one of crisis in the international legal order. In contrast, this chapter suggests that international lawyers should not automatically position ourselves in opposition to this process of change. The idea that international law is primarily committed to achieving certainty is the product of a way of thinking that is characteristic of times that are stable. Yet the assumption that the political and physical worlds that form the backdrop to international law will remain relatively stable is based on the conditions of an era that is passing. In a time of significant geopolitical and physical change, international lawyers need not automatically approach the remaking of international institutions or the withdrawal from treaties, even hard-won multilateral treaties, as necessarily a bad thing. In other words, there is no reason why international lawyers should necessarily defend all existing law and institutions, or see ourselves as guardians of the *status quo*. It is possible to think in strategic, positive, or at least pragmatic terms about the roles that international lawyers might play in a time of transformation.

Keywords International law · Climate change · Geopolitics · Transformation · *Rebus sic stantibus* · Stability

A. Orford (✉)
Melbourne Law School, University of Melbourne, Melbourne, Australia
e-mail: a.orford@unimelb.edu.au

M. Klamberg et al. (eds.), *Reconstructing Power and Hegemony in Public International Law*, https://doi.org/10.1007/978-94-6265-743-4_12

12.1 Introduction

Many international lawyers in the academy and practice are trying to make sense of a world in which established ways of thinking about and practising international law are under challenge, and the situations that international law is called upon to address are changing rapidly. Many of those novel situations raise questions for international lawyers, while also unsettling the grounds on which we might once have based our answers. Yet despite the vertiginous sense this gives that the ground on which we are standing is unstable, the theme of my chapter is simply this: international lawyers do not need to think of such moments of accelerating change only in terms of threats. It is possible to think in strategic, positive, or at least pragmatic terms about the roles that international lawyers might play in a time of transformation.

12.2 Times of Transformation

Characterizing an era as one of legal change and transformation is, of course, a political choice. It makes the abandonment of old legal certainties and the adoption of potentially radical new legal arguments seem plausible and even necessary. With that caveat in mind, I nonetheless find it hard to avoid the sense that in some significant way we are experiencing a period of transformation in international law, and the end of an era that began in the early 1990s.

The 1990s was a period of great ambition in international law. The United States and its allies took advantage of the new geopolitical situation by engaging in the process of remaking international law in the image of a liberal and capitalist form of internationalism. It was an era in which many new multilateral treaties were concluded, often accompanied by the creation of new international courts and tribunals. One of the most significant developments during that period was the US-led negotiation of ambitious new multilateral and regional trade agreements, particularly the creation in 1996 of the World Trade Organization with its compulsory dispute settlement system. Existing forms of investment protection were also consolidated and expanded during the 1990s, with the negotiation of many new bilateral investment treaties and other broad-reaching agreements such as the Energy Charter Treaty and the North American Free Trade Agreement. Many of the bilateral and multilateral treaties that are now in force were concluded in the two decades between 1990 and 2010. In addition, that period saw the creation of various new international courts and tribunals as part of specialized regimes, including the International Tribunal for the Law of the Sea, which commenced operations in 1997, and the adoption in 1998 of the Rome Statute establishing the International Criminal Court (ICC).

There were two key conditions contributing to that expansion in the ambition and reach of international law during the post-Cold War period. The first was that with the ending of the Cold War and the break-up of the Soviet Union, the United States was the sole remaining superpower, with the resulting capacity to exercise a degree of control over the development and uses of international law. The second was that international legal innovations took place against the backdrop of what appeared to be a relatively stable natural world.

Fast-forward to the mid-2020s, and those conditions have changed, with significant effects on the stability of international law in general, and on the agreements and institutions negotiated during the 1990s in particular. The assumption that the international order would continue to be shaped in the image of the United States began to be unsettled in the first decades of the twenty-first century, with the resurgence of a more assertive Russia, the economic growth of China, and the emergence of the BRICS and other South-South alliances as significant players in the development of international law. In addition, the acceleration of changes caused by global warming, including the frequency of tropical cyclones, extreme rainfall and flooding, drought, desertification, temperature rise, ocean acidification, sea level rise, and water salinization,[1] means that it is no longer realistic to assume that the natural world will remain relatively stable and that any legal transformations will be driven primarily by economic and political choices.

The combined impact of geopolitical and physical change has put pressure on mechanisms for modifying or withdrawing from existing international legal commitments and institutions. Indeed, when I began teaching international law in the early 1990s, I spent very little time on the details of treaty termination and withdrawal. Today, it is impossible to teach an international law course without discussing the legal effects of unsigning, withdrawing from, suspending, or terminating treaties. Even the once arcane doctrine of *rebus sic stantibus* (governing treaty termination due to a fundamental change of circumstances) is now undergoing a 'renaissance', at least according to one legal commentator.[2]

12.3 Change and the Role of International Lawyers

This moment of withdrawing from and terminating treaties is viewed negatively by many international lawyers. Numerous legal scholars have treated the critique of or withdrawal from particular international legal regimes as pathological and evidence of a broader crisis, in contrast to the decision to join such regimes, which is seen as a legitimate exercise of sovereignty. Law journals are awash with articles diagnosing the current situation of international law with titles that invoke backlash, a threat to the rule of law, and even tragedy.[3]

In contrast, I want to suggest that international lawyers should not automatically position ourselves in opposition to this process of change, including of termination and withdrawal from treaties and institutions, in a time of physical and geopolitical transformation. In other words, there is no reason why international lawyers should

[1] *See generally*, Intergovernmental Panel on Climate Change 2023.

[2] Kulaga 2020, p. 477.

[3] *See further* the literature discussed in Orford 2021b, p. 3.

necessarily defend all existing law and institutions, or see ourselves as guardians of the *status quo.*

A strong version of this argument is captured in the familiar axiom 'never let a serious crisis go to waste' (attributed to either Winston Churchill or Rahm Emanuel). That assumes a very strategic role and sensibility for international lawyers, which may be true for some of us. But a more modest version of this argument would simply be that it is the role of lawyers to engage with change.

In domestic law, we understand that contracts can be terminated. Commercial law transactions commonly envisage that the relationship can or will come to an end and make provision for that to occur. We understand that cases can be overturned. We understand that legislation can be reformed. We do not see processes of law reform as a threat to the rule of law. The only field that is designed to inhibit legal change is constitutional law (and even then domestic constitutions allow for referenda or other mechanisms for change). Should international lawyers approach treaties more restrictively than constitutions?

When laws are the product of great democratic assemblies gathered together to agree on a constitution or draft a significant piece of legislation, the reluctance to reopen those texts might be understandable. Yet very few international agreements are the result of such processes. As Christian Joerges argues, it is a mistake to 'treat the results of political negotiations as though they were the results of an assembly drawn up to convene a constitution'.[4] There are many treaties that are the result of negotiations involving states with extremely different levels of bargaining power, subject to varying degrees of pressure, sometimes falling just short of coercion, leading to agreements that transfer authority over key questions of politics, security, economics or social welfare to international adjudicators or experts, and in which the negotiating texts are not made public until very late in the process, if at all. There is no obvious reason why international lawyers should automatically approach withdrawal from or termination of all treaties, even hard-won multilateral treaties, as necessarily a bad thing.

And, of course, international law does provide mechanisms for terminating or withdrawing from treaties, for the creation of new custom, and for the progressive development of international law. Focusing upon treaties, most contain provisions addressing issues of termination and withdrawal. And if a treaty does not, international lawyers fall back on the regime established under the Vienna Convention on the Law of Treaties (VCLT) and the broader doctrines of customary international law that it codified or developed. One of the doctrines that appears likely to gain increasing attention in a time of change is the doctrine of fundamental change of circumstances or of *rebus sic stantibus*, included in Article 62 of the VCLT. That ground may be invoked for terminating or withdrawing from a treaty where a fundamental change has occurred with regard to circumstances existing at the time of the conclusion of a treaty, that change was not foreseen by the parties, the existence of those circumstances constituted an essential basis of the consent of the parties to be

[4] Joerges 2014, pp. 985, 991.

bound, and the effect of the change is radically to transform the extent of obligations still to be performed under the treaty.[5]

The International Law Commission explained the inclusion of this provision in the draft text that formed the basis of the VCLT as follows:

> A treaty may remain in force for a long time and its stipulations come to place an undue burden on one of the parties as a result of a fundamental change of circumstances. Then, if the other party were obdurate in opposing any change, the fact that international law recognized no legal means of terminating or modifying the treaty otherwise than through a further agreement between the same parties might impose a serious strain on the relations between the States concerned. … [F]ailing any agreement, one party may be left powerless under the treaty to obtain any legal relief from outmoded and burdensome provisions. It is in these cases that the *rebus sic stantibus* doctrine could serve a purpose as a lever to induce a spirit of compromise in the other party.[6]

The idea that the doctrine of *rebus sic stantibus* could serve 'as a lever to induce a spirit of compromise in the other party' is in obvious tension with the doctrine of *pacta sunt servanda* (or agreements must be kept), which is often treated as the foundational principle of international law. The two principles seem to embody different visions of international law. One – *pacta sunt servanda* – seems to envisage a legal system that prioritizes predictability and stability, whereas the other – *rebus sic stantibus* – seems to envisage a system that can address change and uncertainty.[7]

Throughout history, greater weight has been given to the doctrine of *pacta sunt servanda* in periods of political and social stability, when the priority is certainty and the idea that treaties must always be performed. And greater weight has been given to the doctrine of *rebus sic stantibus* in times of dynamism or transformation in the diplomatic order, when states are faced with changes to fundamental national interests that make withdrawing from or terminating treaties appear necessary if peace is to be maintained.[8] For example, *rebus sic stantibus* was frequently referred to during the interwar period, in the context of broader debates about 'peaceful change'.[9] We are again seeing growing references to *rebus sic stantibus* in debates over treaty termination in the context of rapid changes resulting from great power rivalry and accelerating climate change, in which the balance of interests of state parties to numerous existing treaties are being unsettled and the doctrine offers one means of 'adjusting treaty regimes in an orderly fashion'.[10] As that longer history shows, both principles appear necessary to maintain the international legal order.

---

[5] Vienna Convention on the Law of Treaties, opened for signature 23 May 1969, 1155 UNTS 331 (entered into force 27 January 1980) (VCLT), Article 62.

[6] International Law Commission 1966, pp. 172, 258.

[7] Bederman 1988, pp. 1–2.

[8] Ibid.

[9] Owada 2007.

[10] For analyses arguing for the relevance of the doctrine in the context of climate change, *see* Reisman 2021, p. 211; French and Scott 2018, pp. 677, 701–703; Morgandi and Bartels 2023, pp. 145, 159–166. For an analysis arguing for the relevance of the doctrine in relation to terminating the TRIPS Agreement, *see* Orford 2023, p. 3.

The idea that international law is primarily committed to achieving certainty is the product of a way of thinking that is characteristic of times that are stable. Yet as I have suggested, the assumption that the political and physical worlds will remain relatively stable is based on the conditions of an era that is passing. In the current context of a rapidly changing climate and the new geopolitical situation to which it is giving rise, the balance of interests of states parties to existing treaties may be radically unsettled. That will lead to contentious situations. In that context, lawyers will increasingly be called upon to think about how international law can contribute to maintaining or adjusting relations and regimes in a peaceful and orderly fashion. Doctrines such as *rebus sic stantibus* and other mechanisms for accommodating legal change are likely to play an increasingly important role in legal work. Although international lawyers often express concern about treaty termination or institutional exit, provisions enabling termination or exit can be understood as 'risk management tools',[11] or at least as techniques for channelling potential military conflicts into less destructive means of dispute settlement.

How then might changes in geopolitical and physical conditions require international lawyers to think more pragmatically and productively about corresponding changes in international law?

12.4 Geopolitical Transformations: From a Unipolar to a Multipolar International Order

The move from a world in which there is one single superpower (with which many of the most powerful states have been allied) to a world of competing superpowers is already having significant implications for international lawyers and international law. Competing versions of hegemonic international law are structuring the field of academic and professional practice. In many ways, this returns the field to a situation which is familiar to lawyers who studied or practiced during the Cold War.

In the aftermath of the global catastrophe of World War II, many of the treaties that structured the international legal order of the twentieth century were agreed, including the United Nations Charter, the General Agreement on Tariffs and Trade, the Genocide Convention, and the Refugee Convention. Yet the period from the 1950s through to the 1980s was one of struggle over the weight to be given to competing principles in the resulting legal order—on the one hand, to principles of sovereign equality, territorial integrity, and self-determination that were relied upon by many states as a means of defending their interests against regional hegemons, and, on the other, the right of regional powers to create military and economic alliances, intervene in defence of collective values, or resort to force in collective self-defence under Article 51 of the UN Charter. During the Cold War, both the United States and the USSR drew on broader alliances to gain a degree of legitimacy and success in their attempts at creating spheres of influence, and both used military power to

[11] Helfer 2020, p. 624.

secure networks of economic and trading relations. The balance of power between the two, as much as any commitment to legal principles of sovereign equality and non-intervention, served as a central means of constraining the scale of such projects. The idea of sovereign equality was in constant tension with attempts by superpowers to remake international law in ways that gave them greater freedom of movement and action and allowed them to maintain spheres of influence. The law relating to the use of force was the key site of this struggle.

With the end of the Cold War, states allied with the United States shifted position. For many, it seemed to make sense to support legal arguments that expanded the ability to resort to force. We can think here of the expanded readings of collective self-defence, the flirtation with doctrines of humanitarian intervention authorizing unilateral or collective resort to force to prevent genocide or respond to massive human rights abuses where the Security Council was blocked, and an unwillingness to confront occupations where allied states were the occupiers. As the Harvard law professor Detlev Vagts wrote back in 2001, 'it can be convenient for the hegemon to have a body of law to work with, provided that it is suitably adapted'.[12]

However, in the context of the return to a multipolar world, those expanded interpretations of international law authoring resort to force or justifying the imposition of sanctions and trade embargoes can just as easily end up empowering regional hegemons with which our states are not allied to do the same thing in different circumstances.[13] The overall effect is to consolidate forms of legal argument that enable the use of force to repress dissent and impose control over people and territory, and the coercive creation or maintenance of extended regional spheres of influence. In terms of states, the losers in that game will be middle powers and less powerful states—in other words, most states that are not military or economic superpowers. In such a context, as non-aligned states have long insisted, the means for resisting military and economic coercion remain the familiar mechanisms of supporting the peaceful settlement of international disputes, creating increased pressure for disarmament, resisting the creation and maintenance of foreign military bases, establishing nuclear-free zones, resisting the attempt to expand the legal grounds for resorting to military force, committing to the peaceful use of the world's oceans and outer space, and mounting robust challenges to illegal occupation and annexation of territories.[14]

Indeed, as we move deeper into an era of rival superpowers, it will be central to the legitimacy of international law that states and their legal advisors take the same position on the foundational questions relating to the use of force, annexation, occupation, and economic coercion in relation to states with which they are not allied as they take when it comes to their allies (or the allies of their allies). International lawyers may well want to be able to point to a robust body of jurisprudence on these questions in a future where superpowers are competing for control over what they

---

[12] Vagts 2001, pp. 843, 848.

[13] *See* the discussion in Orford 2021a, p. 149.

[14] Ibid. On the foundational nature of the final item in that list, that is, the prohibition of annexations, *see* Brunk and Hakimi 2024, p. 417.

see as their rightful spheres of influence, from Eastern Europe to the South China Sea to the Middle East and North Africa.[15]

To date, however, that is not the direction in which things appear to be heading. To take one example, many Western states have expressed their view of the importance of third-party interventions in support of Ukraine's case against the Russian Federation before the International Court of Justice (ICJ), brought under the Genocide Convention. Those states have taken a position in support of Ukraine because of the shared understanding that it is important to have the Court articulate the legal principles at stake in a case of illegal invasion and occupation. In that context, recourse to the ICJ is seen as offering an avenue to address questions that the Security Council is unable to take on, because of the operation of the veto power. However, the Russian case is one involving invasion and attempted annexation by a state that is not a Western ally. Many Western states have responded in the past much more cautiously to the use of force by the United States,[16] and to the involvement of the ICJ and the ICC in the context of the war in Gaza.

12.5 Transformations in the Natural World

The second major change to which I have referred concerns the stability of the natural world, as the consequences of climate change begin to accelerate. The relative stability of the natural world has been taken as given until very recently. As Davor Vidas and his colleagues have argued in the context of the law of the sea, our international legal structures have been created over the past centuries based on the premise that the physical world is stable.[17] However, in the context of global warming, 'we are heading for a change in the relatively stable ice–sea–land conditions as generally experienced over the past six to seven thousand years—a key overall circumstance that has contributed to perceptions of enduring general stability, on which various aspects of international law are based'.[18]

The projected pace at which profound change is likely to occur will require a great deal of flexibility and creativity from international lawyers. We are already seeing the climatization of international law, with climate change becoming an issue that generalist international lawyers will need to engage with across almost all fields. Advisory opinions on climate change have been delivered by the International Tribunal on the Law of the Sea, the ICJ, and the Inter-American Court of Human Rights, and climate change is also playing a central role in international trade and investment litigation, in human rights cases before regional and international human rights bodies, as a question of peace and security before the Security Council, and emerging on the agenda at the ICC with the push to create a crime of ecocide.

---

[15] Orford 2021a.

[16] *See* Kotova and Tzouvala 2022, p. 710.

[17] Vidas et al. 2020, pp. 22, 36.

[18] Ibid.

Climate change does not fit neatly with many of those areas of international law, just as it does not fit neatly with many areas of domestic law. Climate litigation is challenging lawyers and traditional legal frameworks across the board. This is because existing legal regimes, particularly in capitalist market economies, are largely not designed around precautionary or prevention principles. In addition, the scope and scale of climate change, and the potential loss and damage it will cause, will necessarily test and disrupt conventional ideas about standing, jurisdiction, causality, and the attribution of responsibility. Overall, the degree of transformation in the natural world that has for so long been taken for granted as a relatively stable basis of law and politics will require a great deal of agility from international lawyers, and the ability to be open to rethinking inherited positions.

12.6 Conclusion

The sense of coherence and consensus that shaped international law during the two decades after the end of the Cold War was the product of the conditions I discussed in opening—the existence of a single superpower and a stable natural world. It seems unlikely that we will experience those conditions again, at least in the near future. The resulting legal situation is going to be messy, because our legal frameworks were developed in a different context of natural and therefore political stability, in which we did not have to think about loss, damage, and vulnerability to disaster on this scale. We will be faced with massive geopolitical and geographical changes, in which the balance of interests of states will also change rapidly.

Under such conditions, situations will be contentious, and disputes will be inevitable. And we will be challenged, perhaps even forced, to rethink fundamental questions of representation, national interest, security, and survival, and to reflect on whether existing legal frameworks and concepts are adequate to the situation in which we find ourselves. In that context, international lawyers will need to adopt a different orientation towards change. We will be called upon to think creatively about how to readjust and revisit existing obligations where necessary, in ways that are just, that avert a complete breakdown of existing relations, and that, hopefully, contribute to the continued survival of life on the planet.

References

Bederman DJ (1988) The 1871 London Declaration, Rebus Sic Stantibus and a Primitivist View of the Law of Nations. American Journal of International Law 82:1–2

Brunk I, Hakimi M (2024) The Prohibition of Annexations and the Foundations of Modern International Law. American Journal of International Law 118:417

French D, Scott KN (2018) International Environmental Law. In: Bowman MJ, Kritsiotis D (eds) Conceptual and Contextual Perspectives on the Modern Law of Treaties. Cambridge University Press, Cambridge

Helfer LR (2020) Terminating Treaties. In: Hollis DB (ed) The Oxford Guide to Treaties, 2nd edn. Oxford University Press, Oxford

Intergovernmental Panel on Climate Change (2023) Synthesis Report of the IPCC Sixth Assessment Report. https://www.ipcc.ch/report/ar6/syr/downloads/report/IPCC_AR6_SYR_LongerReport.pdf. Accessed 15 February 2025

Joerges C (2014) Europe's Economic Constitution in Crisis and the Emergence of a New Constitutional Constellation. German Law Journal 15:985, 991

Kotova A, Tzouvala N (2022) In Defense of Comparisons: Russia and the Transmutations of Imperialism in International Law. American Journal of International Law 116:710

Kulaga J (2020) A Renaissance of the Doctrine of *Rebus Sic Stantibus*? International and Comparative Law Quarterly 69:477

Morgandi T, Bartels L (2023) Exiting the Energy Charter Treaty under the law of treaties. King's Law Journal 34:145, 159–166

Orford A (2021a) Regional Order, Geopolitics, and the Future of International Law. Current Legal Problems 74:149

Orford A (2021b) The Crisis of Liberal Internationalism and the Future of International Law. Australian Year Book of International Law 38:3

Orford A (2023) Why It's Time to Terminate the TRIPS Agreement. Australian Year Book of International Law 41:3

Owada H (2007) Peaceful Change. In: Max Planck Encyclopedia of International Law. Oxford University Press, Oxford

Reisman DAA (2021) *Rebus sic stantibus* as a Stabilizing Doctrine in the Climate Crisis. Climate Law 11:211

Vagts D (2001) Hegemonic International Law. American Journal of International Law 95:843, 848

Vidas D et al (2020) Climate Change and the Anthropocene: Implications for the Development of the Law of the Sea. In: Johansen E et al (eds) The Law of the Sea and Climate Change: Solutions and Constraints. Cambridge University Press, Cambridge

Anne Orford is Melbourne Laureate Professor and Michael D Kirby Chair of International Law at Melbourne Law School, and Visiting Professor of Law and John Harvey Gregory Lecturer on World Organization at Harvard Law School. She researches and teaches in the areas of international law, international dispute settlement, international economic law, climate change, and the history and theory of international law. She is a Member of the Permanent Court of Arbitration, a Fellow of the Academy of the Social Sciences in Australia, and a past President of the Australian and New Zealand Society of International Law. She has been a Visiting Legal Fellow at the Australian Department of Foreign Affairs and Trade and an international expert adviser on climate change and international law to the Pacific Islands Forum. In addition to visiting at Harvard Law School since 2019, she has been a Visiting Professor of Law at Université Paris 1 (Panthéon-Sorbonne), Hedda Andersson Visiting Chair at Lund University, the Raoul Wallenberg Visiting Chair in Human Rights and Humanitarian Law at the Raoul Wallenberg Institute, Torgny Segerstedt Visiting Professor at the University of Gothenburg, Senior Emile Noël Research Fellow at NYU School of Law, and the Olof Palme Visiting Professor at Stockholm University. She presented a Special Course at the Hague Academy of International Law in 2021, and was elected to the Institut de Droit International in 2025.

Chapter 13
Problems in Teaching Public International Law

Iain Cameron

Contents

Abstract One of the contributions of critical legal scholarship is to encourage the writer to reflect over what they are doing and why. The nature and experience of international law means that a teacher and researcher can often be assailed with self-doubt. Why enthuse young people for a subject which seems to weave between excusing the (mis)use of power and building a (unrealistic) utopia? Why research about the limits the law places on state action when powerful states seem to be able to ignore these limits? This chapter consists of my personal reflections about why it is worthwhile teaching and researching international law. If there are no critical teachers and researchers, one leaves a "walk-over" to those opinion-builders from both democratic and non-democratic states who advance an authoritarian vision of international politics. Moreover, learning to think critically about international law helps us to understand better other legal subjects close to politics (constitutional law, EU law etc.) where the law is open, horizontally formed and can be subject to rapid change.

Keywords International law · Critical legal studies · Constitutional law · Teaching

---

I. Cameron (✉)
Uppsala University, Uppsala, Sweden
e-mail: Iain.Cameron@jur.uu.se

M. Klamberg et al. (eds.), *Reconstructing Power and Hegemony in Public International Law*, https://doi.org/10.1007/978-94-6265-743-4_13

13.1 Introduction

Professor Pål Wrange has had a long and distinguished career as teacher, researcher, and legal adviser to the Swedish Foreign Ministry. We began as doctoral students around the same time, Pål in Stockholm and I in Uppsala, and our paths have continued to cross throughout our careers. This chapter, written in homage to Pål, consists of my personal reflections about an issue that Pål (and many others) has brooded over, namely *why* teach and research international law. I use as a point of departure two of Pål's publications, his monumental doctoral dissertation, *Impartial or uninvolved*[1] and one of his many articles, *An Open Letter to My Students.*[2]

13.2 Pål's Reflections

Pål mentions how he was influenced by his early encounters with critical legal scholarship. Pål begins his thesis by briefly discussing if international law has any practical relevance, in the sense of influencing state behavior. He expresses the view that it does: as a common language or mode for states to do things. It is not only "a framework for contemplating and legitimizing international action" but also serves as "a container of values and principles which should be inherent in any nation's foreign policy." Even at this minimum level, international law thus merits academic research and discussion. As international law has this ethical dimension ("should"), Pål notes that it is then necessary to pose the following question: is it *good*? This, in turn, requires asking: Good according to what criteria?

It is, Pål concludes, a good thing, in that it makes international interaction more predictable, and forces states to phrase their claims in a language of generally applicable norms (if you claim the right to do this, you must accept that other states may also do so). Although far from perfect, such a framework is in general more beneficial for the weak. However, to do this job adequately, the law has to be internally coherent and plausible (at least to the community of international lawyers). Moreover, there is a time dimension here. The Foreign Ministry legal adviser, who is making state practices, continually has to react: s/he has to "think fast." There is a need for academic work afterwards to try to make this reactive practice more consistent and coherent. If one does not apply an explicit theoretical framework to this task, one ends up with an implicit theoretical framework. Thus, there is a need for academic work to get the underlying values (or lack thereof) out in the open, to compare to the past and draw out the implications for the future.

As to the issue of teaching, Pål notes that he planned his career, even his life, around the notion that international law is useful. Personally, he has obtained a sense of fulfilment in teaching, though he has experienced (periodic?) self-doubt as to what he has been doing. He notes, however, that at the end of the day, there is a pragmatic

[1] Wrange 2007, pp. 38–52.
[2] Wrange 1996.

need to explain to students what makes law work, and when—particularly as the bad guys are still out there, happily exploiting (or creating) uncertainties in the law. At the very least, students need to know what constitutes a bad legal argument in international law, and why.

13.3 My Own Views

I agree with all Pål's points, which he makes simply but with a praiseworthy openness. Like Pål, I was impressed, and, initially, rather confounded, when I read Martti Koskenniemi's thesis *From Apology to Utopia.* I was two-thirds into the process of writing my own doctoral thesis. At this stage in the work, the last thing a doctoral student needs, or wants, is something fundamentally new which has the potential to call into question the work they have already done. Apart from its quality (Oh no! Is it something like this that we are expected to produce?), the book was also a comprehensive rubbishing of the "classical" approach to the subject of public international law. This was the approach I had been taught in the UK, and this was the approach I had encountered in my contacts with other Swedish international lawyers, both academic and practicing. Simply put, it was that international law was not that different from other parts of law. The task of the researcher was finding out what the law was in any given situation. Courts did this, as did legal advisers and academic lawyers. International law was admittedly formed (largely) in a horizontal (contractual) fashion by states themselves, rather than in a (largely) vertical fashion by the legislature, but the nature of the exercise was essentially the same. As the international legal order was more chaotic and unclear—an anarchic society, in Bull's memorable phrase—the task of the academic international lawyer was in some way more noble, as s/he sought to bring more order and predictability (and justice) into the process by methodically gathering evidence of customary international law and/or state practice indicating the "correct" way to apply a vague treaty provision. This was admittedly a highly subjective exercise but the idea was that it was to be done as transparently and (hopefully) objectively as possible.

However, the first impression I got from reading *From Apology to Utopia* was that there were major problems involved in the exercise of dutifully gathering evidence of state practice and *opinion juris* in order to demonstrate what the content of customary international law was in a given area. Even the—relatively speaking—more solid exercise of showing the "correct" interpretation of a treaty was subject to methodological objections. An ascending argument (appealing to idealistic values) would always be met by a descending argument (the cold reality of state interests). There was no objective point of equilibrium to be obtained on the spectrum running from ascending to descending. In the absence of binding dispute settlement, or at least some form of third-party authoritative interpretation, states would be free to (and would continue to) make their arguments *ad infinitum.* The job of an international lawyer working for a foreign ministry was, like that of a company lawyer, to make whatever arguments s/he could think of to advance the interests of the state employing them. The academic lawyer could be either an apologist or a utopian, or sometimes one and sometimes the other, but either way, was a (largely irrelevant) commentator.

Deeper study showed that this skepticism toward the classical approach international law did not begin with Koskenniemi, although his criticism was particularly well-supported and elegantly expressed. In any event, like Pål, I drew the initial impression from my encounters with critical legal thinking in international law that academic research in international law was fairly pointless, and that teaching international law (which was what had drawn me to the profession in the first place) was a cynical exercise. What was the point of enthusing young people to devote time to a subject which holds out hope for humanity—peace, justice, human rights, sustainability—but in fact is merely a smokescreen for the naked exercise of power?

Like Pål, and for similar reasons, I drew the pragmatic conclusion that at the end of the day, there was nonetheless a need for both qualitative research and qualitative teaching in international law. Like Pål, I was also attracted by a more critical approach than that with which I was taught. The first part of my thesis rested on the relatively solid case law of the European Court of Human Rights (ECtHR) dealing with national security—undoubtedly case law with a political dimension, but still possible to study as "hard law." The second part of my thesis rested on a comparative study of national legislation and case law in one particular area: criminal jurisdiction. In both parts, the critical legal scholarship I had read made me cautious of drawing conclusions as to whether international law placed any limits on state freedom of action. But this did not mean that I had to rip it all up and start again. And though a consensus among the profession seemed to be a pretty thin basis on which to found a subject, it turned out that the rest of social science, and quite a lot of natural science, seems ultimately to be based on the same thing.

I would like to add some further reflections and explain a little of how I have reconciled myself with international law.

13.4 The Joy of Painting on a Big Canvas

What attracted me to a career in academia was primarily teaching. This interest has—so far—stuck with me, and, at the time of writing, I am 66 years old. Some people who choose an academic career regard teaching as a necessary evil: the old joke that the university would be so much better without all these bloody students. A teacher expecting *all* his or her students to be bright-eyed and bushy-tailed will undoubtedly be disappointed, but at least in Uppsala, the majority (in term 1, see below) are sufficiently interested to make it a rewarding experience.

What attracted me to public international law was the "big issues"—justice, human rights, peace etc.—and the natural connections these have to both political science and philosophy. These connections are also present in constitutional law, and nowadays in EU law as well—which provides an alternative career path for an idealistic lawyer.

Most theses in law in Swedish universities are monographs, involving a deep dive into a difficult but usually narrowly defined topic. The author must show that s/he has a very thorough command of the details. This applies particularly for a person who wants to deal with the big issues, who can be likened to a painter who wants to paint abstract art. In order to convince colleagues and critics that s/he can paint large and abstract, the painter finds that it is usually best to first show that s/he can paint from reality and in detail. The legitimacy to branch out and write about the big things comes from how well one can show handling of the small things. But we are what we do. A lawyer who has gone through a long period in the "small world" of legal painting can easily lose the ability to "paint big and abstract." At that point, the lawyer has become so conditioned that s/he may no longer feel comfortable with "big issues" at all.

13.5 International Law and Constitutional Law

A theme for both parts of my thesis, and indeed most of my subsequent research, was the meeting between international law and national law, and the tensions and synergies it can produce. International law enters into the national legal system via the constitutional gate but then permeates into other legal subjects: procedural law, criminal law or administrative law (tax law, police law, social welfare law etc.). I developed an interest in following a big international law issue into the dense jungles of national law (and vice versa). International human rights, a particular interest of mine, I think become "real" only when they are actually applied, and respected, at the national level. Human rights issues can arise in many different ways, and this involves knowing, often quite a lot, about the national procedural and administrative context in which a claim against the state arises. I think that a human rights lawyer who *only* knows the UN supervisory bodies' case law (often a one-sided "wish list for Santa Claus") or even the more balanced—and so, more operative—case law of the ECtHR, is of little practical use to a litigant or potential litigant in Sweden.

In order to have any chance of obtaining a job as a permanent lecturer at a Swedish law faculty, one has to have a doctorate in law. At the time I was accepted as a doctoral student (1988, before the Swedish membership in the EC/EU in 1995), doctoral students from other jurisdictions were not accepted to study any subject other than international law. However, there was little room for employing teachers in international law. The Swedish law degree is four and a half years long,[3] but then—as now—the obligatory undergraduate course in public international law consisted of only four weeks' full-time study (6 ECTS).

I was very lucky in my choice of doctoral supervisor, Professor Nils Jareborg, one of the wisest men I know. I was also lucky in my timing. I completed my doctoral dissertation in May 1991. The Uppsala law degree, and the teaching of it, was entirely reformed around that time, with a first intake in September 1992. A need for several new lecturers arose—not in international law, but in constitutional

[3] There is no requirement to get a bachelor's degree at college first. Thus, most Swedish law students begin their studies straight out of high school.

law. I had taught constitutional law in Hull, where I began my academic career. Moreover, I had followed the course in Swedish constitutional law in Uppsala, then taught by the redoubtable Staffan Rylander, who was also one of the main architects of the teaching reform. On Nils and Staffan's recommendation, my colleagues were prepared to let me try my hand at teaching Swedish constitutional law, despite the obvious differences between this subject and British constitutional law.

I found Swedish constitutional law to be fascinating. It was full of big issues, too. Moreover, the field was wide open, because few had been writing in it for the last fifty years. Like international law, its application was, in some areas, dependent on politics. In other words, some breaches of it were not sanctioned, or at least you seemed to be able to get away with some things, depending on the circumstances. However, whereas international law could, and frequently did, suffer from a Zen-like uncertainty (above the head no sky, below the feet no ground), disappearing to a large extent when you needed it most, constitutional law rested on a bit more solid ground (though the *grundnorm*, too, can disappear when you go looking for it).

Since 1992, I have done the great majority of my teaching in the obligatory undergraduate course in constitutional law. As in all Swedish law faculties, it is held in term 1, during which students also have a short course in legal method. We use problem-based scenarios and have many obligatory seminars (about two per week). Most of the students I meet in term 1 are, relatively speaking, curious and enthusiastic. Teaching them is both challenging (you do not know where they will end up next) and rewarding (you literally see their knowledge and ability to think critically develop before your eyes). The students are interested in learning, even if they start the course thinking that the best way to do this is to memorize the notes taken by last term's students and helpfully integrated and made available online (curse you, Google Docs!).The more gifted students realize fairly quickly that memorizing someone else's notes does not help you when a factor changes in a scenario (which they have an annoying tendency to do).

I have also taught optional (elective) courses in both international law and constitutional law. My experience of these has been more mixed. Some of my most enjoyable and rewarding teaching experiences have been when I taught international law to small groups of highly dedicated students who participated in the Telders International Law Moot Court Competition, which ran for over thirty years and consisted of a hypothetical dispute before the International Court of Justice (ICJ), taking place at the ICJ in the Hague. The openness of much international law means that it is possible to construct plausible scenarios where the potential arguments are evenly balanced on both sides. Many of these students developed a deep and profound knowledge of international law, good critical analysis capacity, and impressive abilities to think fast. I stopped teaching these elective courses in international law fifteen years ago, in order to leave more room for elective courses in constitutional law, taught in English (most of my time still being devoted to term 1 teaching in Swedish). This experience was much more mixed. For every dedicated, interested, final-year student, there were three—Swedish and exchange students—who had simply ended up, more or less involuntarily, on the course. These students tend to be neither curious nor enthusiastic about constitutional law; they seemed to simply want the certificate at the end of the course. Teaching them was less rewarding and more of a struggle.

Anyway, teaching leads naturally to research, and so my research largely became research into Swedish constitutional law. I have kept up my interests in certain international law issues. There are areas which now span the two subjects (and EU law), most obviously European human rights law. But there are also a surprisingly large number of areas, such as sanctions law, which benefit from this double (or triple) perspective.

13.6 Positive and Negative Aspects of Teaching and Researching International Law

Researchers in each legal subject naturally tend to think that their own subject is the most interesting part of the law—otherwise they would not be studying it. The way that law is taught in Sweden, with one course read intensively at a time, reinforces the impression of self-contained teaching regimes which are largely indifferent to each other. Each subject can claim it is "central." Procedural lawyers can point out that things often come down to obtaining a remedy before the ordinary or administrative courts, and this in turn places focus on how one goes about choosing what remedy to seek, the evidence which has to be adduced, and the burden of proof. Criminal lawyers and contract lawyers can both claim that their subjects are the essence of law. Experts in jurisprudence can assert their superiority due to the level of sophistication of their understanding of the nature of law, even if practitioners have a disturbing tendency to be able to do just fine without them. And so on. What does international law bring to this mix?

The first thing is that international lawyers in Sweden have had something of an uphill struggle in being accepted into the fold of law at all. Writing in the early 1920s, in the context of the (misplaced) optimism in the League of Nations, Lundstedt noted that in the field of international law, there are "no real legal rules by which the agreements can obtain legal effect, nor any legal rules at all, on which the state's rights can be supported. There is nothing here but the chimera of natural law with rights and obligations in the sense of legal consciousness to work with."[4] The dualism of the Swedish legal order, and its approach to legal interpretation, has also worked to de-emphasize the role of international law. The preparatory legislative works of a law were (and are) the main source of guidance when it came to interpreting the law: these were comprehensive and there was no need (and democratically speaking, no reason) for going outside of these.

One option is to flee to political science. There is a growing literature with double perspectives: law and international relations. However, although the two disciplines have a lot to learn from one another, in my experience political scientists are less interested in law than lawyers are interested in political science. So, political scientists are not waiting to accept refugee international lawyers with open arms. One is, for the most part, stuck with one's colleagues in other legal disciplines. The real

[4] Lundstedt 1924, p. 20.

or perceived skepticism of one's legal colleagues can make international lawyers particularly apologetic. They are undoubtedly especially prone to soul searching. This is not surprising. If the proverbial man or woman on the street thinks about international law at all, they are likely to do so only when it is spectacularly broken. International law seems, from this simple perspective, to be subject to periodic crises. There was a brief period ("the end of history") after the collapse of the Soviet Union when the US was the only superpower and we in the West could fool ourselves into believing that there was a consensus on the value of a rule-based international order. It turned out that this was due only to the temporary weakness of Russia, and the fact that the government of the People's Republic of China (PRC) did not yet feel strong enough to show its authoritarian (and imperialistic) hand. But even during this period, some of the states with the greatest interest in maintaining this rule-based (Western) order were guilty of acts seriously undermining it. The US "war against terror" after the al-Qaida attacks on September 11, 2001, saw the US discarding several fundamental rules of international law: justifying torture, kidnapping, and indefinite secret detention, invading Afghanistan (with a pretty thin self-defense argument), and invading Iraq with no real legal argument at all. The UK's government at the time joined in the attack on Iraq, despite massive popular protests against it.

It seems that no sooner have we got over this than Russia reminds us that it is not on the same page as the West at all on the most basic rule of international law, the prohibition of seizing other states' territory through the threat or use of force. I write "the West" as an ideological grouping rather than a geographical one. Most of the non-aligned world, most of the states in Africa, Latin America, and Asia, do not support Russia's war of aggression in Ukraine, but they do not seem to care about it, really. The short-lived unipolar world is gone. The second most powerful state in the world, the PRC, is facilitating Russia's war of aggression, as well as being engaged in its own threats of force against Taiwan, and empire building in the Pacific—literally, in the construction of islands, which it then fortifies. International law means little to dictatorships—not surprising, because law itself means little (except as an instrument of power). Most disturbingly, the USA under Trump also seems to have abandoned its previous attachment to the rule-based international order.

It is thus easy to get depressed as international lawyer, at least when it comes to that huge gap at the heart of the subject, namely the use of force. Maybe the common language is not as common as we might want to think?[5] One can of course stress Henkin's approach, "that most international law is followed most of the time,"[6] but there is still something unsatisfactory in a legal system which disappears when you need it most.[7]

[5] International lawyers can miss the fact that a common language might be being used, but that the words refer to quite different things. For illuminating discussions, *see* Roberts 2017.

[6] Henkin 1979.

[7] Although it is little consolation, a number of US constitutional lawyers are nowadays also ridden with self-doubt about how legal their subject is, or rather, has become, with a Supreme Court that is departing from long-accepted case law for—allegedly—naked political reasons. Wegman 2024.

13.7 A Continued Value in Teaching and Researching International Law?

Nonetheless—and although the hour is dark—the need for international law and good international lawyers is as great or greater than ever before. Authoritarian states, at least those which regard themselves as strong, are not interested in a "rule-based international order." For example, Russian spokesmen sometimes show a chilling and open total disregard of the law, a good example being Medvedev, who (in)famously declared that humanitarian law did not apply to Russia because it had the biggest nuclear arsenal in the world.[8] At the same time, Russia seems to think that some things such as spheres of influence (as discussed during the Yalta conference) are binding international law, when they patently are not.[9] However, most of the time, Russia continues to make legal arguments that are comprehensible to the West, though these often involve absurdly straining the facts (the Russian minority in eastern Ukraine is being subject to genocide, the Russian attack on Ukraine is anticipatory self-defense against the imminent release of biological weapons of mass destruction). Ludicrous though these arguments may be, the West needs (quick-thinking) international lawyers to counter them, as well as to constantly monitor the stream of disinformation coming from Russia and its "useful idiots" in Western states. So, even if one considers that the value of international law is only at a minimum level of a "common language structuring diplomacy," there is still a need to maintain the integrity of the language and its normal meaning. A common historical origin long ago, or the presence of a "kin-minority," does not mean that a more powerful state is free to take bits or all of a neighboring state. There was and is no "genocide" going on in eastern Ukraine. Deliberately targeting civilians and civilian infrastructure is a war crime, not "self-defense against terrorists."[10]

The same applies to Chinese "legal" arguments. Building permanent structures on the high seas or in other states' exclusive economic zones and unilaterally extending your maritime boundaries on the basis of "historic title" are violations of the laws of the sea.[11]

Naturally, in advancing the cause of international law, Western states are, or should be, bound by the same rules they are insisting upon applying to others—otherwise

[8] Reuters, Russia's Medvedev warns United States: messing with a nuclear power is folly, 6 July 2022. https://www.reuters.com/world/russias-medvedev-warns-united-states-messing-with-nuclear-power-is-folly-2022-07-06/.

[9] Malksöö 2015. Although the USA, under Trump, also shows a disturbing backward tendency towards spheres of influence.

[10] On March 17, 2023, the ICC issued warrants for the arrest of Vladimir Putin and two senior Russian military officials, Situation in Ukraine: ICC judges issue arrest warrants against Vladimir Vladimirovich Putin and Maria Alekseyevna Lvova-Belova, International Criminal Court News, 17 March 2023, [https://www.icc-cpi.int/news/situation-ukraine-icc-judges-issue-arrest-warrants-against-vladimir-vladimirovich-putin-and].

[11] The South China Sea Arbitration (The Republic of Philippines v. The People's Republic of China), PCA, 2016.

the law loses all legitimacy. Deliberately starving civilian populations and using indiscriminate munitions in built-up civilian areas are war crimes, too.[12]

After war, comes—hopefully—peace. If and when a degree of sanity is restored in the Russian leadership, peace and reconciliation between Ukraine and Russia will require a treaty. An agreement will have to be drafted by international lawyers, although right now it is not clear how much influence (if any) the EU, and even the Ukraine, will have over the final product.

The same applies more generally if and when the deeply fragmented international community begins properly confronting the threats looming to the very existence of humanity: de-escalating the risk of nuclear war, regulating biological and autonomous weapons systems, preparing better for future pandemics and climate change, to name just the most pressing concerns. One can only go so far with voluntary systems of self-regulation. Even when these can cover part of the area, they will have to be supplemented by explicit (and binding) agreements between states. If there is to be any pre-regulation of technological developments which have high positive and negative potential for mankind—instead of just inventing the thing and hoping it all works out (artificial intelligence, genetic engineering etc.)—this will have to occur in the form of a treaty. Treaties will also be required (and at the present time are being finalized) between like-minded states to solve, or at least diminish, the more mundane but still pressing problems of plastics in the oceans and tax dodging by transnational corporations. Nor is the hand of international law seen only in environmental and tax matters. Globalization has meant that very large subjects heavily connected to money have significant international law aspects: international contract law, international banking law, international patent law, etc. Its permeation of the legal system means that there is, quite simply, too much of it to be ignored.

13.8 Concluding Remarks

Speaking personally, I have in my own career been most impressed by the academic lawyers who can do both theory and practice, and who can do both detailed and abstract "legal painting." I have developed a lot of respect for Pål's knowledge and views during my career. As is evident from this chapter, I agree with Pål on the continued value of teaching and researching international law. If taught in a reflective way, the subject can give students the necessary critical perspective to cope with other areas where the law is open, horizontally formed, and subject to rapid change. The political dimension is always present in international law. Although the main focus for a lawyer should always be on the "truth" issue—what has happened and what is the applicable law—it is useful for the international lawyer to review the power issue too, to ask him-/herself: who *wins* from making (or not making) this particular legal

[12] Following Hamas' terrorist attack on Israel on September 2023, and Israel's subsequent attack on and blockade of the territory of Gaza, the ICC has issued warrants for the leaders of Hamas as well as the Prime Minister and Defence Minister of Israel.

argument? A good international lawyer can cope with the openness of international law—the feeling of being adrift on a sea of competing principles—and give useful advice on both policy and law. It turns out that the skills developed in international law are also particularly useful in dealing with other legal subjects with a strong political dimension.

References

Bull H (1977) The Anarchical Society: A Study of Order in World Politics. London, Macmillan Press

Henkin L (1979) How Nations Behave, 2nd ed. New York, Colombia University Press

Koskenniemi M (1989) From Apology to Utopia: the Structure of International Legal Argument. Finnish Lawyers Publishing Co, Helsinki

Lundstedt W (1924) Folkrätten och Genèvepolitiken [International Law and the Politics of Geneva]. Uppsala, Almqvist och Wiksell

Mälksoo L (2015) Russian Approaches to International Law. Oxford, OUP

Roberts A (2017) Is International Law International? Oxford, OUP

Wegman J (2024), The Crisis in Teaching Constitutional Law, New York Times, 26 February 2024, https://www.nytimes.com/2024/02/26/opinion/constitutional-law-crisis-supreme-court.html Accessed 18 February 2025

Wrange P (1996) An Open Letter to My Students: Theory, Practice and Life in International Law. Nordic Journal of International Law 65:573-578

Wrange P (2007) Impartial or uninvolved? The anatomy of 20th Century doctrine on the Law of neutrality. Stockholm (academic dissertation).

Iain Cameron is Professor in Public International Law at Uppsala University. His research interests lie in the general fields of constitutional law, constitutional EU law and international law, more specifically in human rights/civil liberties, international criminal law and police/security issues. Since 2005, he has been one of the two Swedish members of the Commission on Democracy through Law (Venice Commission).

Chapter 14
Karl Olivecrona and the Legal Realist Support for Nazi Germany

Mats Deland

Contents

Abstract This chapter follows the political and theoretical choices made by the Swedish law professor Karl Olivecrona. In 1940, following the publication of his main work, *Law as Fact* (1939), Olivecrona chose to take the side of Nazi Germany. Through a couple of pamphlets, one of them widely translated and distributed in occupied western Europe, Olivecrona argued for political adjustment to the 'New Europe' allegedly created by the Third Reich. Traditionally, this position has been explained by his allegiance to the radical neo-Kantian philosophy of legal realism. However, as pointed out in the chapter, his colleagues chose a completely different political path from the same philosophical foundations. Through a comparison between Olivecrona's main principles and the legal philosophies of Hans Kelsen and Carl Schmitt—like Olivecrona, critics of legal positivism—it is instead suggested that the choice to support the Nazi war of aggression originated in a radical critique of the world order created after the Versailles Peace Treaty and a disbelief in the rule of international law. His was one of several choices in a world in turmoil, logically coherent with his legal theory but not its logical consequence.

Keywords Karl Olivecrona · Axel Hägerström · Vilhelm Lundstedt · Hans Kelsen · Carl Schmitt · Legal realism · Legal positivism · Non-consequentialism · Nazism · Lund University

M. Deland (✉)
Mid Sweden University, Sundsvall, Sweden
e-mail: mats.deland@gmail.com

M. Klamberg et al. (eds.), *Reconstructing Power and Hegemony in Public International Law*, https://doi.org/10.1007/978-94-6265-743-4_14

14.1 Introduction

The essence of critical theory is, as Max Horkheimer famously claimed, that it strives to break the dichotomy between theory and facts, and to situate the researcher as both a product of and an active influence on the structures of human culture, in its historical sequence.[1] A critical theory of law thus has to question both its object of study and the role of the law scholar within society, as it evolves and with the hindsight of its inner possibilities. This points to the inherent political character of law. Never has that been more pronounced than in the Age of Extremes, the conflict-ridden 20th century.[2] Hannah Arendt once said that totalitarian rule is characterized by the degradation of law understood as justice and legality in favour of the laws of nature and history.[3] This *Rechtsstaat* argument points to the influence of modernity and reason as a major factor behind the irrationalism of totalitarian governance. Her argument is repeated in a range of different variations in postwar philosophy.[4] However, even disregarding its normative content, it points to an important difficulty within the understanding of international law and its relation to the violence underpinning it. To what extent is law a result of violence and to what extent does it protect from violence?

The archetypical understanding of law within Nazi Germany, as exemplified by its *Kronjurist* Carl Schmitt, had other origins.[5] The political theology of Schmitt, developed during the early years of the Weimar republic, was derived from Catholicism and aimed, as it were, to assess the possibilities to overcome the challenges of parliamentarism and mass politics.[6] The Nazi state subsequently developed into the four-headed hydra of Franz Neumann's *Behemoth*, and its legal structure into Ernst Fraenkel's *Dual State*, divided between prerogative and normative law, or perhaps between attempts to rule by law and total contempt for the law. However, from the outset, the opposition to the Weimar republic largely drew on monarchist themes, and the possibilities to re-instate the divinely instated ruler as the one who decides over the state of the exception, as Schmitt would have it—even if it had to be in a secular version, such as the *Reichspräsident*.[7] The resolution to the crisis of modernity would thus be to return to pre-modern—or rather: early modern—political forms.[8]

---

[1] Horkheimer 2002, pp. 200–201.

[2] I borrow the concept from Hobsbawm 1994.

[3] Arendt 2017, p. 608.

[4] *Cf.* Horkheimer and Adorno 1947; Rubenstein 1975; Bauman 1989.

[5] The label comes from a Nazi daily, which gave him this honorary title on 11 May 1933, that is a few months after the Nazi takeover in Germany. A *Kronjurist* is an attorney general, but the title was given to Schmitt only honorarily (and, increasingly, dishonorarily, by the exiled opposition), after his role in the June 1934 repressive measures against the Sturmabteilung leadership). *See* Balakrishnan 2000, p. 182.

[6] On the Christian (Catholic) origins of Carl Schmitt's conception of law, *see* Falk 2022.

[7] Neumann 2009; Fraenkel 2010. The famous line about the exception is also the first line of Schmitt's work *Politische Theologie* (1920), *see* Balakrishnan 2000, p. 36.

[8] Scholz-Karl 2021.

At the same time, if support for fascism had come only from monarchist reaction, it would hardly have prevailed. This chapter will study the choice of a liberal-conservative legal scholar, the Swedish legal realist Karl Olivecrona, professor of procedural law in Lund from 1933, to side with the Nazis in their war of conquest. This happened at the height of Nazi conquests, after the successful invasions of Denmark, Norway, Belgium, the Netherlands, Luxembourg and France during spring 1940—that is, at the point when the military threat against Sweden was most pronounced. Not until October 1943, following the arrival of thousands of Danish Jewish refugees to Swedish shores (but a year after the departure of the ship Donau from Oslo, taking almost all the remaining Norwegian Jews towards their destruction in Auschwitz), did he publish an op-ed where he declared his objection to the anti-Jewish policy. However, he never officially backed down from his earlier views.[9] There are parallels here with Schmitt, who after the war protested the crimes against humanity, but implicitly defended the war of conquest (as if it could be divorced from the annihilation policy).[10] The interesting thing about Olivecrona's case, though, is that he arrived at his conclusions without disclosing strong anti-democratic or racist views, at least not stronger than what could be found among many liberals or liberal-conservatives at the time, including the anti-Nazi ones. Even to his main biographer, Stockholm legal philosopher Torben Spaak, his choice remains a puzzle.[11] I will here try to present some contours of an explanation, comparing with the contemporary interventions of Carl Schmitt and Hans Kelsen. This reveals both similarities and differences in the legal universe of legal realism, but also the main political alternatives in a conflicted world—alternatives that co-existed within legal realism.

14.2 The Uppsala School and Carl Schmitt at the Onset of Fordism

Olivecrona was a prominent exponent of the Scandinavian legal realism school. Together with Vilhelm Lundstedt, professor of civil law in Uppsala, and the Dane (Copenhagen) Alf Ross (who was also inspired by British linguistic philosophy), he represents the first and most prominent generation of this school. The Scandinavian legal realists were inspired by the neo-Kantian Uppsala school of philosophy, most prominently represented by Axel Hägerström and Adolf Phalén, who wrote their most important works around the turn of the century. The Uppsala school was, according to the historian of ideas Svante Nordin, author of the most important comprehensive work on the tendency, influenced by the German Marburg school, but had some originality.[12] Hägerström also discussed legal concepts, such as the concepts of Roman Law (1927 and 1941), in order to disclose their origin in ancient

[9] Olivecrona 1943. *Cf.* Oredsson 1996, p. 184.

[10] Schmitt 2011c, p. 127–128.

[11] Spaak 2014, p. 28.

[12] Nordin 1983, pp. 27–30.

religious rituals.[13] The main idea of the Uppsala school concerned the non-existing truth claim of ethical or moral values—which were instead explained psychologically as mere feelings—and the legal offshoot criticized legal concepts in the same way, as mere remains of magical thinking.[14] Both Hägerström and the legal realists were thus modernists and enemies of conservatism.

Although the Uppsala school was a modernist reaction to the old quasi-Hegelian Swedish state philosophy of Christopher Jacob Boström, the legal offshoot directed critique against both natural rights philosophy and 19th century legal positivism such as that developed in Germany by Georg Jellinek.[15] However, it also criticized the sociological and historical schools and generally all versions of the Will theory (the idea that the legal system in the last instance is founded on someone's intention, such as the will of the ruler or the state as an organization or organism) for being only half-hearted attempts to eradicate the magical or sacral content from legal concepts.[16] The programme of the school was mostly negative, and clearly in the Enlightenment tradition. However, it is important to understand that the legal realists were not positivists (except in a very trivial sense)—they were part of the reaction against legal positivism that dominated the years between the wars. One can also say that they represented an understanding of law conditioned by mass politics, emergent Fordism and an intensive codification of international law.[17]

Historically, one can understand the Uppsala school and its legal branch as an exponent of the democratization of the state and society. It was part of the social-liberal, radical-republican (constitutional) movement that had been created in the 1880s and came of age in the years before the first world war. The legal realists have, as already suggested, been seen as paving the way for the particular kind of Fordism that was created in Sweden beginning in the early 1930s.[18] One of its main figures, Vilhelm Lundstedt, for instance, argued against strengthened anti-strike laws in the 1920s and his overarching hypothesis was that the whole legal structure over time developed in accordance with contemporary conceptions of social utility, different in different ages.[19] Without any formalist tendencies, the realists conceived law as a machinery that worked more or less independent of human intentions. The machine metaphor for the legal structure had been introduced already by Hägerström, who

[13] Hägerström 1927; 1941.

[14] Nordin 1983, pp. 118–119.

[15] Nordin 1983, pp. 50–53.

[16] *See* Lundstedt 1929.

[17] The concept of Fordism, understood as the socioeconomic formations that combined the needs of mass production and mass consumption into stable governing regimes in a medium-term perspective, was derived from the famous 'prison notebooks' written by the communist leader Antonio Gramsci in the 1930s. Its modern use within the regulation school of political economy (and beyond) was spearheaded in Aglietta 1976.

[18] The Swedish version of Fordism, the 'people's home', was created after the coalition between the Social Democrats and the Peasant League party in May 1933. The law professor Vilhelm Lundstedt was a Social Democratic member of the second chamber of the Swedish parliament (*Riksdagen*) 1929–1948.

[19] Nordin 1983, pp. 120–121; Källström 1986, pp. 60–65.

conceived of legal functionaries as merely its 'cogs'.[20] It can hardly be more Fordist than that.

The no-nonsense appearance of legal realism contrasts starkly with the reliance on political mythology among Carl Schmitt and his colleagues.[21] Where the Swedes criticized liberal lawyers for not being vigilant enough against mythological elements, Schmitt saw the desacralization of law as a threat against both the state and the people that provided its corporal organism.[22] The legal realists basically purported a consensus ideology—not only in the form of Lundstedt's naive reliance on the tendency of law to work towards a vaguely defined social utility, but also in the overall idea that it is advantageous to rely as much as possible on the human ability to see the world as it is, without the help of religious or other mythological concepts.[23] In the work of Carl Schmitt, on the other hand, the focus is famously on conflict, and the division between friend and enemy.[24]

However, there are also similarities and points of convergence. The legal realists were outright hostile to the Versailles Peace Treaty and the position given to Germany in the world order of the League of Nations.[25] There were two reasons for this view. One was obviously sympathy with the plight endured by Germany, particularly after the Ruhr occupation in 1923. From a small-state perspective, the sympathy was focused on the party that appeared as the bullied one. The other reason was a general lack of confidence in international law.[26] Without effective sanctions from an external authority, the international system built around the League of Nations and the Versailles and Locarno treaties could only be anarchic, and although the realists did not deny that a network of international law was in existence, and quite effectively so, as an important part of the international economic system, this necessarily presupposed that it was not in the interest of the (economically and militarily) stronger nations to break the rules. If they did, no one would be able to stop them or, for that matter, come after them afterwards.

For Carl Schmitt, the development within international law was another threat to the sovereignty of the European nations. Whereas internal forces—mass politics, the unions and the parties, but also the international corporations—were threatening the integrity of the state from within, supra-state organizations that were part of the post-war order under the League of Nations represented another, external threat.[27] In 1941, he presented a solution, a new kind of political entity, the *Reich*, which could integrate larger areas into economic and political projects that entailed modernization

---

[20] Spaak 2014, pp. 264.

[21] On Carl Schmitt's ideas of political mythology, *see* Finchelstein 2022, pp. 94–112.

[22] Nordin 1983, pp. 46–49; Balakrishnan 2000, pp. 23–25.

[23] Nordin 1983, pp. 120–121.

[24] Schmitt 2010.

[25] Nordin 1983, pp. 122–123; Lundstedt 1924a.

[26] *Cf.* Lundstedt 1937.

[27] Koskenniemi 2001, pp. 426–427, emphasizes the homogeneity between the Schmittean concepts of national and international politics.

in communication and production techniques.[28] Naturally, this in its turn meant the breaking of the rules of international law. However, the main problem for Schmitt was the lack of order both within and without the states, and in the longer run, the threat against sovereignty as such. For the legal realists, the problem of order was only found at the international level. They did not fear the revolution; what they theorized was continuity.

14.3 The Pro-Nazi Intervention

Olivecrona presented his views on Nazi Germany mainly in two pamphlets, published in 1940 and 1941, respectively. However, this intervention was preceded by the publication in 1939 of his major opus, *Law as Fact*, a book of about 200 pages, originally in English, dealing with the philosophical consequences of legal realism. This book was also his first larger work, published when he was 42 years of age. The next, thoroughly revised, edition of the book in English did not appear until 1971, but already in 1940 Swedish and German editions were published, both with four extra pages dealing with the war that had broken out in the meanwhile.[29] To understand his position, we need to start with this treatise. It is obvious that it was conceived as a reaction to Hans Kelsen's book, *Reine Rechtslehre* (The Pure Theory of Law), which had been published already in 1934. Olivecrona knew Kelsen personally, he had in fact had him over for dinner during the latter's short lecture trip to Sweden in March 1933, which he—as a well-known defender of the Weimar constitution—undertook in part for security reasons following the *Machtübernahme.* Shortly after his visit, Kelsen was deposed as professor in Cologne, leaving for Geneva and subsequently the USA.[30] However, his lectures were translated into Swedish from lecture notes and published through the Fahlbeck Foundation in Lund, of which Olivecrona was the accountant.[31] In this way, the Swedish public was presented with Kelsen's ideas, in the major political science journal *Statsvetenskaplig tidskrift*, almost a year before his book was even published.[32] If Olivecrona was as uncomfortable with Kelsen's theories as he appears in his book, he kept his views to himself for quite a long while.

Olivecrona's argument was based on a very narrow interpretation of Kelsen. The idea that a legal rule would have—by itself—a 'binding power', as Kelsen (and legal positivists in general) would have it, was impossible, according to Olivecrona. That,

---

[28] Schmitt 2011b; *Cf.* Balakrishnan 2000, pp. 237–238.

[29] The Swedish edition was published simultaneously in occupied Denmark, where the German edition was also printed.

[30] Famously, Schmitt was one of few law professors who did not sign a simultaneous letter of protest against the deposition.

[31] Kelsen 1933.

[32] Bindreiter 2018. Interestingly, it seems that an animated argument did in fact take place during the dinner, but not with Olivecrona—Kelsen argued with the young philosopher Konrad Marc-Wogau.

he said, would amount to sheer magic.[33] Instead, as he saw it, a legal rule is better seen as (in most cases) an 'independent imperative', a prescription to act (or not act) in a certain way but without any inherent binding power.[34] The only way a rule could have any influence had to be through 'psychological pressure'—either directly through the sanction system, the system of organized violence, or indirectly through propaganda and the continuous influence of upbringing and adjustment running through the whole of society.[35] Lacking any direct connection between rule and sanction (as not all crimes are punished), the best a society could do was to cater for a 'certain order'.[36] Although obviously modelled on the penal system, this conception would, according to Olivecrona, be valid for the entire legal system (*rättssystem*).

According to Olivecrona, the legal system was never, and never could be, anything else than organized violence and the consequences that this violence would bring to bear on the rest of society. In other words, although rules could have an effect in the 'world of time and space', through the psychological effects of utterances that are associated with certain acts and sanctions, these effects would always be purely external, never the effects of the rules themselves. Olivecrona objected against Kelsen's system of legal immanence (which had been construed with the intention to reserve a place for law outside of politics) with a legal social psychology—where Schmitt instead had objected with the hyperpolarization of law.[37] Olivecrona in fact avoided politics as much as possible, stating that the basic tools of legal practice—rules upheld by organized violence and propaganda—were the same in democracies and dictatorships.[38] There is no talk about the threats of mass politics and parliamentarism. On the contrary, Olivecrona was at pains to normalize revolutionary change as just another kind of legal practice, that, he admitted, demanded a larger amount of violence than normal legal practice, but on the other hand, soon returns to normalcy again.[39] Like Schmitt, he considered the Nazi takeover as one among many revolutions in world history, on a par with the French and the Russian. It is never stated explicitly, but this could to some extent explain his view of the Nazi regime as just a temporary violent outburst before normalcy would return.[40] In the addendum to the Swedish and German versions of his book, he in fact asked for a 'new spirit'—though regardless of which side would win.[41]

The two pamphlets are surprisingly unpolitical. In *England eller Tyskland* (England or Germany) (1940), Olivecrona argued for some of the ideas that Carl Schmitt developed in his pamphlet *Die Wendung zum diskriminierende Kriegsbegriffes* (The Turn to the Discriminatory Concept of War) (1938)—though without

[33] Olivecrona 1940a, pp. 18–20.
[34] Olivecrona 1940a, p. 35.
[35] Olivecrona 1940a, p. 168.
[36] Olivecrona 1940a, p. 129.
[37] Koskenniemi 2001, pp. 238–249.
[38] Olivecrona 1940a, p. 38.
[39] Olivecrona 1940a, p. 78.
[40] *Cf.* Suuronen 2021.
[41] Olivecrona 1940a, p. 198.

even mentioning Schmitt. Instead of discussing the asymmetry arising from the capacity of the League of Nations to decide the legality of recourse to armed conflict, as Schmitt did, he focused on the German war aims and presented them as a rational solution to the political and economic problems that had existed in Europe in the period between the wars. One important difference is that where Schmitt, whose paper had been published at a conference already in 1937, before the pre-war German annexations, presented the League of Nations' sanctions policy as ruling out the right to neutrality, Olivecrona, writing during Germany's war against western Europe, instead condemned small-state neutrality as wasteful and anachronistic. Why should the peoples of the small states bleed for something that was not resilient anyway?[42] The main argument of his pamphlet was that England (which he saw as the sole upholder and beneficiary of the Versailles Peace Treaty—the pamphlet was finished in August 1940, after the fall of France) was simply too weak to hold its own ground and that the League of Nations therefore had been its guarantee of having a war coalition ready for the next war. This was an idea that had imploded.[43] The German conquest of the other countries had, he conceded, caused a fair amount of irritation among the conquered, but the bigger picture was more important.[44] He argued that a European unification (under German leadership) would be a rational adjustment to a new global situation where blocs had been formed also on other continents (the USA, the Soviet Union, the expanding Japanese empire), thus prefiguring the multipole *Grossraum* theory that Schmitt would present one year later.[45] In his next pamphlet, *Europa och Amerika* (Europe and America) (1941), he developed the idea of the larger blocs further, explicitly comparing it with the American Monroe Doctrine of 1823.[46] In this pamphlet, he also discussed the need for popular homogeneity by digressing on the 'ugly spot' of the United States, the former slaves, who were now forming a population that '[could] not be included into society'. 'They are and will remain an alien race.' Jews are not mentioned in any of his works, but it is anyone's guess to what extent this was a disguised way to discuss the Nazi policy against the Jews.[47]

14.4 The General Pro-Nazi Environment

Olivecrona was one of the 'four professors' from Swedish universities who came out in support of Nazi Germany (not counting German academics residing in Sweden), the others being the German linguist Erik Rooth, the historian Gottfrid Carlsson and

[42] Schmitt 2011a, pp. 65–67; Olivecrona 1940b, pp. 36–38.

[43] Olivecrona 1940b, pp. 14–18, 36–38.

[44] Olivecrona 1940b, p. 28.

[45] Olivecrona 1940b, pp. 41–43.

[46] Olivecrona 1941b, p. 7.

[47] Olivecrona 1941b, p. 15.

the ethnologist Hugo Odeberg, who was also the chair of the friendship society Riksföreningen Sverige-Tyskland (RST).[48] In addition to writing the two pamphlets (and the addendum to *Law as Fact*), Olivecrona took part in a symposium in Germany, organized by the RST. Olivecrona was a member of this society and, according to Per Engdahl, was also a member of the Nazi party Sveriges Nationella Förbund and briefly of Engdahl's splinter organization (1941) Svensk Opposition. However, he is only to be found in the membership list of the RST.[49] The proceedings of the symposium, which apart from Olivecrona and a Danish professor only involved active Swedish national socialist activists (from Svensk Opposition), were published in Germany.[50] It goes without saying that a Swedish professor of law who openly supported the German war aims was a propaganda asset and there is a strange oversight in the literature of the impressive range of translated editions that was published by German or other foreign publishers, many of them in occupied countries. *England eller Tyskland* was translated into English, French, German, Italian, Spanish, Norwegian, Portuguese, Romanian, Dutch, Danish and Finnish in 1941, whereas the Swedish editions were also published in Copenhagen and Helsinki, according to the international Worldcat library catalogue. However, the next pamphlet, *Europa och Amerika,* seems only to have been translated into German and Danish (where it had been circulated in paper copies already in 1940). It is obvious that Olivecrona's main accomplishment was not his intervention in the Swedish discussion, but the support he—through these translations—gave to the German occupation authorities and generally to the war effort in western Europe in the beginning of the war.[51] It can be noted that there were no translations into Slavic languages, maybe because the argument of international cooperation would have less influence in areas that the Germans considered as their own *Hinterland* from the 19th century Berlin and Vienna empires. As far as I know, apart from a brief mention of the Italian translation in Sverker Oredsson's book about Lund University during the Second World War, there is no research into the influence of these translations, or of the incomes derived from them, so we can only guess at the importance of this aspect. Some translations were published by local publishers, but most were published by the Department of *Wirtschaftspropaganda* in Berlin. A superficial investigation shows no trace of any propaganda activities in German archives, beyond an attempt to recruit Olivecrona for a propaganda presentation in Copenhagen in 1942.[52]

---

48 Oredsson 1996, pp. 88–118, 125.

49 Hübinette 2002, p. 263. The information of his membership in SNF and SO comes from Engdahl himself (personal communication with Hübinette, who kindly agreed to help me with this information).

50 Hatt et al. 1943. The German edition was a translation of the Norwegian original.

51 Oredsson 1996, p. 98, who wrote his book long before the Worldcat catalogue was available, however mentions the Italian translation and suggests an influence beyond the Swedish border for Olivecrona.

52 Dr Tietze (Die Deutsche Arbeitsfront NS-Gemeinschaft Kraft durch Freude Zentralbüro) to Deutsche Volkbildungswerk, NSDAP Reichsleitung 4 July 1941, Betr. Veranstaltungen 'Schleswig-Holstein—Brücke zum Norden', Bundesarchiv DBFU NS 15/32, fol. 1, Bundesarchiv-Lichterfelde. The aim of the letter was to get clearance to invite the listed foreigners, from Sweden, Denmark and

14.5 The Critique and Concession

I will only briefly touch on the critique that Olivecrona received for his intervention. Apart from the symposium mentioned above, the most politically charged episode was a lecture on Marxist state theory that he held at the Nazi venue Manhem in Stockholm in October 1941. A Social Democratic daily accused him of participating in celebrations of the Quisling government (the puppet regime in occupied Norway), accusations that he denied.[53] He also took part in a debate in the Swedish daily *Dagens Nyheter*. This happened after a book by his wife, Birgit Lange, was critically reviewed by the liberal publicist Ivar Harrie.[54] She had presented more or less the same ideas as his in an essayistic form. When Olivecrona wrote a long article in defence of his wife, Eli F. Heckscher, professor of economic history and chair of the Swedish branch of World Jewish Congress, took the opportunity to ask directly about his opinion about the character of the Nazi state and its war of conquest.[55] In another long article, Olivecrona still refrained from discussing the actual policy of Nazi Germany. Instead, he made his usual comparison with the Versailles peace 'injustices' and expressed his hope that the situation would be better after the ongoing war, as 'Germany after a victory will not have to worry about either England or France'. At the same time, he placed the blame on the nationalists of the conquered countries, and particularly 'the illusion that some kind of legal order and thereby safety could be established between sovereign states'. Heckscher closed the discussion by recommending Olivecrona to read Hermann Rausching's book about Hitler's table talks (which was banned in Sweden at the time).[56] In an editorial, *Dagens Nyheter* also underlined that Olivecrona said very little about what kind of society he hoped to see under German leadership.[57] In a review of the Swedish translation of *Law as Fact* a couple of months later, the reviewer Olle Holmberg pointed out that Olivecrona was, after all, talking about a state where Himmler and Streicher were among the ones calling the shots.[58]

Norway, for a lecture tour. Only after that would they be contacted by the party official (*Gauleiter*) in Schleswig-Holstein. There is no indication if Olivecrona ever got an invitation. The chosen subject of the talks would have been 'Wo stehen die Schweden?' (Where do the Swedes stand?), which of course was borderline traitorous. However, it provides some insight into what the Germans involved thought Olivecrona was ready for.

[53] Jackson 1941, for Olivecrona's reply, *see* Olivecrona 1941a. The main speaker at the event was Per Engdahl, who spoke on 'The Invasion of Norway'.

[54] Olivecrona's cooperation with the belletrist Lange, who in a couple of her war-time novels expressed his thoughts in a less formal way, is very interesting, but something that I leave out of this chapter. The inspiration was obviously mutual, as Olivecrona thanked Lange for psychological insights and the concept '*appellsystem*' (appellation system) regarding how law influences behaviour. The only time Olivecrona is mentioned in Klas Åmark's standard work on Sweden during the Second World War and the Holocaust is as the husband of Lange. *See* Åmark, 2016, p. 449.

[55] Olivecrona 1940c; Heckscher 1940a.

[56] Olivecrona 1940d; Heckscher 1940b.

[57] Unsigned editorial 1940.

[58] O. H-g. 1940.

There are other examples of critics, such as Erik Blomberg, Ludvig Nordström, and his colleagues, the philosopher Ingemar Hedenius and the political scientist Herbert Tingsten. However, the most serious critique at a personal level—as pointed out also by his biographer Torben Spaak—was probably that delivered by his fellow legal realist law professor, Vilhelm Lundstedt. In June 1941, Lundstedt gave an interview to the liberal and strongly anti-Nazi daily *Göteborgs Handels- och Sjöfarts-Tidning*, where he emphasized that the philosophy of Axel Hägerström could and should not be used as a foundation for Nazism. He mentioned that he had consulted Hägerström's widow (Hägerström had passed away before the war, in 1939) who, reportedly, '[was] despondent at the thought, that something so absurd could happen, that after his death someone would want to try to use his writings for a "social order", that he himself distanced himself from as much as he could'.[59] The interview, as Torben Spaak shows, led to a brief exchange of letters, when Olivecrona wrote to Lundstedt that the answers given in the interview could be interpreted as an attack on the views put forward by himself. Lundstedt more or less confirmed this suspicion but at the same time pointed out that others had also suggested a connection between Hägerström's philosophy—dismissively labelled 'value nihilism' by the professor of pedagogy John Landquist—and what happened on the continent. Olivecrona in his second and final letter maintained that such a connection with what he called the 'German Revolution' in fact existed and that he stood by his contention that Europe should unite under German leadership.[60]

Not until October 1943 did he back away from his support for Germany. In a letter to the daily *Aftonbladet*—during the war a daily newspaper clearly siding with Germany—he distanced himself from the manhunt of Jews that had started in occupied Denmark, and which at that time had brought thousands of Jewish refugees to Swedish shores. However, the letter did not contain any excuses for his previous declarations about the future of Europe. On the contrary, he maintained:

> The alternative is that, as I see it, Europe becomes a huge Balkan, squeezed between the Anglo-Saxon world power and the Russian, maybe squeezed in part or as a whole into the latter. There is such a world of difference between this condition and that which could be created in a collaborative Europe, that all those national antagonisms, that are in the way now, should recede.

He also expressed understanding for German measures against the Jews, although not the means applied:

> As far as I understand, it is necessary to get the Jewish question out of the way by assimilation. But precisely these persecutions work in the opposite way. They weld the Jews together, and the streams of refugees sooner or later will threaten to bring forth new waves of antisemitism also in other countries that previously have been rather unaffected thereof.

The main problem, however, remained that the project of uniting Europe was at risk:

> First and foremost, however, it has been disastrous that the program of European unity on the German part has been combined with the persecution of the Jews. This has made the

---

[59] Unsigned 1941.

[60] Spaak 2014, pp. 23–25.

> understanding between Germans and other people almost impossible. In order to become so engulfed by the belief that the Jews are such a danger, that they have to be eradicated, in my view one has to assume a corrupted grasp of reality. Among most people this belief does not exist, and because of that the extermination war produces the strongest possible reluctance. So, the unification programme will be rejected at the same time as the persecutions. From this also follows, that violence and oppression is used, where persuasion and co-operation on an equal basis should have been preferred.[61]

The general public was naturally less than impressed by this late concession. Conservative *Svenska Dagbladet* (citing the anti-Nazi journal *Nordens Frihet*) and Germany-friendly *Stockholms-Tidningen* both pointed out that what Olivecrona said was late in the day and could not be accepted as sincere (stopping short, though, of calling him an opportunist).[62] Social Democratic *Arbetet* from Malmö asked why he had not reacted against the deportations of the Polish and Norwegian Jews.[63] In *Göteborgs Handels- och Sjöfarts-Tidning*, the sociologist Torgny T:son Segerstedt pointed out that the actions against the Danish Jews were not only preceded by similar oppression in other countries, but also motivated and explained by Nazi ideology.[64] Segerstedt was of course aware that Olivecrona in *England eller Tyskland* had argued that 'the ideologies are something secondary. The people and the geography are more important.'[65]

A year later, Olivecrona was criticized in *Lundagård*, the journal of the student organization of Lund University. The literature history student Jöran Mjöberg pointed out that the students themselves had a largely passive attitude toward Nazi and fascist influences within their own ranks. He particularly recalled that many of them had argued for Nazism, also from positions of trust (probably meaning the student bodies, including the editors of *Lundagård*), and that for the moment they had not been touched. It seems that Mjöberg, without explicitly saying so, was arguing for some form of de-Nazification of Swedish universities.[66] Olivecrona, not mentioned by name in the text, responded with a long article. The main part of his article was devoted to arguing that revenge against former supporters of the Nazi-German cause was mainly reminiscent of how the Nazis themselves had dealt with dissidents. However, he also conceded that it had been a 'huge, inexcusable wrong [on his part] to put the question of ideologies to the side'.[67] After the medical student Lennart Jacobsson in a subsequent article more explicitly asked for a de-Nazification, Olivecrona just as explicitly declared that he would not back down from his general view of the Nazi-German cause (which at that point was conducting its last major military offensive in the Ardennes):

---

[61] Olivecrona 1943.

[62] Unsigned 1943a.

[63] Unsigned 1943b.

[64] T. T:son S. 1943.

[65] Olivecrona 1940b, p. 46, *Cf.* Spaak 2014, p. 25.

[66] Mjöberg 1944. Among those who actually had to leave posts were Odeberg, who was deposed at inspector of the student body Värmlands nation (after protests from Norwegian students). Oredsson 1996, pp. 199–200.

[67] Olivecrona 1944a, p. 223.

> I could never concede to the one-sided and largely false picture of Germany in the hate propaganda. If I would write anything about national socialism or any other social form it would be a purely scientific enquiry about its preconditions and significance. All revolutions are full of horrors, the German as well as the French or the Russian. Personally, I have seen it thus, that the faults over time could have been overcome if Germany would have endured and a European organization had been realized on the basis of co-operation.[68]

14.6 A Nazi or Just a Confused Liberal?

Obviously, it is hard to argue that Olivecrona's pro-German (and thus also pro-Nazi) stance was an oversight. He was aware of the persecution of his own German colleagues—among them Hans Kelsen, who he knew personally and who was sacked and had to flee to Switzerland not long after his visit to Sweden in March 1933. Naturally, Olivecrona was also aware of the fact that all Jews in Germany, including fellow law scholars, lost their positions within the state and at universities already in spring 1933. The historian Sverker Oredsson joins with the war-time critique and argues that Olivecrona's position was the result of his interpretation of Hägerström's philosophy, and furthermore, that his support for Nazi Germany exposed the philosophy to intensive critique from the anti-Nazi majority among scholars and intellectuals.[69] As goes without saying, these two aspects could be conflated, and the philosophical critique largely focuses on the rather unsentimental view of the relation between law and violence in the philosophy of both Hägerström and Olivecrona. However, the realist position is not unique in this respect. As already mentioned, the philosophy developed by Hägerström was a variant of the neo-Kantian reaction against the idealist philosophies that had accompanied the transition from absolutist to constitutional and republican rule in central and western Europe. Within the Anglo-Saxon countries, which had left absolutism behind at an earlier stage (1649/1688 and 1776, respectively), natural law and utilitarian moralism could prevail to a larger extent, and still does (with consequences for international law). However, the difference between these variants was not at all as important as the difference between 19th century idealism and organicism and what would come later. Also, modernist law largely prevailed in the fascist and communist totalitarian states, although legal practices were something completely different in those cases.

The legal scholar Wilhelm M. Grewe, who was partly influenced by Schmitt, in his standard work on the history of international law concluded that the most important legal change in the period between the wars was the introduction of what Schmitt labelled as the 'discriminatory concept of war'.[70] That is, with the introduction of the League of Nations Covenant, and later the Kellogg-Briand Pact of 1928, war was formally outlawed as an instrument of international politics. The large number of ratifying signatories to the pact confirmed that a fundamental change had taken place,

[68] Olivecrona 1944b, p. 269.

[69] Oredsson 1996, pp. 217–218.

[70] Grewe 2000, pp. 619–621.

although reservations—not least the British one—conveyed the opposite message.[71] All of this followed logically from the Versailles Peace Treaty, where the German emperor was accused of being the perpetrator of an illegal war.[72]

Schmitt was not alone in interpreting this arrangement as a way to mobilize international support for a policy intended to keep Germany in the position of a second-rate power for as long as possible. John Maynard Keynes had warned of the consequences of the peace treaty, and we know that not only Olivecrona but also his left-wing liberal tutor Hägerström and his Social Democratic colleague Vilhelm Lundstedt had the same concerns regarding how Germany was treated.[73]

In fact, if we compare the views of Lundstedt with those of Olivecrona before and during the war, the differences are small. Lundstedt was a Social Democrat, but an outlier among them. During the Spanish civil war, he was one of few Social Democrats to support the non-intervention policy. Although, as he conceded in April 1938, it was obvious that the Axis powers made a mockery of the policy, there was no reason to 'let oneself be guided by one's feelings'.[74] In a lecture he held a couple of days later at a student society in Uppsala, Lundstedt—after once more condemning the sanction policy of the League of Nations—expressed understanding for the recent German annexation of Austria. In both cases, he underlined the importance of strict Swedish neutrality.[75] Towards the end of the war, however, he returned to discussing the Versailles Treaty and argued against overly harsh punishments and revenge against the Germans for the many war crimes that had been perpetrated (also questioning the concept of war crimes).[76] He furthermore warned, already in 1942, that too much emphasis on punishment would motivate the German people to continue the war.[77] It may be noted that Lundstedt also, like Olivecrona, used the Germany-friendly daily newspaper *Aftonbladet* as a publishing venue—Lundstedt even for many years legally defended the owner of *Aftonbladet*, industrialist and speculator Torsten Kreuger, in the so-called Högbrofors case, a case of financial crime that was negotiated from 1932 to Kreuger's death in 1960.[78] However, at the same time, in 1935, he joined a large number of Scandinavian intellectuals to campaign—in vain—for the release of the German communist prisoners Rudolf Klaus and Albert Kayser, as well as doing so on his own in 1936, when he tried to argue for the release of the (later to be beheaded) communist leader Edgar André in a letter directed to Hitler himself.[79] It can be noted that Lundstedt after the war dropped the neutrality issue and argued

[71] Schmitt 2011b, p. 92–93.

[72] On this case, Schabas 2018.

[73] Mindus 2009, p. 200; Lundstedt 1924b, pp. 37–40.

[74] Unsigned 1938.

[75] Lundstedt 1938.

[76] Unsigned 1943c.

[77] Lundstedt 1942.

[78] *See, e.g.*, F N 1938.

[79] Unsigned 1935; Lundstedt 1936.

for European unity—though under Anglo-American leadership, against the Soviet Union.[80]

So, what are we to make of this? Obviously, there is no direct connection between the (liberal) philosophy of Hägerström and the pro-German (and consequently, pro-Nazi) position of Olivecrona. Olivecrona made a radical interpretation of Hägerström's philosophy, but the conclusion that only might—in the meaning (ability of) supreme violence—in the long run would guarantee the existence of a society ruled by law, is hardly very controversial. As Torben Spaak points out, his contribution is in line with Hägerström's argument, although he also makes a unique non-consequential version that holds its ground philosophically.[81] There is, however, as Mikael Nilsson proposes, no intrinsic utilitarian content in the philosophy of legal realism.[82] According to Lundstedt, the aim of the legal machinery that he described was what he called 'social utility', though he was not very clear about how this utility should be defined and even less on how it would come about. A more useful description of Hägerström's philosophy, and the philosophy of legal realism, is probably that it simply did not have any ideological content. It was a purely critical (non-idealist) philosophy and Olivecrona was probably honest when he, to the astonishment of many others, at the beginning of what the Germans themselves would describe as a war of world views said that ideologies were not very important. He later conceded that he was wrong. Partly, however, this may reflect an attempt to distance himself from the representatives of organized Nazism, who were never impressive personalities in the Nordic countries even when they, as in Norway, reached political power (his contacts with Per Engdahl, an historian, are an exception). It should probably also be kept in mind that in neighbouring Denmark, the national government under the Social Democrat Thorwald Stauning remained in (sharply restricted) power during the entire period of Olivecrona's intervention, thus giving an example of the pragmatic view that he made himself the voice for, regardless of how controversial it would appear to the postwar world. There are parallels between Olivecrona's ideas and the 'Theory of the Racket society' that Max Horkheimer developed at around the same time. Both noted the attenuation of mediating layers between law and violence in contemporary society. However, their conclusions—acquiescence vs. resistance—were very different.[83]

References

Aglietta M (1976) A Theory of Capitalist Regulation: The US Experience. Verso, London

80 Lundstedt 1947. *See also* Lundstedt 1948.

81 Spaak 2014, p. 276.

82 Nilsson 2022, pp. 63–64.

83 Horkheimer 1985, pp. 287–291. The Racket Theory was never clearly spelled out, although fragments were integrated into both *The Dialectic of Enlightenment* (1944/1947) and *Eclipse of Reason* (1947). Contemporary discussion derives largely from posthumously published texts, such as that mentioned above. *Cf.* Gansinger 2023, pp. 153–176.

Åmark K (2016) Att bo granne med ondskan [Living with Evil as a Neighbour]. Bonniers förlag, Stockholm
Arendt H (2017) The Origins of Totalitarianism (1951). Penguin, Milton Keynes
Balakrishnan G (2000) The Enemy. An intellectual portrait of Carl Schmitt. Verso, London
Bauman Z (1989) Modernity and the Holocaust. Cornell University Press, Ithaca (NY)
Bindreiter U (2018) Hans Kelsens föreläsningsresor till Sverige (1933) och Finland (1953) [Hans Kelsen's lecture voyages in Sweden (1933) and Finland (1953)]. Statsvetenskaplig Tidskrift 120:69–95
Falk H (2022) The modern Epimetheus: Carl Schmitt's katechontism as reactionary chronopolitics. Frontiers of Political Science 4:1–16 https://doi.org/10.3389/fpos.2022.957094 (Accessed 30 March 2025)
Finchelstein F (2022) Fascist Mythologies. The history and politics of unreason in Borges, Freud, and Schmitt. Columbia University Press, New York (NY)
F N (1938) Professor Lundstedt och rättvisan [Professor Lundstedt and Justice]. Arbetaren 4 May
Fraenkel E (2010) The Dual State, A Contribution to the Theory of Dictatorship (1941). The Lawbook Exchange Ltd, Clark (NJ)
Jackson (1941) Olivecrona på gästspel hos Manhem, Hjältemodigt att vara landsförrädare sade nazist [Olivecrona: A guest performance with Manhem. Heroic to be a traitor, said the Nazi]. Socialdemokraten 17 October
Gansinger S (2013) Trägheit als Fortschritt: Neumann und Horkheimer zum normativen Potenzial des Rechts [Inertia as Progress: Neumann and Horkheimer on the Normative Potential of Law]. In: Heimrath S et al. (eds) Zeitliche Dimensionen und Kritische Theorie(n) des Rechts [Temporal Dimensions and Critical Theories of Law]. Franz Steiner Verlag, Stuttgart, pp. 153–176.
Grewe W G (2000) The Epochs of International Law (1984 Byers M trans.). De Gruyter, London
Hägerström A (1927) Der römische Obligationsbegriff im Lichte der allgemeinen römischen Rechtsanschauung 1 [The Roman Concept of Obligation in light of the General Roman Legal View 1]. Almqvist & Wiksell, Uppsala
Hägerström A (1941) Der römische Obligationsbegriff im Lichte der allgemeinen römischen Rechtsanschauung 2 [The Roman Concept of Obligation in light of the General Roman Legal View 2]. Skrifter utgivna av Kungliga Humanistiska vetenskapssamfundet i Uppsala 35, Uppsala
Hatt G et al (1943) Der Norden und Europa, vorträge von Gudmund Hatt, John Weibull, Per Engdahl, Nora Torulf, Rutger Essén, Karl Olivecrona [The North and Europe, lectures by Gudmund Hatt, John Weibull, Per Engdahl, Nora Torulf, Rutger Essén, Karl Olivecrona]. Essener Verlagsanstalt, Essen
Heckscher E F (1940a) Öppen fråga till professor Karl Olivecrona [Open question to professor Karl Olivecrona]. Dagens Nyheter 28 June
Heckscher E F (1940b) [Without heading]. Dagens Nyheter 6 July
Hobsbawm E (1994) The Age of Extremes: The Short Twentieth Century, 1914–1991. Pantheon Books, New York (NY)
Horkheimer M (1985) Die Rackets und der Geist (1943) [The Rackets and the Spirit]. In: Horkheimer M (ed) Gesammelte Schriften 12. S Fischer, Frankfurt am Main
Horkheimer M (2002) Traditional and Critical Theory (1937). In: O'Connell MJ (trans.), Horkheimer M (ed) Critical Theory, Selected Essays. Continuum, New York (NY)
Horkheimer M, Adorno TW (1947) Dialektik der Aufklärung, Philosophische Fragmente [Dialectic of Enlightenment, Philosophical Fragments]. Querido Verlag NV., Amsterdam
Hübinette T (2002) Den svenska nationalsocialismen. Medlemmar och sympatisörer 1931-45 [The Swedish National Socialism, Members and sympathizers 1931–45]. Carlsson förlag, Stockholm
Källström S (1986) Den gode nihilisten. Axel Hägerström och striderna kring Uppsalafilosofin [Axel Hägerström and the battles over the Uppsala school]. Rabén & Sjögren, Kristianstad
Kelsen, H (1933) Den rena rättsläran. Dess metod och grundbegrepp [The pure theory of law. Its method and basic concepts]. Statsvetenskaplig Tidskrift 36:193–244
Koskenniemi M (2001) The Gentle Civilizer of Nations: The Rise and Fall of International Law 1870–1960. Cambridge University Press, Cambridge (UK)

Lundstedt V (1924a) Vägen till fred [The road to peace]. Tidens förlag, Stockholm
Lundstedt V (1924b) Folkrätten och Genèvepolitiken, Föredrag hållet vid Uppsala Studenters Allmänna Diskussionsförenings offentliga diskussion den 21 november 1924 [Public international law and the Geneva politics. Lecture held at the Uppsala students' public debate association, public discussion 21 November 1924]. Almqvist & Wiksells förlag, Uppsala
Lundstedt V (1929) Den historiska rättspositivismen med särskild hänsyn till Bergbohms lära [Historical legal positivism with due regard to Bergbohm's tenets]. AB Lundequistska bokhandeln, Uppsala
Lundstedt V (1936) Professor Lundstedt till försvar för Edgar André. Inlaga till Hitler personligen [Professor Lundstedt to the defence of Edgar André. Letter to Hitler personally]. Norrskensflamman 15 August
Lundstedt V (1937) Folkrätten: en livsfara för folken [Public international law: A mortal danger for the peoples]. Natur & Kultur, Stockholm
Lundstedt V (1938) Ett nytt krig—nya revolutioner. Professor Lundstedt om utrikespolitiken [A new war—new revolutions. Professor Lundstedt on foreign policy]. Aftonbladet 23 April
Lundstedt V (1942) Att sätta ett folk i strykklass. Av professor Vilhelm Lundstedt [To cause injustice to a people. By Professor Wilhelm Lundstedt]. Aftonbladet 17 November
Lundstedt V (1947) Prof. Lundstedt: Europeiskt statsförbund måste vara diktaturfritt [Prof. Lundstedt: A European confederation must be free of dictators]. Arbetaren 23 October
Lundstedt V (1948) Europas demokratier—förenen eder! [European democracies: unite!]. Natur & Kultur, Stockholm
Mindus P (2009) A Real Mind: The Life and Work of Axel Hägerström. Springer, Dordrecht
Mjöberg J (1944) Den eviga fronten [The eternal front]. Lundagård 25: 193–194
Neumann F (2009) Behemoth, The Structure and Practice of National Socialism, 1933–1944 (1942). Ivan R. Dee, Chicago
Nilsson M (2022) Historiemissbrukarna, Ett korrektur till lögnerna och villfarelserna om Sverige under andra världskriget [The abusers of history. A correction of the lies and delusions about Sweden during World War II]. Tankesmedjan Tiden, Stockholm
Nordin S (1983) Från Hägerström till Hedenius: Den moderna svenska filosofin [From Hägerström to Hedenius: Modern Swedish philosophy]. Doxa, Lund
O. H-g (1940) Det monopoliserade våldet [Violence monopolized]. Dagens Nyheter 31 August
Olivecrona K (1940a) Om lagen och staten. Ejnar Munksgaard [On law and the State]. Copenhagen / C W K Gleerup, Lund
Olivecrona K (1940b) England eller Tyskland [England or Germany]. C W K Gleerup, Lund
Olivecrona K (1940c) Öppet brev till d:r Ivar Harrie [Open letter to Dr. Ivar Harrie]. Dagens Nyheter 27 June
Olivecrona K (1940d) Öppet svar till professor Eli Heckscher [Open letter to professor Eli Heckscher]. Dagens Nyheter 6 July
Olivecrona K (1941a) Hr Olivecrona och Quisling [Mr Olivecrona and Quisling]. Dagens Nyheter 20 October
Olivecrona K (1941b) Europa och Amerika [Europe and America]. Sundqvist & Emond, Lund
Oliverona K (1943) Judeförföljelserna i Danmark Från professor Karl Olivecrona i Lund har AB mottagit följande [The persecution of Jews in Denmark From professor Karl Olivecrona in Lund AB has received the following]. Aftonbladet 8 October
Olivecrona K (1944a) Var går fronten? En insändare av Karl Olivecrona [Where is the front? Letter to the editor from Karl Olivecrona]. Lundagård 25:223–225
Olivecrona K (1944b) Karl Olivecrona. Lundagård 25:269–270
Oredsson S (1996) Lunds universitet under andra världskriget, Motsättningar, debatter och hjälpinsatser [University of Lund during World War II, Controversies, debates and aid efforts]. Lunds universitetshistoriska sällskap, Lund
Rubenstein R L (1975) The Cunning of History: Mass Death and the American Future. Harper and Row, New York (NY)
Schabas W A (2018) The Trial of the Kaiser. Oxford University Press, Oxford

Schmitt C (2010) Det politiska som begrepp (1932) [The political as a concept]. Daidalos, Göteborg
Schmitt C (2011a) The Turn to the Discriminating Concept of War (1937). In: Nunan T (trans.), Schmitt C (ed) Writings on War. Polity Press, Cambridge (UK)
Schmitt C (2011b) The Grossraum Order of International Law with a Ban on Intervention for Spatially Foreign Powers: A contribution to the concept of Reich in International Law (1939–1941) (1941). In: Nunan T (trans.), Schmitt C (ed) Writings on War. Polity Press, Cambridge (UK)
Schmitt C (2011c) The International Crime of the War of Aggression and the Principle 'Nullum crimen, nulla poena sine lege' (1945). In: Nunan T (trans.) Schmitt C (ed) Writings on War. Polity Press, Cambridge (UK)
Scholz-Karl J (2021) Behind the theoretical debate between Hans Kelsen and Carl Schmitt: the nineteenth century constitutionalism and German public law. UNIO-EU Law Journal 7:4–17
Spaak T (2014) A Critical Appraisal of Karl Olivecrona's Legal Philosophy. Springer International, London
Suuronen V (2021) Carl Schmitt as a theorist of the 1933 Nazi revolution: The difficult task of rethinking and recultivating traditional concepts. Contemporary Political Theory 20:341–363
T. T:son S. (1943) Individ och gemenskap [Individual and community]. Göteborgs Handels- och Sjöfarts-Tidning 19 October
Unsigned (1935) Tysk demonstration mot petitionärer. Representanter för svensk kultur fingo ej företräde hos prins av Wied. Aktion mot Hitlers dödsdomar [German demonstration against petitioners. Representatives of Swedish culture were not given priority by the Prince of Wied. Action against Hitler's death sentences]. Arbetet 13 December
Unsigned (1938) Noninterventionsskojet fördömes [The non-intervention nonsense is condemned]. Arbetaren 20 April
Unsigned editorial (1940) Politisk mytologi [Political mythology]. Dagens Nyheter 7 July
Unsigned (1941) Filosofi på Östra Hamngatan. Samtal om Hägerström, diktaturen och demokratien [Philosophy on Östra Hamngatan. Conversation about Hägerström, dictatorship and democracy]. Göteborgs Handels- och Sjöfarts-Tidning 27 June
Unsigned (1943a) Från den politiska fronten [From the political front]. Svenska Dagbladet 17 October
Unsigned on Lund page (1943b) Varför just nu? [Why right now?]. Arbetet 19 October
Unsigned editorial (1943c) Prof. Lundstedt om 'krigsförbrytelser' [Prof. Lundstedt on 'war crimes']. Aftonbladet 20 December

Mats Deland in an associate professor in history and holds a PhD in economic history. Currently, he works as a lecturer in history at Mid Sweden University in Sundsvall, and as a research assistant at the Department of Sociology at Södertörn University. His research concerns urban history, Holocaust and genocide studies, the far right, the history of international humanitarian law, the study of authoritarian attitudes and critical theory.

Chapter 15
The Charismatic Educators of International Investment Law

David Schneiderman

Contents

Abstract International investment treaty law and arbitration is a field that is fraught with conflict. Arising out of the post-Cold War geopolitical environment, states in both the Northern and Southern hemispheres have signed onto muscular legal constraints that protect foreign investors. Measures that diminish the value of an investment and that run afoul of protections associated with classical property, contract, and due process rights entitle investors to sue for damages before privatized dispute resolution panels. An investment arbitration community has blossomed alongside the spread of investment treaty disciplines. Among its constituent members are teachers who write, advise, and take part in the field of international investment arbitration, both inside and outside of universities. Taking my cue from the work of Max Weber, this chapter describes these teachers as "charismatic educators" who offer leadership via legal education as a means of training and recruiting newer generations who will fight on behalf of investment law's ideals. In performing this function, they offer justifications for the regime by having recourse to their own authority and expertise. We learn that legal educators play a substantial role in the upkeep of investment law's machinery while maintaining an intimate relationship to its practice.

Keywords International law · Investment law · Legal education · Charisma · Sociology of law · Max Weber

---

This essay draws upon an analysis, supported by modest empirical evidence, that is more fully developed in Schneiderman 2025.

D. Schneiderman (✉)
Faculty of Law and Department of Political Science (courtesy), University of Toronto, Toronto, Canada
e-mail: david.schneiderman@utoronto.ca

M. Klamberg et al. (eds.), *Reconstructing Power and Hegemony in Public International Law*, https://doi.org/10.1007/978-94-6265-743-4_15

15.1 Introduction

There are few subjects in international law more politically fraught than international investment law.[1] This regime emerged out of the post-Cold War geopolitical environment, one in which there were claimed to be "no alternatives" but to nourish free markets by promoting privatization, deregulation, and debt reduction. States in both the Northern and Southern hemispheres signed onto the muscular legal constraints represented by investment law in order to protect foreign investors and their investments. Measures that diminish the value of an investment and that run afoul of protections associated with traditional property, contract, and due process rights entitle investors to sue for damages before privatized dispute resolution panels. An investment arbitration community has blossomed alongside the spread of investment treaty disciplines.[2] Among its constituent members are legal educators who teach, write about, and even participate in, the field of international investment arbitration.

This chapter takes its cue from the work of Max Weber, the legally trained German academic, considered one of the founders of modern social science.[3] Weber's questions and methods generate avenues for inquiring into the state of legal education in the field of international investment law. Weber famously developed the heuristic of "ideal types". He described these as a "one-sided *accentuation* of *one* or *a number* of viewpoints".[4] The ideal type is a method by which one can hypothesize about selected "empirical regularities" of social reality that help to "guide the formulation of hypotheses" about the motivation for social action.[5] Raymond Aron's portrayal of Weberian ideal types best captures this essay's ambition: an attempt to make "more intelligible" the conditions for social action than is "the experience of those who live[ ]it".[6]

Yet another insight drawn from Weber's work concerns the role of legal educators in the rise of modern law.[7] Various modes of knowledge are spread and promoted by experts whom Weber associated, generally, with "bureaucracy". Legal education proved to be central to his account of the spread of formally rational law.[8] Alongside the rise of rational law came a need for increased professional training. This kind of "specialized, i.e. rational, training is an ineluctable requirement", Weber maintained.[9] As legal professionals were the principal agents for the spread of modern law in the

---

[1] *See* Schneiderman 2016.

[2] Hirsch 2020, pp. 719–720.

[3] Weber is described as being ranked "among the founders of modern social science". *See* Derman 2012, p. 179.

[4] Weber 1904, pp. 124–125 (emphasis in original).

[5] Swedberg 2018, p. 188 (referring to "causal adequacy"); Turner and Factor 1994, p. 154 (referring to a "kind of causal knowledge").

[6] Aron 1970, p. 245, and Weber 1904, p. 125.

[7] Weber 1920b, p. 74.

[8] Weber 1920a, p. 207. *See* discussion in Gephart 2015, Chapter VIII.

[9] Weber 1978, p. 775.

Occident,[10] legal training provided by both academics and professionals served as the means by which Western legal institutions and norms proliferated.[11] Largely elided in much of the literature on investment law is the role that legal scholars and practitioners play in promoting and preserving international investment law.

The ideal typical investment law educator exploits their charisma—"seiz[ing] the task for which he is destined and demands that others obey and follow him"—in order to recruit followers to their cause. They are, Weber might say, engaged in "charismatic education".[12] In developing the concept of charisma, Weber originally had in mind religious leaders who successfully recruit followers. More salient to our task is Weber's discussion of how the medium- to long-term success of such movements is explained. In order to maintain followers over time, successors to charismatic rule are compelled to recruit followers by "routinizing" administration. I argue below that legal education provides a platform for charismatic rule to train and recruit the next generation of lawyers who will continue the fight on behalf of investment law's disciplinary effects. It is to a discussion of charisma and its routinization that I turn first, before considering how investment law professionals are engaged in charismatic education.

15.2 Charisma's Routinization

Charisma has been described as a "buzzword beloved by sociologists" as well as others in various academic fields.[13] This is so much the case that it has "become a fixture of modern social science".[14] Weber described this "ideal type" as appealing to authority or expertise in order to justify rule over others. Most readers of Weber understand charismatic leadership to have been overtaken by the rule of rational bureaucratic staff. For this reason, it may seem an inapt category to describe investment law educators.[15] However, even if religious leadership prompted thinking about charismatic rule, Weber insisted that this form of domination was generalizable across society.[16] When coupled with Weber's notion of bureaucratic "routinization"—a process that ensures that the successors to charismatic authority can continue to govern– we arrive at the notion of "charismatic education", discussed in the next section.

[10] Weber 1920a, p. 215.

[11] Weber 2009, p. 152; Bendix 1962, pp. 85–87.

[12] Weber 1978, pp. 458, 1143.

[13] Derman 2012, p. 176.

[14] Derman 2012, p. 177.

[15] Weber 1978, p. 216 credits Rudolf Sohm for having worked out charisma in early Christianity. Others credit Eduard Meyer for having a more sustained influence on Weber. *See* Ghosh 2014, p. 307; Tenbruck 1987.

[16] Weber 1978, p. 1112. *See* Ghosh 2014, pp. 305–317, and Smith 2013, p. 28, on the generalizability of charisma.

The "pure" type of charismatic rule is unbounded. It is also extraordinary and upends traditional norms.[17] No external law or precedent constrains its dominion. Further, it is not connected to markets or addressed to economic subjects.[18] Due to their exceptional or exemplary quality,[19] charismatic rulers exercise unrestrained discretion to declare how followers are to be governed. Models for charismatic rule have extended beyond Jesus Christ or Muhammad to any number of prophetic figures, politicians, thinkers, and leaders.[20] The "charismatic type", writes Mommsen, "could in principle appear in the most varied historical formations and in different epochs, including the modern one".[21] Such exceptional powers are extended by Weber even to those possessing "legal wisdom",[22] though this may take "irrational" forms. This is because charisma typically has none of the features associated with formally rational rule (usually preoccupied with ends-means calculations) that is part of everyday modern life.[23] However, charismatic leadership, because it breaks with tradition, promotes innovation (for example, codification can be inaugurated by the "charismatic creator of law", says Gephart).[24] The "pure type" of charismatic rule, though having a religious pedigree,[25] is not the focus of this discussion. Instead, what is pertinent is its normalization over successive generations.[26] What is of consequence is the movement, described by Weber, towards the "routinization of charisma".[27]

In order for this form of rule to endure beyond its original phase, a community of believers will devise modes of succession and techniques for recruiting new

---

[17] Weber 1978, pp. 244 (charismatic authority "repudiates the past, and is in this sense a specifically revolutionary force"), 1115; Tenbruck 1987, p. 253 ("it always takes the form of revolutionary missions prizing apart the normality of hardened traditions and customs, only for itself to become unavoidably frozen within patterns of normal everyday").

[18] Weber 2019, p. 377.

[19] Weber 1978, p. 241 ("he is considered extraordinary and treated as endowed with supernatural, superhuman, or at least specifically exceptional powers or qualities").

[20] Mommsen 1987, p. 45. *See, for example*, Weber 1978, p. 118, where Weber mentions the American "robber capitalist", Henry Villard, who managed to secure an enormous loan to "stage a raid" on Northern Pacific Railway shares on the basis of "reputation" alone. It turns out that Villard was known to Weber through his network of family connections, *see* Roth 2002, p. 513.

[21] Mommsen 1987, p. 46.

[22] Weber 2019, p. 374.

[23] Due to the problem of succession, Weber 1978, p. 1123, writes that it is "the fate of charisma to recede with the development of permanent institutional structures". Charisma hardly wins in a contest with rationally formal rule, maintains Anter 2014, p. 66 ("legal-rational rule has proved itself to be incomparably stronger").

[24] Gephart 2015, p. 92.

[25] Resting on a sense of "loyalty and obligation", it "always has a religious aura" in Weber 1978, p. 1122.

[26] Bendix 1962, p. 300. "For such is the fate of any authority of this kind", writes Freund 1968 at p. 244, "sooner or later it returns to a traditional or legal form of government".

[27] On "pure charisma" in contrast to "legitimate charisma" or "charisma of office" *see* Bensman and Givant 1975, p. 577. On "institutional charisma", *see* Shils 1965, p. 206. If pressed, one could point to notables who built the regime (e.g., Hermann Abs, Arron Broches) or the first generation of investment arbitrators, who are now its elder statesmen (e.g., Charles N. Brower, Emmanuel Gaillard, Jan Paulsson, Stephen Schwebel), as charismatics.

believers.[28] Weber describes the need for both "education" and "tests of eligibility" in order to sustain this form of rule.[29] Charisma becomes "routinized", more rational or legal, more fixated on generating revenue (via fees, for instance), and preoccupied with ensuring the continued recruitment and promotion of successors together with the support of an administrative staff.[30] Weber describes this process as calling for, in all instances, a "striving for security", the "legitimization" of rule, and economic opportunity for followers.[31] What is emphasized is the need to recruit and train new disciples in order that charismatic rule can be reproduced.

In the next section, I turn to the question of whether this account of charisma, beyond the moment of its origin, captures the methods by which investment law gets routinized via education. Recall that Weber contemplates that forms of legal rule can exhibit charismatic leadership. Even legal rule, Weber writes, is "never purely legal".[32] It can also be charismatic "in a negative sense", giving rise to failure that can "ruin" or "shatter" the prestige of any government.[33] To what extent are functions associated with rule by investment law and arbitration well represented by the routinization of charisma?[34]

15.3 Charismatic Education

Dezalay and Garth laid the foundation for the future socio-legal study of international arbitration in their pathbreaking contribution, *Dealing in Virtue*.[35] The authors undertook approximately 400 interviews with lawyers who served as commercial arbitrators, some of whom would move on to staff investment tribunals. Some were described as the "grand old men" of arbitration, who acted as "private judges" and who displayed an "aura of charisma".[36] Their professional trajectories were described as having a "glorious past". Arbitrators were encouraged to enter the field not to "make a living", but as a "duty".[37] In this early period, "a limited, small group

---

[28] Weber 2019, p. 379. Describing the first generation of Puritans who settled at Massachusetts Bay, Morgan 1955, p. 35, mentions the "irony of a situation in which a chosen people cannot find enough chosen people to prolong its existence".

[29] Weber 2019, p. 383.

[30] Weber 2019, pp. 384–385.

[31] Weber 2019, p. 387.

[32] Weber 2019, p. 401. This is consistent with Weber's observation that charismatic rule rarely appears in its "pure" form.

[33] Weber 2019, p. 401, namely, losing faith in rule.

[34] Weber 2019, p. 406 (emphasis in original).

[35] Dezalay and Garth 1996. Shultz 2016, p. 531 describes the work as "one of the most cited, most influential books on international arbitration, one of the most popular in the field".

[36] Dezalay and Garth 1996, pp. 6, 36.

[37] Dezalay and Garth 1996, p. 34. This might represent the influence of Weber's distinction of living "for", rather than living "from" (making a living from) politics in Weber 1919, p. 319.

of impeccable, outstanding professionals—characters known around the world"—populated the field. At that time, arbitrators exhibited a pre-bureaucratic and "personally detached" style of administration. The "lord of older social structures who was moved by personal sympathy … by grace and gratitude"—Weber's description of personalized rule—had yet to be replaced by technocratic rule.[38]

Today the field is "crowd[ed]" with fewer "outstanding personalit[ies]".[39] The older generation of arbitrators are charged with having relied on their charisma instead of better explaining themselves.[40] For this reason, one interviewee, whom they describe as one of the "stars of the next generation",[41] could say that the "time has come" for Weber's "routinization of charisma".[42] This appears to have occurred in the US foreign policy establishment, where the exercise of charisma has become routinized via "bureaucratic institutions".[43]

Can one say the same thing about investment arbitration? Just as Dezalay's and Garth's interviewees describe the commercial arbitration field as being dominated by a "mafia" or "club",[44] the field of investment arbitration has been described as governed by a "club" of eighteen arbitrators (though membership has enlarged with time).[45] This is mainly a group of repeat players who make their home in capital-exporting states.[46] Those with different profiles or the wrong connections are ineligible to join the club. Those who enter its antechambers grow, as described by Puig, into "central" figures in the arbitration industry, having the power to impose "their political preferences".[47] These same investment law notables have an outsized influence on the legal training that takes place both inside and outside of academic institutions. Schultz describes arbitrator preferences as promoting a version of "right-wing laissez-faire politics".[48] It is a sensibility, reports Waibel, that is united by a "common ethos of investor protection".[49] It is not unreasonable to expect to see this same value system transmitted to new inductees who are expected to participate in the field's routinization.

Weber's formulation for the type of instruction that is required to recruit successors to charismatic rule is "charismatic education".[50] This form of education anticipates

---

38 Weber 1978, p. 975.

39 Dezalay and Garth 1996, p. 36.

40 Though, Garth 2021, p. 39 adds, "charisma is far from eliminated from the field" of arbitration (meaning, I presume, both commercial and investment arbitration).

41 Dezalay and Garth 2012, p. 2335.

42 Dezalay and Garth 1996, pp. 36–37.

43 Dezalay and Garth 2008, p. 720.

44 Dezalay and Garth 1996, p. 10.

45 *See* Gaillard 2015, p. 201.

46 Puig 2014, pp. 416, 419.

47 Puig 2014, p. 422.

48 Schultz 2020, p. 257.

49 Waibel 2015, p. 164.

50 Weber 1978, p. 1144. Bourdieu 1990, p. 122, describes professorial charisma as an "oxymoron" and, elsewhere, a "paradox" (at p. 66).

that the "gifts" originally wielded by charismatics can be "taught and learned".[51] Of course, the borders between charismatic education and what Weber calls "rationalized specialized training" are "fluid".[52] This is because professional training requires knowledge that can only be transmitted by specialized insiders.[53] Investment law educators will naturally draw upon the reason-giving of dominant arbitral thinking as resources for legal training. In other words, they will transmit values concerning the law and politics of economic development that are predominant in arbitral decision-making.[54]

The elite centers for investment law education reveal something about the routinized charisma at work in this field. As Koskenniemi acknowledges, "the culture of international law has grown around a limited number of academic centers".[55] One cannot be expected to enter an international legal profession "without an LLM or doctorate from one of a handful of law schools in Anglophone world, or maybe Paris".[56] There is only the "well-known, but narrow academic pathway" for entering the international legal profession, Koskenniemi insists.[57] Roberts' empirical study of international lawyering confirms the hegemony of elite centers for training in the Global North. The "legal academics at elite schools in core states are prone to be highly influential in constituting the transnational field of international law", despite the high cost of entry into these institutions.[58]

Viewpoints transmitted to students will not be uniformly supportive of all aspects of the regime. Instead, there likely will be disagreement, representing "insider" or "outsider" perspectives.[59] Kennedy adopts these ideal-typical antinomies in his analysis of those who participate in the field of global governance. For Kennedy, these "postures of engagement" represent the difference between those who welcome management by global technocrats (insiders) and those who diagnose global governance as entrenching practices of domination (outsiders). The aim of the former is "reform" and that of the latter is "rupture". These binary positions, reflected within and across disciplinary divides, more often lie on a "continuum", Kennedy admits and, over time, they become more "fluid".[60]

In the politically fraught field of investment law, one is expected to take sides. As a consequence, there is likely to be less fluidity between insiders and outsiders. Reflecting on my own experience, I can say that outsiders are mostly unwelcome.

---

[51] Weber 1978, p. 1143.

[52] Weber 1978, p. 1143.

[53] Weber 1978, p. 1145.

[54] For insights into how arbitrators think about policies for economic development, *see* Tucker 2018, pp. 62–77.

[55] Koskenniemi 2017a, p. xiii.

[56] Koskenniemi 2017a, p. xiii.

[57] Koskenniemi 2017a, p. xiii.

[58] Roberts 2017, p. 68.

[59] *See* Roberts and St John 2023, who describe officials participating in reform of ISDS at UNCITRAL Working Group III as being either insiders or outsiders.

[60] Kennedy 2016, pp. 106–107 and Table 3.1.

They are treated as illegitimate interlopers, often ignored and, when detected, their scholarly output is treated with harsh, even intemperate, scrutiny.[61] New entrants to the field are taught, early on, that there are professional disadvantages to being labelled an outsider. They are also taught about the many advantages of joining the club of insiders, including the opportunity to benefit both reputationally and financially. Instructors, like the pure type of charismatic, will be "deeply convinced of the correctness of the[ir] ultimate ideals".[62] When the presence of adjunct (non-full-time) professors in delivering investment law education is added to this mix—most of whom are gainfully employed in the arbitration industry—it comes as no surprise that an insider perspective emerges as more prominent in elite legal education.[63]

The most influential scholars in the field of investment law will be expected to author doctrinal scholarship. Garth observes that, if "[s]cholarly publication is one of the key criteria for admission to the field", then scholarship will tend to be more prudent, if not timid, about reform. Their publications, Garth adds, "rarely take strong stands on major issues for fear that the writer will scare some potential appointing parties or even lead to disqualification for bias".[64] In their empirical study of investment arbitration scholarship, Ridi and Schultz conclude that, if you want to be an authority in investment law, you must "[w]rite doctrinal scholarship".[65] Their scholarly influence extends beyond the classroom—insiders are not mere teachers—but can have direct effect on evolving investment law jurisprudence.[66] This is because investment law scholars are plugged into a network of power and authority that can make material their interpretive preferences. Having 'invested' their intellectual resources, investment law scholars are not expected to take a stand opposed to the regime. Should they propose reform, it usually involves only minor tinkering with some doctrinal or procedural issue.

It turns out that the routinization of charisma in the investment law field produces a form of charismatic education that maintains a close relationship to practice and ensures the maintenance of investment law's machinery. Successful recruits will learn that by investing in investment law, they can earn dazzling returns.[67] They can

[61] *See, for example,* Brower and Blanchard 2014. Outsiders will be accused of being "ideological" by those who are, themselves, behaving ideologically. *See, for instance,* Collins 2009, p. 232, reviewing Schneiderman 1998. I characterize these authors as exhibiting a "paranoid style" in Schneiderman 2016.

[62] Mommsen 1987, p. 40.

[63] A more detailed empirical inquiry into the profiles of investment law educators can be found in Schneiderman 2025.

[64] Garth 2018, p. 158. Moreover, he writes, "[t]alented individuals seek to master and operate within the rules of the field to gain entry into that world—which allows one to claim to be practicing virtue and to gain generous financial and prestige rewards. Critics have generally kept their criticisms within bounds, arguing in favor of the basic tenets of the system while pushing for a point of entry for a new expertise, perspective, or individual who will enhance that legitimacy (and perhaps new markets)." *See* Garth 2018, p. 164.

[65] Ridi and Schultz 2021, p. 237.

[66] Dezalay and Garth 2017, p. 138.

[67] Bourdieu 1991, p. 195; Bourdieu 1988, p. 98.

join their teachers as "privileged table companions".[68] Moreover, they are taught that by removing disputes from local courts and elevating them to the international level, states can reliably be disciplined should they run afoul of the regime's diktats—it offers the best means of vindicating the interests of foreign investors and their home states.[69] Novices are instructed that they can contribute to the exceptional and unprecedented practice of investment law,[70] "the most important effort so far to remove questions previously under domestic jurisdiction … onto the global level".[71] These "strategies of succession"[72] ensure that the newly enlisted will continue to be seduced by investment law's allure.[73]

It should be acknowledged that investment law scholarship has become more interdisciplinary since its dizzying take-off in the 1990s. Yet it remains the case that doctrinal scholarship, together with legal education's cozy relationship with the field's practitioners, has been the consistent and dominant feature contributing to the regime's durability. This means that investment law educators will continue to instruct new entrants in the virtues, but few of the vices, of this sub-field of international law.

15.4 Conclusion

Weber's portrayal of ideal-typical legal education was modelled upon the continental education prevalent in his own time.[74] This was an autonomous and scientific discipline—an "intrajuristic" field—in which educators would train new entrants in the intricacies of legal history, procedure, and codification.[75] The rise of formal legal education accompanied the spread of rationally formal law administered by disinterested officials (a bureaucracy) who applied the law without emotion or passion. Cultivated in this Weberian model of legal education is an image of legal reasoning

---

[68] Weber 1978, p. 1122.

[69] They are instructed that more international law is preferred over less. This is because international law makes the world "a better place … so international lawyers have to advocate their field, have to extol the virtues of international law", says Schultz 2016, p. 532.

[70] Recalling Weber 1978, p. 244 (on charismatic authority's "revolutionary force").

[71] Koskenniemi 2017b, p. 209. These disputes are "decided in abstraction from local conflicts or political priorities". For a discussion of how apex courts have responded to the constitutional challenge posed by removal of disputes from national constitutional contexts, *see* Schneiderman 2024.

[72] Bourdieu 1988, p. 195.

[73] *Cf.* Wrange 2015, p. 214, who claims that international law is "irrational" because it prioritizes "international investors over people".

[74] The form of legal positivism that Weber promoted, writes Cotterrell 1983, p. 88, "far from being the natural mode of legal thought in modern societies, appears increasingly to have been the product of particular historical conditions and the preserve of a particular tradition of Continent European scholarship in law".

[75] Weber 1978, p. 789. Weber attributes to this type of law teaching an orientation directed "less toward the practical needs of the groups concerned than to the uninhibited intellectualism of scholars". On Weber's legal training, *see* Whimster 2017, p. 275.

as "a method for reaching correct legal results" that is not influenced by "ethical and political" concerns.[76] The romance of disinterested scholars toiling away in their cloisters, training technically proficient lawyers, continues to circulate—as do complaints about scholarly irrelevance.[77] If professional legal education serves business interests, they will say, it is driven not by corporate profits but by logical and professional concerns. For many teaching in the investment law field, the image of detached scholarship and teaching has been abandoned in favor of unqualified, even enthusiastic, support. The "fantasy image" of disinterestedness is no longer persuasive.[78]

Cultivating a more diverse range of teaching and scholarship appears to be one available corrective. Pluralism in the range of viewpoints presented to students in both teaching and instructional resources can provide an antidote. Investment law teachers can also show more humility and honesty about the objectives secured by the regime: the promotion of economic development, good governance, and the rule of law have proven to be elusive regime by-products.[79] The universalizing of the particular case (the promotion of rules authored by the Global North) and the suppression of difference (of Global South voices and choices) requires urgent attention,[80] as does candor about the complicity of investment law academics in the production of power in the modern world.[81]

While practice helps to develop expertise, participating in the regime's ongoing maintenance proves to be problematic in a field as politically riven as this one, particularly as genuine alternatives are not being developed and reform proposals appear only sporadically and are overly modest. In other words, what is called for is a more scholarly approach to the subject, bringing tools of analysis from other fields of law (contract or constitutional law) or other cognate fields (like political philosophy or sociology). This is a call for intellectual pluralism rather than the cramped, practice-oriented pedagogy that tends to dominate investment law education. Professor Pål Wrange understood this better than most. He cared immensely about a pluralist, and critical, legal education.[82] It is fitting to dedicate this essay in his honor.

---

[76] *See* Kennedy 2004, p. 36. Weber had a clear-eyed view of the state of university education, as opposed to his ideal-typical description, in his lecture on "Science as Profession and Vocation" in Weber 1919.

[77] For a realistic assessment, *see* Llewellyn 1960, p. 349 (academic lawyers have the time to "dig", "ruminate", and "dream"). On academic irrelevance, *see* Tamanaha 2012, p. 56.

[78] Bourdieu 2024, pp. 70–71.

[79] On development, *see* Schneiderman 2022, pp. 27–29, and on good governance and the rule of law, *see* Sattorova 2023.

[80] Kennedy 1985, p. 380.

[81] Bourdieu 1988, p. xiii–ix. Bourdieu associates this with sociological "reflexivity" or "epistemological vigilance".

[82] Wrange 1996, p. 575 ("students should be able to critically reflect on the [international legal] order that they will inherit"). I had the good fortune of teaching investment law modules in Professor Wrange's course on International Law and the Global Economy at Stockholm University over the course of two years. This course traversed a wide range of the norms and institutions established and

References

Anter A (2014) Max Weber's Theory of The Modern State: Origins, Structure and Significance. Palgrave Macmillan, London

Aron R (1970) Main Currents in Sociological Thought II. Anchor Books, Garden City, New York

Bendix R (1962) Max Weber: An Intellectual Portrait. Anchor Books, New York

Bensman J, Givant M (1975) Charisma and Modernity: The Use and Abuse of a Concept. Social Research 42:570–614

Bourdieu P (1988) Homo Academicus. Translated by Peter Collier. Stanford University Press, Stanford

Bourdieu P (1991) Language and Symbolic Power. Translated by Gino Raymond and Matthew Adamson. Harvard University Press, Cambridge

Bourdieu P (1998) Practical Reason: On the Theory of Action. Stanford University Press, Stanford

Bourdieu P (2024) The Interest in Disinterestedness: Lectures at the Collège de France, 1987–1989. Translated by Peter Collier. Polity Press, Cambridge

Bourdieu P, Passeron JC (1990) Reproduction in Education, Society and Culture, 2nd ed. Translated by Richard Nice. Sage Publications, London

Brower CN, Blanchard S (2014) What's in a Meme? The Truth About Investor-State Arbitration: Why It Need Not, and Must Not, be Repossessed by States. Columbia Journal of Transnational Law 52:689–777

Collins D (2009) Book Review: Constitutionalizing Economic Globalization: Investment Rules and Democracy's Promise by David Schneiderman. The Cambridge Law Journal 68(1):231–233

Cotterrell R (1983) Legality and Political Legitimacy in the Sociology of Max Weber. In: Sugarman D (ed) Legality, Ideology and the State. Academic Press, London, pp. 61–94

Derman J (2012) Max Weber in Politics and Social Thought: From Charisma to Canonization. Cambridge University Press, Cambridge

Dezalay Y, Garth BG (1996) Dealing in Virtue: International Commercial Arbitration and the Construction of a Transnational Legal Order. University of Chicago Press, Chicago

Dezalay Y, Garth BG (2008) Law, Lawyers, and Empire. In: Grossberg M, Tomlins C (eds) The Cambridge History of Law in America, Volume III: The Twentieth Century and After (1920–). Cambridge University Press, Cambridge, pp. 718–757

Dezalay Y, Garth BG (2012) Corporate Law Firms, NGOs, and Issues of Legitimacy for a Global Legal Order. Fordham Law Review 80(6):2309–2345

Dezalay Y, Garth BG (2017) Assessing the Autonomy of Learned Law. In: Desautels-Stein J, Tomlins C (eds) Searching for Contemporary Legal Thought. Cambridge University Press, Cambridge, pp. 137–154

Freund J (1968) The Sociology of Max Weber. Translated by Mary Ilford. Random House

Gaillard E (2015) Sociology of International Arbitration. In: Caron DD et al (eds) Practising Virtue: Inside International Arbitration. Oxford University Press, Oxford, pp. 187–203

Garth BG (2018) Book Review Essay: One Window into the State of Insiders' Arbitration Scholarship. Journal of World Trade & Investment 19:155–164

Garth BG (2021) Dealing in Virtue: A Perspective from Almost 25 Years Later. In: Lim CL (ed) The Cambridge Companion to International Arbitration. Cambridge University Press, Cambridge, pp. 38–58

Gephart W (2015) Law, Culture, and Society: Max Weber's Comparative Cultural Sociology of Law. Translated by Johannes Nanz. Vittorio Klostermann, Frankfurt am Main

Ghosh P (2014) Max Weber and The Protestant Ethic: Twin Histories. Oxford University Press, Oxford

regulated by international economic law and was designed for instruct students to think critically about the course subject matter.

Halliday S, Schmidt P (2009) Yves Dezalay and Bryant Garth and Dealing in Virtue. In: Halliday S, Schmidt P (eds) Conducting Law and Society Research: Reflections on Methods and Practices. Cambridge University Press, Cambridge, pp. 200–213

Hirsch M (2020) The Sociological Dimension of International Arbitration: The Investment Arbitration Culture. In: Schultz T, Ortino F (eds) The Oxford Handbook of International Arbitration. Oxford University Press, Oxford, pp. 717–739

Kennedy, David (1985) International Legal Education. Harvard International Law Journal 26: 361-84

Kennedy David (2016) A World of Struggle: How Power, Law, and Expertise Shape Global Political Economy. Princeton University Press, Princeton

Kennedy Duncan (2004) Legal Education and the Reproduction of Hierarchy: A Polemic Against the System, A Critical Edition. New York University Press, New York

Koskenniemi M (2017a) Foreword. In: Roberts A (ed) Is International Law International? Oxford University Press, Oxford

Koskenniemi M (2017b) International Law as "Global Governance." In: Desautels-Stein J, Tomlins C (eds) Searching for Contemporary Legal Thought. Cambridge University Press, Cambridge, pp. 199–218

Llewellyn KN (1960) The Common Law Tradition: Deciding Appeals. Little, Brown, Boston

Mommsen W (1987) Personal Conduct and Societal Change: Towards a Reconstruction of Max Weber's Concept of History. In: Lash S, Whimster S (eds) Max Weber, Rationality and Modernity. Allen & Unwin, London, pp. 35–51

Puig S (2014) Social Capital in the Arbitration Market. European Journal of International Law 25(2):387–424

Roberts A, St John T (2023) The Originality of Outsiders: Innovation in the Investment Treaty System. The European Journal of International Law 33(4):1153–1181

Ridi N, Schultz T (2021) Empirically Mapping Investment Arbitration Scholarship: Networks, Authorities, and the Research Front. In: Gómez KF (ed) Private Actors in International Investment Law: European Yearbook in International Economic Law, pp. 209–241

Roberts A (2017) Is International Law International? Oxford University Press, Oxford

Roth G (2002) Max Weber: Family History, Economic Policy, Exchange Reform. International Journal of Politics, Culture and Society 15(3):509–520

Sattorova M (2023) The Impact of Investment Protection Standards on the Rule of Law: Strengthening or Weakening the Domestic Rule of Law? In: Reinisch A, Schill SW (eds) Investment Protection Standards and the Rule of Law. Oxford University Press, Oxford, pp. 353–370

Schneiderman D (2016) The Paranoid Style of Investment Lawyers and Arbitrators: Investment Law Norm Entrepreneurs and their Critics. In: Lim CL (ed) Alternative Visions of International on Foreign Investment: Essays in Honour of M. Sornarajah. Cambridge University Press, Cambridge, pp. 131–155

Schneiderman D (2022) Investment Law's Alibis: Colonialism, Imperialism, Debt and Development. Cambridge University Press, Cambridge

Schneiderman D (2024) Constitutional Review and International Investment Law: Deference or Defiance? Oxford University Press, Oxford

Schneiderman D (2025) A Sociology of International Investment Law: Themes from Max Weber. (forthcoming, Oxford University Press, Oxford)

Schultz T (2016) Celebrating 20 Years of 'Dealing in Virtue'. Journal of International Dispute Settlement 7:531–533

Schultz T (2020) The Ethos of Arbitration. In: Schultz T, Ortino F (eds) The Oxford Handbook of International Arbitration. Oxford University Press, Oxford, pp. 235–259

Shils E (1965) Charisma, Order, and Status. American Sociological Review 30:199–213

Swedberg R (2018) How to Use Max Weber's Ideal Type in Sociological Analysis. Journal of Classical Sociology 18:181–196

Tamanaha BZ (2012) Failing Law Schools. The University of Chicago Press, Chicago

Tenbruck FH (1987) Max Weber and Eduard Meyer. In: Mommsen WJ, Osterhammel J (eds) Max Weber and His Contemporaries. Unwin Hyman, London, pp. 234–267

Tucker T (2018) Judge Knot: How the Crusade for Investor Rights Tangles Our Democracies and Economies. Anthem Press, London

Turner S, Factor R (1994) Max Weber: The Lawyer as Social Thinker. Routledge, London

Waibel, M (2015) Interpretive Communities in International Law. In: Bianchi A et al (eds) Interpretation in International Law. Oxford University Press, Oxford, pp. 147–165

Weber M (1895) "Roman" and "Germanic" Law. International Journal of the Sociology of Law 13:237–246

Weber M (1904) The "Objectivity" of Knowledge in Social Science and Social Policy. In: Bruun HH, Whimster S (2010) Max Weber: Complete Methodological Writings. Routledge, London, pp. 100–138

Weber M (1919) The Profession and Vocation of Politics.' In: Weber M (1994) Political Writings. Edited by Peter Lassman and Ronal Speirs. Cambridge University Press, Cambridge, pp. 309–369

Weber M (1920a) Prefatory Remarks to Collected Essays in the Sociology of Religion. In: Weber M (2009) The Protestant Ethic and the Spirit of Capitalism with Other Writings on the Rise of the West, 4th ed. Translated by Stephen Kalberg. Oxford University Press, Oxford, pp. 205–220

Weber M (1920b) The Protestant Ethic and the Spirit of Capitalism. In: Weber M (2009) The Protestant Ethic and the Spirit of Capitalism with Other Writings on the Rise of the West, 4th ed. Translated by Stephen Kalberg. Oxford University Press, Oxford, pp. 61–159

Weber M (1978) Economy and Society: An Outline of Interpretive Sociology. Translated and edited by Guenther Roth and Claus Wittich. University of California Press, Berkeley (2 volumes)

Weber M (2019) Economy and Society: A New Translation. Translated by Keith Tribe. Harvard University Press, Cambridge, Mass

Whimster S (2017) Max Weber's Roman Agrarian History: Jurisprudence, Property, Civilization. In: Gephart W, Witte D (eds) Recht als Kultur? Beiträge zu Max Webers Soziologie des Rechts [Law as Culture? Contributions to Max Weber's Sociology of Law]. Vittorio Klostermann, Frankfurt am Main, pp. 229–277

Wrange P (1996) An Open Letter to my Students: Theory, Practice and Life in International Law. Nordic Journal of International Law 65:573–578

Wrange P (2015) Land, Development and the Irrationality of International Law. Scandinavian Studies in Law 60:187–220

David Schneiderman is Professor of Law and Political Science (courtesy) at the University of Toronto where he teaches courses on Canadian, US, and comparative constitutional law and international investment law. He has been visiting Professor of Law at numerous universities, including Stockholm University, Georgetown University, and Columbia University. He is the author of over 80 articles and book chapters and, in addition, the author or editor of over a dozen books. Among them are *Constitutionalizing Economic Globalization: Investment Rules and Democracy's Promise* (Cambridge UP 2008), *Resisting Economic Globalization: Critical Theory and International Investment Law* (Palgrave 2013), *Investment Law's Alibis: Colonialism, Imperialism, Debt and Development* (Cambridge UP 2022), *Rethinking Investment Law* (co-edited with Gus Van Harten) (Oxford UP 2023), and *Constitutional Review and International Investment Law: Deference or Defiance?* (Oxford UP 2024).

Part IV
The Politics of Historicizing International Law

Chapter 16
Historicizing International Law

Jens Bartelson

Contents

Abstract In recent decades, international law has undergone a historical turn. While the attempts to historicize the subject matter of international law have been productive, they have also spurred intense controversies, with some international lawyers claiming that contextualization and historicization threaten the critical purchase and autonomy of international law. This essay revisits this debate, arguing that the relationship between law and history should be subjected to historical inquiry rather than futile attempts at principled resolution. Only once the historicity of international law is fully acknowledged can international law reclaim its critical purchase and worldmaking potentials without recourse to transhistorical meanings or principles.

Keywords International law · History · Contextualism · Genetic fallacy · Genealogy · Historicity

16.1 Introduction

In recent decades, academic international relations and international law have undergone historical turns with profound and sometimes destabilizing effects on their disciplinary identity. Propelled by a selective uptake of insights from the linguistic turn in philosophy, attempts to historicize core concepts and theories of international

I would like to thank Lars Vetle Handeland, Mark Klamberg, and Anne Orford for their valuable comments on earlier drafts of this chapter.

J. Bartelson (✉)
Department of Political Science, Lund University, Lund, Sweden
e-mail: jens.bartelson@svet.lu.se

M. Klamberg et al. (eds.), *Reconstructing Power and Hegemony in Public International Law*, https://doi.org/10.1007/978-94-6265-743-4_16

relations and international law have spilled over into contestations of their traditional claims to validity and scientific authority. To academic international relations, the historical turn has implied that concepts, institutions, and practices long believed to be foundational features of the international realm have become recast as historically contingent and mutable, giving rise to a booming subfield devoted to their exploration.[1] Although largely simultaneous developments in international law have been even more productive in terms of scholarly output, they have also generated considerable debate among historians of international law and international lawyers, where some of the latter have viewed contextualization and historicization as potential threats to the normative purchase and relative autonomy of their discipline.[2] Given the inherently normative character of international law, that such tension would arise is hardly surprising. But what is at stake in this debate and how can it be resolved?

In this essay, I will revisit this debate and propose a resolution by contesting its underlying assumptions about the relationship between law and history. Although aspects of this relationship have been thoroughly analyzed already, with the many complex connections between these fields underlined, the present chapter aims to discuss this relationship in more principled and philosophical terms.[3] Arguably, the tensions generated by the historical turn in international law are instances of a more general conflict between genesis and validity in the social and human sciences, not least in the study of political thought. As Martin Jay has argued: "[t]here is no more contentious and perennial issue in the history of Western thought…that the genesis of an idea or value in a specific context, and its claim to validity beyond it."[4] At the heart of this issue is the idea that accounts of origin are logically distinct from those of validity and hence that trying to answer questions of validity with reference to accounts of origin amounts to committing a *genetic fallacy*. As Morris Cohen and Ernst Nagel once characterized this fallacy, it rests on the "supposition that an actual history of any science, art, or social institution can take the place of a logical analysis of its structure".[5] Thus, it would seem that the historical turn poses no threat to the normative purchase and autonomy of international law, as long as historians avoid committing such fallacies by making unwarranted inferences from historical accounts of the emergence of a given concept or theory to judgments about its validity. Yet, as the recent debate between international lawyers and historians indicates, these tasks are difficult to distinguish in practice. Whereas lawyers often invoke the past to vindicate norms and settle disputes in the present, historians sometimes invoke the past to dispute the outcome of these activities. However unproductive the ensuing discussions might seem from an analytical perspective, they point to the extent to

[1] As indicated by the appearance of handbooks summarizing the state of the art of historically oriented international relations and international law, *see* de Carvalho et al. 2021; Bukovansky et al. 2023.

[2] As for the first indications of productivity, *see* Fassbender et al. 2012. Some of the critical interventions include Koskenniemi 2014; Orford 2013, 2017, 2021a; Benton 2018; Fitzmaurice 2018. For an overview, *see* Brett 2021.

[3] *See, for example,* Borda 2021; Petrović 2016; Ploeg et al. 2022.

[4] Jay 2022, p. 1.

[5] *See* Cohen & Nagel 1934, pp. 389–390.

which questions of origin and validity are interdependent. As Jay has noted: "the relationship between genesis and validity is not necessarily adversarial. What might be called a dialectical relationship between the two terms is also possible, with truth claims actually more dependent on concrete embeddedness than on abstract detachment."[6] But if this is true, it follows that it would be futile to resolve the dispute between international lawyers and historians by distinguishing more sharply between questions of genesis and validity and enforcing a stricter division of labor between these fields, especially as invoking the past in support of present positions is part of what international legal theory and practice are all about.[7] Hence, if questions of genesis and validity are connected and condition each other in the human sciences in general and in law in particular, we would perhaps be better off studying how the relationship between law and history has been configured in the past before passing premature judgments on how it ought *ideally* to be conceived in the present. And, as I will argue, doing this is less a matter of finding the appropriate historical method that caters to the needs of historians and lawyers alike, and more a matter of a progressive problem shift that permits us to acknowledge the *historicity* of international law and thereby reclaim its critical purchase and worldmaking potentials in the present. Although both historians and lawyers have tried to bring such a problem shift about, I believe that the underlying philosophical tension between genesis and validity has remained largely unresolved by their efforts. In the next section, I will revisit this debate before sketching the terms of its resolution.

16.2 International Law and the Historical Turn

When the historical turn first gained momentum in international law, it was closely aligned with a critique of power. Pioneering works such as *The Gentle Civilizer of Nations* by Martti Koskenniemi or *Imperialism, Sovereignty, and the Making of International Law* by Anthony Anghie were not reconstructing the past of international law for its own sake but aimed to expose existing inequalities of power and wealth to facilitate their abolition.[8] For example, the *Gentle Civilizer* aimed at making the "present situation clearer to us and to sharpen our ability to act in the professional contexts that are open to us as we engage in our practices and projects. In this sense, it is also a political act".[9] Or, as Anghie had it: "if we understand how colonialism has shaped the fundamental structures of international law, then it might become possible…to rethink a system of international law that might in some way make good on its promise to further international justice."[10] These critical ambitions were later downplayed by historians like Lauren Benton and Andrew Fitzmaurice,

[6] Jay 2022, p. 8.
[7] Lobban 2022.
[8] Koskenniemi 2001; Anghie 2007.
[9] Koskenniemi 2001, p. 10.
[10] Anghie 2007, p. 12.

in favor of scholarly concerns with historical explanations and understanding.[11] This provoked pushback from historically oriented international lawyers who wanted to further cultivate the critical potentials of international legal history. There are two main sticking points in the ensuing debate:

The first of these concerns the problem of *anachronism.* To Anne Orford, the adaption of contextualist methods—in her rendering derived from the early statements of Quentin Skinner—in the history of international law brought a prohibition against anachronism that was hard to reconcile with the spirit of legal reasoning. This prohibition, along with the separation of past and present it presupposes, made legal reasoning difficult if not impossible, as the latter presupposes precisely that meaning can move across time: "[i]nternational legal scholarship is necessarily anachronic, because the operation of modern law is not governed solely by a chronological sense of time in which events and texts are confined to their proper place in a historical and linear progression from then to now."[12] It is the different views of time and anachronism "that [mark] the point at which international law and contextual intellectual history part company".[13]

To Orford, this partition had occurred when intellectual historians started to "challenge accounts of the past offered by international lawyers on methodological grounds".[14] This led to a situation in which historians claim that "reconstructing historical contexts can offer us a verifiable means of interpreting past legal texts, practices, and institutions" which "can offer us new foundations for grounding our arguments about the real history of a regime, the origins of international law, or the meaning of a past text".[15] What Orford argues against is not the historical turn per se, but the ambition of contextually oriented historians to "complete and correct the flawed scholarship of international lawyers".[16] To her, this ambition was but a consequence of their insistence that meaning derives from contexts. This implies that "[a]ll past texts are essentially historical, and their meaning can only be understood by locating them within the temporal context in which they were authored".[17] Hence, contextualism comes with a commitment against writing historical narratives on a grand scale by "assembling material from different periods into arguments that were not structured around linear histories".[18]

In Orford's view, contextualist historians had developed their methods in conscious contrast to other methods of interpretation by offering "narratives about moments in European history that witnessed the emergence of contextualist method" and presenting these as instances where scientific progress and contextualism were

---

[11] *See, for example,* Benton 2009, Benton and Ford 2016; Fitzmaurice 2014.

[12] Orford 2013, p. 175.

[13] Orford 2017, p. 302.

[14] Orford 2021a, p. 4.

[15] Ibid., p. 7.

[16] Ibid., p. 70.

[17] Ibid., p. 82.

[18] Ibid., p. 84.

"politically superior because [they resist] the false claims of those in authority".[19] To this, they added a way of characterizing legal scholarship and lawyers that did not abide by humanist or contextualist precepts in the past as scholastic or metaphysical, which has meant that "[i]nternational legal scholars are presented as symbols and champions of ahistorical or traditional thinking, who defend the status quo through appealing to continuity and tradition".[20] But to Orford, this way of historicizing international law lacks critical bite, as few international lawyers believe that "contemporary international law is timeless, natural, universal and ahistorical", which contextualist historians have assumed.[21] Rather, "there are very few lawyers today for whom the idea that international law is political and a human creation is novel. Such arguments are already an entrenched part of the argumentative field of international law."[22] Thus, to Orford, international law has already come to terms with its own historicity and incorporated these insights into its self-understanding. So, although Orford is not opposed to the use of contextualist methods, she believes that they cannot offer "reliably corrective and impartial interventions in contemporary debates about international law", as international law is no longer based on the kind of metaphysical claims and timeless principles that contextualism was invented to refute.[23]

The second problem concerns the threat allegedly posed by *relativism* to the critical purchase of international law. To Koskenniemi, although contextualist methods might be necessary to make sense of the past, "regardless of the merits of placing historical subjects in their local contexts, critical legal history ought not rest content with this".[24] Apart from the insurmountable difficulties of delimiting the appropriate context for interpreting a given text, the main problem with contextualism is its "relativist and anti-critical nature".[25] This is so, because "it may come to shield past ideas from criticisms that always appear a methodologically suspect 'presentism'".[26] Rather than hiding behind methodological precepts, we should accept that the validity of our historical accounts depends on "how they contribute to emancipation today".[27] To Koskenniemi, the historical turn has given rise to the danger that history "loses its critical edge by limiting its focus to the field's internal divisions and transformations without the ambition to expose law's complicity in the world's injustices".[28] In contrast to a narrow focus on context, attention to "the *longue durée* of structural causality…will help the past speak to the present".[29] Thus, in practice, a history of

[19] Ibid., p. 173.
[20] Ibid., p. 174.
[21] Ibid., p. 250.
[22] Ibid., p. 251.
[23] Ibid., p. 177.
[24] Koskenniemi 2014, p. 123.
[25] Ibid., p. 128.
[26] Ibid., p. 129.
[27] Ibid.
[28] Koskenniemi 2021a, p. 55.
[29] Ibid., p. 63.

international law will be a "history of how law has been used to justify, support, and occasionally critique power is about shifting perceptions of justice and injustice and the accumulation of experiences with which we today form our expectations for the future".[30] From this perspective, contextualism threatens to undermine the critical purchase of international law by relativizing its claims to validity, thereby making it impossible to justify any particular critical stance with reference to a desired future.

The above criticisms identify contextualist methods—however they are defined—as the main source of tensions between international law and history, implying that these tensions could be resolved with a different historical method that would avoid relativism by allowing a certain amount of anachronism. The precepts of contextualism must be supplemented or replaced with principles of historical reconstruction that make it possible to harness legal history for more progressive purposes lest the autonomy of international law be sacrificed on the altar of historicism.

Unsurprisingly, historians at the receiving end of this criticism disagree with this diagnosis and the ensuing prescriptions. Both Lauren Benton and Andrew Fitzmaurice have pointed out that contextualism narrowly defined is neither representative nor exhaustive of recent scholarship in the history of international law. As Benton has argued, this criticism rests on a distorted reception of the *oeuvre* of Quentin Skinner and a misguided belief that the policing of anachronism is what the historical turn in international law has been all about. The historical turn has produced a wide variety of scholarship, some of it best characterized as the study of global legal politics.[31] In a similar vein, Fitzmaurice has claimed that "[v]igilance about imposing present concepts upon the understanding of the past does not preclude achieving an understanding of how the present is constituted by the past, nor is it anachronistic to understand how the terms of political discourse in the present draw upon the past while they are at the same time incessantly reinterpreting the past".[32] Indeed, the critiques of anachronism by contextualist historians "are driven by a concern with the present: namely, with limiting the manipulation of the past for political purposes".[33] Lastly, to Ian Hunter, the many criticisms leveled against contextualism boil down to a single contention, "namely, that ideas or texts cannot be wholly explicated in terms of their historical context because access to context itself has ideational or transcendental conditions".[34] To refute this point, Hunter sets out to contextualize contextualism itself by emphasizing its affinities with earlier modes of contextualist historiography and *their* irreconcilable opposition to quests of transhistorical and transcendental meaning in the past. When responding to these criticisms in her book *International Law and the Politics of History*, Orford sought to substantiate the claim that Skinner's work was indeed based on the tenets of contextualism described above, and, perhaps more importantly, representative of a long-standing but ultimately futile effort to cast

---

[30] Koskenniemi 2021b, p. 13.

[31] Benton 2018.

[32] Fitzmaurice 2018, p. 14.

[33] Ibid, p. 15.

[34] Hunter 2019, p. 186.

lawyers as representatives of a metaphysical and scholastic tradition of thought inherently opposed to the emancipatory spirit of contextualism.[35] As she argued, if we were to apply Skinner's argument "to legal concepts…there is no understanding to be gained about any legal concept…by considering its development, evolution, transformation, application, or interpretation over time".[36] Although this might be true of the first generation of contextualists, Orford was fully aware that this would not apply to those historians—notably David Armitage—who self-consciously expanded the scope of contextualist methods beyond singular contexts to study history in the *longue durée*.[37] Hence, although neither exhaustive of the methods available for studying the history of international law nor necessarily antithetical to its critical ambitions, early and *prima facie* orthodox versions of contextualism became the weapon of choice for historians eager to patronize lawyers. This appropriation—rather than contextualism itself—helps account for the sometimes conservative upshot of the resulting histories.

16.3 The Historicity of International Law

From this, it would follow that relativism and the policing of anachronism would be less of a problem if historians stayed on their turf, and that their work perhaps would be more useful if they were willing to consider the development of legal thought *across* isolated contexts and without debunking purposes. This much is also conceded by Orford, when she states that "[t]he arguments made on this book about the limits of empiricist historical method should not upset those historians whose professional commitment is to produce an accurate or verifiable account of the past rather than having any specific form of engagement with the present".[38] But to Orford, such detachment is difficult to attain in practice as "the advocacy of a particular historical method is inevitably bound up with a particular struggle for the meaning of law".[39] Thus, a mere appeal to the genetic fallacy cannot resolve the tension between history and law, as the latter sometimes must assume that the validity of a given proposition hinges on its origin—as is the case with legal positivism—or when establishing precedents based on past practices. Thus, legal reasoning presupposes some degree of continuity between past and present. As Natasha Wheatley has aptly put it, "[l]aw trades on a belief in its transtemporality—a belief in its capacity to rise above and ward off history by digesting history's shifting forms into enduring categories and principles".[40] This predicament is in no way exclusive to law, but an instance of a general interdependence between past and present usually subsumed under the

[35] Orford 2021a, pp. 135–157.

[36] Ibid., p. 141.

[37] *See, for example*, Armitage 2012.

[38] Orford 2021a, p. 11.

[39] Ibid., p. 10.

[40] Wheatley 2021, p. 326.

heading of *historicity* in the human sciences, that is, the recognition that *all human knowledge is historically situated*.[41] This goes for history as well. Hence, neither international law nor historiography can hope to escape history, whether its own or in general terms. From the vantage point of historicity, it is not only the case that the reconstruction of the past is contingent on the present (something which the above interlocutors willingly concede), but also that the present vantage point from which such a reconstruction is undertaken is *itself* contingent upon history. From this point of view, the genetic fallacy looks less like a fallacy and more like an inescapable predicament of historical writing, especially as the temporal intertwining of the questions of genesis and validity also seems to be integral to the possibility of legal reasoning. In this final section, I will elaborate on the implications of the historicity of international law and history, arguing that the recognition of historicity necessitates a progressive problem shift rather than a methodological reorientation in order to get the relationship between law and history straight on *philosophical* as opposed to legal or historical terms.

However, let us start with the methodological ways of handling this predicament. Granted that contextualism is not exhaustive of the options available, perhaps other methods could deliver the critical purchase desired by Koskenniemi and Orford, without thereby sacrificing history on the altar of legal reasoning. Indeed, some such proposals have recently been made. To Annabel Brett, the ultimate source of tension between international law and history is not so much the commitment to contextual interpretation as such but rather that more hardboiled versions of contextualism tend to *reduce* legal thought to mere expressions of power, thus depriving it of its autonomy vis-à-vis politics and political thought.[42] Hence, one way to resolve this tension would be to relax the explanatory ambitions of contextualism in favor of a more open-ended and genealogical approach that would allow meaning to migrate across contexts in ways more conducive to critical legal theorizing. In contrast to contextualism, a genealogical approach is not content to expose the mere historical contingency of concepts, practices, and institutions. Orthodox genealogical accounts characteristically invoke the past in order to denaturalize and problematize features taken for granted and regarded as unproblematic in the present.[43] As Kate Purcell has reminded us: "[t]o trace the genealogies of contemporary international law is one way in which we might cultivate this critical ethos with its emancipatory potential." Such genealogies "might show us how not to be governed by (or govern by) the particular and limited forms of knowledge—including historical knowledge—that characterize power in contemporary international law".[44] And as Ben Golder has recently pointed out, such a genealogical approach would provide an alternative way of reconstructing the history of international law that is inherently critical insofar as

[41] Hartog 2015, Ruin 2018.

[42] Brett 2021a.

[43] *See, for example,* Bevir 2008, Lane 2012, Srinivasan 2019.

[44] Purcell 2020, p. 35.

it prompts inquiries into "how the categories of the historical and legal are assembled—what they presuppose and reproduce, what they remainder and occlude".[45] But as Orford has objected, genealogy "presupposes that its intended audience is committed to metaphysical ideas or believes that particular moral values are transcendent and universal".[46] Absent such beliefs, genealogy would fall into the same trap as contextualist methods by presupposing that the now uncontentious is still contentious. It therefore seems that the encounter between history and law has run its course, as it, according to Orford, "has shored up the idea that historiography offers a master set of methods for interpreting the past, and that history can offer us a new foundation for formalist arguments about the meaning of the law".[47]

This brings me to my concluding point. If, despite their limitations, genealogies of international law can help us historicize the categories of law and history and their meanings, the final step would be to subject the *relationship* between law and history to historical inquiry: how has the past been invoked to support or debunk legal concepts and theories, and how have legal concepts and theories informed the reconstruction of the past? And how are the same connections between law and history connections between past and present forged and reinforced in our present? Answering these questions would amount to turning the "double historicism" identified by Koskenniemi, "where the role of history within a legal culture or consciousness appears itself an aspect of the history of that culture and consciousness", into a full-blown research program.[48] To some extent, this interdependence between law and history is acknowledged by Orford, when she points out that: "[t]he recognition that international law is politics all the way down is not the end of the story, but the beginning of a new chapter…The return of history into this story is valuable, but only if it can allow us to experience that sense of choice and responsibility anew."[49] According to Orford's account, this was but a case of Othering, as the "encounter with international law enabled the (re)constitution of history as a discipline committed to verifiability, impartiality, and the liberating effects of humanist method".[50] Absent other suitable enemies, the historiography of international law was singled out for target practice by contextualists in their relentless struggle against timeless truths and metaphysical principles. To Orford, however, all of this was Quixotic.

Although this might be true, a systematic emphasis on the historicity of international law would shift the quarrel between lawyers and historians described above to a higher terrain, where the logical interdependence between past and present would be the starting point of inquiry rather than an apple of discord and an obstacle to intellectual progress. Once the historicity of international law *and* its history is acknowledged by lawyers and historians alike, histories of international law will become indispensable to understanding the limits and possibilities of international

45 Golder 2023, p. 11.
46 Orford 2024, p. 778.
47 Orford 2021a, p. 320.
48 Koskenniemi 2021a, p. 56.
49 Orford 2021a, p. 320.
50 Orford 2021b, p. 189.

law as a practice of worldmaking. Although these histories are likely to be supportive or debunking of identifiable legal concepts and theories in the present, it is obvious that these histories would have to be reconstructed from the vantage point of present concerns that are equally historically contingent and open to historicization. If there is no transhistorical vantage point outside history from which such reconstructions can be undertaken and validated, presentism is not only inevitable but also desirable. Consequently, critical histories of international law would require attention to how historical accounts have been tailored to corroborate legal theories as much as to how legal theories have furnished the starting points for the construction of such histories. For example, in my *War in International Thought*, I tried to show how conjectural histories of the violent origins of the state were invoked by early modern international lawyers in support of their attempts to regulate the use of force among polities, and how assumptions that such violence is a productive force in human affairs constituted the starting point for narrating the very same histories.[51] Thus, the stories of how the state and international law came into being were based on a productive circularity between these entities so that it was not possible to imagine one without the other. Likewise, Claire Vergerio has shown in detail how the works of Alberico Gentili were reappropriated by late nineteenth- and early twentieth-century international lawyers, with profound implications for the ways in which the laws of war have been understood and justified since that point in time.[52] These accounts tell us how histories have been recounted based on the same concepts and theories they intended to justify, but also how these concepts and theories have been used to remake the world in their image, thereby indicating the extent to which the double bind between international law and history has been used to *escape* history for what look like undesirable ends in our present.[53] But what if international law stays within history while becoming reflexive about its historicity? If international law and history are indeed mutually implicating and reinforcing, inventing pasts and imagining future possibilities are better viewed as integral aspects of the same process of worldmaking through law. Hence, rather than subverting the critical potentials of international law, historicizing the connection between past and present in the history of international law would seem to liberate international law from the need to justify its critical claims and emancipatory potentials with reference to anything beyond its own Janus-faced ability to integrate experience and expectation recursively *by means* of a hermeneutic circularity that leads lawyers and historians away from their mutual suspicions.

References

Anghie A (2007) Imperialism, Sovereignty and the Making of International Law. Cambridge University Press, Cambridge

---

[51] Bartelson 2017.

[52] Vergerio 2022.

[53] *Compare* Wheatley 2021, p. 329.

Armitage D (2012) What's the Big Idea? Intellectual History and the longue durée. History of European Ideas, 38:493–507
Bartelson J (2017) War in International Thought. Cambridge University Press, Cambridge
Benton L (2009) A Search for Sovereignty: Law and geography in European empires, 1400–1900. Cambridge University Press, Cambridge
Benton L (2019) Beyond Anachronism: Histories of International Law and Global Legal Politics. Journal of the History of International Law/Revue d'histoire du droit international 21:7–40
Benton L, Ford L (2016) Rage for Order: The British Empire and the origins of international law, 1800–1850. Harvard University Press, Cambridge, MA
Bevir M (2008) What is Genealogy? Journal of the Philosophy of History 2:263–275
Borda A Z (2021) Histories Written by International Criminal Courts and Tribunals: Developing a Responsible History Framework. Springer Nature, Cham
Brett A (2021) Between History, Politics and Law: History of Political Thought and the History of International Law. In: Brett A et al (eds) History, Politics, Law: Thinking Through the International. Cambridge University Press, Cambridge, pp. 19–48
Bukovansky M et al (eds) (2023). The Oxford Handbook of History and International Relations. Oxford University Press, Oxford
Cohen MR, Nagel E (1934) Logic and Scientific Method. Harcourt Brace and Co, New York
de Carvalho B et al (eds) (2021) Routledge Handbook of Historical International Relations. Routledge, London
Fassbender B et al (eds) (2012). The Oxford Handbook of the History of International Law. Oxford University Press, Oxford
Fitzmaurice A (2014) Sovereignty, Property and Empire, 1500–2000. Cambridge University Press, Cambridge
Fitzmaurice A (2018) Context in the History of International Law. Journal of the History of International Law/Revue d'histoire du droit international 20:5–30
Golder B (2023) International Law and the Politics of Genealogy. Global Intellectual History 9(6):1–15
Hartog F (2015) Regimes of Historicity: Presentism and Experiences of Time. Columbia University Press, New York
Hunter I (2019) The Contest over Context in Intellectual History. History and Theory 58:185–209
Jay M (2022) Genesis and Validity: The Theory and Practice of Intellectual History. University of Pennsylvania Press, Philadelphia
Koskenniemi M (2001) The Gentle Civilizer of Nations: The Rise and Fall of International Law 1870–1960. Cambridge University Press, Cambridge
Koskenniemi M (2014) Vitoria and Us. Rechtsgeschichte-Legal History 22: 119–138
Koskenniemi M (2021a) The Past According to International Law: A Practice of History and Histories of a Practice. In: Brett A et al (eds) History, Politics, Law: Thinking Through the International. Cambridge University Press, Cambridge, pp. 49–68
Koskenniemi M (2021b). To the Uttermost Parts of the Earth: Legal Imagination and International Power 1300–1870. Cambridge University Press, Cambridge
Lane M (2012) Doing our Own Thinking for Ourselves: On Quentin Skinner's Genealogical Turn. Journal of the History of Ideas 73:71–82
Lobban M (2022) Law and History, History and Law. In: Bourke R, Skinner Q (eds) History in the Humanities and Social Sciences. Cambridge University Press, Cambridge, pp. 20–48
Orford A (2013) On International Legal Method. London Review of International Law 1:166–197
Orford A (2017) International Law and the Limits of History. In: Werner W et al (eds) The Law of International Lawyers: Reading Martti Koskenniemi. Cambridge University Press, Cambridge, pp. 297–320
Orford A (2021a) International Law and the Politics of History. Cambridge University Press, Cambridge
Orford A (2021b) The Politics and Protocols of Interdisciplinary Encounters. Temple International and Comparative Law Journal 36:173–199

Orford A (2024) What is the History of International Law For? Global Intellectual History 9:760–782
Petrović V (2016) The Emergence of Historical Forensic Expertise: Clio takes the stand. Routledge, London and New York
Purcell K (2020) On the Uses and Advantages of Genealogy for International Law. Leiden Journal of International Law 33:13–35
Ruin H (2018) Historicity and the Hermeneutic Predicament: From Yorck to Derrida. In: Zahavi D (ed) The Oxford Handbook of the History of Phenomenology. Oxford University Press, Oxford, pp. 717–733
Srinivasan A (2019) Genealogy, Epistemology and Worldmaking. In: Proceedings of the Aristotelian Society 119:127–156
van der Ploeg K et al (eds) (2022) International Law and Time. Narratives and Techniques. Springer Nature, Cham
Vergerio C (2022) War, States, and International Order: Alberico Gentili and the Foundational Myth of the Laws of War. Cambridge University Press, Cambridge
Wheatley N (2021) Law and the Time of Angels: International Law's Method Wars and the Affective Life of Disciplines. History and Theory 60:311–330

Jens Bartelson is Professor of Political Science at Lund University. His fields of interest include international relations and the history of international thought. Jens Bartelson has published extensively on core concepts in international thought and their history. He is the author of Becoming International (Cambridge University Press, 2023), War in International Thought (Cambridge University Press, 2017, winner of the Best Book Award of the ISA Theory Section), Visions of World Community (Cambridge University Press, 2009), The Critique of the State (Cambridge University Press, 2001), A Genealogy of Sovereignty (Cambridge University Press, 1995), as well as of numerous articles in leading journals across the human, legal, and social sciences.

Chapter 17
Clausewitz and the Development of International Law

Ove Bring

Contents

Abstract The doctrine of military theorist Carl von Clausewitz is situated in the landscape of international law at the time of post-Napoleonic thought. The Clausewitzian thesis that war is a continuation of politics by other means was expressed in the posthumous treatise *On War,* published in its entirety in 1834. Clausewitz argued for the necessity of absolute and total war, although he, during the process of writing, came to the conclusion that limited war was an option. Theoretically, he may have been influenced by the then-current doctrine of international law and the *jus in bello* positions of the Swiss author Vattel and others, but most likely he was aware of the *jus contra bellum* positions of the emerging peace movement. In general, he downgraded the importance of international law and peace policy and stuck to his hardline thesis. Nevertheless, due to the perceived anti-humanitarian harshness of his main thought, his position provoked an antithesis of Hegelian nature that was in tune with the liberal societal attitudes at the time. This in turn led to a kind of synthesis through later humanitarian regulation of armed conflict: the Lieber Code of 1863 during the American Civil War, the first Geneva Convention of 1864 and the Declaration of St. Petersburg of 1868. The Laws of War had come into being and would be further developed.

Keywords Total war · Limited war · *Jus in bello* · *Jus ad bellum* · Chivalry · Peaceful solutions · Arbitration

---

O. Bring (✉)
Stockholm University, Stockholm, Sweden
e-mail: ove.bring@outlook.com

M. Klamberg et al. (eds.), *Reconstructing Power and Hegemony in Public International Law*, https://doi.org/10.1007/978-94-6265-743-4_17

17.1 Introduction

The views of Carl von Clausewitz (1780–1831), the Prussian staff officer, military historian and theorist who gained his military experiences during the Napoleonic wars, will be presented in this contribution dedicated to Pål Wrange. Clausewitz is famous for his treatise *On War* (*Vom Kriege*), published posthumously in 1832–1834.[1] He is best remembered for his dictum that war is a continuation of politics by other means and that politics and war form an indivisible whole—and for his observations on the necessity of total war. He is read by modern historians and military experts who take an interest in his views on strategy and tactics.

Pål Wrange might be interested in Clausewitz as a military philosopher. Pål's doctoral thesis of 2007, *Impartial or Uninvolved?, The Anatomy of 20th Century Doctrine on the Law of Neutrality*, shows a great interest in and knowledge of theory. Pål uses the regime of truths as a recurring point of analysis in his chapters on 20th century authors, starting with Karl Strupp and Nicolas Politis. Pål also refers to Friedrich Hegel, who died in 1831, the same year as Clausewitz. Hegel is of manifest importance in relation to the book *Vom Kriege*. Hegel's theory of truth, that the real is rational and 'the true is the whole', boils down to his dialectic development process of thesis, antithesis and synthesis. Clausewitz's position on what he saw as a matter of facts (that politics and war form an indivisible whole) could be perceived as a provocative thesis that became confronted with an antithesis expressing the radical need for change (voiced by the emerging peace movement), with the resulting synthesis of a compromise (considerations of humanitarian restrictions in warfare limited by military necessity).[2]

The 1976 English version of *Vom Kriege*, translated and edited by Michael Howard and Peter Paret (see footnote 1) has been criticized for softening up Clausewitz's brutal language on the characteristics of war, thereby adapting to the likely expectations of a modern liberal readership. Modern writing on Clausewitz is, in general, more respectful than critical, and, as to language, more well-disposed than brutally realistic. However, Clausewitz was a harsh realist—in modern parlance situated somewhere between Morgenthau and Mearsheimer.

---

[1] The modern version in English of *On War* (*Vom Kriege)* is edited and translated by Michael Howard and Peter Paret and was first published by the Princeton University Press in 1976 and again in 1984. I have used and quoted from a later Howard/Paret edition published in 1993. In a few cases, I have chosen to quote from Anatol Rapoport's 1968 Penguin Classics edition of *On War*, using a reprint from 1984. The translation in the Penguin edition was done by a Colonel J. J. Graham in 1908.

[2] Reactions against war as such started already in 1815 through what later would become the international peace movement (see below), and Martti Koskenniemi has in the *Gentle Civilizer of Nations* shown how reformist lawyers in Brussels, Amsterdam and London around 1870 took the initiative to 'civilize' current political attitudes towards a functioning international society. An international law journal was founded in Brussels in 1868 and the organizations *Institut de droit international* and *International Law Association* were set in motion in 1873. The new intellectual climate produced an agenda of arbitration and peaceful settlement of disputes. *See* Koskenniemi 2002, pp. 11–41.

Clausewitz saw war as an unavoidable phenomenon in international relations. Still, he made a distinction between judicious and injudicious war: hostilities should only be started for a good reason. However, it has often been said that he dismissed international law as being of no consequence in the relations between states. Of course, it has to be admitted that when Clausewitz died, or when his book was published *in toto* in 1834, international law was in an early stage of development. The present text will take a closer look on Clausewitz's attitude towards international law, including the belatedly emerging prohibition on aggression, and what is today called the Law of Armed Conflict (LOAC) or International Humanitarian Law applicable in Armed Conflict (IHL).

17.2 The Position of International Law in the Early 1800s

Emmerich de Vattel of Switzerland, with experience as a diplomat in the service of Saxony, published his *Le Droit des Gens* in 1758—a book that would prove to be influential well into the following century. Vattel made a distinction between just and unjust wars, at the same time seeing the possibility of war being just, or at least could being waged *bona fide*, on both sides. Consequently, he was not prepared to outlaw war as such. However, he argued that a sovereign who waged an unjust war should be heavily punished and repay the evil done.[3] Vattel recognized the existence of legal norms applicable on the battlefield to moderate the severity of war. He rejected all suggestions that the end justifies the means and that might is right. He recognized the need for collective action against aggressors that upset the balance of power. Although he, and many of his successors, paid lip service to a foundation of natural law, Vattel was modern in the sense that his argumentation was adapted to state practice and the diplomatic needs of 'civilized' states.

Le Droit des Gens attained a wide circulation, was translated into many languages and published in Leiden, Amsterdam, Basel, London, Dublin, Paris, New York and other places. It was especially popular in the United States, where it was used by both diplomatic service and universities.

At the end of the 1700s and first half of the 1800s, the doctrine of international law was further developed. In 1780, Johan Jacob Moser, a professor at the University of Tübingen, published the last volume in a collection on diplomatic practice. In 1789, Georg Friedrich de Martens, a professor at the University of Göttingen, published his *Précis du droit des gens moderne de l'Europe fondé sur les traités et l'usage.* Both Moser and Martens advocated a positivist and voluntarist approach: law was linked to state practice and the will of states. According to Martens, every state was entitled to take military action if a disruption of the balance of power might threaten its independence.[4] Johan Ludwig Klüber continued in this realistic spirit

[3] Nussbaum 1958, p. 158. Vattel 1916, Book III, Chapter 3, paras 34 and 49. *Cf.* Boucher 1998, pp. 265–267.

[4] Koskenniemi 2002, p. 20.

with his *Europäisches Völkerrecht* of 1821, also published in French. These writers were inspired by the frequently cited Vattel, who held that international law was not superior to states but rather a useful tool between states.[5]

This was the core of the international law doctrine published during Clausewitz's life. He could not have been expected to follow this discourse, or know any details about it, but he should have been familiar with his fellow Prussian countryman in Austrian Imperial service, Friedrich von Gentz, and his book *Fragmente aus den neuesten Geschichte des politischen Gleichgewichts in Europa* (1806). Von Gentz was heavily disturbed by Napoleon's upheaval of the European traditional balance and expressed the need for national self-determination, balance of power, equality of states, peaceful coexistence and joint action against peacebreakers. As a consequence, he supported normative development towards a prohibition against the first use of force in relations between states. However, in light of his later association with Metternich and the post-1815 big power doctrine of armed intervention against revolutionary movements in other states, his commitment to a genuine *jus contra bellum* approach can be doubted.

Vattel died in 1767, but his views on war were still in vogue during Clausewitz's time. Vattel did not, as we have seen, outlaw war as such. He acknowledged the intermittent necessity of war. He accepted the legal importance of then-current state practices. He was a voluntarist. In many situations, there was a right to go to war, a *jus ad bellum*, but he advocated humanitarian restrictions in warfare, a *jus in bello*. How, then, did Clausewitz's writings relate to these concepts?

17.3 Clausewitz and *Jus ad Bellum*

As a theorist on strategy and tactics, Clausewitz was not overtly interested in normative propositions of a legal nature. His pronouncement that war is a continuation of politics by other means implies a certain normality of political decision-making crossing the border between peace and war. His thesis may give the impression of belonging to another age, but in 2014 President Putin's failed politics (to support a Russian-friendly president in Kyiv) led to new politics (a decision to conquer the Crimea) that in 2022 was followed by further military decision-making (the full-scale invasion of Ukraine). War was a continuation of politics by other means.

When Clausewitz in his chapters on strategy emphasizes 'moral factors' or 'moral elements', he does not mean international morality in foreign policy, but the morale of soldiers as a positive factor in combat. He refers to the 'troop's national feeling'—enthusiasm, fanatical zeal, faith and general temper—as a general good, but above all as a valid factor in mountain warfare 'where every man, down to the individual soldier, is on his own'.[6] Also, there is a need for a professional pride (*esprit de corps*)

[5] O'Connell 2012, p. 278.

[6] Howard and Paret 1993, p. 218, quoting from *On War*, Book Three, Chapter Four.

which forms, he argues, 'the bond between the various natural forces that activate the military virtue'.[7]

However, this approach is related only to combat and its efficiency, not to the idea of a just war. The concept of *bellum justum* was introduced by Roman lawyers (Cicero, Livy), followed up by religious philosophers (St Augustine, Thomas Aquinas) and later developed by Grotius, Pufendorf, Locke and, to a certain extent, Kant.[8] Clausewitz should have been somewhat aware of the just war doctrine. However, he did not seem to acknowledge that a communal spirit will increase if the soldiers feel that they are fighting for a right cause, to defend their country or to save others from massacres (humanitarian intervention). Soldiers would feel proud to belong to an army that offers protection to innocent civilians—children, women and old people. A psychological awareness of doing the morally right thing increases self-esteem and combat value.

Anatol Rapoport has written, in the introduction to the older Penguin edition of *On War,* that many soldiers during the French revolution, belonging to the revolutionary French army, felt 'that they were carrying the Rights-of-Man on the points of their bayonets across Europe'. Their successes kept their 'martial elan at a high pitch', and this was later of benefit to the imperial *Grand Armée.*[9] There was a feeling of being involved in a *bellum justum.*

Of course, it has to be admitted that Clausewitz had no reason to argue in line with just war thinking, with a norm condemning the first use of force. During his time, there was no such norm. Not until the First Hague Peace Conference of 1899 was a first legal step taken in this direction. A system for peaceful solution of conflicts was instituted and further developed at the Second Hague Peace Conference of 1907. Even if Clausewitz could not be expected to foresee this legal development, he should have been aware of the emerging political peace movement in the United States and Europe in 1815–1830 (to which we will return later).

What he says about the possibilities for one party in a political conflict to perform a military attack on another shows that he does not envisage any political or legal restrictions whatsoever in such a situation. In his Eighth Book on military planning, he writes:

> No one starts a war – or rather, no one in his senses ought to do so – without first being clear in his mind what he intends to achieve by that war and how he intends to conduct it. The former is its political purpose; the latter its operational objective.[10]

In an earlier chapter on strategy and the parties to the conflict, he writes that one of the parties must of necessity be the aggressor:

> Politically, only one can be the aggressor: there can be no war if both parties seek to defend themselves. The aggressor has a positive aim, while the defender's aim is merely negative. Positive action is therefore proper to the former, since it is the only means by which he can

[7] Ibid. p. 219 f.

[8] *See*, for each of the mentioned names, Boucher 1998, Index.

[9] Rapoport 1984 in his Editor's introduction to *On War,* p. 20.

[10] Howard and Paret 1993, p. 700.

> achieve his ends. Consequently when conditions are equal for both parties the attacker ought to act, since his is the positive aim.[11]

In a chapter on the strategic relationship between attack and defence, it is underlined that among factors crucial to success, *surprise* is the most prominent one, either through the attack as such or through the unexpected large deployment of troops in a certain area. In the Eighth Book, it is added that a war of aggression, using a favourable early moment for attack, is the best option when the passage of time will only serve the enemy. Here, one is reminded of the Six-Day War, when Israel in June 1967 attacked the Egyptian airfields sooner rather than later.

Clausewitz outlines different examples of his own, including this one:

> Let us suppose a small state which is involved in a contest [a political conflict] with a very superior power, and foresees that with each year its position will become worse: should it not, if war is inevitable, make use of the time when its situation is furthest from the worst? Then it must attack ....[12]

Clausewitz was here probably thinking of Frederick the Great of Prussia, who in 1756 was threatened by a Franco-Austrian-Russian coalition that was ready to crush him. He decided to forestall his enemies, in particular the Empress Maria Theresia in Vienna, and successfully invaded Saxony and thereby unleashed the Seven Years War (1756–1763).

Nothing in *On War* indicates that Clausewitz took an interest in the moral question whether the belligerents were in a position to justify their action. He accepted and sanctioned 'the first use of force', which would later be prohibited. In a sense, he deplored the belligerents that, from a military perspective, found themselves in a less favourable 'second use' situation, acting in self-defence.

17.4 Clausewitz and *Jus in Bello*

After the Enlightenment, there was a certain knowledge among the intellectual elite of the legal and philosophical thought produced through the centuries. In the tradition of natural law, a number of thinkers had proclaimed the need for humanitarian restrictions in warfare: Alberico Gentili in 1598, Hugo Grotius in 1625, Samuel Pufendorf in 1673 and others. Their books were translated and republished in a number of editions over time. Grotius and his predecessor Gentili laid the foundation for a *jus in bello*, including an element of human rights ideology with regard to the protection of civilians and prisoners of war. It has always been the case that 'laws of war' and 'individual rights' coalesce to a certain extent.

Pufendorf contributed to the emerging notion that man possessed certain fundamental rights in a state of nature—and when civil society came into being, these rights remained protected by natural law. This position was reaffirmed and further

[11] Ibid. p. 253.

[12] Rapoport 1984, p. 398, quoting from *On War*, Book Eight, Chapter Five.

developed in the writings of John Locke. He argued, in *Two Treatises of Government* (1689–1690), that natural law produced fundamental individual rights that clearly restricted the freedom of rulers.

Vattel, in fact, put less emphasis on natural law and introduced a balance between sovereigns/governments and individuals/peoples. On the other hand, when he discussed the responsibility of a ruler for an unjust war, he also argued in terms of *jus in bello:*

> He [the sovereign] is responsible for all the evils and all the horrors of the war. The bloodshed, the desolation of families, the pillaging, the acts of violence, the devastations and conflagrations are all his work and his crime.[13]

As already noted, Vattel argued that the guilty sovereign should repay the evil done and must 'even submit to punishment', although he did not clarify who could inflict the punishment.[14]

We do not know how much Clausewitz knew about the doctrine of international law. We cannot expect him to be well-informed, but he should have been aware of the main tenets of discussion, including the issue of humanity in warfare. He ought to have had an informed view on humanitarian restrictions in warfare.

In the very beginning of the first chapter in *Vom Kriege*, war is defined as an act of force 'to compel our enemy to do our will'. Thereafter, follows this often quoted and controversial statement:

> Attached to force are certain self-imposed, imperceptible limitations hardly worth mentioning, known as international law and custom, but they scarcely weaken it.[15]

An older translation classified the 'restrictions' as 'almost imperceptible'.[16] That wording would indicate that Clausewitz does not deny the existence of international law as such; he admits that law accompanies the acts of war, but such 'self-imposed restrictions' are 'almost imperceptible' and do not essentially impair the power of force.

Also, Clausewitz admits that wars of civilized nations tend to be less cruel and destructive than those of 'savages'.[17] Civilized nations may not put their prisoners to death or devastate towns and countryside—but that is, according to Clausewitz, an effect of social conditions, not an intellectual choice. He does not see the practice of civilized countries as linked to legal developments.

Clausewitz shows no interest in emerging human rights or laws of war, but at one point condemns certain warfighting in the past, by Tartars and others, as 'unnecessary barbarity'. Here, he comes close to the modern concept of 'unnecessary suffering',[18]

---

[13] Nussbaum 1958, p. 159, quoting from Vattel, *Le Droit des Gens,* Book III, Chapter 3.

[14] Ibid. p. 158.

[15] Howard and Paret 1993, p. 83, quoting from *On War,* Book One, Chapter One.

[16] The 1908 translation of Graham in Rapoport 1984, p. 101. A Swedish translation coincides with the Rapoport edition. *See* Martenson et al. 2002, p. 29: 'knappt nämnvärda begränsningar ... i form av folkrättsliga regler' (limitations barely worth mentioning ... in the form of international law rules).

[17] Howard and Paret 1993, p. 84.

[18] Ibid. p. 714.

a concept that in the medieval practice of chivalry translated into a prohibition of poisoned weapons.

Clausewitz rejects any ideas of philanthropists or legal reformers to introduce a 'principle of moderation' in warfare as a 'logical absurdity'. The 'mistakes which come from kindness are the very worst'.

> The maximum use of force is in no way incompatible with the simultaneous use of the intellect. If one side uses force without compunction, undeterred by the bloodshed it involves, while the other side refrains, the first will gain the upper hand.[19]

He further argues that the constant technical developments, the invention of gunpowder and the improvement in the construction of firearms are sufficient proofs that 'the tendency to destroy the adversary which lies at the bottom of the conception of war is in no way changed or modified through the progress of civilization'.[20]

Clausewitz continuously repeated his statement that war is an act of violence 'pushed to its utmost bounds', without any restrictions. However, such restrictions were later to come, at the international military conference in St. Petersburg in 1868. It was then declared that weapons causing human suffering not required for putting soldiers out of combat should be prohibited. This general declaration was followed by a concrete prohibition. The prohibition concerned the use of small explosive bullets of a magnitude to hit human targets, which then detonated in the human body. Thus, the principle of unnecessary suffering was introduced in the emerging laws of war. At that time, Clausewitz had been dead for thirty-seven years.

17.5 Rules of Chivalry

Even if Clausewitz had a point when he did not detect any binding legal rules restricting warfare, he should have been aware of an earlier quasi-customary law development. It should have been possible for him to accept rules of chivalry from the later Middle Ages—notions of a gentlemanly conduct that would lend themselves to be applicable also in his own time.[21] These rules were brought forward and commented upon by legal writers of the Renaissance, such as Francisco de Vitoria (d. 1546), Alberico Gentili (d. 1608), Francisco Suárez (d. 1617) and Hugo Grotius (d. 1645).

The rules of chivalry were based on military custom and royal ordinances of war issued by the rulers of late medieval Europe. These customary norms were not initially

[19] Ibid. p. 84.

[20] Rapoport 1984, p. 103.

[21] An example of gentlemanly conduct, although not concerning warfare as such, is pictured by the Spanish painter Velasquéz in his famous painting 'The capitulation of Breda' from 1635. The victorious Spanish general receives the keys to the conquered city from the hands of its burgomaster, and the victor does this with a friendly smile expressing compassion with another human being. Obviously, such human behaviour does not contradict Clausewitz's insistence that war requires 'the utmost use of force'.

a body of law governing the relations of nations, but 'a body of norms governing the conduct of warring men',[22] of relevance in particular to the nobility, knights and military commanders. Notions of duty and honour were important. The chivalric code of conduct required that a knight defeated in battle be given quarter rather than being killed, and be treated as a gentleman when taken prisoner. Chivalry involved such humane and noble principles as aid for the weak and helpless: protection of old people, young children and women (in particular those confined by childbirth). Those who took no part in the hostilities should not be imprisoned.

The French philosopher, author and early feminist Christine de Pisans (d. circa 1430), who compiled the rules of chivalry in 1408–1409, argued that not only was the killing of prisoners prohibited, but there was an obligation to accord them humane treatment. Moreover, she advocated the death penalty for soldiers committing pillage and proclaimed a prohibition on poisonous weapons, which she considered so inhumane as to be against the law of war for Christians.[23]

Ordinances of War issued by the armies of England in 1640 and Scotland in 1643 prohibited the killing of an enemy who had surrendered. In other words, a right to quarter was instituted.[24] Such norms were observed because chivalric honour required obedience of them. A breach of the code of conduct meant dishonour and shame but no general application of the rules can be expected to have occurred. Privileged treatment was often reserved for knights and leaders. Gentili lamented that, in practice, soldiers were slain, whereas wealthy leaders could rely on relatives paying ransom to free them.[25]

Clausewitz does not refer to chivalry, although he mentions one of the norms in question: the non-killing of prisoners. He writes that 'if, then, civilized nations do not put their prisoners to death or devastate cities and countries, it is because intelligence plays a larger part in their methods of warfare and has taught them more effective ways of using force than the crude expression of instinct'.[26]

With regard to 'rude acts', torture has always been part of the history of man. In 1819, Walter Scott published his famous novel *Ivanhoe* (set in late 12th century's England), which included aspects of chivalry and torture. Isaac, the Jew, is in the hands of a Norman knight and threatened by terrible torture if he does not deliver amounts of gold or silver. "Have mercy on me, noble knight!", said Isaac, "I am old, and poor, and helpless."[27] However, ideas of chivalry are non-existent in this situation and cannot help him.

Clausewitz must have reflected on the interrogation needs with regard to enemy prisoners. In his chapter 'Intelligence in War', he notes:

---

[22] Meron 2002, p. 10.

[23] Meron 2002, p. 116.

[24] Ibid. pp. 151–152.

[25] Ibid. p. 73.

[26] Howard and Paret 1993, p. 85.

[27] Scott 2000, p. 181.

> Many intelligence reports in war are contradictory; even more are false, and most are uncertain. What one could easily ask of an [intelligence] officer is that he should possess a standard of judgement, which he can gain only from knowledge of men and affairs and from common sense. He should be guided by the laws of probability.[28]

Nothing is said about physical pressure in interrogations. Torture is neither recommended nor prohibited. On the other hand, *Vom Kriege* was not written as a manual for the armed forces.

Walter Scott's *Ivanhoe* presents an interesting and positive picture of chivalry.[29] Scott, who died in 1832, was widely read during Clausewitz's time (and later), and his historic novels were translated into most European languages. Even if Clausewitz had not read *Ivanhoe*, he should have known of the notion of chivalry.

17.6 The Search for Peaceful Solutions to Conflicts

No legal obligation to seek a peaceful solution of disputes threatening international peace and security existed during Clausewitz's lifetime—or later in the 1800s—although such a norm (of a somewhat vague character) did emerge through the Hague Conventions of 1899 and 1907. On the other hand, already at the end of the Napoleonic wars, Quakers and other religious groupings had started a peace movement in the USA. In 1815, William Low Dodge formed a peace organization in New York, and in 1828 William Ladd assembled various groups in a central organization, *the American Peace Society*. A similar development followed in Europe, inspired by the American example. National peace organizations were founded in Great Britain (1816), France (1821) and Switzerland (1830). The first World Peace Congress was held in London in 1843. International arbitration was soon put forward as a method where states, before a conflict between them was a fact, agreed in a treaty to submit any peace-threatening dispute to impartial settlement. How did Carl von Clausewitz react to this development?

The answer is: he did not! He was not interested in the prevention of wars, although he underlined the need for a good reason to start one. He probably saw international conflicts as an unavoidable phenomenon due to geopolitical reasons. It was not his task to take into account methods for peaceful settlement. He focused on war as such.

---

[28] Ibid. p. 136.

[29] The hero Ivanhoe sees chivalry only as the pursuit of glory in combat. The 'fair maiden' Rebecca, who is imprisoned with Ivanhoe in a Norman castle under attack by Saxons, is not content with this bellicose attitude and wants a more humanitarian approach. When the Saxon attackers, who are the presumptive rescuers of them both, hurl the defenders into the moat, Rebecca exclaims: 'O men, if you are indeed men, spare them who can resist no longer'. Ivanhoe does not respond positively to this but later reinterprets and expands on 'the laws of chivalry'. He now includes among the noblest aspirations of knights the protection of the weak: 'Chivalry! Why, maiden, it is the nurse of pure and high affection—the stay of the oppressed, the redresser of grievances, the curb of the power of the tyrant.' For page references to Scott's work, *see* Bring 2009, pp. 14–15.

Clausewitz consistently argued that the enemy fighting forces must be annihilated, *i.e.*, be put in such a situation that they could not continue their resistance. The enemy territory had to be conquered, occupied or controlled, in order to prevent recruitment of additional military units. Annihilation (*Vernichtung*) is the fundamental principle in war and the total defeat of the enemy will best be accomplished in decisive battles. However, annihilation could also be accomplished in other situations where enemy troops were assembled in big numbers. This kind of advice, on how to achieve complete victory, seems to be directed only at the aggressor, which is in a situation to choose between different options of attack. As a consequence, this approach of Clausewitz will find itself in total contradiction with the peaceful settlement approach, aimed at prevention of the outbreak of hostilities.

Clausewitz asserts in the first chapter of *Vom Kriege,* a chapter he regards as finalized, that the purpose of war is to make the enemy 'utterly defenceless', though this is not true in a war of self-defence, where it is enough to stop the enemy from fulfilling its aggressive intentions. Thus, the annihilation principle is not without exceptions.

Clausewitz also admits that a war can be ended before the enemy is defenceless and that, at that point, peace negotiations or arbitration proceedings may take place. The idea of the peace movement was that arbitration should prevent war, not terminate it, though the latter outcome was nevertheless acceptable to peace activists under certain circumstances.

Overall, Clausewitz did not look upon *Vom Kriege* as a completed and finished piece of work. He had made notes on revisions and additions and wanted to make clear that there were two kinds of war: *limited war,* where the purpose of hostilities was to create a space for peace negotiations, and *total war,* where the purpose was to make the enemy completely defenceless in order to be able to *dictate* the terms of a peace treaty.

These options for states were also inconsistent with the idea that states should enter into arbitration agreements early on, to prevent a later outbreak of war. This idea of prevention was inspired by a treaty of 1794 concluded between the former enemy states of the USA and the UK—the so-called Jay Treaty, named after an American diplomat. The first US President George Washington, in office between 1789 and 1797, had realized the advantages of preventive arbitration agreements.

In the legal doctrine, Emmerich de Vattel was an early spokesman for peaceful settlement of disputes, through multilateral negotiations, enquiry commissions or arbitration, but at the same time he warned states from using legal proceedings in cases where their basic security interests were threatened. Had Clausewitz known about this warning, he would surely have agreed with it.

17.7 Concluding Remarks

Many commentators on Clausewitz convey the impression that he denies the very existence of international law. This is an overstatement. I will quote again a sentence from the first page of his book, this time with some important words in italics. To the question 'What is war?', he answers 'An act of force to compel our enemy to do our will'. Thereafter, he states the following:

> Attached to force *are certain* self-imposed, imperceptible *limitations* hardly worth mentioning, known as *international law and custom,* but they scarcely weaken it.

These limitations may have been difficult to perceive, but they did exist. What Clausewitz did not realize was that he was referring to a nascent platform of legal development. Two pages later, he recognizes that, according to custom, 'civilized nations do not put their prisoners to death or devastate cities and countries'.[30] This practice could be seen as reflecting an *opinio juris* and thus be labelled customary international law. This is not Clausewitz's view—but he does not deny the existence of international law as such. However, he rightly describes its scope and range as extremely limited at the time.

In fact, Clausewitz's views were in line with the rudimentary international law of the time. Of course, his principle of annihilation negates current IHL and the UN Charter obligation of peaceful settlement of serious disputes. His acceptance of 'total war' and its consequence of 'total subjection' of one party to the conflict is also in contradiction with the said UN Charter obligation (Article 33).

Clausewitz's military profession probably made him insensitive to or unaware of the emerging principles of international law, and he cannot retroactively be blamed for that. That his line of thought would come into conflict with later developments of *jus in bello* is shown by the two fundamental statements repeated throughout his book: that there are no limits restricting the use of force in war and that the enemy fighting forces must be annihilated.

It seems that Clausewitz's main contribution to legal development lies in his triggering of the Hegelian dialectics already referred to. His thesis of total war (rejecting 'kindness' and 'moderation' in warfare) provoked an antithesis, a position taken *inter alia* by the early peace movement (war should ideally be abolished, but where that is not possible, it should at least be regulated). This in turn led to a synthesis of later legal regulations and international agreements (the US Lieber Code of 1863, the first Red Cross Convention of 1864, the St. Petersburg Declaration of 1868, the unratified Brussels Declaration of 1874 and the 1899 Hague Conventions). The humanitarian law of armed conflicts had come to stay.

---

[30] Michael Howard's and Peter Paret's edition of *On War,* p. 85. The earlier quotation from p. 83.

References

Boucher D (1998) Political Theories of International Relations. Oxford University Press, Oxford
Bring O (2009) Humanitarian Law and Literature, Vol. 10, Yearbook of International Humanitarian Law 2007. T.M.C. Asser Press, The Hague, p. 14 ff
de Vattel, E (1916) Le Droit des Gens, Ou Principes de la Lois Naturelle [The Law of Nations or the Principles of Natural Law]. Translated by Charles G. Fenwick. Carnegie Classics of International Law, Clarendon Press, Oxford
Howard M, Paret P (eds) (1993) Carl von Clausewitz, On War. Alfred A. Knopf, New York and Toronto
Koskenniemi M (2002) The Gentle Civilizer of Nations. The Rise and Fall of International Law 1870–1960. Cambridge University Press, Cambridge
Martensson H, Böhme K-R, Johansson A W (eds) (2002) Carl von Clausewitz, Om kriget [On war]. Bonniers, Stockholm
Meron T (2002) Henry's Wars and Shakespeare's Laws. Perspectives on the Law of War in the Later Middle Ages. Oxford University Press, Oxford
Nussbaum A (1958) A Concise History of the Law of Nations. Macmillan, New York
O'Connell M E (2012) Peace and War. In: Fassbender B, Peters A, The Oxford Handbook of the History of International Law. Oxford University Press, Oxford
Rapoport A (ed) (1968/1984) Carl von Clausewitz, On War. Penguin Classics, London
Scott W (2000) Ivanhoe. Penguin Classics, London

Ove Bring is Professor Emeritus of International Law, Stockholm University and the Swedish Defence University, Stockholm. Formerly Legal Adviser at the Swedish Ministry for Foreign Affairs (1982–1993). Professor of Public International Law at Uppsala University (1993–1998), thereafter positions in Stockholm as above.

Chapter 18
Uses and Misuses of History in International Criminal Justice and Intertemporal Law

Mark Klamberg

Contents

Abstract This chapter will discuss two phenomena in the field of international criminal justice which both relate to time: the politics of historical truth-seeking and intertemporal law. The concept of truth may be given either a broad or a narrow meaning. Broad in the sense of seeking to set the historical record of a broader course of events straight, or narrow, by merely focus on the individual responsibility of a defendant. The middle ground would be to acknowledge that although the task of judges is narrow, atrocity trials may, as a side effect, contribute to writing historical narratives. The intertemporality of law deals with the dilemma that a court's pronouncement of a legal rule does not necessarily mean that the legal rule came into existence at that same point in time. The cause of this phenomenon is that international courts do not create binding legal precedents. Thus, it is difficult to pinpoint when a specific rule was established. It is not enough that an international court pronounces what appears to be a new rule. For the rule to be binding, we have to search for state consent, in one form or another, or create a fiction that such consent existed when the rule was pronounced.

Keywords International criminal law · War crimes · Truth-seeking · Intertemporal law · Corporate accountability

---

M. Klamberg (✉)
Stockholm University, Stockholm, Sweden
e-mail: mark.klamberg@juridicum.su.se

M. Klamberg et al. (eds.), *Reconstructing Power and Hegemony in Public International Law*, https://doi.org/10.1007/978-94-6265-743-4_18

18.1 Introduction

International lawyers have been accused of "misusing" history, either by selective use of history or by smuggling normative judgments in the form of historical narrative.[1] This has informed a new wave of revisionist international law histories where contextualist scholarship seeks to provide reinterpretations of canonical texts and mainstream understandings. This chapter will discuss two phenomena which relate to history and time: the politics of historical truth-seeking and intertemporal law. This will be illustrated by the *Nouri* case.

The *Nouri* case before the Stockholm District Court related to mass executions in Iran in 1988. The District Court judgment from 2022 raises the problem of timestamping, as the responsibility of the defendant was adjudicated more than 30 years after the event, during a period of rapid evolution in international law. The trial raised questions about legal constructs that either did not exist or were not fully defined when the acts were committed. Nouri was convicted on 14 July 2022 by the Stockholm District Court—a conviction upheld by the Svea Court of Appeal on 19 December 2023—for involvement in show trials and mass executions in 1988 of members of the People's Mojahedin Organization of Iran ("PMOI") and members of left-wing groups.[2] The Supreme Court denied leave to appeal on 6 March 2024, which rendered the Court of Appeal judgment final and meant it entered into force.[3] The prosecutor's indictment contained two charges, one relating to each group of victims. The mass executions happened in the context of the end of the Iran–Iraq war, where the PMOI had, jointly with Iraqi armed forces, fought against Iran. The executed prisoners had been captured several years earlier and had not themselves been involved in the war. The Stockholm District Court still found a nexus between the Iran–Iraq war and the execution of the PMOI members. As a result, Nouri was convicted under the first charge for having committed a crime against international law (a war crime). In contrast, as the left-wing groups were not involved in the Iran–Iraq war, Nouri was prosecuted and convicted under the second charge for murder.

The passage of time not only impacts on availability of witnesses and their memory, it also raises questions about to what extent present-day trials may (or may not) contribute to creating a historical record and to what extent current understandings of international law should be applicable to what happened at the time of the alleged crimes.

---

[1] Orford 2021, pp. 76 and 79; Bederman 2007, pp. 45–46.

[2] Sweden, Stockholm District Court, *Prosecutor v. Nouri*, Judgment, 14 July 2022, B 15255-19.

[3] Sweden, Supreme Court of Sweden, *Prosecutor v. Nouri*, Decision, 6 March 2024, B 204-24.

18.2 The Politics of Historical Truth-Seeking

When thinking about the relationship between the broader creation of historical accounts outside of the courtroom on the one hand and truth-seeking as part of a trial on the other, one could describe these as two potential directions of influence. The first direction of influence would be when court findings are subsequently used by historians and relevant stakeholders and actors (such as politicians, journalists, parties to a conflict, the general public) to describe a course of events. The second and opposite direction of influence would be how historical accounts are collected, presented as evidence and used before a court. This can be introduced into the trial record by the parties during their pleadings, during witness testimony or by experts heard by the court.

Wilson argues that although international criminal trials are indispensable for creating a historical account of an armed conflict, the reverse is not always true. Historical accounts produced by historians and political scientists are not always indispensable to international criminal trials.[4]

Starting with how international criminal trials may contribute (or not) to creating a historical record, the public perception is often that courts and trials have the function of establishing the truth. A lawyer would rather say that the mission is more modest: to determine what can be proven based on the evidence presented at trial.[5] Nevertheless, trials may still contribute to establishing the truth. However, the concept of truth may be given either a broad or a narrow meaning. There are certainly reasons courts dealing with atrocity crimes should seek to establish truth in its broad sense. Setting the historical record straight may be a necessary precondition for reconciliation and the avoidance of future conflicts. Further, international crimes are often conducted by groups, not individuals, in specific settings, sometimes over extended periods. This drives the judges to engage in broad fact-finding.[6] As the British prosecutor Shawcross expressed at Nuremberg:

> This tribunal … will provide a contemporary touchstone and an authoritative and impartial record to which future historians may turn for truth, and future politicians for warning.[7]

Scholars in the field of memory studies emphasize how the law may certify historical knowledge and claims about historical truths while excluding ineligible accounts.[8] There is also the "politics of memory, that is the political means by which events are

---

[4] Wilson 2011, p. 69.

[5] ICTY, *The Prosecutor v. Milomir Stakić*, T. Ch., Judgment, 31 July 2003, IT-97-24-T, para 20, paras 20–21; Zammit Borda, 2021, pp. xiii and 22.

[6] Wilson 2011, p. 69; Klamberg 2013, p. 500.

[7] Trial of the Major War Criminals before the International Military Tribunal, Volumes 1–42, published at Nuremberg 1947 reprinted 1995 by William S. Hein & Co. Buffalo, New York (Trial of the Major War Criminals before the International Military Tribunal), vol. 3, p. 92.

[8] Zammit Borda 2021, p. 2.

classified, commemorated, or discarded to influence community values and attitudes."[9] Following this logic, criminal trials should engage in "collective pedagogy"[10] challenging that "the sole purpose of a trial should be to render justice narrowly conceived."[11]

There are several convincing counterarguments to why courts lack the capacity to create a historical record. Judges act under time constraints and are tasked with issuing stable decisions upon which action is taken. Historians, on the other hand, are not subject to constraints of promptness and finality; they are free to modify their findings. Further, even if the limits of legal relevancy are enlarged, matters relevant to a full historical account will remain legally irrelevant. Additionally, seekers of genuine historical knowledge prefer to explore a wide range of possibilities and approach their subject matter from multiple perspectives instead of depending on two contrary accounts. Polarization becomes a straitjacket for historians. The best that can be expected of international criminal tribunals and courts is to provide fragmentary material that may assist subsequent historical research.[12]

Moreover, a historical record involves broader and collective events, whereas criminal procedure focuses on the criminal responsibility of an individual. To focus on individual responsibility, to separate the culpable from the non-culpable and thus lessen collective guilt, is arguably an essential part of the rationale of international criminal trials.[13] The creation of a historical record could even counter the aim of individualizing the guilt and responsibility for atrocities committed during a conflict.[14] As Hannah Arendt stated at the Eichmann trial:[15]

> The purpose of the trial is to render justice and nothing else; even the noblest of ulterior purposes … can only distract from the law's main business: to weigh the charges brought against the accused, to render judgment and to mete out punishment.[16]

Buruma went even further when he wrote "when the court of law is used for history lessons, then the risk of show trials cannot be far off."[17] There is a potential middle ground between the broad and the narrow approaches to truth-finding.[18] Some would argue that in any trial relating to mass atrocities, one "can hardly avoid creating a

---

[9] Belavusau and Gliszczyńska-Grabias 2017, p. 2.

[10] Douglas 2001, p. 2.

[11] Ibid. p. 110.

[12] Damaška 2008, p. 338. *See also* Klamberg 2013, p. 500, and Zammit Borda 2021, pp. 235–238.

[13] ICC, *The Prosecutor v. Gaddafi et al.*, PT. Ch. I, Decision to Terminate the Case Against Muammar Mohammed Abu Minyar Gaddafi, 22 November 2011, ICC-01/11-01/11-28, p. 4: "the purpose of criminal proceedings is to determine individual criminal responsibility."

[14] Klamberg 2013, p. 500.

[15] Supreme Court of Israel, *Attorney General of the Government of Israel v. Eichmann*, Judgment, 29 May 1962.

[16] Arendt 1963, p. 232.

[17] Buruma 1994, p. 142.

[18] Zammit Borda 2021, pp. 3–5, 59–72.

historical record, regardless of the wishes of its protagonists."[19] Such trials "contribute to writing historical narratives as a rule rather than an exception."[20] Moreover, there is a growing recognition of victims' right to truth as a complementary endeavor to the rendering of justice.[21] However, it is conceivable that a trial does not produce only one historical account; several historical narratives may emerge from a trial,[22] as the *Nouri* proceedings show. One can portray the production of historical narratives as a "negotiated process"[23] or maybe even as "negotiated history."

Turning to how a historical record may be used (or not) in a trial and the *Nouri* case: the Iranian regime and PMOI were and are political opponents and as such their rivalry is not only about formal control of state institutions but also about the historical narrative. Both want to portray themselves as the true and natural representatives of the Iranian people while vilifying the other, and in this context, I acknowledge that the Iranian regime is one of the most oppressive and authoritarian in the world. In view of the Ruhollah Khomeini's and fellow Islamists' seizure of the government, following the 1979 revolution, the PMOI was persecuted and marginalized within Iran, its leaders went into exile, first in Paris (1981–1986), later in Iraq (1986–2013), and currently in Albania (2018–). Although the PMOI has sought to portray itself as involved in a struggle between Iranian parties, albeit an uneven one, the Islamist regime has portrayed the PMOI as an agent of foreign powers. This arguably became most contentious during the Iran–Iraq war, when the PMOI had its headquarters in Iraq and fought with military means from bases in Iraq against the armed forces of Iran. The Islamist regime was keen to lump Iraq and the PMOI together in an international armed conflict, portraying the PMOI as traitors against their own country and people, whereas the PMOI rather saw itself as engaged in a civil war. The irony is that Nouri, on one side, and the victims belonging to the PMOI group, on the other, involuntarily had a legal interest before the Stockholm District Court to reverse these opposing historical narratives. I will explain why.

International humanitarian law (IHL)—and consequently also international criminal law (ICL)—has separate legal frameworks depending on whether a situation is characterized as an international armed conflict (IAC) or a non-international armed conflict (NIAC). The applicable law in IACs provides for more restrictions on the belligerent parties and a wider scope of criminalized behavior compared with the applicable law in NIACs. Thus, from the perspective of the prosecution and the victims (i.e., the PMOI), the road to getting Nouri convicted would be much easier if the district court first classified the PMOI's military encounters with the armed forces of Iran as part of an IAC. In contrast, Nouri's prospect of being acquitted would increase if the court classified the conflict as a NIAC. That is why Nouri and

[19] Gaynor 2012, p. 1262.

[20] *Compare with* Aksenova 2017, p. 54, noting that she makes this statement in relation to tribunals as opposed to domestic courts. However, the same reasoning may also apply to domestic courts, *see* Zammit Borda 2021, p. 31.

[21] Zammit Borda 2021, p. 8.

[22] Ibid. p. 21.

[23] Ibid. p. 28.

the PMOI in the context of the trial were pressured to acquire interests that the court would make factual findings opposite to the historical narratives that they otherwise would entertain.

Turning to the pleadings during the trial, whereas the prosecution argued that the alleged crimes were committed in the context of an IAC, Nouri conceded that there was an IAC between Iran and Iraq and that the PMOI attacks against Iran originated from bases in Iraq. However, he disputed that the PMOI attacks were part of the IAC between Iran and Iraq.[24] In other words, Nouri argued in favor of a factual finding on a crucial matter that would increase the likelihood of getting him convicted. The trial involved several groups of victims represented by different lawyers. In addition to the victims' representative appointed by the Swedish state, the PMOI had a privately appointed legal representative. The latter group of victims argued that the PMOI was not engaged in an IAC with Iran; instead, it should be characterized as a NIAC that started in 1981. In other words, this group of victims argued in favor of a factual finding on a crucial matter that would decrease the likelihood of getting the defendant convicted. Both Nouri and the PMOI victims were caught in opposing historical narratives that went beyond their immediate interests in the trial. Ultimately, the court ruled in favor of the prosecution, finding that the alleged conduct occurred in the context of an IAC, which provided the basis for Nouri being convicted.

18.3 Intertemporal Law

The intertemporality of law deals with the dilemma that a court's pronouncement of a legal rule does not necessarily mean that the legal rule came into existence at that same point in time. This will be illustrated by two questions: (1) How does the passage of time impact on the choice of legal tests and standards? (2) How can you pinpoint when customary international law in the field of IHL changes such that this has an impact on the applicable law relevant for a case?

The alleged conduct in the *Nouri* case occurred in 1988, just before the turn to the 1990s, arguably the most rapid period of evolution in the field of international criminal law. Could the legal tests and standards adopted in the 1990s apply to the *Nouri* case? Or would the parties be trapped in the time of legal austerity, when almost nothing happened, from the Nuremberg trial until the establishment of the UN ad hoc tribunals in the 1990s? To answer these questions, we must first consider the nature of international law sources.

As international lawyers, we are taught and we teach that the primary sources of international law are derived from states, in the form of either treaties, customary international law, or general principles of law.[25] In contrast, case law from international courts may merely serve "as subsidiary means for the determination of

[24] *Nouri* 2022, above n 3, p. 26.

[25] Statute of the International Court of Justice, San Francisco, 26 June 1945, 1 UNTS XVI, Article 38(1).

rules of law."[26] In other words, the traditional approach is that judges may only find existing rules—they cannot create international law. However, this perception should be nuanced. Case law from international tribunals and courts often has a more prominent role than the International Court of Justice (ICJ) statute at first suggests. Courts often cite their own cases more than treaty provisions, and scholars follow suit.[27] Case law from international courts is relevant for domestic trials provided that 1) domestic courts are under an obligation to apply sources of international law, such as treaty law and/or customary international law, and 2) the international judgments have accurately identified and interpreted the relevant rules of international law. One can debate whether international judgments are binding on domestic courts, but at the very least, they have persuasive authority.[28]

The *Nouri* case raised an interesting dilemma: there was a need for the Stockholm District Court to determine whether the alleged acts occurred in the context of an IAC or a NIAC, as the conflict involved two states as well as an armed non-state actor. In essence, this is a question about the scope of protection under IHL. One alternative would be to apply the *effective control test* first elaborated upon in the *Nicaragua* judgment at the ICJ from 1986.[29] Another would be to use the *overall control test* from the *Tadić* decision of 1999 at the International Criminal Tribunal for the Former Yugoslavia (ICTY).[30] For acts committed after 1999, this appears to be a straightforward matter. However, as the alleged crimes in the *Nouri* case occurred in 1988, the Stockholm District Court had to ponder whether it could apply the *overall control test* in relation to events occurring 11 years before the test was adopted by the ICTY. If one holds that these tests only came into existence once they were pronounced by the relevant international tribunal or court, the Stockholm District Court would arguably need to reject the *overall control test* from 1999 and fall back on the *effective control test* from 1986. The alternative view would be that *overall control* existed as a standard already before the *Tadić* decision. The assumption would be that the ICTY trial chamber did not create the standard—it found a pre-existing standard. The *overall control* standard is more lenient than the *effective control* standard. Thus, if the court opted for the first standard, it would make the remainder of the case much easier for the prosecution. The Stockholm District Court opted for the *overall control* standard without elaborating on the reasons.[31]

[26] Ibid. Article 38(1)(d).

[27] Klamberg 2013, pp. 36–43; Lo Giacco 2019.

[28] *Compare with* ICTR, *The Prosecutor v. Joseph Kanyabashi*, T. Ch., Decision on the Defence Motion on Jurisdiction, 18 June 1997, ICTR-96-15-T, para 8. *See also* Jones and Powles 2003, 141, para 4.1.17; Klamberg 2013, p. 42.

[29] ICJ, *Military and Paramilitary Activities in and against Nicaragua (Nicaragua v. United States of America)*, Judgment, 27 June 1986, ICJ Reports 1986:14, para 115. Upheld in ICJ, *Application of The Convention on the Prevention and Punishment of the Crime of Genocide (Bosnia and Herzegovina v. Serbia and Montenegro)*, Judgment, 26 February 2007, ICJ Reports 2007:43, para 405.

[30] ICTY, *The Prosecutor v. Duško Tadić*, A. Ch., Judgment, 15 July 1999, IT-94-1-A, paras 88–91, 120, 122, 131, and repeated in ICC, *Situation in Georgia*, PT. Ch. I, Decision on the Prosecutor's request for authorization of an investigation, 27 January 2016, ICC-01/15-12, para 27.

[31] *Nouri* 2022, above n 3, para 59.

However, the court was well-aware of the dilemma. Two experts were called to trial to give their views on the matter, supporting the conclusion that neither the ICJ nor the ICTY can create rules of international law—they can only find existing rules.

This begs the question: where do the *effective control* and *overall control* standards come from if they are not created by judges? There was no treaty prescribing either of the standards; the ILC draft articles were adopted in 2001.[32] It appears that the *Tadić* Appeals Chamber did make a survey and found guidance from national case law and the European Court of Human Rights before reaching its conclusion, although some of this case law was from the mid-1990s, after the events in *Nouri*.[33] The fact that the 1988 mass executions in Iran occurred in a period between two key legal decisions—one at the ICJ and the other at the ICTY—did not create a legal limbo or major incoherence.

Turning to the question of pinpointing when customary international law changes, we may start with the 1946 Nuremberg judgment. Although the judgment is often described as the ultimate peak in the progress of international law, with an indisputable impact and legacy, the trial and judgment had real legal flaws.[34] The most obvious relate to the legal basis for criminalizing crimes against humanity and to some extent crimes against peace at the time when the acts were committed. It was less problematic as regards war crimes, considering the existence of the Hague Conventions on land warfare from 1899 and 1907, and the 1929 Geneva Convention on the treatment of prisoners of war. It is also somewhat straightforward to argue why crimes against peace were criminalized at the outbreak of the Second World War, considering that the Kellogg-Briand Pact was adopted in 1928. The real problem related to crimes against humanity is the view that there was no treaty criminalizing such acts at the time of their commission, not even a human rights treaty. Such treaties were first adopted only in the post-war period. This is ultimately a question of whether the Nuremberg tribunal applied existing law or created new law—it was arguably a process involving both practices. Instead of further repeating the flaws of the Nuremberg judgment, this chapter will look at the politics of creating international law and the difficulties in timestamping certain concepts of international law as "law." The process of timestamping involves not only courts: beyond states, scholars and non-governmental organizations such as the International Committee of the Red Cross (ICRC) are also relevant actors and stakeholders. Another way of describing "timestamping" is to frame it in terms of an "intertemporal rule". When there are two substantive legal rules which differ in temporality, the intertemporal

---

[32] Article 8 of the ILC draft is an attempt to codify when a state is responsible for the actions of a private actor, a legal issue distinct from the one in *Tadić* and *Nouri*. *See* Draft Articles on "Responsibility of States for internationally wrongful acts" with commentaries, International Law Commission, 2001, p. 48: "But the legal issues and the factual situation in the *Tadić* case were different from those facing the Court in [the *Nicaragua* case]. The tribunal's mandate is directed to issues of individual criminal responsibility, not State responsibility, and the question in that case concerned not responsibility but the applicable rules of international humanitarian law."

[33] *Tadić* 1999, above n 32, paras 124–131.

[34] Trial of the Major War Criminals, vol. 22 (Judgment).

rule will decide which of the two is applicable.[35] One understanding of this rule, in line with the 1928 *Island of Palmas* award, provides the following:

> a juridical fact must be appreciated in the light of the law contemporary with it, and not of the law in force at the time when a dispute in regard to it arises or falls to be settled[36]

Moreover, Wheatley explains that time must feature in any discussion of customary international law in at least three ways:

> First, time is an important element in the creation of customary international law, because evidence of state practice and *opinio juris* only emerges over time. ... Secondly, we need the element of time to explain the possibility of change, because custom cannot say incompatible things on the same subject at the same time. ... Finally, we must, ... be aware of the influence of the passage of time ... in the evolution of the rules of international law.[37]

Crawford describes it as a dilemma: "new customary international law rules can only come into existence if we deceive ourselves into believing they existed all along."[38] By using the example of customary international law on the continental shelf, he suggests that we should abandon the idea of a "momentary" legal system, where we can write a textbook definitively stating what international law was on a specific day. Instead, he argues that we cannot tell what the law is on a specific day except after the fact. A court deciding on the applicable law needs to consider the whole body of material that was relevant to a legal rule, including the international reactions to it, not just the material evidence from the day when it may came into force.[39]

This can be applied to the *Nouri* trial and the legal basis for the charges, Chapter 22 Section 6 of the Swedish Criminal Code. The first paragraph, which is relevant here, had the following wording:

> A person guilty of a serious violation of a treaty or agreement with a foreign power or an infraction of a generally recognised principle or tenet relating to international humanitarian law concerning armed conflicts shall be sentenced for crime against international law to imprisonment for at most four years. Serious violations shall be understood to include, *inter alia...*

A second paragraph listed seven acts, constituting a non-exhaustive list of criminalized acts. The words *inter alia* in the first paragraph and the reference to treaties and customary international law relating to IHL made the provision open-ended. This forces courts to investigate the content of treaties and customary international law to determine the scope of criminalized behaviour. This makes the provision dynamic in the sense that the criminal scope adapts whenever Sweden joins a new treaty relating to IHL or customary international law evolves.

As indicated above, the scope of IHL is more far-reaching in IACs than in NIACs. Some of the rules were constructed in the mid-1990s and late 1990s by international

---

[35] Wheatley 2021, pp. 486–487. See reference to Crawford and Viles 2002.

[36] *Island of Palmas* (Netherlands v USA) (1928) 2 RIAA 829, p. 845.

[37] Wheatley 2021, pp. 487–488.

[38] Crawford 2014, p. 78.

[39] Crawford 2014, p. 77–81.

tribunals and courts, relating to acts committed in the 1990s—in other words, international courts made pronouncements on events and acts that occurred *after* Nouri's crimes. Organizations such as the ICRC, experts, and scholars argued in the early 1990s that these acts were not criminalized if committed in a NIAC.[40] This may appear strange considering that Common Article 3 of the 1949 Geneva Conventions (CA3) clearly prohibits certain acts during NIACs. However, CA3 contains neither the phrase "grave breaches" nor the phrase "war crimes." Grave breaches were mentioned only in the context of IACs and only these were subject to an explicit obligation for states to criminalize and prosecute.[41] Similarly, the defendant argued in the *Tadić* case that "prohibitions [under customary international law] do not entail individual criminal responsibility when breaches are committed in internal armed conflicts."[42] Nevertheless, the ICTY Appeals Chamber found in a paradigmatic decision in 1995 that war crimes in the sense of "serious violations of the law and customs of war," as provided in Article 3 of the ICTY Statute, applied in NIACs.[43] However, this paradigmatic decision in *Tadić* related to acts committed in 1992, 4 years after the alleged acts in *Nouri*—could one assume that the law was the same? In a sense, the Stockholm District Court was asked whether one could antedate certain international law concepts from the 1990s into the 1980s.

The timestamping of when an international law concept became law may not only determine the outcome in specific cases. It arguably also raises grander questions: how does time play into the validity of an international legal norm and who actually creates international law, is it courts or states?

Due to the evolutionary process of customary international law, Bring has made the argument that "serious violation" in Chapter 22 Section 6 of the Swedish Criminal Code only criminalizes acts committed in NIACs after 2010 and it is only after that date they may be sanctioned as such.[44] The reason for setting the year to 2010 would be that the Swedish review of the 2005 ICRC study on customary international law[45] was completed in 2010, and it was only at that time that Sweden accepted the relevant norms as part of customary international law.[46] A similar argument was made in the

---

[40] International Committee of the Red Cross (1993) Some Preliminary Remarks by the International Committee of the Red Cross on the Setting-Up of an International Tribunal for the Prosecution of Persons Responsible for Serious Violations of International Humanitarian Law Committed on the Territory of the Former Yugoslavia. In: Morris V and Scharf M (eds) An Insider's Guide to the International Criminal Tribunal for the Former Yugoslavia: A Documentary History and Analysis, Vol. 2, Transnational Publishers, New York, pp. 391–398, para 4; Commission of Experts 1994, paras 42, 52–54; Fenrick 1989, p. 259, footnote 9.

[41] First Geneva Convention, Article 49; Second Geneva Convention, Article 50; Third Geneva Convention, Article 129; Fourth Geneva Convention, Article 146 and Additional Protocol I, Articles 85, 86.

[42] ICTY, *The Prosecutor v. Duško Tadić*, A. Ch., Decision on the Defence Motion for Interlocutory Appeal on Jurisdiction, 2 October 1995, IT-94-1, para 128.

[43] Ibid. paras 84, 89–93; Abi-Saab 2001, p. 116.

[44] Bring 2020; response by Klamberg 2021; rebuttal by Bring 2021.

[45] Henckaerts and Doswald-Beck 2005.

[46] Folkrättskommittén 2010; Bring 2020.

Nouri case.[47] If this argument is accepted, it would not only prevent prosecution for war crimes in the *Nouri* case but also render the conclusion that prior convictions in Swedish courts relating to war crimes committed before 2010[48] were erroneous and persons now in prison should have been acquitted.

The counterargument, in favour of war crimes being criminalized in NIACs already from 1998, would be as follows: even though customary international law has evolved over time, the method of determining when a customary norm becomes binding upon a state (Sweden) cannot be based on when the concerned state (Sweden) accepts a particular practice, as long as the practice is supported by general practice and *opinio juris* of states. States that have been silent during such a process are also bound by customary rules when they have been established. In order to determine at what point in time a specific customary rule was established and became binding, one needs to examine the general practice and *opinio juris* of states at the time.[49] I have elsewhere argued that rather than undergoing a sudden shift in the 1990s, the process of criminalizing war crimes in NIACs was gradual, starting already with the Lieber code, the inclusion of CA3 in the four Geneva Conventions, the adoption of Additional Protocol II, changes in national military manuals and domestic criminal legislation, resolutions by the UN Security Council, and cases. There is sufficient state practice and *opinio juris* that violations of IHL in NIACs should have been criminalized already in the early 1990s, possibly earlier.[50]

18.4 Conclusions

Even though judicial proceedings have the narrow task of examining what can be proven based on the evidence presented, trials may still contribute to establishing truth in its broad sense and creating a historical record. This is arguably true both for paradigmatic cases such as that against Nazi-Germany's leaders in Nuremberg and for international crime trials in domestic settings.

The historical truth and legal rules are obviously social constructs with various stakeholders having vested interests in a court's findings on such matters. What is fascinating is that the same actor may have conflicting interests, and the desired historical account may come in conflict with determination of guilt, as illustrated in the *Nouri* case. Both Nouri and the PMOI victims were caught in opposing historical narratives that went beyond their immediate interests in the trial.

Turning to the intertemporality of law, this might be a problem unique to international law as a system where international courts do not create binding legal precedents. This makes it difficult to pinpoint when a specific rule was established. It is

[47] *Nouri* 2022, above n 3, p. 27.

[48] *See, for example* Stockholm District Court, *Prosecutor v. Arklöv*, Judgment, 18 December 2006, B 4084-04, relating to crimes committed by the Swedish citizen Arklöv in Bosnia in July 1993.

[49] Orakhelashvili 2019, pp. 33–35.

[50] Klamberg 2022, pp. 907–926.

not enough that an international court pronounces what appears to be a new rule. In order for the rule to be binding, we have to search for state consent in one form or another—or create a fiction that such consent existed at the time when the rule was pronounced. The best lawyers and courts can do is to strive for methodological stringency and transparency in how they arrive at a certain conclusion.

References

Abi-Saab G (2001) The Concept of War Crimes. In: Yee S, Tieya W (eds) International Law in the Post-Cold War World: essays in memorial of Li Haopei, Routledge, London, pp. 99–118

Aksenova M (2017) The Role of International Criminal Trbunals in Shaping the Historical Accounts of Genocide. Belavusau U and Gliszczyńska-Grabias A (eds.), Law and Memory: Towards Legal Governance of History, Cambridge University Press, Cambridge

Arendt H (1963) Eichmann in Jerusalem: A Report on the Banality of Evil. The Viking Press, New York

Bederman D K (2007) Foreign Office International Legal History. In: Craven M, Fitzmaurice M, Vogiatzi M (eds), Time, History, and International Law, Martinus Nijhoff, Leiden

Belavusau U, Gliszczyńska-Grabias A (2017) Memory Laws: Mapping a New Subject in Comparative Law and Transitional Justice. In: Belavusau U, Gliszczyńska-Grabias, A (eds), Law and Memory: Towards Legal Governance of History, Cambridge University Press, Cambridge

Bring O (2020) Domstolarna saknar en hållbar och konsistent linje [The Courts Lack a Tenable and Consistent Approach]. Advokaten: Tidskrift för Sveriges advokatsamfund 86(7):44–47

Bring O (2021) Klambergs och min metod kan båda vara tillämpliga [Both Klamberg's and My Approach May Be Applicable]. Advokaten: Tidskrift för Sveriges advokatsamfund 87(7):50–51

Buruma I (1994) The Wages of Guilt: Memories of War in Germany and Japan, 1st edn. Farrar, Straus, and Giroux, New York

Crawford J (2014) Chance, Order, Change: The Course of International Law, Chance, Order, Change: The Course of International Law, The Hague Academy of International Law: General Course on Public International Law

Crawford J, Viles T (2002) International Law on a Given Day. In; Crawford J, International Law as an Open System: Selected Essays, Cameron May, London

Damaška M (2008) What is the Point of International Criminal Justice? Chicago-Kent Law Review 83(1):329–365

Douglas L (2001) The Memory of Judgment: Making Law and History in the Trials of the Holocaust. Yale University Press, New Haven

Fenrick W J (1989) The Prosecution of War Criminals in Canada. Dalhousie Law Journal 12(2):256–297

Folkrättskommittén (2010) Folkrätt i väpnad konflikt - svensk tolkning och tillämpning [International Law in Armed Conflict - Swedish Interpretation and Implementation], SOU 2010:72

Gaynor, F (2012) Uneasy Partners - Evidence, Truth and History in International Trials. Journal of International Criminal Justice 10(5):1257–1275

Henckaerts J-M, Doswald-Beck, L (eds) (2005) ICRC, Customary International Humanitarian Law. Cambridge University Press, Cambridge

Jones J R W D, Powles S (2003) International Criminal Practice, 3rd edn. Transnational Publishers, Inc. and Oxford University Press, Ardsley and Oxford

Klamberg M (2013) Evidence in International Criminal Trials: Confronting Legal Gaps and the Reconstruction of Disputed Events. Martinus Nijhoff Publishers, Leiden

Klamberg M (2021) Har svenska domstolar dömt fel i mål om krigsförbrytelser? [Have Swedish Courts Ruled Wrongly in War Crime Trials?]. Advokaten: Tidskrift för Sveriges advokatsamfund 87(6):36–37

Klamberg M (2022) Prosecuting Corporate Executives for War Crimes in Sudan. New York University Journal of International Law and Politics 54(3):887–939

Lo Giacco L (2019) Citing Matters: An Analysis of the Use of Judicial Decisions in International Criminal Law Adjudication through the Lens of Law-Making. Lund University, Lund

Morris V and Scharf M (eds) (1993) An Insider's Guide to the International Criminal Tribunal for the Former Yugoslavia: A Documentary History and Analysis, Vol. 2, Transnational Publishers, New York

Orakhelashvili A (2019) Akehurst's Modern Introduction to International Law, 8th edn. Routledge, London and New York

Orford A (2021) International Law and the Politics of History. Cambridge University Press, Cambridge

Wheatley S (2021) Revisiting the Doctrine of Intertemporal Law. Oxford Journal of Legal Studies, 41(2):484–509

Wilson R A (2011), Writing History in International Criminal Trials, Cambridge University Press, Cambridge

Zammit Borda A (2021) Histories Written by International Criminal Courts and Tribunals. T.M.C. Asser Press I Springer, The Hague

Mark Klamberg is Professor in Public International Law at Stockholm University and Deputy Director at the Stockholm Center for International Law and Justice (SCILJ). He has the following affiliations and appointments: research fellow with the Centre for International Law Research and Policy (CILRAP), fellow with the American University Washington College of Law, Washington D.C., nonresident Senior Fellow with the Atlantic Council, Washington D.C., expert to the Consultative Council at the National School of Judges of Ukraine, expert for OSCE ad hoc missions as part of its human dimensions mechanism (also known as the Moscow mechanism), and board member for the Raoul Wallenberg Institute of Human Rights and Humanitarian Law, Lund. He did his post doc at the University of Oxford, Institute for European and Comparative Law, and has been a scholar-in-residence at the School of International Service (SIS), American University, Washington D.C., and Senior Fellow at the Carter School of Peace and Conflict Resolution, George Mason University, Arlington.

Chapter 19
State Sovereignty and the Origins of International Legal Formalism

Martti Koskenniemi

Contents

Abstract This essay explores the historical and intellectual context of the late-19th century that led public international law to adopt a formalist focus on the sovereign will of states. The discussion of the work of four German-speaking academics—Carl Wilhelm von Gerber, Georg Jellinek, Carl Menger and Max Weber—situates the rise of modern "public international law" within the debates concerning the specialization of different types of social science—namely those of public law, economics, and sociology. The essay highlights the impact of the methodological separation of these disciplines on the formalist orientation of international law. The analysis underscores the tension between legal abstraction and empirical social phenomena, revealing the challenges of thinking about international governance by focusing exclusively on the principles of sovereignty and the rule of law.

Keywords Georg Jellinek · Max Weber · Carl Wilhelm von Gerber · Carl Menger · Sovereignty · Statehood · Legal formalism · Economics · Sociology

---

M. Koskenniemi (✉)
University of Helsinki, Helsinki, Finland
e-mail: martti.koskenniemi@helsinki.fi

M. Klamberg et al. (eds.), *Reconstructing Power and Hegemony in Public International Law*, https://doi.org/10.1007/978-94-6265-743-4_19

19.1 The Weight of Sovereignty

'States are sovereign.' 'International law is based on State sovereignty.' 'Sovereign States are the only original subjects of international law.' Statements like these could be gathered *ad infinitum* from international law texts—official documents and writings of lawyers and diplomats. Although sovereignty has been the object of persistent criticism from the very inception of the field in the late 19th century, even critics have tended to presume the great importance of sovereignty in the international world, and that its holder is the (modern) State. No better authority can be cited for this proposition than Lassa Oppenheim in the first edition of his *International Law* of 1904:

> ...the science of politics has learned to distinguish between sovereignty of the State and sovereignty of the organ which exercises the power of the State. The majority of publicists teach nowadays that [none of those organs] is originally Sovereign in a State, but the State itself. Sovereignty, we say nowadays, is a natural attribute of every State as a State.[1]

This sentence makes two important points—namely that there is a history to 'sovereignty' in the course of which the holder of that attribute has changed from a person or a group to an abstraction, namely the State, and that we know this owing to the 'science of politics' as represented by 'the majority of publicists'. Oppenheim had received his legal training in Germany, where the legal academy had long been oriented in a historical direction whose excesses had—by the end of the century—become the subject of criticism. One legacy of those debates has been the centrality of 'doctrine', or the teachings of 'publicists', for what we think international law is or should be. The idea of a system of contractual relations between States, understood as 'legal subjects' whose sovereignty meant that they could only be bound by their 'will', was part of the globalization of so-called 'classical legal thought', as developed by late 19th century German public lawyers.[2] Here is a famous statement of its key ideas by the Permanent Court of International Justice in the *Lotus* case in 1927:

> International law governs relations between independent States. The rules of law binding upon States therefore emanate from their own free will as expressed in conventions or by usages generally accepted as expressing principles of law and established in order to regulate the relations between these co-existing independent communities or with a view to the achievement of common aims. Restrictions upon the independence of States cannot therefore be presumed.[3]

This made official the view of international law as an effect of what sovereign States have willed or not willed, what kinds of conventions or usages they have established and how to interpret those, how to derive general principles from them and collect

---

[1] Oppenheim 1905, pp. 106–107.

[2] On classical legal thought, *see, e.g.*, Kennedy 2006, pp. 25–37.

[3] Case of the S.S. Lotus, Permanent Court of International Justice, P.C.I.J. (ser. A) No. 10 (1927), para 44.

them into something coherent—perhaps representing shared values or purposes—that may be called a 'system', within which professional specialization could become possible.

The *Lotus* principle has, of course, been severely critiqued over the course of the decades. Many later lawyers have been extremely reluctant to accept the central position of 'sovereign States' for understanding the world and have suggested alternative frames based either on individualist humanism or some idea of a 'moral community' or an 'international society'. Their influence has remained marginal, however, and most proposals have been forgotten almost as soon as they have been presented. However, one significant caveat should be noted. All of this describes a distinctly 'European' way of thinking about international law. Postwar writings and attitudes in the United States regarding the role of law in the global world have developed in a totally different direction and it is possible to question the official commitment of lawyers from the developing countries to this way of thinking, which has been subtly complicit in the formation and maintenance of the extremely unequal system of distributing material and spiritual values in the world.[4]

I have elsewhere argued about international law as a 'German discipline'.[5] My intention here is to support that provocation by examining the writings of four German-speaking academics from the late 19th and early 20th centuries who contributed greatly to the organization of the social science academy as well as to thinking about the modern 'sovereign State'. Through this division of labour, legal science came to understand the State as a 'legal subject' whose 'will' would be available in legal texts that it would be the task of lawyers to interpret and organize into a legal system. I will suggest, briefly and tentatively, that the view of 'State sovereignty' that became an important part of the conceptual arsenal of this effort, gave international law a *formalist orientation* that not only compelled it to refrain from substantive engagement with the injustices of the world, but also allowed it to become an instrument to perpetuate them. I want to argue, paraphrasing Marx, that the 19th century idea of State sovereignty *weighs like a nightmare on the brains of the living.*

19.2 The Challenge of "Society"

The most important academic work regarding the law of nations in the early part of the 19th century was produced at German universities.[6] Predominant among them was Göttingen, where Georg Friedrich von Martens had provided a new beginning for the 'public law of Europe' with his massive treaty collection, his practical teaching on the laws of diplomacy and his widely translated textbook on modern European law

[4] The contrast between European and US approaches in a theme running through Kennedy and Koskenniemi 2023.

[5] Koskenniemi 2011, pp. 47–72.

[6] *See* Koskenniemi 2021, pp. 873–950.

of nations.[7] Unlike his predecessors, von Martens refrained from basing his views on philosophical speculation about natural law. Instead, he began *in medias res*, first providing a list of the States existing in Europe and then describing the law in terms of the treaties concluded and customary practices adopted by them. For von Martens, the regular conduct of diplomatic relations between European nations constituted the daily management of a legal system—the system of 'modern European law of nations'. The work was anti-revolutionary, pragmatic and widely regarded as the most reliable account of its subject-matter.[8]

By mid-century, owing to Hegelian influences, and especially after the liberal disappointments in 1848, the type of 'positivism' represented by von Martens had become old-fashioned. Academics were keen to reject the view of the law of nations simply as a mirror image of official diplomacy and wished to imbue it with cosmopolitan ideas and objectives. One post-1848 proposal was to focus on the 'social question', which was becoming an increasingly Europe-wide concern. Lorenz von Stein's important writings began to grapple with the rise of social movements in France. His *Socialismus und Communismus des heutigen Frankreichs* (1842) was the first German study to take French socialism seriously and 'had a profound effect on German intellectual life'.[9] In a three-volume expansion of that work, *Geschichte der sozialen Bewegung in Frankreich* (1850), Stein began to engage more deeply with the challenges of governing a society that led its life separately from the institutions of the state.[10] For Stein, industrialization and urbanization had given rise to social classes and mass movements that could—and should—be studied per se. For that purpose, the received *Staatslehre* and public law showed themselves inadequate, having nothing meaningful to say about mass poverty, for instance, or the formation of class interests that resulted from the unequal division of property.[11] The most important public lawyer of the mid-century, Robert von Mohl, had even suggested the development of a new type of public law for that purpose, a *Gesellschaftsrecht*. Both von Stein and von Mohl also insisted that this would be a public law reaching beyond the limits of the domestic state. Whereas von Stein wrote of international institutions as managers of social problems of largely international scope, von Mohl suggested that it was now time for international lawyers to develop a doctrine of 'international society'—*Lehre von der internationalen Gemeinschaft*.[12] This was to be treated as one of the social formations that had emerged in recent times through

[7] Von Martens 1785, 1789, 1801, 1821.

[8] *See, e.g.,* Koskenniemi 2008, pp. 189–207, 2021, pp. 938–939.

[9] Siclovan 2014, p. 30. *See also* Richter (1970), p. 17.

[10] Von Stein 1850. A general statement of von Stein's position was also included in volume 2, von Stein 1852, published separately, later, as von Stein 1956.

[11] Ibid. at 24.

[12] Von Mohl 1860, p. 580. von Mohl published his work before Tönnies had made his influential distinction between *Gemeinschaft* and *Gesellschaft*—that is, 'community' and 'society', *see* Tönnies 2001. However, that work did not become widely used until the 1920s. Because both von Stein and von Mohl advocated a science of society, and both wrote about 'social formations' (*Gesellschaftliche Kreise*), I have preferred to use the translation 'international society'.

the actions of groups, corporations, social classes, associations of states and other transnational types of collective activity.

But the idea of an international 'society' with a transnational law covering important social problems shared by most European nations remained a late-liberal dream only. It could not withstand the strong push towards the consolidation of the idea of the nation-state. I have elsewhere described the criticisms of the idea of a 'law of society' and the turn among constitutional and public lawyers to renew the public law of Europe by investing it with a civilizational vocabulary and a set of developmental ideas.[13] A leading protagonist in the movement that eventually led to the foundation of the *Institut de droit international* in 1873 was Johann Caspar Bluntschli, the successor of von Mohl in Heidelberg, the drafter of the statute of the *Institut* and its eventual president. Bluntschli was well-known for his organic ideas about public and constitutional law, his internationalism and his advocacy of *Menschenrechte*.[14] He was also an adamant opponent of the introduction of the vocabulary of 'society' into legal thinking. Together with the Prussian nationalist Heinrich von Treitschke, he viewed statehood as the basic structure and organizational form of modern life. There were individuals, and there were States, he argued, and whatever common activity there existed in the space between them could without difficulty always be understood either as a form of private association or as a function of public law.[15] However, his writings were also critiqued for their superficial and occasionally frankly eccentric humanism. Though he was an efficient organizer and ideologue for the first generation of professional internationalist lawyers, his reasonings were regarded as insufficiently 'juridical' to be taken into account in the renewal of public law in its domestic and international contexts.

19.3 The Formalism of Sovereignty: Gerber

The great turn toward 'juridical' thinking about statehood was connected to the gradual consolidation of 'German public law' (*Deutsches Staatsrecht*) through the constitutional changes of 1866 and 1871. Here arose both a formal notion of the State as a 'juridical person' and an autonomous legal science devoted to a formal analysis of the constitution. In his *Grundzüge des Deutschen Staatsrechts* (1865, third edition 1880), Carl Wilhelm von Gerber gave a concise account of such legal science, in sharp contrast to what he suggested had been frequently amateurish efforts to derive public law from purely historical studies, or from political reasoning in the form of

[13] Koskenniemi 2024, pp. 107–127.

[14] *See further*, Koskenniemi 2002, pp. 42–47.

[15] Bluntschli 1856, pp. 229–266.

abstract speculations—'*Vorspiel im philosophischen Himmel*', he called them.[16] Nor did he think that studies often labelled 'positivist' amounted to more than statistical analyses of elements of state power. As a conservative supporter of constitutional monarchy, he was especially critical of the efforts of post-1848 public lawyers to think of the State as an organism, with an analogy from natural sciences: a passive function of the actions of its various elements. No, for Gerber, a State was a person, a juridical person that consolidated the legal conscience of a people in the monarch, whose will it expressed in the daily operation of its various organs.[17] A properly juridical science of public law (*Staatsrecht*) would concentrate on analysing the relations of authority and subordination, expressed in relations between a dominant and a subordinated will, within and beyond particular States.[18]

von Gerber had commenced his career as a systematiser of private law and many elements of his earlier work were preserved, in a modified form, in his treatise—and still remain today in the largely contractual understanding of a law among States. In the introduction to his main work, widely applauded by readers for its clarity and coherence, von Gerber stressed that the tasks of a properly juridical science were the exposition of the elements of the public law (*Staatsrecht*) of a specific State, as well as the systematic presentation of those elements.[19] This did not mean, he explained, that the jurist was limited to interpreting and arranging positive laws. The point was to derive larger principles from positive laws—but not from history or philosophy—that would also be used to fill the 'gaps' in positive legislation.[20]

For our purposes, the crucial thesis that von Gerber put forward was the view of the State as a 'person' and its 'will' as the origin of its norms—abstractions he readily conceded were products of legal science as it departed from its naturalist heritage. It was precisely the personhood of the State that explained its authority: '*Der Staatsgewalt ist die Willensmacht eines persönlich gedachten sittlichen Organismus.*'[21] To speak of 'State will' was meaningful only if the State was conceived as a person—with the understanding that this will was concretely present in the monarch who might be constitutionally expected to involve the estates in its formation.[22] State will was not an arbitrary 'want', however. Its direction and content were received

---

[16] Von Gerber 1880, p. 238. *See further* pp. 217–223. This was of course a reflection of the political changes from the aftermath of the liberal disappointment of 1848 that prompted philosophical-political speculation about State law in general (*allgemeine Staatslehre*) and that ended with the establishment of the imperial constitution in 1871.

[17] For a critique of the organic theory, *see* von Gerber 1880, pp. 217–225 (Annex I), and on 'State as a juridical person', pp. 225–235 (Annex II).

[18] It would not, then, extend to cover other fields of law such as administrative law or criminal or procedural law, for example, von Gerber 1880, pp. 235–243 (Annex III). Translating *Staatsrecht* involves all kinds of difficulty. The literal translation, state law, does not convey the significance that the field has had for what in other countries is usually called either 'public law' or 'constitutional law'.

[19] Von Gerber 1880, pp. v–vii.

[20] Von Gerber 1880, p. 238.

[21] Von Gerber 1880, p. 19.

[22] Von Gerber 1880, p. 19n1.

from the ethical essence of statehood—a view that von Gerber borrowed from older ideas about *Staatszweck* (State purpose). The highest legal authority would always be the State itself; it was the State that was sovereign and this sovereignty was precisely an expression of the fact that nothing other than the State's own will could act as a motivation for its action. Talk about 'princely sovereignty' or 'national sovereignty' was merely political posturing.[23]

Despite his conservative commitment to the imperial constitution, von Gerber did not argue that sovereignty meant limitless authority. The State was to respect the ethical essence of the people that gave substance to its *telos*, its objects. These included acquired rights as well as other *Volksrechte*. These were no subjective rights, however, but aspects of objective law limiting State power. von Gerber took pains to argue that these were not just 'reflexive rights', freedoms constituted by absence of regulation, but products of the spiritual ethos of the people, positive parts of State will. That von Gerber did not recognize citizens but only 'subjects', subordinated to the *Staatsgewalt*, was, he explained somewhat disingenuously, not a limitation of their rights, but an act of generosity (*Wohlthat*) that guaranteed their membership in the nation.[24]

von Gerber's *Grundzüge* became the founding work for a new generation of *Staatsrechtler* in Germany and set the tone for a doctrine of public law that insisted on its autonomy from history, philosophy and politics and was keen to stress its professional and scientific ambitions. The rejection of the older 'organic' or 'political' views (such as Bluntschli's) was not, von Gerber explained, meant as a declaration of war on that approach. Rather, it was based on the wish to draw a clear line between natural sciences (where organic explanations were frequent) and legal science, which concentrated on conceptual construction, focusing on the State as a legal person and the law as a product of its will. Both approaches were legitimate, but they represented different standpoints. In an analogous way, the social sciences, history and politics examined the factual basis of the law, whereas legal science examined *the law itself*.[25]

19.4 Statehood Both Social and Legal: Jellinek

In 1882, the period's most brilliant public lawyer, Georg Jellinek, wrote that it had been von Gerber who 'finally' brought the discussion of public law on a properly juridical basis.[26] He then followed the older jurist in a series of wide-ranging studies, covering the whole area of state sciences (*Staatslehre*), including international law, to which he devoted a study on the legal nature of treaties (*Die rechtliche Natur der Staatenverträge*, 1880). Unlike von Gerber, however, Jellinek was a keen participant in the period's intensive debates on the character and qualities of the humanities and

[23] Von Gerber 1880, p. 22.
[24] Von Gerber 1880, p. 50.
[25] Von Gerber 1880, p. 224.
[26] Jellinek 1882, p. 4. Also Jellinek 1892, pp. 4–5.

social sciences, *Cultur- und Geisteswissenschaften,* and keen to connect the legal study of statehood to the social developments in the empire during the crisis period of the 1890s.

Jellinek wanted to argue that although the legal study and the social study of statehood had the same *object*, the two sciences were to be distinguished by the *method* with which they approached it. Human behaviour could be studied from a wide variety of standpoints—psychological, anthropological, historical, economic, as well as legal and social. Each used a specific method. Some would focus on individuals, others on larger groups or types of behaviour, some on single periods or locations, others generalized more widely. Some—such as linguistics or aesthetics—proceeded without assuming any unifying will in their object, others—such as law or social science—concentrated on activities with a collective purpose.[27] The State was an institution with a purpose, a *Staatszweck*, as generations of German public lawyers had called it. As such, it could become an object of research in social sciences (*allgemeine Soziallehre des Staates*) as well as public law (*allgemeine Staatsrechtslehre*).[28]

At the core of Jellinek's oeuvre stands the view of statehood as a human enterprise, a social and a legal phenomenon with a purpose and a collective 'will' with which it aims to realize that purpose. Nevertheless, it was not an aspect of empirical reality (nobody had ever *seen* a State). It belonged to the cultural world; it was an interpretation projected on certain institutional activities, a 'conceptual scheme'.[29] The question for the sociological and legal scholar was never 'what is a State?', but instead 'how should one [as a sociologist or a lawyer] *think about statehood*?' The former would take a historical-political perspective and study the rise, formation and decomposition of States as well as the conditions and effects of statehood.[30] For the sociologist, the State was an instrument of rule, of *Herrschaft*. For the jurists, again, it was a 'complex of legal relationships' akin to concepts such as 'property', 'sale', 'loan' or 'contract'—an abstraction whose meaning was received from the function it served and which united it with the collective will of the community.[31] All law was about human will and public law was about the will of the State as a human community, directed to the realization of State purpose (*Staatszweck*) that united the people into a '*unitas rerum*'.[32] To fulfil its instrumental role, the State had to be able

---

[27] Jellinek 1905, pp. 3–4.

[28] Jellinek 1905, p. 11. Jellinek distinguished between two forms of State science (*Staatslehre*): social study of statehood (*soziale Staatslehre*) and the legal science of statehood (*Staatsrechtslehre*). In addition, following a long German tradition, he considered there to be a practical State science, namely 'politics' (*Politik*), Jellinek 1905, pp. 9–13. Although much of his discussion of the difference between the social and legal sciences followed the familiar German debates on the difference between natural sciences and *Geisteswissenchaften*, Jellinek preferred the expression 'cultural sciences' for the latter in reference to the writings of Wilhelm Rickert, id, 3n1.

[29] '*Ein begriffliches Schemen*', Jellinek 1882, p. 24.

[30] Jellinek 1905, pp. 19, 131–132.

[31] Jellinek 1892, p. 15.

[32] Jellinek 1892, p. 23.

to rule by making its will effective against that of others, and to have that capacity, it needed to be conceived as a legal subject.[33]

As a legal subject, the State was both a lawmaker and itself bound by the obligations that it had created. Jellinek's 'autolimitation doctrine' (*Selbstverpflichtung*) combined his voluntarism with the view of States as sovereign legal subjects. If law was not present in things themselves, as taught by naturalism, then its presence reflected authoritative will. If States were sovereign, and if sovereignty meant that a State was not subordinated to any external will, then State law had to be based on self-limitation. 'Sovereignty is thus the property of a State owing to which it can only be legally bound by its own will.'[34] There was nothing scandalous or illogical in self-limitation. It had always been a banal part of the law reflected, for example, in the unproblematic assumption of the validity (and, usually, efficiency) of constitutional and administrative laws. And in terms very different from Gerber, Jellinek explained that the relation between the State and its citizens was a *legal* relationship; it was an essential aspect of the rule of law that a State was bound by the rights it granted to its citizens.[35] All this was simply part of what Jellinek, like Max Weber, called the 'rationalization process', which characterized the State as a modern institution.[36]

Nor did Jellinek associate sovereignty with omnipotence. There was no such omnipotence in the social world. Sovereignty meant both not being bound by the will of any other entity and having the ability of self-determination (*Selbsbestimmung*). 'According to its positive side, sovereignty consists in the exclusive ability of public authority to give its ruling will the capacity to bind all sides of a legal order and thus to determine all aspects of its own legal order.'[37] This was not to be confused with empirical State power (*Staatsgewalt*). Sovereignty was a purely formal concept (*i.e.*, it did not have a predetermined substance) that juristic thinking projected on legal relationships that were binding on all sides—the State as a lawmaker and the State as subject to law in its relationships to its citizens, corporations and other States.[38]

Like von Gerber, Jellinek drew a sharp contrast between a social theory of statehood and a 'legal' theory of statehood. However, unlike the older professor, he insisted that lawyers needed to know how social, political and historical phenomena contributed to State purposes in a world of change. New laws were needed—customs

[33] Jellinek 1882, pp. 31–32.

[34] Jellinek 1882, p. 34. The explanation that Jellinek gave for autolimitation varied over the course of time. In the early work on treaties, he went through a long series of philosophical, psychological and pragmatic arguments to the effect that all obligations are in one way or another self-imposed. Although in that work he finally landed on the explanation that States were bound owing to the 'natural living conditions' in the international world that compelled States to stick to their word, in later texts he returned to the Kantian categorical imperative for which free will reflected normatively on itself, Jellinek 1880, pp. 9–45. *See further* Kersten 2021, pp. 263–265.

[35] In other words, the State granted to the citizens the quality of 'legal subjects', creating them as subjects of legally recognized will, whereas the subjects recognized their being bound by the laws of the state, *see* Jellinek 1892. *See further* Jouanjan 2008, pp. 393–397.

[36] Jellinek 1905, p. 346.

[37] Jellinek 1905, p. 467.

[38] Jellinek 1905, pp. 470–471.

arise, crystallize and fall to desuetude. Political changes affected the interpretation of norms. The social and the legal were different but not wholly independent from each other. Jellinek connected the two realms ('power' and 'validity') in the famous doctrine of the 'normative power of facts' (*die normative Kraft des Faktischen*). Things that had existed for a long time tended to be consecrated as law. This did not take place automatically; facts turned into law through psychological attitudes and convictions (*Überzeugung*).[39] The human psyche was inclined to think of existing states of affair as legally proper as well.

However, Jellinek's psychological conception of law also suggested to him that modern jurists had too rapidly discarded the significance of natural law, ethical convictions and political ideologies that often challenged existing facts and the prevailing legal order.[40] There was always room for new rules and new readings of old rules. People did not simply accept existing facts because they were there. Political struggle often focused on the legitimation (*Legitimierung*) of State law.[41] These two arguments—the normative power of facts and the search for legitimation of State power—departed greatly from the kind of formalism that von Gerber had put forward and constituted an altogether more sophisticated construction. They also created an intellectually unstable ground from which Jellinek retreated to a more conventional focus on the normative meaning of formal-legal texts.

In the end, consciousness of the powers of historical factuality and countervailing political ideologies did nothing to undermine the proper juristic task, namely the 'clear construction of legal concepts' (*klare juristische Durchdringung des Rechtsbegriffes*).[42] If law was a 'conceptual frame', then it was up to legal science to translate into valid legal concepts the social transformations that affected peoples' views about valid norms and authoritative institutions. The focus was not on things or phenomena in themselves, but in their *normative relationships* to human objectives and needs. The objectivity of legal science lay in the fact that, given the fluidity of social and political life, the jurist was to abstract from it legal concepts 'in a sharp, determinate, and solid way and so as to be strictly limited against each other'.[43] Still, law was a human and practical science, not a natural science. Its conceptions resulted from close observation of real phenomena, but these were not like the facts of natural science. They rested 'within the subjective world'.[44] Although generalizations were possible, and frequent, they still depended on evaluative assumptions about what, in each experience of a phenomenon, was significant and generalizable, and what was a mere historical accident.[45] Hence legal concepts were best seen as approximations, as *types* that abstracted relevant features from phenomena in view of what seemed *legally significant* in them. In public law, one would look for *typical features*

[39] Jellinek 1905, p. 334.
[40] Jellinek 1905, pp. 336–345.
[41] Jellinek 1905, p. 345.
[42] Jellinek 1882, pp. 11, 12.
[43] Jellinek 1882, p. 14.
[44] Jellinek 1892, pp. 22–25.
[45] Jellinek 1882, pp. 12–14.

of State life.[46] For example, as Jellinek showed in his study of composite States, even legal notions (such as 'federation') were derived inductively—they existed only as 'empirical types', as generalizations that accentuated the typical features of a phenomenon.[47] Nevertheless, from these concepts it would then be possible to derive legal principles, and the entirety would then be amenable for presentation in a systemic way as, for example, 'the law (or doctrine) of federations'.

The distinction that Jellinek made between law in its doctrinal substance (*dogmatischen Gehalt*)[48] and the empirical problems of politics, history and social sciences, offered for future generations of legal scholars a sophisticated, autonomous concept of legal science that contrasted with older ways of thinking about the human social and cultural world. For this science, statehood was an abstraction that enabled thinking about a group of people in a territory as a 'legal person'. This personhood followed from the attribution to it of a certain number of purposes that enabled conceptualizing these people as having a collective 'will' (for the fulfilment of those purposes) and a unity that made it possible to attribute the actions of some people to that (juridical) person, as its 'organs'. Through such processes of abstraction and imputation, the State would emerge as a *legal subject* with the ability to create and extinguish legal relationships both within and outside its territorial and personal sphere.[49] Because all of this operated in the realm of pure form, nothing about it prejudiced the specific rights or powers that States had—thus enabling the striking everyday phenomenon that a State could be 'sovereign' both when it lived in hermetic isolation and when it had donated all its rights and powers to an international institution.[50] A world of the greatest inequality could—and would—still be described as one of 'sovereign equals'.

This otherwise elegant structure contained two fragile points. One was its psychological orientation that never proceeded to explain the access it supposedly had to other minds, the beliefs and willing of people, what made them think or want something as valid law or authoritative order. How were jurists supposed to find out what people held or did not hold as 'valid'? Could the turn toward psychology be merely a reaction to an unwillingness to pursue the naturalist line of seeking to determine what was 'right' or 'good' or 'natural', so that people had reason to regard it as such, independently of what they actually thought about it? The second problem involved the 'normative power of fact'. It is one thing to assert the likely truth that effective facts do tend to become accepted as normatively meaningful—but quite another to determine what this process involves, and when, in a single case, the boundary from pure factuality to 'norm' has been crossed. This is a question about the meaning of facts (normative or not?) and as people project such meaning differently—which Jellinek knew when he discussed the process of political critique—how would the

---

46 Jellinek 1905, pp. 32–33.

47 Jellinek 1882, p. 14.

48 Jellinek 1892, p. 17.

49 Jellinek 1892, pp. 26–31.

50 '*Aus dem Souveränitätsbegriff, der rein formaler Natur ist, folgt an sich nichts für den Inhalt der Staatsgewalt*', Jellinek 1905, p. 470.

jurist know which side to stand on? Such were precisely the kinds of questions that were pursued in the other parts of the social science academy, to which Jellinek insisted there was reason for jurists to keep healthy distance.

19.5 The Calculus of Statehood: Menger

At the time when Jellinek was developing his views about statehood as a social and legal phenomenon, another professor at the Vienna Faculty of Law and State was focusing on the same world of human activity, seeking also to abstract from its law-like regularities so as to provide a properly theoretical foundation for his discipline. He ended up with a wholly different concept of statehood. Carl Menger may have conceived his work as a contribution to the study of 'economical behaviour', but his assumptions about how to do this in a scientific manner resembled Jellinek's and would eventually rival his public law. This was a time of intense scientific and cultural creativity at the University of Vienna, where academics were focused on trying to understand the complexities of modern society through empirical and positivist methods that would be analogous, though not identical, with the natural sciences. Jellinek and Menger read the modern world somewhat differently—one aiming at a proper 'juridical' understanding, the other trying to develop 'economics' into a theoretical science. That difference of perspective provided them with different methodological tools—and, as Jellinek explained, it would be precisely those methodologies that would establish the specificity of the disciplines of which they would become widely respected authorities.

Both Viennese academics insisted on a proper division of labour between different social sciences and humanities disciplines and rejected shallow syncretism. Both were critical of purely empirical-historical methods that were unable to reach generalizable conclusions from individual cases. They respected historical studies and recognized the contribution that these had made to their fields earlier in the century. However, they now wanted to assert the independence of their fields from the historicism predominance in the German-language academy. To do this, both began with a subjectivist lens, focusing on individuals' purposes or needs. Both then addressed the difficulty of generalizing from that starting point by resorting to the notion of 'types', empirical or logical patterns of behaviour not binding in the manner of causality but nevertheless representative of truths in their respective fields. Menger even insisted that an 'exact theoretical' method was shared by all sciences, one that would identify certain basic elements of empirical reality that could be used to generate universally applicable 'exact laws'.[51]

In his explicitly methodological work of 1883, Menger provided an exposé of his 'exact-theoretical' approach and his spontaneous theory of social institutions, including law. The discussion circled around the kind of 'strictness' that

[51] Menger 1985, pp. 59–61.

can be expected of empirical versus theoretical research in economics. Empirical-realistic research (including the historical research against which he polemicized), he concluded, could only ever attain what he called 'real types' and 'exact laws', which had exceptions owing to the nature of the induction on which they were based. It enabled the formation of '...*real types*, basic forms of real phenomena, within the typical image of which, however, a more or less broad scope is given for particularities...[and to link them together into] *empirical laws*, theoretical knowledge, which make us aware of the actual regularities (though they are by no means guaranteed to be without exception) in the succession and coexistence of real phenomena'.[52] He then contrasted this with 'strict types' and 'strict laws' (also called 'natural laws') that operated in the natural sciences but also—which was his main argument—in theoretical economics. These were laws based on the identification of basic elements that were not, and were not expected to be, realized in the empirical world but would react in relation to each other and to the wholes that they formed in a way that was logically sound. Therefore, they allowed the formation of exceptionless 'strict types' and necessarily true 'strict laws'. His theoretical economics was, we would say today, focused on building logical 'models' that enabled the assessment of real conditions without, however, being exactly realized anywhere. This he contrasted with both historical economics and 'practical' economics (*i.e.*, economic policy).[53]

And what would those 'basic elements' be, from which typical forms of behaviour could be abstracted in the form of 'strict laws'?[54] Menger's first large treatise *Principles of National Economy* (*Grundsätze der Volkwirtschaftslehre*), from 1871, sought to answer that question. It identified three basic facts of human behaviour: actions of individuals, needs of individuals and "goods" (*Güter*)—things that satisfy the needs of individuals. Society was, for Menger, best understood in terms of the needs and actions of individuals. Like Jellinek, Menger believed that the feature that best allowed explaining human behaviour was the incessant search for the 'good'. But Menger's 'good' did not emerge from the 'will' of a people, it did not exist in any specifiable *Staatszweck* (State purpose). It arose from whatever brought 'satisfaction' to an individual. Therefore, his *Principles of Economics* was organized so as to describe the 'strict' (or natural) laws that linked different kinds of 'goods' to each other and to the ultimate fulfilment of the needs of individuals as consumers.[55]

The relationship between human needs or requirements (*Bedürfnis*), the foundation of economic activity, and specific goods as well as goods of higher orders was sometimes a little confusedly described by Menger as 'empirical', sometimes as

---

[52] Menger 1985, p. 57.

[53] Menger 1985, pp. 54–65.

[54] Menger sometimes spoke of 'strict' laws and sometimes of 'natural' ones. Either way, his 'analytical composite method' is very close to that put forward by Samuel Pufendorf as he was seeking the invariable core of human nature to found his natural law, in his principal treatise *De iure naturae et gentium* (1672).

[55] He distinguished between goods of the first order, that would enable the immediate satisfaction of a need, goods of the second order, that could be used to produce a first-order good, and upwards to goods of a third and fourth order and so on, measured by the distance that each good had from the immediate satisfaction of an individual need, Menger 2007.

'causal'. It is best to think of these relationships within a utilitarian means-ends frame, a kind of updated (Aristotelian) natural law.[56] Menger was an essentialist. His point was to juxtapose the 'real' (natural) needs of human beings to their merely imagined needs, to discover those 'definite laws of phenomena that condition the outcome of the economic activity of men and are entirely independent of the human will'.[57] Four elements accounted for how something became a 'good' (a thing capable of fulfilling a need): a need; an object capable of fulfilling this need; the subject's knowledge that the object has this property, and the ability of the subject to command the object so as to satisfy the need.[58] The concepts of the 'good' and of 'need' provided the basis for theories of 'value', 'exchange', 'price', 'use and exchange value', 'commodity' and 'money', each building on the foundational idea that 'value' (unlike 'price', which was just a subjective approximation) reflected the (objective) needs of the individual and that it was the task of an 'exact-theoretical science" to explain this relationship in terms of an invariable law. Two consequences followed—first, that the focus of economics was *not* to be on production, land or labour but on the needs of the individual (customer), and second, that when the value to an individual was to be measured, emphasis was to be on 'the importance of the final, marginal unit of a good'.[59]

Menger's individualism challenged traditional *Nationalökonomie* that focused on 'national wealth' as an independent object of research. This was nothing but 'a complex composite of the wealth of the members of society'.[60] This also contrasted with public law to the extent the latter operated with the collective personality of the 'nation'. For, as he explained, '[t]he nation as such is not a large subject that has needs, that works, practices economy…' National economy is the 'result of all the innumerable individual economic efforts in a nation'.[61] Menger's methodological individualism led him to stress the spontaneous origin of social institutions. He began exactly as Jellinek had done in *Allgemeine Staatslehre*, by distinguishing between *voluntary action*, oriented towards specific collective purposes, and *spontaneous action*, not so oriented. Jellinek's theory of statehood focused on the former. As the

56 For a discussion of Menger's essentialism, *see especially* Alter 1990, pp. 161–186; Caldwell 2003, pp. 21–23. For an exhaustive review, *see* Turowski 2023, pp. 1–20.

57 Menger 2007, p. 48. For the distinction between objective needs and those people merely imagined, *see* Menger 2007, p. 53. The problems created by Menger's essentialism in its relationship with his subjective theory of value is discussed at length in Alter 1990, pp. 161–183.

58 Menger 2007, p. 52. Goods existed in a first, second, third order, and so on, with successively greater distance from the first order that was the immediate source of satisfaction of a need. If bread is a first-order good, then grain is a second-order good, the bakery, including machinery, and the land are third-order goods, and so on. Much of the science of economics is about the analysis of how the value attributed by the individual to that first-order good is to be distributed to the higher-order goods that help to produce it (pp. 56–57). But each of these only has goods character to the extent that it actually contributes to serving that need. If it does not, then it is no longer an 'economic good'.

59 Wasserman 2019, p. 25. For Menger's famous treatment of the 'water/diamond' paradox, *see* Menger 2007, pp. 140–141.

60 Menger 2007, p. 113.

61 Menger 1985, p. 93.

heart of a modern public law, 'State will' was directed at the realization of certain *Staatszwecke*. By contrast, Menger was interested in the question 'How can it be that institutions which serve the common welfare and are extremely significant for its development come into being without a common will directed towards establishing them?'[62] From this, he developed his theory of spontaneous social orders: 'Language, religion, law, even the state itself [in addition to economic markets] are already met with in epochs of history where we cannot properly speak of purposeful activity of the community as such, directed at establishing them.'[63]

Like Jellinek, Menger rejected older organic views of society that had taken the physiological analogy too far. This could, in his view, at best be used as a metaphor for the rise and operation of certain human institutions. Part of the human social world does emerge from 'purposeful activity'.[64] However, when considered from their earliest origin, it was possible to find that '[l]aw, language the state, money, markets, all these social structures in the various empirical forms and in their constant change are in no small extent the unintended consequences of social development'.[65] They resulted neither from organic processes nor from agreement or legislative fiat. They were effects of spontaneous efforts by individuals to fulfil their needs. How to put this in a theoretical understanding? Money was his favourite example. Money did not have its origin in any agreement or in intervention by a public power, he claimed. It was born out of 'reciprocal conditioning' and 'mutual causation'. When an individual 'becomes aware of his economic interest, he is led by this interest, without any agreement, without any legislative compulsion, and even without regard to the public interest, to give his commodities, in exchange for other saleable commodities'.[66]

Menger gave a similar explanation to the rise of public institutions such as the State. Families did not join together in the earliest epochs by express agreement, but simply by recognizing that it was in the interests of the weak to submit to the strong for protection, or for neighbours to join together to produce their livelihood.[67] Of course, such a supposition had no empirical grounding. It was put forward as conjecture, not unlike Enlightenment histories such as those of Adam Smith.[68] Law, too, he suggested, had emerged everywhere in a thoroughly spontaneous process, based on no express agreement or legislative fiat, supported only by the gradual realization by individuals of their need for rules. Drawing partial support from Savigny, this founder of neoclassical economics speculated that: 'in the beginnings of society [everybody] is directly aware of the significance of rules for his well being. Every individual

[62] Menger 1985, p. 146.

[63] Menger 1985, p. 146. By contrast, Jellinek made an express distinction between language and law precisely on the basis of the presence of a common will in the latter.

[64] Menger 1985, p. 132.

[65] Menger 1985, p. 147.

[66] Menger 2007, p. 260.

[67] Menger 1985, p. 157.

[68] Menger defended his conjectures by arguing that what he was interested in was the primaeval origin of social institutions such as money, statehood or law, dating so far back in time that no historical records existed and that 'empirical-realistic' history therefore had nothing to work with.

recognizes that he is benefited in *his* interests by their observation on their part of the members of society.'[69] As people adhere to rules, they will gradually be socialized in community. Compliance is secured by linking the rules with a 'sanctified tradition' supposedly 'handed down from generation to generation'.[70] Unfortunately, the development of customary rules was often disturbed by the ambitions of legislators enacting new rules, as mere 'statutes' would often signal the emergence of despotic rule. This led Menger to indict the unholy alliance of Enlightenment rationalism with the cosmopolitanism of lawyers.

> ...the learned juristic class [had] turned away from the study of their own national character and one-sidedly moved in mental spheres of the developed law of other nations and of abstract law theories. They lacked not only *understanding* of the unintended wisdom of national law, but also *feeling* for it.[71]

Though Menger claimed that his interest was only in developing a theoretical study of 'economizing behaviour', he had no scruples in extending his methodological individualism and his essentialism beyond activities we would conventionally regard as 'economic'. However much his 'empirical' assumptions about the origins of money, statehood or law neglected or were contradicted by standard histories, the assumption that human action was always best understood in terms of the search of appropriated 'goods' for satisfaction of needs pushed its way into most areas of life.[72]

Menger's view of statehood as an unintended result of private efforts to satisfy needs directly challenged Jellinek's purpose-oriented abstraction. Jellinek admired the creation of American statehood, for example, as the deliberate effort to construct a republic with basic protections of civil rights. For Menger, States were merely incidental instruments for individual satisfaction of needs. He had nothing to say about rights beyond what was needed to ensure a system of exchanges that would allow individuals to get the goods they needed. Both were critics of 18th century rationalism as applied to government and society, yet both were also complete products of some aspect of the dialectic of enlightenment. Jellinek saw humans as free to create their conceptual and normative worlds in accordance with their understanding and will. Menger invited them into the production and exchange of goods for the satisfaction of their needs.

Menger's main works, his *Principles of Economics* (*Grundsätze der Volkwirtschaftslehre*) of 1871 and the *Investigations on Method of Social Sciences* (*Untersuchungen über die Methode der Sozial-wissenschaften und der politischen Oekonomie*) of 1883, were key contributions to the *Methodenstreit* among German and Austrian economic writers in the 1870s and 1880s. That struggle led to the virtual demise of historical economics and the domination of Menger's 'exact-theoretical' perspective that aimed to explain social phenomena based on their conformity to

---

69 Menger 1985, p. 226 (emphasis in original).

70 Menger 1985, pp. 227–228.

71 Menger 1985, pp. 231–232 (emphasis in original).

72 Menger defended his assumptions by observing that the 'origins' he was interested in extended so far into the past that no written sources existed, and therefore no countervailing evidence was available.

laws of needs satisfaction. The works were eventually greeted as founding documents of the 'marginalist revolution'. However, Menger's naturalist construction of objective needs was also extendable into an all-encompassing social theory that could explain the basic features of public institutions such as statehood in view of the material resources available at each moment for enterprising individuals to figure out new solutions for satisfaction of their needs.[73] Instead of the expression of a will, law became a set of instrumentalities spontaneously developed within a community. This was a conservative view that looked back to older natural law, which supposed an essential harmony of interests between individuals in a community where conflict signalled misunderstanding or lack of knowledge about how realize the 'general equilibrium' where everyone's needs would be optimally satisfied.

19.6 The Powers of Statehood: Weber

By the time Jellinek published his *Allgemeine Staatslehre* (1900), he had moved to Heidelberg where he had encountered a younger colleague, Max Weber, with whom he shared an interest in the methodology of social and cultural sciences.[74] Like Menger, both men aimed to proceed further than purely historical description but were also critical of older organic theories or efforts to seek social causalities in general concepts such as 'national feeling' or 'capitalism', for example. As Jellinek put it, 'social phenomena are never only products of general forces, but above all also achievements of determined individuals'.[75] And as Weber wrote at the outset of his *Economy and Society* (*Wirtschaft und Gesellschaft*): '[a]ction, in the sense of meaningful and comprehensive orientation of one's behaviour, is for us always the behaviour of one or more *individual* persons.'[76] They, like Menger, accepted that it was this empirical heterogeneity of the historical foundation of society that limited generalization to typical, instead of absolutely invariable, forms of social action. Making express reference to Menger, and operating with what Jellinek called 'empirical types', Weber sketched his view of 'ideal types': generalizations on the basis of individual instances sufficiently representative to be used as heuristic devices in the study of converging individual meanings or forms action.[77] However, neither

[73] Menger's reliance on active, problem-solving individuals is highlighted in Milford 1990, pp. 218–219.

[74] Weber was not an enthusiast about method, but he continued the *Methodenstreit* between the historical school and the positivists. It is well-known that Weber was in many ways influenced by Jellinek. For analyses, *see* Breuer 1999; Anter 2014; Kelly 2003, pp. 93–108.

[75] Jellinek 1905, 27.

[76] Weber 2019, p. 89.

[77] For Jellinek, an 'ideal type' denoted the complete, original or teleologically 'full' specimen of a type whereas an 'empirical type' did not have that normative sense as it was composed as the 'standard case', Jellinek 1905, pp. 33–35. Weber, on the other hand, used 'ideal type' to refer to a 'one-sided accentuation of one or a number of viewpoints…into an internally consistent mental image' that is 'utopian' to the extent that it can be used as a heuristic tool to measure empirical

Jellinek nor Weber shared Menger's essentialism or his assumption about social institutions as by-products or unintended consequences of the ways in which individuals sought to satisfy their needs. As Weber argued in his famous 'objectivity' essay, no cultural processes were reducible exclusively to economic causes, not even economic processes.[78]

Like Jellinek, Weber insisted on a sharp difference between their respective fields, law and sociology. The two had distinct 'points of view' (*Betrachtungsweise*) on human behaviour. Weber had trained as a lawyer, and his understanding of law was greatly influenced by the historicist tradition.[79] Above all, he viewed modern law in terms of its formal rationality, a quality that was the result of a long historical process enshrined in the institutions of the contract (private law) and bureaucratic formalism (public law). To work as a lawyer was to ask the question about valid law: 'What normative meaning ought to be attributed in correct logic to a verbal pattern having the form of a legal proposition?' He contrasted this sharply with the sociological point of view that would focus on 'what actually happens in a community owing to the probability that persons participating in the communal activity ... orient their own conduct towards these norms'.[80] Whereas legal science operated with textual materials and looked for the 'correct meaning of [legal] propositions' within 'a system which is logically coherent, i.e. free from internal contradictions', sociology was concerned with 'human activities as they actually take place'.[81] Despite their differing standpoints, both the lawyer and the sociologist would seek to maintain objectivity, constituted by the distance to what Jellinek called 'politics' and Weber 'value judgment'.

Still, both scholars were aware that evaluative discourses occasionally penetrated their work. It entered the assumptions of the scientists themselves and it was embedded in the objects they studied. There was no absolutely 'objective scientific analysis of cultural life...independent of special and one-sided points of view'.[82] Like all cultural activity, science was influenced by differing perceptions about what constituted a significant and useful object of research.[83] But, as Weber famously added, values were also a causally influential factor in social life itself and thus perfectly appropriate, indeed necessary, objects of research. One cannot judge individuals' life goals but they can still be subjected to research as influential elements determining social action. After all, 'a "goal" is...the idea of a result that becomes the cause of an action...and we shall take it into account, as we take into account *any* cause that contributes or may contribute to a *significant* result'.[84] Jellinek, too,

deviations. As a 'concept', it is not found as such, but 'leads away from reality', Weber 2012, pp. 125, 127, and Weber 1980, p. 4.

[78] Weber 2012, p. 113.

[79] For the von Jhering influence, *see especially* Turner and Factor 1994.

[80] Weber 1954, p. 11, 1980, p. 181.

[81] Weber 1954, pp. 11–12, 1980, p. 181.

[82] Weber 2012, p. 113.

[83] Weber 2012, pp. 105, 113.

[84] Weber 2012, pp. 120–121.

realized that law involved more than dispassionate scientific work, practical politics, namely 'a compromise between different conflicting interests'.[85] Further, he was adamant that in studying human associations such as the 'State', one could not ignore their functional character, the fact that they are set up to advance human purposes.[86] Whereas Weber wished to include all that subjective and evaluative material as part of dispassionate scientific analysis, Jellinek held that law had no business in engaging with those purposes. They were to be taken note of, but it was not the law's business to adjudicate in relation to them. His *Staatsrechtslehre* was no *Staatszwecklehre*.[87] As we have seen, Jellinek recognized the political significance of legal arguments operating through the conservative pull of factuality and the ethical-psychological push to critique the status quo.[88] Still, he could accept only two ways in which such debates should affect legal research: first, the politically impossible could not be a proper object of legal research, and there was to be a presumption in favour of lawfulness in the acts of the highest State organs. For the rest, engagement with politics was to engage with 'art' (*Kunstlehre*), not science.[89]

Weber never produced his planned sociology of statehood. Nevertheless, his views on the matter are to be found in scattered writings.[90] Like Jellinek, he regarded the State as a conceptual framework, not an element intrinsic to the world. It was a heuristic device to make sense of an 'infinite number of diffuse and discrete human actions and acts of acquiescence and relationships recognized in practice and legally'. He noted that this 'practical idea of what a state is runs parallel to the theoretical ideal type that is constructed for cognitive purposes; and the two show a constant tendency to shade off into one another'.[91] Weber's definition of the State is famous. A State is an entity that can make a successful claim to 'the monopoly of legitimate physical violence'.[92] For the purposes of his systematic sociology, he defined it somewhat more concretely as an 'institutionally organised political enterprise... [whose] administrative staff can lay claim to a monopoly of legitimate physical force in the execution of its orders'.[93]

To understand modern statehood in the Weberian sense, attention had to be drawn to both the external empirical fact of someone having a 'monopoly of physical force' and the internal, 'subjective' sense that this was a 'legitimate' arrangement.[94] Weber defined the State in terms of the *means* available to a certain type of rulership, not its objective. Whatever the *Staaszweck*, it was the monopoly of violence that was

[85] Jellinek 1905, p. 333.

[86] Jellinek 1892, p. 31.

[87] Jouanjan 2008, p. 393.

[88] Jellinek 1905, p. 345.

[89] Jellinek 1905, pp. 13–19, 14.

[90] *See further* Anter 2014.

[91] Weber 2012, p. 130.

[92] Weber 1994, pp. 310–311.

[93] Weber 2019, pp. 135–136.

[94] For Weber's famous theory of the forms of (traditional, charismatic and rational-legal) legitimacy, *see* Weber 1980, pp. 122–176, 1994, pp. 311–312.

decisive. Still, a State was not 'pure' power—it also needed to be recognized as 'legitimate'. Like Jellinek, Weber understood legitimacy in terms of the subjective beliefs (*inneren Rechtsfertigungsgründe*) of the governed. However, unlike his legal colleague, he was interested in examining its sources—namely the famous manner in which tradition, charisma and the pursuit of legal rationality produced those subjective beliefs, to which he gave the name 'legitimacy'.[95] As the meaning of a certain type of legitimate rule or *Herrschaft*, a State was neither an objective fact (of economic power, for instance) imposing itself on human beings nor the consequence of some theory (or historical stages, for instance) about social life.[96] Where Weber penetrated further than Jellinek was precisely in the way his analysis combined a minute description of the historical circumstances of the modern State with an outline of the subjective perspectives from which contemporaries experienced them.

This led Weber to think about modernity as the result of a long rationalization process in which law played an important role. He famously had much to say about the effects of formal legal rationality in different historical periods. He discussed the way its underlying notion of contractual 'freedom' had worked to uphold capitalist economic relations and the calculability of economic activities that techniques of rational administration of the modern state had made possible.[97] But also, like Jellinek, he pointed to the way in which substantive natural law concepts had emerged time and again to challenge existing formal legalities.[98] Weber's complex analyses of the interplay of formal and substantive legal rationality in fact developed into a critique of the key aspects of modern society itself. An aspect of his 'tragic' perspective is the endless oscillation that inhabitants of the modern world experience between being captured in faceless bureaucratic formalism with the only refuge available in occasional interventions by a substantive legal rationality that tends to collapse into evaluative arbitrariness ('Kadi justice').[99]

In comparison with Weber's extensive and deep analyses of the operations of the legal order, including the role of the juristic class, Jellinek's insistence on the proper tasks of legal science as conceptual and systematic work over 'valid norms' seems narrow and materially impoverished—to say nothing about Menger's conjectural histories regarding the rise of spontaneous orders. As Stefan Breuer has shown, even if Jellinek's 'social' study of statehood includes a discussion of the justifications of statehood, and the idea of 'recognition' by citizenry enters the legal study as well, confining the latter to an exercise on valid norms and their systematization does not allow any material research into what such 'recognition' might entail and how to

[95] Weber 1980, p. 822.

[96] In other words, Weber rejected both the Marxist and the 'pure' historicist frames of explanation, both contemporary rivals to his work. *See* the very useful Beiser 2011, pp. 511–567.

[97] On how formal contractual equality benefits 'propertied classes', *see, e.g.,* Weber 1980, p. 419. On how the formal bureaucratic rationality guarantees the calculability of economic transactions in capitalism, *see* Weber 1980, pp. 825–826.

[98] Weber 1954, pp. 292–300.

[99] *See, e.g.*, Trubek 1986, pp. 573–604.

determine whether it is present in a particular case.[100] Similar considerations apply to Jelinek's theory of the 'normative power of facts', which he used in order to link legal systems and statehood itself into the world of empirical behaviour. Though the rise of customary law and the emergence of an entity in the form of a 'State' may be vitally connected to the consolidation of a set of facts on the ground, he suggests no independent 'legal' way to ascertain this process. In some ways, the initial distinction between the legal standpoint and the social one is broken down into the assumption that law 'emerges' from social power—yet the process of that emergence tends to remain a mystery.

19.7 Conclusion: Law's Sovereignty Between Economy and Society

The above sketch of the writings of four German-language academics working in social sciences and law has aimed to illuminate a moment in European intellectual history when it seemed that methodological specialization was the right way to deepen the analysis and management of modern life. There was, first of all, conceptual work to carry out. What was this elusive thing, 'society', and how should its relationship to the modern bureaucratic State be understood? What should the roles of the individual and the collective be in explaining and understanding modern institutions? And what was that entity—the 'State'—and how should it be studied? Older biological or mechanistic theories might serve as analogies, but often appeared quite deceptive. The general Science of the State (*Allgemeine Staatslehre*) that arose from the amalgam between German historicism and principles of public law had its most significant representative in Georg Jellinek, who explained statehood as a central fact of modern life and as an instrument of individual purposes that crystallized in the legislative will of the State, understood as a juridical person. Its 'sovereignty' meant that it was bound by no other will than its own—a reaffirmation of the liberal-constitutionalist legalism that had had a rough ride since the disappointment of 1848. The legacy of that view reached the 20th and the 21st century in the legal voluntarism that forms the mainstay of public international law in its distinct 'European' version.

> No real 'fact' [*Sein*] is identified by legal norms. It is not the task of jurisprudence to determine the 'in-itself' of the State. Instead, it seeks to organize what is given by reference to specific purposes under a firm perspective and to subordinate the result to an evaluation by the abstract norms of the law.[101]

This is international law in its formalist mode, which has long had a bad reputation owing to its supposed ignorance about what takes place in the 'real world'. The construction of the State as a 'legal person' with a 'will' that is 'sovereign' in the sense that it cannot be bound by any other will than its own has been attacked a

[100] Breuer 1999, p. 17.

[101] Jellinek 1905, p. 132.

thousand times as utterly fictitious and illogical, as well as morally and politically pernicious. But Jellinek knew that the accusation about fictitiousness was often based on a naïve epistemology; the State was not a fiction, but an abstraction, a concept with which the world's phenomena could be grasped and engaged with. And as for its claimed negative social consequences, well, its character as a legal person in reciprocal legal relationship with its subjects and other States actually made it possible to conceive of the world in rule-of-law terms. Neither Menger nor Weber went beyond a rather unilateral *Herrschaftsverband*, the construction found also in Gerber's *Grundzüge*.

However, economics and sociology have their formalisms as well, which have tried to distance them from their historical and empirical objects. In economics, the choice has been either to pursue Menger's Aristotelianism, that assumed an essential hierarchy of needs (something a lawyer immediately interprets as one type of natural law), or to move into abstracting typical features of the world into (formal, preferably mathematical) models, perhaps in view of an abstract 'general equilibrium'. And what are efforts in empirical sociology doing to understand human (or state) behaviour by rational choice and game theory other than operating with formal models? Any pursuit of knowledge about the world through a system of propositions requires, as Weber recognized, 'the formation of clear concepts' whose very clarity is in opposition to the opaqueness of the social world.[102]

The late 19th century was a moment of intense innovation in the field of *Geisteswissenchaften*, of humanities and social sciences. My interest has been to glance at a moment when the modern university was being professionalized, with the emergence of an increasingly functional understanding of academic work. It would no longer only train the social skills of the sons of privileged families. The university was to assist in the increase of the cultural and material wealth that characterized the ambitious agendas flaunted by domestic leaders across Europe. In Germany, and elsewhere, public law (*Staatsrecht*), economics and sociology would justify the hierarchical ordering of societies in such a way as to make possible the efficient employment and distribution of domestic resources for the ostensible purpose of the general good. The contribution of sovereign statehood in this process lay in its very formality, which allowed it to spread into a universally applicable intellectual cornerstone of an emerging international order.

My own prior work has been on (public) international law—how it emerged in this period and received the character that it did, including how the notion of sovereignty was consolidated at the centre of its formal arsenal. It was both an invaluable instrument for the attainment of the kinds of purposes of which the above four German academics wrote and an object of relentless criticism in view of all the destruction wrought by it in its later history. International legal science has been at the heart of these debates. In two earlier works, I have tried to characterize the structure of this 'science' and its disciplinary and professional pedigree from 1870 to 1960. I have pointed out the intellectual influences, resources and problems inherent to that structure and described its use as part of the international law profession's ideological

[102] Weber 2012, p. 100n1.

agenda through the 20th and into the 21st century. [103]The present sketch—it is no more than that—has returned to the origins of this same 'public international law', enquiring about the debates among German-language academics in the final years of 19th century. Said debates ended up giving us three disciplinary fields and forms of professional practice focused on the same object—human action in society—but produced quite differing images of it, as well as often contradictory proposals on how to manage it. Public law, economics and sociology developed into specialist institutions, authoritative texts, methodological orientations and political biases. Although my four protagonists were aware that all kinds of struggles penetrated the world they studied, they hoped in some way to stay out of them, so as to produce useful but impartial expert insight for the ruling elites of their countries.

More than any other jurist at the time, Jellinek was aware of the roles of power and ideology in the government of the modern State. How to understand and learn to govern it in a successful way? And what might 'success', in terms of rulership in an increasingly competitive international environment, mean? Glancing sideways, he saw both the rise of an economic doctrine building upon neo-naturalist ideas about a humanity in search of material gratification and an exposé of proliferating human meanings connected to increasingly complex social relations no longer embedded in a world held together by tradition. What would be the role of public law in such a world? Jellinek accepted that statehood and law were human products designed to advance human purposes but refrained from examining how they had come about or what they should be. Public law was neither history nor policy advice. Economic policy was hugely important, and complex, but to think that ruling would be all about satisfaction of material needs must have appeared to Jellinek old-fashioned and ideologically repulsive. To know more about domination (*Herrschaft*) was absolutely imperative, but law could not remain merely its mirror image. To examine the sources of (public) authority, it did not suffice to list the psychological conditions of legitimacy. Thus, there was a role of law—of formal, public law of the kind that recognized statehood as an element of human proposes, understood *Herrschaft* as a *Körperschaft*, and described the relations between the rulers and the ruled in terms of mutual rights and obligations, available from codes of law enacted in a formal process and available for systemic exposition and critique through a 'juridical method'.

It was with this methodological choice that Jellinek was able to carve out a field between economics and sociology for understanding the governance of modern States under principles of the 'rule of law'. That choice came at a cost. The 'rigorous' distinction between legal norms, social facts and political values could not be maintained, not even by Jellinek himself, and even less in the real world of legal and political conflicts between social and economic actors with real stakes. Conceptual exercises regarding valid norms supposedly emerging from the 'will' of States enshrined the basic principles of classical legal thought but, despite the sophistication with which it was done, also its problems. How to know the 'will' of a State, and who was to be the judge of this? Later jurists in the Weimar period, such as Hermann Heller, Rudolf Smend and Carl Schmitt, would no longer trust law's formality as the structure to hold

[103] Koskenniemi 2005, 2002.

together a society in crisis. They would penetrate much deeper into the 'normative power of facts' that Jellinek had recognized superficially, using insights from Weber, in particular, to debate the contours of the 'legitimacy' of specific governmental policies. These efforts never extended to international law, where a Machiavellian realism and political economy have offered much more important instruments for rulership than public international law, with a formal sovereignty inherited from Wilhelminian Germany.

References

Alter M (1990) Carl Menger and the Origins of Austrian Economics. Westview

Anter A (2014) Max Weber's Theory of the Modern State. Origins, Structure and Significance. Palgrave

Beiser F C (2011) Max Weber and the End of the Historicist Tradition. In: Beiser (ed) The German Historicist Tradition, pp. 511–567

Bluntschli J C (1856) Über die neuen Begründungen der Gesellschaft und des Gesellschaftsrechts [On the New Foundations of the Society and Societal Law]. 3 Kritische Überschau der Deutschen Gesetzgebung und Rechtswissenschaft: 229–266

Breuer S (1999) Georg Jellinek und Max Weber. Von der sozialen zur soziologischen Staatslehre [Georg Jellinek and Max Weber. From the social to the sociological theory of statehood/State science]. Nomos, Baden-Baden

Caldwell B (2003) Hayek's Challenge—An Intellectual Biography of F A Hayek. Chicago University Press

Jellinek G (1880) Die rechtliche Natur der Staatenverträge [The Legal Nature of International Treaties]

Jellinek G (1882) Die Lehre von den Staatenverbindungen [The Doctrine of Federations]. Vienna

Jellinek G (1892) System der subjektiven öffentlichen Rechte [System of Subjective Public Rights]

Jellinek G (1905) Allgemeine Staatslehre [General Science of Statehood], 2nd edn. Berlin

Jouanjan O (2008) Philosophische Verwicklungen in der Rechtswissenschaft: zur Geschichte des deutschen juristischen Denkens im 19. Jahrhundert [Philosophical Entanglements in Jurisprudence: on the History of German Legal Thought in the 19th century]. Zeitschrift der Savigny-Stiftung für Rechtsgeschichte 125.

Kelly D (2003) The State of the Political: Conceptions of Politics and the State in the Thought of Max Weber, Carl Schmitt and Franz Neumann. Oxford, pp. 93–108

Kennedy D (2006) The Three Globalizations of Law. In: Trubek D, Santos A (eds) The New Law and Economics. Critical Perspectives. Cambridge University Press, Cambridge

Kennedy D, Koskenniemi M (2023) Of Law and the World. Critical Conversations on Power, History, and Political Economy. Harvard University Press, Cambridge, Mass

Kersten J (2021) The Normative Power of the Factual: Georg Jellinek's Phenomenological Theory of Reflective Legal Positivism. In: Spaak T, Mindus P (eds) The Cambridge Companion to Legal Positivism

Koskenniemi M (2002) The Gentle Civilizer of Nations. The Rise and Fall of International Law 1870–1960

Koskenniemi M (2005) From Apology to Utopia: The Structure of International Legal Argument. Cambridge University Press (2nd ed)

Koskenniemi M (2008) Into Positivism: Georg Friedrich von Martens (1756–1821) and Modern International Law. 15 Constellations: 189–207

Koskenniemi M (2011) Between Coordination and Constitution: International Law as German Discipline, 14 Redescriptions: Yearbook of Political Thought and Conceptual History, pp. 47–72

Koskenniemi M (2021) To the Uttermost Parts of the Earth. Legal Imagination and International Power 1300–1870. Cambridge University Press, Cambridge, pp. 873–950
Koskenniemi M (2024) The Law of International Society: A Road Not Taken. 74 University of Toronto Law Journal, Supplement 1:107–127
Menger C (1895) Investigations into the Method of the Social Sciences, with special reference to Economics. NYU Press 1985
Menger C (2007) Principles of Economics. von Mises Institute
Milford K (1990) Menger's Methodology. 22 History of Political Economy
Oppenheim L (1905) International Law. Vol I: Peace, Longmans, Green and Co, London
Richter B (1970) Völkerrecht, Aussenpolitik und international Verwaltung bei Lorenz von Stein [International Law, Foreign Policy and International Administration with Lorenz von Stein]. Hansischer Gildenverl, Hamburg
Siclovan D (2014) Lorenz Stein and German Socialism 1835–1872. PhD dissertation, King's College
Tönnies F (2001) Community and Civil Society. In: Harris J (ed), Harris J & Hollis M (translation). Cambridge University Press, Cambridge
Trubek D M (1986) Max Weber's Tragic Modernism and the Study of Law in Society. Law & Society Review 20:573–604
Turner S P, Factor R A (1994) Max Weber. The Lawyer as Social Thinker. Routledge
Turowski K (2023) Menger's Philosophical Influences. In: Sielska A et al. (eds) Mengerian Economics. Elgar
von Gerber C W (1880) Grundzüge des Deutschen Staatsrechts [Fundamentals of German Public Law] (3. Aufl.)
von Martens G F (1785,1789, 1801, 1821) Précis du droit des gens moderne de l'Europe fondé sur les traités et l'usage [Textbook on the modern law of nations of Europe based on treaties and usage]. Gottingue
von Mohl R (1860) Die Pflege der internationalen Gemeinschaft als Aufgabe des Völkerrechts [The Maintenance of the International Community as a Task of International Law]. In: Mohl: Staatsrecht, Völkerrecht und Politik, 3 vols. Laupp, Tübingen
von Stein L (1850) Geschichte der sozialen Bewegung in Frankreich, Erster Band: Der Begriff der Gesellschaft und die Gesetze ihre Bewegung [History of the Social Movement in France, Volume I: The Concept of Society and the Laws of its Movement]. Otto Wingan, Leipzig
von Stein L (1852) System der Staatswissenschaften: Die Gesellschaftslehre [System of Political Science: Social Theory], Abteilung I
von Stein L (1956) Begriff und Wesen der Gesellschaft [Concept and Nature of Society]. Springer, Cologne
Wasserman J (2019) The Marginal Revolutionaries. How Austrian Economists fought the World of Ideas. Yale University Press, New Haven
Weber M (1954) On Law in Economy and Society. Max Rheinstein (ed). Harvard University Press
Weber M (1980) Wirtschaft und Gesellschaft [Economy and Society], 5th edn. Mohr, Tübingen
Weber M (1994) The Profession and Vocation of Politics. In: Weber M, Political Writings. Cambridge University Press
Weber M (2012) The Objectivity of Knowledge in Social Science and Social Policy. In: Bruun H H, Whimster S (eds) Max Weber, Collected Methodological Essays
Weber M (2019) Economy and Society (A New Translation by Keith Tribe). Harvard University Press

Martti Koskenniemi is Professor Emeritus of International Law at the University of Helsinki. He has been member of the Finnish diplomatic service and of the International Law Commission (UN). He is a Corresponding Fellow of the British Academy and a Member of the American Academy of Arts and Sciences. His main publications include From Apology to Utopia; The Structure of International Legal Argument (1989/2005), The Gentle Civilizer of Nations: The Rise and Fall of International Law 1870–1960 (2001) and To the Uttermost Parts of the Earth: Legal Imagination and International Power (2021). His most recent publication is a joint work with Professor David Kennedy (Harvard), Of Law and the World. Critical Conversations on Power, History and Political Economy (2023).

Part V
International Law as an Instrument and Part of Warfare

Chapter 20
The Key Role of International Law in Contemporary Conflicts: Challenges and Prospects

Ola Engdahl

Contents

Abstract This article discusses the key role of international law in the context of Russia's full-scale invasion of Ukraine. International law cannot, on its own, prevent conflicts. However, it provides a framework for peaceful dispute resolution, accountability, and compensation. Despite clear violations of international law, including the UN Charter and international humanitarian law, international law remains relevant and plays a crucial role in conflict management and post-conflict reconstruction. The article provides examples of methods for securing compliance with international law, such as the use of sanctions, the implementation of individual criminal responsibility, and institutions for settlement of disputes. A well-known critique against international law is the lack of effective compliance mechanisms, compared with national legal systems. There are inherent challenges in any consent-based system with few supranational institutions to enforce compliance. However, there is room for political solutions and new initiatives, supported by broad state consensus, that could serve as models for handling similar situations in the future.

Keywords Aggression · Crimes · Responsibility · Accountability · Sanctions · Institutions

O. Engdahl (✉)
Ministry for Foreign Affairs, Stockholm, Sweden
e-mail: ola.engdahl@gov.se

M. Klamberg et al. (eds.), *Reconstructing Power and Hegemony in Public International Law*, https://doi.org/10.1007/978-94-6265-743-4_20

20.1 Introduction[1]

It might be argued that international law is at a critical stage in light of clear and obvious violations of the UN Charter and international humanitarian law. Does the full-scale invasion of Ukraine by Russia, a permanent member of the Security Council, challenge the international law system? Is international law still relevant?[2]

At the same time, we see an increasingly important role for international law regarding the settlement of disputes as well as the adjudication of individual criminal responsibility, as evidenced by a rising number of cases in international courts and tribunals. We also witness efforts aiming to secure the compliance and accountability of States and the criminal responsibility of individuals. These efforts operate to implement central norms of international law, and it is obvious that international law has a key role to play in contemporary conflicts—from conflict prevention to accountability and post-conflict reconstruction.

Russia's full-scale invasion and the ensuing war in Ukraine raise a host of international law questions and have prompted international law initiatives, providing examples of the key role of international law in contemporary conflicts. The purpose of this contribution is to study the continued relevance of international law also after a serious violation of one of its most central norms: the prohibition on the use of force. This article describes how international law permeates all stages of conflict and how it is fundamental in assessing State behaviour, settling disputes, and providing for accountability. This will be done by recourse to a set of examples relating to conflict prevention, State responsibility, settlement of disputes, and individual criminal responsibility in relation to the Russian aggression against Ukraine. The article will not provide an in-depth analysis of the legal rules at play, but rather take account of old and new legal avenues to overcome inherent challenges of implementing international law and show the strength of international law in critical new situations.

It has been a true joy to contribute to this book in honour of Pål Wrange. Pål's vast production of comprehensive analyses of various areas of international law, in his previous position at the Ministry for Foreign Affairs, continues to be a source of great value to all of us at the legal department. Personally, I deeply value the opportunities to discuss matters of international law with Pål.

[1] The article includes events up to 1 January 2025.

[2] Allott 2022.

20.2 Challenges and Prospects

International law comprises rules of responsibility for States for internationally wrongful acts.[3] A State responsible for an internationally wrongful act is under an obligation to cease that act and guarantee non-repetition.[4] A responsible State is also under an obligation to make full reparation for the injury caused by the wrongful acts.[5] Injured States may invoke the responsibility of the responsible State and may also exercise countermeasures to induce compliance with international law.[6]

Some acts entail an individual criminal responsibility under international law. Based on a notion of universality, States may exercise jurisdiction over individuals suspected of serious international crimes even if a connection of nationality or territoriality is lacking.[7] International courts and tribunals may also under certain circumstances exercise jurisdiction over individuals allegedly responsible for committing such crimes.[8]

A well-known critique against international law is the lack of effective compliance mechanisms, compared with national legal systems. A consent-based system with few supranational institutions includes inherent challenges when it comes to implementing the rules on conflict prevention, settlement of disputes, compliance, and accountability. However, within the international law system, there is room for political solutions to overcome practical challenges. The full-scale invasion of Ukraine by Russia, a permanent member of the Security Council, is a case in point where the implementation of international law is hampered, but where new initiatives rooted in broad support among States provide new prospects that may even stand model for other situations where the implementation of international law is challenged.[9]

20.2.1 Conflict Prevention

The UN Charter is a key instrument of conflict prevention. It is based on the notion of sovereign equality between States.[10] It includes explicit obligations on the settlement

[3] International Law Commission, Articles on Responsibility of States for Internationally Wrongful Acts, reproduced in International Law Commission 2001, pp. 26 *et seq* (ILC Articles on State Responsibility).

[4] Ibid. Article 30 (Cessation and non-repetition).

[5] Ibid. Article 31 (Reparation).

[6] Ibid. Article 42 (Invocation of responsibility by an injured State) and Articles 49–53 on Countermeasures.

[7] *See* The Princeton Principles on Universal Jurisdiction, 2001. https://www.icj.org/resource/princeton-principles-on-universal-jurisdiction/. Accessed 23 February 2025.

[8] *See, e.g.*, Rome Statute of the International Criminal Court, opened for signature 17 July 1998, 2187 UNTS 3 (entered into force 1 July 2002) (Rome Statute), Article 5.

[9] UNGA 2022b.

[10] Charter of the United Nations, opened for signature 26 June 1945 (entered into force 24 October 1945) (UN Charter), Article 2.1.

of disputes with peaceful means. A core provision is the prohibition on the use of force. The Charter also contains rules on non-intervention.[11]

The UN Charter stipulates that parties to any dispute, the continuance of which is likely to endanger the maintenance of international peace and security, shall, first of all, seek a solution by peaceful means.[12] This is an overall legal obligation incumbent on States in relation to conflicts that are at risk of developing into a threat to international peace and security. Moreover, among the purposes of the UN is the furtherance of international law and justice.[13]

The UN Security Council is charged with primary responsibility for the maintenance of international peace and security and with powers to decide on enforcement actions if it finds that a situation constitutes a threat to international peace and security. The powers of the Security Council are unprecedented but require that none of the permanent members of the Council opposes an action or decision.[14]

If the Security Council is unable to act, the General Assembly may make recommendations on a question relating to international peace and security, but it lacks the power to decide on enforcement measures or adopt resolutions of a legally binding nature.[15] On 27 February 2022, the Security Council decided to call an emergency session of the General Assembly, taking into account that the lack of unanimity of its permanent members prevented it from exercising its primary responsibility for the maintenance of international peace and security.[16]

There is only one exception in the Charter where a State may use force unilaterally. All States have the right to use force in self-defence if an armed attack occurs.[17] Article 51 does not define what constitutes an armed attack, but some guidance can be sought from the General Assembly Resolution from 1974 on the definition of aggression. The definition of aggression includes situations like "[t]he invasion or attack by the armed forces of a state of the territory of another state" and "[b]ombardment by the armed forces of a State against the territory of another state or the use of any weapons by a state against the territory of another state".[18]

States may also use force if it is based on a resolution from the Security Council stipulating the ramifications of such use.[19]

---

[11] Ibid. Article 2.4. Article 2.7 is directed at the organisation but has been interpreted, together with Article 2.4, as directed also at Member States.

[12] Ibid. Article 33.

[13] Ibid. Article 1.1.

[14] Ibid. Article 27(3) as it has been interpreted in practice.

[15] Ibid. Articles 11 and 12. *See also* ICJ, *Certain Expenses of the United Nations*, Advisory Opinion, 20 July 1962, 1962 ICJ Reports 151, pp. 164–165.

[16] UNSC 2022a.

[17] UN Charter, above n. 10, Article 51.

[18] UNGA 1974.

[19] UN Charter, above n. 10, Articles 42 and 25.

20.2.2 Full-Scale Invasion of Ukraine

On 24 February 2022, Russia began its full-scale invasion of Ukraine. According to the president of Russia, in a speech delivered on the day of the invasion, the reasons for the military invasion were: "[T]o protect people who have been subjected to bullying and genocide by the Kiev regime for eight years. And for this we will strive for the demilitarisation and denazification of Ukraine, as well as bringing to justice those who committed numerous, bloody crimes against civilians, including citizens of the Russian Federation."[20]

To do so, Russia launched a "special operation", basing this on a right of self-defence in accordance with Article 51 of the UN Charter and in pursuance of the treaties of friendship and mutual assistance with the Donetsk People's Republic and the Luhansk People's Republic.[21]

Russia thus sought to justify the invasion based on arguments lending support from international law. First, a right of self-defence is claimed by Russia, although without providing any details on how it applies to the situation. There is no claim of Russia being subject of an armed attack. Rather, the argument seems to be based on a need to protect its nationals. Although there is some support in practice for the argument of self-defence to rescue nationals when they are being threatened in the territory of another State, this constitutes a limited exception to the prohibition on the use of force and the facts in this case do not in any way support such an argument.[22]

The facts supporting the second argument put forward by Russia are flawed and the argument does not carry any weight in this situation but may, under other circumstances, be valid and legal. A State may invite the military forces of other States, either ad hoc or based on agreements stipulating criteria for such invitation. Only a State, and the proper authority of the State, can invite foreign military forces onto its territory.[23] The Donetsk People's Republic and the Luhansk People's Republic are areas that are part of Ukraine territory. The fact that Russia, as the only State, recognised these areas as independent States the day before the invasion does not in any way alter the fact that they are still part of Ukraine. Only Ukraine has the power to invite foreign military forces onto its territory, including these areas.

There has been overwhelming support for the condemnation of the Russian military invasion on 24 February 2022. An initial draft resolution in the Security Council deploring the Russian aggression against Ukraine was vetoed by Russia.[24] The Security Council will continue to be blocked as long as the aggressor State is ready to use its veto on any decision relating to Russia or Ukraine.[25]

---

[20] UNSC 2022b.

[21] Ibid.

[22] Ruys 2010; Nolte and Randelzhofer 2012.

[23] *See, e.g.*, Gray 2018, pp. 84–107. *See also* Fox 2015.

[24] https://news.un.org/en/story/2022/02/1112802. Accessed 23 February 2025.

[25] UN Charter, above n. 10, Article 27(3).

In an Emergency Special Session, the General Assembly adopted a resolution condemning the aggression against Ukraine.[26] The General Assembly, with the support of 141 States, "[r]eaffirmed its commitment to the sovereignty, independence, unity and territorial integrity of Ukraine within its internationally recognized borders, extending to its territorial waters".[27] It deplored the aggression by the Russian Federation in violation of Article 2(4) of the Charter and demanded that Russia immediately cease its use of force against Ukraine and withdraw all of its military forces from Ukrainian territory.

The General Assembly recalled its resolution in 1970 approving the Declaration on Friendly Relations and reaffirmed the principles therein on *inter alia* that the territory of a State shall not be the object of acquisition by another State resulting from the threat or use of force. It also recalled its Resolution 3314 from 1974 defining aggression as the use of armed force by a State against the sovereignty, territorial integrity, or political independence of another State or in any other manner inconsistent with the UN Charter.

The fact that an act of aggression has been committed, and is ongoing, raises the question of what avenues international law provides in the face of a clear violation of a peremptory norm. The rules on judicial settlement, arbitration, or other forms of settlement of disputes continue to be relevant. Ukraine has in fact resorted to various legal institutions to reach judicial settlement and decisions by international courts showing that Russia is in breach of international law.

20.2.3 State Responsibility for Wrongful Acts

The rules on State responsibility stipulate that every internationally wrongful act of a State entails the international responsibility of that State. A State has committed a wrongful act when a conduct attributable to it constitutes a breach of one of its international obligations. As an additional condition, the conduct must not fall within one of the circumstances precluding wrongfulness.[28]

The full-scale invasion is clearly attributed to Russia.[29] It violates its international obligation regarding the prohibition on the use of force. Its justification for the use of force may be traced to two of the circumstances precluding wrongfulness: consent and the right of self-defence. As noted above, neither of these justifications precludes the wrongfulness of the full-scale invasion in this case.[30]

A State responsible for an international wrongful act must cease that act and offer appropriate assurances and guarantees of non-repetition. It must moreover make full reparation for the injury caused by the internationally wrongful act. Such

---

[26] UNGA 2022a.

[27] Ibid.

[28] ILC Articles on State Responsibility, above n. 3, Articles 1 and 2 and Chapter V.

[29] Ibid. Article 4: "The conduct of any State organ is considered an act of that State [...]".

[30] Ibid. Articles 20, 21.

injury includes any damage, whether material or moral, caused by the internationally wrongful act of the State.[31]

An injured State may invoke the responsibility of the other State and may, after giving notice of its claim to that State, specify the conduct that the responsible State should take to cease the wrongful act and what form reparation should take.[32]

It should be noted that rules on State responsibility include obligations for all States to cooperate to bring to an end, through lawful means, any serious breach of an obligation under a peremptory norm of general international law. No State shall recognise as lawful a situation created by such a breach, nor render aid or assistance in maintaining that situation.[33]

Russia has clearly not ceased its wrongful act. The act has been labelled an act of aggression by the General Assembly. The prohibition of aggression is generally agreed on as being a peremptory norm of general international law.[34] The Security Council has the power to decide on enforcement actions aiming to prevent the continuance of the illegal act. Resolutions by the Security Council may also take the form of sanctions to induce a State to cease its illegal behaviour.

When the Security Council is blocked, States, other than the injured State, can resort to sanctions in the form of retorsions, to induce a State in breach of international law to end its behaviour. Whether other States than an injured State may take countermeasures against a State responsible for a wrongful act is currently a matter of debate.[35]

20.2.4 Settlement of Disputes

Ukraine has sought to settle disputes with Russia through peaceful means by resorting to international courts. International law obviously plays a key role before an international court or tribunal. However, solving a dispute before an international court requires that the Court has jurisdiction over the case at hand. In the relationship between Ukraine and Russia, it has been necessary for Ukraine to find a particular basis for jurisdiction in international agreements to which both Russia and Ukraine are parties in order to bring a case before a court or tribunal.

On 26 February 2022, Ukraine filed an application, instituting proceedings against Russia before the *International Court of Justice* (ICJ) concerning "a dispute … relating to the interpretation, application and fulfilment of the 1948 Convention on

[31] Ibid. Articles 29–31.

[32] Ibid. Chapter II.

[33] Ibid.

[34] International Law Commission 2001, p. 112, Article 40 Commentary, para 4.

[35] Ibid. p. 137, Article 54 Commentary.

the Prevention and Punishment of the Crime of Genocide".[36] Ukraine also submitted a request for the indication of provisional measures.[37]

The ICJ found that it had *prima facie* jurisdiction pursuant to Article IX of the Genocide Convention and indicated the following provisional measures: 1) "The Russian Federation shall immediately suspend the military operations that it commenced on 24 February 2022 in the territory of Ukraine", 2) "The Russian Federation shall ensure that any military or irregular armed units which may be directed or supported by it, as well as any organizations and persons which may be subject to its control or direction, take no steps in furtherance of the military operations referred to in point 1 above" and 3) "Both Parties shall refrain from any action which might aggravate or extend the dispute before the Court or make it more difficult to resolve."[38]

The Court also reaffirmed that orders on provisional measures have binding effect and "thus create international legal obligations for any party to whom the provisional measures are addressed".[39]

In a judgment in February 2024, the ICJ rejected the first preliminary objection by the Russian Federation and found that, on the date of application, there was a dispute under the Genocide Convention.[40] The Court thereafter considered two aspects of the dispute.

In relation to the first aspect of the dispute, the Court declared, contrary to the allegations of the Respondent, that the Applicant has not committed genocide. By such a request, Ukraine did not seek to invoke the international responsibility of the Russian Federation for an internationally wrongful act attributable to that State; it sought a judicial finding that it had itself not committed the wrongful acts that the Russian Federation had—falsely, in Ukraine's view—imputed to it in public statements.

The ICJ noted that the second aspect of the dispute was fundamentally different in nature from the first. Ukraine sought to invoke the international responsibility of the Russian Federation by imputing internationally wrongful conduct to it. The claims for reparation submitted by Ukraine were part of that second aspect. The Court found that it had jurisdiction to entertain the first aspect of the dispute, whereas the other

---

[36] ICJ, *Allegations of Genocide under the Convention on the Prevention and Punishment of the Crime of Genocide, (Ukraine v. Russian Federation)*, Application Instituting Proceedings, 27 February 2022.

[37] ICJ, *Allegations of Genocide under the Convention on the Prevention and Punishment of the Crime of Genocide (Ukraine v. Russian Federation)*, Request for the Indication of Provisional Measures, 27 February 2022.

[38] ICJ, *Allegations of Genocide under the Convention on the Prevention and Punishment of the Crime of Genocide (Ukraine v. Russian Federation)*, Provisional Measures, Order of 16 March 2022, 2022 ICJ Reports 211.

[39] Ibid. para 84.

[40] ICJ, *Allegations of Genocide under the Convention on the Prevention and Punishment of the Crime of Genocide (Ukraine v. Russian Federation)*, Preliminary Objections, Judgment, 2 February 2024.

aspect did not concern a question of violation of the Genocide Convention and was dismissed. Thirty-two States intervened in the case, which is pending.

Ukraine also initiated an inter-State complaint before the European Court of Human Rights (ECtHR) claiming "that the Russian Federation unlawfully invaded Ukraine and that its invasion and occupation of parts of Ukraine were ongoing and that the Russian Federation was engaged in targeted, indiscriminate and disproportionate attacks against civilians and their property across Ukraine in breach of all applicable norms of international law".[41]

On 28 February 2022, it filed a request for interim measures. The Court indicated on 1 March 2022, to the Government of the Russian Federation, that it was:

> to refrain from military attacks against civilians and civilian objects, including residential premises, emergency vehicles and other specially protected civilian objects such as schools and hospitals, and to ensure immediately the safety of the medical establishments, personnel and emergency vehicles within the territory under attack or siege by Russian troops.[42]

On 1 and 4 March 2022, the Court indicated additional interim measures to the Russian Federation that "in accordance with their engagements under the Convention, notably in respect of Articles 2, 3 and 8, they should ensure unimpeded access of the civilian population to safe evacuation routes, healthcare, food and other essential supplies, rapid and unconstrained passage of humanitarian aid and movement of humanitarian workers".[43]

Further, on 1 April 2022, the Court said that the evacuation routes should allow civilians to seek refuge in safer regions of Ukraine and that the measures indicated on 1 March 2022 also included "any and all attacks against civilians, including with the use of any form of prohibited weapons, measures targeting particular civilians due to their status, as well as the destruction of civilian objects under the control of Russian forces".[44] The Ukrainian Government has complained that the Russian Federation is responsible for numerous violations of the European Convention on Human Rights. The case is pending.

International courts provide the institutional framework for States to comply with the obligation to settle their disputes by peaceful means. Courts and tribunals often have the power to order provisional measures with a binding effect on the parties to the dispute. This may include measures that could be of particular importance when lives are at stake.[45]

Several international treaties include compromissory clauses stipulating forms for settling a dispute on the interpretation or application of a treaty. The Genocide

---

[41] ECtHR, *Ukraine v. Russia (X)*, Application No 11055/22.

[42] ECtHR 2022a. Including this case, there are currently four inter-State cases lodged by Ukraine against Russia, covering also the period from 2014 and invasion of Crimea, and approximately 8,500 individual complaints related to the events in Crimea, eastern Ukraine, and the Sea of Azov.

[43] ECtHR 2022b.

[44] Ibid.

[45] It should be noted that Ukraine had already initiated proceedings against Russia before the ICJ, the ECtHR, and the International Tribunal for the Law of the Sea relating to the illegal annexation of Crimea. However, this paper will be limited to proceedings related to the full-scale invasion of 2022.

Convention includes a provision on dispute settlement and thus provides a potential basis to refer the dispute to the ICJ. This is not the case with all treaties and to refer a dispute to the ICJ may therefore not be a way forward in all instances.

20.2.5 Compliance and Accountability

Sanctions are a tool often used by the Security Council to induce a State to cease its wrongful acts. Such sanctions may take the form of binding decisions applicable to all States. When the Security Council is prevented from acting, it may still be possible for States to decide on sanctions. It should be noted that sanctions as such are not a legal concept. Generally, from an international law perspective, it is rather a question of retorsion, i.e., unfriendly acts within the confines of existing legal obligations. A question raised concerning sanctions directed against Russia by third states is whether they could also include countermeasures—measures that are normally illegal but may be resorted to, under certain circumstances, to induce a State responsible for a wrongful act to cease that act.

In response to the military aggression against Ukraine, the EU expanded its sanctions.[46] A number of sanctions have thereafter been adopted, including the immobilisation of Russian central bank assets. This sparked a discussion on immunity, countermeasures, and peremptory norms and is evidence of the critical importance of international law in all stages of conflict.[47]

It is, however, incumbent on Russia to make full reparation for the injury caused by the full-scale invasion. In November 2022, the General Assembly adopted a resolution on remedy and reparation for aggression against Ukraine.[48] The Assembly recognised "that the Russian Federation must be held to account for any violations of international law in or against Ukraine, including its aggression in violation of the Charter of the United Nations, as well as any violations of international humanitarian law and international human rights law, and that it must bear the legal consequences of all of its internationally wrongful acts, including making reparation for the injury, including any damage, caused by such acts".[49]

The General Assembly recommended "the creation by Member States, in cooperation with Ukraine, of an international register of damage to serve as a record, in

[46] It added a significant number of individuals and organisations to the sanctions list and adopted unprecedented measures with the aim of weakening Russia's economic base, depriving it of critical technologies and markets, and significantly curtailing its ability to wage war. https://finance.ec.europa.eu/eu-and-world/sanctions-restrictive-measures/sanctions-adopted-following-russias-military-aggression-against-ukraine_en. Accessed 23 February 2025.

[47] *See, e.g.*, European Parliamentary Research Service 2024; Franchini 2024. Generally, on third-party counter measures, *see* Dawidowicz 2017.

[48] UNGA 2022b.

[49] Ibid. para 2.

documentary form, of evidence and claims information on damage, loss or injury to all natural and legal persons concerned, as well as the State of Ukraine".[50]

In March 2023, a *Register of Damage* was created under the auspices of the Council of Europe. The Register will function as a record of eligible claims seeking compensation for the damage, loss, and injury caused by the Russian aggression. Eligible claims must meet three criteria: occurred on or after 24 February 2022; occurred in the territory of Ukraine, within its internationally recognised borders, including territorial waters; and caused by the internationally wrongful acts of the Russian Federation in or against Ukraine.[51] The register will receive claims and categorise, classify and organise them. However, it will not examine or evaluate the claims. This is planned to be the task for a future compensation mechanism.

As a further implementation of the General Assembly resolution on remedy and reparation for the aggression against Ukraine, a preparatory meeting on an international instrument has been held to establish a *claims commission* for Ukraine. The purpose of a future claims commission is to "examine claims for compensation submitted to and recorded in the Register of Damage for Ukraine, assess such claims and evidence, and determine the amount of compensation due in each case".[52]

The creation of a Register of Damage and the current work on a claims commission are important measures to take stock of damages and claims, providing a tool for future claims of compensation by Russia for its internationally wrongful acts. These are not measures of realisation of claims, which continues to be a challenge, but are nevertheless evidence of how international law plays a crucial role in pursuing accountability and post-conflict reconstruction.

The implementation of the non-binding resolution of the General Assembly is evidence of a political will among a majority of States to establish international institutions to pursue reparation for Russia's wrongful acts. It is international legal requirements that provide the basis for these measures. International law is in itself a tool for States to induce Russia to cease its actions and compensate the damage.

20.2.6 Individual Criminal Responsibility

The claims by Ukraine before international courts, relating to the situation after 24 February 2022, have thus far concerned the Genocide Convention and the European Convention on Human Rights. State responsibility for violations of international humanitarian law and the law of occupation may be addressed in relation to alleged violations of human rights in armed conflict. War crimes, however, carry individual criminal responsibility under international law. This is the case also for crimes against humanity, genocide, and the crime of aggression. Although war crimes

[50] Ibid. para 4.

[51] RD4U 2024.

[52] *See* https://rd4u.coe.int/en/-/first-preparatory-meeting-on-an-international-instrument-to-establish-a-claims-commission-for-ukraine. Accessed 23 February 2025. *See also* Giorgetti et al. 2022.

presuppose acts with a nexus to an armed conflict, crimes of genocide and crimes against humanity can be committed in times of peace or times of war. International crimes can be investigated and prosecuted by the Ukraine authorities. Such crimes also fall in the category of universal jurisdiction that could be exercised by third States.

War crimes, crimes against humanity, genocide, and crimes of aggression are crimes in the Rome Statute of the International Criminal Court (ICC). Russia is not a member of the ICC. On 1 January 2025, the Rome Statute entered into force for Ukraine.[53] Ukraine lodged a declaration accepting the jurisdiction of the ICC in 2013 and extended the time of the ICC jurisdiction through another declaration in 2014.[54] The ICC also derived jurisdiction over the situation in Ukraine through referral. In a Statement on 28 February 2022, the ICC Prosecutor sought authorisation to open an investigation into the situation in Ukraine. The Prosecutor indicated that active investigations by the Office of the Prosecutor (OTP) would significantly be sped up if a State party would refer the situation to the OTP. Shortly after, the OTP received referrals from 39 States parties to the Rome Statute.[55]

The ICC thus has jurisdiction over the situation in Ukraine. The ICC Pre-Trial Chamber has thus far issued warrants of arrest for six Russian individuals concerning war crimes and crimes against humanity.[56] The Pre-Trial Chamber recently confirmed the obligation of States parties to co-operate with the Court and arrest the wanted individuals whenever they are present in their territories.[57]

Regarding the situation in Ukraine, the Court does not exercise jurisdiction over the crime of aggression. This fact led to an initiative to establish a separate tribunal for the crime of aggression. A number of States are involved in exploring the possibilities of a special tribunal for the crime of aggression against Ukraine. The need to create a forum to exercise jurisdiction over those responsible for the crime of aggression and the possible ways to do so also sparked academic debate.[58] Different models have been proposed linked to certain legal considerations, such as immunities of the so-called troika.

[53] https://www.icc-cpi.int/news/icc-welcomes-ukraine-new-state-party. Accessed 23 February 2025.

[54] https://www.icc-cpi.int/sites/default/files/itemsDocuments/997/declarationRecognitionJuristiction09-04-2014.pdf. Accessed 23 February 2025. *See also* https://www.icc-cpi.int/sites/default/files/iccdocs/other/Ukraine_Art_12-3_declaration_08092015.pdf. Accessed 23 February 2025.

[55] After Lithuania referred the situation in Ukraine on 1 March 2022, 38 other States followed on 2 March 2022. https://www.icc-cpi.int/news/statement-icc-prosecutor-karim-aa-khan-qc-situation-ukraine-receipt-referrals-39-states. Accessed 23 February 2025.

[56] https://www.icc-cpi.int/situations/ukraine. Accessed 23 February 2025.

[57] *See* ICC, *Situation in Ukraine*, PT. Ch. II, Finding under article 87(7) of the Rome Statute on the non-compliance by Mongolia with the request by the Court to cooperate in the arrest and surrender of Vladimir Vladimirovich Putin and referral to the Assembly of States Parties, ICC-01/22-90, 25 October 2024. Pre-Trial Chamber II of the ICC found that by failing to arrest Mr Putin while he was on its territory and surrender him to the Court, Mongolia had failed to comply with its obligations.

[58] *See, for example*, Kress et al. 2023; Corell 2023; Hathaway et al. 2023.

The Council of Europe has become involved and the Committee of Ministers supported the ongoing work on a tribunal.[59] The Parliamentary Assembly gave its support in a resolution in June 2024, stating that:

> [t]he Assembly calls for consultations to be started as soon as possible on the draft agreement between the Council of Europe and the Government of Ukraine on the establishment of a special tribunal for the crime of aggression of the Russian Federation against Ukraine, including its statute, and on a possible draft enlarged partial agreement governing the modalities of support to such a tribunal, its financing and other administrative matters.[60]

The European Commission had already launched an International Centre for the Prosecution of the Crime of Aggression in Ukraine, which started operations in July 2023.[61] The centre is to coordinate the collection of evidence. It is connected to the Joint Investigative Team within Eurojust (the European criminal justice agency for judicial cooperation and investigation).

Individual criminal responsibility is primarily a question for national jurisdictions. However, it is apparent that international law plays a significant role in prosecuting individuals suspected of international crimes. It is through arrest warrants from the ICC that a majority of States have an obligation to detain any of the individuals, if they are within their territory. The work on a special tribunal for the crime of aggression is evidence of State co-operation to seek ways to implement the criminal responsibility of those with the greatest responsibility. In the meantime, a special centre is coordinating the collection of evidence.

20.3 The Key Role of International Law: Challenges and Prospects

International law plays a critical role in all stages of contemporary conflicts: before, during, and after. States often seek to justify their actions in accordance with international law and seldom, if ever, is there an argument that international law does not apply at all to a situation of conflict.

International law establishes obligations on States to refrain from solving their conflicts with other than peaceful means. It includes a clear prohibition on the use of force. International law as such cannot prevent conflicts from occurring. This requires political will and institutions designed to prevent conflicts from happening. The UN is one such institution, with a strong potential to prevent the outbreak of conflicts. The obvious challenge in this conflict is that one of the permanent members of the Security Council is the aggressor, thus effectively limiting the possibilities for the Security Council to act.

---

[59] Committee of Ministers 2024.

[60] Parliamentary Assembly 2024.

[61] https://www.eurojust.europa.eu/news/history-making-international-centre-prosecution-crime-aggression-against-ukraine-starts-operations-at-eurojust. Accessed 23 February 2025.

The General Assembly may also address issues relating to the maintenance of international peace and security, albeit with a limited mandate. Even though it lacks enforcement powers, it may recognise a situation as a violation of international law and recommend that the aggressor State cease its violation. It may also provide recommendations for third States in this respect.

International law is not challenged, but the international system includes inherent challenges to induce compliance, even in the event of obvious and serious violations. This is not necessarily evidence that new rules are needed. Sometimes it could be a challenging question to assess whether a State is responsible for a wrongful act. However, this is not the case regarding the Russian aggression against Ukraine. International law offers possibilities for peaceful settlement and provides a framework for compliance, including cessation, non-repetition, and compensation.

International law provides a system in which it is possible to establish responsibility for wrongful acts for States and criminal responsibility for individuals. In the face of clear violations of peremptory norms, States have shown a will to overcome and work around institutional obstacles to establish responsibility and provide avenues for accountability and compensation. International law thus provides a bulwark against a world where might is right. Even though the system of international law faces many challenges, it is in the interest of all States that the norms agreed upon are respected and fulfilled.

References

Allott P (2022) Anarchy and Anachronism: An Existential Challenge for International Law. EJIL:Talk! https://www.ejiltalk.org/anarchy-and-anachronism-an-existential-challenge-for-international-law/. Accessed 23 February 2025

Committee of Ministers, Council of Europe (2024) 133rd Session of the Committee of Ministers (Strasbourg, 17 May 2024)—2. United around our values—a. Council of Europe response to the full-scale aggression of the Russian Federation against Ukraine, CM/Del/Dec(2024)133/2a. https://search.coe.int/cm?i=0900001680afa985. Accessed 6 May 2025

Corell H (2023) A Special Tribunal for Ukraine on the Crime of Aggression—The Role of the U.N. General Assembly. Just Security. https://www.justsecurity.org/85116/a-special-tribunal-for-ukraine-on-the-crime-of-aggression-the-role-of-the-u-n-general-assembly/. Accessed 23 February 2025

Dawidowicz M (2017) Third-Party Countermeasures in International Law, Cambridge University Press

ECtHR (2022a) Press Release issued by the Registrar of the Court. *Inter-State case Ukraine v. Russia (X)*: receipt of completed application form and notification to respondent State. ECHR 220, 28 June 2022

ECtHR (2022b) Press Release issued by the Registrar of the Court. Expansion of interim measures in relation to Russian military action in Ukraine. ECHR 116, 1 April 2022

European Parliamentary Research Service (2024) Legal options for confiscation of Russian state assets to support the reconstruction of Ukraine, https://www.europarl.europa.eu/RegData/etudes/STUD/2024/759602/EPRS_STU(2024)759602_EN.pdf. Accessed 23 February 2025

Fox GH (2015) Intervention by Invitation. In: Weller M (ed) The Oxford Handbook of the Use of Force in International Law. Oxford University Press

Franchini D (2024) Immobilised Assets, Extraordinary Profits: The EU Council Decision on Russia's Central Bank Reserves and Its Legal Challenges. EJIL:Talk! https://www.ejiltalk.org/immobilised-assets-extraordinary-profits-the-eu-council-decision-on-russias-central-bank-reserves-and-its-legal-challenges/ Accessed 23 February 2025
Giorgetti C et al (2022) Launching an International Claims Commission for Ukraine. EJIL:Talk! https://www.ejiltalk.org/launching-an-international-claims-commission-for-ukraine/. Accessed 23 February 2025
Gray C (2018) International Law and the Use of Force, 4th edn. Oxford University Press
Hathaway OA et al. (2023) The Legal Authority to Create a Special Tribunal to Try the Crime of Aggression Upon the Request of the UN General Assembly. Just Security. https://www.justsecurity.org/86450/the-legal-authority-to-create-a-special-tribunal-to-try-the-crime-of-aggression-upon-the-request-of-the-un-general-assembly/. Accessed 23 February 2025
International Law Commission (2001) Yearbook of the International Law Commission 2001, Volume II (Part Two). A/CN.4/SER.A/2001/Add.1 (Part 2). https://legal.un.org/ilc/publications/yearbooks/english/ilc_2001_v2_p2.pdf. Accessed 1 March 2025
Kress C et al. (2023) The Ukraine War and the Crime of Aggression: How to Fill the Gaps in the International Legal System. Just Security. https://www.justsecurity.org/84783/the-ukraine-war-and-the-crime-of-aggression-how-to-fill-the-gaps-in-the-international-legal-system/. Accessed 23 February 2025
Nolte G, Randelzhofer A (2012) Article 51. In: Simma B et al (eds) The Charter of the United Nations: A Commentary, Volume II, 3rd edn. Oxford University Press
Parliamentary Assembly, Council of Europe (2024) The role of sanctions in countering the Russian Federation's war of aggression against Ukraine, Resolution 2557. https://pace.coe.int/en/files/33684/html. Accessed 6 May 2025
RD4U (2024) Rules Governing the Submission, Processing and Recording of Claims. RD4U-Board(2024)04-Rev1-EN. https://rd4u.coe.int/en/documents. Accessed 23 February 2025
Ruys T (2010) 'Armed Attack' and Article 51 of the UN Charter: Evolutions in Customary Law and Practice. Cambridge University Press
UN General Assembly (1974) Definition of Aggression, Resolution 3314 (XXIX), UN Doc. A/RES/3314(XXIX)
UN General Assembly (2022a) Aggression against Ukraine, Resolution ES-11/1, UN Doc. A/RES/ES-11/1
UN General Assembly (2022b) Furtherance of remedy and reparation for aggression against Ukraine, Resolution ES-11/5, UN Doc. A/RES/ES-11/5
UN Security Council (2022a) Resolution 2623, UN Doc. S/RES/2623
UN Security Council (2022b) Annex to the letter dated 24 February 2022 from the Permanent Representative of the Russian Federation to the United Nations addressed to the Secretary-General, UN Doc. S/2022/154

Ola Engdahl is the Principal Legal Adviser at the Swedish Ministry for Foreign Affairs. In that capacity, he advises on issues of general international law. He has been an expert in several Governmental Inquiries on subjects such as terrorism, implementation of international humanitarian law, the crime of aggression, space law, and other issues in the field of military and civil defense. Ola Engdahl is Associate Professor at Stockholm University and has published mainly with a focus on the law of the UN Charter, international humanitarian law, human rights law, and the law of peace operations. He is the author of *Protection of Personnel in Peace Operations* and has also written several articles on the law of peace operations and matters of general international law.

Chapter 21
'Hybrid' Naval Warfare and Its Intended Legal Implications?

Said Mahmoudi

Contents

Abstract The increasing sabotage and unfriendly, illegal or even terrorist activities against vessels or port facilities in marine areas have occasioned intensive discourse on 'hybrid' naval warfare. Using all possible means—not only weapons—in an armed conflict to damage an enemy's interests has long been considered an option in any war. However, the current use of the expression 'hybrid warfare' denotes methods and means that have become more available due to recent technological developments. As regards hybrid naval warfare, the main legal issue is whether these developments necessitate revision of two main branches of international law, namely the law of the sea and the law of armed conflict. The present hypothesis is that international law is still sufficiently equipped with the rules necessary for addressing the challenges of a hybrid naval war. Any attempt to expand the possibility of use of force in international relations under the pretext of new threats should be discouraged.

Keywords Hybrid warfare · Marine areas · Blurred definitions · Self-defence · Countermeasures

An earlier version of this text was the basis of the author's speech at the conference 'Hybrid Naval Warfare through the Lens of Maritime Security Law', held in Tallinn, Estonia, on 11–12 May 2023.

S. Mahmoudi (✉)
Stockholm University, Stockholm, Sweden
e-mail: Said.Mahmoudi@juridicum.su.se

Luleå Technical University, Luleå, Sweden

M. Klamberg et al. (eds.), *Reconstructing Power and Hegemony in Public International Law*, https://doi.org/10.1007/978-94-6265-743-4_21

21.1 Introduction

'Hybrid warfare' has become a buzzword among military professionals, social scientists, security experts and, more recently, international law scholars. The insertion of 'hybrid' before the term 'warfare'[1] has prompted some to try to elaborate the content of this combination and analyse its legal implications. The relevant discourse in international law has predominantly concerned the constituent elements of 'hybrid' warfare and the possible need to develop international law in this area.

The proposed definitions of hybrid warfare and hence also hybrid naval warfare have varied tremendously. The common feature is reference to a combination of conventional military operations, the use of irregular military/paramilitary forces, non-state actors' terrorist or criminal activities, economic, social and informational means, or some of these elements.[2] A common view has been that 'hybrid warfare' implies a *grey* area, a space short of clear-cut military action where the aggressor creates enough ambiguity to reach its strategic objectives without an open offensive.[3] Reference to *grey* area here implies that the legal situation is not considered to be sufficiently clear. Consequently, a frequent question is whether international law must be revised or updated to meet the challenges of this 'new' form of warfare. This paper seeks to address this specific question.

21.1.1 Proposed Definitions of Hybrid Warfare

To address this question, the proposed definitions of hybrid warfare have generally adopted a very broad scope. Sometimes, this is stretched to include practically anything. For instance, an editorial about hybrid warfare published in the Swedish daily *Svenska Dagbladet* on 22 September 2024 insinuated that a planned concert by the Shanghai Symphonic Orchestra in the city of Uppsala should be considered an act of hybrid warfare by China against Sweden![4]

The various definitions offered can be twofold. *A first group* includes activities to disturb, discredit or distress an adversary, or more often to inflict damage on its various interests. They may be covert, short-lived, hit-and-run operations such as dissemination of false information or propaganda, terrorist attacks, use of explosives, kidnapping and so forth. A second group can also be overt measures. An example relevant to maritime activities is unwarranted vessel boarding services. Some have included in this latter group, e.g., the establishment of platforms, artificial islands and other constructions in disputed marine areas; or laying submarine pipelines

[1] As an early reference to 'hybrid warfare' in the current discourse, *see* Hoffman 2007.

[2] As regards hybrid naval warfare from military and strategic perspectives, *see* Murphy et al. 2016. For an international law overview, *see* Lott 2022; Lott 2024; Shelest 2018.

[3] Stavridis 2016, pp. 30–33.

[4] The example confirms what many other observers have also noted. Käihkö, e.g., writes: 'In its evolved form, hybrid war is a buzzword that can mean almost anything.' *See* Käihkö 2021, p. 126.

in such areas; enacting national laws to justify claims on neighbouring territories or disputed geographical zones. One recent example is Russia's decision to send asylum seekers to Finland, which led the Finnish government to adopt a regulation to close its borders.[5] Another example is Poland's decision in October 2024 to bar asylum seekers from claiming asylum in the country after crossing the border with neighboring Belarus, as the mass ingress of asylum seekers from Belarus is considered part of a 'hybrid war' aiming to destabilize the EU.[6] Yet another example is Russia's threat in May 2024 to adjust its maritime borders with Lithuania in the Gulf of Finland which Russia formally justified by sea-level changes and the need to adjust the Russian baselines.[7]

The response to such unfriendly or criminal/illegal measures, particularly if carried out by non-state actors, depends on establishing whether they constitute solely criminal or antagonistic acts. In that case, the mechanism of reciprocity and the victim state's criminal law rules can provide an appropriate legal response. If the unfriendly or illegal measure can be attributed to a state and is at the same time a breach of an international legal obligation entailing state responsibility, countermeasures short of use of force as defined in Article 22 of the International Law Commission's Draft Articles on State Responsibility would be the appropriate and legal means for reaction. Thus, if the victim state cannot with certainty establish who the perpetrator is or which state is in fact behind the criminal or damaging act, reactions may normally at best be confined to clandestine, retaliatory measures against the assumed perpetrating entity. This has been practiced regularly, for instance in relations between Iran on the one hand and Israel, the littoral Arab states of the Persian Gulf, the UK and the United States on the other.[8]

The second group of definitions encompasses activities involving use of force either as a claimed law enforcement measure of a state or as an armed attack in the sense of Article 51 of the UN Charter, or an 'armed' attack by a terrorist organization. Legal responses to such scenarios are—at least theoretically—well-defined.

---

[5] Reuters (2023) More asylum seekers rushed to Finland from Russia before border reclosure. https://www.reuters.com/world/europe/more-asylum-seekers-rush-finland-russia-before-border-closure-2023-12-15. Accessed 19 February 2025.

[6] Politico (2024) Poland to suspend right to asylum as 'hybrid war' escalates on Belarus border. https://www.politico.eu/article/poland-donald-tusk-asylum-right-border-migration-belarus-russia-hybrid-war-eu/. Accessed 19 February 2025.

[7] Politico (2024) Russia mysteriously deletes threat to redraw Baltic Sea border. https://www.politico.eu/article/russia-defense-ministry-change-baltic-sea-border-finland-latvia/. Accessed 19 February 2025. As regards Russia's view on changing or challenging maritime borders in general, *see* The Maritime Executive (2022) Russia's New Maritime Doctrine: 'Hybrid War with the Collective West'. The Maritime Executive, p. 3. https://maritime-executive.com/index.php/editorials/russia-s-new-maritime-doctrine-hybrid-war-with-the-collective-west. Accessed 19 February 2025.

[8] As an example, note a series of explosions on oil tankers in May 2019 https://apnews.com/article/f8ed00420d42476292a106d26d33ede9 and in June the same year https://apnews.com/article/d67714ab8ac344a3b3af19cea1c20192, both in the Persian Gulf. Note also the seizure of a Panama-flagged ship in the Persian Gulf in August 2021 by suspected Iranian agents. *See* The Guardian (2019) A visual guide to the Gulf tanker attacks. https://www.theguardian.com/world/2019/jun/13/a-visual-guide-to-the-gulf-tanker-attacks. Accessed 19 February 2025.

The concept of hybrid warfare is used irrespective of whether the source of the threat or actual damage to a state's interests is known, as in the case of Russia's operation in Crimea in 2014 and China's construction of platforms in disputed maritime areas in the South China Sea[9], or not, as in the case of Nord Stream pipeline sabotage in the Baltic Sea in September 2022.[10] What is characterized as a 'grey' area in international law often relates to the second scenario, i.e., some degree of force, particularly by irregular/paramilitary forces: below the legal threshold of war but enough for the aggressor to achieve its objectives.

21.1.2 Criminal and Enforcement Jurisdiction of the Coastal State

Possible questions regarding the victim state's appropriate response relate to i) *the extent* of the coastal state's criminal jurisdiction (as regards criminal acts in areas that are under a state's jurisdiction or control), and ii) *the nature* of the military force used by 'the aggressor'. To answer these questions, rules of both the law of the sea and the law of naval warfare must be considered.

With respect to the extent of a state's criminal jurisdiction, it definitely applies in the whole territory of the state, including its internal and territorial waters. However, the exercise of such jurisdiction in the state's exclusive economic zone (EEZ) and on its continental shelf is subject to the limitations in the 1982 United Nations Law of the Sea Convention (the LOS Convention).

A recent case that illustrates uncertainty in this area is the Nord Stream pipeline explosions in the Swedish EEZ. Here, the Swedish military and security authorities took the firm position that Swedish criminal law was applicable, and that they had exclusive jurisdiction to investigate the crime as regards these explosions. As a result, the Swedish Coast Guard maintained the prosecutor's ban on navigation within a radius of five nautical miles from the positions of the damaged pipelines for over a week.[11] The prohibition applied to all vessels, including foreign ships, and any violation could entail penalty.

---

[9] For a background summary of these operations, *see* Ball 2023.

[10] For a comprehensive analysis of the legal aspects of this sabotage, *see* Koivurova and Winkel 2024, pp. 195–221. Recent publications in the Swedish press (e.g. Dagens Nyheter, 14 August 2024, https://www.dn.se/varlden/tre-ukrainska-dykare-misstanks-for-sabotaget-av-nord-stream/ ; Svenska Dagbladet, 14 August 2024 https://www.svd.se/a/o3Ke4R/ukrainsk-grupp-planerade-sabotaget-pa-fyllan) refer to leaked information from the German police investigation and claim that a Ukrainian special commando blew up the Russian-owned Nord Stream pipelines in the Baltic Sea in September 2022. The same information adds that the said sabotage was approved by Ukrainian President Zelenskyy. For a recent analysis of Russia's hybrid warfare, *see* Bilal A (2024) Russia's hybrid war against the West. NATO Review. https://www.nato.int/docu/review/articles/2024/04/26/russias-hybrid-war-against-the-west/index.html. Accessed 19 February 2025.

[11] That decision of the prosecutor was short, without any details. https://www.aklagare.se/nyheter-press/pressmeddelanden/2022/oktober/uppdatering-i-arende-om-nord-stream/. More details about the decision to ban navigation and the extent of the area closed to any sort of navigation was

It is interesting to note that the Swedish Ministry for Foreign Affairs announced no formal position on this matter,[12] nor did any other country publicly protest the decision of the Swedish prosecutor.

The legality of the Swedish authorities' decision to restrict freedom of navigation for foreign ships in the Swedish EEZ in this case, without getting support for it from the International Maritime Organization, is questionable.

21.1.3 The Nature of the Force Used

The second question, i.e., the nature of the force used by the aggressor, relates to the need to respond with force to the actor that has inflicted damage on a state's interests. This applies when the source of damage is known. If the source is clearly a state and the generally accepted conditions of 'armed attack' are fulfilled,[13] the victim state may invoke the right to use force in self-defence. Even when the source of damage is a non-state actor, the victim state may use force in self-defence under the conditions that the International Court of Justice and the International Law Commission have pronounced.[14]

The more probable scenario of hybrid warfare is that the force does not reach the generally accepted level of an 'armed attack' entitling the victim state to self-defence in the sense of UN Charter Article 51. A typical example is the case of the People's Republic of China in the South China Sea. In addition to its navy, China has a Coast Guard and also a maritime militia of civilian-manned fishing vessels. It employs all three forces to maintain its sovereignty in disputed maritime areas of the South China Sea.[15] The relevant question will be how to establish the point at which the action of a Coast Guard or maritime militia vessel constitutes an 'armed attack'.[16] Current international law permits the victim state to use force as an enforcement measure if

published in the media in early October 2022. See, e.g. Svenska Dagbladet, 3 October 2022 https://www.skd.se/2022-10-03/svensk-aklagare-sparrar-av-havet-vid-gaslackor/.

[12] Generally, the case was treated as a matter of high national security and was therefore mainly under the control of the Swedish Armed Forces, in cooperation with the Swedish Coast Guard, the Swedish Maritime Administration, the Swedish Security Service, and the Swedish Prosecution Authority. The Ministry for Foreign Affairs seemed to have had no or a marginal role in dealing with the matter.

[13] The level of magnitude—threshold—for the use of force as discussed by the International Court of Justice in the Nicaragua Case, and the transborder character of such use, are given as two main conditions. *See* Mahmoudi 2021, pp. 284–286.

[14] Ibid. pp. 286–287, 353–355.

[15] Haines 2016, p. 443. He adds: 'Chinese coastguard vessels, which are ostensibly deployed on constabulary tasks, are effectively operating as warships in all but name, while claiming civilian status.' As regards the interplay between enforcement measures and naval warfare or the blurred border between enforcement measures and military operations, *see* Hoffman et al. 2024.

[16] Haines 2016, p. 443.

the attack or the damaging effect of the act has taken place in its territory, including territorial waters and, under certain conditions, in its EEZ or on its continental shelf.[17]

However, the accepted level of force for characterizing the incident as an 'armed' attack is not seldom challenged by advocates of more force in international relations. They lower the threshold for when the action of a vessel, e.g., a coast guard or maritime militia ship, constitutes an armed attack. They suggest that the law on the conduct of hostilities at sea should begin to develop in ways that might accommodate the hybrid characteristic of contemporary conflict and permit self-defence even when a military attack is not an 'armed' attack *stricto sensu.*[18]

Efforts to expand the possibility to use force, either by re-interpreting the prohibition of the use of force as enshrined in the UN Charter Article 2(4) or by simply justifying the need for force by introducing new concepts, should be seen as problematic. The concept of hybrid warfare has the potential of providing for such an expansion, at least in response to cases of limited paramilitary attacks. Since 2015 and following the Russian annexation of Crimea, NATO has at its annual high-level meetings regularly discussed hybrid threats and hybrid activities that aim to create ambiguities and blur the lines between peace, crisis and conflict, and has referred to Article 5 in the Washington Treaty.[19] It has underlined its preparedness to use force according to this provision also if a certain event is designated as hybrid warfare.[20]

The question is whether the emergence of 'grey' areas such as employment of irregular maritime forces in operations whose objective is the same as or similar to that of a conventional use of force in an armed attack must be considered in the context of the law of armed conflicts and warrants a revision of that law. If the matter is seen as a *jus ad bellum* issue, the answer will be in the negative.

21.2 Updating the Law of Armed Conflict

Seen from the perspective of *jus in bello* and the conduct of war at sea, the 1994 San Remo Manual[21] is certainly a reliable collection of rules, despite containing no reference to hybrid naval warfare. The question is whether this type of warfare, and

---

[17] Concerning the EEZ and continental shelf, the coastal state's enforcement measures must as a rule be limited to issues related to the coastal state's jurisdiction in those areas enumerated in the LOS Convention Parts V & VI, particularly Arts 56 and 77. For a useful study on the risk of sabotage in the EEZ as a part of a hybrid war, *see* Schaller 2024.

[18] This is the position that seems to be advocated by, e.g., Haines. *See* Haines 2016, pp. 446–447.

[19] *See,* e.g., Kotman 2021, p. 2.

[20] The latest declaration is the Washington Summit Declaration dated 10 July 2024. Its point 13 proclaims: 'We reiterate that hybrid operations against Allies could reach the level of an armed attack and could lead the North Atlantic Council to invoke Article 5 of the Washington Treaty.' https://www.nato.int/cps/en/natohq/official_texts_227678.htm. Accessed 19 February 2025.

[21] For the text of the manual, *see* https://ihl-databases.icrc.org/en/ihl-treaties/san-remo-manual-1994.

particularly the existence of irregular maritime forces assumed to be an important part of such warfare, justifies any review of the law.

Proponents of a review of the existing law argue that the traditional understanding of warfare primarily focuses on conventional military conflict and is therefore no longer sufficient to address the complexities of the contemporary security environment.[22] According to them, such a review may shed light on the relevance of some basic principles of international humanitarian law, such as that of distinction in cases of interaction between warships, coast guard vessels and militia ships participating in hybrid naval warfare. The opposite view is that all forms of warfare are in essence hybrid, a concept that blurs the line between war and peace. As such, it presents nothing new and cannot contribute to better understanding or policymaking.[23] The need for updating the law is thus debatable.

21.3 Concluding Reflections

The concept of hybrid warfare and hence hybrid naval warfare still lacks a generally accepted definition. Its use is almost always based on the subjective assessment of the user. This has led to the proliferation of expansive definitions that include a very broad range of activities, most of which are already properly regulated in international law. What is needed is a precise and exclusive definition to avoid ambiguity. The problem of ambiguity is not a concern of lawyers alone; military strategists and political decision-makers also consider ambiguity an obstacle to a better understanding of modern warfare.[24]

The existing relevant international law, i.e., the law of the sea and the law of armed conflict, is largely sufficient to accommodate necessary adjustments to cover hybrid naval warfare. Lott rightly observes: 'Although rapid developments in technology have made it now possible to adopt more sophisticated means of hybrid warfare, including cyber warfare, states should still principally be able to classify any incidents of hybrid warfare under either the ramifications of armed conflict or peacetime law enforcement operations.' His correct conclusion is: 'Any new legal framework for hybrid naval warfare that falls between the laws of peace and war would risk creating additional ambiguities in assessing the legality of the aggressor's actions in the so-called grey area.'[25]

Arguably, subsequent practice of states parties to the LOS Convention has already influenced the expanded scope of flag and coastal state jurisdiction in some areas.

---

[22] Haines 2016, p. 446.

[23] Käihkö 2016, p. 623; *see also* Lott 2020.

[24] The problem is elaborately described in Stoker and Whiteside 2020, pp. 13–48. *See also* Robert Person et al., who notes that 'To date, there is no consensus … about how to define hybrid war. The result is a myriad of definitions that vary so widely in their core elements as to render the term "hybrid war" nearly useless—even if the underlying concept remains relevant…' Person et al. 2024, p. 1754.

[25] Lott 2020.

Sweden's reaction to the Nord Stream blasts in its EEZ may be taken as a move to increase coastal-state criminal and enforcement jurisdiction in that zone against many foreign activities normally termed hybrid naval warfare.

Hybrid warfare can be considered a useful alternative to conventional armed conflicts that usually involve all types of force.[26] This was implied by the 'Gerasimov' doctrine, which seemed to be the theoretical basis of the Russian operations in Crimea. Accordingly, grey-zone conflicts 'envisage a shift from use of force in war to use of nonviolent means below the threshold of war'. The doctrine is attributed to Valery Gerasimov, Chief of the General Staff of the Federal Russian Armed Forces, who has argued that 'the focus of applied methods of conflict has altered in the direction of the broad use of political, economic, informational, humanitarian, and other non-military measures—applied in coordination with the protest potential of the population'. In that sense, he maintains, such 'warfare' as a low-intensive and often non-military operation is to be preferred because many lives are saved, and state and non-state actors gain strategic advantages without resorting to full-scale conventional warfare. According to Gerasimov, the general perception is that the techniques used in a hybrid war are such that 'they create an effect short of war, and the adversary cannot retaliate due to the absence of legitimacy for a military attack'.[27] However, another aspect of the increased occurrence of hybrid warfare is to invoke it as an excuse to expand the legal possibility of more use of military force in international relations, and this should definitely be considered a negative development.

The fact is that the great majority of the operations thus far included in the concept of hybrid warfare, including those exercised in a maritime zone, are covered by existing international rules and relevant national laws that fall outside the UN Charter provisions relating to the use of force and its prohibition. The appropriate reaction to such operations is a more effective application of those rules and laws, without unduly increasing the possibilities of states to use force, which would be contrary to the aspirations of the drafters of the UN Charter.

In summary, the answer to the question posed at the beginning of this paper is that there is, at least presently, no need to adopt new international agreements governing hybrid naval warfare and grey-zone conflict. Possible adjustments to the San Remo Manual, review of national laws in the light of such adjustments, emerging state practice, and decisions of international courts and tribunals relating to operations that can arguably be considered examples of hybrid warfare, will provide sufficient grounds for legally addressing such warfare.[28]

---

[26] The doctrine is elaborated in Gerasimov 2016, p. 24; *Cf.* Käihkö 2021, pp. 117–120.

[27] *See*, e.g., Jamal Nasir (2021) Hybrid War: Challenges & Response. https://strafasia.com/hybrid-war-challenges-response/#google_vignette. Accessed 19 February 2025.

[28] *Cf.* Lott 2020.

References

Ball J (2023) The Changing Face of Conflict: What is Hybrid Warfare? Global Security Review. https://globalsecurityreview.com/hybrid-and-non-linear-warfare-systematically-erases-the-divide-between-war-peace. Accessed 19 February 2025

Gerasimov V (2016) The Value of Science Is in the Foresight: New Challenges Demand Rethinking the Forms and Methods of Carrying Out Combat Operations. Military Review 96(1):24

Haines S (2016) War at sea: Nineteenth-century laws for twenty-first-century wars? International Review of the Red Cross 98

Hoffman, FG (2007) Conflict in the 21st Century: The Rise of Hybrid Wars. Potomac Institute for Policy Studies

Hoffman F et al (2024) The Future of Hybrid Warfare. Center for Strategic & International Studies. https://www.csis.org/analysis/future-hybrid-warfare. Accessed 19 February 2025

Käihkö I (2016) All krigföring är av hybrid natur [All warfare is hybrid in nature]. Statsvetenskaplig tidskrift 118:623

Käihkö I (2021) The Evolution of Hybrid War: Implications for Strategy and the Military Profession. Parameters 51(3):126

Kotman T (2021) Maritime Hybrid Threat. https://www.marseccoe.org/wp-content/uploads/2021/08/Maritime-Hybrid-Threat.pdf. Accessed 19 February 2025

Kovurova T, Winkel T (2024) The Nord Stream Pipelines from the Viewpoint of Law and Geopolitics. In: Lott A (ed) (2024) Maritime Security Law in Hybrid Warfare. Nijhoff, Leiden

Lott A (2020) Implications of Hybrid Warfare for the Order of the Oceans. Center for International Maritime Security. https://cimsec.org/implications-of-hybrid-warfare-for-the-order-of-the-oceans/. Accessed 19 February 2025

Lott A (2022) Hybrid Threats and the Law of the Sea: Use of Force and Discriminatory Navigational Restrictions in Straits. Brill | Nijhoff, Leiden

Lott A (2024) Maritime Security Law in Hybrid Warfare. Nijhoff, Leiden

Mahmoudi S (2021) Self-Defence and Unwilling or Unable States. Recueil des cours 422:284–286

Murphy M et al (2016) Hybrid Maritime Warfare and the Baltic Sea Region. Center for Military Studies, University of Copenhagen https://cms.polsci.ku.dk/publikationer/Hybrid_Maritime_Warfare_and_the_Baltic_Sea_Region.pdf. Accessed 19 February 2025

Person R et al (2024) Back to the future: the persistent problems of hybrid war. International Affairs 100:1754

Schaller C (2024) Critical Maritime Infrastructure and the Regime of the EEZ: A Blank Cheque for saboteurs? EJIL:Talk! https://www.ejiltalk.org/critical-maritime-infrastructure-and-the-regime-of-the-eez-a-blank-cheque-for-saboteurs/. Accessed 19 February 2025

Shelest H (2018) Hybrid Warfare on the Sea. "https://prismua.org/en/гібридна-війна-на-морі/". Accessed 19 February 2025

Stavridis J (2016) Maritime Hybrid Warfare is Coming. Proceedings of the United States Naval Institute 142(12):30–33

Stoker D, Whiteside G (2020) Blurred Lines: Grey-Zone Conflict and Hybrid War—Two Failures of American Strategic Thinking. Naval War College Review 73(1):13–48

Said Mahmoudi , born 1948 in Tehran, Iran, is Professor Emeritus in International Law at the Law Faculty of Stockholm University and Guest Professor at Luleå University of Technology. He served as diplomat in Sweden between 1974 and 1979. He got his PhD from Stockholm University 1987 with a dissertation on the law of deep seabed mining. Between 2009 and 2011 he acted as dean of the Law Faculty of Stockholm University. His main fields of research interest are law of the sea, international environmental law, the law of State immunity, and use of force. He has authored seven books, edited eight books and published some 80 articles on various international law issues in Swedish and English. He gave a course on self-defence and "unable or unwilling" States at the Hague Academy of International Law in 2019.

Chapter 22
Of Legal Cars Leaving Political Factories

Sarah M. H. Nouwen

Contents

Abstract This chapter covers three journeys of law and politics. We begin with a trip to an event organized to promote an International Criminal Court bill in Uganda, during which I met Pål Wrange as a courageous driver and top-class doctrinal scholar. The main journey is that of a special War Crimes Court, which travelled away from the peace agreement that had given rise to it. Although the travellers presented it as law leaving politics behind, they in fact still travelled a political route, just a different one: they, for instance, prioritised one understanding of rule of law ('accountability') over another ('legal certainty'). The War Crimes Court's journey illustrates the journey that the field of transitional justice has made: from justice around a political compromise to criminal justice trying to avoid compromise. The third is Pål's journey back to academia and to critical international law. May that journey continue, even after retirement.

Keywords Law-politics · International criminal court · Uganda · Transitional justice · International donors · Amnesty · Critical international law

22.1 A Ugandan Ride

'That train has left the station' is the usual expression. However, my first encounter with Pål Wrange was when he gave me a ride in his car. Unfazed by Uganda's relentless traffic, he calmly drove us from Mbuya Hill to Entebbe. It was 5 September

S. M. H. Nouwen (✉)
European University Institute, Florence, Italy
e-mail: smhn3@cam.ac.uk

University of Cambridge, Cambridge, UK

M. Klamberg et al. (eds.), *Reconstructing Power and Hegemony in Public International Law*, https://doi.org/10.1007/978-94-6265-743-4_22

2008. We were on our way to an event organized by the Ugandan Coalition on the International Criminal Court (ICC): 'The Domestication of the Rome Statute in Africa: Challenges and Prospects'. Pål went as a consultant, advising the donor community on accountability; I went as a PhD student, researching the impact of the ICC's intervention on Uganda's legal system. Pål came up with ingenious doctrinal solutions to real obstacles: could the International Criminal Court Act—then still a bill—be retroactively applied in domestic trials of members of the Lord's Resistance Army (LRA)?[1] I observed the dynamics of the meeting: Western-funded NGOs convening Ugandan parliamentarians to persuade them to prioritize and adopt the ICC Bill. The donor community had very concrete ideas of what 'democracy', 'good governance' and 'rule of law' looked like: adopt this bill—the more like the Rome Statute (ideally incorporating even more human rights norms),[2] the better.

More than in previous years, international law was in the Ugandan air.[3] It had not been in December 2003, when Uganda referred the 'Situation concerning the Lord's Resistance Army' to the ICC: that referral was the initiative of those in control of Uganda's military and security services, not of Ugandan lawyers. But during the Juba peace talks, which had started in 2006, it became apparent that the only way to *end* the ICC's involvement—and thus to obtain the LRA's agreement to a peace accord—was to have investigations and prosecutions under Ugandan law. The Juba Peace Agreement envisaged a 'Special Division of the High Court'—later also known as 'the War Crimes Court' and 'the International Crimes Division'—to 'try individuals who are alleged to have committed serious crimes during the conflict'.[4] Genuine domestic proceedings could render the ICC's case inadmissible on the basis of the Rome Statute's principle of complementarity.[5] Suddenly, the Ugandan legal system had become relevant to a situation that Ugandan lawyers had previously mostly left to the military and politicians. Western diplomats and NGOs were not entirely sure: some did not want to support a process that could deprive the ICC of its promising first case; others saw the positive impact that the ceasefire had had on the humanitarian situation in northern Uganda and wanted to give peace a chance. Even those pro-ICC saw the developments as an opportunity to push through Uganda's ICC Bill, which could facilitate co-operation with the ICC. At the time of the conference that Pål and I attended, the mediation team of the Juba peace talks was still trying to persuade LRA leader Joseph Kony to sign the Final Peace Agreement.

---

[1] He discusses this and many other legal questions related to Ugandan investigations and prosecutions of international crimes in Wrange 2008.

[2] *See, generally,* Mégret 2011.

[3] The sources of the facts of this account are provided in Nouwen 2013, Chapter 3.

[4] Agreement on Accountability and Reconciliation between the Government of the Republic of Uganda and the Lord's Resistance Army/Movement, Juba, 29 June 2007. https://ucdpged.uu.se/peaceagreements/fulltext/Uga%2020070629.pdf. Accessed 11 June 2025. *See also* Annexure to the Agreement on Accountability and Reconciliation, Juba, 19 February 2008, clauses 7 and 10. https://peacemaker.un.org/en/node/9467. Accessed 11 June 2025.

[5] Rome Statute of the International Criminal Court, opened for signature 17 July 1998, 2187 UNTS 3 (entered into force 1 July 2002), article 17.

But the legal car left the political factory of the Juba peace talks: encouraged by foreign donors, some Ugandan lawyers began implementing the part of the peace agreement on accountability and reconciliation, even in the absence of a signature under the Final Peace Agreement and domestic legislation giving effect to the agreement. In their view, this was a chance for the Ugandan legal system to make a contribution to peace—and to obtain donor funding for a special court, including buildings, cars, drivers, and training abroad. (Some of their colleagues, however, feared that all the attention for and investment in a 'special' division would come at a cost to the ordinary justice system.) In the Juba Peace Agreement's Accountability and Reconciliation Agreement and its Annexure, the Special Division of the High Court was only one component of a complex transitional justice puzzle. Other components of the puzzle were to be resolved by the legislature and executive: which laws the Special Division would apply; how the Amnesty Act 2000 would be dealt with; which alternative sanctions would apply and how formal and 'traditional justice' would interact. At the heart of the transitional-justice puzzle was a political compromise: the LRA would give up its armed struggle and be tried domestically, but the punishment would be in accordance with northern Ugandan 'traditional justice' mechanisms, focused on reconciliation and reparation rather than retribution.

The focus of the Ugandan legal sector and Western donors on only one aspect of the peace agreement meant that the political compromise was lost out of sight. Joseph Kony was still to sign the agreement, but budgets already envisaged radio jingles announcing the 'War Crimes Court'. When asked about the potential impact of such jingles on the peace process, the lawyer in the lead of establishing the special court, the Principal Judge, answered: 'For political questions, you are with the wrong people here.' In his view, the legal car had left the political factory of the Juba peace talks. In fact, however, the legal car was still on a political route; it was only on a different political route than the one envisaged in the Juba peace talks.

In the end, Kony did not sign the Final Peace Agreement. Northern Uganda remained relatively peaceful thanks to the LRA having moved out during the Juba peace talks, but the LRA continued to wreak havoc in neighbouring countries, with deadly consequences. The Special Division was created, externally funded and, like many of its international counterparts, desperately needed a first case.[6] When LRA member Thomas Kwoyelo wanted to rely on the Amnesty Act, like more than 26,000 members of armed groups before him, the Ugandan Supreme Court came up with an argument as to why the Act could not apply to international crimes—an argument that undermined the legal certainty of the thousands of amnesties granted before—so that he could be tried by the War Crimes Court.[7] Once again, international donors had very concrete ideas of what the 'rule of law' required: Kwoyelo on trial—at all costs.[8] One Ugandan lawyer commented on how the Ugandan and international supporters of the War Crimes Court were willing to sacrifice the legal certainty of

[6] *See* Nouwen and Becker 2017 on the phenomenon of 'being a Tadić'.

[7] Supreme Court of Uganda, *Uganda v. Thomas Kwoyelo,* Constitutional Appeal No. 1 of 2012, 8 April 2015.

[8] *Cf.* Nouwen 2012.

26,000 people who had already benefited from an amnesty under the Amnesty Act just to prosecute Kwoyelo: 'They fell every man to get their man'.

Legislation to provide for alternative sanctions or the interaction of formal and traditional justice never materialized. The Special Division had become unmoored from the transitional justice context from which it originated; it had become an ordinary criminal court—albeit with extraordinary donor funding—focusing on international crimes. In October 2024, fifteen years after his arrest, Kwoyelo was convicted to 40 years in jail—15 years more than his superior Dominic Ongwen, who had been tried by the ICC.

22.2 The Ride of Transitional Justice

The Ugandan experience is emblematic of the 2000s. Whereas criminal accountability had initially been transitional justice's most inaccessible route, it had, by the 2000s, become the discourse's most cherished mechanism. Transitional justice was no longer inherently about justice involving compromises; it became criminal justice with special add-ons (truth commissions, reparations, vetting, institutional reform).[9] And whereas international criminal justice in the 1990s was still justified as a tool to pursue peace (recall that the Security Council created the tribunals for the former Yugoslavia and Rwanda under Chapter VII of the UN Charter), it had, by the 2000s, been emancipated.[10] Indeed, the spirit became one of 'If not peace, then justice'.[11] Many international criminal lawyers critical of transitional justice as 'compromised justice' would celebrate this development. But the Ugandan experience illustrates that what is gained in criminal justice can be lost in terms of transition: there has been no transition in terms of government, in terms of ending the violence by the LRA or in terms of reckoning with the northern Ugandan experience of the decades-long war. This is not to say that the Special Division on its own could have achieved any such transition. But it has been evident that it could not contribute to this by going alone, leaving the peace agreement behind. The transformation of what was envisaged as a transitional justice court into a purely criminal court, broken free from the political compromise that led to its creation, illustrates the challenges of judicialized transitional justice. More than a decade later, Colombia would struggle with the challenge of having handed over a political compromise—the peace agreement with the FARC—to legal professionals who are cautious with deviating from ordinary

[9] Jain and Nouwen 2025.

[10] Mégret 2008.

[11] Rubin 2006.

criminal justice, leading to accusations by the FARC of the government reneging on the peace agreement.[12]

22.3 Pål's Onward Ride

After the event in Entebbe, Pål drove home to Kampala. His onward journey took him back to Sweden, back to academia, and to 'critical international law'. Wrange works with a broad understanding of critical international law, encompassing—in his terminology—C1 (critical in the sense of criticism) and C2 (critical in the sense of critique). No matter which C, he has always been interested in the political aspect of the law. At the time of his retirement, the 2020s, many hope that courts will do what politicians have failed to do—think about South Africa's case against Israel and the climate change hearings before the International Court of Justice. Thus, even when Pål has retired, it will be important to continue assessing the politics of the legal: which solutions are reinforced, which ones eliminated? Who wins, who loses?

References

Jain N, Nouwen S (2025) Overture to a Battle: Transitional Justice from 1975-2000. In: von Bernstorff J et al (eds) The Battle for International Law II. Oxford University Press (forthcoming, on file with author)

Mégret F (2008) A Special Tribunal for Lebanon: The UN Security Council and the Emancipation of International Criminal Justice. Leiden Journal of International Law 21(2):485–512

Mégret F (2011) Too Much of a Good Thing? Implementation and the Uses of Complementarity. In: Stahn C, El Zeidy M (eds) The International Criminal Court and Complementarity: From Theory to Practice. Cambridge University Press, Cambridge, pp. 361–390

Nouwen S (2012) The ICC's Intervention in Uganda: Which Rule of Law Does It Promote? In: Zürn M et al (eds), Rule of Law Dynamics. Cambridge University Press, New York, pp. 278–304

Nouwen S (2013) Complementarity in the Line of Fire: The Catalysing Effect of the International Criminal Court in Uganda and Sudan. Cambridge University Press, Cambridge

Nouwen S, Becker M (2017) Tadić v. Prosecutor, International Criminal Tribunal for the Former Yugoslavia. In: Bjorge E, Miles C (eds) Landmark Cases in Public International Law. Hart, Oxford and Portland, pp. 377–407

Rubin E (2006) If Not Peace, Then Justice. New York Times. http://www.nytimes.com/2006/04/02/magazine/02darfur.html?ex=1144641600&en=585d2ee57ddf337f&ei=5070&emc=eta1. Accessed 11 June 2025

Wrange P (2008) The Agreement and the Annexure on Accountability and Reconciliation between the Government of Uganda and the Lord's Resistance Army/Movement—A Legal and Pragmatic Commentary. Uganda Living Law Journal 6:42–128. https://papers.ssrn.com/sol3/papers.cfm?abstract_id=2558561. Accessed 11 June 2025

[12] Congress of the Republic of Colombia: Audiencia Pública Seguridad Jurídica de Firmantes del Acuerdo de Paz—Últimas Actuaciones JEP [Public Hearing on Legal Security of Signatories of the Peace Agreement—Latest Actions of the JEP] (June 2024). https://www.youtube.com/watch?v=buO-399tIuU. Accessed 11 June 2025.

Sarah Nouwen is professor of Public International Law at the European University Institute and Editor in Chief of the European Journal of International Law. She is on leave from the University of Cambridge, where she is also a Professor of International Law and was for many years Co-Deputy Director of the Lauterpacht Centre for International Law and a Fellow of Pembroke College. Prior to assuming her academic roles, Nouwen worked in international diplomacy: at the Dutch mission to the United Nations, at the Netherlands Embassy in Khartoum, and as a Senior Legal Advisor to the African Union High Level Implementation Panel in Sudan. She also served as a consultant for the UK Department of International Development in Darfur and worked with an NGO in Senegal on microfinance. Her article 'As You Set out for Ithaka: Practical, Epistemological, Ethical, and Existential Questions about Socio-Legal Empirical Research in Conflict' won the Leiden Journal prize for the best article published in 2013–2016.

Chapter 23
Responsibility and Accountability for Environmental Destruction in Relation to Armed Conflicts: The Case of Ukraine

Marie Jacobsson

Contents

Abstract This chapter addresses the legal framework and potential processes regarding the responsibility for environmental destruction in relation to an armed conflict, with a special focus on the environmental consequences of the war against Ukraine. It does so in a generic manner with the aim of illustrating that the legal aftermath of harm to the environment in relation to armed conflicts is likely to take a more prominent role than ever before. Accountability for environmental damage in Ukraine as a result of the Russian aggression will take many forms, from individual to State responsibility. It will go beyond the law of armed conflict and include other areas, such as environmental law, human rights law, and criminal law. It also shows that claims to reparation and compensation in interstate conflicts will be accompanied by civil and criminal law proceedings pursued by both individuals and legal entities. Pursuing claims is part of a legitimate lawfare and needs due processes, as distinct from parallel political agreements that aim at ending hostilities.

Keywords Ukraine · Aggression · Law of armed conflict · EcoZagroza · Environmental crimes · Ecocide · Damage · Responsibility · Accountability ·

M. Jacobsson (✉)
University of Lund, Lund, Sweden
e-mail: marie.g.jacobsson@outlook.com; marie.jacobsson@jur.lu.se

M. Klamberg et al. (eds.), *Reconstructing Power and Hegemony in Public International Law*, https://doi.org/10.1007/978-94-6265-743-4_23

International Law Commission · Protection of the environment in relation to armed conflicts · Lawfare

23.1 Introduction

Since the large-scale Russian invasion of Ukraine began on 24 February 2022, the Ministry of Ecology and Natural Resources in Ukraine has collected information on the environmental damage caused by Russia's war of aggression against Ukraine. This turned out to be a foresighted initiative and must be seen as part of Ukraine's overall ambition to hold Russia accountable for its aggression against Ukraine. It is yet another example of Ukraine's legitimate "lawfare" to counter the hostile Russian actions that started already in 2014.[1] The environmental destruction that has taken place and continues to take place in Ukraine is appalling and goes far beyond what can be labelled as "collateral damage".[2] A few months into the large-scale invasion, on 12 May 2022, the Ministry of Ecology and Natural Resources launched an official web resource and a mobile app called EcoZagroza ("environmental threat" in Ukrainian). According to the Ministry: *"[t]he application features an interactive map of Ukraine with monitoring data on air quality and radiation levels, as well as information on the environmental crimes committed by the Russian occupiers. The app users can also report the environmental crimes they have witnessed."*[3] The use of the EcoZagroza[4] app has expanded almost exponentially since its launch in 2022.

Developments after 1 March 2025 are not considered in the chapter.

[1] *See, e.g.*, the interview with Mykola Gnatovsky, Professor of international law at the University of Kyiv, then a special advisor to the Foreign Ministry of Ukraine, https://www.justiceinfo.net/en/90566-ukraine-momentum-tribunal-aggression.html. For a broader recapitulation of Ukraine's lawfare, *see* Goldenziel 2022, pp. 1–15.

[2] For an early and preliminary report, *see* UNEP 2022. Even if "collateral damage" is not a proper legal term, its meaning is reflected in Article 51(5)(b) of the 1977 Additional Protocol I, which prohibits an attack that may be expected to cause incidental loss of civilian life, injury to civilians, damage to civilian objects, or a combination thereof, which would be excessive in relation to the concrete and direct military advantage anticipate. It is most often reflected in Military Manuals. According to the ICRC IHL database, the Russian Federation's Combat Manual (2005) states that "causing severe suffering or damage, which is excessive for the achievement of a military objective is prohibited". The rule is also reflected in Ukraine's Manual on the Application of IHL Rules, Ministry of Defence, 11 September 2004, § 2.1.8. Excerpts from the Manuals can be found on the ICRC IHL databases, *see* https://ihl-databases.icrc.org/en/customary-ihl/v2/rule14. Accessed 16 February 2025. It is worth recalling that the environment is not in itself a military objective.

[3] This quotation stems from the web page of the Ministry of Ecology and Natural Resources when the application was launched in 2022. Today, the updated EcoZagroza is presented as an official resource of the Ministry of Environment, developed with the support of the Ministry of Digital Transformation of Ukraine. It is a standardized form for automatic collection and recording of information about environmental threats in real time, with geographic reference to the area. https://ecozagroza.gov.ua/en. Accessed 16 February 2025.

[4] https://ecozagroza.gov.ua/en/feed. Accessed 16 February 2025.

An important step in the direction of (what I would label) "environmental accountability" was the inclusion of the point "immediate protection of the environment" as part of President Zelensky's peace plan, initially presented to the G20 Summit on 15 November 2022.[5] Point 8 of the peace plan reads:

> *The huge damage to the environment and wildlife was caused by Russian invasion: burned forests, mined fields, polluted waters, killed animals. Just the environmental damage caused by the Russians' blowing up of the Kakhovka hydroelectric power plant dam has been approximately $1.5 billion – but it is hard to put numbers to the damages that changed the ecosystem for decades to come. And that is a challenge for the whole world.*[6]

However, it should be underlined that point 8 is not the only point that is related to the environment. Apart from the fundamental requirement of the peace plan—namely, the withdrawal of Russian troops and the cessation of hostilities (point 6)—Zelensky's peace plan also contains points on radiation and nuclear safety, food security, energy security, and justice (points 1, 2, 3, and 7, respectively)—all of which are directly related to the protection and restoration of the environment.

As a result of the inclusion of environmental protection in the peace plan, the Office of the President established at High-Level Working Group on the Environmental Consequences of War. It was Co-Chaired by Andriy Yermak, Head of the Office of the President, and Margot Wallström, former Minister of Foreign Affairs of Sweden. The High-Level Working Group was asked to look into the environmental damage resulting from the war, assess how justice could be strengthened, and recommend steps towards green reconstruction and recovery. The result was the report, *An Environmental Compact for Ukraine*, containing 50 recommendations.[7] Ensuring accountability "for the massive environmental destruction wrought by Russian forces" is one of the three priorities.[8] Twenty-four of the 50 recommendations in the report directly address accountability. They address steps that should be taken by Ukrainian authorities, such as encouraging Ukraine's Prosecutor-General to develop a comprehensive strategy for the prosecutions of wartime environmental damage, training of judges, and capacity-building of investigators and prosecutors regarding environmental crimes. It also encourages European and other States to investigate and prosecute war crimes. It recommends that Ukraine ratify the Rome

---

[5] https://www.president.gov.ua/en/news/ukrayina-zavzhdi-bula-liderom-mirotvorchih-zusil-yaksho-rosi-79141. Accessed 16 February 2025. The details of the recent Victory Plan, presented by President Zelensky during his visit to the United States around 24 September 2024, are not available.

[6] https://war.ukraine.ua/faq/zelenskyys-10-point-peace-plan/. Accessed 16 February 2025.

[7] *See* https://www.president.gov.ua/storage/j-files-storage/01/24/69/cc0dab040b3207268e5c8fb5275b22e4_1707492952.pdf; https://www.president.gov.ua/en/news/ukrayina-zavzhdi-bula-liderom-mirotvorchih-zusil-yaksho-rosi-79141. Accessed 16 February 2025. The Report was presented on 9 February 2024.

[8] Ibid. Priority 2: Ensure Accountability, pp. 8–11.

Statute of the International Criminal Court (ICC).[9] The recommendations stress the need to ensure that the investigations of Russian crimes include an environmental emphasis in the context of the work done by Eurojust (the European Union Agency for Criminal Justice Cooperation) and to establish an international mechanism for reparation for damage, loss, or injury for Ukraine.[10] Furthermore, some of the recommendations focus on the environmental consequences for individuals and their right to "reparations". It requests a focus on environmental aspects in international human rights investigations, including within existing mechanisms, such as the Independent International Commission of Inquiry on Ukraine established by the UN Human Rights Council.[11] Some of the suggestions already existed in an embryonic form, whereas others most likely got pushed forward by the recommendations. Recommendation 20, that Ukraine should seek an advisory opinion from the International Court of Justice to clarify the rights, responsibilities, and liabilities in regard to environmental crimes and other violations in the contexts of conflict, had not been officially discussed before.

Thus, it is clear that Zelensky's peace plan from 2022 extends beyond responsibility for breaches of the law of armed conflict (LOAC). As expected, it also covers Russia's responsibility for the environmental consequences of the act of aggression *per se*. At the same time, it must be noted that the devastating environmental consequences of the war of aggression against Ukraine did not start with the invasion on 24 February 2022, but already with the aggression against Ukraine in 2014. However, the effects and scale of the impact since the commencement of the large-scale invasion on 24 February 2022 are of a different magnitude and raise new questions of accountability for the environmental consequences of the war.

[9] Ukraine has since ratified the Rome Statute on 25 October 2024, in force on 1 January 2025. https://www.president.gov.ua/en/news/z-1-sichnya-2025-roku-ukrayina-stane-125-yu-derzhavoyu-uchas-94061. Accessed 16 February 2025. *See also* https://asp.icc-cpi.int/sites/default/files/asp_docs/2025-Bureau2-Agenda-Decisions.pdf. Accessed 16 February 2025; https://treaties.un.org/Pages/ViewDetails.aspx?src=TREATY&mtdsg_no=XVIII-10&chapter=18&clang=_en#EndDec. Accessed 16 February 2025.

[10] Environmental Compact, Recommendations 9–22.

[11] Independent International Commission of Inquiry on Ukraine established by the UN Human Rights Council, https://www.ohchr.org/en/hr-bodies/hrc/iicihr-ukraine/index. Accessed 16 February 2025. Other international human rights investigations were also mentioned: the UN Human Rights Monitoring Mission in Ukraine and the OSCE Moscow Mechanism. The connection between human rights and the environmental consequences of the war is not addressed in these human rights-oriented reports, https://www.ohchr.org/en/countries/ukraine/our-presence, https://www.osce.org/permanent-council/567358. Accessed 16 February 2025.

23.2 Historical Notes

Historically, the legal protection of the environment in relation to armed conflicts has been rather weak. In fact, older treaties did not refer to the environment at all.[12] The only relevant legal protection of the environment came indirectly through the rules on property rights and natural resources. The first provision on the protection of the environment as such came in the 1976 ENMOD convention.[13] It was followed by some provisions in the First Additional Protocol 1977 to the Geneva Conventions of 12 August 1949.[14] The provisions came as a result of the negative impact on the environment during the Vietnam War in the 1960s and 1970s. Since then, the international community has slowly started to realize the environmental consequences of modern means and methods of warfare. Following the reports revealing the Agent Orange defoliation in Vietnam, shocking images of environmental destruction in other conflicts—such as the Iraq war against Kuwait, where 600 oil wells were set on fire by retreating Iraqi forces—made their way through the media landscape. Similarly, subsequent armed conflicts in the Former Republic of Yugoslavia, Kosovo, Iraq, Sierra Leone, Lebanon, and Liberia have all demonstrated the high environmental costs for war-torn societies. Both the conflicts in the Democratic Republic of the Congo and Mali bear witness to the connection between a conflict, natural resources, and impact on the climate, whereas the military coup in Myanmar resulted in modern environmental considerations being ignored. The wars in Yemen and in Gaza have caused different, but considerable, environmental harm to the detriment of the land, sea, and people who live in the region,[15] and are reported to have long-term effects due to carbon emissions.[16]

---

[12] A list of treaties and declarations relevant to the conduct of hostilities, dating from 1899 to 1948 are listed in International Law Commission 2015, pp. 135–185, *see in particular* pp. 157 *et seq.*

[13] The ENMOD Convention regulates military or any other hostile use of environmental modification techniques. The Convention provides that such use is prohibited if it has widespread, long-lasting, or severe effects as the means of destruction, damage, or injury to any other State Party. *See* Convention on the Prohibition of Military or Any Other Hostile Use of Environmental Modification Techniques, opened for signature 10 December 1976, 1108 UNTS 152 (entered into force 5 October 1978) (ENMOD) article 1(1).

[14] Articles 35 and 55 directly address damage to the environment, Protocol Additional to the Geneva Conventions of 12 August 1949, and relating to the Protection of Victims of International Armed Conflicts (Additional Protocol I), 1977, 1125 UNTS 3. *See* section 23.3 *below.*

[15] The war in Gaza is reported to have an unprecedented environmental impact, *see, e.g.,* the early assessment by UNEP on the environmental impact of the conflict in Gaza. This includes impacts on environmental management and waste disposal systems; energy, fuel and associated infrastructure; destruction of buildings and conflict-related debris; marine and terrestrial environments; and air quality. *See* UNEP 2024a. For the early preliminary report on the war against Ukraine, *see* UNEP 2022. For reports on Yemen, *see, e.g.*, Mohammed 2023. For further references, *see, for example,* the reports by UNEP https://www.unep.org/topics/disasters-and-conflicts and by the Conflict and Environmental Observatory, CEOBS, https://ceobs.org/countries/yemen. Accessed 16 February 2025.

[16] *See, e.g.*, Saber 2024.

Even if the legal analysis of regulations related to the protection of the environment have been focused on the rules and provisions found in the law of armed conflict, which is primarily applicable during an armed conflict, it should be noted that such a narrow view is not sufficient from either a legal or an environmental perspective. Not only is there a need to examine what preventative measures that need to be taken to protect the environment—there is also a need to repair and restore the damaged or affected environment and sort out questions relating to liability and responsibility. Hence, applicable law extends beyond the realm of the law of armed conflict. This was recognized by the United Nations International Law Commission (ILC) when it decided to include the topic "Protection of the environment in relation to armed conflicts" in its long-term programme of work in 2011. The purpose was to analyse the topic from a wider perspective than the law of armed conflict.[17]

23.3 The Law of Armed Conflict and the Environment—A Brief Recapitulation

So, how far does the law allow harm to the environment during an armed conflict? Perhaps not as far as many may imagine. It would go beyond the purpose of this chapter to analyse the details of the law of armed conflicts, but a very brief recapitulation may serve a purpose.[18]

As previously mentioned, the law of armed conflicts contains a limited number of articles that directly address protection of the environment. The "environment" as such is not even mentioned in the 1907 Hague Conventions or the 1949 Geneva Conventions. This is perhaps not surprising, as the idea of the "environment" as used today does not appear in the international context until the 1960s.

The LOAC rules are very basic: The natural environment is a civilian object, and as such may not be attacked unless it has become a military objective. The environment must not be modified and used a weapon. Likewise, attacks on the natural environment by means of reprisals are prohibited. All the customary law principles of the law of armed conflict apply: distinction, proportionality, and precautions in attack, as well as the rules of military necessity and humanitarian considerations (including

---

[17] International Law Commission 2011, para 365. For the preparatory work and background, *see* the syllabus to the topic in Annex V, pp. 211–221. Two years later, the Commission decided to include the topic in its Programme of work and appointed a Special Rapporteur—*see* International Law Commission 2013, p. 78, para 167. The first Special Rapporteur was Marie G. Jacobsson, Sweden, followed by Marja Lehto, Finland, who led the work to conclusion in 2022.

[18] A summary of the legal framework with references can be found in the Preliminary report on the protection of the environment in relation to armed conflicts, by Marie G. Jacobsson, Special Rapporteur, *see* International Law Commission 2014, pp. 205–238. For a comprehensive analysis, *see* the Draft principles on protection of the environment in relation to armed conflicts, with commentaries 2022. https://legal.un.org/ilc/texts/instruments/english/commentaries/8_7_2022.pdf. Accessed 16 February 2025. *See also* the Guidelines on the Protection of the Natural Environment in Armed Conflict: Rules and Recommendations Relating to the Protection of the Natural Environment under International Humanitarian Law, with Commentary, ICRC, Geneva, September 2020.

the Martens Clause). Irrespective of those principles, the belligerents must show due regard to the protection and preservation of the natural environment.[19]

The first reference to the environment is found in the Convention on the Prohibition of Military or Any Other Hostile Use of Environmental Modification Techniques (the ENMOD Convention), Article 1(1). The purpose of the Convention is to prohibit hostile use of the environment as a means of warfare. Article 1(1) reads:

> Each State Party to this Convention undertakes not to engage in military or any other hostile use of environmental modification techniques having widespread, long-lasting or severe effects as the means of destruction, damage or injury to any other State Party.[20]

A few years later, in 1980, a specific prohibition "to make forests or other kinds of plant cover the object of attack by incendiary weapons except when such natural elements are used to cover, conceal or camouflage combatants or other military objectives, or are themselves military objectives" was included in the third Protocol to the Conventional Weapons Convention.[21]

The basic rules for the general protection of the environment are reflected in Article 35 of the Additional Protocol I. It recalls that "the right of the Parties to the conflict to choose methods or means of warfare is not unlimited" and provides that "[I]t is prohibited to employ methods or means of warfare which are intended, or may be expected, to cause widespread, long-term and severe damage to the natural environment".[22]

The other explicit reference to the protection of the environment is found in Article 55, para 1 of Additional Protocol I. It reads:

> 1. Care shall be taken in warfare to protect the natural environment against widespread, long-term and severe damage. This protection includes a prohibition of the use of methods or means of warfare which are intended or may be expected to cause such damage to the natural environment and thereby to prejudice the health or survival of the population.
>
> 2. Attacks against the natural environment by way of reprisals are prohibited.[23]

The difference between the cumulative requirement in Article 35 of Additional Protocol I and the non-cumulative formulation in Article I in the ENMOD Convention is notable and well-known.

Other articles in Additional Protocol I indirectly aim to address the environmental consequences of war. One of the most important articles, Article 56, concerns the

[19] In context of the law of armed conflict, references are made to the "natural environment", not "the environment", whereas the ILC in its work on the Protection of the environment in relation to armed conflicts simply refers to "the environment".

[20] ENMOD, above n. 13.

[21] Convention on Prohibitions or Restrictions of the Use of Certain Conventional Weapons Which May Be Deemed Excessively Injurious or to Have Indiscriminate Effects, in Protocol III (Protocol on Prohibitions or Restrictions on the Use of Incendiary Weapons Geneva), 10 October 1980. 1342 UNTS 137; Annex III, article 2, para 2. The provision was considered to be a part of the regulation on the protection of civilians and civilian objects.

[22] Additional Protocol I, above n. 14, Article 35, Basic rules, paras 1 and 3, respectively.

[23] Ibid. Article 55.

protection of works and installations containing dangerous forces and provides *inter alia* that:

> Works or installations containing dangerous forces, namely dams, dykes and nuclear electrical generating stations, shall not be made the object of attack, even where these objects are military objectives, if such attack may cause the release of dangerous forces and consequent severe losses among the civilian population. Other military objectives located at or in the vicinity of these works or installations shall not be made the object of attack if such attack may cause the release of dangerous forces from the works or installations and consequent severe losses among the civilian population.[24]

Article 56 consists of two elements: a primary prohibition and a limited exception to the prohibition. Even the exception comes with caveats. The rule is quite unique in the LOAC context as it clearly states that even if a dam, dyke, or a nuclear power station could be considered a military objective, particularly restrictive rules apply before it may be targeted.[25] It has been underlined that *"[t]he absence of a radioactive leak or severe civilian losses does not preclude the unlawfulness of the attack, if perpetrated despite the risk of such an outcome."*[26] Launching an attack against such work and installations containing dangerous forces as defined in Article 57, para 2 (*a*) (iii); amounts to a grave breach of the Geneva Conventions and the Protocol.[27]

In addition, the Rome Statute contains a directly relevant provision on the protection of the environment during armed conflict. Its Article 8 (with the heading "War crimes") includes among serious violations of the laws and customs applicable in international armed conflict within the established framework of international law, the act of:

> Intentionally launching an attack in the knowledge that such attack will cause incidental loss of life or injury to civilians or damage to civilian objects or widespread, long-term and severe damage to the natural environment which would be clearly excessive in relation to the concrete and direct overall military advantage anticipated.[28]

In areas under occupation, the laws and responsibilities of occupation law apply. This imposes a clear obligation to ensure public order and security on the one hand, and civil life, including the welfare of the local population, on the other (Article

---

[24] Ibid. Article 56, para 1 (Protection of works and installations containing dangerous forces).

[25] These rules are found in Article 56, paras 2–4 and include a specific prohibition on reprisals in para 4.

[26] Dannenbaum 2022.

[27] Rome Statute of the International Criminal Court, opened for signature 17 July 1998, 2187 UNTS 3 (entered into force 1 July 2002) (Rome Statute), article 85(3)(b).

[28] Ibid. Article 8 (2)(b)(iv). Humle has noted that a caveat must be made with this provision (and several other provisions in the Rome Statute). The reason is that it imports a standard of military necessity much higher than that traditionally understood by international humanitarian law (IHL) for the purposes of securing accountability for war crimes (i.e., serious violations). Furthermore, the references to "clearly excessive" and "overall military advantage" are not the standards within international humanitarian law. These were compromises at the Rome Conference so as to ensure that ICC judges do not apply the standard too strictly and put themselves in the military commanders' shoes ex-post facto. *See* Humle 2004.

43 of the 1907 Hague Regulations).[29] When analysing the legal framework on the protection of the environment in situations of occupation, the ILC Special Rapporteur on the *Protection of the environment in relation to armed conflicts* submitted that "the occupying State has a general obligation to respect the environment of the occupied territory and to take environmental considerations into account in the administration of such territory".[30]

23.4 The Work of the International Law Commission

This brings us to the work of the International Law Commission on the topic *Protection of the environment in relation to armed conflicts* 2011–2022.

The International Law Commission had previously addressed the applicability of treaties in armed conflicts in the topic *Effects of armed conflicts on treaties*, which was adopted by the Commission in 2011.[31] It was recognized that the classical distinction between the law of peace and the law of war was no longer apt to reflect the post-World War II developments whereby international law was codified in multilateral treaties. Hence, the *Draft articles on the effects of armed conflicts on treaties* start from the presumption that "[t]he existence of an armed conflict does not *ipso facto* terminate or suspend the operation of treaties" either "between States parties to the conflict" or "between a State party to the conflict and a State that is not."[32] The articles furthermore contain "an indicative list of treaties, the subject matter of which involves an implication that they remain in operation, in whole or in part, during armed conflict". The list ("the Annex") includes treaties on the international protection of human rights, the international protection of the environment, as well as international watercourses and aquifers and their related installations and facilities. It also includes treaties on international criminal justice.[33] This means that the Commission had drawn the conclusion that also treaties not directly written for the situation of armed conflict may continue to be applicable, in whole or in part, during armed conflicts.

---

[29] *See, e.g.*, Humle 2020, pp. 203–241. For an updated analysis of the law applicable during occupation, *see* Part Four, Principles applicable in situations of occupation, of the Draft principles on protection of the environment in relation to armed conflicts, with commentaries 2022 which will appear in Yearbook of the International Law Commission, 2022, Vol. II, Part Two. The text can now be found in the ILC Report on the work of the seventy-third session (2022). *See* UNGA 2022a, pp. 90–187, also available as a separate file at https://legal.un.org/ilc/reports/2022/english/chp5.pdf.

[30] *See* UNGA 2018, p. 27, para 50.

[31] International Law Commission 2011, p. 106, para 95.

[32] Ibid. p. 107, Article 3, General principle, reads: "The existence of an armed conflict does not *ipso facto* terminate or suspend the operation of treaties:

(a) as between States parties to the conflict;

(b) as between a State party to the conflict and a State that is not."

[33] Ibid. Article 7 and the Annex.

The Commission held lengthy discussions on category (g) in the Annex, namely *Treaties relating to the international protection of the environment*. The reason was its connection to the use of nuclear weapons. The discussions should be seen in light of the International Court of Justice Advisory Opinion in the *Legality of the Threat or Use of Nuclear Weapons Case*. The Commission refers to how the Court there analysed the question and formulated the Court's general position by stating that "[t]he existence of the general obligation of States to ensure that activities within their jurisdiction and control respect the environment of other States or of areas beyond national control is now part of the corpus of international law relating to the environment." It then continued by saying: "However, the Court is of the view that the issue is not whether the treaties relating to the protection of the environment are or are not applicable during an armed conflict, but rather whether the obligations stemming from these treaties were intended to be obligations of total restraint during military conflict."[34] The Court recalled that: "States must take environmental considerations into account when assessing what is necessary and proportionate in the pursuit of legitimate military objectives. Respect for the environment is one of the elements that go to assessing whether an action is in conformity with the principles of necessity and proportionality."[35] The Court recalled Article 35, para 3, and Article 55 of Additional Protocol I and concluded that: "Taken together, these provisions embody a general obligation to protect the natural environment against widespread, long-term and severe environmental damage; the prohibition of methods and means of warfare which are intended, or may be expected, to cause such damage; and the prohibition of attacks against the natural environment by way of reprisals. These are powerful constraints for all the States having subscribed to these provisions."[36]

At this stage, the ILC was careful not to draw overly large and sweeping conclusions from the Court's formulations in these sensitively worded (and much debated) paragraphs of the Advisory Opinion on Nuclear Weapons. On several other occasions, the Commission elaborated more explicitly with respect to the Court's judgments or Orders relating to the protection of the environment.[37]

Apart from the *Draft articles on the effects of armed conflicts on treaties*, other topics were also of significance when the Commission addressed the *Protection of the environment in relation to armed conflicts*. They included the work the Commission did on the fragmentation of international law, 2006; the law of transboundary aquifers, 2008; the prevention of transboundary harm from hazardous activities, 2001; the allocation of loss in the case of transboundary harm arising out of hazardous activities, 2006; and the law of the non-navigational uses of international watercourses, 1994.[38]

---

[34] ICJ, *Legality of the Threat or Use of Nuclear Weapons, Advisory Opinion*, 8 July 1996, 1996 ICJ Reports 226, paras 29–31.

[35] Ibid. para 30.

[36] Ibid. para 31.

[37] For an overview, *see* Sender 2024.

[38] Jacobsson and Lehto 2020, pp. 27–46.

Of particular importance is the work on the responsibility of States for internationally wrongful acts.[39]

The International Law Commission concluded its substantive work on the *Protection of the environment in relation to armed conflicts* in 2022.[40] The Commission adopted 27 principles (the PERAC principles) with a temporal scope that covers the periods before, during, and after armed conflicts, and presented them to the UN General Assembly. As suggested by the Commission, the United Nations General Assembly took note of the principles and attached them to an UNGA resolution.[41] Built on the UNGA resolution, the United Nations Environmental Assembly adopted a resolution in which it invited States to "take note of the International Law Commission's principles on protection of the environment in relation to armed conflicts, as applicable".[42]

The ILC PERAC principles reflect the urgent need to enhance the protection of the environment in relation to armed conflicts. Apart from reflecting the applicable law of armed conflict, including occupation, they also include innovative principles relating to the operation and liability of business enterprises.[43] The Martens Clause is clearly reflected. The principles further include remnants of war, with a separate principle on remnants of war at sea remaining, as well as the important principle on sharing and granting access to information. State responsibility is reflected as a generally applicable principle.[44]

23.5 Ecocide

Ecocide is not a new term in and of itself. In fact, it was used already more than 50 years ago (including by former Swedish Prime Minister Olof Palme), but it is not yet a term with an accepted definition under international law. In 2020, an initiative to make ecocide a crime under international criminal law by including it in the Statute of the International Criminal Court was taken by the Stop Ecocide Foundation. An independent expert panel was convened and elaborated a definition of the crime of ecocide to be included as Article 8 *ter* of the Rome Statute.[45] This idea was later

[39] International Law Commission 2001, pp. 20 *et seq.*

[40] Draft principles on protection of the environment in relation to armed conflicts, with commentaries, 2022, which will appear in the forthcoming Yearbook of the International Law Commission, 2022, Vol. II, Part Two. Until then, they can be found in UNGA 2022a.

[41] UNGA 2022b.

[42] UNEP 2024b.

[43] *See, in particular*, UNGA 2019, pp. 32–44, paras 67–92.

[44] UNGA 2022a, Principle 9.

[45] This was an initiative by the Stop Ecocide Foundation which convened an Independent Expert Panel for the Legal Definition of Ecocide. https://www.stopecocide.earth/expert-drafting-panel. Accessed 16 February 2025. The Panel has suggested a definition that includes the following wording: "*For the purpose of this Statute, "ecocide" means unlawful or wanton acts committed with knowledge that there is a substantial likelihood of severe and either widespread or long-term*

reflected in a formal proposal by Vanuatu, co-sponsored by Fiji and Samoa, to include "ecocide" in the Rome Statute. Vanuatu had aired this idea already in 2019, but the formal proposal came in 2024. It is clear from the statement by Vanuatu that its objective was to include ecocide as an international crime in general, not a crime relating to the law of armed conflict as such. This does not take away the importance of the initiative, but it will not, in this context, assist in analysis of the possible connection between the crime of ecocide and (environmental) war crimes.

However, ecocide exists as a crime in the national legislations of many States, including those of Ukraine and Russia.[46] Technically, this means that a person under the jurisdiction of these States may be indicted for the crime of ecocide as defined in their national legislation.[47]

23.6 Responsibility and Accountability

For obvious reasons, the law of armed conflict, *jus in bello*, applies during or as a result of an armed conflict. The State involved has a legal responsibility to ensure that the law of warfare is implemented and upheld by its armed forces. A breach of this obligation is a breach of international law and entails State responsibility.

Therefore, the law applicable during armed conflict does not give a sufficient answer if we want to address accountability. We need to revert to the wider circle of international law, *and* we need to make a distinction between the responsibility of a State and the criminal responsibility of an individual.

Needless to say, a military aggression against another State is a breach of international law and entails the responsibility of the aggressor State. Such a breach *(jus ad bellum)* is independent of any breaches of the law of armed conflict—the *jus in bello*. This is reflected in Principle 9 of the International Law Commission's *Draft principles on the protection of the environment in relation to armed conflicts*.[48] The principle makes clear that "an internationally wrongful act of a State, in relation to an armed conflict, that causes damage to the environment entails the international responsibility of that State, which is under an obligation to make full reparation for such damage, including damage to the environment in and of itself." The draft

---

damage to the environment being caused by those acts." https://static1.squarespace.com/static/5ca2608ab914493c64ef1f6d/t/60d7479cf8e7e5461534dd07/1624721314430/SE+Foundation+Commentary+and+core+text+revised+%281%29.pdf. Accessed 16 February 2025.

[46] Article 441 of Section XX of the Criminal Code of Ukraine and Russian Criminal Code, article 358. https://ecojurisprudence.org/initiatives/criminal-code-russian-federation/. Accessed 16 February 2025.

[47] Point 8 of President Zelensky's Peace Plan from 2022, is described as implying the "[t]he eighth challenge is ecocide, the need for immediate protection of environment".

[48] Principle 9 State Responsibility, in Draft principles on protection of the environment in relation to armed conflicts, with commentaries, 2022, which will appear in forthcoming Yearbook of the International Law Commission, 2022, Vol. II, Part Two. Until then they can be found in UNGA 2022a.

principles are without prejudice to the rules on the responsibility of States and the rules on individual criminal responsibility. State responsibility and individual criminal responsibility do not exclude each other. They co-exist, and if the State has not fulfilled its obligations under the law of armed conflict, it is responsible for its breaches, irrespective of an individual's responsibility under criminal law which can result in criminal proceedings in accordance with the rule of law.

The commentary to Principle 9 explains that the paragraph reaffirms the applicability of this principle to internationally wrongful acts in relation to armed conflict that cause environmental damage, including damage caused to the environment in and of itself. Para 1 has been modelled on Articles 1 and 31, para 1, of the *Articles on the responsibility of States for internationally wrongful acts.* The legal link is obvious.

An aggressor State will always be obliged to make reparations to the State that it is the object of its aggression. Such reparations can take different forms, but the aggressor State cannot be relieved of its responsibility. There is no statute of limitation.[49] It is most likely that a State that is subject to an aggression will demand reparation from the aggressor State in accordance with international law. In the case of damage to the environment, it is likely to be a request for full reparation.

When accountability for damage to the environment in Ukraine is discussed, a variety of terms are used, including war crimes, grave breaches or serious violations of international humanitarian law, ecocide, and environmental war crimes. Some are legal concepts, others are not. War crime is the most encompassing term; it has come to cover most breaches of the law of armed conflicts in international and non-international armed conflicts. Grave breaches of international humanitarian law are the most severe breaches of international humanitarian law applicable in an international armed conflict. States are bound to act; they cannot remain passive if a grave breach has been committed. They must search for the perpetrator and adjudicate or extradite the suspect. "Environmental war crimes" is not a proper legal term. It is used to indicate that a crime that has environmental consequences or environmental consequences can amount to a war crime. It is, as pointed out by one experienced authority, "a new territory".[50] This is further evidenced by the fact that the ICC Office of the Prosecutor (OTP) in its Policy Paper on Environmental Crimes simply refers to "environmental crimes".[51]

[49] It has been reported that the reference to State responsibility was a contentious issue when the UNEA III Resolution on Environmental assistance and recovery in areas affected by armed conflict was adopted in March 2024. *See* UNEP 2024b. For information about the contentious issue of state responsibility, *see* https://ceobs.org/unea-6-passes-resolution-on-environmental-assistance-and-recovery-in-areas-affected-by-armed-conflict/. Accessed 16 February 2025.

[50] Payne 2024.

[51] ICC OTP 2024.

23.7 Turning to the Responsibility of Environmental Damages

The obligations to pay war reparations date back to ancient times.[52] The term "war reparations" is not defined in international law. Historically, it was a way for the victor to ensure that the cost of the war was covered. Although this chapter will not address the history of war reparations, it is worth recalling that the modern term "war reparations" is often included in peace treaties or peace settlements. In such situations, the parties involved in the armed conflict may undertake not to pursue claims.[53] War reparations negotiated between States may include reparations to individuals. There is no right under international humanitarian law for an individual to obtain compensation. However, we have seen a parallel development in the context of human rights, whereby individuals turn to human rights courts also for claims related to situations of armed conflict.

There are relatively few examples of war reparation processes relating to the environmental consequences of an armed conflict. One important example is the United Nations Compensation Commission, set up by the United Nations Security Council as a consequence of the Iraq-Kuwait war 1990–1991. The Commission evaluated a number of claims related to environmental destruction.[54] According to the Final Report of the Governing Council of the Commission, the environmental claims turned out to be uniquely complex in terms of volume and content, but also in terms of the challenges posed from a legal standpoint.[55] The Commission received 168 environmental claims from 12 Governments and when the processing of all environmental claims was concluded in June 2005, 109 environmental claims resulted in awards of USD 5.3 billion.[56] The Governing Council established a Follow-up Programme for Environmental Awards to monitor both the financial and the technical implementation. The Final Report, which was presented more than 20 years after the Commission was established, reveals how difficult it is to assess environmental damage and environmental claims.

As a result of an agreement after the termination of the Eritrea-Ethiopia war (1998–2000), a Claims Commission was established. It had a mandate to settle war-related claims for loss, damage, and injury resulting from violation of international

[52] Sullo and Wyatt 2015. *See also* d'Argent 2002.

[53] The Governments of Great Britain and Argentina, respectively undertook "not to pursue any claim against the other, including nationals of the other, in respect of loss or damage arising from the hostilities and all other actions in and around the Falkland Islands, South Georgia and the South Sandwich Islands before 1989." Joint statement issued at Madrid on 19 October 1989 by the delegations of the Republic of Argentina and the United Kingdom of Great Britain and Northern Ireland, para 3. https://faolex.fao.org/docs/pdf/bi-24305.pdf. Accessed 16 February 2025.

[54] https://uncc.ch/uncc-glance. Accessed 16 February 2025. For a detailed overview, *see* Payne and Sand 2011.

[55] UNSC 2022, pp. 13–14, para 73.

[56] Ibid. paras 174–175.

law.[57] The case concerned claims related to both *jus ad bellum* and *jus in bello* and included claims for environmental damages. Both parties' claims regarding environmental damages were rejected by the Commission. The Commission took the view that the claim by Ethiopia regarding *"[t]he allegations and evidence of destruction of environmental resources also fall well below the standard of widespread and long-lasting environmental damage required for liability under international humanitarian law"* due to lack of proof.[58]

The International Court of Justice has on several occasions held that compensation is due for damage caused to the environment as a consequence of an international wrongful act. In its judgment on the reparation phase in the *Armed Activities on the Territory of the Congo (Democratic Republic of the Congo* v. *Uganda) case,*[59] the Court referred back to its earlier judgment, stating that *"it is consistent with the principles of international law governing the consequences of internationally wrongful acts, including the principle of full reparation, to hold that compensation is due for damage caused to the environment, in and of itself"* and that *"damage to the environment, and the consequent impairment or loss of the ability of the environment to provide goods and services, is compensable under international law"*.[60]

The Court also held that it is for the Court to decide whether there is a sufficient causal nexus between the wrongful act and the injury suffered.[61] The formulation stems from the *Certain Activities Carried Out by Nicaragua in the Border Area* case, whereby the Court had found that *"[t]he damage may be due to several concurrent causes, or the state of science regarding the causal link between the wrongful act and the damage may be uncertain. These are difficulties that must be addressed as and when they arise in light of the facts of the case at hand and the evidence presented to the Court. Ultimately, it is for the Court to decide whether there is a sufficient causal nexus between the wrongful act and the injury suffered."*[62]

As noted in other contexts, environmental considerations are often part of modern peace agreements.[63] An interesting legal development can be found in the 2016 Peace Agreement entered between the Government of Colombia and Fuerzas Armadas Revolucionarias de Colombia (Revolutionary Armed Forces of Colombia or FARC), whereby Colombia's Jurisdicción Especial para la Paz (JEP) developed a system of

[57] The Governments of Ethiopia and Eritrea agreed on the 2000 "Algiers Agreement" to establish two commissions: a Boundary Commission and a Claims Commission.

[58] Permanent Court of Arbitration, Case 2001-02 *Eritrea-Ethiopia Claims Commission.* https://pca-cpa.org/en/cases/71/. Accessed 15 March 2025. For a comprehensive recapitulation of the Eritrea-Ethiopia Claims Commission, *see* Murphy et al. 2013.

[59] ICJ, *Armed Activities on the Territory of the Congo (Democratic Republic of the Congo* v. *Uganda),* Reparations, Judgment, 2022 I.C.J. Reports 13, para 348.

[60] ICJ, *Certain Activities Carried Out by Nicaragua in the Border Area (Costa Rica v. Nicaragua),* Compensation, Judgment, 2018 I.C.J. Reports 2018 (I), p. 28, paras 41 and 42.

[61] ICJ, *Armed Activities on the Territory of the Congo (Democratic Republic of the Congo* v. *Uganda),* Reparations, Judgment, 2022 I.C.J. Reports, p. 13, para 349. The Court's quotation is from *Certain Activities Carried Out by Nicaragua in the Border Area,* ibid. p. 26, para 34.

[62] Ibid.

[63] International Law Commission 2016, pp. 297–298, paras 154–160.

legal processes in the context of transitional justice. During the processes, the JEP has elaborated on the direct environmental protection under international humanitarian law and international criminal law, as outlined in Articles 35(3) and 55 of Additional Protocol I and Article 8(2)(b)(iv) of the Rome Statute, when addressing individual accountability.[64]

The emerging trend that also individuals who have lost their relatives, have been injured, or have had their property destroyed may request compensation from the aggressor State, is likely to grow stronger. The demands will be based on human rights law, environmental law, and civil law and we may expect numerous legal processes of this kind in the future.

None of these cases will be of a legally uncomplicated character. Facts and evidence will have to be presented to a court or tribunal and tried in a proper procedure. Analysis based on the best available science and expert opinions from all thinkable sources need to be evaluated and assessed—irrespective of the character of the process.[65] The cases referred to above serve as examples of that. This is also the case with the events taking place in Ukraine. It is therefore of particular importance that Ukraine at an early stage started to register and assemble data on the environmental damage as a result of the Russian war against Ukraine. This has facilitated for the international community in taking further steps to assist Ukraine in demanding reparations. One of the most prominent examples is the establishment of the Register of Damage Caused by the Aggression of the Russian Federation Against Ukraine through an Enlarged Partial Agreement, performed by the Council of Europe Summit. It stated: *"The Register will serve as a record of evidence and claims for damage, loss or injury caused to all natural and legal persons concerned, as well as the State of Ukraine by Russia's internationally wrongful acts in or against Ukraine. It is a first step towards an international compensation mechanism for victims of this aggression."*[66]

For claims to be recorded in the Register, they must relate to damage, loss, or injury that occurred on or after 24 February 2022 and in the territory of Ukraine, within its internationally recognized borders, including territorial waters, and was caused by the internationally wrongful acts of the Russian Federation in or against Ukraine. At this stage, the Damage Register will not examine or evaluate claims it receives on their merit, assess their value, or order any payments. This is left for a future Compensation Commission once established. The requirement that the damage, loss, or injury must have occurred on or after 24 February 2022, does not

[64] Sjöstedt 2025, pp. 24–44. Information about the JEP can be found on https://www.jep.gov.co/Paginas/Inicio.aspx. Accessed 16 February 2025.

[65] This is illustrated by Payne 2024, p. 3, where she notes that the "list of the fields of expertise that were necessary to understand the environmental consequences of war illustrates both the complexity of the task and the advisors that can help prosecutors, defense counsel, and judiciary do their jobs".

[66] Register of Damage Caused by the Aggression of the Russian Federation Against Ukraine through an Enlarged Partial Agreement established by the Council of Europe Summit. https://rd4u.coe.int/en/mandate-and-functions. Accessed 16 February 2025. It is notable that damage of the environment is not addressed in the Reports from the Independent International Commission of Inquiry on Ukraine. https://www.ohchr.org/en/hr-bodies/hrc/iicihr-ukraine/index. Accessed 16 February 2025.

relieve the Russian Federation of its obligations under the law of State responsibility to make reparations for its internationally wrongful act against Ukraine that started already in 2014 with the illegal occupation of Crimea and the activities under Russian control in the Eastern parts of Ukraine. Likewise, the time limit set cannot prevent individuals and companies from pursuing claims related to the period that started already eight years earlier with the Russian aggression and illegal occupation of certain areas in Ukraine in other fora.

It is clear that the need to restore justice for Ukraine and hold the Russian Federation accountable is of utmost importance for the international community. It involves and concerns other States, as evidenced by the 32 interventions by States in the ongoing ICJ case on *Allegations of Genocide under the Convention on the Prevention and Punishment of the Crime of Genocide (Ukraine v. Russian Federation).*[67] Several initiatives, based on UN General Assembly Resolutions, have been initiated covering investigation and prosecution of international crimes, including the crime of aggression, establishment of structures for compensation of damage, and the promotion of international dialogue on accountability for Ukraine.[68] This will also include environmental harm.

23.8 Concluding Remarks

The most recent annual report (as of 31 December 2023) on the total cost of reconstruction and recovery in Ukraine is estimated to be $486 billion over the next decade.[69] A year later, we can expect that the cost of reconstruction will have become considerably higher. The Ministry of Ecology and Natural Resources of Ukraine estimates that the consequences of military actions and impact on the environment amount to 2,696 billion hryvnia (equivalent to more than 65 billion USD), as reported

[67] ICJ, *Allegations of Genocide under the Convention on the Prevention and Punishment of the Crime of Genocide (Ukraine v. Russian Federation).* https://www.icj-cij.org/case/182. Accessed 15 March 2025.

[68] Most of the efforts are summarized in the Political Declaration on Restoring Justice for Ukraine, The Hague, 2 April 2024. https://www.government.nl/ministries/ministry-of-foreign-affairs/activiteiten/restoring-justice-for-ukraine-conference. Accessed 16 February 2025.

[69] https://www.worldbank.org/en/news/press-release/2024/02/15/updated-ukraine-recovery-and-reconstruction-needs-assessment-released. Accessed 15 March 2025. The report is available in full: Third Rapid Damage and Needs Assessment (RDNA) February 2022–December 2023. https://documents1.worldbank.org/curated/en/099021324115085807/pdf/P1801741bea12c012189ca16d95d8c2556a.pdf. Political Declaration on Restoring Justice for Ukraine, The Hague, 2 April 2024. https://www.government.nl/ministries/ministry-of-foreign-affairs/activiteiten/restoring-justice-for-ukraine-conference. Accessed 16 February 2025.

in the app EcoZagroza.[70] Immobilized Russian assets would not be enough to cover this cost.[71]

Accountability for environmental damage in Ukraine as a result of the Russian aggression will take many forms, from individual to State responsibility. It will cover traditional claims and it will reflect recent case law and embrace the development in several areas of international law, such as environmental law and human rights. There is no statute of limitation for claims under international law, which means that Ukraine's claims against Russia will not disappear unless the two States agree not to pursue further claims against each other. Even if this was to be the case, breaches of international humanitarian law, human rights law, and economic claims from individuals and companies will remain. States can agree not to pursue claims against each other, which may include a commitment on behalf of nationals and residents. However, they cannot prevent criminal law cases in domestic courts and individuals from pursuing liability (tort) claims, unless they agree to modify their national legislation. Even if this were to be done, they can only do this in as far as their national jurisdiction reaches. Hence, they cannot prevent other States' criminal proceedings (including those under universal jurisdiction) or cases that the ICC has opened against individuals.

How much of the reparations under the law of State responsibility and how many of the individual claims to be presented will concern environmental damage is difficult to predict. However, it is likely that claims for environmental damage will make up a prominent share, either as separate claims or as part of other categories of claims. The legitimate lawfare initiated by Ukraine is not only a bilateral matter between Ukraine and the Russian Federation. It is a matter for the international community as a whole and for a rules-based international order.

References

Dannenbaum T (2022) The attack at the Zaporizhzhia Nuclear Plant and Additional Protocol 1. Articles of War, Lieber Institute West Point. https://lieber.westpoint.edu/attack-zaporizhzhia-nuclear-plant/. Accessed 1 March 2025

D'Argent P (2002) Les réparations de guerre en droit international public: la responsabilité internationale des états à l'épreuve de la guerre [War reparations in public international law. The international responsibility of States put to the test by war]. Bruylant Brussels

Goldenziel J (2022) An Alternative to Zombieing: Lawfare between Russia and Ukraine and the Future of International Law. Cornell Law Review Online 108(1):1–15

Humle K (2004) War Torn Environment: Interpreting the Legal Threshold. Martinus Nijhoff Publishers, Leiden

Humle K (2020) Enhancing Environmental Protection During Armed Conflicts. Goettingen Journal of International Law 10(1): 203–241

---

[70] https://ecozagroza.gov.ua/en. Accessed 15 March 2025.

[71] https://neighbourhood-enlargement.ec.europa.eu/news/first-transfer-eu15-billion-proceeds-immobilised-russian-assets-made-available-support-ukraine-today-2024-07-26_en. Accessed 16 February 2025.

ICC OTP (2024) Draft Policy on Environmental Crimes under the Rome Statute. https://www.icc-cpi.int/sites/default/files/2024-12/2024-12-18-OTP-Policy-Environmental-Crime.pdf. Accessed 1 March 2025
International Law Commission (2001) Yearbook of the International Law Commission 2001, Volume II Part Two. A/CN.4/SER.A/2001/Add.1 (Part 2). https://legal.un.org/ilc/publications/yearbooks/english/ilc_2001_v2_p2.pdf. Accessed 1 March 2025
International Law Commission (2011) Yearbook of the International Law Commission 2011, Volume II Part Two. A/CN.4/SER.A/2011/Add.1 (Part 2). https://legal.un.org/ilc/publications/yearbooks/english/ilc_2011_v2_p2.pdf. Accessed 1 March 2025
International Law Commission (2013) Yearbook of the International Law Commission 2013, Volume II Part Two. A/CN.4/SER.A/2013/Add.1 (Part 2). https://legal.un.org/ilc/publications/yearbooks/english/ilc_2013_v2_p2.pdf. Accessed 1 March 2025
International Law Commission (2014) Yearbook of the International Law Commission2014 , Preliminary report on the protection of the environment in relation to armed conflicts, by Marie G. Jacobsson, Volume II Part One. A/CN.4/SER.A/2014/Add.1 (Part 1). https://legal.un.org/ilc/publications/yearbooks/english/ilc_2014_v2_p1.pdf. Accessed 1 March 2025
International Law Commission (2015) Protection of the Environment in Relation to Armed Conflicts, Second report on the protection of the environment in relation to armed conflicts, by Marie G. Jacobsson, Special Rapporteur, Doc. A/CN.4/685. https://legal.un.org/ilc/publications/yearbooks/english/ilc_2015_v2_p1.pdf. Accessed 1 March 2025
International Law Commission (2016) Third report on the protection of the environment in relation to armed conflicts, by Marie G. Jacobsson, Yearbook of the International Law Commission 2016, Volume II Part One. A/CN.4/SER.A/2016/Add.1 (Part 1). https://legal.un.org/ilc/publications/yearbooks/english/ilc_2016_v2_p1.pdf. Accessed 1 March 2025
Jacobsson M, Lehto M (2020) Protection of the Environment in Relation to Armed Conflicts—An Overview of the International Law Commission's Ongoing Work. Goettingen Journal of International Law 10 (1):27–46
Mohammed S (2023) Yemen's Environmental Crisis: The Forgotten Fallout of an Enduring Conflict. Arab Reform Initiative, Environmental Policies Series. https://www.arab-reform.net/publication/yemens-environmental-crisis-the-forgotten-fallout-of-an-enduring-conflict/. Accessed 1 March 2025
Murphy S et al (2013) Litigating War: Mass Civil Injury and the Eritrea-Ethiopia Claims Commission. Oxford University Press
Payne C R, Sand P H (2011) Gulf War reparations and the UN Compensation Commission environmental liability. Oxford University Press
Payne P (2024) Comment on OTP Environmental Crimes Policy. https://iucn.org/sites/default/files/2024-04/icc_submission_cymie_payne1.pdf. Accessed 1 March 2025
Saber A (2024) The Price of Victory in the Gaza War: Women, Climate, and Peace. Wilson Center. https://www.wilsoncenter.org/blog-post/price-victory-gaza-war-women-climate-and-peace. Accessed 1 March 2025
Sender O (2024) International Law-Making by the International Court of Justice and International Law Commission: Partnership for Purpose in a Decentralized Legal Order. Cambridge University Press
Sjöstedt B (2025) Protecting War's Unseen Environmental Damage. Nordic Journal of International Law 94: 24–44
Sullo P, Wyatt J (2015) War Reparations. In: Max Planck Encyclopedia of Public International Law. https://opil.ouplaw.com/home/MPIL. Accessed 12 February 2025
UNEP (2022) The Environmental Impact of the Conflict in Ukraine: A Preliminary Review. Nairobi, Kenya. https://www.unep.org/resources/report/environmental-impact-conflict-ukraine-preliminary-review. Accessed 16 February 2025
UNEP (2024a) Environmental Impact of the Conflict in Gaza: Preliminary Assessment of Environmental Impacts. Nairobi, Kenya. https://www.un.org/unispal/wp-content/uploads/2024/06/environmental_impact_conflict_Gaza.pdf. Accessed 1 March 2025

UNEP (2024b) Environmental assistance and recovery in areas affected by armed conflict, UN Doc. EA.6/Res.12. https://docs.un.org/en/UNEP/EA.6/RES.12. Accessed 1 March 2025

UNGA (2018) First report on protection of the environment in relation to armed conflicts by Marja Lehto, Special Rapporteur, UN Doc. A/CN.4/720. https://docs.un.org/en/A/CN.4/720. Accessed 1 March 2025

UNGA (2019) Second report on protection of the environment in relation to armed conflicts by Marja Lehto, Special Rapporteur, UN Doc. A/CN.4/728. https://docs.un.org/en/A/CN.4/728. Accessed 1 March 2025

UNGA (2022a) Report of the International Law Commission, Seventy-third session, UN Doc. A/77/10. https://documents.un.org/doc/undoc/gen/g22/448/48/pdf/g2244848.pdf. Accessed 1 March 2025

UNGA (2022b) Protection of the environment in relation to armed conflicts, UN Doc. A/RES/77/104. https://docs.un.org/en/A/RES/77/104. Accessed 1 March 2025

UNSC (2022) Letter dated 10 February 2022 from the President of the Governing Council of the United Nations Compensation Commission addressed to the President of the Security Council, Annex, UN Doc. S/2022/104. https://docs.un.org/en/S/2022/104. Accessed 1 March 2025

Marie Jacobsson is Associate Professor at the Faculty of Law, Lund University Before her retirement she was Ambassador and the Principal Legal Adviser on International Law to the Swedish Ministry for Foreign Affairs. She was a Member of the United Nations International Law Commission 2007–2016 and the first Special Rapporteur on the topic Protection of the environment in relation to armed conflicts 2013–2016. She now works as an independent consultant on international law. Her ongoing assignments also include Member of the PCA and Chair of Stockholm Centre for International Law and Justice. Her research interests lie in public international law, in particular in matters relating to peace and security, the law of armed conflict, law of the sea, and polar law.

Chapter 24
Minorities' Aspiration to Self-Determination as a Major Cause of Conflict in Europe: Does It Shape International Law Towards a Right to Remedial Secession?

Katinka Svanberg

Contents

This chapter draws on conclusions from the author's research project *Self-determination as the Main Cause of Conflict in Europe in the Last 100 Years*, supported by Stiftelsen för rättsvetenskaplig forskning [Foundation for Jurisprudential Research], https://srf.wallenberg.org/.

K. Svanberg (✉)
Stockholm University Law Faculty, Stockholm, Sweden
e-mail: lilykatinka.svanberg@gmail.com

M. Klamberg et al. (eds.), *Reconstructing Power and Hegemony in Public International Law*, https://doi.org/10.1007/978-94-6265-743-4_24

Abstract Post-colonial self-determination in the 21st century centers on new groups seeking to assert self-determination. I examine the hypothesis that minorities' pursuit of self-determination is a significant cause of European conflicts. Traditionally, minorities have fallen outside the scope of self-determination. I utilize the Responsibility to Protect (R2P) and the Friendly Relations Declaration's savings clause to determine whether a severely oppressed minority might advance to "remedial secession", proposing that threshold criteria be established within a framework connected to the large-scale atrocity crimes inherent to the R2P doctrine. A case study of military conflicts in Europe over the last 100 years is utilized, as minorities' aspirations to self-determination have consistently fueled conflict since US President Woodrow Wilson included them in his Fourteen Points for Peace. Drawing on the case study, I present a framework for addressing disintegrative conflicts over secession by minority groups. The urgency of the subject is underscored by two contemporary cases, where great powers' aspirations to become empires manipulate the right to self-determination to serve their strategic interests: Russia's President Putin's government's support for separatists aiming to reintegrate lost territories and the American President Trump's assertion that Greenland should be incorporated into the United States.

Keywords Remedial secession · Self-determination · Minority · R2P · Atrocity crimes · Ukraine · Autonomy

24.1 Introduction

This chapter continues my work from 10 years ago in my dissertation, "The UNSC Serving in a Legal Capacity—a Study of UNSC's Interventions Under Chapter VIII in the UN Charter for the Right to Democracy", on internal self-determination. Professor Wrange was one of my supervisors, providing excellent advice on methodology and engaging in inspiring discussions.[1] Thus, I examine whether claims of external self-determination destabilize Europe and how this affects the interpretation of the right to external self-determination in the form of secession. Three key questions will be addressed: (1) Can minorities achieve status as "peoples" under UN Charter Article 1(2), and what conditions might justify such reclassification? (2) How can secessionist claims be managed to prevent history from repeating itself? (3) What modes of self-determination should be available?

Ethnicity-based persecution leading to self-determination claims has arguably been a primary driver of conflict in Europe from the 1920s to the 2020s, to quote

[1] Svanberg 2014.

from the preamble of the Framework Convention for the Protection of National Minorities:

> Considering that the upheavals of European history have shown that the protection of national minorities is essential to the stability, democratic security, and peace in this continent.[2]

The right to self-determination as a legal principle traces its roots to Europe after WWI, when the fall of several great empires and the redrawing of the European map prompted self-determination claims from minorities, ultimately leading to WWII. The end of the Cold War in the early 1990s, marked by the collapse of Soviet-controlled communist dictatorships in Eastern Europe and the disintegration of the Soviet Union (USSR), resulted in a similar redrawing of Europe's map as after WWI. This period posed similar challenges to those of the interwar period, with dissatisfied minorities finding themselves in newly formed states. Much like in the 1930s, a wave of nationalism, separatism, xenophobia, and religious intolerance is once again sweeping across Europe, in the wake of economic stagnation and recession.[3] In the 21st century, Russia has militarily supported Russian minorities to break away from state formations, including in Georgia, Ukraine, and Moldova,[4] to merge with Russia. The dangers of such a Russian policy, a scary reminiscence of the German 1930s policies to collect all Germans in a Third Reich, were highlighted in 2022, when the ethnic conflict over the Donetsk and Luhansk territories inside Ukraine triggered a full-scale invasion by Russia of Ukraine, with an attempt to seize the whole of Ukraine. It created concern over direct military confrontation between Russia and NATO, when the United States Biden administration, the EU, and NATO sent advanced weapons and economic support to Ukraine, based on its right to collective self-defense. The new US Trump administration marked a shift in US policy in 2025, pursuing a peace plan based on negotiations and suggesting that Ukraine might have to cede territory for peace. Also, Trump reiterated his call for Greenland to become US territory, at a moment when its Indigenous population strives towards independence under established processes for colonial peoples and territories in the UN Charter. As history tends to repeat itself, Europe's history of minority conflicts shows the need for an inclusive regional study to assess implications from a self-determination perspective.

---

[2] Framework Convention for the Protection of National Minorities, ETS 157, 1 February 1995.

[3] *E.g.*, new DNA-based methods have contributed to increasing individuals' interest in ethnic origin, mirroring the interest in race biology in the 1920s and 30s.The Swedish State Institute for Racial Biology in Uppsala was one of the earliest race biology institutes in Europe, established in 1922. The pseudo-medicine phrenology also became popular, as a justification for European superiority. Today, individuals order DNA analyses through database services providing information not only on ancestry, but also on ethnicity and race.

[4] Svanberg and Bring 2019, p. 409.

24.2 Normative Background

A central norm in the area of statehood is self-determination, a norm that was spelled out for the first time in Article 1(2) of the UN Charter:

> To develop friendly relations among nations based on respect for the principle of equal rights and self-determination of peoples.[5]

The preparatory works of the UN Charter emphasize that this principle has two complementary parts: external and internal self-determination.[6]

External self-determination is the right of peoples to rule themselves, free from foreign domination and interference. External self-determination equals sovereignty for a people in a state, but can also lead to secessionist claims.[7] The other side is *internal self-determination*, the right of a people to govern themselves within a state. The committee that drafted Article 1(2) at the San Francisco Conference in 1945 found:

> [W]hat is intended by para 2 is to proclaim the equal rights of peoples as such, consequently, their right to self-determination. Equality of rights, therefore, extends in the Charter to States, nations, and peoples.[8]

The Belgian delegate noticed that there was "confusion" regarding its interpretation:

> ...the word "peoples" means national groups which do not identify themselves with the population of a State...Thus, it would be dangerous to put forth the peoples' right of self-determination as a basis for the friendly relations between the nations. This would open the door to inadmissible interventions [...].[9]

A juridical interpretation of the principle of the right to self-determination cannot ignore the defining features of a people, traditionally identified using anthropological and historical criteria such as ethnicity, race, language, culture, religion, history, and affiliation with a geographic area. The case for self-determination is particularly compelling when the people in question have a historically established state or other political entity.

The broad, largely undefined principle of self-determination in the UN Charter has since been enriched with normative content through customary international law (CIL) and treaties, as well as through several important UN documents such as General Assembly (UNGA) and Security Council (UNSC) resolutions, along with

[5] Charter of the United Nations, opened for signature 26 June 1945 (entered into force 24 October 1945) (UN Charter), Article 1(2). Self-determination is also referred to in Article 55 of the UN Charter but here it has a primarily declaratory character.

[6] *See* the Report of the Rapporteur of Committee 1 to Commission I, referenced in UNCIO 1945, Vol. 6, p. 455: "The Committee understands that the principle of equal rights of peoples and that of self-determination are two complementary parts of one standard of conduct".

[7] Hilpold, 2017, p. 302.

[8] *See* Report of Rapporteur, Subcommittee, I/1/A, UNCIO doc., 1945, Vol. 6, p. 704.

[9] Belgian Delegation Amendment to Para 2 of Chapter I, UNCIO doc., UNCIO 1945, Vol. 6, p. 300.

the UN International Covenant on Civil and Political Rights (ICCPR) and the International Covenant on Economic, Social and Cultural Rights (ESCR) from 1966, which have influenced the practices of the UN and its member states.[10] Self-determination possesses a dual character, as it is also a fundamental human right, *see* ICCPR Article 1 and ESCR Article 1.[11] In humanitarian law, Additional Protocol I to the Geneva Conventions refers to self-determination in Article 1(4),[12] extending the application of the protocol to armed conflicts where people are fighting colonial domination, alien occupation, or racist regimes while exercising their right to self-determination.

The complexity of the principle of self-determination arises from the fact that not all peoples are recognized in CIL as bearers of the right, but only certain categories. These include people in sovereign states, colonial peoples, and those under foreign domination, whereas Indigenous peoples and racial majorities denied government access hold a right to internal self-determination.[13] Furthermore, depending on the classification of peoples recognized as bearers, they can access different modes for exercising their rights.[14] The formulation of the right to self-determination in the UN Charter has evolved into a principle that is not static or limited to specific categories of peoples or circumstances. It has emerged as an overarching principle sufficiently ambiguous to allow for variable interpretations and applications. Hence, new groups of "peoples" may be included.

24.2.1 Minorities

International law does not offer any exact definition of what constitutes a minority.[15] The most widely accepted theoretical definition is one that Francesco Capotorti, Special Rapporteur of the Sub-Commission on Prevention of Discrimination and Protection of Minorities, made in his work on minority rights in Article 27 of ICCPR:

> A group which is numerically inferior to the rest of the population of a State and in a non-dominant position, whose members possess ethnic, religious or linguistic characteristics which differ from those of the rest of the population and who, if only implicitly, maintain a sense of solidarity, directed towards preserving their culture, traditions, religion or language.[16]

---

[10] Svanberg 2014, p. 190.

[11] International Covenant on Civil and Political Rights, opened for signature 16 December 1966, 999 UNTS 171 (entered into force 23 March 1976) (ICCPR); International Covenant on Economic, Social and Cultural Rights, opened for signature 19 December 1966, 999 UNTS 3 (entered into force 3 January 1976) (ICESCR).

[12] Protocol Additional to the Geneva Conventions Of 12 August 1949, and Relating to the Protection of Victims of International Armed Conflicts, opened for signature 8 June 1977, 1125 UNTS 3 (entered into force 7 December 1978) (Additional Protocol I).

[13] Cassese 1995, p. 244.

[14] Ibid.

[15] Petričušić 2005, p. 1.

[16] UN Special Rapporteur Capotorti 1979, p. 96, para 568.

There is no direct exclusion of a "minority" from the ambit of self-determination.[17] This may be intentional. As the preparatory works of the UN Charter suggest, there was a terminological indeterminacy regarding the juridical distinction between peoples, nations, and minorities.[18] Yet, the application of self-determination to minority groups remains one of the most contested issues.

Minorities have been denied self-determination rights since the *Åland Islands* case in 1920–1921, when the League of Nations International Committee of Jurists decided against the right to secession from Finland for the Swedish minority living in the Åland Islands to form a union with Sweden, shortly after Finland gained independence from Russia in 1917.[19] This landmark opinion established the principle that minorities do not possess a right to self-determination; they are considered a numerically inferior group and thus not regarded as a "people". The *Åland Islands* Opinion continues to be cited to support that minorities lack the right to self-determination, including in the more recent judgment *Reference re. Secession of Quebec*.[20] Self-determination claims from minorities pose a threat that could destabilize and fragment the Westphalian order of sovereign nation-states, which serves as a cornerstone of international law, based on fundamental principles in the UN Charter, such as Article 2(1) on the sovereign equality of states, Article 2(7) on the principle of non-intervention in the domestic affairs of states, and Article 2(4) on the prohibition on the threat or use of force, against the territorial integrity or political independence of any state.

Minorities are to rely on the minority rights established in Article 27 of the ICCPR (1966), the UN Declaration on the Rights of Persons Belonging to National or Ethnic, Religious, and Linguistic Minorities (1992), and the Framework Convention for the Protection of National Minorities (1995). Minority rights are human rights aimed at integration rather than separation. When exercised within states, they offer a lower level of protection, as enforcement depends on the domestic judiciary and the rule of law. They are group rights. The right to self-determination generally holds stronger protection because it is recognized as a fundamental, partially *jus cogens* right at its core, which consequently garners more international attention and can lead to calls for independence. A pressing issue in contemporary public international law is how to address minorities' aspirations to self-determination. An interpretation that excludes minorities altogether may no longer be valid today.[21]

---

[17] Knop 2004, p. 104.

[18] *See* n. 8-9-10 above.

[19] Report Presented to the Council of the League of Nations by the Commission of Rapporteurs, LN Council Doc. B 7. 21/68/106 (1921), p. 318 [The Ålands Islands Opinion].

[20] Supreme Court of Canada, *Reference re. Secession of Quebec*, Judgment, 20 August 1998, Case No 25506, 2 SCR 217, para 109.

[21] Shelton 2011, pp. 60, 72.

24.2.2 Remedial Secession

Remedial secession refers to the concept that a distinct group within a state may unilaterally declare independence as a remedy for severe injustices, such as systemic human rights violations or denial of meaningful self-governance. It is used as a last resort.[22] There are different theories regarding remedial secession. I view it as a legal extension of the right to self-determination, referred to as an "ascriptive" theory of secession.[23] A more proper term would be "remedial self-determination", to position it as a subcategory of the principle of self-determination. To assist the reader, I here use the term "remedial secession" because others use it. However, "remedial secession" is broader, and can be seen as more of a political concept existing outside the ambit of public international law, as shown in the findings of the International Court of Justice (ICJ) in *Accordance with International Law of the Unilateral Declaration of Independence in Respect of Kosovo*.[24] This is the view that secession for a minority is more of a practical measure, unregulated by law.

"The main conceptual framework comes from the situation when a people are not having their security protected by their parent state, which then fits into what is known as the 'Remedial Right to Secede'", according to Ed Brown.[25] Already, John Locke used his social contract theory, described in the *Second Treatise Concerning Civil Government*, to frame the idea that if a group has its rights abused by the sovereign, they have a right to look for a new sovereign.[26] Although this could be achieved through democracy or revolution, this could also include creating a new sovereign by establishing a new state.[27] It means that if the government is not upholding its side of the social contract, providing security to its citizens—including the individuals within a secessionist entity—the government forfeits its legitimacy, paving the way for secession and making a stronger case for recognition of the secessionist territory.[28]

The idea of remedial secession is often discussed in doctrinal works as a topical issue, based on the Kosovo precedent.[29] However, it is a concept dating back to the *Åland Islands* Opinion, when the Swedish minority—being the majority in the Ålands Islands—wanted to separate from the newly independent Finland and join Sweden, as Finland had been part of Sweden between the Middle Ages and 1809, when lost to Russia. The League of Nations Council appointed the Commission of Rapporteurs to advise on the resolution of the *Åland Islands* question on the merits:

---

[22] Walter et al. 2014.

[23] Bolton et al. 2010, p. 4.

[24] ICJ, *Accordance with International Law of the Unilateral Declaration of Independence in Respect of Kosovo*, Advisory Opinion, 22 July 2010, 2010 ICJ Reports 403, para 81. *See also* Newman and Visoka 2019, pp. 215–231.

[25] Brown 2020; Buchanan 1997, p. 35.

[26] Locke 1689, Chapter 3, §§ 149, 155, 168, 207–210, 220–231, 240–243.

[27] Buchanan 1997, p. 37.

[28] Ibid.

[29] Adimassu 2021; Sterio 2013.

"The Aalanders have neither been persecuted nor oppressed by Finland."[30] They found that a state that guarantees its minorities protection and preservation "to practice freely their religion and to cultivate their language" shall have territorial integrity.[31] This prompts the Commission to ask the rhetorical question: "What reasons would there be for allowing a minority to separate itself from the State to which it is united, if this State gives it the guarantees which it is within its rights in demanding?"[32] Thus, the idea of remedial secession was established in the 1920s, at the same time as national minorities became a hot topic in Europe[33], as I will return to in section 24.3.1 in the case-study.

Decades later, the foundations for remedial secession emerged through developments in international law and scholarship. Buchheit first significantly developed the theoretical framework, introducing the term "remedial secession" and considering it *lex lata*.[34] The post-Cold War redrawing of maps, along with subsequent ethnic conflicts, prompted scholars like Cassese to argue that severe human rights violations could justify secession.[35] A milestone was the Supreme Court of Canada's 1998 *Reference re. Secession of Quebec* ruling.[36] Following Quebec's 1995 referendum, the Court established that self-determination applies to nations rather than minorities, unless they face oppression. Despite ruling against Quebec's unilateral secession due to its French minority's adequate representation in government, the Court acknowledged that remedial secession might be justified under colonial rule, foreign occupation, or denial of meaningful governance participation, following the *Åsland Island* precedent.[37]

In the 2000s, the Venice Commission's report, "Safeguarding the Human Rights of Minorities", supported remedial secession while emphasizing its exceptional nature.[38] Kosovo's 2008 independence declaration and subsequent ICJ advisory opinion brought significant attention to the doctrine, but ultimately, the ICJ avoided addressing secession rights directly:

> The Court is not required by the question it has been asked to take a position on whether international law conferred a positive entitlement on Kosovo unilaterally to declare its independence or, a fortiori, on whether international law generally confers an entitlement on entities situated within a State unilaterally to break away from it.[39]

---

[30] Ibid.

[31] Ibid.

[32] Report Presented to the Council of the League of Nations by the Commission of Rapporteurs, LN Council Doc. B 7. 21/68/106 (1921), p. 318 [The Aaland Islands Opinion]

[33] See in Chapter 24.3.1, *infra.*

[34] Buchheit 1978, p. 18f.

[35] Cassese 1995.

[36] *Reference re. Secession of Quebec*, above n. 19, para 109.

[37] Bayefsky 2021.

[38] Report adopted by the Venice Commission at its 47th Plenary Meeting (Venice, 6-7 July 2001) CDL-INF (2001) 14, at http://www.venice.coe.int/. Accessed 25 Nov.2025.

[39] ICJ, *Accordance with International Law of the Unilateral Declaration of Independence in Respect of Kosovo*, above n.23, para 56.

Interest in remedial secession then declined, as Russia began invoking the doctrine to support separatists in neighboring states, with academic scholarship expressing pessimism.[40] In the 2020s, "remedial secession" became even less in fashion, due to the Russian invasion of Ukraine, putting the spotlight on the disruptiveness of self-determination claims from minorities. It also shows the bias from Western liberal European states regarding when a minority has a right to remedial secession. Crawford has emphasized that although remedial secession has gained some recognition in theory, its status as a right in international law remains uncertain.[41]

I propose to merge two important normative developments to support a right to "remedial self-determination".

1. The *Responsibility to Protect (R2P) doctrine.* It has become widely acknowledged and reiterated in documents and actions by the UN, regional organizations, and Global North states, and is considered an evolving principle in international law.[42] It is based on the premise that sovereignty entails a responsibility to protect populations from mass atrocities, ultimately by military means, as described in the *Report of Responsibility to Protect: The International Commission on Intervention and State Sovereignty* (2001), para 2.29:

   > [t]hat intervention for human protection purposes, including military intervention in extreme cases, is supportable when major harm to civilians is occurring or imminently apprehended, and the state in question is unable or unwilling to end the harm or is itself the perpetrator.[43]

2. *The Friendly Relations Declaration* (FRD) in para 7, its so-called "savings clause", shows that a state's territorial integrity is conditioned on:

   > Compliance with the principle of self-determination of peoples, and…thus possessed of a government representing the whole people belonging to the territory without distinction as to race, creed, or colour.

The savings clause is used to support racial majorities' right to internal self-determination through government access, but can be read to open for secession as a last resort for racial and religious groups excluded from representation in a government.[44]

A question left unanswered is what degree of oppression would open for remedial secession. I propose that threshold criteria that connect to the atrocity crimes inherent to the R2P doctrine act as a trigger for intervention.[45] Those crimes are genocide, crimes against humanity, and war crimes, as defined in the Rome Statute.[46]

---

[40] Getachew 2019; Sterio 2018.

[41] Crawford 2009.

[42] *See, e.g.*, UNGA 2005, World Summit Outcome Document, GA Res. 60/1, 25 Oct.2005, Article 138 and 139. *See also* Svanberg 2024.

[43] Evans and Sahnoun 2001, para 2.29.

[44] Cassese 1995, p. 181.

[45] Svanberg 2024, p. 116.

[46] *See* UN Secretary General 2024; and the ACT Group's Proposal on a Responsibility Not to Veto, in Svanberg and Bring 2019, p. 300.

24.3 Case Study

24.3.1 *The Interwar Period to WWII: Minorities in the Diaspora*

In 1918, US President Woodrow Wilson presented his famous "Fourteen Points" for European peace, stressing that the interests of people and minorities must be met.[47] This inspired minorities' claims to self-determination, at a point in the redrawing of Europe's map after WWI when several great empires had collapsed (the Ottoman, Russian, Austro-Hungarian, and German Empires). The peacemakers at Versailles drew new borders, creating nations aimed at ethnic homogeneity in the belief that this would substantially decrease violence between different nationalities. This was illusional, to quote Historian M. MacMillan: "The possibilities for dividing up peoples were unending, especially in central Europe, where history had left a rich mix of religions, languages, and cultures."[48] Instead, it paved the way for ethnic unrest. Probably, the *Åland Islands* Opinion from 1920, denying a right to secession from Finland for the Swedish minority living in the Åland Islands, was due to the need to stem an avalanche of independence claims in Europe.[49]

The new European map, unfortunately, laid the foundation to support populist nationalists who demanded changed borders and states based on "people" and "race". The most dangerous example was Adolf Hitler and National Socialism's aim to unite all Germans in a Third Reich, which resonated with large German minorities in the diaspora. The Russian Empire comprised a multitude of nationalities, languages, ethnic groups, and religions, which became the USSR, initially made up of Russia, Ukraine, Byelorussia, and the Transcaucasian republics of Armenia, Azerbaijan, and Georgia.[50] Lenin's position was that after the revolution, all nationalities would be free to become part of the Soviet Union or be independent.[51] The Soviet Union, despite initially acknowledging constituent republics' secession rights, forced millions of people into a federation while paradoxically championing self-determination as a legal norm to combat imperialism and build support among non-Russian nationalities.[52]

Zionism is an ethnocultural nationalist movement that emerged in Europe in the late 19th century, aimed to establish a national home for the Jewish people through the colonization of Palestine, a region corresponding to the Land of Israel in Judaism.[53] It

[47] *See* Woodrow Wilson's address to Congress on 8 January 1918. https://www.archives.gov/milestone-documents/president-woodrow-wilsons-14-points. Accessed 9 May 2025.

[48] MacMillan 2003, p. 12.

[49] The Aaland Islands Opinion, above n.31.

[50] Davis 2022.

[51] Low 1958, pp. 130–139.

[52] Tunander 2008, pp. 164-184.

[53] *See Zionism,* https://www.britannica.com/topic/Zionism. Accessed 23 February 2025.

emerged in Central and Eastern Europe as a reaction to antisemitism. From 1917, the Balfour Declaration had the British Mandate for Palestine privilege Jewish settlers.[54]

Significant German populations resided outside post-Versailles Germany, particularly in Czechoslovakia (3.2–3.5 million), Romania (745,000–800,000), Poland (740,000–800,000), and the USSR (1.2 million). These communities faced various forms of discrimination and persecution, such as language and cultural restrictions, and economic discrimination. German minorities across Eastern Europe experienced discrimination, which Nazi propaganda exploited to justify territorial expansion under the "*Lebensraum*" concept, creating a German Empire with German hegemony, based on racism.[55] When Jewish immigration increased in Europe, at the time of the Great Depression, these were parameters that research shows had a significant effect on antisemitism.[56] Europe's Jewish population, approximately 9.5 million in the 1930s, concentrated in Eastern and Central Europe, suffered during the Holocaust, with an unbelievable 6 million killed. The dispersion of minorities across new national borders and their persecution emerged as a critical factor that led to World War II.

24.4 Post-WWII: The Incorporation of Self-Determination in the UN Charter

After World War II, modern international law emerged with the UN Charter's peace imperative, explicitly articulating self-determination as a foundational purpose in Article 1(2). Pivotal developments included the codification of human rights and the establishment of individual criminal responsibility for atrocity crimes.[57] The Nuremberg Tribunal established a precedent that war crimes, crimes against humanity, and acts of aggression constitute international crimes that carry individual criminal responsibility, a principle that was subsequently affirmed by the 1946 Tokyo Tribunal.[58] These juridical innovations formed the conceptual framework for later international criminal tribunals and the International Criminal Court (ICC). Significantly, the Nuremberg indictments did reference genocide, but as part

[54] *See* the 1917 Balfour Declaration at https://avalon.law.yale.edu/20th_century/balfour.asp. Accessed 9 May 2025.

[55] Those ideas built on wrongful interpretations of social-Darwinism and Friedrich Ratzel's concept of states as "living organisms". Philosophers like Johann Gottlieb Fichte argued for German cultural uniqueness in *Addresses to the German Nation* 1808. The 19th-century pseudoscientific racial biology, like Arthur de Gobineau's *Essay on the Inequality of Human Races* (1853), Hans F.K. Günther's "*Rassenkunde des deutschen Volkes*" [Racial Studies of the German People] (1922), and Karl Haushofer's geopolitical theories influenced Nazi expansionism.

[56] Brunstein and King 2004, p. 50.

[57] Evans 2009, p. 8.

[58] The Nuremberg Tribunal was created by the London Agreement of 8 August 1945. The International Military Tribunal for the Far East was set up by an order from US General Douglas McArthur dated 19 January 1946.

of "crimes against humanity". Only later, through the Convention on the Prevention and Punishment of the Crime of Genocide, 1948, was genocide classified as a separate crime.

Europe again underwent extensive border changes. Stalin's communism appeared to be the big gainer in WWII, making occupied territories in Central and Eastern Europe into satellite states. Germany was split into West Germany and East Germany, losing eastern territories to Poland and the USSR. Poland shifted westward, gaining former German territories, but lost eastern areas to the USSR, which annexed the Baltic states, got Eastern Poland, and annexed parts of Finland, northern East Prussia (Kaliningrad), and Ruthenia from Czechoslovakia. Italy lost territories to Yugoslavia and Greece. The new Communist Empire in Eastern Europe prompted Winston Churchill to deliver his famous "Iron Curtain" speech at Westminster College in Missouri in 1946.[59]

The Holocaust and Nazi Germany's aggression had significant consequences for German minorities. In Czechoslovakia, approximately 3 million Sudeten Germans (29.5% of the population) were expelled after WWII, being held accountable for Nazi atrocities, reducing their numbers to 200,000–300,000.[60] Similar forced expulsions of ethnic Germans occurred across Eastern Europe, as described by Harvey M. Coverley, Deputy Land Commissioner for Wuerttemberg-Baden:

> The bulk of these people were forcibly expelled from their former homelands because they were German racial minorities... With few exceptions, property-less, rootless, and homeless, dependent entirely upon daily wages or public relief for existence. To make this situation more bitter, many of these unfortunates were proprietors of businesses or farms in their former homes, and many occupied positions as teachers, officials, lawyers, or engineers.[61]

The UN remained unresponsive to the post-WWII ethnic cleansing of German minorities through forced deportations. The prevailing interpretation of the newly adopted UN Charter Art 1(2) aligned with the *Åland Islands* Opinion, excluding minorities from self-determination.

24.4.1 The Founding of Israel

Seldom is the Holocaust committed against the Jewish population in Europe cited as the first case in modern international law where severe persecution was a decisive factor in the right of the Jewish people to establish their own state, rather this has been largely denied or downplayed in the literature.[62] The British mandate over Palestine had 1939, shifted its focus to an independent Palestinian state through a White Paper favoring Arab interests, which made it much harder for Jews to immigrate. In 1945–1946, there were post-war reconsiderations. The Anglo-American Committee

---

[59] Ward 1968.

[60] Guzi et al. 2021. p. 4.

[61] Coverly 1950, p. 138.

[62] Friesel 1996. However, some share my view, see e.g. Kleinman 2002.

of Inquiry, which involved the US in the planning, recommended allowing Jewish refugees into Palestine, as there were 300,000 Jewish Holocaust survivors in European refugee camps.[63] In 1947, Britain referred the Palestine question to the UN and announced its intention to withdraw from Palestine. The UN Special Committee on Palestine (UNSCOP) proposed a two-state solution. The UNGA adopted Resolution 181 (II), the Partition Plan, in November 1947, allocating about 60% of the territory to the State of Israel and 40% to an Arab state, whereas the area surrounding Jerusalem would remain a corpus separatum administered by the UN. The Jewish leadership accepted the UN Partition Plan, but the Arabs of Palestine and all independent Arab countries opposed it. Following the vote, violence escalated, leading to the 1948 Arab-Israeli War after Israel declared independence on May 14, 1948. By the end of the war, the State of Israel controlled all of the territory that the UN had proposed for a Jewish state, and nearly 60% of the land suggested for an Arab state.[64]

The establishment of Israel marks the first instance where atrocity crimes facilitated independence. Although Jews maintained historic territorial claims and had established a state there 3,000 years ago, most had lived in the diaspora as minorities. Public awareness of Nazi death camps strongly validated the Zionist argument that Jewish safety necessitated a sovereign homeland.[65] Growing consciousness of the Holocaust influenced American support for partition and the swift recognition of Israel, with survivors constituting a significant portion of early immigrants. Self-determination represented a core purpose of the new UN, and Jews qualified as a people through shared religion, ethnicity, historical nationhood, and territorial claims. Although multiple factors contributed to Israel's establishment—including Zionist migration, the conclusion of the British Mandate, and post-war geopolitical shifts—other peoples with defined ancestral territories, including Kurds, Uyghurs, Tamils, and Baloch, remain unrecognized. This suggests that the Holocaust's unprecedented persecution significantly influenced the UNGA's two-thirds majority vote establishing Israel, presenting overlooked implications for remedial self-determination.[66]

---

63 Cohen, Sharon Kangisser 2013, p. 35.

64 UNGA 1951.

65 Holocaust Survivors and the Establishment of the State of Israel (May 14, 1948). In: Holocaust Encyclopedia, United States Holocaust Museum, https://encyclopedia.ushmm.org/content/en/article/postwar-refugee-crisis-and-the-establishment-of-the-state-of-israel#:~:text=In%20the%20aftermath%20of%20the,State%20of%20Israel%20was%20established. Accessed 19 May 2025.

66 Yakobson 2008.

24.5 The Cold War

24.5.1 Hungary and Czechoslovakia

The Cold War deep-frosted Europe. Very few military conflicts erupted, with public revolts against communist governments in Hungary in 1956 and Czechoslovakia in 1968 being crushed by a Soviet-led Warsaw Pact invasion. The West condemned these invasions for violating the principle of external self-determination—the right of peoples to govern themselves freely without outside interference. This principle was central to the original intention behind self-determination for peoples in sovereign states.

24.5.2 Divided Islands: Cyprus and Northern Ireland

Cyprus was a British colony that gained independence in 1960 through a power-sharing agreement between Greek and Turkish Cypriots. Intercommunal violence erupted in 1963–1964, prompting the deployment of UN peacekeepers. Following a Greek-sponsored coup in 1974 aimed at the integration of Cyprus with Greece, Turkey invaded Northern Cyprus, displacing approximately 200,000 Greek Cypriots to the north and 50,000 Turkish Cypriots to the south. The UN peacekeeping mission UNFICYP's mandate expanded significantly after this, as the island was effectively partitioned following the Turkish military intervention. The island remains divided, with roughly 75% of its 1.2 million population in the Greek community and 25% in the Turkish community. The declaration of the Turkish Republic of Northern Cyprus in 1983 spurred UNSC Resolution 550, which required collective non-recognition. Despite Cyprus's EU accession in 2004 (with EU law suspended in the north), UN-sponsored reunification talks stalled in 2017. Türkiye and Turkish Cypriots are advocating for permanent partition and international recognition. Resolution efforts continue through the UN framework involving the guarantor powers Greece, Türkiye, and Britain.[67] The UN and EU maintain recognition of the Republic of Cyprus's sovereignty over the entire island, considering the north to be illegally occupied.[68]

The Northern Ireland conflict, characterized as an ethnic-nationalist and sectarian low-level conflict, originated in British colonization, with Northern Ireland remaining within the United Kingdom (UK) following Irish independence in 1922. It manifested as Protestant-Catholic tensions aligned with political divisions: Unionists (predominantly Protestant) supporting UK membership versus Republicans (predominantly Catholic) advocating Irish unification, finding the division of Ireland by the British illegal. The partition of Ireland was considered to go against the will of the majority

---

[67] UN Secretary General (2025).

[68] Tindall 2023; James Ker-Lindsay et al. 2011, p. 15.

of its people, meaning that the Northern Ireland state was neither legitimate nor democratic.[69] The conflict resulted in over 3,500 fatalities, 52% civilians. Civil rights protests against Catholic discrimination in the late 1960s precipitated violent confrontation and British military intervention. Republican paramilitaries, notably the Provisional Irish Revolution Army (IRA), conducted an armed campaign through bombings and assassinations, in a "guerrilla" warfare style against the Protestants and British rulers. The 1972 "Bloody Sunday" incident saw British forces kill fourteen unarmed civilians. The peace process started in 1985, culminating in the 1998 Belfast ("Good Friday") Agreement. It established consociational power-sharing governance structures.[70] Although Northern Ireland remained within the UK, the agreement provided mechanisms for potential Irish reunification through concurrent referenda in both jurisdictions. The agreement facilitated peace, reconciliation, and weapons decommissioning.[71] Brexit introduced complications through the Northern Ireland Protocol (later Windsor Protocol) regarding UK-EU border controls. The 2021 census revealed a demographic shift, with Catholics outnumbering Protestants for the first time since 1921.[72] Following governmental collapse in 2022 and subsequent restoration, nationalist parties proposed reunification referenda to be held in the 2020s, facing unionist opposition.[73]

Religious and ethnic divisions define both conflicts.[74] Despite peace accords, both territories navigate processes of potential reunification or separation. Given the histories of external military occupation, voluntary reunification emerges as the legally preferable option per principles of self-determination: the right of an occupied people to regain independence.

24.6 Post-Cold War 1990–2007

The conclusion of the Cold War paralleled developments after World War II. The collapse of communism in Eastern Europe triggered the dissolution of both the USSR and Yugoslavia, resulting in the emergence of new states. Previously suppressed ethnic conflicts erupted when border changes left minority populations unexpectedly within foreign jurisdictions.

---

[69] Deutsch 2002.

[70] UK Government 1998.

[71] Deutsch 2002, p. 105

[72] The 2021 Northern Ireland Census was conducted by the Northern Ireland Statistics and Research Agency (NISRA) on 21 Mar.2021. The census counted 1,903,175 people living in Northern Ireland.

[73] Rosher and Hayward 2023.

[74] Approximately 29–30% of Northern Ireland's population identifies as Irish only, whereas approximately 40–42% identify as British only. In Cyprus, Turkish Cypriots and Greek Cypriots identify as belonging to different religious and ethnic minorities.

24.6.1 The Breakup of the Yugoslavian Federation: Slovenia, Croatia, Bosnia, Kosovo Conflicts

The Yugoslavian state (1918–1991) disintegrated violently when Slovenia and Croatia declared independence in 1991. Yugoslavia had existed as a nation-state for 73 years, emerging at the end of WWI with the collapse of the Austro-Hungarian Empire, and became a Socialist Republic in 1945, the Federal Republic of Yugoslavia (FRY). The Federal Republic of Yugoslavia's violent dissolution began with military conflict, as the republics of Slovenia and Croatia fought for their independence. The inherent issue was that within Croatia and Bosnia, the populations comprised several ethnic minorities. The EU, then known as the EC, recognized these republics in 1992 after its Badinter Commission provided legal advice indicating that Slovenia met the criteria for recognition, whereas Croatia and Bosnia did not satisfy the standards for minority protection.

In Bosnia, ethnic tensions escalated. The population consisted mainly of three ethnic and religious groups: Bosniaks, predominantly Muslim (44%), Serbians, predominantly Serbian-Orthodox (31%), and Croats, predominantly Catholic (18%).[75] A referendum for independence, boycotted by Bosnian Serbs, triggered military conflict. Serbian forces, backed by Belgrade, sought territorial control through a policy of ethnic cleansing. Bosnian Croats pursued similar ethno-territorial objectives, using a policy of ethnic cleansing. Thus Serbs and Croats aimed to possibly annex Bosnian territory. The 1992–1995 conflict resulted in approximately 100,000–110,000 fatalities and 2.2 million refugees. The UNSC authorized NATO airstrikes, which intensified after the Srebrenica genocide, (S/RES 836, 1993). This contributed to the 1995 Dayton Accords, which established a consociational governance model for Bosnia under an international security force supervision.[76] The International Criminal Tribunal for the former Yugoslavia (ICTY), established under UNSC Resolution 826 (1993), prosecuted genocide, war crimes, and crimes against humanity. It was the first criminal tribunal after the Nuremberg and Tokyo Tribunals.[77]

The break-up of FRY is a remarkable example of how minorities can succeed in a claim to self-determination. Two issues distinguish this precedent. First, the right to secession for republics in a dissolving federation was conditioned on the seceding republic maintaining its borders per the *uti possidetis* principle, which previously

[75] Svanberg and Bring 2019, p. 101.

[76] Consociationalism is a form of power-sharing in deeply divided societies, typically designed to manage conflict in places with significant ethnic, religious, or linguistic divisions. It was theorized by political scientist Arend Lijphart in his work Democracy in Plural Societies: A Comparative Exploration, 1977. In Bosnia it resulted in powersharing between the three dominant ethnic groups, Bosniaks, Serbs and Croats, Szazs 1997, p. 759.

[77] Szazs 1997, p. 765.

applied to colonial territories seeking independence.[78] Its relevance is evidenced by its practice during the dissolution of the former USSR, FRY, and Czechoslovakia, relying on the former internal administrative lines as interstate frontiers.[79] Second, the oppression and escalating international crimes that took place during the secessionist wars, which the ICTY is evidence of, paved the way for remedial secession. The atrocities also stopped any further fragmentation of Bosnia, as the principle of no fruits of aggression and international criminal responsibility was applied against the separatists and their backers Serbia and Croatia, accused of aggression and atrocity crimes. However, in 1994 Croatia signed the "Washington Agreement" ending hostilities.

Kosovo, a Serbian province with a 90% Kosovar-Albanian population, lost its constitutional autonomy in 1989 under FRY President Milosevic. Despite Kosovo declaring independence in 1990, international recognition was withheld. The non-violent resistance strategy initially employed by Kosovo Albanians proved ineffective against increasing state repression. In the late 1990s, systemic discrimination escalated into armed conflict between Serbian forces and the Kosovo Liberation Army, which attacked Serbian police and military.[80] Following civilian massacres at Račak and mass displacement of approximately 400,000 Kosovar-Albanians, Western powers perceived an imminent "humanitarian crisis if not genocide", while the UNSC adopted several resolutions trying to solve the situation without the use of force.[81] The failed Rambouillet Agreement, which proposed interim autonomy with a status referendum and NATO security presence, precipitated NATO's 1999 so-called "humanitarian intervention": a bombing campaign against Serbia, performed without UNSC authorization due to Russian and Chinese opposition. The intervention's legality is quite disputed in international legal scholarship.[82] Concurrently with military operations, the ICTY indicted Milosevic in the first prosecution of a sitting head of state during ongoing hostilities.[83] In 2001, after losing elections, he was handed over by the new authorities to the ICTY as a condition of having sanctions lifted from Serbia. However, the sitting President of Kosovo, Hashim Thaçi, the

---

[78] ICJ, *Case Concerning the Frontier Dispute, (Burkino Faso/Republic of Mali)*, Judgment, 22 December 1986, 1986 ICJ Reports 565, para 20, where the ICJ confirmed that *uti possidetis* had developed into a general concept of CIL.

[79] Ratner 1996, p. 595.

[80] Svanberg and Bring 2019, p. 404.

[81] Hughes 2013, p. 1002. The UNSC adopted resolutions 1160 (1998), 1199 (1998), and 1203 (1998).

[82] Amnéus 2008, p. 346.

[83] The UN Nations International Criminal Tribunal for the Former Yugoslavia writes on their webite at https://www.icty.org/en/content/slobodan-milo%C5%A1evi%C4%87-trial-prosecutions-case "The Tribunal demonstrated that not even the president of a country could use his position of high office to claim immunity from prosecution, and that societies need not live for decades in denial about the role their highest leaders played in committing crimes...a barrier against malign attempts to revise history." However, some doubts were cast on the procedure as Milosevics was allowed to represent himself, and that he died some weeks before any judgement, in the tribunals detention center (but presumably of natural causes), why the judgement could not be delivered.

former leader of the Kosovo Liberation Army, along with three other senior government officials, was recently indicted on charges of crimes against humanity and war crimes by the Kosovo Specialist Chambers. Following his resignation, he was transferred to The Hague for trial, accused of committing crimes against humanity and war crimes during and after the war. The trial commenced in 2023.[84]

After a month of NATO strikes, Kosovo was placed under indefinite international UN territorial administration by mandatory UNSC Resolution 1244 (1999), which provided for a NATO military force (KFOR) to maintain security. International standards were established, requiring a stable, multi-ethnic self-government before the administration could conclude, with Kosovo's final status to be determined through negotiations between Serbia and Kosovo. The majority of Kosovar-Albanians returned, but ethnic violence against the remaining Serbian minority increased. Following failed status negotiations, Kosovo's Albanian-majority parliament unilaterally declared independence in 2008, despite Serbia's constitutional claim over the territory.[85] The ICJ's 2010 advisory opinion *Accordance with International Law of the Unilateral Declaration of Independence in Respect of Kosovo,* deliberately avoided addressing self-determination, focusing narrowly on the declaration's legal status as an act, rather than addressing whether there was a positive right to declare independence.[86] The impression was that the ICJ found independence declarations unregulated by law.[87] To date, over 100 states have recognized Kosovo.

Kosovo represents an exceptional case of remedial secession justified through humanitarian intervention. The Independent International Commission on Kosovo characterized NATO's intervention as "illegal but legitimate", a position echoed by numerous scholars.[88] Although Kosovo should be seen in the context of Milosevic's brutal rule of FRY and its dissolution, it raised concerns for an unfortunate precedent, indeed, subsequently invoked by Russia to legitimize military interventions and territorial changes in neighboring states.[89]

[84] *See* the case of *Hashim Thaçi et al.* (KSC-BC-2020-06) at https://www.scp-ks.org/en/cases/hashim-thaci-et-al. Accessed 15 May 2025.

[85] International Crisis Group 2009, p. 5.

[86] ICJ, *Accordance with International Law of the Unilateral Declaration of Independence in Respect of Kosovo*, above n. 23, para 84.

[87] Christakis 2011, p.73, where he cited Burundi's submission to the ICJ in the Kosovo Case that unilateral declarations were "unregulated by law". The quote comes from Burundi's Verbatim Record (CR 2009/28) where they argued that international law does not regulate certain aspects of state creation.

[88] Amnéus 2008 p. 348, finds "[t]he opposition from many states to diminish its presidential value", *but see*, Téson 2009, Cassese 1999.

[89] Ingimundarson 2022.

24.6.2 Transnistria

Transnistria is a separatist enclave in Moldova, occupying 12% of Moldovan territory, that declared independence in 1990. Transnistria's population is approximately 360–400.000, with Russians making up two-thirds, alongside Moldovan and Ukrainian minorities.[90] Following the dissolution of the USSR, tensions between the Moldovan government and the breakaway region of Transnistria escalated into a military conflict in 1992, just a year after Moldova was recognized as an independent state in 1991.[91] The former Soviet 14th Guards Army, already present, supported the separatists with weapons, training, and direct military action. Since the ceasefire in 1992, Russia has maintained 1,500 troops as peacekeepers. Transnistria remains internationally unrecognized, despite having de facto independence, having held a referendum in 2006 where a majority voted for independence. Settlement proposals have ranged from federalization to reintegration, but Transnistrian authorities have sought membership in the Russian Federation, following the annexation of Crimea. The continued Russian military presence in Transnistria remains a point of international dispute, with calls for Russia to fulfill its commitment from 1999 to withdraw its troops from Transnistria.[92] The war in Ukraine and Moldova's pursuit of EU membership heighten the potential for Russian intervention.[93]

Transnistria seems to lack a valid case for secession because there was neither severe oppression nor atrocities committed by Moldovan authorities before the 1992 conflict, and the territory does not have a prior status as an autonomous republic within the USSR.

24.6.3 Chechnya

The predominantly Muslim, ethnically homogeneous Chechen Republic had a population of 1.3 million in 1989 (approximately 750,000 ethnic Chechens) and has historically resisted Russian rule since the 19th century conquest. Following the dissolution of the USSR in 1991, the Chechen-Ingush ASSR split into separate republics within the Russian Federation. Chechnya's secessionist ambitions were fueled by historical grievances, including Stalin's 1944 mass deportation of the entire Chechen population to Central Asia based on false accusations of Nazi collaboration. Thirty percent perished before the group was allowed to return in 1957.[94]

---

[90] Verseck 2025.

[91] Rosa 2021.

[92] *See* NATO Brussel Summit 2018, where NATO member states called on Russia to respect the internationally recognized borders of Moldova, Ukraine, and Georgia.

[93] Special Eurasia 2024.

[94] Williams 2000, p. 101.

Two secessionist wars were fought against Russia, motivated by its repressive history, strong clan structures, and Islamic identity.[95] In 1991, Chechens declared independence of the Chechen Republic of Ichkeria, followed by the First Chechen War (1994–1996). This was an insurgency against Russian forces attempting to regain control of Chechnya. The Russians faced a military defeat, which would mean their withdrawal and the Chechens' de facto independence. Initially, the West supported independence,[96] viewing the Chechens as oppressed, despite terrorism being pioneered by the Chechen fighters already in the first war.[97] The Second Chechen War (1999–2003) was portrayed by Russia as a counter-terrorist operation rather than anti-secessionism, coincided with the separatists' radicalization towards jihadism and post-9/11 anti-terrorism sentiments. The Chechen cause lost legitimacy following significant terrorist attacks in Russia, including the Moscow theater siege and the Beslan school massacre, which collectively resulted in over 1,000 civilian deaths.[98]

Since 2007, Ramzan Kadyrov's pro-Russian regime has maintained peace through state-sanctioned force and substantial Russian economic support, with Chechnya retaining its status as an autonomous republic.[99] The conflicts led to approximately 160,000 fatalities.[100] International support for secession diminished significantly after 9/11, when global counterterrorism norms bolstered Russia's position, as did Chechnya's retention of its autonomous republic status.

24.7 Imperialism Revisited with the Beginning of a "Cold War II" 2008–2025

From 2008, a new era could be said to have begun, marked by the resurgence of old great power rivalries, such as between Russia and the Western powers, at a time when the "war on terrorism" was winding down. "This 'Cold War II' phenomenon is when

[95] Lapidus 1998.

[96] Swedish Parliament 2001.

[97] In Budyonnovsk in June 1995, 195 terrorists took around 1,500 civilians hostage in the village, 129 people were killed and 415 injured.

[98] In 2002, in the Dubrovka Theatre in Moscow, a group of terrorists under the command of Chechens took nearly 1,000 spectators hostage. The terrorists threatened to blow up the building unless Putin began withdrawing Russian troops from Chechnya. Tactical units stormed the theatre using a poisonous narcotic gas. All the terrorists were killed, and 130 of the hostages also died of the gas. In 2004, Russia witnessed several large terrorist attacks, the worst in Beslan when about 1,200 people, children, teachers and parents, present on the opening school day, were taken hostages in the siege of a school. The terrorists demanded that Putin withdraw forces from Chechnya. The siege ended in a battle between the hostage takers and the Russian security force, with 330 hostages killed. The Beslan attack was preceded by a series of terrorist acts including the blowing up of two Russia's civilian planes, *see* Gidadhubli 2004, pp. 4704–4706.

[99] Wilhelmsen 2020, pp. 27–41.

[100] Ibid.

the unipolar world run by the US is replaced by tension and superpower rivalry", to cite historian Professor Niall Ferguson.[101] From a European perspective, the most significant event has been Russia's intervention in Georgia and Ukraine in a partly successful plan to carve up their territories in the attempt to "protect" minorities through their incorporation into the Russian Federation. Russia's assertion of its old place as a superpower could also be traced to its intervention in the Syrian war in 2012, as well as its creeping aspirations to collect Russian minorities back into "Mother Russia". Azerbaijan took advantage of this imperial climate to throw out Armenians from Nagorno-Karabakh.

24.7.1 *The Georgian Conflict—South Ossetia and Abkhazia*

In South Ossetia, the Russian majority declared independence from Georgia in 1991, intending to unite with Russia. This declaration led to a prolonged conflict between the separatists and Georgia from 1992 to 2008. The 1992 Dagomys Agreement facilitated the deployment of peacekeeping forces from both Georgia and Russia.[102] Despite this peace process, the South Ossetians established state structures and a parliament. After the election of Georgia's pro-Western President Saakashvili in 2004, who advocated for NATO membership and territorial reintegration, tensions escalated. In 2008, Georgia, Moldova, and Ukraine enhanced their ties with the EU through the Eastern Partnership, which prompted additional unrest. The UNSC adopted Resolution 1808 (2008), reaffirming Georgia's sovereignty. Subsequently, Georgia launched an offensive to retake South Ossetia, which the Organization for Security and Co-operation in Europe (OSCE) later confirmed as the initial attack.[103] Russian forces immediately intervened, citing the Kosovo precedent and the R2P doctrine, and using distributed Russian passports to justify intervention.[104] The Russian ambassador explained at the UNSC: "[t]he aim of that operation is to ensure that we protect Russian citizens who are in that region […]. Force will be used only in accordance with Article 51 of the Charter, in exercise of the right to self-defense by the Russian Federation."[105] After five days, Russia assumed control. In 2014, Russia drafted the *Treaty of Alliance and Integration*, aimed at legalizing South Ossetia's integration with Russia.[106]

Despite a ceasefire, human rights violations persisted. South Ossetian forces allegedly destroyed ethnic Georgian villages, displacing 192,000 people. In 2021, the European Court of Human Rights ruled that Russia exercised "direct control"

---

[101] Robinson, *Cold War II: Niall Ferguson, On the Emerging Conflict With China*, Interview in Uncommon Knowledge, Hoover Institute (2023).

[102] Dunn et al. 2014, p. 413.

[103] Roy 2008, p. 1147.

[104] Dunn et al. 2014, p. 411.

[105] U.N. Doc. S/PV.5953 2008, p. 9.

[106] Svanberg and Bring 2019, p.410.

over the separatist regions and was responsible for war crimes, including failure to prevent civilian killings, looting, and arson.[107] In 2022, the ICC issued arrest warrants for three Russian nationals over war crimes against ethnic Georgians, though commentators criticized the move as insufficient.[108] As in the case of Transnistria, and later Ukraine, Russia justified support for separatists under the pretext of protecting Russian minorities.[109] Like in Ukraine in 2022, they used self-defense arguments. In 2021, South Ossetia's population had changed its ethnic composition to approximately 89.9% Ossetians, 7,4% Georgians, 1.1% Russians.

Abkhazia is a former autonomous Soviet republic with a large Indigenous population of Abkhaz, another Caucasian mountain people. They had become decimated in the 1980's when ethnic Georgians had moved in and made up 45% of the population in 1989.[110] When Georgia declared independence, Abkhazians (who had voted to remain in the USSR) proposed a federation. Instead, war erupted in 1992, with the Georgian army being dispatched. Despite demographic disadvantages, Abkhazian forces prevailed and expelled Georgia's fighters, ending the war in 1993 and declaring de facto independence.[111]

A fact-finding mission dispatched by the UN in October 1993 reported numerous serious human rights violations perpetrated by both sides. The Human Rights Watch reported ruthless ethnic cleansing, war crimes, and acts of genocide, committed primarily by the Abkhazians and its anti-Georgian military coalition, comprising Caucasian, Chechen, Armenian, Cossack, and Russian forces.[112] Atrocities were also committed by Russian and Georgian forces.[113] Approximately 5,000 ethnic Georgians and 4,000 Abkhaz were reported killed or missing, and 250,000 Georgians became refugees after acts of ethnic cleansing. The conflict became frozen. In 1999, the Abkhazians formally declared independence, based on a referendum in 1994, but conflict cycles occurred in 1998 and 2008, alongside systematic "passportization" of Abkhazians by the Russians.[114]

The 2008 South Ossetia war immediately spread to Abkhazia, which allegedly implemented a mutual defense pact. An estimated 9,000 Russian soldiers entered Abkhazia, allegedly to reinforce the Russian peacekeepers in the republic. Together with Abkhazians, they acted to clear Abkhazia of the Georgian military. After a weekend of bombing, Georgian forces and civilians had evacuated the last part of

[107] ECtHR, *Georgia v. Russia (II)*, Judgment (Merits), 21 January 2021, Application No 38263/08.

[108] ICC OTP 2015.

[109] Marxsen 2014, p. 374.

[110] Hewitt 2009, p. 187.

[111] Ibid. p. 190.

[112] Council of Europe, Recommendation 1305 (1996) on the humanitarian situation of the displaced persons in Georgia, [https://web.archive.org/web/20140407080334/http://assembly.coe.int/documents/adoptedtext/ta96/erec1305.htm]. Accessed 20 Mar.2025. The United Nations General Assembly adopted Resolution 62/249 by 14 votes to 11, 105 abstentions. A/RES/62/249 (8 May 2008).

[113] Anderson et al. 1995.

[114] Ibid.

Abkhazia by 12 August.[115] Russia recognized the independence of Abkhazia and South Ossetia in August 2008, immediately following the war.[116] This was followed by the annulment of the 1994 ceasefire agreement and the termination of the UN and OSCE monitoring missions.[117] The Parliament of Georgia passed a resolution declaring Abkhazia a Russian-occupied territory.[118]

With support from the Russian military, South Ossetia and Abkhazia de facto seceded from Georgia in 2008, culminating in Moscow's formal recognition and subsequent military-economic integration via the Treaty of Alliance and Integration (2014).[119] Putin justified intervention using R2P rhetoric, suggesting parallels with Western interventionism.[120] Though Georgia has effectively ceded control, it maintains territorial claims, together with the UN, OSCE, NATO, and the US, considering these territories to be under Russian occupation.[121] Security analysts identify Russian strategic objectives: terminating Georgian sovereignty, preventing NATO expansion, and deterring similar aspirations among post-Soviet states.[122] However, competing perspectives exist: emphasizing Stalin's arbitrary border demarcations and minority rights as paving the way for today's situation in former USSR republics.[123]

24.7.2 Ukraine Background

Ukraine declared independence in 1991. It has a population of 48 million, including 17.8% ethnic Russians (2001 census), constituting Russia's largest diaspora, concentrated in eastern and southern regions.[124] This demographic distribution has contributed to persistent regional and ethnic divisions.[125] Ukraine experienced fragmented governance under Lithuanian, Polish, Russian, and Cossack rule from the 14th to the 18th century, before falling under predominantly Russian

[115] Ibid.

[116] Gerrits and Bader 2016, p. 297.

[117] Ibid. p. 300.

[118] Parliament of Georgia 2008.

[119] In 2014 (Abkhazia) and 2015 (South Ossetia), Russia signed new treaties with the two regions that promise a new level of integration and that, following the annexation of Crimea earlier in 2014, have been criticized for amounting to "de facto annexation", to quote Gerrits and Bader 2016, p. 302.

[120] Cohen and Hamilton 2011.

[121] Hafkin 2010, p. 219.

[122] Cohen and Hamilton 2011.

[123] Hewitt 2009, p. 188.

[124] This figure combines non-Ukrainian-born residents and Ukrainian-born individuals declaring Russian ethnicity.

[125] *See* https://www.britannica.com/summary/Ukraine. Accessed 12 March 2025. General results of the census on national composition of population, 2001 Ukrainian Census Statistics Committee, Archived from the original on July 6 2007, https://2001.ukrcensus.gov.ua/eng/results/general/nationality/. Accessed 21 May 2025.

control. Following World War I, most Ukrainian lands became a Soviet republic.[126] Ukraine became independent in 1991 after USSR dissolution. Restrictions on Russian language and cultural rights have occurred in Ukraine since 1991, which has contributed to separatist movements. The 2013 abandonment of EU association agreements under Russian pressure precipitated the Maidan protests from Ukrainians, which culminated in pro-Russian President Yanukovych's resignation, followed by ethnic Russian unrest.

24.7.3 Crimea and Sevastopol

The Crimean Peninsula has historically belonged to Russia. In 1944, the peninsula saw the deportation of all Indigenous Crimean Tatars by the Stalin government, based on accusations of being Nazi collaborators and likely targeted for religious reasons, being predominantly Muslim.[127] Within the USSR, President Nikita Khrushchev transferred the Crimean ASSR to Ukraine in 1954, although the Russian fleet maintained its base in Sevastopol. Crimea, a popular resort, has a population of approximately 2 million, comprising 60–80% ethnic Russians, 20–25% Ukrainians, and a smaller Tatar minority (defining the exact numbers of the Crimean population is challenging due to bias).[128] Its autonomous status within Ukraine was restricted in 1995.

Ukraine's 2014 governmental crisis, when the pro-Russian President Yanukovych was ousted, led to an uprising in Crimea in February 2014. The Crimean separatists took control, supported by Russian military forces already stationed at the Sevastopol naval base, without direct military confrontation with the Ukrainian army. The Crimean parliament declared independence in March 2014, after a referendum reporting 96% approval (83% turnout). International condemnation followed, citing procedural irregularities and the pre-existing Russian military presence.[129] Russia incorporated Crimea and Sevastopol into the Russian Federation on March 18 2014, citing Kosovo's independence as precedent.[130] The UNGA declared the annexation illegal and called for non-recognition, as did a UNSC draft resolution declaring that the referendum in Crimea "has no validity", though this was defeated by a Russian veto.[131] Large parts of the international community, the UN, the EU, the European Council, and the US have continued to consider Russia's takeover as illegal, as it

[126] Hewitt 2009, p. 188.

[127] This accusation was largely based on the work of Islamic Committees, which were Nazi-created offices tasked with supporting the German authorities during occupation but also used to advocate for Crimean Tatar interests.

[128] https://www.britannica.com/summary/Ukraine. Accessed 14 May 2025.

[129] The referendum was condemned by Ukraine, the EU, Canada, and the US, among others.

[130] Mamlyuk 2015, p. 479.

[131] UNGA 2014. The GA resolution 68/262 was adopted by 100 votes. The UNSC draft resolution, S/2014/189, (15 March 2014) would have been adopted by 13 votes, *see* UNSC 2014a.

contravenes the Budapest Memorandum on sovereignty and territorial integrity of Ukraine from 1994, to which Russia is a signatory.[132] The annexation led to the G8 suspending Russia from the group.[133] Subsequent legal proceedings included the European Court of Human Rights' 2024 judgement finding systematic human rights violations in Crimea,[134] and the ICJ's determination under *International Convention on the Elimination of All Forms of Racial Discrimination* that Russia discriminated against 12,000 Crimean Tatars and Ukrainian speakers.[135]

24.7.4 Conflict in the Donbas in Ukraine: Donetsk and Luhansk 2014–2022

The Donbas region in eastern Ukraine is heavily industrialized and has approximately 6 million residents, predominantly Russian-speaking.[136] Economic decline and events in Crimea fueled separatist movements in Donetsk and Luhansk. In spring 2014, violence escalated. On April 15, 2014, the Ukrainian government announced the start of an "anti-terror operation" and deployed its armed forces to the Donetsk and Luhansk regions. Russia, while denying direct involvement, provided secret military, economic, and political support to the separatists who seized control of parts of these territories. The ICC later classified this as "an international armed conflict between Ukraine and the Russian Federation".[137] Following unrecognized referendums in May 2014, the self-declared "Donetsk and Luhansk People's Republics" claimed independence, but remained unrecognized by almost all states, including Russia. The two Minsk Accords I–II (2014–2015), attempting to resolve the conflict by granting partial autonomy to these regions within Ukraine, were endorsed by UNSC Resolution 2202 (2015), but ultimately failed. During the first eight years

---

[132] GA res. A/C.3.7/l/L.26 (31 Oct. 2016), Situation of human rights in the Autonomous Republic of Crimea and the city of Sevastopol (Ukraine), 70 in favor, 77 states abstained and 26 voted against. See also, Situation of human rights in the Autonomous Republic of Crimea and the city of Sevastopol, Ukraine, A/C.3/72/L.42, (31 Oct. 2017).

[133] Svanberg and Bring 2019, p.414.

[134] *Ukraine v. Russia (re Crimea) [GC]*—20958/14 and 38334/18, Judgment 25.6.2024 [GC], [https://hudoc.echr.coe.int/eng#{%22itemid%22:[%22002-14347%22]]. Accessed 1 Apr.2025.

[135] *International Convention on the Elimination of All Forms of Racial Discrimination*, United Nations, Treaty Series, vol. 660, p. 195, 21 Dec. 1965, ICJ, *Application of the International Convention for the Suppression of the Financing of Terrorism and of the International Convention on the Elimination of All Forms of Racial Discrimination (Ukraine v. Russian Federation)*, Judgment, 31 January 2024.

[136] The majority of Donbas residents spoke Russian, though exact ethnic demographics in 2014 are unclear.

[137] Report on Preliminary Examination Activities 2016, para 169.

of conflict, approximately 30,000 people died, with millions requiring humanitarian assistance or becoming displaced.[138]

In the winter of 2022, after Russia positioned approximately 190,000 troops near Ukraine's borders, the Russian Duma officially recognized Donetsk and Luhansk as independent states on February 21, 2022. The recognition was used by President Putin as an invitation to defend them in collective self-defense under Article 51 in the UN Charter. He also referred to R2P, claiming the population in the Republics of Donbas had suffered subjugation and acts of genocide for eight years, to support the military intervention into Ukraine on 24 February 2022.[139] Although those claims were likely greatly exaggerated, the US State Department, Amnesty International, and the UN have also made allegations of Ukrainian forces' human rights abuses and the Ukrainian government's inaction to prosecute them in the Donbas region.[140] However, the separatists and Russian forces are likewise accused of many atrocities—more than the Ukrainians—including the downing of a passenger jet belonging to Malaysian Airlines.[141] In 2020, the ICC Prosecutor in the preliminary examination found there was a reasonable basis to believe that a broad range of conduct constituting war crimes and crimes against humanity had been committed in Eastern Ukraine since 2014.[142] As Ukraine was not a State Party to the Rome Statute until 1 January 2025, the preliminary examination was triggered by Ukraine's declarations of acceptance of *ad hoc* jurisdiction of the Court.[143]

---

[138] Approximately 2 million people were internally displaced, 730,000 fled to Russia. UN Human Rights Monitoring Mission in Ukraine (HRMMU), https://www.ohchr.org/en/countries/ukraine. Accessed 11 Mar.2025.

[139] Annex to the letter dated 24 February 2022 from the Permanent Representative of the Russian Federation to the United Nations addressed to the Secretary-General, S/2022/154 (24 Feb.2022).

[140] There were significant deficiencies in investigations into human rights abuses committed by Government forces, resulting in a climate of impunity in Ukraine, 2017, *see* Human Rights Report, US Department of State, (2017), Ukraine, Report on the Human Rights Situation in Ukraine, Office of the United Nations High Commissioner for Human Rights, (Nov.16 2017-Feb.15, 2018). The Ukrainian "Azov" Battalion has caused controversy for alleged human rights abuses, and over its association with far-right groups and neo-Nazi ideology, Jones 2018 See Amnesty International and Human Rights Watch 2016: UN OHCHR 2016.

[141] The UNSC adopted S/RES 2166 (2014), which demanded that those responsible for the incident be held to account. The ECHR was seized by the Netherlands' inter-State application against the Russian Federation regarding the downing of Flight MH17, *Joint Statement ten years since the downing of Malaysia Airlines Flight MH17*, US Mission to the OSCE, (18 July 2024)

[142] Marchuk and Wanigasuriya 2020.

[143] In 2015, the Government of Ukraine lodged a second declaration under Article 12(3) of the Statute accepting the exercise of jurisdiction of the ICC in relation to alleged crimes committed on its territory from 20 February 2014 onwards. *The International Criminal Court welcomes Ukraine as a new State Party*, Press release, 17 July 2025, https://www.icc-cpi.int/news/international-criminal-court-welcomes-ukraine-new-state-party. Acessed 28 November 2025.

24.7.5 The Russian Invasion of Ukraine 2022

On February 24 2022, Putin launched a "special military operation" across Ukraine, aiming to capture Kyiv and install a pro-Moscow government. Strong Ukrainian resistance under President Zelensky thwarted this initial strategy, instead, it has led to a prolonged war. The conflict has become Europe's deadliest since World War II, with up to 1 million casualties (including civilians) and approximately 10 million displaced persons.[144] The invasion is widely condemned internationally as an act of aggression in violation of Art 2(4) in the UN Charter and severe sanctions have been imposed on Russia.[145] The UNSC adopted resolution S/RES/ 2623 (Feb. 27, 2022), calling for an *Emergency Special Session of the UNGA* because a Russian veto deadlocked the Council.[146] The UNGA resolution deplored Russia's invasion of Ukraine and demanded a full withdrawal of Russian forces and a reversal of its decision to recognize the self-declared People's Republics of Donetsk and Luhansk,[147] seen as a pretext for invasion.[148]

Putin's letter to the UNGA (originally an address to the Russian people) outlined Russia's official rationale for its Ukraine invasion. First, the threat of Ukraine joining NATO was cited, but then emphasis was placed on the alleged persecution of Russian minorities in Donbas and their right to self-determination and to collective self-defense, framing the intervention as Russia's Responsibility to Protect the suffering of Russian minorities:

> The People's Republic of Donbas appealed to Russia for help. In accordance with Article 51 (Chapter VII) of the Charter of the United Nations, I have decided to conduct a special military operation with the approval of the Federation Council of Russia and under the treaties on friendship and mutual assistance with the Donetsk People's Republic and the Lugansk People's Republic, as ratified by the Federal Assembly on 22 February this year. Its purpose is to protect people who have been subjected to abuse and genocide by the Kiev regime for eight years. To this end, we will seek the demilitarization and de-Nazification of Ukraine, as well as the prosecution of those who have committed numerous bloody crimes against civilians, including citizens of the Russian Federation.[149]

Further, Putin stressed the right to self-determination:

> ... the right of nations to self-determination as enshrined in Article 1 of the Charter of the United Nations. Our policy is based on freedom, the freedom of choice for all to determine their future... And we consider it important that all peoples living on the territory of today's

---

[144] *After three years of war, Ukrainians need peace and aid*, UNCHR, Press release 18 February 2025, https://ukraine.un.org/en/289506-unhcr-after-three-years-war-ukrainians-need-peace-and-aid#:~:text=UNHCR%2C%20the%20UN%20Refugee%20Agency,continue%20to%20receive%20protection%20abroad. Accessed 26 November 2025.

[145] *See* UNGA 2022, adopted with 141–5–35 (for–against–abstentions).

[146] UNSC 2022b, recorded votes of 11 in favor to 1 against (Russian Federation), with 3 abstentions. A thorough analysis of the Russian aggression is discussed elsewhere in this volume.

[147] G.A. Res. ES-11/1.

[148] Ibid. para 5-6.

[149] Annex to the letter dated 24 February 2022 from the Permanent Representative of the Russian Federation to the United Nations addressed to the Secretary-General, S/2022/154 (24 Feb.2022).

> Ukraine, all those who want to exercise this right – the right to choose – should have the right to do so... In 2014, Russia was obligated to protect the residents of Crimea and Sevastopol from those you call nationalists. The people of Crimea and Sevastopol made their choice to be with their historic homeland, with Russia, and we supported that.[150]

Despite Putin's claims to respect post-Soviet states' sovereignty,[151] his actions suggest aims beyond the Donbas republics, toward annexing more territories with Russian minorities, and could even be read as an attempt to seize the whole of Ukraine, as a former USSR republic! The attempted occupation and potential installation of a puppet regime raises concerns about Ukraine's forced integration into Russia, which would be contrary to its right to external self-determination. Putin's speech echoes an implicit reference to earlier NATO humanitarian operations in Kosovo, Libya, and the US-led coalition in Syria. This is twisted, as Putin's address explicitly condemns those interventions as Western hegemony.[152] Western legal scholars have repudiated Putin's R2P claims as an abuse of humanitarian intervention, "abusing R2P language to justify intervention".[153] Hilpold described it as "Orwellian 'Newspeak' in an attempt to justify an intervention that has no roots in large-scale human rights abuses".[154]

During the first three years of the war, Europe, the US, and Canada, through NATO, supported Ukraine with weapons, materiel, financing, and draconian economic sanctions against Russia, but stopped short of direct military involvement. The Trump administration initiated a major policy change in 2025.[155] President Trump used humanitarian concerns in his call for peace negotiations, blaming his Ukrainian and Russian counterparts equally for the war, which he said claimed the lives of far too many "young, beautiful people, Russians, and Ukrainians".[156] In November 2025, as Russia gained ground, the Trump administration unveiled a 28-point peace plan demanding severe Ukrainian concessions such as: territorial losses, military restrictions, and permanent exclusion from NATO. Despite initial resistance from Kyiv and its European allies, mounting battlefield losses, a governmental corruption scandal, and American pressure to end US support, the Ukrainian government negotiated a revised plan of 19 points with the US delegation in the Fall of 2025, but territorial issues and Ukraine's future in NATO were deferred to future meetings. Polling indicates that Ukrainian public opinion remains divided.[157]

---

150 Ibid.

151 Ibid. p. 6: "We respect and will continue to respect all the newly formed countries of the former Soviet Union. We respect and will continue to respect their sovereignty."

152 Ibid.

153 Kersten 2014.

154 Hilpold 2023, p. 427.

155 NATO support included military equipment, financial aid, and economic sanctions.

156 Trump's attitude could be seen as implicit R2P references, Svanberg 2024, p.71–72, Nerozzi, 2025.

157 *Russia-Ukraine 'peace plan': What's the latest version after US-Kyiv talks?*, 27 November 2025, https://www.aljazeera.com/news/2025/11/26/russia-ukraine-peace-plan-whats-the-latest-version-after-us-kyiv-talks. Januta 2025.

The current US approach employs humanitarian rationales to advocate for Ukrainian territorial concessions, legitimizing remedial secession in Russian-occupied areas, with R2P being implicitly applied to justify territorial adjustments. If great powers use minorities to build empires, this would set a dangerous precedent, reminiscent of Nazi Germany's expansionism, such territorial claims contradict the UN Charter Article 1(2)'s drafting history, to cite the Rapporteur at the San Francisco conference:

> an essential element of the principle [of self-determination] is the free and genuine expression of the will of the people, which avoids cases of the alleged expression of the popular will, such as those used for their own ends by Germany and Italy in later years.[158]

Nevertheless, pragmatic humanitarian considerations necessitate addressing the conflict's devastating toll and protecting the region's significant Russian minority post-war will be daunting. Autonomous and consociational governance structures for Crimea, Donetsk, and Luhansk within Ukraine's sovereign borders could prevent the forced population displacements observed in comparable conflicts.

24.7.6 Nagorno-Karabakh

The predominantly Armenian enclave of Nagorno-Karabakh has deep historical roots dating back to the 3rd to 7th centuries. In 1809, it was ceded from Persia to Russia. At that time, the five districts comprising modern Nagorno-Karabakh were 90.8% Armenian. Following the Sovietization of Armenia and Azerbaijan, Karabakh remained within the Azerbaijan SSR, with broad regional autonomy. After the USSR's dissolution, Nagorno-Karabakh sought to transfer to Armenia, but this request was denied. Shortly thereafter, ethnic violence against Armenians began. The region declared independence as the Republic of Artsakh in 1990, followed by a referendum in 1991, which received 99.8% support in the enclave; the 22.4% Azerbaijani population boycotted it.[159] Soon, an ethnic, religious, and territorial conflict began between Armenia and Azerbaijan, resulting in Armenian occupation of the region. In 1993, the UNSC adopted resolutions supporting the territorial integrity of Azerbaijan, demanding the immediate withdrawal of Armenian forces, and leading to a ceasefire being established in 1994.[160] Now, Armenia was in control of most of the enclave. The war had resulted in the displacement of approximately 725,000 Azerbaijanis and 300,000–500,000 Armenians.[161] International mediation has long been

---

[158] Report of Rapporteur of Committee 1 to Commission I, (June 13, 1945), UNCIO Doc., vol. 6, p. 455.

[159] https://www.britannica.com/place/Nagorno-Karabakh. Accessed 9 May 2025.

[160] UNSC 1993a; UNSC 1993b; UNSC 1993c. The Bishkek Protocol on the Cessation of Armed Conflict in and Around Nagorno-Karabakh, Armenia-Azerbaijan-Republic of Artsakh-Russian Federation-Kyrgyzstan, May 5, 1994.

[161] Omidi 2022, p. 169.

carried out by the OSCE Minsk Group. In 2008, the UNGA demanded the immediate withdrawal of Armenian occupying forces, but the conflict remained frozen.[162]

In 2020, a second full-scale war erupted in Nagorno-Karabakh, initiated by an Azerbaijani offensive supported by Türkiye, resulting in an Azerbaijani victory. An armistice was established through a tripartite ceasefire agreement, in which Russia played a significant role. Azerbaijan regained control over a third of the Nagorno-Karabakh territory. Russian peacekeepers were deployed. In December 2022, Azerbaijan blockaded the region despite humanitarian concerns and ICJ provisional measures after an Armenian referral.[163] International efforts to condemn the blockade failed in the UNSC due to opposition from several states.[164] On 19 September 2023, Azerbaijani troops launched a large-scale military offensive that overran the Republic of Artsakh in one day, leading to its surrender. Azerbaijan termed the offensive a "local counter-terrorism measure in its sovereign territory". The attack resulted in the exodus of approximately 100,000 Armenians—nearly the entire population in Nagorno-Karabakh—with the republic officially dissolving on January 1, 2024.[165]

Despite this forced transfer of a population, the international community's response remained limited. The UNSC failed to adopt resolutions, likely due to Russian opposition and Europe's dependence on Azerbaijani oil due to the Ukraine war. Some UNSC members, including Germany and the US, invoked R2P principles, drawing parallels to Kosovo (1998–1999).[166] The ICJ, in its Provisional Measures, emphasized that the *International Convention on the Elimination of All Forms of Racial Discrimination* requires the forced expulsion to be reversed, albeit without calling it "ethnic cleansing" or genocide.[167] The European Parliament characterized events as ethnic cleansing, but the EU did not adopt any sanctions.[168] The European Court of Human Rights ordered Azerbaijan to honor its convention obligations regarding the right to life and the prohibition of torture.[169] After Armenia became a party to the ICC, a complaint accusing Azerbaijani officials of crimes against humanity was filed on behalf of two of the victims.[170] Notably, international institutions primarily employed judicial rather than coercive mechanisms. This approach

[162] UNGA A/62/PV.86,62 Sess.(2008). The co-chairs of the Minsk Group, Russia, France, US, voted against.

[163] Application of International Convention on Elimination of All Forms of Racial Discrimination (Armenia v. Azerbaijan), Provisional Measures, Order of 22 February 2023, 2023 ICJ Reports 14.

[164] Kucera 2023.

[165] ICJ, *Application of the International Convention on Elimination of All Forms of Racial Discrimination (Armenia v. Azerbaijan)*, Provisional Measures, Order of 17 November 2023, ICJ Reports 619 (*Armenia v. Azerbaijan*, Order of 17 November 2023), para 26.

[166] Tatikyan 2023a, Tatikyan 2023b.

[167] *Armenia v. Azerbaijan*, Order of 17 November 2023, above n. 158.

[168] Avedissian 2021, p. 34.

[169] Interim measures issued by the European Court of Human Rights, Interim Measures in the Case of Armenia v. Azerbaijan, App. No. 42521/22, Eur. Ct. H.R. (Sept. 22, 2022). Application of the International Convention on the Elimination of All Forms of Racial Discrimination (Armenia v. Azerbaijan), Provisional Measures, Order of 7 December 2021, ICJ Reports 2021, p. 359.

[170] Center for Truth & Justice 2024.

prioritized minority rights discourse over self-determination claims, despite evidence of ethnic cleansing and the Armenian minority belonging to a people previously subjected to the second-largest genocide in the 20th century.[171]

24.8 Two Peaceful Aspirations to Secede 2017–2025

Two territories belonging to Western Europe have chosen a peaceful path to secession, but their efforts have not yet succeeded. Their claims stem from different legal grounds, and in the case of Greenland, US President Trump's claims on the island add an extra dimension.

24.8.1 Catalonia

The rich and industrialized region of Catalonia, an autonomous community within Spain, which has been part of Spain since medieval times, held a referendum on independence in 2017 with 3 million voters. Catalonian separatism dates back to the 16th century. In the region the language Catalan is spoken. The Spanish Government declared the referendum illegal and temporarily dissolved its self-government. The Constitutional Court decided that the republic could not secede from Spain. The EU and most states also opposed its right to secession.[172] No military conflict erupted. The regional politicians who led the secessionists were charged with treason in the Spanish Supreme Court, which sentenced them to between 9 and 13 years in prison, finding them guilty of sedition.[173] In 2021, they were pardoned by Spain's Prime Minister.

Catalonia is similar to the judgements on Åland and Quebec, how minorities cannot claim a right to secession if the parent state is a democracy and respects human rights.

24.8.2 Greenland

Greenland, the world's largest non-continental island, is an example not only of the right to internal self-determination for Indigenous peoples, with its Inuit population (among 56,000 residents). It is an example of *saltwater colonialism* that has

[171] The Armenian genocide (1915–1916) claimed between 1.2 and 1.5 million lives. See The Armenian Genocide. In: Holocaust Encyclopedia. https://encyclopedia.ushmm.org/content/en/article/the-armenian-genocide-1915-16-overview. Accessed 20 April 2025.

[172] Fernández Alles 2018, p. 179.

[173] Minder 2019.

not received proper attention until late, having been a Danish colony since the 1700s. Only in 2009 did Greenland gain real self-government following a 75% referendum approval.[174] This arrangement maintains Danish sovereignty, while allowing for potential independence through a future referendum and Danish parliamentary approval, though some argue a constitutional amendment would be required.[175] The Self-Government Act's preamble significantly recognized Greenlanders as "a people according to international law" with self-determination rights.[176]

President Trump's claims on Greenland in 2025 revived international attention to the island's status and intensified debate about its future. American interest in buying it dates back to 1917, and the WWII occupation and continued military presence through NATO bases.[177] Trump's statements to buy or in any other manner, take over Greenland, coincided with Greenlandic elections, where independence featured prominently. Due to its colonial status, some have rightly argued that under international law, Greenland already has a right of external self-determination and could make a unilateral declaration of independence, based on UN Charter Chapter XI (Non-Self-Governing Territories) and subsequent decolonization frameworks.[178] These provide referendums held in the territory to choose between independence, integration, or association options. In a referendum on future status, the alternatives "association or integration" would give Greenlanders the option to become part of the US or stay with Denmark. Both the Greenlandic and Danish governments rejected Trump's claims to acquire Greenland as violations of self-determination principles. However, Greenland is not ruling out closer cooperation with the US. The historical underdevelopment of Greenland and its dependency relationship have arguably negatively impacted its economy.[179] Economic self-determination is one part of the right to self-determination, where a people have a right to their natural resources, to prevent a colonial power from stealing or exploiting dependent peoples, see ICCPR Article 47 and IESCR, Article 25, to quote Professor Wrange: "For sure, in principle the right of self-determination requires that the people are allowed to 'freely pursue their economic, social and cultural development" [180] This effectively appears to bar the buy of Greenland by the US in the purpose to enrich itself from Greenland's natural resources as Greenland could be a rich source for rare earth minerals and energy.[181]

---

174 Statsministeriet (Danish Government) 2025.

175 Nielsen 2024.

176 Ackrén 2019, p. 2.

177 Jacobsen and Olsvig 2024, p. 107.

178 Hartmann 2025.

179 Oslund 2015.

180 Demirjian 2025.

181 Wrange 2019, p. 27

24.9 Conclusions

24.9.1 A Paradigm for If and How a Minority Could Achieve Self-Determination

A clear paradigm is needed to determine: a) when a minority can upgrade towards self-determination and b) what forms of self-determination are available. The Montevideo Convention on the Rights and Duties of States (1933) established four key criteria for statehood that can be applied by analogy: a permanent population, a defined territory, a functioning government, and the capacity to enter into relations with other States.[182] This is combined with the uti possidetis principle in CIL, that newly independent states should preserve the existing territorial borders of their former colonial administrators. The idea is to maintain stability in newly independent countries, often applied during periods of decolonization or the dissolution of Federations. Thus, the uti possidetis could be used to maintain existing territorial boundaries *within a state*. Taken together with the Montevideo criteria, they can provide legal standards for evaluating minority self-determination claims. If a minority group has strong historical ties to a specific territory and exhibits ethnic, cultural, and/or religious characteristics, these factors should qualify them for internal self-determination rights within that defined territory. This draws direct parallels to the Montevideo statehood criteria, but applied at a sub-state level and highlights that the uti possidetis principle hinders further fragmentation but at the same time acknowledges internal self-determination rights on a defined territory.

The proposed approach builds on UN Resolution 1541(XV) from 1960, which established self-determination options for colonial peoples and is accepted as CIL. For minorities, a careful step-by-step process should include: first, respecting basic minority rights; second, implementing self-government or power-sharing for significant minority groups living in a defined territory. If the parent state continues to be repressive, the minority gains the right to a fair, internationally observed referendum, with the choice of self-government (autonomy within existing states). However, as a last resort, full sovereignty (independence) could be used when the survival of the people is endangered, in cases of genocide or large-scale crimes against humanity. However, the third option in UNGA Resolution 1541 (integration or association with another state) would be excluded, to prevent the exploitation for territorial gains by neighboring states. This certified process ensures that minority self-determination follows a pattern already established in CIL. In cases of extreme persecution (large-scale genocide or ethnic cleansing risk), minorities should be automatically granted external self-determination rights, supported by the *Åland Islands* and *Quebec* precedents. Under such circumstances, the elevation of minorities to the level of self-determination makes Article 1(4) of Additional Protocol I to the Geneva Conventions applicable, allowing minorities to seek international support, including asking

[182] Montevideo Convention on Rights and Duties of States, opened for signature 26 December 1933, 165 LNTS 19 (entered into force 26 December 1934), Article 1.

for potential R2P intervention. Conversely, if separatists commit atrocity crimes, legitimacy is forfeited and their right to any self-determination claim is scrapped.

24.9.2 Overall Conclusions

The case study reveals that ethnic minority claims to self-determination have driven nearly all European military conflicts over the past century. However, secession rights have been granted in only one-third of cases (4 of 12): the FRY dissolution, Kosovo, Israel, and Northern Ireland's referendum provisions. The case study also reveals that classification as a "people" upgrades a group to the right to self-determination but does not in itself give an immediate right to independence. Minorities remain outside the ambit of self-determination. Their status can only be upgraded if they are victims of severe and persistent atrocity crimes perpetrated by the parent state.

Russian-backed separatist movements in former USSR Republics, the unrecognized Turkish Cypriot government, and Armenia's occupation of Nagorno-Karabakh demonstrate that minority claims supported by a neighboring state are consistently subordinated to principles of non-use of force, territorial integrity, *uti possidetis*, and prohibition on occupation. Thus, external intervention and military support typically undermine the legitimacy of secessionist claims. The *uti possidetis* is applied to internal provincial borders, which have hindered secession by Chechnya, Catalonia, and Nagorno-Karabakh. Azerbaijan's employment of starvation tactics and ethnic cleansing in 2022–2023 could potentially satisfy the humanitarian intervention threshold established in Kosovo, suggesting its limited precedential value when the political will is lacking.

Nevertheless, the case study demonstrates that only the most severe international delicts can justify legitimate remedial secession claims, corresponding with R2P's atrocity crime thresholds. Genocide seems particularly influential when it occurs alongside other atrocity crimes because genocide and ethnic cleansing are crimes targeted at a people or minority. Thus, Israel represents the first case of remedial secession, distinctively featuring the Holocaust genocide. It is distinguished by Jews being a people (but a significant minority in Europe), with ancient territorial claims that resurfaced during the planning for the British mandate of Palestine's post-colonial transition. The FRY dissolution demonstrates how federal government atrocity crimes enabled constituent republics to secede, using an analogy to the secession of colonial territories, application of the *uti possidetis* principle, and the right to secede within pre-existing borders. It meant that they fall under Article 1(4) of the Geneva Protocol I, framing their actions as a legal struggle for self-determination and their right to receive support. Kosovo initially appeared to establish precedent for minority remedial secession following genocide and ethnic cleansing, triggering NATO humanitarian intervention seemingly enabling the R2P threshold. Still, the ICJ in its Advisory Opinion on Kosovo's unilateral declaration of independence, deliberately avoided articulating guidance on secession. No European minority has since received legal approval to secede, even when citing atrocities. Nor has the risk of repetition of historical genocides (Armenian, Chechen) proven sufficient for contemporary secession claims. The Northern Ireland conflict's lower intensity distinguishes it from cases involving systematic large-scale atrocity crimes. Instead, the long-lasting ethno-nationalist, sectarian violence targeting civilians led to a political agreement on power-sharing, with mechanisms for potential future status changes, but without immediate territorial changes. The solution reflects attentiveness to the Irish population's right to self-determination before partition, as one people, and the right of a people under foreign domination to regain independence.

When separatists commit atrocity crimes (as in Bosnia, Ukraine, and Georgia), their claims are delegitimized, particularly if coordinated with the former parent state's forces, in a quest for renewed integration. However, Ossetians and Abkhazians are Indigenous peoples, why they have a right to internal self-determination with self-government measures, but not the right to secede. Although, the threshold for remedial secession could have been reached when the Ossetians and Abkhazians were forcely displaced and partly transferred, in the armed conflicts with Georgia, and their indigenous self-government forcibly revoked. The situation bears close similarity to that of Kosovo and could potentially legitimize remedial secession, under the claim they were not safe within Georgia, but PIL does never allow a merger with another state, why Russia's invasion is a violation of Art.2(4) in the UN Charter, not R2P. Surprisingly, terrorist tactics receive inconsistent international responses in secession contexts—delegitimizing Chechen independence but not preventing agreements in Northern Ireland or international support for Kosovo. The crime of aggression delegitimizes remedial secession, as in the case of Russia's invasion of its neighbors, in attempts at annexing territory, and Turkey's invasion of Southern Cyprus or Serbia's of Bosnia.[183] Thus, attempts to use coercion against Greenland's Indigenous population to dominate it are illegal. As colonial people, the Inuit have the right to choose independence without domination or exploitation. Their colonial and Indigenous status also gives them the right to freely exploit their natural resources, in economic self-determination under ICCPR Article 47 and IECSR Article 25.[184]

The overall conclusion to be drawn is that the international community generally rejects external self-determination for minorities. Sovereignty considerations typically outweigh even atrocity crimes when minorities retain participation capabilities in state governance, relying on the *Åland Islands* Opinion from over 100 years ago. Genocide stands as the exception, as its intent to exterminate a group fundamentally precludes their continued existence within the parent state.

Finally, a warning about territorial borders: when empires or federations break up, failing to maintain their internal borders, or to preserve the autonomous status or self-governance that minorities historically enjoyed, nor consulting them, creates serious risks—something President Woodrow Wilson warned about after WWI. Evidenced by the case study, disregard for the wishes of minorities in the drawing of new borders has contributed to basically all conflicts in Europe, including two world wars.

---

[183] Wrange 2010, p. 591.

[184] Wrange 2019, pp. 3–29.

References

Ackrén M (2019) Referendums in Greenland - From Home Rule to Self-Government. Fédéralisme Régionalisme 19:2. https://popups.uliege.be/1374-3864/index.php?id=1892, Accessed 5 August 2025

Adimassu Y (2021) The Essence of Remedial Secession: From the Perspectives of Human Right and Preservation of Natural Resources. Beijing Law Review 12:1252–1267

Alakashenko S (2024) Have Western Sanctions Against Russia Been Effective?, New Euroasian Strategy Center. https://nestcentre.org/have-western-sanctions-against-russia-been-effective/. Accessed 9 August 2025

Amnesty International, Human Rights Watch (2016) You Don't Exist, Arbitrary Detentions, Enforced Disappearances, and Torture in Eastern Ukraine. https://www.amnesty.nl/content/uploads/2016/07/ukrainian_report.pdf. Accessed 1 April 2025

Amnéus D (2008) Responsibility to Protect by Military Means—Emerging Norms on Humanitarian Intervention. Department of Law, Stockholm University, Stockholm

Anderson et al. (1995) Georgia/Abkhazia: Violations of the Laws of War and Russia's Role of the Conflict. Human Rights Watch Arms Project 7(7)

Avedissian K (2021) The Failure of the European Union to Address the Threat of Ethnic Cleansing of Armenians in Nagorno-Karabakh. Genocide Studies International 15(1):34–44

Bayefsky A (2021) Self-Determination in International Law, Quebec and Lessons Learned: Legal Opinions Selected and Introduced. Brill, Leiden

Bolton G, McGivern L, Steele S (2010) Editorial Introduction: Secession, Sovereignty, and the Quest for Legitimacy. St Antony's International Review 6:1:3–15

Brown E (2020) The United Nations, Self-Determination, State Failure and Secession. In: Avgustine JR (ed) United Nations: Friend or Foe of Self-Determination? E-International Relations

Brunstein W, King RD (2004) Anti-Semitism in Europe Before the Holocaust. International Political Science Review 25(1):35–53

Buchanan A (1997) Theories of Secession. Philosophy and Public Affairs 26(1):31–61

Buchheit L C (1978) Secession: The Legitimacy of self-determination. Yale University Press, New Haven and London

Cassese A (1995) Self-Determination of Peoples—A Legal Reappraisal. Oxford University Press, Oxford

Cassese A (1999) Ex Iniuria Ius Oritur: Are We Moving Towards International Legitimation of Forcible Humanitarian Countermeasures in the World Community? European Journal of International Law 10:1–25

Center for Truth & Justice (2024) The Planning, Inciting, Ordering, Instigating, and Implementing of Genocide by President Ilham Aliyev and other High Ranking Officials. https://www.cftjustice.org/wp-content/uploads/2024/04/ICC-Communication-NEW-IND.pdf. Accessed 16 March 2025

Cleaver T (2025) Tatar: Region's developments prove right a two-state Cyprus. Cyprus Mail. https://cyprus-mail.com/2025/02/17/tatar-regions-developments-prove-right-a-two-state-cyprus. Accessed 9 May 2025

Cohen A, Hamilton RE (2011) The Russian Military and the Georgia War: Lessons and Implications. Strategic Studies Institute, US Army War College

Cohen S K (2013) Choosing a Heim: Survivors of the Holocaust and Post-War Immigration, European Judaism: A Journal for the New Europe 46: 2: 32–54.

Council of Europe Parliamentary Assembly (1996) Humanitarian situation of the displaced persons in Georgia, Recommendation 1305. https://pace.coe.int/en/files/15339. Accessed 14 May 2025

Coverly HM (1950) Danger on the Right in Germany. Current History 18(103):138–143

Crawford J (2009) The Creation of States in International Law, 2nd edn. Oxford University Press

Christakis T (2011) The ICJ Advisory Opinion on Kosovo: Has International Law Something to Say about Secession? Leiden Journal of International Law 24:1, 73–86

Davis J (2022) The birth of the Soviet Union and the death of the Russian Revolution. JSTOR Daily 21. https://daily.jstor.org/the-birth-of-the-soviet-union-and-the-death-of-the-russian-revolution/. Accessed 18 March 2025
Demirjian K (2025) Why Does Trump Want Greenland? Here's What to Know. New York Times, 28 March 2025, https://www.nytimes.com/article/trump-greenland-why.html. Accessed 21 May 2025
Deutsch R (2002) The Good Friday Agreement: Assessing Its Implementation 1998-2001. Nordic Irish Studies 1:95–109
Dunn EC, Bobick MS (2014) The Empire Strikes Back: War without War and Occupation without Occupation in the Russian Sphere of Influence. American Ethnologist 41(3):405–413
Evans G (2009) The Responsibility to Protect: Ending Mass Atrocity Crimes Once and for All. Irish Studies in International Affairs 20:7–13
Evans G, Sahnoun M (2001) The R2P: Report of Responsibility to Protect: The International Commission on Intervention and State Sovereignty. International Development Research Centre, Ottawa
Fernández Alles JJ (2018) Spanish Constitutional Jurisprudence: Secession in Catalonia. Journal of Comparative Law 13(1):179
Fichte JG (1808) Addresses to the German Nation. Ed. Gregory Moore, Cambridge University, Cambridge.
Friesel E (1996) The Holocaust: Factor in the Birth of Israel? Yad Vashem. Jerusalem: 519–544
Gerrits WM, Bader, (2016) Russian patronage over Abkhazia and South Ossetia: implications for conflict resolution, East European Politics, 32:3:297
Getachew A (2019) Worldmaking after Empire: The Rise and Fall of Self-Determination. Princeton University Press, Princeton
Gidadhubli RG (2004) Russia after Beslan. Economic and Political Weekly 39–43:4704–4706
Guzi M et al. (2021) Old Sins Cast Long Shadows: The Long-Term Impact of the Resettlement of the Sudetenland on Residential Migration. Journal of Urban Economics 126
Hafkin G (2010) The Russo-Georgian War of 2008: Developing the Law of Unauthorized Humanitarian Intervention after Kosovo. Boston University International Law Journal 28(1):219
Hartmann J (2025) Denmark can't prevent Greenland from becoming part of the US: Commentary. Arctic Today, https://www.arctictoday.com/opinion-danish-politicians-cannot-prevent-greenland-from-becoming-part-of-the-us/. Accessed 21 May 2025
Hewitt G (2009) Abkhazia and Georgia: Time for a Reassessment. Brown Journal of World Affairs 15(2):183–196
Hilpold P (2017) Self-determination and Autonomy: Between Secession and Internal Self-determination. International Journal on Minority and Group Rights 24:302–335
Hilpold P (2023) Justifying the Unjustifiable: Russia's Aggression against Ukraine, International Law, and Carl Schmitt's "Theory of the Greater Space" ("Großraumtheorie"). Chinese Journal of International Law 22.3:409–433
Hughes J (2013) Russia and the Secession of Kosovo: Power, Norms and the Failure of Multilateralism. Europe-Asia Studies 65:992–1016
ICC OTP (2015) Situation in Georgia, Summary of the Prosecution's Request for authorisation of an investigation pursuant to article 15. https://www.icc-cpi.int/sites/default/files/iccdocs/otp/Art_15_Application_Summary-ENG.pdf. Accessed 14 May 2025
ICC OTP (2016) Report on Preliminary Examination Activities 2016. https://www.icc-cpi.int/sites/default/files/iccdocs/otp/161114-otp-rep-PE_ENG.pdf. Accessed 1 April 2025
Ingimundarson V (2022) The 'Kosovo Precedent': Russia's Justification of Military Interventions and Territorial Revisions in Georgia and Ukraine. LSE IDEAS. https://www.lse.ac.uk/ideas/Assets/Documents/updates/2022-SU-Valur-RussKosovo.pdf. Accessed 1 April 2025
International Crisis Group (2009) Belgrade and the Kosovo Serbs Before Independence
Jacobsen M, Olsvig S (2024) From Peary to Pompeo: The History of United States' Securitizations of Greenland. In: M Jacobsen et al (eds) Greenland in Arctic Security: (De)Securitization Dynamics under Climatic Thaw and Geopolitical Freeze, pp. 107–148. University of Michigan Press

Januta A (2025) Temporary ceasefire or redrawing borders?—what 'territorial concessions mean to Ukraine, Russia and the US. Kyiv Independent. https://kyivindependent.com/temporary-ceasefire-or-redrawing-borders-what-territorial-concessions-mean-to-russia-ukraine-and-the-us. Accessed 16 March 2025
Jones SG (2018) The Rise of Far-Right Extremism in the United States. Center for Strategic and International Studies
Ker-Lindsay J et al. (2011) An Island in Europe: The EU and the Transformation of Cyprus. In: Ker-Lindsay J (ed), The Cyprus Problem: What Everyone Needs to Know? L.B. Tauris, London
Kersten M (2014) Does Russia Have a "Responsibility to Protect" Ukraine? Don't Buy It. The Globe and Mail. https://www.theglobeandmail.com/opinion/does-russia-have-a-responsibility-to-protect-ukraine-dont-buy-it/article17271450. Accessed 25 January 2024
Kleinman T (2002) Did the Holocaust Play a Role in the Establishment of the State of Israel? Oral history Project. University of California, Santa Barbara
Knop K (2004) Diversity and Self-Determination in International Law. Cambridge University Press, Cambridge
Krylov A (1992) The Georgian–Abkhazian conflict, The Security of the Caspian Sea region, SIPRI, 16:281–294
Kucera J (2023) UN Security Council opts not to issue statement on Karabakh blockade. Eurasianet. https://eurasianet.org/un-security-council-opts-not-to-issue-statement-on-karabakh-blockade. Accessed 8 April 2025
Lapidus GW (1998) Contested Sovereignty: The Tragedy of Chechnya. International Security 23(1):5–49
Locke J (1689) Two Treatises of Government: The Works of John Locke. A New Edition, Corrected (1823) In Ten Volumes. Vol. V. Thomas Tegg; W. Sharpe and Son; G. Offor; G. and 1133 J. Robinson; J. Evans and Co. London
Low AD (1958) Lenin on the Question of Nationality. Bookman Associates, London
MacMillan M (2003) Paris 1919: Six Months that Changed the World. Random House, New York
Mamlyuk BN (2015) The Ukraine Crisis, Cold War II, and International Law. German Law Journal 16(3):479. SSRN: https://ssrn.com/abstract=2627417, Accessed 7 April 2025
Marchuk I, Wanigasuriya A (2020) The ICC concludes its preliminary examination in Crimea and Donbas: What's next for the situation in Ukraine? EJIL:Talk! https://www.ejiltalk.org/the-icc-concludes-its-preliminary-examination-in-crimea-and-donbas-whats-next-for-the-situation-in-ukraine. Accessed 11 March 2025
Mark RA (2008) National Self-Determination, as Understood by Lenin and the Bolsheviks. Lithuanian Historical Studies 13(1):21–39
Marxsen C (2014) The Crimea Crises: An International Law Perspective. Zeitschrift für ausländisches öffentliches Recht und Völkerrecht 74:367–399
Minder R (2019) Trial of Catalan Independence Leaders Ends in Spain. The New York Times. https://www.nytimes.com/2019/06/12/world/europe/spain-catalan-leaders-trial.html. Accessed 10 May 2025
Morelli VL (2019) Cyprus: Reunification Proving Elusive. Congressional Research Service. https://sgp.fas.org/crs/row/R41136.pdf. Accessed 10 May 2025
NATO (2018) Brussels Summit Declaration: Issued by the Heads of State and Government participating in the meeting of the North Atlantic Council in Brussels 11–12 July 2018, Press Release (2018) 074. https://www.nato.int/cps/en/natohq/official_texts_156624.htm. Accessed 14 May 2025
Nerozzi (2025) Trump wants a peace in Ukraine, no matter what a deal looks like, Politico. https://www.politico.com/news/2025/11/25/trump-wants-peace-in-ukraine-no-matter-what-a-deal-looks-like-00668136. Accessed 1 December 2025
Newman E, Visoka G (2019) Kosovo 20 Years On: Implications for International Order. The Brown Journal of World Affairs 26:215–231
Nielsen R S (2024) Selvstændighedsbestemmelsen i selvstyreloven for Grønland i et stats- og folkeretligt perspektiv [The Right to Independence in the Self-government Law for Greenland

in a State and International Law Perspective]. SSRN https://papers.ssrn.com/sol3/papers.cfm?abstract_id=4995489. Accessed 21 May 2025
Omidi A (2022) Analyzing the Compatibility of the Remedial Right of Secession with Regard to the Nagorno-Karabakh Conflict. Region 11(2):167–192
Oslund K (2015) Scarcity in the Arctic: A Colonial Construct? RCC Perspectives 2:29–36
Parliament of Georgia (2008) Resolution of the Parliament of Georgia of the Occupation of Georgian Territories by the Russian Federation, 28 August 2008. https://rrc.ge/law/dadg_2008_28_08_E.htm. Accessed 9 May 2025
Petričušić A (2005) The Rights of Minorities in International Law: Tracing Developments in Normative Arrangements of International Organizations. Croatian International Relations Review I:38/39:1
Ratner SR (1996) Uti Possidetis and the Borders of New States. American Journal of International Law 90(4):590–624
Robinson P (2023) Cold War II: Sir Niall Ferguson, On the Emerging Conflict With China, Interview in Uncommon Knowledge, Hoover Institute, https://www.hoover.org/research/cold-war-ii-niall-ferguson-emerging-conflict-china, Accessed 1 January 2025
Rosa V (2021) The Transnistrian Conflict: 30 Years Searching for a Settlement. SCEEUS Reports on Human Rights and Security, No. 4
Rosher B, Hayward K (2023) The Good Friday Agreement at 25: a Matter of Trust. UK in a Changing Europe. https://ukandeu.ac.uk/the-good-friday-belfast-agreement-at-25-a-matter-of-trust. Accessed 5 March 2025
Roy A (2008) Russia Resurgent? Moscow's Campaign to 'Coerce Georgia to Peace. International Affairs 84:1145–1171
Shelton D (2011) Self-determination in Regional Human Rights Law: From Kosovo to Cameroon. American Journal of International Law 105:60
Special Eurasia (2024) Transnistria Asks Russia's Protection from Moldova: Why Matters? Geopolitical Report ISSN 2785-2598 39(9). https://www.specialeurasia.com/2024/02/28/transnistria-russia-moldova/. Accessed 14 May 2025
Statsministeriet (Danish Government) (2025) Greenland. https://english.stm.dk/the-prime-ministers-office/the-unity-of-the-realm/greenland. Accessed 26 Mar 2025
Sterio M (2013) The Right to Self-determination Under International Law: "Selfistans", Secession and the Rule of the Great Powers. Routledge, London
Sterio M (2018) Session in International Law—a New Framework. Routledge, London
Svanberg K (2024) R.I.P. R2P and Yet it Moves: It is Premature to Declare the Responsibility to Protect Dead No, It Needs CPR in the Dark Ages of the 2020s! South Carolina Journal of International Law and Business 21(1):1–116, https://scholarcommons.sc.edu/scjilb/vol21/iss1/1/
Svanberg K, Bring O (2019) FN-stadgan och Världspolitiken Om FN:s roll i en föränderlig värld [The UN Charter in World Politics,the UN in a Changing World], 5th edn. Norstedts Juridik, Stockholm
Svanberg K (2014) FN:s säkerhetsråd i rättens tjänst—en studie av säkerhetsrådets ingripande under kap. VII i FN-stadgan för rätten till demokrati [The UNSC Serving in a Legal Capacity—a Study of UNSC's Interventions Under Chapter VII in the UN Charter for the Right to Democracy]. Jure, Stockholm
Swedish Parliament (2001) Kriget i Tjetjenien [War in Chechnya]. Parliamentary Motion 2001/02:U230. https://data.riksdagen.se/dokument/GP02U230. Accessed 20 March 2025
Szazs P (1997) The Dayton Accord: The Balkan Peace Agreement. Cornell International Law Journal 30:759
Tatikyan S (2023a) International Community Must Prevent Azerbaijan's Creeping Ethnic Cleansing in Nagorno-Karabakh. EVN Report
Tatikyan S (2023b) Can the International Community Reverse the Ethnic Cleansing of Armenians of Nagorno-Karabakh? Part 2. EVN Report

Téson FR (2009) Kosovo: a Powerful Precedent for the Doctrine of Humanitarian Intervention. Amsterdam Law Forum 1(2):42–48
Tindall T (2023) Citizens without States: The Implications of Non-Recognition for People in de Facto States. ODI
Tunander, O (2008). Geopolitics of the North: Geopolitik of the Weak: A Post-Cold War Return to Rudolf Kjellén. Cooperation and Conflict, 43(2):164–184
UK Government (1998) The Belfast Agreement: An Agreement Reached at the Multi-Party Talks on Northern Ireland, Cm 3883. https://assets.publishing.service.gov.uk/media/619500728fa8f5037d67b678/The_Belfast_Agreement_An_Agreement_Reached_at_the_Multi-Party_Talks_on_Northern_Ireland.pdf. Accessed 9 May 2025
UNCIO (1945) Documents of the United Nations Conference on International Organization, Volume VI
UN General Assembly (1951) General Progress Report and Supplementary Report of the United Nations Conciliation Commission for Palestine, Covering the Period from 11 December 1949 to 23 October 1950, Supplement No. 18, UN Doc. A/1367/Rev.1
UN General Assembly (2005) 2005 World Summit Outcome Document, UN Doc. A/RES/60/1
UN General Assembly (2008a) Status of internally displaced persons and refugees from Abkhazia, Georgia, UN Doc. A/RES/62/249
UN General Assembly (2008b) Sixty-second session, 86th plenary meeting, UN Doc. A/62/PV.86
UN General Assembly (2014) Territorial integrity of Ukraine, UN Doc. A/RES/68/262
UN General Assembly (2016) Third Committee, Situation of human rights in the Autonomous Republic of Crimea and the city of Sevastopol (Ukraine), UN Doc. A/C.3/71/L.26
UN General Assembly (2017), Third Committee, Situation of human rights in the Autonomous Republic of Crimea and the city of Sevastopol, Ukraine, UN Doc. A/C.3/72/L.42
UN General Assembly (2022) Aggression against Ukraine, Resolution ES-11/1, UN Doc. A/RES/ES-11/1
UN OHCHR (2016) Report on the human rights situation in Ukraine 16 February to 15 May 2016. https://ukraine.ohchr.org/en/14-periodic-report-EN. Accessed 9 May 2025
UN OHCHR (2018) Report on the human rights situation in Ukraine 16 November 2017 to 15 February 2018. https://ukraine.ohchr.org/en/21-periodic-report-EN. Accessed 9 May 2025
UN Secretary General (2024) Responsibility to protect: the commitment to prevent and protect populations from atrocity crimes, Report of the Secretary-General, UN Doc. A/78/901-S/2024/434
UN Secretary General (2025) Report of the Secretary-General on his mission of good offices in Cyprus, UN Doc. S/2025/7/Rev.1
UN Security Council (1993) Resolution 836, UN Doc. S/Res/836
UN Security Council (1993a) Resolution 822, UN Doc. S/RES/822
UN Security Council (1993b) Resolution 853, UN Doc. S/RES/853
UN Security Council (1993c) Resolution 884, UN Doc. S/RES/884
UN Security Council (2008) 5953rd meeting, 10 August 2008, UN Doc. S/PV.5953
UN Security Council (2014a) Draft Resolution 189, UN Doc. S/2014/189
UN Security Council (2014b) Resolution 2166, UN Doc. S/RES/2166
UN Security Council (2022a) Annex to the letter dated 24 February 2022 from the Permanent Representative of the Russian Federation to the United Nations addressed to the Secretary-General, UN Doc. S/2022/154
UN Security Council (2022b) Resolution 2623, UN Doc. S/RES/2623
UN Special Rapporteur Capotorti (1979) Study on the Rights of Persons Belonging to Ethnic, Religious and Linguistic Minorities, UN Doc. E/CN.4/Sub.2/384/Rev.1
US Mission to the OSCE (2024) Joint Statement Ten years since the downing of Malaysia Airlines Flight MH17. https://osce.usmission.gov/joint-statement-ten-years-since-the-downing-of-malaysia-airlines-flight-mh17/. Accessed 9 May 2025
US State Department (2017) Ukraine 2017 Human Rights Report. https://www.state.gov/reports/2017-country-reports-on-human-rights-practices/ukraine/. Accessed 9 May 2025

Van Hulle K, van der Tas L (2001) European Union—Individual Accounts. In: Ordelheide D (ed) Transnational Accounting, 2nd edn. Palgrave, Basingstoke

Verseck K (2025) Breakaway Transnistria is Russia's Stronghold in Moldova, DW. https://www.dw.com/en/breakaway-transnistria-is-russias-stronghold-in-moldova/a-74159854. Accessed 10 August 2025

Walter C et al. (2014) Self-Determination and Secession in International Law. Oxford University Press, Oxford

Ward JK (1968) Winston Churchill and the 'Iron Curtain' Speech. The History Teacher 1(2):5–63

Wilhelmsen J (2020) Exclusion and Inclusion: The Core of Chechen Mobilization to Jihad. Perspectives on Terrorism 14(2):27–41

Williams BG (2000) Commemorating 'The Deportation' in Post-Soviet Chechnya: The Role of Memorialization and Collective Memory in the 1994-1996 and 1999-2000 Russo-Chechen Wars, History and Memory 12(1):101–134

Wrange P (2010) The Crime of Aggression and Complementarity. In: Bellelli R (ed) International Criminal Justice: Law and Practice from the Rome Statute to Its Review. Ashgate

Wrange P (2019) Self-Determination, Occupation and the Authority to Exploit Natural Resources: Trajectories from Four European Judgments on Western Sahara. Israel Law Review 52(1):3–29s

Yakobson, A Rubinstein A (2008) Israel and the Family of Nations: The Jewish Nation-State and Human Rights, Routledge

Lily Katinka Svanberg holds LL.D. and LL.M. degrees from Stockholm University Law Faculty, as well as an LL.M. from New York University. She is an Australian Government of Education Laureate Fellow at Melbourne University. She has served as an international postdoctoral researcher at the University of Miami and as a visiting lecturer at West Virginia University and Senior University Lecturer at Stockholm University. Her research interests include international peace and security, the right to self-determination, treaty law, and maritime security.

Chapter 25
The Vanishing Point of Interpretation: Recognising the Limits to Reconciling the Concurrent Applications of International Human Rights Law and International Humanitarian Law

Sally Longworth

Contents

Abstract This chapter explores the underlying philosophies of international human rights law (IHRL) and international humanitarian law (IHL), to critically consider the limits to reconciliation of the two fields. Although there are significant crossovers between IHRL and IHL, there is a finite point where the two bodies cannot meet—namely, the role that the protection of human rights plays in the international architecture for peace and the concept of military necessity at the heart of IHL. Understanding this is important for ensuring that the two fields can be applied faithfully to their terms of protection and assists those seeking to establish peace to use all the tools available to them to the best effect. The protections under IHRL and IHL have proven time and again to be essential in armed conflict and understanding the difference between the two does not undermine that. Although IHL may not strive for peace, it does not apply in a vacuum. It is one tool in the toolbox that, used effectively together with others, might ultimately help in the mending of broken fissures.

Keywords International human rights law · International humanitarian law · Peace · Humanity · Military necessity · Interpretation

S. Longworth (✉)
Stockholm University, Stockholm, Sweden
e-mail: sally.longworth@juridicum.se

M. Klamberg et al. (eds.), *Reconstructing Power and Hegemony in Public International Law*, https://doi.org/10.1007/978-94-6265-743-4_25

25.1 Introduction

Since the drafting of the Geneva Conventions of 1949, questions have been raised about the relationship between international humanitarian law (IHL) and international human rights law (IHRL).[1] Considerable scholarship has been dedicated to exploring the subject,[2] including in Pål Wrange's work.[3] A basic question arises of how one body of law that protects individuals from being arbitrarily deprived of their lives can be reconciled with a body of law under which it is not unlawful to carry out an attack that results in civilians deaths, if those deaths are not excessive in relation to the direct military advantage gained. This and similar questions have led to significant development in our understanding of the similarities and differences between the fields, and how they can apply at the same time. It is generally accepted today that IHL provides protection complementary to that of IHRL. Older understandings of the operation of *lex specialis* (IHL) as displacing the *lex generalis* (IHRL) have now been solidly disproven, even if there remains disparity in the finer details of how specific norms should be interpreted in a given situation.[4] The current emphasis on complementarity between the two fields does not, however, address a fundamental discomfort that has been present since the developments in the post-World War II structures in the architecture for peace, where IHRL and IHL were key. Can the two bodies of law really be fully reconciled? Faith in this architecture has been significantly undermined with the full-scale invasion of Ukraine by Russia on 22 February 2022 and the outbreak of hostilities between Israel and Hamas following the attack by Hamas on 7 October 2023. Calls for peace in these armed conflicts are often accompanied by references to IHL. It is here that the essential mismatch between the two fields of law is revealed. Although both are essential in the framework preventing 'total war', as seen in the twentieth century, the philosophical foundations of the two bodies are fundamentally different, suggesting that the two can never be fully reconciled.

Understanding this difference is essential in order that the two bodies of law can be applied faithfully to their terms of protection. It does not question the essential protection offered by the two fields of law to individuals in the extreme situation of armed conflict. Rather, it clarifies the legal framework applicable and enables those that sue for peace to have recourse to the best tools available to them.

---

[1] *See, for example*, Kolb 2013.

[2] *See, for example*, Doswald-Beck 2011; Forrest et al. 2012; Kolb and Gaggioli 2013; De Wet and Kleffner 2014; Clapham 2015; Murray et al. 2016; Fortin, 2017; Bohrer et al. 2020; Sassoli 2020; Kolb et al. 2022.

[3] *See, for example*, Wrange 2018, 2019a. *See also* Wrange 2019b, pp. 107–126.

[4] *See further* Fortin 2022, pp. 345–350. *See also* d'Aspremont and Tranchez 2013, pp. 224–225.

25.2 Understanding the Philosophical Underpinnings of the Two Fields

The historical developments of both IHL and IHRL have long roots. IHL lawyers highlight ancient rules regulating warfare, such as the 5th century BCE treatise 'The Art of War' by Sun Tzu.[5] Although the modern development of IHRL is often considered to start with the drafting of the United Nations Charter 1945 (UN Charter)[6] and Universal Declaration on Human Rights 1948 (UDHR),[7] older historical roots in developments from the League of Nations, the abolition movement of the 1800s, the Age of Enlightenment belief in natural rights, the revolutions in France and the United States in the late 1700s with the recognition of the 'rights of Man', and ancient religious texts highlighting the sanctity of life are also a part of the tale.[8]

The modern development of these two bodies of law displays critical differences between their philosophical bases. IHL aims to limit the impact of hostilities on those who do not or no longer participate in a conflict.[9] IHL also limits the rights of parties to a conflict to use armed force only to the extent necessary to achieve the aim of the conflict, which is to weaken the military forces of the enemy.[10] This is recognised in preamble para 6 of the 1899 Convention (II) with Respect to the Laws and Customs of War on Land and its annex (1899 Hague Regulations) and preamble para 5 of the 1907 Convention (IV) respecting the Laws and Customs of War on Land and its annex, put succinctly as the provisions of IHL being 'inspired by the desire to diminish the evils of war', but only 'as far as military requirements permit'.[11]

The provisions of IHL thus include exceptions to certain requirements and provide that parties to an armed conflict may take measures that tip the balance of otherwise humanitarian considerations, if they are considered necessary to achieve their aim

[5] Tzu 2010. Wilson 2017, pp. 563–564, highlights that this body of law was historically more commonly referred to as 'the Laws of War' or 'the Law of Armed Conflict'. It was only in 1981 in the Conventional Weapons Convention that reference to 'international humanitarian law' first appeared in a treaty. This is not the only terminology that changed in the modern development of IHL. The introduction of the term 'armed conflict' as opposed to 'war' in the Geneva Conventions of 1949 is a further example. *See further* Crawford et al. 2023, pp. 214–215. *See also* Alexander 2015, pp. 109–138.

[6] Charter of the United Nations, 24 October 1945, 1 UNTS XVI.

[7] UNGA (1948) Universal Declaration of Human Rights, Resolution 217 A(III), UN Doc. A/RES/3/217A.

[8] *See further* Ishay 2008 and Moyn 2010. *See also* Alston 2013.

[9] O'Connell 2021, pp. 44–46, paras 2.33–2.37; Dinstein 2016, pp. 8–12.

[10] Declaration Renouncing the Use, in Time of War, of Explosive Projectiles Under 400 Grammes Weight, Saint Petersburg, 29 November (11 December) 1868, preamble para 2 (St Petersburg Declaration 1868).

[11] Convention (II) with Respect to the Laws and Customs of War on Land and its annex: Regulations concerning the Laws and Customs of War on Land, The Hague, 29 July 1899, preamble para 5; Convention (IV) respecting the Laws and Customs of War on Land and its annex: Regulations concerning the Laws and Customs of War on Land, The Hague, 18 October 1907.

militarily. A clear example of this is seen in the protection of cultural property.[12] Article 4.1 of the 1954 Hague Convention for the Protection of Cultural Property sets out the obligation of State parties to 'respect cultural property situated within their own territory as well as within the territory of other High Contracting Parties by refraining from any use of the property and its immediate surroundings or of the appliances in use for its protection for purposes which are likely to expose it to destruction or damage in the event of armed conflict; and by refraining from any act of hostility directed against such property'. Article 4.2 then provides that the obligations in Article 4.1 may be waived only in cases where military necessity imperatively requires such a waiver. Article 6 of the 1999 Second Protocol to The Hague Convention then goes on to define the meaning of imperative military necessity applicable in this context.[13]

The balance between military necessity and humanity, reflected throughout the treaty provisions and customary rules,[14] reveals something about the philosophical basis of IHL—that military force may be necessary at times. This is also recognised in the preamble of the 1899 Hague Regulations that 'while seeking to preserve peace and prevent armed conflicts among nations, it is likewise necessary to have regard to cases where an appeal to arms' may be impossible to avert.[15]

In contrast, the link between the protection of human rights and the prevention of armed conflict is included in the first and second paragraphs of the preamble of the UN Charter.[16] The purpose of ensuring human rights are protected as a means to ensure peace is also highlighted in the preamble of the UDHR, according to which the protection of human rights is 'essential, if man is not to be compelled to have recourse, as a last resort, to rebellion against tyranny and oppression'.[17] Whereas IHRL strives to ensure that recourse to armed conflict is not necessary, IHL explicitly recognises that this level of armed force may indeed be necessary. This therefore marks a finite point where the two bodies cannot be fully reconciled.

---

[12] Convention for the Protection of Cultural Property in the Event of Armed Conflict 1954, 249 UNTS 240, Article 4.

[13] *See also* Protocol Additional to the Geneva Conventions of 12 August 1949, and Relating to the Protection of Victims of International Armed Conflicts 1977, 1125 UNTS 3 (API), Articles 56(1) and (2) as a further example.

[14] *See further* Francis Lieber, 'Instructions for the Government of Armies of the United States in the Field', 24 April 1863, principle 14; API, Article 1(2). *See further* Dörmann et al. 2016, para 32, and Coupland 2001.

[15] 1899 Hague Regulations, preamble para 1. *See also* 1907 Convention (IV) respecting the Laws and Customs of War on Land and its annex, preamble para 1.

[16] UN Charter, preamble para 1. *See further* Articles 1(1) and 1(3).

[17] UDHR, preamble para 3. *See also* para 1. The UDHR is referenced in the International Covenant on Civil and Political Rights 1966, 999 UNTS 171 (ICCPR), preamble para 3, Convention for the Protection of Human Rights and Fundamental Freedoms, as amended by Protocols Nos. 11 and 14, 1950, ETS 5 (ECHR), preamble para 1, American Convention on Human Rights 1969, O.A.S. Treaty Series No. 36, 1144 UNTS 123 (ACHR), preamble para 3, and African Charter on Human and Peoples' Rights 1981, OAU Doc. CAB/LEG/67/3 rev. 5, 1520 UNTS 217 (ACHPR), preamble para 3.

25.3 Placing This Understanding in Context

As important as it is to understand the philosophical differences between IHRL and IHL, that understanding needs to be placed in the broader context of the fundamental principles enshrined in both bodies of law. These include, for example, the principles of human dignity and humane treatment. The fundamental principles were described by the International Criminal Tribunal for the former Yugoslavia ('ICTY') in *Prosecutor v. Furundzija* as 'the basic underpinning and indeed the very *raison d'être* of international humanitarian law and human rights law'.[18] Both IHL and IHRL also stand out in the field of international law as aiming to provide protection for individuals.[19]

These similarities are made more apparent in the dominance of 'international humanitarian law' as a way to reference the field of law that governs the conduct of hostilities and protections against the effects of hostilities during armed conflict. Crawford et al. highlight that this reference to 'humanitarian' came after the agreement of the Geneva Convention of 1949 with the publication of the first International Committee of the Red Cross Commentary to Geneva Convention I in 1952.[20] References to 'international humanitarian law' grew more and more common in the 1990s, with the trend continuing to this day; this is now the main way in which the field is referred to in scholarship and by international organisations.[21] This change in the language coincides with the growth in academic research and case law analysing the relationship between IHRL and IHL, which has predominately emphasised the complementary protections between the two fields.[22] Critical approaches argue that reference to 'IHL' primarily subjects the conduct of warfare to humanitarian considerations, rather than the principle of military necessity.[23] Others argue that broad references to 'military advantage' included in IHL provisions have allowed scholars

---

[18] ICTY, *Prosecutor v. Furundžija*, T. Ch., Judgment, 10 December 1998, IT-95-17/1-T, para 183. *See also* UN Commission on Human Rights, Sub-Commission on the Promotion and Protection of Human Rights 'Working paper on the relationship between human rights law and international humanitarian law by Françoise Hampson and Ibrahim Salama', UN Doc. E/CN.4/Sub.2/2005/14, 21 June 2005, para 3.

[19] *See, for example*, API, preamble para 3, and Protocol Additional to the Geneva Conventions of 12 August 1949, and Relating to the Protection of Victims of Non-International Armed Conflicts, 1125 UNTS 609 (APII), preamble paras 3 and 4. *See further* APII, preamble paras 1 and 2. However, the normative structures of protection differ greatly. *See further* Longworth 2022, pp. 48–54, and Hill-Cawthorne 2017.

[20] Crawford et al. 2023, pp. 205–207. *See also* Wilson 2017, pp. 567–568.

[21] Crawford et al. 2023, pp. 205–207.

[22] *See* n. 1. *See also* ECtHR Press Unit, 'Factsheet—Armed conflicts', January 2023, https://www.echr.coe.int/documents/d/echr/FS_Armed_conflicts_ENG, accessed 5 March 2025, for examples of case law relating to the ECHR. Cases before the ECtHR regarding the violation of human rights in armed conflict have grown significantly in recent years, including inter-State applications. *See further* https://www.echr.coe.int/inter-state-applications, accessed 5 March 2025.

[23] *See, for example*, Wilson 2017, p. 577, and Alexander 2015, pp. 122–123. *See also* De Koker 2018.

and practitioners to broaden the interpretation of this term to such a point as to violate fundamental protections of humanity, such as the principle of distinction.[24]

Both bodies of law also require transparency and accountability in the exercise of the extreme power that is armed force against individuals. Under IHRL, this is evident in the obligation to protect human rights,[25] procedural obligations relating to violations of human rights,[26] and the right to an effective remedy.[27] It is also evident in the operation of specific rights, such as the right to freedom of expression.[28] IHL also requires measures of accountability and transparency in fulfilling the obligations to respect and ensure respect for IHL,[29] and States are obliged to investigate and, where appropriate, prosecute alleged grave breaches and serious violations of IHL.[30] IHL includes some complementary protections to ensure a plurality of voices in society, for instance through prohibition of adverse distinction based on political and other opinions,[31] and protection of journalists.[32] Further, Article 70 of Geneva Convention IV Relative to the Protection of Civilian Persons in Time of War 1949 prohibits the Occupying Power from arresting, prosecuting or convicting protected persons 'for acts committed or for opinions expressed before the occupation, or during a temporary interruption thereof, with the exception of breaches of the laws and customs of war'. Furthermore, the provisions requiring access to information relating to individuals in the hands of the adverse party to the conflict serve a transparency function by ensuring that protection obligations are upheld.[33]

IHRL also recognises that the use of armed force, including military force, may be a 'necessary' and lawful interference with specific human rights in a given context.

---

[24] Soni 2024.

[25] *See, for example,* UN Human Rights Committee (2004) General Comment No. 31 (2004) on The Nature of the Legal Obligation Imposed on State Parties to the Covenant. UN Doc CCPR/C/21/Rev.1/Add. 13, para 8.

[26] *See, for example,* ECtHR, *Al-Skeini and Others v. the United Kingdom,* Application no. 55721/07, Grand Chamber Judgment, 7 July 2011, and ECtHR, *Jaloud v. The Netherlands,* Application No. 47708/08, Grand Chamber Judgment, 20 November 2014.

[27] *See* ICCPR, Article 2(3); ECHR, Article 13; ACHR, Article 25. *See further* Musila 2006.

[28] UN Commission for Human Rights (1994) Promotion and protection of the right to freedom of expression: Report of the Special Rapporteur, Mr Abid Hussain, pursuant to Commission on Human Rights resolution 1993/45. UN Doc E/CN.4/1995/32, para 14.

[29] Common Article 1 to the Geneva Conventions of 1949; Dörmann et al. 2016, paras 146, 151, 154–156.

[30] Convention for the Amelioration of the Condition of the Wounded and Sick in Armed Forces in the Field 1949, 75 UNTS 31 (GCI), Article 49; Convention for the Amelioration of the Condition of Wounded, Sick and Shipwrecked Members of Armed Forces at Sea 1949, 75 UNTS 8 (GCII), Article 50; Convention relative to the Treatment of Prisoners of War 1949, 75 UNTS 135 (GCIII), Article 129; Convention Relative to the Protection of Civilian Persons in Time of War 1949, 75 UNTS 287 (GCIV), Article 146; API, Article 87; Henckaerts and Doswald-Beck 2005, Rule 158 (Prosecution of War Crimes). *See further* Lubell et al. 2019, paras 12–16.

[31] GCI, Articles 3 and 12(2); GCII, Articles 3 and 12(2); GCIII, Articles 3 and 16; GCIV, Articles 3, 13 and 27(3); API, Article 9(1), and APII, Article 2(1).

[32] API, Article 79. *See further* GCIII, Article 4(4).

[33] *See further* Longworth 2022, pp. 306–319.

Indeed, the use of armed force may even be necessary for the protection of the rights of others. This may include the lawful deprivation of the lives of some individuals, if the conditions that such force is absolutely necessary for life to be deprived in a non-arbitrary way are met.[34] A number of treaties recognise that certain rights may be derogated in emergency situations such as armed conflict.[35] However, the overarching aim in the State derogating is to bring about or return to a situation of peace. So, although accommodating extreme use of State power, including military force, may be necessary, the aim in exercising such power is to enable a return to a situation where that force is not necessary. This is demonstrated in the requirements that derogations must be only temporary and only to the extent strictly required by the exigencies of the situation.[36] Even in situations of emergency, the State must still make every effort to preserve and safeguard the values of a democratic society.[37] Other human rights treaties reference their application in times of armed conflict.[38] But, as the UN Human Rights Committee noted:

> Wars and other acts of mass violence continue to be a scourge of humanity resulting in the loss of many thousands of lives every year. Efforts to avert the risks of war and any other armed conflict, and to strengthen international peace and security, are among the most important safeguards of the right to life.[39]

Thus, the use of military necessity can only be accommodated to a limited extent within this framework.

---

[34] *See further* UN Human Rights Committee (2019) General Comment No. 36 (2019) on Article 6 of the International Covenant on Civil and Political Rights, on the Right to Life. UN Doc CCPR/C/GC/36, paras 12–13 and 21–22. *See also* the example of the ECtHR, *Giulani and Gaggio v. Italy,* Application no. 23458/02, Judgment, 24 March 2011. *See further* Council of Europe/European Court of Human Rights, 'Guide on Article 2 of the European Convention of Human Rights: Right to life', updated on 31 August 2024, paras 104–199, https://ks.echr.coe.int/documents/d/echr-ks/guide_art_2_eng, accessed 5 March 2025.

[35] ICCPR, Article 4; ECHR, Article 15; ACHR, Article 29.

[36] UN Human Rights Committee (2001) General Comment No. 29 (2001) on Article 4 of the International Covenant on Civil and Political Rights, on States of Emergency. UN Doc CCPR/C/21/Rev.1/Add.11; Council of Europe/European Court of Human Rights, 'Guide on Article 15 of the European Convention of Human Rights', updated on 31 August 2024, https://ks.echr.coe.int/documents/d/echr-ks/guide_art_15_eng, accessed 5 March 2025; Inter-American Court of Human Rights (IACtHR), *Habeas corpus in Emergency Situations (Arts. 27(2), 25(1) and 7(6) American Convention on Human Rights),* Advisory Opinion OC-8/87 of January 30, 1987, Series A No. 8.

[37] ECtHR, *Mehmet Hasan Altan, v. Turkey*, Application no. 13237/17, Judgment, 20 March 2018, para 210; ECtHR, *Şahin Alpay v. Turkey*, Application no. 16528/17, Judgment, 20 March 2018, para 180; IACtHR, *Habeas Corpus in Emergency Situations*, n. 36, para 20. *See also* UN Human Rights Committee, General Comment No. 29, 2001, n. 36, para 1.

[38] *See, for example,* Convention on the Rights of the Child 1990, 1577 UNTS 3, Article 38, and Convention on the Rights of Persons with Disabilities 2006, 2515 UNTS 3, preamble para u and Article 11.

[39] UN Human Rights Committee 2019, para 69.

25.4 What Difference Does This Make?

Recognising the differences between the two bodies of law assists in understanding what IHL does for individuals caught in the midst of armed conflict. Indeed, it may aid understanding of why international human rights courts and monitoring bodies have grappled with determining how these two fields of law apply at the same time. Although calls for adherence to IHL as a means to bring about peace are somewhat misplaced, IHL does provide essential protections to individuals in armed conflict, laying a foundation enabling the forging of a path towards an eventual more sustainable peace. But it is not in itself a path to peace.

Research has highlighted, however, that compliance with IHL can facilitate peace processes and strengthen the chance of lasting peace.[40] In addition, IHL imposes a number of obligations once a cessation of hostilities has been reached. These are linked to the restoration of peace. One of the most well-known is the obligation under Article 6(5) of Additional Protocol II to the Geneva Conventions 1977 applicable in non-international armed conflicts, which provides that at the end of hostilities, the authorities in power shall endeavour to grant the broadest possible amnesty to persons who have participated in the armed conflict and those deprived of their liberty for reasons related to the armed conflict.[41] In international armed conflicts, Article 17(4) of Geneva Convention I for the Amelioration of the Condition of the Wounded and Sick in Armed Forces in the Field 1949 provides that, at the end of the hostilities, the Official Graves Registration Services shall, through the Information Bureau, exchange lists showing the exact locations and markings of graves, together with particulars of the dead interred therein, if this has not already taken place.[42] This obligation is not only linked to the right of the families to know the fate of their relatives,[43] but also to broader national healing processes, as well as establishing historical records and understandings, all of which are ultimately connected to establishing conditions for a secure peace.[44] Prisoners of war (POWs) should also be released and repatriated without delay after the cessation of active hostilities.[45] The 2020 Commentary to Geneva Convention III relative to the Treatment of Prisoners of War 1949 notes that repatriation of POWs is one of the measures taken in the efforts to return to peace.[46] In both international armed conflicts and non-international armed conflicts, there are also obligations to investigate and prosecute

[40] *See, for example,* Bellal and Casey-Maslen 2011; Hofmann 2012. *See also* ICRC 2019.

[41] *See also* Henckaerts and Doswald-Beck 2005, Rule 159 (Amnesty).

[42] GCI, Article 17(4).

[43] Dörmann et al. 2016, para 1716.

[44] Gavshon, D, 2015, p. 278. *See also* 290–291 on returning the remains, and Henckaerts, JM and Doswald-Beck, L, 2005, Rule 114 (Return of the Remains and Personal Effects of the Dead) as a further example of obligations aimed at creating conditions for a secure peace.

[45] GCIII, Article 118(1). *See further* Articles 118(2) and (3). *See also* Article 119 on the details for the procedure of repatriation.

[46] Dörmann et al. 2021, para 4444.

war crimes after a conflict,[47] a requirement clearly aimed at upholding the rule of law and ensuring accountability in the long-term interest of ensuring sustainable peace.[48]

IHL does not contain any goal for the parties to strive for peace. However, it does not apply on its own, in a vacuum. It is one tool in the toolbox that, used effectively together with others, might ultimately help mend broken fissures.[49] That is why concerns that IHL is in crisis are so concerning for the overarching goal of international peace and security.[50]

Strengthening our understanding in this area should ultimately contribute to upholding the fundamental principles evident in both IHL and IHRL, such as protection, human dignity and humanity. This is demonstrated in the growing body of case law from international human rights monitoring bodies, as well as the number of UN inquiries and fact-finding missions with mandates to consider both IHL and IHRL.[51] As more and more bodies consider the normative relationship between IHRL and IHL, greater understanding is achieved on the substance of the overlapping norms under the respective legal frameworks. This in turn generates a more systematic understanding and contributes to a more unified approach.[52] That said—and as highlighted in this piece—there cannot be a perfect match between all these various norms. What must be borne in mind is, as Andrew Clapham observed, 'how the one branch at the heart of the investigation is impacted by the other branch', as opposed to looking for 'a theory of everything'.[53]

[47] *See further* Henckaerts and Doswald-Beck 2005, Rule 161 (International Cooperation in Criminal Proceedings).

[48] *See further* UN Human Rights Council (2021a) Accountability: Prosecuting and punishing gross violations of human rights and serious violations of international humanitarian law in the context of transitional justice processes', Report of the Special Rapporteur on the promotion of truth, justice, reparation and guarantees of non-recurrence. UN Doc A/HRC/48/60, paras 18–27.

[49] *See* Fortin 2022, p. 353.

[50] UN Charter, Article 1(1).

[51] *See, for example*, UN Human Rights Council (2022) Situation of human rights in Ukraine stemming from the Russian aggression, Resolution 49/1. UN Doc A/HRC/RES/49/1, para 11; UN Human Rights Council (2021b) Ensuring respect for international human rights law and international humanitarian law in the Occupied Palestinian Territory, including East Jerusalem, and in Israel, Resolution S-30/1. UN Doc A/HRC/RES/S-30/1, para 1; UN Human Rights Council (2023) Responding to the human rights and humanitarian crisis caused by the ongoing armed conflict in the Sudan, Resolution 54/2. UN Doc A/HRC/RES/54/2, para 18; UN Human Rights Council (2024) Situation of human rights in the Syrian Arab Republic, Resolution 55/22. UN Doc A/HRC/RES/55/22, paras 2 and 20.

[52] Maduro 2007, pp. 3 and 12.

[53] Clapham 2015,p. 705.

25.5 Conclusion

The philosophy behind IHRL is that protecting human rights will contribute to establishing peace. On the other hand, IHL—though it shares humanity and dignity as philosophical starting points—does not strive for peace. These foundational differences go on to shape the normative contents of the laws and are therefore never fully reconciled when they apply at the same time in the same space.[54] This does not, however, undermine the protections under these bodies of law. The reality of armed conflict has shown time and time again just how essential they are. But understanding this difference may aid those seeking to establish peace to use all the tools available to them to the best effect.

Although the base-level difference in the philosophical underpinnings between IHRL and IHL may seem obvious on its face, understanding it is important for the interpretation of the two bodies of law, particularly in situations where they both apply. Whereas upholding IHRL will in an ideal world act as one of the protections against armed conflict breaking out, upholding IHL once the peace has been broken is not a means for achieving peace per se. Rather, it encompasses the critical protections and limitations applicable in such extreme circumstances, and contributes to establishing a situation where peace can be facilitated.

References

Alexander A (2015) A Short History of International Humanitarian Law. European Journal of International Law 26:109–138

Alston P (2013) Does the Past Matter? On the Origins of Human Rights. Harvard Law Review 126(7):2043–2082

Bellal A, Casey-Maslen S (2011) Rules of Engagement: Protecting Civilians Through Dialogue with Non-State Actors. Geneva Academy of International Humanitarian Law and Human Rights, Geneva

Bohrer Z, Dill J, Duffy H (eds) (2020) Law Applicable to Armed Conflict. Cambridge University Press, Cambridge

Clapham A (2015) The Complex Relationship between the Geneva Conventions and International Human Rights Treaties. In: Clapham A, Gaeta P, Sassòli M (eds) The 1949 Geneva Conventions: A Commentary. Oxford University Press, Oxford, pp. 701–735

Coupland R (2001) Humanity: What Is It and How Does It Influence International Law? International Review of the Red Cross 83(844):969–989

Council of Europe/European Court of Human Rights, 'Guide on Article 2 of the European Convention of Human Rights: Right to life', updated on 31 August 2024, paras 104–199, https://ks.echr.coe.int/documents/d/echr-ks/guide_art_2_eng

Council of Europe/European Court of Human Rights, 'Guide on Article 15 of the European Convention of Human Rights', updated on 31 August 2024, https://ks.echr.coe.int/documents/d/echr-ks/guide_art_15_eng

Crawford E, Lukin A, Mowbray J (2023) The Terminology of the Law of Warfare: A Linguistic Analysis of State Practice, Journal of International Humanitarian Legal Studies, 14: pp. 197–222

[54] *See also* Milanovic 2011.

d'Aspremont J, Tranchez E (2015) The Question for a Non-Conflictual Coexistence of International Human Rights law and Humanitarian Law: Which Role for the Lex Specialis Principle?. In: Kolb R and Gaggioli G (eds) (2013) Research Handbook on Human Rights and Humanitarian Law. Edward Elgar Publishing, Cheltenham, UK, Northampton, MA, pp. 223–250

De Koker C (2018) The European Court of Human Rights' Approach to Armed Conflict and Humanitarian Law: Ivory Tower or Pas de Deux? In: De Hert, P, Smis, S, Holvoet, M (eds) Convergences and Divergences Between International Human Rights, International Humanitarian and International Criminal Law. Cambridge University Press, Cambridge, pp. 195–222

de Wet E, Kleffner J (eds) (2014) Convergence and Conflicts of Human Rights and International Humanitarian Law in Military Operations. Pretoria University Law Press, Pretoria

Dinstein Y (2016) The Conduct of Hostilities under the Law of International Armed Conflict, 3rd ed. Cambridge University Press, Cambridge

Dörmann K, Lijnzaad L, Sassòli M, Spoerri P (editorial committee) (2016) Commentary on the First Geneva Convention: Convention (I) for the Amelioration of the Condition of the Wounded and Sick in Armed Forces in the Field, 2nd ed. Cambridge University Press, Cambridge

Dörmann K, Lijnzaad L, Sassòli M, Spoerri P (editorial committee) (2021) Commentary on the Third Geneva Convention: Convention (III) Relative to the Treatment of Prisoners of War, 2nd ed. Cambridge University Press, Cambridge

Doswald-Beck L (2011) Human Rights in Times of Conflict and Terrorism. Oxford University Press, Oxford

European Court of Human Rights, Press Unit, 'Factsheet—Armed conflicts', January 2023, https://www.echr.coe.int/documents/d/echr/FS_Armed_conflicts_ENG

Forrest Martin F, Schnably S J, Wilson R, Simon J, Tushnet M (2012) International Human Rights and Humanitarian Law: Treaties, Cases, and Analysis. Cambridge University Press, Cambridge

Fortin K (2017) The Accountability of Armed Groups under Human Rights Law. Oxford University Press, Oxford

Fortin K (2022) The Relationship Between International Human Rights Law and International Humanitarian Law: Taking Stock at the End of 2022? Netherlands Quarterly of Human Rights 40(4):343–353

Gavshon D (2015) The Dead. In: Clapham, A, Gaeta, P, Sassòli, M (eds) The 1949 Geneva Conventions: A Commentary. Oxford University Press, Oxford, pp. 277–296

Henckaerts J M, Doswald-Beck L (2005) Customary International Humanitarian Law, Volume I: Rules. Cambridge University Press, Cambridge

Hill-Cawthorne L (2017) Rights under International Humanitarian Law. European Journal of International Law 28(4):1187–1215

Hofmann C (2012) Reasoning with Rebels: International NGOs' Approach to Engaging Armed Groups. German Institute for International and Security Affairs, Berlin

International Committee of the Red Cross and Red Crescent (2019) Displacement in Times of Armed Conflict: How International Humanitarian Law Protects in War, and Why It Matters. ICRC, Geneva

Ishay M R (2008) The History of Human Rights: From Ancient Times to the Globalization Era. University of California Press, Berkely, Los Angeles and London

Kolb R (2013) Human Rights Law and International Humanitarian Law Between 1945 and the Aftermath of the Tehran Conference of 1968: In: Kolb R, Gaggioli G (eds) (2013) Research Handbook on Human Rights and Humanitarian Law. Edward Elgar Publishing, Cheltenham, UK, Northampton, MA, pp. 35–52

Kolb R, Gaggioli G (eds) (2013) Research Handbook on Human Rights and Humanitarian Law. Edward Elgar Publishing, Cheltenham, UK, Northampton, MA

Kolb R, Gaggoli G, Kilibarda P (2022) Research Handbook on Human Rights and Humanitarian Law: Further Reflections and Perspectives. Edward Elgar Publishing, Cheltenham, UK, Northampton, MA

Lieber F (1863) Instructions for the Government of Armies of the United States in the Field, 24 April 1863

Longworth S (2022) The Silence Between Spaces: Freedom of Expression in Armed Conflict. Stockholm University, Stockholm

Lubell N, Pejic J, Simmons C (2019) 'Guidelines on Investigating Violations of International Humanitarian Law: Law, Policy, and Good Practice', International Committee of the Red Cross and Red Crescent, Geneva

Milanovic M (2011) Norm Conflicts, International Humanitarian Law, and Human Rights Law. In: Ben-Naftali, O (ed) International Humanitarian Law and International Human Rights Law. Oxford University Press, Oxford, pp. 95–125

Moyn S (2010) The Last Utopia. Harvard University Press, MA

Murray D, Wilmshurst E, Hampson F, Garraway C, Lubell N, Akande D (eds) (2016) Practitioners' Guide to Human Rights Law in Armed Conflict. Oxford University Press, Oxford

Musila G M (2006) The Right to An Effective Remedy Under the African Charter on Human and Peoples' Rights. African Human Rights Law Journal 6(2):442–464

O'Connell M E (2021) Historical Development and Legal Basis. In: Fleck D (ed.) The Handbook of International Humanitarian Law. 4th ed., Oxford University Press, Oxford, pp. 10–4

Poiares Maduro M (2007) Interpreting European Law: Judicial Adjudication in a Context of Constitutional Pluralism. European Journal of Legal Studies 1(2):1–21

Sassoli M (2020) International Humanitarian Law and International Human Rights Law. In: Saul B, Akande D (eds) The Oxford Guide to International Humanitarian Law. Oxford University Press, Oxford, pp. 381–402

Soni S (2024) Proportionality *in Bello*: A Case Against Indirect Military Advantage. Journal of International Humanitarian Studies (published online ahead of print) 2024:1–20

Tzu S (2010) The Art of War. Capstone Publishing, Chichester

Wilson P (2017) The Myth of International Humanitarian Law. International Affairs 93(3):563–579

Wrange P (2018) Authority, Legitimacy and Military Violence: De Facto Combatant Privilege of Non-State Armed Groups through Amnesty. In: Deland M, Klamberg M, Wrange P (eds), International Humanitarian Law and Justice: Historical and Sociological Perspectives. Routledge, Abingdon, pp. 60–75

Wrange P (2019a) Protecting which peace for whom against what? A conceptual analysis of collective security. In: Bailliet C M (ed) Research Handbook on International Law and Peace. Edward Elgar Publishing, Cheltenham, UK, Northampton, MA, pp. 107–126

Wrange P (2019b) Self-Determination, Occupation and the Authority to Exploit Natural Resources: Trajectories from Four European Judgments on Western Sahara. Israel Law Review 52(1):3–29

UN Commission for Human Rights, 'Promotion and protection of the right to freedom of expression: Report of the Special Rapporteur, Mr Abid Hussain, pursuant to Commission on Human Rights resolution 1993/45', UN Doc. E/CN.4/1995/32, 14 December 1994

UN Commission on Human Rights, Sub-Commission on the Promotion and Protection of Human Rights 'Working paper on the relationship between human rights law and international humanitarian law by Françoise Hampson and Ibrahim Salama', UN Doc. E/CN.4/Sub.2/2005/14, 21 June 2005

UN Human Rights Committee, General Comment No. 36, 'Article 6: right to life', UN Doc. CCPR/C/GC/36, 3 September 2019

UN Human Rights Committee, 'General Comment No. 29: State of Emergency (Article 4)', UN Doc. CCPR/C/21/Rev.1/Add.11, 31 August 2001

UN Human Rights Council, Resolution S-30/1, 'Ensuring respect for international human rights law and international humanitarian law in the Occupied Palestinian Territory, including East Jerusalem, and in Israel', UN Doc. A/HRC/RES/S-30/1, 28 May 2021

UN Human Rights Council, 'Accountability: Prosecuting and punishing gross violations of human rights and serious violations of international humanitarian law in the context of transitional justice processes', Report of the Special Rapporteur on the promotion of truth, justice, reparation and guarantees of non-recurrence, UN Doc. A/HRC/48/60, 9 July 2021

UN Human Rights Council, Resolution 49/1, 'Situation of human rights in Ukraine stemming from the Russian aggression', UN Doc. A/HRC/RES/49/1, 7 March 2022

UN Human Rights Council, Resolution 54/2, 'Responding to the human rights and humanitarian crisis caused by the ongoing armed conflict in the Sudan', UN Doc. A/HRC/RES/54/2, 12 October 2023
UN Human Rights Council, Resolution 55/22, 'Situation of human rights in the Syrian Arab Republic', UN Doc. A/HRC/RES/55/22, 9 April 2024
UN General Assembly, Resolution 217 A(III), 'Universal Declaration of Human Rights', UN Doc. A/RES/3/217A, 10 December 1948

Dr. Sally Longworth, LL.M is a post-doctoral researcher at Stockholm University Center on Global Governance and researcher in public international law at the Swedish Defence Research Agency. Her research focuses on the relationship between international human rights law, international humanitarian law, international criminal law, and international peace and security. Previously, she worked as a Senior Lecturer in international law at Stockholm University Faculty of Law and as a Lecturer and Researcher in international law at the Swedish Defence University. Sally defended her PhD thesis on the relationship between international human rights law and international humanitarian law in regards to the right to freedom of expression in armed conflict in October 2022. She has an LL.M in international human rights law from Lund University, an LL.B in European, comparative and international law from the University of Sheffield, and was called to the Bar of England and Wales in 2010.

Chapter 26
Economic Lawfare and WTO Law

Joachim Åhman

Contents

Abstract In this chapter, I use a model of "economic lawfare" to explore how WTO members may interact with WTO law strategically to achieve security objectives. The model contains three types of interactions: application, conversion, and modification. Application implies that a State applies or enforces existing laws consistent with their stated purposes. Conversion means that a State uses laws serving purposes other than security protection to achieve security objectives. Modification implies formal changes to laws to achieve security objectives. I identify certain key WTO provisions for each type and discuss how members can interact with them. The main conclusion is that there are many possibilities for members to engage in economic lawfare through the application and conversion of WTO law, but not through modification. It is also argued that the model of "economic lawfare" is a valuable analytical tool that can be developed further to better understand how States can use, and are using, international economic law to protect security interests.

Keywords National security · Economic lawfare · WTO law · GATT 1994 · Trade · Goods · Application · Conversion · Modification

---

J. Åhman (✉)
University of Gothenburg, Gothenburg, Sweden
e-mail: joachim.ahman@law.gu.se

M. Klamberg et al. (eds.), *Reconstructing Power and Hegemony in Public International Law*, https://doi.org/10.1007/978-94-6265-743-4_26

26.1 Introduction

As long as law—national and international—has existed, it has been possible for actors to use it as an instrument to achieve different objectives. One way of doing this is to participate in the processes when laws are created, modified, or repealed. Another is to use strategic litigation in different fora or to use legal argumentation outside courts to influence the behavior of other actors. There is always certain leeway in how the law can be interpreted and applied, which can be used for many purposes. This is nothing new, but from a scientific perspective the extent to which these issues have been studied in different legal contexts may differ.

One area that has received particular attention during the last two decades is how States use law instead of force to achieve security objectives. As an alternative to "warfare", States may engage in "lawfare". The term "lawfare" was introduced to a wider audience in 2001, in a text written by Charles J. Dunlap, Jr., Colonel in the United States Air Force.[1] In his later writings, he defined the term as a "strategy of using—or misusing—law as a substitute for traditional military means to achieve an operational objective".[2] Scholars in international law have picked up and developed this concept.[3] They have explored different aspects of using law as an instrument of war, and more broadly to achieve other security objectives. Research on lawfare has focused on regimes like international humanitarian law, human rights law, and the law of the sea.[4] However, despite the strong connection between national security and international trade, less research has been done on lawfare in international economic law.

In a recent article, Victor A. Ferguson uses insights from international relations literature on economic statecraft and from international law literature on lawfare to develop a basic model of "economic lawfare". He defines this specific type of lawfare as "the use (or misuse) of *legal instruments* that affect international commerce in order to achieve *security objectives*".[5] According to Ferguson, it involves "governments strategically interacting with laws that govern international commerce in order to facilitate or obstruct international economic transactions that generate security externalities".[6] As part of economic lawfare, Ferguson identifies three types of interactions/pathways: *application*, *conversion*, and *modification*.[7] *Application* implies that a State applies or enforces existing laws consistent with their stated purposes. *Conversion* implies that a State uses laws serving other purposes than security protection to achieve security objectives. In this case, the application is plausibly consistent with the letter of the law, but not necessarily its purpose. *Modification* implies formal

[1] Dunlap 2001.

[2] Dunlap 2005, p. 95; Dunlap 2008, p. 146.

[3] *E.g.*, Kennedy 2012; Kittrie 2016.

[4] *E.g.*, Kotzambasis 2018; Ahmad Qureshi 2019; Trachtman 2016; Goldenziel 2021.

[5] Ferguson 2022, p. 7.

[6] Ibid. p. 8.

[7] Ibid. p. 9. Ferguson describes a fourth type of interaction: the use of nonlegal instruments. However, this is not included in the concept of economic lawfare.

changes to laws to achieve security objectives. It involves the introduction of new rules, amendments to existing rules, and the repeal of existing rules.

In international economic law, the law of the World Trade Organization (WTO) constitutes the main regulatory framework. Hence, if States want to engage in economic lawfare, they will often interact with WTO law in one way or another. In this chapter, I will use Ferguson's definition and model of economic lawfare as an inspiration to explore possibilities for WTO members to interact with WTO law strategically to achieve security objectives. The focus will be on the most important agreement on international trade in goods, the General Agreement on Tariffs and Trade 1994 (GATT 1994). I will give examples of provisions that I consider to be of particular interest and describe what possible interactions could look like. In Section 26.2, I will examine possible interactions through application, in Section 26.3, possible interactions through conversion, and, in Section 26.4, possible interactions through modification. Lastly, in Section 26.5, I will provide some concluding remarks.

26.2 Economic Lawfare Through Application of WTO Law

The first type of interaction in Ferguson's model is economic lawfare through the application of law. According to him, this implies that States "openly use laws that are explicitly designed to manage the security externalities arising from economic exchange".[8] As examples, he mentions decisions to block foreign investments on national security grounds and to penalize actors that violate legislation on sanctions. The definition includes two elements. One is that the State is *open* with the purpose of the interaction: to achieve security objectives. The other is that the law is *explicitly designed* to make it possible for the State to achieve such objectives.

In a WTO context, the closest one comes to this type of interaction is the possibility to invoke Article XXI of the GATT 1994. The article contains the so-called "security exceptions" and is the only provision in the agreement explicitly referring to the security interests of the members.[9] If a member wants to adopt a measure that is inconsistent with another GATT 1994 provision—such as the prohibitions against discrimination in Articles I and III or the prohibition against quantitative restrictions in Article XI—the measure is allowed if it fulfills the requirements in Article XXI. For a long time, WTO members relied on the provision when adopting trade-restrictive

---

[8] Ibid.

[9] There are a few other provisions in WTO law mentioning security interests in relation to trade in goods: Article 1.10 of the Import Licensing Agreement; the preamble and Article 2.2 of the Agreement on Technical Barriers to Trade; and Article III:1 of the Government Procurement Agreement. Basically, these provisions do not allow trade-restrictive measures which are not already allowed under Article XXI of the GATT 1994. There are also certain provisions mentioning security interests in relation to trade in services and intellectual property rights: Article XIV*bis* of the General Agreement on Trade in Services and Article 73 of the Agreement on Trade-Related Aspects of Intellectual Property Rights.

measures but did not invoke it in dispute settlement.[10] Recently, however, there have been a few cases when the provision has been invoked by members and interpreted by dispute settlement panels.[11]

One of the key parts of the provision—Article XXI:(b)(iii)—says that nothing in the GATT 1994 shall be construed "to prevent any contracting party from taking any action which it considers necessary for the protection of its essential security interests ... taken in time of war or other emergency in international relations". Some WTO members, like Russia and the United States, have argued that the expression "which it considers" implies that it is entirely up to the member itself to decide which measures are necessary to protect security interests (the provision is "self-judging" or "non-justiciable"). However, this view has been rejected by WTO dispute settlement panels.

Further case law is needed to clarify these limits, but Article XXI can unambiguously justify the adoption of many types of trade-restrictive measures to achieve security objectives. Hence, invoking the provision can be seen as the most straightforward way for members to engage in economic lawfare through the application of WTO law.

As mentioned above, there are no other provisions in the GATT 1994 which are explicitly designed to make it possible for WTO members to achieve security objectives. However, some provisions do not have this explicit design but can still be used in line with their purposes to achieve such objectives. One example is the WTO rules on tariff concessions in Article II of the GATT 1994. The main rule is that members are allowed to use regular tariffs (customs duties) if they are not discriminatory. At the same time, members are encouraged to cut and "bind" tariffs, which means that they agree not to raise a tariff above a certain level. The applied tariff can be lower than the bound level, but the member is allowed to raise the tariff to the bound level.[12] The possibility not to bind a tariff, to raise a tariff to the bound level, or to apply a low or no tariff are legal tools that can be used for many purposes. As long as the aforementioned rules are observed, WTO law allows members to change tariff levels for any reason.[13] Hence, this is a provision which does not explicitly mention security objectives but which can be used to achieve such objectives. If a member openly states that there are security interests behind the change of a tariff level on a certain product, it is not a case of economic lawfare through conversion. Even though this type of interaction does not seem to fit entirely into Ferguson's

---

[10] Van Damme 2022, p. 714.

[11] Panel Report, Russia—Measures Concerning Traffic in Transit, adopted 26 April 2019, WT/DS512/R; Panel Report, United States—Origin Marking Requirement, WT/DS597/R (appealed); Panel Report, United States—Certain Measures on Steel and Aluminium Products, WT/DS564/R (appealed). Regarding security exceptions and intellectual property rights, *see also* Panel Report, Saudi Arabia—Measures Concerning the Protection of Intellectual Property Rights, WT/DS567/R (withdrawn).

[12] Matsushita et al. 2015, p. 224.

[13] Economic liberals, like Adam Smith, have argued that trade barriers—e.g., high tariffs—can be justified on national security grounds. *See* Collins 2022, pp. 284–285.

definition of lawfare through application, I would argue that it is reasonable to place it in that category.

26.3 Economic Lawfare through Conversion of WTO Law

The second type of interaction in Ferguson's model is economic lawfare through the conversion of law. This implies that laws that are not explicitly designed to make it possible for States to achieve security objectives are used to achieve such objectives. Ferguson's definition seems to include two important elements.[14] One is that the State *does not openly admit* that the law is used in this way. The other is that *ambiguities and indeterminacies in legal provisions are exploited*. Hence, the State is formally acting in accordance with the law but the behavior can also be seen as a sort of misuse of the law. The law is not applied in line with the regulatory purpose. The second element is probably the most relevant. For example, when the provisions on tariff concessions in Article II of the GATT 1994, described above, are applied to achieve security objectives, it is usually not a case of exploitation of ambiguities or indeterminacies. It can differ whether the member openly admits the purpose of applying the provisions in a certain way. However, even if the member does not openly admit the purpose, it seems reasonable to treat it as a case of economic lawfare through application, rather than conversion.

If, on the other hand, a State wants to exploit ambiguities and indeterminacies in a provision to achieve security objectives, this would most likely not be done openly. The ambiguities and indeterminacies can make it possible for the State to argue that the interaction is legal and difficult for other actors to argue that it is illegal. It seems that, at least in a WTO context, this type of case will often require that a measure has double purposes: one open and one hidden (to achieve security objectives). The provision will allow the WTO member to take a certain measure for a certain purpose. The member will argue that the measure is taken for this purpose, even though the real purpose is to achieve a security objective. However, to be able to interact with WTO law in this way, it will usually also be necessary for the member to show that the measure can fulfil the open purpose to some extent. I will give two examples: anti-dumping measures and health protection measures.

Anti-dumping measures are regulated in Article VI of the GATT 1994, and the Agreement on Implementation of Article VI of the General Agreement on Tariffs and Trade 1994. In short, dumping entails that an imported product is sold for a price that is lower than the price for which the product is sold in the exporting company's home market (the so-called "normal value"). WTO law does not prohibit dumping. However, if dumping occurs and is causing or threatening to cause material injury to the industry in the importing member, that member has the right to take anti-dumping measures. The logic behind this is that dumping has been considered to be a type of unfair trade practice and that members should be able to take special action against

[14] Ferguson 2022, p. 9.

such behavior.[15] Often, an anti-dumping measure implies that the tariff on certain products from certain members is raised above the bound level. Hence, if Article VI did not allow such a measure, it would have been inconsistent with the provisions on tariff concessions in Article II and the prohibition against discrimination in Article I.

If there is no question that dumping is causing injury, an anti-dumping measure can be a case of economic lawfare through application. A member may, for example, openly admit that a certain industry is important for security reasons and that a perfectly lawful measure is taken to protect that industry against dumping. In such cases, there is no exploitation of ambiguities or indeterminacies. However, the reason the provisions on anti-dumping measures are a good example of a possibility to engage in economic lawfare through conversion is that they are very detailed and complex, especially when it comes to the calculation of the so-called "dumping margin" (the difference between the price of the imported product and the normal value) and the assessment of injury caused to the domestic industry. It has been argued that if a member wants to find a dumping margin causing injury, this is often possible in a dumping investigation.[16] In other words, there is room to exploit ambiguities and indeterminacies in the provisions for the hidden purpose of achieving security objectives. An anti-dumping measure can be a useful tool in economic lawfare, as it can be directed against producers in specific members, which implies that trade relations with other members are not affected.

The other example of WTO provisions which can be used in economic lawfare through conversion relates to the rules on health protection measures. If a member adopts a measure to protect human health and that measure affects international trade, it may be inconsistent with several of the main principles in WTO law. Health requirements may for example imply that producers in one member get a competitive disadvantage compared with producers in other members, which would be inconsistent with the non-discrimination principle in Article I of the GATT 1994. They may also entail that trade with products that are considered to constitute a health risk is banned, which would be inconsistent with the prohibition against quantitative restrictions in Article XI. However, as in the case of measures protecting national security, there is an exception. Article XX(b) allows measures necessary to protect *inter alia* human health. If the requirements in that article are fulfilled, it does not matter whether a measure is inconsistent with other articles in the agreement. The requirements in Article XX(b) are elaborated in the Agreement on the Application of Sanitary and Phytosanitary Measures (the SPS Agreement).

The requirements in Article XX(b) and the SPS Agreement are rather strict in the sense that the member must show that there is a health risk against which the measure can protect. The measure must be based on a scientific risk assessment. Hence, it would not be possible for a member to adopt a measure to achieve security objectives (the hidden purpose) and merely argue that the measure is taken to protect

[15] From an economic point of view, dumping is not necessarily seen as unfair. Instead, it can often be argued that it is the anti-dumping measure that is unfair. *See* Mankiw and Swagel 2005, p. 108.
[16] Prusa 2005, p. 696.

human health (the open purpose). To some extent, the measure must also be able to fulfill the open purpose. At the same time, the agreements allow members to protect themselves against any health risks—and they are free to decide the level of protection.[17] Moreover, members are allowed to adopt measures in situations when there is scientific uncertainty.[18] Thus, it can be argued that these provisions contain ambiguities and indeterminacies which can be exploited to achieve security objectives. In other words, they can be used in economic lawfare through conversion of WTO law.

26.4 Economic Lawfare Through Modification of WTO Law

The third type of interaction in Ferguson's model is economic lawfare through the modification of law. This involves making formal changes to the law. When the law has been changed, the new law can also be used in economic lawfare through application or conversion. According to Ferguson, the main obstacle to this type of interaction is the existence of veto actors, that is actors that can block the modification.[19] In international law, a State must give its consent to be bound by an agreement, which includes consent to changes in existing agreements. Hence, each State is a veto actor. However, if States create an international organization—like the WTO—they can decide the procedures for making changes in the organization's agreements. If a State is a member of the organization, it must accept these procedures.

Article X of the Marrakesh Agreement Establishing the World Trade Organization (the WTO Agreement) contains detailed provisions on how amendments to the WTO agreements can be made. Amendments to certain important provisions require the acceptance of all members. Regarding other provisions, a distinction is made between amendments that would alter the rights and obligations of the members and amendments that would not. The latter type takes effect for all members upon acceptance of two-thirds of the members. The former type also takes effect upon the acceptance of two-thirds of the members, but only for the members accepting the amendment.

If a member wants to interact with WTO law to achieve security objectives, modification is the most difficult type of interaction (compared with application and conversion), and therefore also the least attractive. In a domestic context, it may be possible to influence the legislative process in different ways, and for many legislative changes, it will be sufficient with a single majority in the parliament. The WTO has 166 members.[20] To reach a consensus or a two-thirds majority is difficult,

[17] Du 2010, p. 1102.

[18] Foster 2009.

[19] Ferguson 2022, p. 10.

[20] WTO: Members and Observers, available at https://www.wto.org/english/thewto_e/whatis_e/tif_e/org6_e.htm. Accessed 14 September 2024.

and it is therefore cumbersome and time-consuming to make amendments to the agreements.[21] Of course, a member may still try to put pressure on other members. One example is when the United States recently intimated that it would agree to a reform of the WTO dispute settlement system if other members agreed that national security cannot be reviewed in dispute settlement.[22]

Even though the procedures in Article X of the WTO Agreement are the only formal ways of making changes in WTO law, it should be noted that there is a discussion about changes through interpretation. It follows from Article 3.2 of the Understanding on Rules and Procedures Governing the Settlement of Disputes (the DSU) that, when WTO provisions are interpreted in dispute settlement, they are only supposed to be clarified. Recommendations and rulings cannot add to or diminish the rights and obligations in the agreements. But some members—primarily the United States—have criticized the Appellate Body (the main judicial body in the WTO dispute settlement system) for overstepping its authority.[23] One part of the criticism is that the Appellate Body has made modifications through interpretations. Regardless of whether this criticism is valid or not, it can be observed that it is often difficult to draw the line between clarifying and modifying. The principle *jura novit curia* is applied in WTO dispute settlement.[24] Still, the judicial body can hardly avoid being affected by the legal argumentation of the parties. Hence, if a member wants to engage in economic lawfare through modification (or at least through stretching the limits of clarification), one option is to make strategic legal arguments in dispute settlement proceedings.

However, interpretations are not only made in dispute settlement. Article IX:2 of the WTO Agreement contains rules on authoritative interpretations of WTO provisions. Such interpretations can be adopted by the WTO Ministerial Conference and the General Council by a three-fourths majority of the members. Like interpretations in dispute settlement, they are supposed to clarify the meaning of existing obligations, not modify their contents.[25] According to Article IX, the interpretations should not be used in a manner that would undermine the amendment provisions in Article X. Hence, from an economic lawfare perspective, authoritative interpretations combine the main problem with amendments (the cumbersome and time-consuming process) and the main problem with interpretations in dispute settlement (the fact that they are not supposed to modify the provision).[26] Consequently, it is not a very useful tool for a member that wants to engage in economic lawfare through modification of WTO law.

---

[21] Bronckers 1999, p. 552.

[22] Kho et al. 2023, p. 36.

[23] USTR 2020.

[24] Appellate Body Report, European Communities—Conditions for the Granting of Tariff Preferences to Developing Countries, WT/DS246/AB/R, para 105.

[25] Appellate Body Reports, European Communities—Regime for the Importation, Sale and Distribution of Bananas, Second Recourse to Article 21.5 of the DSU by Ecuador, Recourse to Article 21.5 of the DSU by the United States, adopted 11 and 22 December 2008, WT/DS27/AB/RW2/ECU and WT/DS27/AB/RW/USA, para 383.

[26] Van Damme 2009, pp. 26–30.

26.5 Concluding Remarks

In this chapter, I have used Ferguson's model of economic lawfare as an inspiration to explore how WTO members may interact with WTO law strategically to achieve security objectives. The model contains three types of interactions: application, conversion, and modification. For each type, I have identified certain key WTO provisions and discussed how members can interact with them. The focus has been on trade in goods and the most important agreement in this regard: the GATT 1994. The main conclusion is that there are many possibilities for members to engage in economic lawfare through application and conversion of WTO law, but not through modification. If a member wants to engage in economic lawfare through application—that is, to adopt trade restrictive measures with the open purpose of achieving security objectives—it can often rely on the security exceptions in Article XXI. There is also a possibility to rely on more general provisions, like Article II on tariff concessions. If a member wants to engage in economic lawfare through conversion, it can use the ambiguities and indeterminacies in provisions like Article VI on anti-dumping measures and Article XX(b) on health protection measures. However, the cumbersome and time-consuming process of making amendments to the WTO agreements, and the prohibition against modification through interpretation, make it difficult to engage in economic lawfare through modification.

As described above, lawfare is nowadays a well-established concept that has been discussed, developed, and applied in studies in several legal fields. The model of economic lawfare, however, is more of a novelty. In this chapter, I have explored how the model can be used in relation to the most important regulatory framework in international economic law: WTO law. To some extent, I have also discussed the elements of the model and how they can be understood. Still, I have only scratched the surface. Considering the important connection between trade/investments and security, it can be argued that the model is a valuable analytical tool. Ferguson describes it as a "basic" model. Hence, it can be developed further and applied in relation to WTO law and other areas of international economic law. In future studies, it may help us to better understand how States can interact, and are interacting, with international economic law to achieve security objectives.

References

Ahmad Qureshi W (2019) Lawfare: The Weaponization of International Law. Houston Journal of International Law 42(1):39–85

Bronckers M (1999) Better Rules for a New Millennium: A Warning Against Undemocratic Developments in the WTO. Journal of International Economic Law 2(4):547–566

Collins G M (2022) Adam Smith on the Navigation Acts and Anglo-American Imperial Relations. History of Political Thought 43(2):273–304

Dattu R, Boscariol J (1997) GATT Article XXI, Helms-Burton and the Continuing Abuse of the National Security Exception. Canadian Business Law Journal 28(2):198–209

Du M M (2010) Autonomy in Setting Appropriate Level of Protection under the WTO Law: Rhetoric or Reality? Journal of International Economic Law 13(4):1077–1102
Dunlap C J (2001) Law and Military Interventions: Preserving Humanitarian Values in 21st Century Conflicts. Carr Center for Human Rights Policy, Kennedy School of Government, Harvard University, Washington D.C., November 29
Dunlap C J (2005) Lawfare in Modern Conflicts. The Reporter: The Judge Advocate General's Corps. Keystone Edition 95–101
Dunlap C J (2008) Lawfare Today: A Perspective. Yale Journal of International Affairs 3(1): 146–154
Ferguson V A (2022) Economic Lawfare: The Logic and Dynamics of Using Law to Exercise Economic Power. International Studies Review 24(3):1–30
Foster C E (2009) Precaution, Scientific Development and Scientific Uncertainty under the WTO Agreement on Sanitary and Phytosanitary Measures. Review of European, Comparative & International Environmental Law 18(1):50–58
Goldenziel J (2021) Law as a Battlefield: The U.S., China, and the Global Escalation of Lawfare. Cornell Law Review 106(5):1085–1172
Kennedy D (2012) Lawfare and Warfare. In: Crawford J, Koskenniemi M (eds) The Cambridge Companion to International Law, Cambridge University Press, Cambridge, pp. 158–184
Kho S, McNamara Y, Kirwin S, Davies B (2023) The Conundrum of the Essential Security Exception: Can the WTO Resolve the GATT Article XXI Crisis and Save the Dispute Settlement Mechanism? Working Paper, Geneva Graduate Institute, Centre for Trade and Economic Integration
Kittrie O F (2016) Lawfare: Law as a Weapon of War. Oxford University Press, New York
Kotzambasis Z (2018) Lawfare: A New Tool for Fighting Terrorism? Arizona Journal of International and Comparative Law 35(1):165–194
Mankiw N G, Swagel P L (2005) Antidumping: The Third Rail of Trade Policy. Foreign Affairs 84(4):107–119
Matsushita M, Schoenbaum T J, Mavroidis P C, Hahn M (2015) The World Trade Organization: Law, Practice, and Policy, 3rd edn, Oxford University Press, Oxford
Prusa T J (2005) Anti-dumping: A Growing Problem in International Trade. The World Economy 28(5):633–747
Trachtman J P (2016) Integrating Lawfare and Warfare. Boston College International and Comparative Law Review 39(2):267–282
United States Trade Representative (USTR) (2020) Report on the Appellate Body of the World Trade Organization
Van Damme I (2022) National Security. In: Bethlehem D, McRae D, Neufeld R, Van Damme I (eds) The Oxford Handbook of International Trade Law, 2nd edn, Oxford University Press, Oxford, pp. 713–744
Van Damme I (2009) Treaty Interpretation by the WTO Appellate Body. Oxford University Press, Oxford

Joachim Åhman is a Professor of Public International Law in the Department of Law, University of Gothenburg. His research focuses primarily on international economic law, international organizations, and the relationship between public international law and constitutional law. He has been a visiting research fellow at Columbia Law School. He has published several books in the above-mentioned fields, and articles in leading international journals, such as the Journal of World Trade, European Public Law, and the Journal of International Economic Law.

Part VI
Reconsidering Hegemony, Imperialism and Colonialism

Chapter 27
Carl Schmitt in Russia and China: A Revival for Großraum Analytics in International Law?

Matilda Arvidsson and Gregor Noll

Contents

Abstract In this chapter, we seek to answer the question of if—and if so: how—the Russian and Chinese receptions of the *Großraum* concept developed by Carl Schmitt in 1939/41 intersect and reinforce each other at critical junctures. If they turn out to do so, this will help us understand what the accumulated threat of *Großraum* thinking is today in its competition with liberal modes of thinking non-intervention in international law. We conclude that the pattern of Russian and Chinese practices that we have surveyed is not reducible to a single or clear-cut Schmittian *Großraum* model. On the basis of our survey, a *Großraum* mode of arguing international law cannot be said to have grown to such a degree that it threatens the dominance of liberal accounts of international law. That said, Schmitt's *Großraum* theory remains helpful for understanding, in part, the international legal behavior of Russia, and to some degree also that of China. We suggest that further engagement and analysis are needed.

Keywords Russian international law · Chinese international law · Carl Schmitt · *Großraum* · The *Nomos* of the Earth · War in Ukraine · South China Sea conflict · Nine-dash line

---

M. Arvidsson (✉)
Department of Law and HDK-Valand Academy of Art and Design, Gothenburg University, Gothenburg, Sweden
e-mail: matilda.arvidsson@law.gu.se

G. Noll
Department of Law, Gothenburg University, Gothenburg, Sweden

Swedish Academy of Defense, Stockholm, Sweden
e-mail: gregor.noll@law.gu.se

M. Klamberg et al. (eds.), *Reconstructing Power and Hegemony in Public International Law*, https://doi.org/10.1007/978-94-6265-743-4_27

27.1 Introduction

The past years have seen multiple analyses of contemporary geopolitical conflicts through tropes devised by the German legal scholar Carl Schmitt, setting off yet another wave of interest in Schmittian legal thinking.[1] Much of this recent interest is focused on Schmitt's concept of *Großraum*. Schmitt launched *Großraum*, literally meaning "large space," as a legal concept with a hegemonic central *Reich*—realm—lawfully dominating its regional neighbors without formally annexing or incorporating them.[2] The *Reich* ensures that outside powers do not intervene into the *Großraum*. Schmitt, in devising his *Großraum* concept in international law, launched a principle of non-intervention, alternative to the one by which modern liberal international law operates. This is of interest when considering the military aggression by the Russian Federation (hereafter Russia) against Ukraine and has already boosted the currency of Schmittian analytics. Moreover, in the past decade, the question of Schmitt's influence on the international affairs of the People's Republic of China (hereafter China) has also attracted scholarly attention. In addition, Russia and China have, since their joint declaration on "the Promotion of International Law" of 25 June 2016, followed by their joint statements of March 23, 2021, and of February 4, 2022, sparked considerable debate as to the exact nature of the global governance and international law envisioned by the two powers.[3] Are the Russian and Chinese approaches overlapping to such an extent that it vouchsafes the conclusion that the two powers are jointly introducing a new world order? If so: is Schmitt a common denominator for Russia and China and, to the extent he is, should we be worried about it?

In this chapter, we seek to answer the question of if—and if so: how—the Russian and Chinese receptions of Schmitt's *Großraum* thinking intersect and reinforce each other at critical junctures. If they turn out to do so, this will help us understand what the accumulated threat of *Großraum* thinking is today in its competition with liberal modes of thinking non-intervention in international law.

---

[1] For examples of the recent application of Schmittian thinking in concrete geopolitical contexts, *see* the references in the following section. In an engagement with Schmittian thought as such, Jochen von Bernstorff has argued that Schmitt's advocacy of hegemonically dominated and State-border transcending spaces (*Großräume*) is not a principled contradiction to his then ground-breaking critique of US imperialism in the first half of the 20th century. *See* von Bernstorff 2023, pp. 369–383.

[2] In the field of international relations (IR), regional domination is conceived of a power's "sphere of influence"," something which may come through as similar to Schmitt's understanding. Although IR scholarship is attentive to patterns of power differentials in these spheres, their normative implications are not read in the key of international law, as Schmitt did, for which reason our chapter focuses on the latter. For a current example, *see* Resnick 2022.

[3] The statement on the "Promotion of International Law" is no longer available on the Russia's official website, but can be accessed in full translated into English here: https://www.lawfaremedia.org/article/text-russia-china-joint-declaration-promotion-and-principles-international-law. For the 2021 "Joint Statement by the Foreign Ministers of China and Russia on Certain Aspects of Global Governance in Modern Conditions" *see* https://mid.ru/en/foreign_policy/position_word_order/1418041/. For the 2022 "Joint Statement of the Russian Federation and the People's Republic of China on the International Relations Entering a New Era and the Global Sustainable Development" *see*: http://en.kremlin.ru/supplement/5770.

Our chapter is organized as follows: We first track the persistence of Carl Schmitt's antiliberal *Großraum* international legal thinking in the justification of the Russian Federation's 2022 military intervention into Ukraine, mapping existing research and adding our own contribution to that line of research (Section 27.2). In a second step, we will consider the usefulness of Schmitt's *Großraum* theory to the understanding of international law in the People's Republic of China (Section 27.3). In Section 27.4, we will consider whether the Chinese government actively seeks to establish a *Großraum,* primarily by engaging with conflicting claims in the South China Sea. In Section 27.5, we analyze to what extent the Russian and Chinese *Großraum* analytics overlap and reinforce each other. We conclude that the pattern of Russian and Chinese practices that we have surveyed is not reducible to a single or clear-cut Schmittian *Großraum* model. For that reason, a *Großraum* mode of arguing international law in the context that we are revisiting in this chapter cannot be said to have grown to such a degree that it threatens the dominance of liberal accounts of international law. That said, Schmitt's *Großraum* theory remains helpful for understanding, in part, the international legal behavior of Russia, and to some degree also that of China. We suggest that further engagement and analysis are needed.

27.2 Putin and a Schmittian International Law

How has Schmitt's *Großraum* theory been received in Russian Federation? Either we research the uptake of Schmitt's text among Russian academics or intellectuals,[4] or we focus on the conduct of the Russian Federation and its representatives as a matter of international law. Choosing the latter option, we draw on the example of the Russian 2022 full-scale military intervention in Ukraine. In parallel to arguments on the protection of Russian nationals and intervention by invitation, Vladimir Putin invoked the principle of non-intervention in his speech of 24 February 2022.[5] Putin's aim was to establish a new security order in which the principle of non-intervention played a central role (though most contemporary international lawyers have a quite different understanding of that principle). To grasp what kind of "non-intervention" Putin had in mind, we turn to Schmitt and his *Großraum* analytics. In 1939, Schmitt first published a scholarly text on the *Großraum*—a hard-to-translate term for a larger complex where geography, politics, economy, language, and culture came together, and which was ultimately governed by a *Reich* hegemon. In developing the *Großraum* theory, Schmitt sought to liberate himself from the dominance of geography in earlier German studies of space and geopolitics; his *Großraum* was neither coextensive with

[4] David Lewis offers a broad account of the reception of *Großraum* thinking in Russian debates on geopolitics, highlighting inter alia the role of the notorious Aleksandr Dugin. *See* Lewis 2020, pp. 161–192.

[5] "Address by the President of the Russian Federation," Kremlin official webpage, February 22, 2024: http://en.kremlin.ru/events/president/news/67843. Accessed 12 February 2025.

regions nor with continents: it was present and pursued through social cultural, legal, and military power.

The title of his 1939 monograph was a program in itself: *Völkerrechtliche Großraumordnung mit Interventionsverbot für raumfremde Mächte* or "International legal order of the *Großraum* with a ban on intervention for spatially foreign powers." The 1941 edition of this book was translated into English only in 2011 and remains one of Schmitt's least read and least known texts.[6] It was in this text that Schmitt first unfolded the notion of the *Großraum* into a theory of international law, a scholarly offering just in time for an aggressively expanding Third Reich. After the Second World War, Schmitt embedded a somewhat sanitized version of his *Großraum* theory in his grand narrative of international law's Hobbesian structures *Der Nomos der Erde im Völkerrecht des Jus Publicum Europaeum*, originally published in 1950, and translated into English in 2006 as *The Nomos of the Earth in the Jus Publicum Europaeum.*[7] This latter book has become Schmitt's most well-known and oft-cited text in contemporary international law and scholarship. Most international legal scholars would recognize Schmitt's notion of the *Großraum* from it. In addition, Schmitt nuanced and contextualized his *Großraum* concept in a number of shorter texts published between 1939 and 1969. These appear to be untranslated at the time of writing.[8]

In our chapter, we draw on all these sources when exploring the relevance of Schmitt's original thinking to the contemporary global constellation. The point of our reading is not to establish a creeping association between Putin—or anyone else—and German National Socialism. Schmitt was a member of the German National Socialist Party, and the *Großraum* text from 1939 was his attempt at promoting Third Reich articulations of international law and defining his own interpretive role of this new way of thinking international law. Schmitt's return to *Großraum* thinking in *The Nomos of the Earth* serves to establish the theory as standing on its own—also after the defeat of the Third Reich—and to establish Schmitt himself, as a counterforce and counternarrative to what Schmitt saw as an ahistorical and thinly veiled liberal international legal order prone to instability. This particular Schmittian point and criticism—the anti-liberal critique, although not necessarily its ideological context of emergence—has found contemporary followers in international legal scholarship at both far-left and far-right ends of the political spectrum.

Anyone reading Schmitt's *Großraum* text against Putin's speech of 24 February is struck by how strongly Putin's international legal order resonates with Schmitt's. Putin's speech has been perceived as illogical by some commentators in the West, yet a Schmittian reading easily establishes its logic. Rather than a critique of an ideological nature, our reading seeks to track the elective affinity between Schmitt's and Putin's way of thinking international law in an alternative key. Whereas Schmitt's thinking is quite consistent over the decades, Putin's justifications have been fluctuating over the months that the 2022 intervention into Ukraine has lasted. We choose

[6] Schmitt 2011.

[7] Schmitt 1950, 2006.

[8] Republished in Schmitt 1995 in Section III. on *Großraum und Völkerrecht*, pp. 225-481.

to focus on Putin's 24 February 2022 speech, which is relatively explicit on the motives pursued.[9]

In his 1939 *Großraum* text Schmitt had launched the idea that, rather than the State, it is the *Reich*—the central hegemonic power dominating other States within one of several *Großräume*—that constitutes the primary category of international law. "*Reichs* [sic!]... are the leading and bearing powers, whose political ideas radiate into a certain *Großraum* and which fundamentally exclude the intervention of spatially alien powers into this *Großraum*."[10] Historically, this can be understood as the spheres of interest held either by military force or by proxy by both imperial and other greater powers: it is not only a claim to power by military force, but also builds on dominance on matters cultural, linguistic, and—not the least—commercial relations of trade and trade routes, technology developments, concessions, and straight down to raw extraction and exploitation. What Schmitt did in his 1939 text was to bring some of these historical traits of greater powers together with an authoritarian ideological orientation toward a spatial theory of international law. That theory was normatively underpinning the domination and subjugation of "lesser" peoples within the *Großraum* that Schmitt saw Third Reich Germany as the lawful and natural power of.

Putin arguably put Schmitt's idea to practice when going to war with Ukraine and signaling to the West not to get involved. In his speech of 24 February 2022, Putin states that "an anti-Russia is being created that is hostile to us i*n our own historical territories*" (emphasis added).[11] Putin went on to explain that "[t]oday's events are not connected with the desire to infringe on the interests of Ukraine and the Ukrainian people. They are connected with the protection of Russia itself from those who took Ukraine hostage and are trying to use it against our country and its people."[12] The Schmittian ban on intervention by outside powers featured in an ominous form toward the end of the speech: "Whoever tries to hinder us, and even more so to create threats for our country, for our people, should know that Russia's response will be immediate and will lead you to such consequences that you have never experienced in your history."[13] Indeed, before launching the full-scale war on Ukraine, Putin warned Sweden and Finland, who were not members of the North Atlantic Treaty Organization (NATO) at the time, against entering that organization. This move, which was received as a gross insult by the two States, could be read as Putin exercising his right as the leader of a *Reich* with a *Großraum*—consisting, at the very least, of the former Soviet Union regions and satellite States—instructing

[9] "Address by the President of the Russian Federation," Kremlin official webpage, February 22, 2024: http://en.kremlin.ru/events/president/news/67843. Accessed 12 February 2025.

[10] Schmitt 2011, p. 101.

[11] "Address by the President of the Russian Federation," Kremlin official webpage, February 22, 2024: http://en.kremlin.ru/events/president/news/67843. Accessed 12 February 2025.

[12] "Address by the President of the Russian Federation," Kremlin official webpage, February 22, 2024: http://en.kremlin.ru/events/president/news/67843. Accessed 12 February 2025.

[13] "Address by the President of the Russian Federation," Kremlin official webpage, February 22, 2024: http://en.kremlin.ru/events/president/news/67843. Accessed 12 February 2025.

States at the fringe of his *Großraum* not to subjugate themselves to the powers of another *Reich*, e.g., that of NATO.

Putin's reference to "historical territories" resonates strongly with Schmitt's geographical-political *Großraum* and its relation to a specific *Reich.*[14] In the quote, Putin seems to retain a place for the Ukrainian people, just as Schmitt did for other peoples inhabiting non-dominant *Großraum* states. Schmitt suggested that the empire is best placed to respect other *Großraum* peoples, as the empire itself ultimately rests on the confluence of an imperial people with a given territory. However, as we have already noted, Schmitt's master distinction is that between *Reich* and State. This entails a hierarchized distinction between the master people who sustain the *Reich*—and the other peoples of the *Großraum.* Schmitt chooses not to articulate this hierarchization in his 1939 text. Reading the text today, one is struck by how today's formally egalitarian international law (*Völkerrecht* in German, the law of peoples) is transformed into a sort of *Herrenvölkerrecht*: the international law of the master people of the *Reich.*

Once the concept of the *Reich* is established as a dominant category in this alternative reading of international law, the war in Ukraine changes its character. Here is its Schmittian reading: what the Russian Federation does in its *Großraum* cannot be an unlawful intervention nor a violation of the self-determination of the Ukrainian people. This is so as the very existence of the Ukrainian people is conditioned by Russia's existence. The *Reich's* capacity to organize and dominate its historical territories, of which Ukraine is part, as a *Großraum*, is a capacity fundamental to Putin's and Schmitt's alternative international law. If powers outside Russia's *Großraum* (such as NATO, the US, the European Union (EU), or individual EU Member States) give military aid in the form of equipment and expertise to Ukraine, or project their political ideas into Ukraine, such acts constitute a violation of the non-intervention principle in Putin's and Schmitt's alternative *Großraum* international law. The meaning and applicability of the non-intervention principle, as it is known in mainstream contemporary international law, thus changes in the Schmitt-Putin *Großraum* version from referring to sovereign *State* territory to referring to the much more extensive geographical unit of the *Großraum.*

The world order that Schmitt tried to write forth consists of a number of *Großraum* regions where regionally dominant *Reiche* enter into an equilibrium with each other so that none of them can achieve a universal position of power. According to Schmitt's reasoning, liberal and universalist international law fell apart as soon as the Third Reich restored Germany as a strong player, once again capable of dominating its *Großraum.* This, according to Schmitt, caused conflicts with the powers of the West and East, which had exploited Weimar Germany's weakness by expanding their dominance into Germany's *Großraum* at its cost in the post-Versailles international legal order. Putin uses the very same figure of thought in his speech, stating that the West exploited the weakness of post-Soviet Russia in the nineties and expanded into its sphere. According to Putin, this became possible as the geopolitical order created after World War II—an order Putin describes as "sacred"—was set aside in the 1990s.

---

[14] *See also* Skordas 2022.

That is a spurious argument, because the 1945 UN Charter and the prohibition of the use of force in its Article 2.4 are part of the very same geopolitical order, and Putin himself invokes the UN Charter twice in his speech. If *Reiche* rather than States are seen as the primary actors of international law, the UN Charter slips down the norm hierarchy. Its standards then apply only subject to Russia's hegemonial exercise of power within its *Großraum*. With the help of Schmitt's international legal writing, a worrying coherence in Putin's argument becomes discernible. It is worrying, at least, if we want to uphold international law as being one of formal equality between States, and if we aim to uphold the non-intervention principle of the UN Charter as applicable equally to all States.

Putin's rhetorical strategy in the speech from 2022 is to hold up an "authentic international law" consisting of the outcomes of World War II alongside the UN Charter and contrast it with the "manipulated international law" that the West launched after the Cold War.[15] The exact same figure of thought appears in Schmitt, who also contrasts "authentic" international law with its universalist distortion through liberal democracies. Schmitt points out how the National Socialist government of Germany corrects this distortion by the Third Reich regaining its legitimate role in its *Großraum*. This certainly creates conflicts with the West, but Schmitt implies that such conflicts are necessary to return to authentic international law. In Putin's speech, the conflict between the West and Russia arises at a time when Russia is reclaiming its historically predetermined role in its geopolitical sphere and insists on the rules of an authentic international law. Putin's strategy is, of course, not only rhetorical, and goes beyond his speech of 24 February 2022: it is part of a full-scale war on Ukraine. The coherence in both rhetorical figure of speech and actions by Putin's Russia thus give us reason to worry about the state of international law.

There is more to the story than the war in Ukraine: Developments preceding the 2022 war are also relevant to consider in this context. In 2014, Russia brought about a regional integration effort in the form of the Eurasian Economic Union (EAEU), which operates as an economic union based on the treaty signed in 2014.[16] Its former Soviet Union Member States are the Republic of Armenia, the Republic of Belarus, the Republic of Kazakhstan, the Kyrgyz Republic, and the Russian Federation. Paolo Pizzolo has argued that the EAEU may be read as an attempt to surpass the Westphalian state and to bring about a Schmittian *nomos* of the earth.[17] We argue that the *Großraum* concept offers a narrower and more precise frame of analysis, with Russia forming treaty relations with its "own historical territories" to ensure its position as a *Reich* for a *Großraum* consisting of the former Soviet Union's territories and the economic-military dominance of its Russian center. Although Pizzolo's point about

[15] Therefore, it is unhelpful to point out that Putin's adaptation of *Großraum* thinking risks undermining the "very basics of international law." The point of Putin's Schmittianism is to establish an avowedly more basic version of those basics. *See* Hilpold 2023.

[16] Treaty on the Eurasian Economic Union, signed on 29 May 2014, entry into force: 1 January 2025. Available at https://docs.eaeunion.org/en-us/pages/displaydocument.aspx?s=bef9c798-3978-42f3-9ef2-d0fb3d53b75f&w=632c7868-4ee2-4b21-bc64-1995328e6ef3&l=540294ae-c3c9-4511-9bf8-aaf5d6e0d169&entityid=3610. Accessed 24 September 2024.

[17] Pizzolo 2023.

the EAEU may also apply to, e.g., the European Union (EU)—another economic union based on a treaty—the difference lies in how the EAEU reinserts the unequal power relation of one dominant power—a *Reich* – over, in this case, its former satellite States—its *Großraum* – whereas the EU is structured less obviously toward such asymmetry.

Having touched upon two current examples taken from the international relations of Putin's contemporary Russia, we need to ask: What do we get out of reading Putin against Schmitt's 1939 book and *Großraum* international law? Putin's at times obscure and apodictic rhetoric as well as the acts by the Russian Federation will be easier to understand, we argue, and the next steps to be expected should be more predictable. We can be fairly certain that "non-intervention" in Putin's vocabulary refers to the Schmittian *Großraum* analytics. Putin's perspective on Russia is marked by its premodern history as an empire as much as by its contemporary history as a State. The empire's need for territorial depth is allotted hierarchical primacy, which has repercussions on Putin's reading of international law in our contemporary time. Schmitt, the promoter of another empire and its violent territorial expansion, helps us discern this superordination of imperial international law over the international law of formally equal States.

27.3 A Chinese International Law with Schmittian Characteristics?

If *Großraum* analytics in international law can help us understand Putin's war on Ukraine and his rhetoric in defense of it as a way of translating Schmittian international legal theory into contemporary international legal practice, can China's international legal acts be understood in similar ways? China is, besides Russia, a major international power that contemporary international legal scholars struggle to make sense of through the usual terminology and categorizations in liberal international law. What if Schmitt, and his *Großraum* international law, could be equally of help in analyzing and describing China's acts in developing regional hegemony and domination?

China has no ongoing military conflict of the scale and severity seen in Ukraine. Yet, there are other acts than large-scale belligerent ones that count in terms of how a State conducts itself under international law. Below, we will look at China's position on the South China Sea as an example to see if Schmitt's *Großraum* that can help explain something in terms of Chinese international law. Schmitt's *Großraum* theory rests on there being a number of *Reiche* and *Großräume* locking each other in an equilibrium so that none of them can achieve a universal position of power. If Putin's Russia clearly has the ambition to be one such power, as we have seen in the analysis above, then China may have similar ambitions, albeit working toward fulfilling them in a slightly different key. Russia and China arguably present themselves on the international arena, as well as in their multilateral interactions with other States within their geographical immediacy, as major regionally focused powers with what may be *Reich* ambitions within their respective *Großraum*. Moreover, Russia and China have developed an ever-stronger strategic partnership during the last decade, including in trade relations, collaboration on military technology, and their positions in international law and global governance. This is something that goes well with Schmittian *Großraum* international legal thinking. We note that China has, repeatedly, abstained from criticizing Russia's war on Ukraine in international legal fora. This too goes well with the balancing of powers between *Großraum* regions, where the Schmittian idea of non-intervention becomes an intergovernmental rule.

In immediate proximity to the International Permanent Court of Arbitration's final decision on the dispute brought about by the Philippines regarding China's acts in the South China Sea, in 2016, China and Russia advanced a "Joint Position on international law."[18] At the time, both powers had faced substantial criticism for their non-compliance with international law, not the least in the Russian annexation of Crimea in 2014, and in China's activities in the South China Sea, the latter of which was under arbitration at the time. The criticism also concerned the two States' non-compliance with international human rights law. The Russo-Chinese 2016 Joint Position was largely perceived by the international community as calcifying the Russo-Chinese understanding of the US as a hegemonic power whose invocation of international law is flavored by its imperial claims as a universal power, and by its excessive interventions into Russian and Chinese geopolitical spheres of interests. The US has persistently claimed freedom of navigation in the South China Sea and has a longtime military collaboration with and support for several States neighboring China around the South China Sea—not least Taiwan. This, needless to say, does not sit well with China's geopolitical ambitions for the South China Sea.

Russia and China have, moreover, issued two joint statements of particular interest for the question of the Russo-Chinese receptions of Schmitt's *Großraum* thinking. In 2021, the foreign ministers of China and Russia made a joint statement in which they put forward what scholars have identified as "a nascent proposal for an alternative global governance system."[19] On February 4, 2022, Russia and China released a "Joint Statement of the Russian Federation and the People's Republic of China on the International Relations Entering a New Era and the Global Sustainable Development."[20] The statement was issued just before the Beijing Winter Olympic Games. The Russian full-scale invasion of Ukraine began on February 24, which is just a few days after their end.[21] One paragraph is of particular interest from a *Großraum* analysis perspective:

---

[18] The South China Sea Arbitration (The Republic of Philippines v. The People's Republic of China): https://pca-cpa.org/en/cases/7/. Accessed 12 February 2025. For the Russo-Chinese joint statement: https://archive.mid.ru/en/foreign_policy/news/-/asset_publisher/cKNonkJE02Bw/content/id/2331698. Accessed 12 February 2025.

[19] Skordas 2021, p. 298.

[20] http://en.kremlin.ru/supplement/5770. Accessed 12 February 2025.

[21] According to the New York Times, referencing to US intelligence sources, China had asked Russia to postpone its invasion of Ukraine until after the Olympic games: https://www.nytimes.com/2022/03/02/us/politics/russia-ukraine-china.html. Accessed 12 February 2025.

> Russia and China stand against attempts by external forces to undermine security and stability in their common adjacent regions, intend to counter interference by outside forces in the internal affairs of sovereign countries under any pretext, oppose colour revolutions, and will increase cooperation in the aforementioned areas.[22]

Both joint statements emphasize the Schmittian idea of non-intervention in the internal affairs of States as well as in the *Großräume*—the "adjacent regions"—of historically important regional powers. The 2022 statement identifies a rise of the Global South and a polycentric and multipolar world order in which international law, in the Russo-Chinese view, serves the "inviolability of the results of the Second World War and established world order."[23] Just as in Putin's 2022 speech, the respective historical victories of the Soviet Union and China and their positions as hegemonic regional powers—or *Reiche*—underscore which theory of international law China and Russia seem to put forward.

China's imperial history has reverberated through the foreign policy of the People's Republic. The question for us is whether the emerging Chinese position in international law consolidates non-intervention as an intergovernmental rule of law or as a norm that separates different *Großräume* from each other. If China chooses Putin's and Schmitt's interpretation—a Chinese variation of the Schmittian *Großraum* thinking—it may just be that contemporary international law is faced by a fundamental challenge.

Whereas Schmitt has been well-read and received in Russia for a long time, his scholarship and theory of international law arrived later to China.[24] Over the past three decades, the literature on the reception of Schmitt in the Chinese context has expanded, driven by the number of translations of Schmitt's text into Chinese and the uses that Chinese scholars make of it.[25] Their focus has been on the internal aspect of State power, with Schmitt being deployed in arguments for a preferred constitutional future for China. Well-rehearsed axioms of Schmittian constitutional theory, such as the "absolute constitution" of a State, the key function of the "friend-enemy" distinction for the political, and the axiom that "sovereign is he who decides the exceptional," are referenced in those intellectual skirmishes between supporters of the status quo, the new left, and liberal reformers in China.[26]

It has been suggested, however, that the Schmittian literature and debate is really a curious sideshow to Chinese reform debates, which remain quintessentially Chinese at their ideational core.[27] This complicates how we imagine the transmission belts moving Schmittian thought eastward. Likewise, the responsibility of Western

[22] https://www.nytimes.com/2022/03/02/us/politics/russia-ukraine-china.html. Accessed 12 February 2025.

[23] https://www.nytimes.com/2022/03/02/us/politics/russia-ukraine-china.html. Accessed 12 February 2025.

[24] On the uptake of Schmitt in Russia, *see*, inter alia, Lewis 2020 and Skordas 2022.

[25] *See*, e.g., Libin and Patapan 2020; Zheng 2016; Lam 2023.

[26] Both Libin's and Patapan's Schmitt Fever and Zheng's monograph subdivide contributions to Chinese debates into three typecast factions. Libin and Patapan 2020; Zheng 2016.

[27] Warning observers away from an overidentification of complex Chinese debates with conceptually isolated Schmittian references, Quélennec 2018.

scholars implicated in the Schmitt renaissances becomes less straightforward to determine if Chinese scholars engage in sovereign bricolage rather than faithful replication of Western ideas, whether liberal or totalitarian.

Although Schmitt's concepts are being argued in contemporary Chinese legal-political debates, we must ask why the concept of *Großraum* is missing in these debates. Schmitt's *Nomos of the Earth* was translated from its original German to Chinese only relatively recently, and the 1939 *Großraum* book remains to be translated. In a sense, it may be too early to judge the impact of Schmitt's writings on international law on the Chinese debates. A first speculation would be that Schmitt's *Großraum* thinking may not add value to the context of China's international legal politics—especially as the arguably central 1939 text is unavailable in Chinese. Yet, there is arguably more to the story than a single book, in this case Schmitt's 1939 *Großraum* text.

China is characterized by a combination of imperially tainted nationalism, its trademark "socialism with Chinese characteristics," its self-declared status as a developing nation, and its exponential economic expansion, as it carves out a special status in international affairs. By and large, Russia and China are different in their reception of Schmittian *Großraum* thinking in international law in the same way that practice is different from theory. Putin is a *Großraum* adept in all but name. In his justification for the 2022 war on Ukraine, he includes no reference to Schmitt, as sovereigns need not acknowledge lessons from their academic teachers. Structurally, however, his 2022 speech reproduces the nuts and bolts of Schmitt's *Großraum* thinking just as the Russian belligerent acts against Ukraine does. By contrast, beyond the joint statements with Russia referred to earlier, Chinese leadership is not on record with positions on international law that are as structurally Schmittian. In China, Schmitt is not received in the presidential office, but in the seminar room. In the latter forum, his concepts are referred to outright, but exactly what these references are justifying against the backdrop of Chinese intellectual debates remains fiendishly difficult to establish. At least at this point, and for the purpose of this chapter. Even if Chinese scholars will include Schmittian *Großraum* analytics into their debates, we still must resist the temptation of equating Chinese conceptions of empire with Schmitt's. To do so would be to make ourselves guilty of a false conceptual universalism that Schmitt is usually deployed against in both left- and right-leaning camps.[28]

For these reasons, we leave aside what Chinese intellectuals and academics *say* when drawing on Schmitt in inter-scholarly debates and focus on what the People's Republic of China *does,* as a State actor, in the field of international law: This is what we will seek to analyze through the admittedly entirely Western lens of Schmittian international legal thinking. In so doing, we read a behavior that is meant to be legible to international lawyers in—as well as outside of—China, through a European thinker whose history of ideas is legible to us as European international law scholars (who

[28] For an analysis of the relations between Schmitt's *Großraumtheorie* and Sinocentric and Japanocentric modes of international legal thought contemporary to it, *see* Hong 2019. Hong's hypothesis is that Schmitt's *Großraumtheorie* and the Japanocentric and Sinocentric orders emerged independently from each other.

have read and know Schmitt's thinking on international law). To argue the relevance of *Großraum* analytics to Chinese conduct, Ryan Mitchell has made a number of observations:

> Beginning early in Xi Jinping's administration, the Party's emphasis on developing its own new forms of internationalism had manifested in a number of major platform announcements (particularly the One Belt, One Road infrastructure investment initiative) and concepts such as calling for the creation of a "community of shared destiny for mankind" (renlei mingyun gongtongti 人类命运共同体). Regional platforms such as the "community of shared destiny" for Asian states, "Asian inter-civilizational dialogue," development of Asian security cooperation, and a "South-South Human Rights Dialogue," have also followed suit. New institutions such as China's Asian International Investment Bank and the Belt and Road Forum add concrete order to these abstract ideas. Meanwhile, China's disputes over the South China Sea, as well as the ongoing dilemma presented by Taiwan, directly present the problem of attempting to transform China's surrounding environment into one consistent with the interests of the Party and the state.[29]

These initiatives reflect a superpower at work, but do they show a Chinese *Reich* safeguarding its *Großraum* from external intervention? Against the backdrop of the Russo-Chinese joint statements mentioned above, we see a rewarding candidate for an analysis driven by that question: the hegemonic domination of the South China Sea. If this form of hegemony bears the traits of a *Großraum* structure, it can be argued that Putin's overt Schmittianism and the Schmittian structures of Chinese international legal politics reinforce each other, thus aggregating to a greater threat to Western-liberal traditions of understanding of international law than we may previously have thought.

27.4 Is the Chinese Government Seeking to Establish a *Großraum*?

The South China Sea dispute is an ongoing multi-State conflict, raising issues under the UN Charter and the law of the seas.[30] The United Nations Convention on the Law of the Sea (UNCLOS) is its primary framework for international legal analysis. This introduces a different logic to the international legal conflict as well as to our analysis. The law of the sea allows, since Grotius' times, for free passage on open waters—the principle of *mare liberum* or freedom of navigation. No power can lay claim to own or control an entire ocean and turn it into a *mare clausum*. Today, the UNCLOS operationalizes when, why, and how national claims over coastal and open waters can be made; it also gives freedom of navigation in the South China Sea.

The disputes over the South China Sea—including incidents of violent attacks by Chinese Coast Guard vessels on non-Chinese fishing boats[31] and non-authorized

---

[29] Martinez Mitchell 2020.

[30] For an introduction to the regulatory framework for the South China Sea dispute, *see*, e.g., Beckman 2013.

[31] For a more recent example: Financial Times 2024, p. 4.

Chinese military presence within other States' waters—hark back to the mid-1700s. They must be read as part of a wider history where international law and Western colonialism have been mutually co-productive and co-constituent. Two World Wars and innumerable territorial disputes later, the area is covered by an intricate series of peace treaties, former colonial borders, and postcolonial legal situations of territorial disputes. Moreover, and relevant to the South China Sea, we have the principle of *uti possidetis juris*. The International Court of Justice has upheld this principle in its decisions, meaning that unilateral historical claims, such as those pursued by China through recourse to newly printed maps depicting historical claims in the South China Sea, do not supersede treaties and postcolonial State boundaries under contemporary international law.[32]

The South China Sea borders Vietnam to the west, the Philippines, Malaysia, and Brunei to the east, Indonesia and Malaysia to the south, and China and Taiwan to the north. It is a major commercial transport route for vessels moving in and out of ports in all the area, as well as for ships *en route* to and from Russia and Singapore. Moreover, the area is considered rich in natural resources, in particular oil and gas. Who will govern the South China Sea—or even parts of it—is, thus, a major geopolitical question. For any reader of Schmitt's scholarly work on international law—including the 1939 *Großraum* text and *The Nomos of the Earth*—this raises a red flag, and the question of how relevant his scholarship may be for analyzing the situation. This is all the more the case as it involves a major international power—China—and postcolonial States which, to varying degrees, have been and continue to be dependent on their great neighbor. For commercial and military reasons, China's surrounding neighbors depend on peaceful regional relations. The only way to back the States' claims under international law is to rely on military support of other major geopolitical players—primarily the US. But keeping the US as a global hegemonial actor out of its South China Sea backyard is exactly what the Chinese government seeks to do.

The UNCLOS gives quite clear and specific answers to questions of claims over oceanic spaces: with a baseline, internal waters, archipelagic waters, territorial waters, territorial sea, contiguous zone, exclusive economic zone, continental shelf, and high seas. These meticulous lines of demarcation offer a great deal of opportunities to act in contestation for States with ambitions that exceed what the UNCLOS permits. China has, in this respect, repeatedly been found to pursue land extensions—e.g., by adding sand on reefs which then become new islands in the South China Sea—and militarizing several of the islands by adding airstrips, cruise missiles, and radar systems on them. In 2016, the Permanent Court of Arbitration at The Hague ruled in favor of the Philippines in a case over the role of historic rights and the source of maritime entitlements in the South China Sea.[33] At the center of that, and many of the other conflicts in the South China Sea, are parts of the Spratly

[32] *See, especially*, the Burkina Faso/Mali case from 1986: https://www.icj-cij.org/case/69. Accessed 12 February 2025.

[33] The South China Sea Arbitration (The Republic of Philippines v. The People's Republic of China), Award In The Matter Of The South China Sea Arbitration before an Arbitral Tribunal Constituted Under Annex VII to the 1982 United Nations Convention on the Law of the Sea between the

Islands, and what is known as the nine-dash line. The latter is the demarcation line for China's territorial claims in the South China Sea.

A very first observation, and without getting into the details of either the conflict or the UNCLOS, is that China's actions in the South China Sea during the last decades are challenging the principle of the *mare liberum*, introducing in its place a Chinese *mare clausum* with little respect given to the UNCLOS, decisions by the Permanent Court of Arbitration, or the UN Commission's investigating aspects of the South China Sea dispute. China is noted to have argued, in the 2009 UN Commission on The Limits of the Continental Shelf, that "China has indisputable sovereignty over the island in the South China Sea" and that this is "widely known by the international community."[34] The map attached to their argument shows an image of a Chinese *mare clausum* South China Sea. However, as the Permanent Court of Arbitration concluded in 2016, to the extent China had historic rights to resources in the waters of the South China Sea, such rights were extinguished to the extent they were incompatible with the exclusive economic zones provided for in the Convention.[35] China continues to challenge this conclusion in both diplomatic relations and its State practice.

Can the acts that China has taken on as part of achieving an ever-greater control over the South China Sea be seen as an exercise of *Großraum* building in the international law of the sea? Is it a structural *Großraum* Schmittianism, like that of Putin's Russia, or is it rather an enactment of a critique of liberal international law along Schmittian lines? The latter would explain China's non-compliance with the UNCLOS, whereas the former would perhaps require some more substantiation before we would feel certain about this line of argument.

There are, moreover, arguments to the contrary of seeing China as developing a *Großraum* international law through its geopolitics in the South China Sea. First, it is hard to identify a clear-cut Schmittian *Großraum* rhetoric or practice in the Chinese claims to the nine-dash line. Such an argument would presuppose that China sees and treats the Philippines, Malaysia, Brunei, Indonesia, Malaysia, and Taiwan as lesser States within its historical *Großraum,* and its peoples as dependent on the culture, language, and people of China, as a *Reich.* That China sees Taiwan as part of its own State is a wholly other thing than seeing it as a lesser people within a *Großraum.* As for the other States, these simply do not have a lesser-State-within-a-*Großraum* relation to China. At least not as far as we can see. Second, China articulates claims under international law to the South China Sea that are arguable (also) in a liberal, non-Schmittian international law. Third, matters are complicated as the *Großraum*—in Schmitt's theorization of it—operates through a tellurian—or earthly—logic. Schmitt makes a baseline distinction between land and sea, emphasizing the impossibility to nomotically appropriate the maritime domain, however much it gets drawn into

Republic of the Philippines and the People's Republic of China, PCA Case Nº 2013-19, 12 July 2016, https://pca-cpa.org/en/cases/7/. Accessed XX Month 2025.

[34] Page 1, paragraph two, of the official translation of China's response to the complaint brought before the UN by Malaysia and Vietnam: https://www.un.org/Depts/los/clcs_new/submissions_files/mysvnm33_09/chn_2009re_mys_vnm_e.pdf. Accessed 12 February 2025.

[35] The South China Sea Arbitration (The Republic of Philippines v. The People's Republic of China), Dispositif, B(2), p. 473.

geopolitical struggles. If nothing else, this latter point seems to make a strong case against an analysis of the South China Sea as a Chinese Schmittian *Großraum.*

Let us then widen the picture. China pursues many more nationalistic and globally expansive interests, of which its activities in the South China Sea are only one leg: the One Belt One Road initiative, mentioned above in the quote from Mitchell, is another example. However, that initiative is only partially consistent with a Schmittian *Großraum*, and would be better analyzed with his *nomos* concept, For Schmitt, *nomos* denotes the arch-act of taking land, typically for the purpose of pasturing or agricultural use. His *nomos* is the foundation of a normatively significant division of the world's landmass for economic exploitation. As Schmitt explained in his later works written during the Cold War, *nomos* also embraces contemporary technological-economical forms of appropriation, typically through the vehicle of development assistance. In a 1962 text inter alia describing the position of the US, he enumerates a plurality of the spaces that it dominates, with the *Großraum* of the Monroe doctrine being only one.[36] All these spaces of domination are "magnetic force fields of human energy and work."[37] It is hard to argue that the dependencies coming along with China's One Belt One Road initiative have the requisite intensity to speak of a *Großraum* appropriation of sorts, making partner countries into vassal States. That said, the One Belt One Road initiative appears to connect well to Schmitt's Cold War-related vision of overlapping force fields, where *Großraum* politics would be but one field, and the pursuit of One Belt One Road another. However, Schmitt's model of force fields is much diluted in comparison to his *Großraum* concept, and adds little, if any, explanatory value compared with, say, a realpolitik understanding of China's international law politics.

In summary: Neither China's acts nor its rhetoric easily lend themselves to a simple matching against Schmitt's international legal theory. In that encounter, Schmitt appears ideologically very particular and surprisingly Western. In resonance with Schmitt, however, China reiterates a critique of liberal international law and the global hegemonic position of the US. Both China and Russia understand the US to actively pursue hegemony, with liberal international law acting as its enabler.[38] Among Chinese international law acts criticizing liberal international law, the best-known is perhaps China's attempts to insert its concept of a "community of a shared destiny for mankind" into UN documents and international legal discourse. This concept puts strong emphasis on sovereign equality, wooing audiences in the Global South.[39] However, Schmitt has no particular interest in wooing the Global South. Instead, he is reaching for a balance among *Großraum* powers, not sovereign equality, even as his particular critique brings together authoritarian States and interests from both the right and the left of the political spectrum. And even if China, in the joint statements with Russia, signed on to Schmittian rhetoric on international law, commentators agree that the joint statements do not form a coherent ideology, but

[36] Schmitt 1995, pp. 604–605.

[37] Ibid. p. 605. Translation by the authors.

[38] As expressed in their joint statements, above n. 3. *See* our explanation above.

[39] Zhang 2018.

remain a mash-up of Russian and Chinese positions that do not necessarily overlap on all counts.[40] We will come back to and develop this further below, when we reflect on what this all means for *Großraum* thinking in international law today.

27.5 Conclusion

We started this chapter by setting out how Schmitt launched the notion of the *Großraum* as a legal concept in 1939. It was a time of much international legal tension, where Schmitt introduced his theory of the *Großraum* with a hegemonic central *Reich* lawfully dominating its regional neighbors, matching the ambitions of the Third Reich. His theory established a principle of "non-intervention" in sharp contrast to the one found in liberal international law and saw the *Reich*—rather than the State—as its central actor. The resurfacing of a scholarly interest in Schmitt's international legal writings combined with the last decade of developments in international relations, focused on Russia and China, is what sparked our interest in this matter. We began with a hunch that there was something Schmittian, and specifically *Großraum* Schmittian, about Russia's and perhaps also China's recent positions on, and acts in, international law.

Following our analysis above, in which we focused on Russia's war on Ukraine and China's actions in the South China Sea, what can we say about the Russian and Chinese receptions of Schmitt's *Großraum* theory in international law? Is there an intersection, do their Schmittian *Großraum* adaptations reinforce each other at critical junctures? And, moreover, are we able to conclude anything substantive on the accumulated threat of *Großraum* thinking today, in its competition with liberal modes of non-intervention in international law?

On Russia, the analysis is clear: Putin is pursuing a Schmittian *Großraum* version of international law in all but words. Both Russian actions and Russian rhetoric on the war in Ukraine are evidence of this. Regarding China, the picture is more complex. China's actions might appear as driven by Schmittian *Großraum* non-interventionism in the South China Sea, with *Großraum*-ish rhetoric in the Russo-Chinese joint statements on international law and global governance. But rather than being Schmittian at their core, Chinese international law acts seem to at times overlap with Schmittian logics and critique of liberal international law.

In conclusion, we see two things: First, *Großraum* thinking is back as a seemingly legitimate item in international law rhetoric and State practice, at least among States whose ambition in international law and governance are like those of Putin's Russia and Xi Jinping's China. Moreover, Schmitt's theories are very much alive and discussed in academic rooms and debates in international law and beyond. In Russia's international relations, we see an implementation of Schmitt's international law theory not just in general but also on the specific question of the *Großraum* and *Reich* in international law. In the case of China, we have seen that *Großraum* thinking

[40] Joint statements, above n. 3.

may be part of a larger turn to Schmitt's critique against liberal international law, yet to argue that China is pursuing a *Großraum* international law politics in the South China Sea is, we find, too far of a stretch. Inter alia, we found that the *Großraum* concept is a bad fit for the predominantly maritime situation obtaining in the South China Sea, and that Schmitt's *nomos* does not add explanatory power to the Chinese domination politics of the One Belt One Road initiative.

Thus, we find Schmitt's *Großraum* theory helpful for understanding, in part, the international legal self-positioning of Russia, and to some degree also that of China. Although we cannot say for sure where these developments will take international law, we can expect at the very least to recognize more of Schmitt's *Großraum* thinking in both State practice and international legal scholarly debates. What is the accumulated threat of such a development? We flag this as a development for international legal scholarship to follow up on, to better determine how worried we should be.

References

Beckman R (2013) The UN Convention on the Law of the Sea and the Maritime Disputes in the South China Sea. American Journal of International Law 107(1):142–163

Financial Times (2024) China Targets Vietnamese fishermen. 3 October 2024

Hilpold P (2023) Justifying the Unjustifiable: Russia's Aggression against Ukraine, International Law, and Carl Schmitt's "Theory of the Greater Space" ('Großraumtheorie'). Chinese Journal of International Law 22:409–433

Hong M (2019) Die Großraumtheorie von Carl Schmitt im Vergleich mit dem ostasiatischen Völkerrechtsverständnis. [Carl Schmitt's Großraum theory in Comparison with Eastern Asian Conceptions of International Law] Duncker & Humblot, Berlin

Lam J (2023) Bringing Bonhoeffer into Dialogue with Schmitt in Contemporary China. International Journal of Public Theology 17:55–73

Lewis D G (2020) Russia's New Authoritarianism. Edinburgh University Press, Edinburgh

Libin X, Patapan H (2020) Schmitt Fever: The Use and Abuse of Carl Schmitt in Contemporary China. International Journal of Constitutional Law 18:130–146

Martinez Mitchell R (2020) Chinese Receptions of Carl Schmitt Since 1929. Penn State Journal of Law and International Affairs 8:181–263

Pizzolo P (2023) Exploring Eurasian Integration through the Lenses of Carl Schmitt: The Eurasian Economic Union as an Example of Schmittian "Great Space." Journal of International Political Theory 19:292–316

Quélennec B (2018) La réception contemporaine de Carl Schmitt et de Leo Strauss en Chine [The contemporary reception of Carl Schmitt and of Leo Strauss in China]. Revue française de science politique 68:130–133

Resnick E N (2022) Interests, Ideologies, and Great Power Spheres of Influence. European Journal of International Relations 28:563–588

Schmitt C (1950) Der Nomos der Erde im Völkerrecht des Jus Publicum Europaeum [The Nomos of the Earth in the Jus Publicum Europaeum]. Duncker&Humblot, Berlin

Schmitt C (1995) Staat, Großraum, Nomos. Arbeiten aus den Jahren 1916-1969 [State, Großraum, Nomos. Work of the years 1916-1969]. Duncker & Humblot, Berlin

Schmitt C (2006) The Nomos of the Earth in the Jus Publicum Europaeum, Telos Press Publishing, Candor N.Y.

Schmitt C (2011) The *Großraum* Order of International Law with a Ban on Intervention for Spatially Foreign Powers: A Contribution to the Concept of *Reich* in International Law (1939-1941). In: Nunan T (ed) Carl Schmitt: Writings on War, p. 76

Skordas A (2021) Authoritarian Global Governance? The Russian-Chinese Joint Statement of March 2021. Zeitschrift für ausländisches öffentliches Recht und Völkerrecht / Heidelberg Journal of International Law 81:293–302

Skordas A (2022) Russia's Eurasian Großraum and its Consequences, Verfassungsblog. https://verfassungsblog.de/russias-eurasian-groraum-and-its-consequences/ Accessed on 12 February 2025

von Bernstorff J (2023) Governing Hegemonic Spaces in Carl Schmitt: Colonialism, Anti-Imperialism and the Großraum Theory. Humanity 14:369–83

Zhang D (2018) The Concept of "Community of Common Destiny" in China's Diplomacy: Meaning, Motives and Implications. Asia & the Pacific Policy Studies 5:196–207

Zheng Q (2016) Carl Schmitt, Mao Zedong and the Politics of Transition. Palgrave Macmillan

Matilda Arvidsson is an Associate Professor in International Law, and Senior Lecturer in Jurisprudence at the Department of Law, University of Gothenburg, Sweden. She has researched and published extensively on international law, jurisprudence, and Law and AI, with a focus on feminist and other critical enquires into the histories, theories and methods of law and the many technological, biological and inanimate entities and relations law seeks to order. She completed her LLD, in international law, at Lund University, Sweden. Dr. Arvidsson is currently a Visiting Researcher at HDK-Valand Academy of Arts and Craft, University of Gothenburg, and holds affiliated positions at Luleå Technical University, Sweden, and the Faculté de Droit de l'Université Catholique de Lille, Paris, France.

Gregor Noll is a Professor of International Law at the Department of Law, University of Gothenburg, Sweden, and a Visiting Researcher at the Swedish Defense University, Stockholm, Sweden. Noll has written extensively on the theory of international law, on migration law, on international humanitarian law as well as on law and AI. He has developed close ties to disciplines such as political theory, the medical sciences, history and demography from an empirical foothold in legal scholarship. He is currently working on apocalyptic law, on shared responsibility and on the Stauffenberg brothers' tyrannicidal exercise of *pouvoir constituant*.

Chapter 28
Tackling Hazardous Dumping or Legitimizing Toxic Colonialism? —Exploring the Role of International Law in Managing Trade in Hazardous Substances

David Langlet

Contents

Abstract Since the 1970s, demands have been made, not least from African states and environmental non-governmental organizations, to prevent 'toxic dumping' of hazardous substances from the global north in developing countries. Spurred by much-publicized cases of hazardous substances being exported from developed to developing states with catastrophic health and environmental effects, legal frameworks addressing different forms of hazardous exports have been put in place. This development has been characterized by conflicts and inconsistencies both between and within groups of developed and developing states. Some actors have been fervent in opposing export of products or substances that are banned or largely unwanted in developed states to the global south. Others have described such policies, in particular when they involve complete bans, as paternalistic and as depriving states in the global south of their sovereignty. The chapter explores how these perspectives have played out in the development of legal responses and how current legal regimes balance sovereign decision-making, economic interests, and environmental and health protection in a policy area fraught with power imbalances and colonial legacies.

Keywords Hazardous trade · Waste export · Prior informed consent · Basel convention · Basel ban · Rotterdam convention

D. Langlet (✉)
Uppsala University, Uppsala, Sweden
e-mail: david.langlet@jur.uu.se

M. Klamberg et al. (eds.), *Reconstructing Power and Hegemony in Public International Law*, https://doi.org/10.1007/978-94-6265-743-4_28

28.1 Introduction

For several decades, shipments of hazardous substances, including many kinds of wastes and chemicals, from industrialized to developing countries have attracted extensive criticism. This has been spurred by recurring scandals when exported substances have caused serious environmental harm and human suffering as well as by continuous problems with pesticides being used without sufficient protection or knowledge and imported waste piling up in open dumps or being managed in harmful ways. Shipments of hazardous substances from industrialized to developing countries have been discussed in terms of 'toxic colonialism'[1] and 'imperialistic exploitation'.[2]

This chapter looks at the development and nature of legal responses to the problems associated with the shipment of hazardous substances from industrialized to developing countries, or from the 'global north' to the 'global south', although these concepts are becoming increasingly blurred. Of particular relevance is what interests have been given priority in the development of international legal mechanisms and what problems they have in fact been designed to address. And, also, whether the legal measures that states have been able to agree upon internationally are designed in a way that allows them to achieve their stated purpose, or if they mainly serve to cloak the perpetuation of the relocation of risk from the rich to the poor?

After first looking at some broader policy initiatives, the chapter's main focus is the two global convention regimes developed to address international shipments of hazardous wastes and chemicals, respectively, i.e., the 1989 Basel Convention and the 1998 Rotterdam Convention.[3] The 2001 Stockholm Convention is only addressed tangentially, as it is not primarily concerned with trade but with the general phasing out of specific persistent organic pollutants.[4] It also covers much fewer substances than the other conventions. Other areas of internation law, such as trade and investment law, are not addressed, although they can have an impact on how flows of hazardous substance and the management of such substances can be regulated.[5] Before looking at the features and the operation of the legal regimes formed by the Basel and Rotterdam Conventions, I will briefly chart the development of legal responses to what has been termed 'toxic exports'.[6]

---

[1] Barsalou and Picard 2018, p. 897.

[2] Strohm 1993, p. 137.

[3] Basel Convention on the Control of Transboundary Movement of Hazardous Wastes and Their Disposal, 1989, 1673 UNTS 57 (Basel Convention); Rotterdam Convention on the Prior Informed Consent Procedure for Certain Hazardous Chemicals and Pesticides in International Trade, 1998, 2244 UNTS 337 (Rotterdam Convention).

[4] Stockholm Convention on Persistent Organic Pollutants, 2001, 2256 UNTS 119 (Stockholm Convention).

[5] On international trade law and its relationship to agreements such as the Basel and Rotterdam Conventions that aim to regulate trade from a health and environmental perspective, *see* Langlet 2009, and on the potential effects of investment law on waste management, *see* Hippolyte 2012; Schneiderman, 2022.

[6] Clapp 2001.

28.2 The Recognition of a Problem

At the 1972 Stockholm Conference on the Human Environment, often seen to mark the birth of modern international environmental law, neither wastes nor chemicals received much attention and neither is referred to in the 26 principles of the Stockholm Declaration.[7] While negative effects of hazardous wastes and chemicals are captured by general references to the just struggle against pollution,[8] and the safeguarding of the air, water, and land,[9] no mention is made of the impact of international trade in such substances.

At the time of the Stockholm Conference, many developing states perceived the increasing calls for environmental standards, not least when linked to trade, as a threat to their economic and social development. In the run-up to the Conference, developing states championed the adoption by the United Nations General Assembly (UNGA) of a resolution stating that 'no environmental policy should adversely affect the present or future development possibilities of the developing countries' and holding that the action plan and proposals submitted to the Stockholm Conference must 'avoid any adverse effects of environmental policies and measures on the economy of the developing countries in all spheres'.[10] Environmental policies tended to be seen as a way for industrialized countries to deny developing ones their right to industrialize or at least as diverting attention away from the urgent economic and social problems facing developing countries.[11]

However, environmental standards set by industrialized countries also had other effects. In the years following the Stockholm Conference, the introduction of environmental standards made waste management increasingly costly and the use of hazardous chemicals became restricted. In Europe and North America, increasing waste generation coupled with regulatory action led to soaring costs for waste management. In combination with declining transportation costs, this made it attractive to 'deal' with waste by shipping it to states with lower environmental standards and lower labour costs.[12] Pesticides were also being exported in large volumes from industrialized to developing states. The latter typically lacked preconditions for safe use and the exported chemicals were often banned from use in the countries of export.[13]

Towards the end of the 1970s, the newly established United Nations Environment Program (UNEP) started to address the ability of developing countries to manage import of hazardous substances. In 1978, the UNEP Governing Council (UNEP GC) instructed the recently set up International Register of Potentially Toxic Chemicals to 'give priority to providing countries with information on legal and administrative

[7] United Nations 1972.

[8] Ibid. p. 4, Principle 6.

[9] Ibid. Principle 2.

[10] UNGA 1971.

[11] Brighton 2017, p. 213.

[12] Chakraborty 2023, p. 147.

[13] *See* Weir and Schapiro 1981; Bull 1982.

limitations, bans and regulations placed on potentially toxic chemicals in producing countries'.[14] The UNGA also adopted a series of resolutions regarding information exchange on banned hazardous chemicals.[15] A 1982 resolution recognized that 'products that have been banned from domestic consumption and/or sale because they have been judged to endanger health and the environment should be sold abroad ... only when a request for such products is received from an importing country or when the consumption of such products is officially permitted in the importing country'.[16]

These attempts to address the broad category of so-called domestically prohibited goods were not followed up by substantive regulatory action.[17] However, a development had started that would result in international legal measures aimed at addressing the risks associated with shipments of hazardous wastes and chemicals from industrialized to developing countries.

In 1984, the UNEP GC adopted a provisional notification scheme for banned and severely restricted chemicals.[18] Three years later, it was replaced by the London Guidelines for the Exchange of Information on Chemicals in International Trade.[19] Due to pressure from pesticide-exporting states, the Guidelines did not stipulate prior consent as a prerequisite for export.[20]

Also in 1987, the so-called Cairo Guidelines and principles for the environmentally sound management (ESM) of hazardous wastes were approved by the UNEP GC.[21] Among the principles was that no export of hazardous waste should be permitted without the prior notification and consent of the prospective states of import and transit.

The same questions were also addressed by the Organisation for Economic Co-operation and Development (OECD). In 1984, the OECD Council recommended exporting member countries to provide information regarding chemicals banned or severely restricted in the exporting country, to enable importing countries to make timely and informed decisions.[22] With respect to waste, the OECD Council took a decision in 1986 according to which member countries were to prohibit movements of hazardous wastes to a final destination in a non-member country without its consent.[23] In 1992, a further decision set up a control system concerning trans-frontier movements of wastes destined for recovery operations classifying wastes as 'green', 'amber' or 'red' and prescribing control measures for the latter two categories.[24]

---

[14] UNEP 1978.

[15] *See, e.g.*, UNGA 1979.

[16] UNGA 1982.

[17] Langlet 2009, p. 66.

[18] UNEP 1984.

[19] UNEP 1987a.

[20] *See* Pallemaerts 1988, p. 66.

[21] UNEP 1987b. *See also* the amendment through UNEP 1989.

[22] OECD 1984.

[23] OECD 1986.

[24] OECD 1992. *See further* Kummer 1995, p. 161 et seq.

28.3 Waste Export—the Basel Regime

When the Cairo Guidelines were adopted in 1987, the UNEP executive director also convened, at the initiative of Switzerland and Hungary, a working group tasked with elaborating a global convention. Based on a draft produced by the group, the Basel Convention was adopted after intensive negotiations at a conference of plenipotentiaries in 1989 and entered into force in 1992. At the conference, many developing countries as well as non-governmental organizations pushed for comprehensive bans on waste export. Among developed states, however, there was widespread resistance towards imposing far-reaching limitations on transboundary shipments, making them illegal or very costly, in particular regarding trade between industrialized countries, but also with respect to shipment to developing states.[25] Some developing countries were also concerned that such bans would undermine their recycling industries.[26]

In the Convention, the parties recognize in the preamble 'the increasing desire for the prohibition of transboundary movements of hazardous wastes and their disposal in other states, especially developing countries' as well as the fact that transboundary movements of hazardous wastes, especially to developing countries, have a high risk of not constituting ESM.[27] It is also explicitly recognized that states have a sovereign right to ban the entry or disposal of foreign wastes in their territories.[28] In its operative part, the Convention is focused on establishing a prohibition on export to states that have explicitly prohibited import of a specific kind of waste and requiring prior informed consent (PIC) for the export of other wastes covered by the Convention.

All parties are to inform the other parties when they prohibit the import for disposal of any 'hazardous wastes and other wastes'. Export of wastes covered by a prohibition may not be permitted to any party that has notified their prohibition.[29] Even when import has not been prohibited, export may only be allowed if the country of import has consented in writing to the specific import.[30] In this way, the Convention can be said to be focused on making effective national import bans and ensuring that shipments for disposal of covered wastes occur only with the consent of the importing country.

Of obvious significance is what wastes are covered by the Convention's requirements, i.e., what counts as 'hazardous wastes and other wastes'. The definition builds on several annexes. At the core is Annex I, which contains a list of categories of waste that are deemed hazardous unless they do not possess any of the hazardous characteristics set out in another annex. By way of example, Annex I includes clinical wastes from medical care and wastes from different kinds of production, as well as wastes having as constituents, e.g., copper, zinc or lead compounds. In practice, the definitions have proven to be fraught with ambiguities and attempts have been made

[25] Langlet 2009, pp. 75–76.

[26] Puthucherril 2020, p. 200.

[27] Basel Convention, above n 3, Preambular paras 7 and 8.

[28] Ibid. Preambular para 6.

[29] Ibid. Article 4.1 (b)

[30] Ibid. Article 4.1 (c).

to make the system easier to apply.[31] Importantly, waste that is defined as hazardous by the domestic legislation of a party of export, import or transit is to be regarded as hazardous waste under the Convention in relation to shipments affecting such a party.[32]

Parties are also generally obliged to ensure that the transboundary movement of hazardous wastes is reduced to the minimum consistent with the environmentally sound and efficient management of such wastes.[33] More specifically, export may not be allowed if the country of export has reason to believe that the wastes in question will not be managed in an environmentally sound manner.[34] What constitutes ESM is subject to a general definition in the Convention, including 'taking all practicable steps' to ensure that the waste is managed in a manner which will protect human health and the environment, but has also been further elaborated in technical guidelines for various categories of wastes.[35]

A common criticism of the Convention, as adopted, was that the lack of a general ban on export of hazardous waste makes it hard to control the flows of waste and easy to avoid most of the Convention's requirements by labelling shipments as destined for recycling rather than disposal.[36] Among African and many Asian countries in particular, the Convention was perceived as failing to include sufficient measures to curb hazardous waste flows to developing states.[37]

This discontent led to both the elaboration of regional agreements and a further push for introducing a ban in the Basel Convention. Most significant among the regional initiatives was the elaboration and adoption in 1991 of the Bamako Convention,[38] which requires its parties to prohibit import of all hazardous waste, for any reason, into Africa from noncontracting parties. As only African states can become parties, it amounts to a ban on import from all states outside Africa.[39] However, much fewer African countries have become parties to the Bamako Convention than to the Basel Convention and major economies like Algeria, Egypt, Nigeria and South Africa are parties only to the latter.[40]

---

[31] Gudofsky 1998; Basel Convention Conference of Parties (1998), Amendment and adoption of annexes to the Convention, Decision No. IV/9.

[32] Basel Convention, above n 3, Article 1(1).

[33] Ibid. Article 4.2 (d).

[34] Ibid. Article 4.2 (e).

[35] *See* 'Adopted Technical Guidelines' at https://www.basel.int/Implementation/TechnicalMatters/DevelopmentofTechnicalGuidelines/TechnicalGuidelines/tabid/8025/Default.aspx. Accessed 3 October 2024.

[36] Lucier and Gareau 2016, p. 498.

[37] Kummer 1995, p. 44.

[38] Bamako Convention on the Ban of the Import into Africa and the Control of Transboundary Movement and Management of Hazardous Wastes within Africa, 1991, 2101 UNTS 177 (Bamako Convention).

[39] Langlet 2009, p. 88.

[40] *See* parties to the Bamako Convention at https://treaties.un.org/pages/showDetails.aspx?objid=080000028009385c. Accessed 5 October 2024.

Continued work for including an export ban in the Basel Convention first resulted in the Conference of the Parties (COP) requesting industrialized states to prohibit export of hazardous waste for disposal to developing states and later a decision prohibiting all transboundary movements of hazardous waste destined for final disposal from OECD to non-OECD states and also to phase out such export of hazardous waste destined for recycling or recovery.[41] However, these COP decisions did not create actual legal obligations. At the third COP meeting, in 1995, the decision was made to formally incorporate a ban into the Convention, the so-called ban amendment.[42] This time, reference was not made to export to non-OECD states, but to states not listed in a new Annex VII. This annex contains members of the OECD, the EU and Lichtenstein. In principle, further parties can be added to the annex, thereby making export to those countries permissible.

However, it took more than 20 years for the ban amendment to enter into force and disputes arose as to the correct interpretation of how many parties had to ratify the amendment for it to take effect.[43] Eventually, it entered into force in late 2019. As of late 2025, it has been ratified or accepted by—and thus applies in relation to—104 of the Convention's 191 parties, including China and the EU, but not Canada, India, Japan or Russia. The USA remains a non-party to the Convention and thus also to its amended version.

With the amendment, the Convention prohibits all transboundary movements from Annex VII parties to states not included in that annex, of hazardous wastes (but not 'other waste' such as wastes collected from households)[44] covered by the Convention and intended for final disposal as well as all transboundary movements from Annex VII parties to non-Annex VII states, of hazardous wastes as defined in the Convention (not by the domestic laws of parties) that are destined for reuse, recycling or recovery operations.[45]

Amendments have also been made to enhance the ability of the Convention to address problems associated with specific categories of wastes. In 2019, the COP decided to change some of the annexes to clarify the scope of plastic wastes presumed to be hazardous and hence subject to the PIC requirement.[46] Due to the ban amendment, plastic waste that is deemed to be hazardous may no longer be exported from Annex VII parties to non-Annex VII states. In 2022, amendments were made to some of the annexes with the purpose of enhancing the control of transboundary movements of e-waste and making all electronic and electrical waste subject to the PIC

[41] Basel Convention Conference of Parties (1992), Decision I/22, Decision No. I/22 and Basel Convention Conference of Parties (1994), Decision II/12, Decision No. II/12.

[42] Basel Convention Conference of Parties (1995), Amendment to the Basel Convention, Decision No. III/1.

[43] *See* Note by the Basel Convention Secretariat (2010), Addressing the interpretation of para 5 of Article 17 of the Convention, UNEP/CHW/OEWG/7/15.

[44] On the meaning of 'other wastes', *see* Basel Convention, above n 3, Article 1.2.

[45] Basel Convention, above n 3, Article 4A.

[46] Basel Convention Conference of Parties (2019), Amendments to Annexes II, VIII and IX to the Basel Convention, Decision No. 14/12. *See further* van der Marel 2022.

requirement.[47] As these amendments only concerned annexes, they did not require ratification or approval.

It should also be noted that parties may not permit shipments of hazardous or other wastes to or from non-parties, such as the USA.[48] However, such trade is permissible if conducted in accordance with agreements or arrangements which do not derogate from the ESM requirements of the Basel Convention and stipulate provisions no less environmentally sound.[49]

28.4 Chemicals Exports—the Rotterdam Regime

In the 1990s, pressure mounted for converting the London Guidelines into a legally binding instrument. In 1995, an international negotiating committee (INC) was set up to prepare such an instrument.[50] Although the G77 group of developing countries proposed that the instrument should ban the export of domestically prohibited chemicals, the mandate for the INC did not mention a ban, and large industrialized countries, including Australia, Canada and the USA, pushed for a narrow mandate.[51] Based on the work of the INC, the Rotterdam Convention was adopted at a diplomatic conference in 1998 and entered into force in 2004.[52] Like the Basel Convention, it provides for PIC as a prerequisite for export of certain hazardous substances. However, whereas the Basel PIC procedure applies to a broad range of wastes, including wastes collected from households, the PIC requirement of the Rotterdam Convention applies only to chemical substances listed in the Convention's Annex III.

As part of the listing process, parties are required to notify the Convention secretariat when they ban or severely restrict a chemical, or take a 'final regulatory action', in the Convention's terminology. In order to be eligible for listing, a substance must have been banned or severely restricted in at least two parties, located in at least two different so-called PIC regions.[53] Actual listing is done through a unanimous decision by the COP based on a recommendation by the Chemical Review Committee (CRC).[54] The CRC is tasked with assessing, inter alia, if the regulatory action taken by the parties leads to an actual reduction of risk or would be expected to result in a significant reduction of risk for human health or the environment. Several other

---

47 Basel Convention Conference of Parties (2021), Amendments to Annexes II, VIII and IX to the Basel Convention, Decision No. 15/18

48 Basel Convention, above n 3, Article 4.5.

49 Ibid. Article 11.

50 UNEP 1995.

51 Pallemaerts 2003, pp. 565–570.

52 Rotterdam Convention, above n 3.

53 The Convention defines seven PIC regions: Africa, Asia, Europe, Latin America and the Caribbean, Near East, North America and the Southwest Pacific.

54 Rotterdam Convention, above n 3, Article 7.

criteria must also be met, including that the regulatory action should have been taken as a consequence of a risk evaluation based on a review of scientific data in the context of the conditions prevailing in the party taking the action.[55] Many notifications of bans and restrictions, in particular by developing country parties, are not deemed to meet the requirements and can therefore not serve as a basis for recommending inclusion of the chemicals in question.[56] For so-called severely hazardous pesticide formulations,[57] a notification by only one party suffices, provided that it is a developing country or a country with an economy in transition and is experiencing specific problems caused by the pesticide.[58] In practice, not many developing countries use their right to propose such pesticides for inclusion.[59]

The fact that listing a substance requires a unanimous decision by the COP, in addition to a recommendation by the CRC, has made the process of adding new substances slow. When the Convention was adopted, Annex III already included 27 chemicals: 22 pesticides and five industrial chemicals. Twenty-six years later, that number had risen to 55 chemicals.[60] In many cases where the CRC has found relevant notifications to meet all criteria, the COP has nonetheless failed to reach consensus for adding the substance to Annex III. At COP 11, in 2022, the parties could only agree on the listing of one chemical out of the seven proposed for listing by the CRC.[61] At the same COP, an attempt was made to add a new annex containing chemicals recommended for inclusion in Annex III but for which consensus has not been reached. The proposal, which was hotly debated and then narrowly defeated in a vote, would make the PIC procedure apply for the listed chemicals among countries that become parties to the new Annex.[62] Continued decision-making only by consensus was supported by, e.g., Argentina, Brazil and China.

It is also noteworthy that a significant number of the chemicals listed in Annex III are also listed in Annex A of the Stockholm Convention on POPs, meaning that its 186 parties have committed to eliminating the production and use of these chemicals.[63] Although a listing under the Stockholm Convention can be subject to exceptions, it still means that a number of the chemicals to which PIC applies according to the Rotterdam Convention are neither to be manufactured nor used according to international law applicable to the vast majority of states.

---

[55] Ibid. Article 5.6 and Annex II.

[56] Jansen and Dubois 2014, p. 116; Langlet 2009, pp. 126–127.

[57] *See* Rotterdam Convention, above n 3, Article 2(d). Severely hazardous pesticide formulation is defined as 'a chemical formulated for pesticidal use that produces severe health or environmental effects observable within a short period of time after single or multiple exposure, under conditions of use'.

[58] Rotterdam Convention, above n 3, Article 6.

[59] Jansen and Dubois 2014, p. 116.

[60] Annex III Chemicals, https://www.pic.int/TheConvention/Chemicals/AnnexIIIChemicals. Accessed 13 December 2024.

[61] Allan et al. 2023, p. 13.

[62] Ibid, p. 20.

[63] Stockholm Convention, above n 4, Annex A, https://www.pops.int/TheConvention/ThePOPs/AllPOPs/tabid/2509/Default.aspx. Accessed 13 December 2024.

After a chemical has been listed, there are important exceptions to the PIC requirement. If a party fails to inform the secretariat whether it consents to future import, a one-year moratorium applies, after which export is allowed.[64] Even in situations where a party has notified the secretariat that it does not consent to import of a listed chemical, export of that substance is allowed if it 'is registered as a chemical in the importing Party' or even on the basis that 'evidence exists that it has previously been used in, or imported into, the importing Party' and that 'no regulatory action to prohibit its use has been taken'. The same applies if explicit consent to the import has been obtained directly by the exporter from a designated national authority of the importing party.[65]

In the fall of 2025, the Convention had 167 parties including essentially all industrialized countries except the USA.[66]

28.5 Discussion and Conclusions

The objective of the Rotterdam Convention is stated as the protection of human health and the environment from potential harm from certain hazardous chemicals as well as contributing to the environmentally sound use of those chemicals, to be done, inter alia, by providing for a national decision-making process.[67] The objective behind the Basel Convention is not quite as clearly stated, but its preamble, including in its first paragraph, refers repeatedly to the risks to human health and the environment caused by transboundary movement of hazardous waste. It is also obvious that neither convention would have existed had it not been for a desire to address the risks to humans and the environment posed by many wastes and chemicals. Still, the PIC mechanisms at the heart of both conventions are far from the most effective means of affording such protection. They are rather designed primarily to enhance the ability of prospective states of import to exercise sovereign control and make informed decisions.[68] The Basel Convention also explicitly recognizes the sovereign right to ban the entry or disposal of foreign wastes. The Rotterdam Convention has no similar recognition regarding the listed chemicals.

It is also striking how much weaker the PIC mechanism of the Rotterdam Convention is, in terms of both coverage and its many exceptions. Here, a market logic is much more prevalent. It is important to note that not only (industrialized) exporters but also (developing) importers of chemicals act to block the adding of substances to the PIC list. The fact that many private standard-setting bodies use the PIC list

[64] Rotterdam Convention, above n 3, Article 11.2.

[65] Ibid.

[66] Status of ratifications, https://www.pic.int/Countries/Statusofratification/PartiesandSignatories/tabid/1072/language/en-US/Default.aspx. Accessed 13 December 2024. On requirements under US law, *see* Langlet 2009, pp. 141–144.

[67] Rotterdam Convention, above n 3, Article 1.

[68] Langlet 2009, p. 191; Strohm 1993, p. 140.

as a basis for defining substances as inconsistent with their standards or labelling schemes seems to have made a listing tantamount to a ban in many respects, in particular for pesticides.[69] In this way, the PIC listing brings us back to the concerns of developing states at the time of the 1972 Stockholm Conference. While in principle helping developing states to exercise control and protect health and environment, the listing of a chemical can also prevent access to important markets for those who, for whatever reason, consider it necessary to use a listed substance, typically in an agricultural setting.

Furthermore, it must be noted that, in practice, a PIC procedure can be a quite ineffective way not only to protect the environment but also to make informed decisions and exercise control. There is no lack of indications of the inability or non-interest of many responsible authorities to make or communicate relevant decisions, or decisions of sufficient quality. Ironically, there are good reasons to believe that the more need a country has for assistance with upholding both environmental and health protection and sovereign control, the less likely it is that a PIC requirement will be an effective instrument.[70] There can be no doubt that strong influence by exporting states has resulted in a regime that allows practices harmful to weaker states.[71]

Under the Basel Convention, export is not to be permitted if the exporting state has reason to believe that the wastes will not be managed in an environmentally sound way. Giving the (industrialized) exporting country the final say, even if the (developing) importing country has given its consent, could easily be characterized as paternalistic.[72] However, to the extent that this is ever an actual problem—exporting states are hardly prone to preventing export when an importing state consents to it—it is reasonably dwarfed by the risks associated with shipments that are not managed in a sound way.

In the case of the Basel Convention, things have taken a significantly different turn through the Basel ban. Although it has been applied by the EU since the 1990s, it only became binding in 2019, and then only to the parties that had ratified the amendment. Still, it signifies an important change in international regulation of hazardous trade. Due to the ban, the Basel Convention has been described as the first global environmental convention with 'an explicit environmental justice component'.[73] The ban operates based on two groups of states, those in the EU, the OECD and Lichtenstein, and all the rest, thus reflecting a classic global north versus global south distinction. In practice, however, both wastes and chemicals are increasingly made or generated in low- and middle-income countries.[74]

Arguably more dramatic than the 'Basel ban' was the decision by China in 2017 to ban plastic waste imports. As China had imported over half of the exported plastic

---

[69] Kinniburgh et al. 2023, p. 440.

[70] Langlet 2009, p. 145; Kinniburgh et al. 2023, p. 439.

[71] Puthucherril 2020, p. 200.

[72] Strohm 1993, p. 144.

[73] Lucier and Gareau 2016, p. 494.

[74] UNEP 2019, p. 2.

waste worldwide, its decision shook up the entire system of plastic waste management, both making exporters find new destinations, such as Malaysia and Turkey, and forcing big generators of plastic waste to process more of it within their own country.[75]

While the idea of protecting developing countries from the dumping of hazardous substance still has merit, operationalizing it has become more complex when the same countries or regions can both struggle to uphold effective control and be significant exporters of hazardous substances. To some extent, the flow of hazardous substances from developed to developing states has been replaced by flows within the global south, typically controlled by local elites.[76] When hazardous waste or very problematic chemicals flow from richer and more technologically advanced regions to poorer regions that face greater challenges in managing the substances in an environmentally sound manner, that is obviously cause for vigilance and legal action. In the case of waste, there is now considerable acceptance of far-reaching restrictions on international shipments in a 'north to south' context. The old resistance by developing states towards environmental standards has, in the case of waste shipments, been replaced by overwhelming support for rather strict standards. However, many challenges remain, not least with mislabelling, smuggling and other illicit practices. Increasing shipments between developing countries call for partly new responses. The regulation of international shipments of chemicals is still fraught with significant conflicts that divide both industrialized and developing states and make effective protection seem more distant.

References

Allan J et al (2023) BRS COPs FINAL. Earth Negotiations Bulletin 15:304

Barsalou O, Picard MH (2018) International environmental law in an era of globalized waste. Chinese Journal of International Law, 17(3):887–906

Brighton C (2017) Unlikely Bedfellows: The Evolution of the Relationship between Environmental Protection and Development. International and Comparative Law Quarterly 66:209–235

Bull D (1982) A Growing Problem: Pesticides and the Third World Poor. Oxfam, Oxford

Chakraborty S (2023) Trade and Management of Waste. In Singh P et al (eds) Green Circular Economy. Springer International Publishing:145–166

Clapp J (2001) Toxic exports. Cornell University Press, Ithaca and London

Gudofsky J L (1998) Transboundary Shipments of Hazardous Waste for Recycling and Recovery Operations. Stanford Journal of International Law 34:219–285

Hippolyte AR (2012) Negative Environmental Sovereignty in the Third World: A Twail Analysis of ICSID's Disregard for Environmental Justice in the South. Available at SSRN 2124645

Jansen K, Dubois M (2014) Global Pesticide Governance by Disclosure: Prior Informed Consent and the Rotterdam Convention. In: Gupta A, Mason M (eds) Transparency in Global Environmental Governance: Critical Perspectives. MIT Press, Cambridge, MA

Kinniburgh F et al (2023) When Private Governance Impedes Multilateralism: The Case of International Pesticide Governance. Regulation & Governance 17(2):425–448

[75] Chakraborty 2023, p. 164.

[76] Puthucherril 2020, p. 200.

Kummer K (1995) International Management of Hazardous Wastes: The Basel Convention and Related Legal Rules. Clarendon Press, Oxford
Langlet D (2003) Prior Informed Consent for Hazardous Chemicals Trade—Implementation in EC Law. European Environmental Law Review 12(11):292–308
Langlet D (2009) Prior Informed Consent and Hazardous Trade: Regulating Trade in Hazardous Goods at the Intersection of Sovereignty, Free Trade and Environmental Protection, 2nd edn. Kluwer Law International, Alphen aan den Rijn
Lucier CA, Gareau BJ (2016) Obstacles to preserving precaution and equity in global hazardous waste regulation: an analysis of contested knowledge in the Basel Convention. International Environmental Agreements 16:493–508
OECD (1984) Recommendation of the Council concerning Information Exchange related to Export of Banned or Severely Restricted Chemicals, OECD/LEGAL/0210
OECD (1986) Decision-Recommendation of the Council on Exports of Hazardous Wastes from the OECD area, OECD/LEGAL/0224
OECD (1992) Decision of the Council on the Control of Transboundary Movements of Wastes Destined for Recovery Operations, C(92)39/FINAL
Pallemaerts M (1988) Developments in International Pesticide Regulation. Environmental Policy and Law 18(3):62–68
Pallemaerts M (2003) Toxics and Transnational law: International and European Regulation of Toxic Substances as Legal Symbolism. Hart Publishing, Oxford
Puthucherril TG (2020) Regulating toxic chemicals, pesticides, and hazardous wastes: A TWAIL approach to the BRS legal regime for a detoxified future. In: Techera EJ et al (eds) Routledge handbook of international environmental law, 2nd edn. Routledge
Schneiderman D (2022) Local resistance: at the margins of investment law. Globalizations 19:897–910
Strohm LA (1993) The Environmental Politics of the International Waste Trade. The Journal of Environment & Development 2(2):129–153
United Nations (1972) Report of the UN Conference on the Human Environment, UN Doc. A/CONF.48/14/Rev.1. https://docs.un.org/A/CONF.48/14/Rev.1. Accessed 15 February 2025
United Nations Environment Programme (1978) Decision of the Governing Council, Decision 6/3B. https://documents.un.org/doc/undoc/gen/n78/225/57/pdf/n7822557.pdf#page=133. Accessed 15 February 2025
United Nations Environment Programme (1984) Decision of the Governing Council, Decision 12/14. https://documents.un.org/doc/undoc/gen/n84/221/41/pdf/n8422141.pdf#page=47. Accessed 15 February 2025
United Nations Environment Programme (1987a) Decision of the Governing Council, Decision 14/27. https://documents.un.org/doc/undoc/gen/n87/232/50/pdf/n8723250.pdf#page=83. Accessed 15 February 2025
United Nations Environment Programme (1987b) Decision of the Governing Council, Decision 14/30. https://documents.un.org/doc/undoc/gen/n87/232/50/pdf/n8723250.pdf#page=87. Accessed 15 February 2025
United Nations Environment Programme (1989) Decision of the Governing Council, Decision 15/30. https://documents.un.org/doc/undoc/gen/n89/227/24/pdf/n8922724.pdf#page=160. Accessed 15 February 2025
United Nations Environment Programme (1995) Decision of the Governing Council, Decision 18/12. https://documents.un.org/doc/undoc/gen/n96/011/60/pdf/n9601160.pdf#page=60. Accessed 15 February 2025
United Nations Environment Programme, Global Chemicals Outlook II, UNEP, 2019
United Nations General Assembly (1971) Development and Environment, Resolution 2849 (XXVI)
United Nations General Assembly (1979) Resolution 4/173
United Nations General Assembly (1982) Protection against products harmful to health and the environment, UN Doc. A/RES/37/137. https://docs.un.org/en/A/RES/37/137. Accessed 15 February 2025

van der Marel ER (2022) Trading Plastic Waste in a Global Economy: Soundly Regulated by the Basel Convention? Journal of Environmental Law 34:3:477–497
Weir D, Schapiro M (1981) Circle of Poison: Pesticides and People in a Hungry World. Institute for food and development policy, Oakland

David Langlet is professor of environmental law at Uppsala University. He has previously held positions as, inter alia, professor of ocean governance law at the University of Gothenburg and research fellow at Oxford University and Christ Church. He is editor-in-chief of the Nordic Environmental Law Journal (NELJ). His research has touched on a wide range of topics in the fields of environmental law, international trade law, and law of the sea. His book 'Prior Informed Consent and Hazardous Trade: Regulating Trade in Hazardous Goods at the Intersection of Sovereignty, Free Trade and Environmental Protection' (Kluwer Law International, 2009) charts the development and compares the mechanisms of the international legal regimes concerning transboundary shipments of respectively waste, chemicals and genetically modified organisms.

Chapter 29
A New UN: The Regrettable Irrelevance of the Security Council

Inger Österdahl

Contents

Abstract The UN Security Council has long been unrepresentative of the international society of states. Simultaneously, the geopolitical balance of power is nearing a tipping point, in favor of states heretofore less well-represented in the Council. The Russian invasion of Ukraine may be the triggering factor, accentuated, possibly, by the recent war between Israel and Hamas in Gaza. This chapter will look at how the UN Security Council so far has, or has not, handled these two serious, possibly defining conflicts, how they might have been dealt with by the UN General Assembly instead or in parallel, and how this all fits into the larger picture of geopolitical change and its potential effects on the UN organization. What will the consequences be for the UN Security Council, the international law underpinning it, and ultimately the UN? The chapter ends with an attempt to picture what kind of new UN might be forming on the horizon.

Keywords UN Security Council · UN General Assembly · Uniting for Peace · Use of force · Aggression · Annexation · Protection of civilians · Geopolitics · BRICS

I. Österdahl (✉)
Uppsala University, Uppsala, Sweden
e-mail: inger.osterdahl@jur.uu.se

M. Klamberg et al. (eds.), *Reconstructing Power and Hegemony in Public International Law*, https://doi.org/10.1007/978-94-6265-743-4_29

29.1 Introduction

The global balance of power is shifting and this is likely ultimately to affect the UN (United Nations) organization. The membership of the UN looks very different today from when the organization was created in 1945. The UN Security Council, for instance, has long been unrepresentative of the global society of states, despite its membership having been expanded once from eleven to fifteen members due to the growing number of UN members. Also, the deep contradictions that characterized the Security Council during the Cold War have come back with renewed strength, making the UN organ with the primary responsibility for the maintenance of international peace and security seem largely unable to fulfil that responsibility, due to its inability to make decisions. The mightier the formerly less well-represented in the UN organization become, the sharper the contradictions will get, and the stronger the tensions between the original institutional design and the current realities of the UN system will be.

This chapter will look at how the UN Security Council so far has, or has not, handled two current armed conflicts, how they might have been handled by the UN General Assembly instead or in parallel, and how this fits into the larger picture of geopolitical change and its potential effects on the UN organization. The cases are the important, serious, possibly defining ones of Russia's invasion of Ukraine and the war between Israel and Hamas in Gaza. Perhaps the handling by the UN of the cases of Ukraine and Gaza is reflective of an ongoing development. Perhaps the handling of these cases may even accelerate a development under way both inside the UN with respect to the division of competence between the Security Council and the General Assembly, and in the world at large with respect to the shifting balance of power globally.

The contents of the resolutions adopted by the Security Council and the General Assembly are briefly explained in order to illustrate the seriousness of the issues involved, the grave consequences of the conflicts for the civilian population, and the challenges to fundamental norms of international law that these conflicts entail. Thus far, the addressees of the UN resolutions have ignored the resolutions and the outside world seems largely unable, or unwilling, to bring about a just peace. The chapter ends with an attempt to picture what kind of new UN might be forming on the horizon.

29.2 Almost All Quiet in the Security Council

29.2.1 Ukraine

Since the full-scale Russian invasion of Ukraine on 24 February 2022, at the time of writing, not a single resolution on this matter has been adopted by the Security Council, except one to call an emergency special session of the General Assembly.[1] Thus, there is not much emanating from the Security Council to comment on—except its silence. A draft resolution was put on the Security Council's table the day after the beginning of the invasion, deploring Russia's aggression and demanding among other things that Russia immediately cease its use of force against Ukraine and that Russia immediately, completely, and unconditionally withdraw all of its military forces from the territory of Ukraine, but this resolution was vetoed by Russia.[2] After the initial invasion by Russia of Ukraine in March 2014, a draft resolution was also put on the Security Council's table, and was vetoed by Russia.[3] In that resolution, the Security Council among other things reaffirmed its commitment to the sovereignty, independence unity, and territorial integrity of Ukraine within its internationally recognized borders, urged all parties to pursue immediately the peaceful resolution of the dispute through direct political dialogue, and called on Ukraine to continue to respect and uphold its obligations under international law and protect the rights of all persons in Ukraine, including the rights of persons belonging to minorities.[4]

29.2.2 Gaza

On the subject of the use of military force in Gaza subsequent to the terror attacks by Hamas in Israel on 7 October 2023, at the time of writing, the Security Council has adopted four resolutions in substance.[5] As there was already an emergency special session going on in the UN General Assembly regarding the situation in Palestine, convened in 1997, there was no need for the Security Council in 2023 to adopt a resolution transferring the matter, or parts of the matter, to the General Assembly to the extent the permanent Security Council members could not agree; parallel handling of the situation in Palestine by the General Assembly was already in existence.[6] In its first resolution adopted in November 2023, the Security Council among other things demanded that all parties comply with their obligations under international

[1] UNSC 2022a (votes: 11–1–3; henceforth referring to: states in favor—against—abstaining). Resolutions adopted up to July 2024 have been included in this chapter.

[2] UNSC 2022b, paras 2–4 (10–1–3).

[3] UNSC 2014 (13–1–1).

[4] Ibid. paras 1–3.

[5] UNSC 2023a (12–0–3); UNSC 2023b (13–0–2); UNSC 2024a (14–0–1); UNSC 2024b (14–0–1).

[6] UNGA 1997.

law, including international humanitarian law, notably with regard to the protection of civilians, especially children; called for urgent and extended humanitarian pauses and corridors throughout the Gaza Strip for a sufficient number of days to enable humanitarian access; called for the immediate and unconditional release of all hostages held by Hamas and other groups; and further called on all parties to refrain from depriving the civilian population in the Gaza Strip of basic services and humanitarian assistance indispensable to their survival.[7]

In its second resolution, adopted in December 2023, which was considerably longer, the Security Council among other things demanded that the parties to the conflict allow and facilitate the use of all available routes to and throughout the entire Gaza Strip, including border crossings, for the provision of humanitarian assistance; requested the Secretary-General, with the objective of expediting the delivery of humanitarian assistance to the civilian population in the Gaza Strip, to appoint a Senior Humanitarian and Reconstruction Coordinator; demanded the immediate and unconditional release of all hostages; and reaffirmed the obligations of all parties under international humanitarian law, including respecting and protecting civilians and taking constant care to spare civilian objects, including such objects critical to the delivery of essential services to the civilian population, and refraining from attacking, destroying, removing or rendering useless objects indispensable to the survival of the civilian population.[8]

In its third resolution, adopted in March 2024, which was briefer than the previous two, expressing in the preamble deep concern about the catastrophic humanitarian situation in the Gaza Strip, the Security Council in the operative paragraphs, among other things, demanded an immediate ceasefire for the month of Ramadan leading to a lasting sustainable ceasefire, demanded the immediate and unconditional release of all hostages, and emphasized the urgent need to expand the flow of humanitarian assistance and reinforce protection of civilians in the entire Gaza Strip.[9]

In its fourth resolution on the current war between Israel and Hamas in Gaza, the Security Council welcomed a new ceasefire proposal announced at the end of May 2024 and urged both parties to fully implement its terms without delay and without conditions.[10] The ceasefire proposal consisted of three different phases to be implemented consecutively.[11] The Security Council further rejected any attempt at demographic or territorial change in the Gaza Strip, including any actions that would reduce the territory of Gaza.[12] The Security Council reiterated its unwavering commitment to the vision of the two-state solution where two democratic states, Israel and Palestine, exist side by side in peace within secure and recognized borders,

---

[7] UNSC 2023a, paras 1–4.

[8] UNSC 2023b, paras 3, 4, 7, 10.

[9] UNSC 2024a, paras 1–2.

[10] UNSC 2024b, para 1.

[11] Ibid. para 2.

[12] Ibid. para 5.

consistent with international law and relevant UN resolutions, and in this regard stressed the importance of unifying the Gaza Strip with the West Bank under the Palestinian Authority.[13]

29.3 More Activity in the General Assembly

29.3.1 Ukraine

In total, more resolutions have been adopted by the General Assembly than by the Security Council with respect to the situations in Ukraine and Gaza, and the resolutions in the General Assembly have generally been more comprehensive. Within the framework of the eleventh and tenth Emergency Special Session, respectively, at the time of writing, the General Assembly has adopted six resolutions on Ukraine since 24 February 2022 and three resolutions on Gaza since 7 October 2023.[14]

After an unsuccessful attempt at having a substantial resolution adopted by the Security Council following the full-scale invasion of Ukraine, the Security Council as we saw adopted a resolution calling for an emergency special session of the General Assembly instead.[15] In its initial resolution, the General Assembly among other things reaffirmed its commitment to the sovereignty, independence, unity, and territorial integrity of Ukraine within its internationally recognized borders, extending to its territorial waters; deplored in the strongest terms the aggression by the Russian Federation against Ukraine in violation of Article 2(4) of the Charter; and demanded that the Russian Federation immediately cease its use of force against Ukraine and refrain from any further unlawful threat or use of force against any Member State.[16]

The General Assembly also demanded, among other things, that the Russian Federation immediately, completely, and unconditionally withdraw all of its military forces from the territory of Ukraine within its internationally recognized borders and immediately and unconditionally reverse the decision related to the status of certain areas of the Donetsk and Luhansk regions of Ukraine.[17] Then, further down the resolution, the General Assembly demanded that all parties, again among other things, allow safe and unhindered access to humanitarian assistance and to protect civilians, condemned all violations of international humanitarian law and violations

[13] Ibid. para 6; *cf. also* International Court of Justice, *Legal Consequences Arising from the Policies and Practices of Israel in the Occupied Palestinian Territory, Including East Jerusalem*, Advisory Opinion, 19 July 2024; UNGA 2024c (124–14–43).

[14] UNGA 2022a (141–5–35); UNGA 2022b (140–5–38); UNGA 2022c (93–24–58); UNGA 2022d (143–5–35); UNGA 2022e (94–14–73); UNGA 2023a (141–7–32); UNGA 2023b (121–14–44); UNGA 2023c (153–10–23); UNGA 2024a (143–9–25); *see also* UNGA 2023d (78–15–79); UNGA 2024b (99–9–60).

[15] UNSC 2022a (11–1–3).

[16] UNGA 2022a, paras 1–3.

[17] Ibid. paras 4, 6.

and abuses of human rights, called upon all parties to respect the relevant provisions of international humanitarian law and international human rights law, and, lastly, demanded that all parties fully comply with their obligations under international humanitarian law to spare the civilian population and civilian objects.[18]

In its second resolution on Ukraine, the General Assembly demanded full respect for and protection of all medical personnel and humanitarian personnel exclusively engaged in medical duties, their means of transport and equipment, as well as hospitals and other medical facilities, and stressed that the sieges of cities in Ukraine, in particular the city of Mariupol, further aggravated the humanitarian situation for the civilian population and hampered evacuation efforts, and therefore demanded that these sieges would end.[19]

Through its third resolution on Ukraine, the General Assembly suspended the rights of membership in the Human Rights Council of the Russian Federation.[20] In its fourth resolution, the General Assembly condemned the organization by the Russian Federation of "illegal so-called referendums" in regions within the internationally recognized borders of Ukraine and the attempted illegal annexation of the Donetsk, Kherson, Luhansk, and Zaporizhzhia regions of Ukraine, following the organization of the aforementioned referendums.[21] The General Assembly called upon all States, international organizations, and United Nations specialized agencies not to recognize any alteration by the Russian Federation of the status of any or all of the Donetsk, Kherson, Luhansk, or Zaporizhzhia regions of Ukraine, and demanded that the Russian Federation immediately and unconditionally reverse its decisions of 21 February and 29 September 2022 related to the status of certain areas of the Donetsk, Kherson, Luhansk, and Zaporizhzhia regions of Ukraine, as they were violations of the territorial integrity and sovereignty of Ukraine and inconsistent with the principles of the Charter of the United Nations, and that it immediately, completely and unconditionally withdraw all of its military forces from the territory of Ukraine within its internationally recognized borders.[22]

In its fifth resolution on Ukraine, the General Assembly recognized that the Russian Federation must be held to account for any violations of international law in or against Ukraine, including its aggression in violation of the Charter of the UN, as well as any violations of international humanitarian law and international human rights law, and that it must bear the legal consequences of all of its internationally wrongful acts, including making reparation for the injury, including any damage, caused by such acts.[23] Furthermore, the General Assembly recognized the need for the establishment, in cooperation with Ukraine, of an international mechanism for reparation for damage, loss, or injury. The General Assembly also recommended the creation by Member States, in cooperation with Ukraine, of an international register

[18] Ibid. paras 9, 11, 12.
[19] UNGA 2022b, paras 4, 8.
[20] UNGA 2022c, para 1.
[21] UNGA 2022d, para 2; *cf. also* Brunk and Hakimi 2024.
[22] Ibid. paras 4–5.
[23] UNGA 2022e, para 2.

of damage caused by internationally wrongful acts of the Russian Federation in or against Ukraine, as well as to promote and coordinate evidence-gathering.[24]

In its sixth resolution on Ukraine, adopted on 23 February 2023, the General Assembly among other things underscored the need to reach, as soon as possible, a comprehensive, just, and lasting peace in Ukraine in line with the principles of the UN Charter.[25] Further down the resolution, the General Assembly embarked on the topic of prisoners of war and demanded that the treatment by the parties to the conflict of all prisoners of war be in accordance with the Geneva Convention III and Additional Protocol I to the Geneva Conventions, and called for the complete exchange of prisoners of war, the release of all unlawfully detained persons, and the return of all internees and of civilians forcibly transferred and deported, including children.[26] In addition to its statement on the accountability of the Russian Federation for any violations of international law in or against Ukraine in its fifth resolution, the General Assembly in its sixth resolution on Ukraine also emphasized the need to ensure individual criminal accountability for the most serious crimes under international law committed on the territory of Ukraine through appropriate, fair, and independent investigations and prosecutions at the national or international level, and to ensure justice for all victims and the prevention of future crimes.[27]

29.3.2 Gaza

The tenth Emergency Special Session of the UN General Assembly, originally convened in 1997 following a request from Qatar, was reconvened when the war between Israel and Hamas broke out in Gaza after the terror attacks by Hamas in Israel on 7 October 2023.[28] Three resolutions on the situation in Gaza have been adopted so far by the General Assembly. Two resolutions focus on the humanitarian situation in Gaza and the protection of civilians whereas the third deals with the membership of the State of Palestine in the UN.[29]

In its first resolution on the situation in Gaza, which is the most comprehensive of the three, the General Assembly called for an immediate, durable, and sustained humanitarian truce leading to a cessation of hostilities.[30] Then, the General Assembly demanded that all parties immediately and fully comply with their obligations under international law, including international humanitarian law and international human rights law, particularly in regard to the protection of civilians and civilian objects, as well as the protection of humanitarian personnel, persons *hors de combat*, and

[24] Ibid. paras 3–4.

[25] UNGA 2023a, para 1.

[26] Ibid. para 6.

[27] Ibid. para 9.

[28] UNGA 2023e.

[29] UNGA 2023b (121–14–44); UNGA 2023c (153–10–23); UNGA 2024a (143–9–25).

[30] UNGA 2023b, para 1.

humanitarian facilities and assets, and to enable and facilitate humanitarian access for essential supplies and services to reach all civilians in need in the Gaza Strip.[31] The General Assembly also demanded the immediate, continuous, sufficient, and unhindered provision of essential goods and services to civilians throughout the Gaza Strip, stressing the imperative, under international humanitarian law, of ensuring that civilians are not deprived of objects indispensable to their survival.[32] Further, the General Assembly, among other things, encouraged the establishment of humanitarian corridors and other initiatives to facilitate the delivery of humanitarian aid to civilians.[33]

Next, the General Assembly also called for the rescinding of the order by Israel for Palestinian civilians and UN staff, as well as humanitarian and medical workers, to evacuate all areas in the Gaza Strip north of the Wadi Gaza and relocate to southern Gaza.[34] The General Assembly, moreover, firmly rejected any attempts at forced transfer of the Palestinian civilian population.[35] The General Assembly ended its first resolution on the situation in Gaza by calling upon all parties to exercise maximum restraint and upon all those with influence on them to work towards this objective, and by reaffirming that a just and lasting solution to the Israeli-Palestinian conflict can only be achieved by peaceful means, based on the relevant UN resolutions and in accordance with international law, and on the basis of the two-state solution.[36] The second resolution adopted by the General Assembly on the situation in Gaza was relatively short.[37] In this resolution, the General Assembly demanded an immediate humanitarian ceasefire.[38]

In its third resolution related to the situation in Gaza, the General Assembly did something unique.[39] The General Assembly decided, "on an exceptional basis and without setting a precedent," to adopt the modalities set out in the annex to the resolution for the participation of the State of Palestine in the sessions and work of the General Assembly and the international conferences convened under the auspices of the Assembly or other organs of the UN, as well as in UN conferences.[40] Thus, the General Assembly, for all practical purposes, made the State of Palestine a member of the UN General Assembly. The State of Palestine does not, its capacity as an observer state—it is pointed out in the annex—have the right to vote in the General Assembly or to put forward its candidature to UN organs.[41]

[31] Ibid. para 2.
[32] Ibid. para 3.
[33] Ibid. para 4.
[34] Ibid. para 5.
[35] Ibid. para 6.
[36] Ibid. paras 12–13.
[37] UNGA 2023c.
[38] Ibid. para 1.
[39] UNGA 2024a.
[40] Ibid. para 3; *see also* UNSC 2024c (12–1–2).
[41] UNGA 2024a, Annex item (l).

29.4 Changing Places

The Security Council has not been able to effectively handle either the war between Russia and Ukraine or the war between Israel and Hamas in Gaza. It is not the first time that the Security Council finds itself in a deadlock after the fall of the Berlin Wall and the end of the Cold War era in 1989. The Security Council was also incapable of dealing with the war in Syria beginning in 2011.[42] In the case of Gaza, the Security Council has tried to shoulder its primary responsibility for the maintenance of international peace and security under the UN Charter, but ineffectually—illustrated not least by its resolution in June 2024 on a peace plan; heeded, it would seem, by no one.[43] The feebleness of the Security Council in the cases of Ukraine and Gaza is all too obvious.

The increasing irrelevance of the Security Council is illustrated among other things by the fact that more matters relating to the maintenance of international peace and security, that rightly should have been dealt with by the Security Council under the UN Charter, are being dealt with by the General Assembly instead.[44] From the point of view of the UN organization, it is good that the matters can still be kept and dealt with within the UN organization at all. It is also good that the General Assembly does what it can, that it is inventive, in the case of Ukraine and Gaza and in other cases, given that the alternative under the reigning circumstances would be no action or almost none on the part of the UN.

From the formal legal point of view, the General Assembly disposes of much weaker instruments of action than the Security Council does. The General Assembly may merely discuss and make recommendations under the UN Charter, except for matters internal to the organization including its budget, whereas the Security Council may make legally binding decisions. Still, the activities of the General Assembly may play an important role in several respects, including from the point of view of international law. For instance, the positions put forward in the discussions and resolutions of the Assembly can contribute to the creation of customary law as a manifestation of both the *opinio juris* of the Member States and state practice. The General Assembly could also, hypothetically, be considered to be able to legitimize certain actions on behalf of the UN that would otherwise be illegal if carried out by the states unilaterally, for instance the international use of armed force.[45] If a two-thirds majority of the General Assembly members could make recommendations whereby the otherwise illegal actions of states would become legal due to being undertaken on behalf of the UN organization, the General Assembly could become an important actor also from the more formal legal point of view.

---

[42] UNSC 2012a (13–2–0); *see also* the futile UNSC 2012b (15–0–0).

[43] UNSC 2024b.

[44] *See* UNGA 1950, para 1.

[45] *Cf.* Carswell 2014, pp. 472–476, on the legitimizing powers of the UNGA under UNGA 1950, adding the necessary condition that the matter has been referred to the UNGA by the Security Council, still through a procedural vote; *cf. also*, *mutatis mutandis*, Hashimi and Cogan 2016; Hashimi 2018; Österdahl 2019.

The political pressure created by large majorities in the General Assembly might also be significant. In today's world, with its sharp divisions between different blocs of states, the voting figures in the General Assembly might be indicative of the relative power of the different blocs, both generally and on specific issues. The West led by the US constitutes one bloc, China and Russia constitutes another, and then there is the Global South, siding with either the West or with China and Russia depending on the issue, but mostly tending to side with China and Russia.[46] The group of countries called the BRICS has expanded its membership with six countries in 2024–25 and could develop into an important organization, perhaps competing with the UN for power, or at least consolidating the collective power of China and Russia together with the Global South, which would make it felt also in the UN General Assembly.[47] What bloc the Global South will side with in the UN General Assembly is and will remain of great political, and ultimately legal, significance.

In comparison with the Security Council, thus, the General Assembly would seem to be increasing in relative importance, whereas the importance of the Security Council would seem to decreasing. Ways of reforming and thereby strengthening the Security Council and making it more up to date, given the current membership composition of the UN compared with that in the early years, have been discussed for some time.[48] It will be interesting to see if the BRICS states and other states in the Global South will insist on membership in the Security Council. It will also be interesting to see how the veto power develops—whether any new member of the Security Council will ever be granted the right of veto or whether any old member of the Security Council will ever voluntarily formally renounce its right of veto.[49]

It would seem less unlikely that the membership of the Security Council would be expanded than that any new member would be granted the right of veto. That any current member would voluntarily formally renounce its right of veto seems almost unthinkable. Whether the Security Council would be strengthened and become a more relevant institution in the UN collective security system through a reform that lets in more members from the Global South, with or without veto power, remains an open question. All things considered, perhaps the BRICS countries will not insist on an expanded membership in the Security Council at all but will regard either Russia and China or the US depending on the issue, but most likely Russia and China, as representing their interests in the Security Council.

---

[46] *Cf.* The Ministry of Foreign Affairs of the Russian Federation (2016) The Declaration of the Russian Federation and the People's Republic of China on the Promotion of International Law. https://archive.mid.ru/en/foreign_policy/news/-/asset_publisher/cKNonkJE02Bw/content/id/2331698. Accessed 28 July 2024. *Cf. also* Österdahl 2015.

[47] Egypt, Ethiopia, Indonesia, Iran, Saudi Arabia, United Arab Emirates; *cf.* Hathaway and Patrick 2024, pp. 15–17.

[48] UNGA 2005, para 153.

[49] *Cf.* UNGA 2022f.

29.5 Conclusion

If the trend continues that the Security Council is deadlocked due to renewed and reinforced geopolitical contradictions, and thereby becomes irrelevant for the maintenance of international peace and security, despite its statutory primary responsibility, the question arises what the future could look like for the UN collective security system more broadly.

The UN General Assembly, with its mere recommendatory powers, will be where the more serious, and thus divisive, issues relating to international peace and security are handled. Regional organizations are becoming more numerous and are likely to become more important, including in the area of peace and security. As the UN Security Council's relevance decreases, the regional organizations might also become more independent as actors in the area of international peace and security. Currently, they have a strictly circumscribed role under the UN Charter where the authorization of the Security Council is necessary before any regional organizations may take enforcement action, for instance. For lack of a functioning Security Council, the UN General Assembly with its relatively limited powers is likely to become the UN counterpart to the regional organizations.

The much-discussed prohibition on the use of force in Article 2(4) of the UN Charter will suffer further if the Security Council and the remaining UN collective security system loses its grip on the Member States. The self-inflicted irrelevance of the Security Council—at least in principle exclusively entitled to use force internationally on behalf of the member states—means the loss of the executive power within the UN collective security system. If no credible executive power exists within the UN system, chances are small that the Member States will renounce their right to use force for the benefit of this de facto non-existent organ. If it is obvious that no Security Council in the UN organization will claim the exclusive right to use force, the states themselves will. If the states have conferred on the UN Security Council a monopoly on the use of force and there is no longer even a theoretical chance that the Security Council will ever be able to agree, even the legal argument that the use of force is prohibited will, unfortunately, be hard to sustain.

These are developments that have been going on for some time. What effects the cases of Ukraine and Gaza will have is as yet unclear, but it is easy to see how they would fit into the picture of a changing geopolitical reality and how they could reinforce and speed up the ongoing shift in the global balance of power and the ensuing consequences for the UN. However, developments may turn out completely differently from what might have been expected. Climate change is adding another large measure of non-foreseeability and uncontrollability to whatever may remain of UN collective security. In any case—and this deserves to be emphasized—a new United Nations is better than no United Nations and perhaps even necessary: nothing is predetermined.

29.6 Post Scriptum

In early 2025 the Security Council adopted a resolution on Ukraine (2774(2025) (10-0-5)), in which the Security Council, in the only operative paragraph, "*[i]mplores]* a swift end to the conflict and further urges a lasting peace between Ukraine and the Russian Federation".

In late 2025 the Security Council in a resolution endorsed President Donald J. Trump's Comprehensive Plan to End the Gaza Conflict (annex 1 to the resolution) (2803(2025) (13-0-2)), and calls on all parties to implement the Comprehensive Plan it in its entirety, including the maintenance of the ceasefire, in good faith and without delay (op. para. 1). The following points in the resolution are particularly noteworthy, among others: the Board of Peace (BoP) established under the Comprehensive Plan is welcomed as a transitional administration with international legal personality that will set the framework, and coordinate funding for, the redevelopment of Gaza pursuant to the Comprehensive Plan (op. para. 2)—"headed and chaired by President Donald J. Trump" and "including Former Prime Minister Tony Blair" (annex 1 para. 9); Member States participating in the BoP and the BoP are authorized to carry out a broad mandate, including the implementation of a transitional governance administration, the reconstruction of Gaza and of economic recovery programs, the coordination and supporting of delivery of public services and administration; and any such additional tasks as may be necessary to support and implement the Comprehensive Plan (op. para. 4); and, finally, Member States working with the BoP and the BoP are authorized to establish a temporary International Stabilization Force (ISF) in Gaza to deploy under unified command acceptable to the BoP, and to use all necessary measures to carry out its mandate, including to help secure border areas, stabilize the security environment in Gaza, protect civilians, including humanitarian operations, train and provide support to the vetted Palestinian police force, and undertake such additional tasks as may be necessary in accordance with the Comprehensive Plan (op. para. 7). As the ISF establishes control and stability, the resolution says, the Israeli Defense Forces (IDF) will withdraw from the Gaza strip based on standards, milestones and timeframes linked to demilitarization that will be agreed between the IDF, ISF, the guarantors, and the United States, save for a security perimeter presence that will remain until Gaza is properly secure from any resurgent terror threat (op. para. 7).

References

Brunk I, Hakimi M (2024) The Prohibition of Annexations and The Foundations of Modern International Law. The American Journal of International Law 118:417–467

Carswell A J (2013) Unblocking the UN Security Council: The Uniting for Peace Resolution. Journal of Conflict & Security Law 18:453–480

Hakimi M, Cogan J K (2016) The Two Codes on the Use of Force. The European Journal of International Law 27:257–291

Hakimi M (2018) The Jus ad Bellum's Regulatory Form. The American Journal of International Law 112:151–190
Hathaway O A, Patrick S (2024) Can the UN Security Council Still Help Keep the Peace? Reassessing its Role, Relevance, and Potential for Reform. https://carnegieendowment.org/posts/2024/07/can-un-security-council-still-help-keep-the-peace?lang=en. Accessed 28 July 2024
Österdahl I (2015) Collective Security in a Changing Geopolitical Landscape. In: Wallensteen P, Bjurner A (eds) Regional Organizations and Peacemaking—Challengers to the UN? Routledge, London and New York, pp. 54–71
Österdahl I (2019) The Gentle Legitimiser of the Action of Others. Zeitschrift für Ausländisches Öffentliches Recht und Völkerrecht 79:699–701
UN Security Council (2025a) Resolution 2774, UN Doc. S/RES/2774
UN Security Council (2025b) Resolution 2803, UN Doc. S/RES/2803
UN Security Council (2024a) Resolution 2728, UN Doc. S/RES/2728
UN Security Council (2024b) Resolution 2735, UN Doc. S/RES/2735
UN Security Council (2024c) Draft resolution, UN Doc. S/2024/312
UN Security Council (2023a) Resolution 2712, UN Doc. S/RES/2712
UN Security Council (2023b) Resolution 2720, UN Doc. S/RES/2720
UN Security Council (2022a) Resolution 2623, UN Doc. S/RES/2623
UN Security Council (2022b) Draft resolution, UN Doc. S/2022/155
UN Security Council (2014) Draft resolution, UN Doc. S/2014/189
UN Security Council (2012a) Draft resolution, UN Doc. S/2012/77
UN Security Council (2012b) Resolution 2042, UN Doc. S/RES/2042
UN General Assembly (1950) Uniting for peace, Resolution 377 (V), A/RES/377 (V)
UN General Assembly (1997) Convening of the session Note by the Secretary-General, Resolution ES-10/1, A/ES-10/1
UN General Assembly (2005) Resolution adopted by the General Assembly on 16 September 2005, Resolution 60/1, A/RES/60/1
UN General Assembly (2022a) Resolution adopted by the General Assembly on 2 March 2022, Resolution ES-11/1, A/RES/ES-11/1
UN General Assembly (2022b) Resolution adopted by the General Assembly on 24 March 2022, Resolution ES-11/2, A/RES/ES-11/2
UN General Assembly (2022c) Resolution adopted by the General Assembly on 7 April 2022, Resolution ES-11/3, A/RES/ES-11/3
UN General Assembly (2022d) Resolution adopted by the General Assembly on 12 October 2022, Resolution ES-11/4, A/RES/ES-11/4
UN General Assembly (2022e) Resolution adopted by the General Assembly on 15 November 2022, Resolution ES-11/5, A/RES/ES-11/5
UN General Assembly (2022f) Resolution adopted by the General Assembly on 26 April 2022, Resolution 76/262, A/RES/76/262
UN General Assembly (2023a) Resolution adopted by the General Assembly on 23 February 2023, Resolution ES-11/6, A/RES/ES-11/6
UN General Assembly (2023b) Resolution adopted by the General Assembly on 27 October 2023, Resolution ES-10/21, A/RES/ES-10/21
UN General Assembly (2023c) Resolution adopted by the General Assembly on 12 December 2023, Resolution ES-10/22, A/RES/ES-10/22
UN General Assembly (2023d) Resolution adopted by the General Assembly on 19 December 2023, Resolution 78/221, A/RES/78/221
UN General Assembly (2023e) Letter dated 19 October from the Permanent Representatives of Jordan and Mauretania to the United Nations addressed to the President of the General Assembly, A/ES-10/958
UN General Assembly (2024a) Resolution adopted by the General Assembly on 10 May 2024, Resolution ES-10/23, A/RES/ES-10/23

UN General Assembly (2024b) Resolution adopted by the General Assembly on 11 July 2024, Resolution 78/316, A/RES/78/316
UN General Assembly (2024c) Resolution adopted by the General Assembly on 18 September 2024, Resolution ES-10/24, A/RES/ES-10/24

Inger Österdahl is Professor of Public International Law at Uppsala University in Sweden. Inger Österdahl is a Professor of Public International Law at the Law Faculty of the University of Uppsala. Her research interests lie in public international law, focusing on the law of international organizations, the law on the use of force, and the relationship between international law and domestic law. Her research interests also lie in Swedish constitutional law, focusing on the law on foreign relations as well as on the law on freedom of information and expression. Prior to joining the Uppsala Law Faculty in 1995, she completed her LL.D. at the University of Uppsala, and LL.M. at the University of Lund. Dr. Österdahl has been a Visiting Scholar at the University of Minnesota Law School and a postdoctoral researcher at the Paris-Panthéon-Assas University.

Chapter 30
The Aggression Against Ukraine—What are the Lessons for a Future World Order?

Hans Corell

Contents

Abstract The chapter describes how the UN Charter prohibits the threat or use of force against the territorial integrity or political independence of any state and the role that the Security Council has in this context. It explains how the General Assembly in the context of the aggression against Ukraine has met in an emergency session, adopted resolutions, condemned the invasion of Ukraine, deplored Russia's aggression, and demanded that Russia immediately cease its use of force against Ukraine and withdraw all of its military forces from the territory of Ukraine. The resolutions were adopted by a great majority of the UN Members, which is crucial

H. Corell (✉)
Stockholm, Sweden
e-mail: hans.corell@havc.se

M. Klamberg et al. (eds.), *Reconstructing Power and Hegemony in Public International Law*, https://doi.org/10.1007/978-94-6265-743-4_30

as a permanent member of the Security Council is committing the violations of the Charter. The chapter also analyses the case referred to the International Court of Justice by Ukraine, the three cases pending before the International Criminal Court and the independent Commission of Inquiry established by the UN Human Rights Council in March 2022. The major challenge with the ICC arrest warrants is to apprehend the suspects. Although the proposal for a special court for the crime of aggression against Ukraine seeks to address the most serious violations committed, it also raises questions about selectivity in international justice. The aggression against Ukraine will have significant effects for the future world order. It is imperative that the international community acts when a permanent member of the UN Security Council is committing flagrant violations of the most basic rules of the Charter of the United Nations.

Keywords Aggression · Crimes against humanity · Criminal responsibility · Damage · Emergency · Genocide · Human rights · Humanitarian · Occupy · Peace · Sanctions · Security · Sovereignty · Veto · War crimes

30.1 The Charter of the United Nations

The Charter of the United Nations was negotiated by a generation that had experienced two world wars.[1] This led to the establishment of the United Nations in 1945 in order, as it is said in the preamble to the Charter, "to save succeeding generations from the scourge of war, which twice during our lifetime has brought untold sorrow to mankind". In the Charter, we then find the following: "to reaffirm our faith in fundamental human rights, in the dignity and worth of the human person, in the equal rights for men and women and for nations large and small." It goes without saying that we must respect this heritage.

The UN has six principal organs. One of these organs is the Security Council. The Council consists of fifteen members, including the following five permanent members: China, France, the Russian Federation, the United Kingdom, and the United States of America. In Article 24 of the Charter, the members of the United Nations confer on the Security Council primary responsibility for the maintenance of international peace and security and agree that, in carrying out its duties under this responsibility, the Security Council acts on their behalf.

Russia's attack on Ukraine on 24 February 2022 was a flagrant violation of the UN Charter by a permanent member of the UN Security Council. Here, particular reference should be made to the basic provision in Article 2, para 4, as well as to Articles 24, 25, and 39 of the Charter. They read:

[1] Charter of the United Nations, signed 26 June 1945, 1 UNTS XVI, entered into force 24 October 1945.

Article 2, para 4

> All Members shall refrain in their international relations from the threat or use of force against the territorial integrity or political independence of any state, or in any other manner inconsistent with the Purposes of the United Nations.

Article 24

1. In order to ensure prompt and effective action by the United Nations, its Members confer on the Security Council primary responsibility for the maintenance of international peace and security, and agree that in carrying out its duties under this responsibility the Security Council acts on their behalf.
2. In discharging these duties the Security Council shall act in accordance with the Purposes and Principles of the United Nations. The specific powers granted to the Security Council for the discharge of these duties are laid down in Chapters VI, VII, VIII, and XII.
3. The Security Council shall submit annual and, when necessary, special reports to the General Assembly for its consideration.

Article 25

> The Members of the United Nations agree to accept and carry out the decisions of the Security Council in accordance with the present Charter.

Article 39

> The Security Council shall determine the existence of any threat to the peace, breach of the peace, or act of aggression and shall make recommendations, or decide what measures shall be taken in accordance with Articles 41 and 42, to maintain or restore international peace and security.

What we are now seeing in Ukraine are obvious violations of these rules. In particular, it is a clear crime of aggression on the part of Russia. We also see crimes against humanity, war crimes and probably also genocide.

The question is then: What has been done? Here, I want to focus on the ensuing measures from an international law perspective. In this context, it is important to bear in mind that one of the purposes of the United Nations is to develop friendly relations among nations based on respect for the principle of equal rights and self-determination of peoples, and to take other appropriate measures to strengthen universal peace (UN Charter Article 1, para 2).

30.2 The UN General Assembly has Acted

30.2.1 Uniting for Peace

The UN General Assembly has become involved in the issue through a very unusual procedure called "Uniting for Peace". The system was introduced by a resolution of the General Assembly in 1950 and means that if the Security Council is prevented from intervening in a very serious situation due to the right of veto, the Security Council can, through a procedural resolution where the veto does not apply, request that the General Assembly be convened for an emergency special session within twenty-four hours.[2]

The most important provision of the resolution reads:

> Resolves that if the Security Council, because of lack of unanimity of the permanent members, fails to exercise its primary responsibility for the maintenance of international peace and security in any case where there appears to be a threat to the peace, breach of the peace, or act of aggression, the General Assembly shall consider the matter immediately with a view to making appropriate recommendations to Members for collective measures, including in the case of a breach of the peace or act of aggression the use of armed force when necessary, to maintain or restore international peace and security. If not in session at the time, the General Assembly may meet in emergency special session within twenty-four hours of the request therefor. Such emergency special session shall be called if requested by the Security Council on the vote of any seven members, or by a majority of the Members of the United Nations.

30.2.2 The Resolution of 2 March 2022

On 27 February 2022, the Security Council adopted a resolution that the General Assembly would hold an emergency special session.[3]

The UN General Assembly acted immediately. The emergency special session was held the next day, and on 2 March 2022, the Assembly adopted a resolution entitled "Aggression against Ukraine".[4]

The resolution condemns the invasion of Ukraine. In the resolution, the General Assembly reaffirms, among other things, its commitment to the sovereignty, independence, unity, and territorial integrity of Ukraine within its internationally recognized borders, extending to its territorial waters. The General Assembly strongly deplores Russia's aggression against Ukraine in violation of Article 2, para 4 of the UN Charter, and demands that Russia immediately cease its use of force against Ukraine and refrain from any further unlawful threat or use of force against any Member State. The General Assembly further demands that Russia immediately, completely, and unconditionally withdraw all of its military forces from within the internationally recognized borders of Ukraine.

The General Assembly also deplores the involvement of Belarus in this unlawful use of force against Ukraine and calls upon the country to abide by its international obligations.

In the vote, 141 states voted for the resolution, five against it, and 35 abstained. The five states that voted against the resolution were Russia, Belarus, Syria, North Korea, and Eritrea. The Assembly's resolutions are not legally binding but can reflect and influence world opinion.

---

[2] UNGA 1950.

[3] UNSC 2022.

[4] UNGA 2022a.

30.2.3 The Resolution of 24 March 2022

On 21 March 2022, the General Assembly resumed the emergency special session, and, on 24 March 2022, it adopted a detailed resolution entitled "Humanitarian consequences of the aggression against Ukraine".[5]

In this resolution, the General Assembly deplores the dire humanitarian consequences of the hostility by Russia in Ukraine, including the besiegement of and shelling and airstrikes in densely populated cities of Ukraine, in particular Mariupol, as well as attacks on civilians, schools and other educational institutions, water and sanitation systems, and medical facilities. Furthermore, it expresses great concern at the deteriorating humanitarian situation in and around Ukraine, in particular at the large number of civilian casualties, including women and children, and the increasing number of internally displaced persons and refugees in need of humanitarian assistance.

The General Assembly also expresses concern that the conflict is leading to increased food insecurity globally, in particular in the least developed countries, as Ukraine and the region are one of the world's most important areas for grain and other agricultural exports.

In fourteen operational clauses, the General Assembly then describes strict requirements for various measures that Russia must implement.

In the vote, 140 states voted for the resolution, five against it, and 38 abstained. The five states that voted against the resolution were the same that voted against the resolution on 2 March 2022.

30.2.4 The Resolution of 7 April 2022

On 7 April 2022, the General Assembly resumed the emergency special session and on the same day adopted a resolution entitled "Suspension of the rights of membership of the Russian Federation in the Human Rights Council".[6] In the resolution, the General Assembly decided to suspend the rights of membership in the Human Rights Council of the Russian Federation.

In the vote, 93 states voted for the resolution, 24 against it, and 50 abstained.

30.2.5 The Resolution of 12 October 2022

On 30 September 2022, President Putin announced that Russia had annexed the four Ukrainian regions of Luhansk, Donetsk, Kherson, and Zaporizhzhia. The decision was based on mock polls which were said to show an overwhelming majority in favor

[5] UNGA 2022b.

[6] UNGA 2022c.

of Russian accession. Parts of these areas are today occupied by Russia in violation of international law. As the annexation as such is against international law, several Western powers and organizations have said that they will not recognize the areas as Russian.

On 11 October 2022, the General Assembly resumed the emergency special session, and, on 12 October 2022, it adopted a resolution entitled "Territorial integrity of Ukraine: defending the principles of the Charter of the United Nations".[7]

In the resolution, the General Assembly condemns the organization by Russia of illegal so-called referendums in regions within the internationally recognized borders of Ukraine and the attempted illegal annexation of the Donetsk, Kherson, Luhansk, and Zaporizhzhia regions of Ukraine, following the organization of the referendums mentioned. It further declares that these unlawful actions by Russia are not valid under international law and that they do not constitute a basis for any change in the status of the regions in Ukraine. The General Assembly demands that Russia immediately, completely, and unconditionally withdraw all its military forces from within the internationally recognized borders of Ukraine.

In the vote, 143 states voted for the resolution. Russia, Belarus, Syria, North Korea, and Nicaragua voted against the resolution, and 35 states abstained.

30.2.6 The Resolution of 14 November 2022

On 14 November 2022, the General Assembly resumed the emergency special session and on the same day adopted a resolution entitled "Furtherance of remedy and reparation for aggression against Ukraine".[8] In the resolution, the General Assembly recalls its resolution 60/147 of 16 December 2005, where the annex contains the basic principles and guidelines on the right to a remedy and reparation for victims of gross violations of international human rights law and serious violations of international humanitarian law.

In the resolution, the General Assembly reaffirms its commitment to the sovereignty, independence, unity, and territorial integrity of Ukraine and its demand that the Russian Federation immediately cease its use of force against Ukraine and immediately, completely fully, and unconditionally withdraw all of its military forces from the territory of Ukraine.

The General Assembly further recognizes that the Russian Federation must be held to account for any violations of international law in or against Ukraine, including its aggression in violation of the UN Charter, as well as any violations of international humanitarian law and international human rights law, and that it must bear the legal consequences of all of its internationally wrongful acts, including making reparations for the injury and any damage caused by such acts. The General Assembly also focuses on compensation for damage and the need for a register of such damage.

---

[7] UNGA 2022d.

[8] UNGA 2022e.

In the vote, 94 states voted for the resolution, 14 states voted against it, and 73 states abstained.

30.2.7 The Resolution of 23 February 2023

On 22 February 2023, the General Assembly resumed the emergency special session and on 23 February 2023, it adopted a detailed resolution entitled "Principles of the Charter of the United Nations underlying a comprehensive, just and lasting peace in Ukraine".[9]

In the resolution, the General Assembly—recalling its relevant resolutions adopted at its eleventh emergency special session—underscores the need to reach, as soon as possible, a comprehensive, just, and lasting peace in Ukraine in line with the principles of the Charter of the United Nations and welcomes and expresses strong support for the efforts of the Secretary-General and Member States to promote such peace, consistent with the Charter, including the principles of sovereign equality and territorial integrity of States.

In the resolution, the General Assembly further reiterates its demand that the Russian Federation immediately, completely, and unconditionally withdraw all of its military forces from within the internationally recognized borders of Ukraine and calls for a cessation of hostilities. It also addresses several other questions relating to attacks on civilian objects, criminal responsibility, food security, energy, finance, the environment, and nuclear security and safety.

In the vote, 141 states voted for the resolution. Russia, Belarus, Syria, North Korea, Eritrea, Mali, and Nicaragua voted against it, and 32 states abstained.

It goes without saying that these resolutions by the General Assembly are of great importance. The four most important resolutions were adopted by a great majority of the UN Members—with between 141 and 143 votes. It is crucial that this kind of determination is demonstrated—in particular as a permanent member of the Security Council is committing the violations of the Charter that have led to the emergency session.

30.3 The Case Before the International Court of Justice

Ukraine has taken Russia to the International Court of Justice (ICJ), which is one of the six principal organs of the UN, objecting to Russia's use of genocide. According to the Genocide Convention, to which both Russia and Ukraine are parties, such a dispute must be resolved by the ICJ.

---

[9] UNGA 2023.

On 16 March 2022, the ICJ made a preliminary decision, which is summarized in three points with the following wording:[10]

> (1) By thirteen votes to two,
>
> The Russian Federation shall immediately suspend the military operations that it commenced on 24 February 2022 in the territory of Ukraine;
>
> (2) By thirteen votes to two,
>
> The Russian Federation shall ensure that any military or irregular armed units which may be directed or supported by it, as well as any organizations and persons which may be subject to its control or direction, take no steps in furtherance of the military operations referred to in point (1) above;
>
> (3) Unanimously,
>
> Both Parties shall refrain from any action which might aggravate or extend the dispute before the Court or make it more difficult to resolve.

The judges who voted against the decision were from China and Russia.

On 2 February 2024, the ICJ delivered a judgment addressing the preliminary objections that the Russian Federation had raised to the jurisdiction of the Court and the admissibility of the Application.[11] The case will proceed to the merits.

30.4 Cases Before the International Criminal Court

The International Criminal Court (ICC) is governed by the Rome Statute of 1998, which entered into force on 1 July 2002. Russia is not a party to the Rome Statute. However, Ukraine has accepted the jurisdiction of the ICC under Article 12 of the Statute. On 21 August 2024, Ukraine's parliament approved a law, signed by President Volodymyr Zelenskyy on 24 August, providing for ratification of the Rome Statute. The ICC can thus hear cases against individuals who have committed crimes against Ukraine. Against this background, there are now three cases before the ICC relating to the situation in Ukraine.

On 17 March 2024, the Pre-Trial Chamber of the ICC issued arrest warrants in relation to Mr. Vladimir Putin, President of the Russian Federation, and Ms. Maria Lvova-Belova, Commissioner for Children's Rights in the Office of the President of the Russian Federation. The Pre-Trial Chamber confirmed that there are reasonable grounds to believe that President Putin and Ms. Lvova-Belova bear criminal responsibility for the unlawful deportation and transfer of Ukrainian children from occupied areas of Ukraine to the Russian Federation.[12]

---

[10] ICJ, *Allegations of Genocide under the Convention on the Prevention and Punishment of the Crime of Genocide (Ukraine v. Russian Federation)*, Provisional Measures, Order, 16 March 2022, 2022 ICJ Reports.

[11] ICJ, *Allegations of Genocide under the Convention on the Prevention and Punishment of the Crime of Genocide (Ukraine v. Russian Federation)*, Preliminary Objections, Judgment, 2 February 2024.

[12] International Criminal Court (2024) Statement by Prosecutor Karim A. A. Khan KC on the issuance of arrest warrants against President Vladimir Putin and Ms Maria

On 5 March 2024, the Pre-Trial Chamber of the ICC issued additional arrest warrants in relation to Sergei Ivanovich Kobylash, a Lieutenant General in the Russian Armed Forces who at the relevant time was Commander of the Long-Range Aviation of the Aerospace Force, and Viktor Nikolayevich Sokolov, an Admiral in the Russian Navy, who at the relevant time was Commander of the Black Sea Fleet. The Pre-Trial Chamber confirmed that there are reasonable grounds to believe that General Kobylash and Admiral Sokolov bear individual criminal responsibility for war crimes and crimes against humanity.[13]

On 25 June 2024, the Pre-Trial Chamber of the ICC issued additional arrest warrants in relation to Sergei Kuzhugetovich Shoigu, Minister of Defense of the Russian Federation at the time of the alleged conduct, and Valery Vasilyevich Gerasimov, Chief of the General Staff of the Russian Federation's Armed Forces, and First Deputy Minister of Defense of the Russian Federation. The Pre-Trial Chamber confirmed that there are reasonable grounds to believe that Mr. Shoigu and General Gerasimov bear individual criminal responsibility for war crimes and crimes against humanity.[14]

The great challenge now is to apprehend these suspects. If a person against whom the ICC has issued an arrest warrant visits a state that is a party to the Rome Statute, this state is obliged to arrest this person for transfer to the ICC. It is against this background that President Putin was not able to visit the BRICS meeting in South Africa in August 2024. However, on 3 September 2024, he was able to travel to Mongolia for a state visit, as Mongolia did not fulfil this obligation.

30.5 An Independent Commission of Inquiry has Submitted Reports

On 4 March 2022, the UN Human Rights Council decided to establish the Independent International Commission of Inquiry (COI) on Ukraine.[15] The commission now consists of the following three human rights experts: Erik Møse (Norway), chairman, Vrinda Grover (India), and Pablo de Greiff (Colombia). Its mandate is to investigate

Lvova-Belova. https://www.icc-cpi.int/news/statement-prosecutor-karim-khan-kc-issuance-arrest-warrants-against-president-vladimir-putin. Accessed 15 February 2025.

[13] International Criminal Court (2024) Statement by SProsecutor Karim A.A. Khan KC on the issuance of arrest warrants in the Situation in Ukraine. https://www.icc-cpi.int/news/statement-prosecutor-karim-aa-khan-kc-issuance-arrest-warrants-situation-ukraine. Accessed 15 February 2025.

[14] International Criminal Court (2024) Statement by Prosecutor Karim A.A. Khan KC on the issuance of arrest warrants in the Situation in Ukraine. https://www.icc-cpi.int/news/statement-prosecutor-karim-aa-khan-kc-issuance-arrest-warrants-situation-ukraine-0. Accessed 15 February 2025.

[15] UN Human Rights Council, Independent International Commission of Inquiry on Ukraine. https://www.ohchr.org/en/hr-bodies/hrc/iicihr-ukraine/index. Accessed 15 February 2025.

all alleged violations and abuses of human rights, violations of international humanitarian law, and related crimes in the context of the aggression against Ukraine by the Russian Federation.

The reports of the commission are horrifying to read. Reference is made to press releases, statements, reports, and the COI mandate on the website.[16] The following quote from the Chair of COI on Ukraine 19 March 2024 can serve as a brief description of the Commission's work:

> The Russian Federation's full-scale invasion of Ukraine has resulted in thousands of casualties, damage, destruction, unbearable suffering, and hardships for the civilian population. More than 10,000 civilians have been killed and close to 20,000 others have been injured during this period, according to OHCHR.
>
> Since the Commission's establishment, our investigations have focused on patterns of violations. The Commission has travelled to Ukraine 26 times and visited 90 settlements. We express our deep gratitude to victims and witnesses, to those who shared with us valuable information, and appreciate the access and information provided by the Government of Ukraine. The Commission regrets that communications addressed to the Russian Federation have remained unanswered.[17]

30.6 A Special Criminal Court May Be Established and Sanctions Against Russia

As mentioned above, there are cases relating to Ukraine before the International Criminal Court (ICC). However, the ICC does not have jurisdiction over the crime of aggression in this case. This is an extremely important issue that needs to be resolved. Discussions are presently taking place in a Task Force established by the UN General Assembly.

One of the methods discussed is a proposal to set up a Special Criminal Court elaborated by Irwin Cotler, former Attorney General of Canada, David Crane, the first Chief Prosecutor of the Special Court for Sierra Leone, and myself, having negotiated the 2002 Agreement between the United Nations and the Government of Sierra Leone on the Establishment of a Special Court for Sierra Leone. It is this court that is the model for our proposal.[18]

This question is presently discussed in a core group under the UN General Assembly. There are different opinions within the group. Some states prefer a court established on the basis of a resolution by the UN General Assembly, whereas others think that the court should be established by another organization, preferably the Council of Europe. There are also states that complain about selectivity in the creation of international criminal courts.

[16] See note 15.

[17] UN Human Rights Council (2024) Update by the Chair of the Independent International Commission of Inquiry on Ukraine, at the 55th session of the Human Rights Council. https://www.ohchr.org/sites/default/files/documents/hrbodies/hrcouncil/coiukraine/20240318-Oral-update-55th-session-EN.pdf. Accessed 15 February 2025.

[18] Corell 2023a.

Extensive sanctions against Russia have been adopted by many states and organizations. Without going into detail here, let me say that the sanctions have taken effect, but suffer from problems. By way of example, reference can be made to an analysis conducted by the European Council.[19]

30.7 NATO

Particular attention must also be paid to the manner in which the North Atlantic Treaty Organization (NATO) is acting in this situation. Here, reference can be made to the declaration "Washington Summit Declaration issued by the NATO Heads of State and Government participating in the meeting of the North Atlantic Council in Washington, D.C. 10 July 2024".[20] Of particular interest in this context are paras 3, 5, 15–20, 23–26, 29–31, and 33. Reference is also made to the six paragraphs under the title "Pledge of Long-Term Security Assistance for Ukraine".

30.8 What are the Lessons for a Future World Order?

30.8.1 Ukraine

What is happening in Ukraine is, as can be seen from the reporting in the media and various surveys, extremely serious. This means that the international community has a responsibility to act with determination to uphold the rule of law at both national and international levels. Russia's behavior towards Ukraine is completely unacceptable. It violates the most basic international law. Moreover, it diverts attention and energy from other issues of paramount importance to international peace and security, such as climate change, population growth, the need to support developing countries, the need to combat transnational crime, and other issues affecting humanity and our global environment.

A very serious matter is the fact that the Russian Federation completely ignores the important resolutions of the UN General Assembly and rulings of the International Court of Justice.

There is also another very serious effect of President Putin's decision on "partial mobilization", as he said in his announcement on 21 September 2022. It is obvious that the Russian troops in Ukraine are committing systematic violations of the laws of war, humanitarian law, and human rights law. The Russian soldiers are therefore

[19] Council of the European Union (2023) Impact of sanctions on the Russian economy. https://www.consilium.europa.eu/en/infographics/impact-sanctions-russian-economy/. Accessed 15 February 2025.

[20] NATO (2024) Washington Summit Declaration. https://www.nato.int/cps/en/natohq/official_texts_227678.htm. Accessed 15 February 2025.

not only risking their lives in an illegal war. They also risk being ordered to commit war crimes, for which they may be brought to justice. No effort can be spared in making Russia stop its war of aggression against Ukraine.

30.8.2 The United Nations

It is obvious that the United Nations must carefully analyze what has happened in this case. The need to reform the UN Security Council is obvious (see below). Of particular importance here is also the Pact for the Future, adopted by the Summit of the Future on 22 September 2024. There are many actions in the Pact focusing on strengthening the United Nations and the United Nations System (see below).

30.8.3 Regional Organizations

An important provision in the UN Charter is Article 52 on regional arrangements or agencies. A basic idea here is that such organizations should be used on the condition that they live up to the UN's purposes and principles. However, there is an important limitation here. It follows from Article 53 of the UN Charter that coercive measures (for example using military force) may not be carried out in accordance with regional agreements or by regional bodies without the consent of the Security Council.

30.8.4 The Need for Reforming the UN Security Council

What is happening in Ukraine now shows once again that it is absolutely necessary to reform the UN Security Council. This matter was also discussed during the Summit of the Future (see below).

There are many ideas about how this should be done. A couple of days before the Summit of the Future, the Global Governance Forum presented an additional proposal of this kind as food for thought: "A Second United Nations Charter: Modernizing the UN for a New Generation."[21]

The lessons from what is happening in Ukraine are extremely serious. As many have said, we have not seen anything of this sort since the Second World War. The systemic attacks on civilians, buildings, and equipment, which are strictly forbidden targets under the laws of war, may feel surreal. These attacks are particularly serious as this is a war of aggression for which those responsible should be brought to justice.

[21] Global Governance Forum (2024) A Second United Nations Charter: Modernizing the UN for a New Generation, https://globalgovernanceforum.org/second-united-nations-charter-modernizing-un-new-generation. Accessed 15 February 2025.

The obvious lesson is that something must be done when a permanent member of the UN Security Council grossly violates the most fundamental rules in the UN Charter. The question is whether this can be done quickly. It is obvious that a major reform of the UN Charter may be made in the future. However, the lesson from what is happening in Ukraine is that a reform of the Security Council must be made immediately. This can be done if the permanent five members of the Security Council realize that they have responsibility for present and coming generations. What is needed here is statesmanship. I have tried to explain this earlier, and my latest contributions describe a reform that could be made without changing even a comma in the UN Charter.[22]

30.8.5 *The Summit of the Future*

Of great importance in this context is the Summit of the Future that was held in New York on 22–23 September 2024. It was "a high-level event, bringing world leaders together to forge a new international consensus on how we deliver a better present and safeguard the future".[23] The result of the event was a resolution adopted by the General Assembly entitled "Pact for the Future" with a "Global Digital Compact" and a "Declaration on Future Generations" as annexes.[24]

The undertakings made in the Pact and its annexes are enormous. However, the reality is that the Summit of the Future resulted in a much-needed outcome, and it is evident that the situation in Ukraine will impact the fulfilment of the 56 actions in the Pact.

The Pact contains several references to the Sustainable Development Goals (SDGs).[25] The problem is that these goals have not been fulfilled as was intended. The Pact underscores that the supervision of the fulfilment of these goals must be more detailed and effective.

For my part, I never miss an opportunity to draw attention to SDG 16:

> Promote peaceful and inclusive societies for sustainable development, provide access to justice for all and build effective, accountable and inclusive institutions at all levels.

Achieving this goal, with its focus on the rule of law and anticorruption, is a precondition for achieving all the other SDGs.

---

[22] Corell 2023b, 2018.

[23] United Nations, Summit of the Future. https://www.un.org/en/summit-of-the-future. Accessed 15 February 2025.

[24] United Nations (2024) Summit of the Future Outcome document. https://www.un.org/sites/un2.un.org/files/sotf-pact_for_the_future_adopted.pdf; UNGA 2024.

[25] United Nations, Department of Economic and Social Affairs, The 17 Goals. https://sdgs.un.org/goals. Accessed 15 February 2025.

Another question that is important to focus on in this context is the responsibility that politicians have for the rule of law. A brief guide for politicians on the rule of law is now freely available on the web for downloading and printing in 26 languages.[26]

30.9 Conclusions

The United Nations General Assembly has acted under the unusual system Uniting for Peace and adopted very important resolutions condemning the behavior of Russia and ordering Russia to withdraw from the territory of Ukraine. The International Court of Justice has decided that the Russian Federation shall immediately suspend the military operations in Ukraine that it commenced on 22 February 2022. The International Criminal Court has issued arrest warrants in relation to several persons, including President Putin; the Court has found that there are reasonable grounds to believe those persons bear individual criminal responsibility for the crimes for which they are suspected. An Independent Commission of Inquiry has issued alarming reports about terrible violations and abuses of human rights, violations of international humanitarian law, and related crimes in the context of the Russian aggression against Ukraine.

The summary conclusion is therefore that the situation in Ukraine is very serious. It is imperative that the international community act against what is happening there now. A permanent member of the United Nations Security Council is in flagrant violation of the most basic rules of the Charter of the United Nations. This will have serious consequences for the entire international system as it developed after the end of the Second World War. In the media, we often find reasoning reminding us of what happened in the 1930s, which led to the Second World War.

References

Corell H (2018) UN Security Council Reform—The Council Must Lead by Example. Max Planck Yearbook of United Nations Law, 22:3–33. https://www.havc.se/res/SelectedMaterial/20191128corellunsecuritycouncilreform.pdf. Accessed 15 February 2025

Corell H (2023a) A Special Tribunal for Ukraine on the Crime of Aggression—The Role of the U.N. General Assembly. Just Security. https://www.justsecurity.org/author/corellhans/. Accessed 15 February 2025

Corell H (2023b) The UN Security Council and the Rule of Law. The Fifth Hilding Eek Memorial Lecture. Nordic Journal of International Law 91(1):1–18

Raoul Wallenberg Institute, The Hague Institute for the Internationalisation of Law (2012) Rule of Law—A guide for politicians. https://rwi.lu.se/download/rule-of-law-a-guide-for-politicians-english-version/. Accessed 15 February 2025

UN General Assembly (1950) Uniting for Peace, Resolution 377(V), UN Doc. A/RES/377(V)

---

[26] Raoul Wallenberg Institute and The Hague Institute for the Internationalisation of Law 2012.

UN General Assembly (2022a) Aggression against Ukraine, Resolution ES-11/1, UN Doc. A/RES/ES-11/1
UN General Assembly (2022b) Humanitarian consequences of the aggression against Ukraine, Resolution ES-11/2, UN Doc. A/RES/ES-11/2
UN General Assembly (2022c) Suspension of the rights of membership of the Russian Federation in the Human Rights Council, Resolution ES-11/3, UN Doc. A/RES/ES-11/3
UN General Assembly (2022d) Territorial integrity of Ukraine: defending the principles of the Charter of the United Nations, Resolution ES-11/4, UN Doc. A/RES/ES-11/4
UN General Assembly (2022e) Furtherance of remedy and reparation for aggression against Ukraine, Resolution ES-11/5, UN Doc. A/RES/ES-11/5
UN General Assembly (2023) Principles of the Charter of the United Nations underlying a comprehensive, just and lasting peace in Ukraine, Resolution ES-11/6, UN Doc. A/RES/ES-11/6
UN General Assembly (2024) The Pact for the Future, Resolution 79/1, UN Doc. A/RES/79/1
UN Security Council (2022) Resolution 2623, UN Doc. S/RES/2623

Hans Corell (Sweden) was Under-Secretary-General for Legal Affairs and the Legal Counsel of the United Nations from March 1994 to March 2004. From 1962 to 1972, he served in the Swedish judiciary. In 1972, he joined the Ministry of Justice where he became Chief Legal Officer in 1981. He was Ambassador and Under-Secretary for Legal and Consular Affairs in the Ministry for Foreign Affairs from 1984 to 1994. Since his retirement from public service in 2004 he is engaged in many different activities in the legal field, inter alia as legal adviser, lecturer, and member of different boards. Among other, he is involved in the work of the International Bar Association and the Stockholm Center for International Law and Justice. He was Chairman of the Board of Trustees of the Raoul Wallenberg Institute of Human Rights and Humanitarian Law at Lund University, Sweden, from 2006–2012.

Chapter 31
Private Authority in International Finance: The Case of Credit Rating Agencies

Kangle Zhang

Contents

Abstract Private actors like credit rating agencies (CRAs) in the financial market possess regulatory authority to the extent of rendering the efforts of states and intergovernmental organisations futile. This chapter examines the source of authority for the CRAs, and in doing so draws attention to the infrastructure of international finance. The authority of CRAs rests in the institutional design of the financial infrastructure, a design that seeks to satisfy the *desire* for credit information in the market. In other words, the CRAs possess an imagined authority. This reveals an important aspect of the financial market: some cornerstones in the financial market architecture are constructed out of a broader desire for those cornerstones, and sometimes herd 'belief' is enough to give them effect. Realising this fictional aspect of the architecture is useful, as it exposes—at least in this aspect—that it is the desire of (those with) capital that the architecture of international finance serves. The chapter proposes that the attempt to better understand, deconstruct, and eventually reconstruct power and hegemony in international finance requires critical examinations of its infrastructure, with an understanding that said infrastructure is made and constantly shaped by political and economic powers through legal means.

Keywords Private authority · Rating · Credit · Financial · Infrastructure · Capital · Distribution

K. Zhang (✉)
Peking University Law School, Beijing, China
e-mail: kangle.m.zhang@gmail.com

M. Klamberg et al. (eds.), *Reconstructing Power and Hegemony in Public International Law*, https://doi.org/10.1007/978-94-6265-743-4_31

31.1 Introduction

In May 2020, the G20 countries established the Debt Service Suspension Initiative (DSSI) to cope with the rising risk of waves of sovereign debt crises.[1] Among the various efforts listed in the Initiative was a call on private creditors to participate. It was soon observed, however, that despite the fallout of the pandemic tipping dozens of nations into fiscal crisis, countries eligible for debt suspension were reluctant to renegotiate their debts with private creditors.[2] One of the most significant reasons was that the world's poorest countries feared such arrangements would trigger downgrades in their credit ratings, and thereby damage their access to financial markets.[3] That is to say, a small number of credit rating agencies (CRAs)—more precisely, Moody's Standard, Poor's and Fitch, the big three—contributed to, if not rendered, the chaos and ineffectiveness of debt relief measures at the time when such measures were most needed.

This was not the first time the big three have attracted much attention. Before the outbreak of the Greece debt crisis, when the International Monetary Fund (IMF) and the European Central Bank were preparing for a support package to prevent that crisis from materialising, the CRAs downgraded Greek bonds.[4] Throughout the crisis and even when deals of rescue packages were reached, the CRAs continued to raise default fears over bonds. These have been criticised for contributing to market panic and worsening the crisis,[5] and led to discussions on the role of ratings and the regulatory use of them in capital markets.[6] Indeed, CRAs have never been far from controversy, at either the international or the domestic level. In examining the causes of the 2007–2008 financial and economic crisis in the US, the Financial Crisis Inquiry Commission (FCIC) detailed how CRAs, by giving their seal of approval, fuelled risks in the financial market. The FCIC Report concluded that 'the failures of credit rating agencies were essential cogs in the wheel of financial destruction'.[7] Dating back further, to the turn of the millennium, the Enron crisis exposed the failure of ratings—Enron's debts were considered above investment grade only days before Enron declared bankruptcy.[8]

These episodes of rating-related chaos reveal the authority of a few CRAs, private actors in international finance that were initially incorporated in the United States and now have local offices on most continents. In other words, some private actors wield such authority that they could deem the efforts of states (in the case of the DSSI) and

---

[1] A record of low-income countries participating in the DSSI is provided by the World Bank and updated weekly. *See* The World Bank 2022.

[2] Wheatley 2020.

[3] Hodgson 2020.

[4] Wachman 2010.

[5] Baum et al. 2016.

[6] Gaillard 2014.

[7] United States of America Financial Crisis Inquiry Commission 2011, p. xxv (hereafter FCIC Report).

[8] United States of America Staff of the Committee on Governmental Affairs 2002, pp. 84–89.

intergovernmental organisations (in the case of the IMF, addressing the Greece debt crisis) futile. The topic of private authority in international finance is undoubtedly familiar. For example, the standard contract of the International Swaps and Derivatives Association (ISDA), a non-profit corporation headquartered in New York City, is the norm for today's over-the-counter derivative market.[9] Private authorities like the ISDA have given rise to discussions on the loss of public regulatory capacity in international finance[10] and on contracts as regulatory instruments in the financial market.[11]

This chapter addresses the making of private authority in international finance, using the example of CRAs. The chapter starts with an overview of the role of CRAs in the financial market and explains the existing arguments regarding the source of the CRAs' authority. After introducing CRAs and some existing work on the source of their authority, the chapter seeks to offer a distinct view of the authority of CRAs by relocating the central focus from the CRAs and legal settings around them to the international financial infrastructure. It approaches the authority issue by investigating the institutional role that CRAs undertake in the contemporary infrastructure of international finance, arguing that the authority of CRAs rests in the institutional design of the financial infrastructure. More specifically, the financial infrastructure is designed to satisfy the *desire* for (determinant) credit information in the market, and CRAs happen to have the role of satisfying that desire. Lastly, the chapter reflects on the infrastructure of international finance, suggesting that various cornerstones of the financial market infrastructure are constructed out of a broader desire for those cornerstones, and sometimes herd 'belief' is enough to give them effect. Realising this fictional aspect—as I have termed it—of international financial infrastructure is useful, as it exposes that it is the desire of (those with) capital that the infrastructure of international finance serves. That is to say: capital power and state backing of that power are embedded in the very design of the international financial infrastructure.

Three caveats are necessary. First, although CRAs and international finance have traditionally been within the purview of either financial regulations or international economic law, this chapter seeks to bring the authority of these private actors into a broader discussion on power and hegemony in international law. As I have argued elsewhere, international finance warrants the critical attention of public international lawyers.[12] Second, the chapter approaches the issue of private authority by examining an overlooked aspect in the existing discussions. Existing studies on the authority of private actors like CRAs or the ISDA tend to focus primarily on these private actors themselves and the mechanisms around them. For example, the ISDA's regulatory authority is generally considered to lie in the convenience it provides in derivatives trading and its lobbying power. In the case of CRAs, both the regulatory license view and the informational value view, which I will get to in Section 31.1.2, concentrate on

[9] Gelpern 2009. *See also* Riles 2011.

[10] Pistor 2019, pp. 144–152.

[11] Gelpern 2025.

[12] Zhang 2020.

the laws concerning CRAs and the actions of CRAs. Not enough attention has been paid to the link between private authorities in international finance and the financial infrastructure. Third, this overlooked aspect of approaching private authority in international finance warrants attention when attempting to understand the power relationships behind the law of international finance. Although the law is typically understood as a set of rules and standards that facilitate financial market operations and avert risks,[13] its role in entrenching the preferences of those in positions of power has not attracted enough attention. A critical arena where the entrenchment of power occurs is the financial infrastructure— the mechanisms designed and built to enable financial dealings. As this chapter shows, it is through that infrastructure that CRAs gain regulatory authority, and the infrastructure is built for those with capital. Effectively, CRAs serve the interest of capital, and the repercussions of ratings for poorer countries are by design not the concern of that infrastructure. Attempts to reconstruct power and hegemony in the field of international finance thus require attention to the financial infrastructure.

31.2 Credit Rating: Mechanisms and Repercussions

Credit rating directly affects the creditworthiness of both financial products and the issuers of these products. Because high ratings signal low credit risk and low ratings signal high credit risk, CRAs could be viewed as regulating the allocation of capital in the financial market.[14] As some term it, CRAs hold 'the key to capital and liquidity', the lifeblood of corporate finance and capitalist economy.[15] They do so by affecting the cost of raising capital and, as a result, the access to capital for sovereign and non-sovereign bond issuers.[16] This section offers an overview of the workings of CRAs in the context of sovereign rating and introduces two main arguments on the source of authority of the CRAs.

31.2.1 Sovereign Rating

Sovereign rating refers to the ratings accorded to the obligations of central governments.[17] Since the inter-war years, CRAs have been carrying out business by conducting sovereign ratings.[18] CRAs assess the ability and willingness of a sovereign debt issuer to make full and timely payments of principal and interest for

[13] Kern et al. 2006.

[14] Cantor and Packer 1996, p. 41.

[15] Statement of Senator Joseph Lieberman, 2002.

[16] Schwarcz 1998.

[17] Cantor and Packer 1996; Kräussl 2005.

[18] Sylla 2002. For a comprehensive recount of sovereign ratings, *see* Gaillard 2012.

the debt in question.[19] The sovereign ratings are part of the bigger pool of information—in which macroeconomic indicators are also included—correlated to sovereign bond yield movements, and affect a government's access to the international capital market.[20] The yield spread is the key channel through which ratings affect the rated country's access to the capital market. This takes place in the following manner. As dollar bond spreads respond to sovereign ratings in that 'sovereign yields tend to rise as ratings decline',[21] the rise of dollar bond yield entails higher costs for the sovereign issuer when raising capital from the international capital market. That is to say, lower ratings (or downgrading of ratings) indicate a higher cost of raising capital from the international market.

For a government, the increase in borrowing costs and the difficulty of accessing international capital markets hurt the economy. This is particularly disastrous for countries facing balance of payment issues. This has been the case for various Latin American countries in the past decades. CRAs play a crucial role in determining the cost of raising capital for a sovereign state, and this role tends to expand in times of crisis when capital is particularly needed in a country. During the not-too-distant European sovereign debt crisis, the downgrading of Greece's sovereign ratings—despite the deal reached by the IMF and the EU to support Greece, as I recounted at the start of the article—was criticised for contributing to a herd mentality in investors' confidence and thus worsening the crisis.[22] Notably, though the herd mentality seems irrational in the sense that broader market perceptions instead of economic fundamentals are the basis of investment decision-making, the nature of the financial market is such that it is rational for individual investors to adopt the herd mentality.

In the specific context of the 1997 Asian financial crisis, economists focused on the impact of sovereign ratings on emerging economies. Their studies capture the effects of ratings and rating changes during a financial crisis in a transnational context. The downgrading of sovereign ratings by the big three during the crisis was considered to have caused 'an increase in the cost of funds', which sent a negative 'signal on the country being downgraded to market participants'. Consequentially, after the downgrading by the rating agencies, it was witnessed that 'the yield spread of East Asian crisis countries' bond denominated in USD with respect to US Treasury bonds of equivalent maturity significantly rose'. Essentially, for the East Asian crisis countries, the downgrades unduly exacerbated 'the cost of borrowing abroad and caused the supply of international capital to them to evaporate'.[23]

Another useful finding of studies on the impact of ratings and rating changes during the Asian financial crisis suggests that negative rating actions have more significant impacts on emerging economies than on high-income economies.[24] As

[19] For an account of why sovereigns borrow, *see* Hammond 2014; Picker and McConnel 1993.

[20] Cantor and Packer 1996, p. 38.

[21] Ibid. p. 43.

[22] Baum et al. 2016. *See also* De Santis 2012.

[23] Ferri et al. 1999.

[24] Elkhoury 2008.

the studies suggest, ratings 'have a substantial influence on the size and volatility of emerging markets lending'[25] and there is 'a highly significant announcement effect when emerging markets' sovereign bonds are put on review with negative outlook'.[26]

31.2.2 The Source of Regulatory Authority: A Debate

Arguments on the source of authority could be categorized into two groups: one group traces it to the information value of ratings, and the other focuses on regulatory delegations to CRAs. According to the informational view, CRAs produce valuable information—both fresh information and clarification of that already existing—to the financial market.[27] The informational value and the reputation of the CRAs derived therefrom are considered the lifeline of the CRAs—a point commonly employed in arguing for that value. Proponents of the informational view suggest that proof of the informational value of the CRAs lies in the fact that market participants react to ratings in rather nuanced ways. Distinct reactions to the ratings of different CRAs have been noted. Also, 'issuers seek ratings even when they expect the ratings to be below investment grade', an observation that boosts the value of the information that issuers obtain from the ratings. In other words, it is considered that the ratings must have some value for issuers to acquire it even when these ratings do not increase the overall revenue for issuing a specific bond.[28]

It is also noted that CRAs are equipped with expertise in rating activities. The expertise refers to the time needed to investigate and analyse available market information, the experience in a particular financial market sector,[29] and the proprietary algorithms and specialised econometric modelling tools. This comparative advantage makes the CRAs producing information the ideal actors for rating activities. The praise of CRAs' analytical resources lends support to the aforementioned suggestions on the role of CRAs in the market. By producing valuable information, the rating agencies function as gatekeepers and intermediaries. And because CRAs are equipped to provide such information, states are inclined to form principal-agent relationships with CRAs.[30]

The regulatory licensing view argues that the regulatory authority of CRAs lies in their capacity to issue regulatory licenses.[31] It is argued that CRAs do not provide

---

[25] Kräussl 2005, p. 379.

[26] Elkhoury 2008. *See also* Ferri et al. 2001; Kim and Wu 2008.

[27] Rhee 2015.

[28] Hill 2004.

[29] Ibid. pp. 73–74.

[30] 'Public regulators ... perceived themselves as lacking essential analytical resources, that is capabilities to cope with financial market uncertainty in a risk-sensitive way. Therefore, public regulators have delegated governance tasks and (quasi-)regulatory authority to specialised risk-measuring agents, namely credit rating agencies.' *See* Kruck 2011, p. 17.

[31] Partnoy 1999.

helpful information in the current financial market.[32] This is the case because regulatory incorporations have caused 'a decline in the information value of credit ratings' and created 'incentives for the agencies to provide inaccurate ratings'. With the ratings incorporated into regulations, market participants pay for the 'regulatory entitlements stemming from the agencies' ratings' instead of the 'informational content of the ratings'.[33] Furthermore, the behavioural reliance on the ratings evolves into regulatory reliance, further promoting regulatory incorporations of CRAs and strengthening their rating authority.

Frank Partnoy is among the first to note the empowerment of CRAs through regulatory incorporations. Partnoy usefully traces the incorporations and dates them to the 1930s.[34] The 1970s was another critical period, as the Securities and Exchange Commission of the US then started using ratings from nationally recognised statistical rating organisations (NRSROs).[35] Partnoy's close examination of regulatory incorporations and the added value to the ratings resulting from such incorporations leads to his assertion of the private CRAs' authority resting in the regulatory incorporations. Furthermore, Partnoy compares the expansion of the rating businesses and the rating accuracy during particular historical periods. As mentioned, Partnoy points out two historical periods in which credit ratings increased in importance, namely the 1930s and the mid-1970s through the 1990s. However, each was 'paradoxically followed by a series of bond defaults demonstrating the rating agencies' serious mistakes in rating bonds'.[36] Partnoy questions the mismatch between the expansion of the business of the rating agencies and the declining rating accuracy. From there, it is suggested that the synchronicity of the expansion of the rating businesses and the regulatory incorporations of the ratings reveals the role of rating agencies as issuers of regulatory licenses.

31.3 The Authority of CRAs: An Imagined Authority

This chapter suggests a distinct view on CRAs' private ordering authority: the authority lies in the *desire* for determinate rating information (on the creditworthiness of financial products in the market). The term 'determinate' is understood as accurate and timely in this context. This source of authority can be understood in three steps. The first concerns the reasons for the emergence of the desire. This desire is a psychological reaction to a combination of, on the one hand, a lack of stable and medium- to long-term credit information in the highly fragmented financial markets and, on the other hand, the prominent financial returns and reduced risks brought by

[32] Partnoy further suggests that if the rating information provided by the CRAs is correct, it is nothing that the market does not already know. Partnoy 2002. *See also* Darbellay 2013.

[33] Partnoy 1999, pp. 623–624.

[34] Ibid.

[35] Partnoy 2002, p. 71.

[36] Partnoy 1999, p. 654.

valuable credit information. In other words, such information is generally desired in a system filled with uncertainty, risk, economic losses and gains, where credit information essentially means financial benefits.

Second, in response to that desire, a specific institutional position—a cornerstone—is created in the financial infrastructure. CRAs fill that institutional position. The cornerstone satisfies the desire formally (instead of substantively) and underpins market operations. For example, borrowers seek ready recognition of the creditworthiness of their bonds; investors look for market-accepted vehicles of risk assessment; financial institutions require some risk charging when measuring the financial products that are sold to individual investors; and regulators seek a regulatory benchmark when looking at the capital adequacy of financial institutions. This cornerstone signals credit information and measures risk levels, and in doing so, it supports the operations involving borrowers, investors, financial institutions and regulators. More importantly, it formally responds to the desire for such information. As CRAs take on this particular role, their ratings become an institutional component in the financial infrastructure. As a result, a market participant may be well aware of the ratings' flaws, but the ratings' institutional role makes them irreplaceable in the market. Adding to this, the herd behaviour in the financial market amplifies the impact of the ratings. As long as a broad range of investors react to the ratings and rating changes, it is an individual participant's rational choice to follow the ratings even in case of doubts over the reliability of the rating information. This explains the continuous reliance on the ratings after each episode of rating-related chaos.

Third, the desire for credit information and the corresponding institutional role of the entity offering that credit information lead to a circle (*the circle*, Figure 31.1). The circle is formed by the established practices of the rating agencies producing rating information and regulatory incorporations. It satisfies the desire for determinate information and equips private CRAs with regulatory authority in the financial market. The desire then reinforces the imagined authority of the CRAs through *the circle*.[37]

The (formation of the) circle is witnessed in the history of CRAs and regulatory incorporation. The investors and regulators searched for credit information in the US market. The investors were in pursuit of accurate and timely information about where it was (relatively) safe to place their money—though over the years, with the change of the CRAs' business model, the ratings evolved to respond to the needs of the borrowers. The regulators needed some basic parameters regarding the creditworthiness of different financial products to promulgate regulations on these products.[38] The letter ratings—which are straightforward—produced by the CRAs offered indicators that responded well to the regulatory needs, and some market

[37] In other words, it is an imagined authority stemming from the desire for such authoritative existence. For a critique of the sovereign authority following the same train of thought, *see* Sherwin 2018.

[38] For instance, in 1930, 'the Federal Reserve began using bond ratings in their examination of the portfolios of member banks. Gustav Osterhus, of the Federal Reserve Bank of New York, devised a system for weighting a bank's entire portfolio based on credit ratings, so that the portfolio's "safety" or "desirability" could be expressed in a single number.'; 'In 1931, the United States

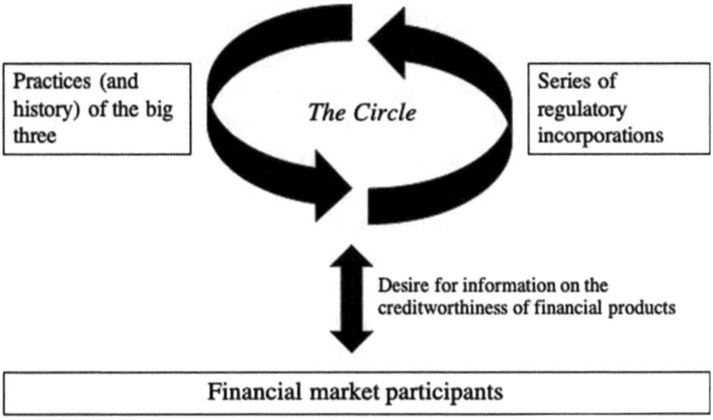

Fig. 31.1 The circle. *Source* The author

participants were already using these ratings.[39] As a result (and as we witnessed in the 1930s and from the mid-1970s to the 1990s), the ratings were incorporated into regulations. Regulatory incorporation, in turn, signalled a recognition of the value of the rating information produced by CRAs, and the use of ratings in the market flourished.

The circle illustrates the psychological appeal that ratings offer to market participants. Reinforced by regulatory incorporations and the praise of the CRAs' proprietary algorithms and specialised econometric modelling tools, the CRAs have been sanctified as having the capability to produce 'scientific' and accurate ratings. Authoritative figures were created, and the market participants look up to these figures and perform ritual practices out of belief in their expertise and authority. As witnessed, 'many institutional investors are encouraged by institutional norms, embedded in guidelines, forms, and practices, to buy securities rated investment grade by one or more NRSROs'.[40]

This chapter's assertion that the authority of ratings lies in the desire for credit information in the financial market and that the CRAs fill an institutional role designed to satisfy this desire is perhaps best exemplified in recent years with the post global financial crisis rating-related regulatory changes in the US. The *Dodd-Frank Wall Street Reform and Consumer Protection Act* signed into US federal law in 2010 called for 'eliminating credit ratings in financial regulation' and led to 'alternative means for evaluating credit'.[41] Section 939A of the *Dodd-Frank Act*

Treasury Department, through the Comptroller of the Currency, adopted credit ratings as proper measures of the quality of the national banks' bond accounts.' Partnoy 2002, p. 70.

[39] Partnoy 1999.

[40] Hill 2004, p. 55.

[41] Soroushian 2016.

requires regulatory references to NRSRO credit ratings to be removed,[42] and for the federal regulators to find alternative means of evaluating credit. The US regulators have, since then, rewritten most of the rules that incorporated the NRSRO ratings and come up with various alternatives, including replacing the credit ratings with 'definitions, regulatory models, and third-party classifications'.[43]

These alternatives seek to replace ratings in the regulations concerned. Still, they neither change nor modify the institutional role created in response to *the desire* for determinate information on the creditworthiness of financial products. In other words, some sort of rating—be it definitions, regulatory models, or third-party classifications—is institutionally required as the cornerstone in the infrastructure of international finance. Furthermore, efforts to bring in third-party classification have given rise to various problems. An example of third-party classification is the OECD country risk classification (CRC). The OECD CRCs were adopted by the US federal bank regulators when implementing the Basel III capital standards. CRCs are linked to the risk-weighting of assets—more specifically, the sovereign and depository institution debt—in capital adequacy assessment. This is problematic because, although the CRCs take over the role of rating agencies in the capital requirement regulations, the CRCs and ratings are designed to measure different risks.[44] Country risk indicators are not sovereign ratings.[45] Another problem that arises with the incorporation of CRCs in Basel III standards in the US is that it creates confusion when assigning risk weights to countries that have different statuses according to different modes of classifications. For example, Cyprus and Malta are in the Eurozone. Thus, the sovereign debt ratings are under the 'euro area umbrella',[46] receiving zero risk weight. However, neither country is a member of the OECD; thus, they are not included in the CRCs. As a result, the sovereign debt of both countries would receive the risk weight of 100% under the standardised US Basel III. The same confusion would apply to risk-weighting on Lithuanian bonds before that country joined the OECD in July 2018. It is my contention that these confusions and problems all arise out of the need to fill an institutional role that satisfies the desire for credit information in the financial market.

31.4 International Financial Infrastructure: A Reflection

The CRAs' source of authority reveals that some cornerstones of the international financial infrastructure are constructed out of a desire for those cornerstones. Some insightful works on the financial market have engaged with different cornerstones

[42] Dodd-Frank Wall Street Reform and Consumer Protection Act, Pub L No 111–203, Section 335(a), 124 Stat 1376, 1540 (2010).

[43] Soroushian 2016, p. 3.

[44] Ibid.

[45] Gaillard 2020.

[46] McCauley and White 1997.

and contributed evidence to this suggestion. In a description of the concept of a 'safe asset' by Anna Gelpern and Erik Gerding, they demonstrate how that concept (as a cornerstone) is artificially constructed and adapted in the financial system. That is to say, the idea of a safe asset is objectified through, among other things, regulatory actions and the herd behaviour of financial market participants. Safe assets could thus be considered a cornerstone produced in a similar manner as credit ratings. One significant aspect of these cornerstones is that they nurture each other. Gelpern and Gerding have illustrated the reinforcement of the concept of safe assets by CRAs through labelling assets that meet the needs of particular constituents with high ratings.[47] As they incisively write:

> For years market participants have been doing their business on the assumption that there are risk-free assets. I believe that this concept is a natural human reaction to the complexity of the world surrounding us. The risk-free theory was welcomed because it made decision making much easier. And we are always looking for simple decisions! Plus, the risk-free methodology turned out to become the cornerstone in different mathematic models for the calculation of the value of any financial asset. From the very beginning a number of sovereign bonds were treated as risk-free financial instruments. Credit rating agencies helped a lot in this understanding with their 'AAA' versus 'BBB' or 'CCC' references.[48]

This narrative also usefully reveals the fictional and psychologically appealing aspects of the financial market. They are fictional, as some cornerstones are artificially created and, in a way, make believe. There is no such thing as determinate credit information, yet market participants look up to the ratings. Similarly, a safe asset is merely a conceptual construction particularly useful for accounting purposes. Admittedly, the economic and political backings of the United States in particular historical contexts have made treasuries a safe asset in international finance, as mostly famously illustrated by Alexander Hamilton, Secretary of the Treasury, in his two reports on public credit.[49] With letter ratings and the easily understandable notion of a safe asset, financial investments and regulatory decisions are much more manageable. And this is undoubtedly psychologically appealing.

The desire for credit information is a natural human reaction to the complex (and often complicated) financial market. The desire for such information, preferably in simplified symbols, will always thrive, even where such information does not exist. As a former team managing director at Moody's stated: 'People expect too much from ratings... [I]nvestment decisions should always be based on much more than just a rating.'[50] Regardless, the desire for such 'determinate' information needs to be satisfied, one way or another. A cornerstone is institutionally designed for this exact purpose, and CRAs have, for a relatively long time, had the role as that cornerstone. The resilience of the ratings, despite their role in leading to financial and economic

---

[47] Gelpern and Gerding 2016. For a similar argument on the concept of safe assets, *see* Gaballero et al. 2017. It is argued in this article that 'safety is an elusive concept, because nothing is ever absolutely safe'.

[48] Storchak 2013.

[49] Hamilton 1790a, 1790b.

[50] Financial Crisis Inquiry Commission 2011, p. 120.

disaster, only highlights the strong desire for credit information in the market. This offers some insight into the construction of international financial infrastructure, and might lead to a better understanding of international finance, global economic disparity and their relation to one another.

Here, an important question arises: whose desire for credit information is satisfied by this cornerstone, constructed and institutionalised in the financial infrastructure? I suggest that only those with capital are in pursuit of credit information. That is to say, the institutional design of the financial infrastructure, often in the legal form through the law of international finance, reinforces the desire of those possessing capital and further enables their pursuit of (more) capital in the financial market.

This might seem intuitive, as CRAs are a product of capital markets serving investors. What is particularly significant is that the institutional role of CRAs in the infrastructure of international finance is intertwined with regulations and other infrastructure segments, to the extent that operations in a whole segment of the capital market rely on CRAs. That is to say: some parts of the broader financial infrastructure are built for (those with) capital. This view contradicts the orthodox understanding of finance—'the science of goal infrastructure', the system structuring economic arrangements and stewarding assets for promoting economic productivity.[51] Instead of being a wholly neutral set of techniques efficiently allocating monetary resources, attracting huge volumes of capital and producing revenue in return, the very infrastructure of finance has particular distributional preferences built into it.

31.5 Concluding Remarks

At a time when the linkages between the routine (and seemingly highly sophisticated) operations in the financial market and the unprecedented income and wealth inequality have attracted much attention,[52] when many efforts are spent to understand the complicity of international law in this deeply unequal world, this chapter attempts to draw attention to the relatively small but significant issue of the private authority in international finance. The chapter points out that the international financial infrastructure around CRAs serves the desires of (those with) capital. In doing so, it seeks to draw attention to that infrastructure (as opposed to the seemingly neutral set of rules and standards) with an understanding that the infrastructure of international finance is made and constantly shaped by political and economic powers through legal means. In the particular case of the CRAs, the authority of this small group of private actors rests in the institutional role that they fulfil. And most importantly, their

[51] Shiller 2012, p. 6. The six basic functions that the financial system serves are, according to Robert Merton and Zvi Bodie: clearing and settling payments; pooling resources and subdividing shares; transferring economic resources; managing risk; generating and providing information; and dealing with incentive problems. Bodie and Merton 1995.

[52] Piketty 2014; Pistor 2019.

institutional role in the financial infrastructure is created to satisfy the desire of (those with) capital. In the domestic financial market of the US, the desire for determinate credit information led to the incorporation of the ratings into domestic regulations. The process of global financial liberalisation further enabled the expansion of the US capital market, where the leading role of the US in international financial law-making enabled the globalisation of the infrastructure around ratings. Effectively, while the infrastructure serves capital power, the states where that power resides consolidate the infrastructure through legal actions in international finance.

This chapter concludes by asking: What are the biases and distributive implications already embedded in the underpinning cornerstones of the international financial infrastructure? It is beyond the scope of this chapter to answer this question, but it is a necessary question in understanding, deconstructing and eventually reconstructing power and hegemony in international finance. Reflections on the embedded distributional preferences in the infrastructures and the roles of states and international law in making those infrastructures are much needed to understand and fight inequality and challenge the financial world's power and hegemony.

References

Baum C et al (2016) Credit Rating Agency Downgrades and the Eurozone Sovereign Debt Crises. Journal of Financial Stability 24:117–131

Bodie Z, Merton R (1995) A Conceptual Framework for Analyzing the Financial Environment. In: Crane D (ed) The Global Financial System: A Functional Perspective. Harvard Business Review Press

Cantor R, Packer F (1996) Determinants and Impact of Sovereign Credit Ratings. Economic Policy Review 10:37–54

Darbellay A (2013) Regulating Credit Rating Agencies. Edward Elgar Publishing Ltd, Cheltenham

De Santis R (2012) The Euro Area Sovereign Debt Crisis, Safe Haven, Credit Rating Agencies and the Spread of the Fever from Greece, Ireland and Portugal. Working Paper Series No 1419 https://www.ecb.europa.eu/pub/pdf/scpwps/ecbwp1419.pdf. Accessed 29 November 2024

Elkhoury M (2008) Credit Rating Agencies and Their Potential Impact on Developing Countries. UNCATD Discussions Papers No 186. UNCTAD/OSG/DP/2008/1. https://unctad.org/en/docs/osgdp20081_en.pdf. Accessed 29 November 2024

Ferri G et al (1999) The Procyclical Role of Rating Agencies: Evidence from the East Asian Crisis. Banca Monte dei Paschi di Siena SpA 28:335–355

Ferri G et al (2001) The Role of Rating Agency Assessments in Less Developed Countries: Impact of the Proposed Basel Guidelines. Journal of Banking & Finance 25:115–148

Gaballero R et al (2017) The Safe Assets Shortage Conundrum. Journal of Economic Perspectives 31:29–46

Gaillard N (2012) A Century of Sovereign Ratings. Springer

Gaillard N (2014) How and Why Credit Rating Agencies Missed the Eurozone Debt Crisis. Capital Markets Law Journal 9:121–136

Gaillard N (2020) Country Risk: The Bane of Foreign Investors. Springer

Gelpern A (2009) Commentary to D. Gorden Smith and Brayden G. King, Contracts as Organisations. Arizona Law Review 51:57–74

Gelpern A (2025) Boilerplate against Bailouts: A Regulatory Ride Fallacy. In: Omarova S et al (ed) Hidden Fallacies in Corporate Law and Financial Regulation: Reframing the Mainstream Narratives. Bloomsbury Publishing
Gelpern A, Gerding E (2016) Inside Safe Assets. Yale Journal on Regulation 33:363–421
Hamilton A (1790a) Report Relative to a Provision for the Support of Public Credit. Treasury Department
Hamilton A (1790b) The Second Report on the Further Provision Necessary for Establishing Public Credit (Report on a National Bank). Treasury Department
Hammond B (2014) Sovereignty and Empty Purse: Banks and Politics in the Civil War. First published 1970, Princeton University Press
Hill C (2004) Regulating the Rating Agencies. Washington University Law Quarterly 82:43–94
Hodgson C (2020) Moody's clashes with UN over G20 debt-relief efforts. Financial Times. https://www.ft.com/content/7d51d373-c12e-4440-a408-e61a939e3a3c. Accessed 29 November 2024
Kern A et al. (2006) Global Governance of Financial Systems: The International Regulation of Systemic Risk. Oxford University Press, New York
Kim SJ, Wu E (2008) Sovereign credit ratings, capital flows and financial sector development in emerging markets. Emerging Markets Review 9:17–39
Kräussl R (2005) Do credit rating agencies add to the dynamics of emerging market crises? Journal of Financial Stability 1:355–385
Kruck A (2011) Private Ratings, Public Regulations: Credit Rating Agencies and Global Financial Governance. Palgrave
McCauley R, White W (1997) The Euro and European Financial Markets. Bank for International Settlements Working Paper No 41. https://ssrn.com/abstract=860646. Accessed 29 November 2024
Partnoy F (1999) The Siskel and Ebert of Financial Markets? Two Thumbs Down for the Credit Rating Agencies. Washington University Law Quarterly 77:619–714
Partnoy F (2002) The Paradox of Credit Ratings. In: Levich R et al. (eds) Ratings, Rating Agencies and the Global Financial System. Springer Science+Business Media
Picker R, McConnel M (1993) When Cities Go Broke: A Conceptual Introduction to Municipal Bankruptcy University of Chicago Law Review 60:425–495
Piketty T (2014) Capital in the Twenty-First Century. Arthur Goldhammer tr, The Belknap Press of Harvard University Press
Pistor K (2019) The Code of Capital: How the Law Creates Wealth and Inequality. Princeton University Press, New Jersey
Rhee R (2015) Why Credit Rating Agencies Exist. Economic Notes, Banca Monte dei Paschi di Siena SpA 44:161–176
Riles A (2011) Collateral Knowledge: Legal Reasoning in the Global Financial Markets. University of Chicago Press, Chicago
Statement of Senator Joseph Lieberman (2002) Rating the Raters: Enron and the Credit Rating Agencies. https://www.hsgac.senate.gov/imo/media/doc/lieberman032002.pdf. Accessed 29 November 2024
Schwarcz S (1998) The Universal Language of Cross-Border Finance. Duke Journal of Comparative and International Law 8:235–254
Sherwin R (2018) Sovereign Imaginaries: Visualizing the Sacred Foundation of Law's Authority. NYLS Legal Studies Research Paper No 3212807. https://papers.ssrn.com/sol3/papers.cfm?abstract_id=3212807. Accessed 29 November 2024
Shiller R (2012) Finance and the Good Society. Princeton University Press, New Jersey
Soroushian J (2016) Credit Ratings in Financial Regulation: What's Changed Since the Dodd-Frank Act? Office of Financial Research Brief Series. https://www.financialresearch.gov/briefs/2016/04/21/credit-ratings-in-financial-regulation/. Accessed 29 November 2024
Storchak S (2013) Risk-Free Assets: An Unreachable Dream or a Must. BIS Papers No72:82–85 https://www.bis.org/publ/bppdf/bispap72o.pdf. Accessed 29 November 2024

Sylla R (2002) An Historical Primer on the Business of Credit Rating. In: Levich R et al (ed) Ratings, Rating Agencies and the Global Financial System. Springer Science+Business Media

The World Bank (2022) COVID 19: Debt Service Suspension Initiative. https://www.worldbank.org/en/topic/debt/brief/covid-19-debt-service-suspension-initiative. Accessed 29 November 2024

United States of America Financial Crisis Inquiry Commission (2011) The Financial Crisis Inquiry Report: Financial Report of the National Commission on the Causes of the Financial and Economic Crisis in the United States. US Government Printing Office

United States of America Staff of the Committee on Governmental Affairs (2002) Financial Oversight of Enron: The SEC and Private-Sector Watchdogs. https://www.govinfo.gov/content/pkg/CPRT-107SPRT82147/pdf/CPRT-107SPRT82147.pdf. Accessed 29 November 2024

Wachman R (2010) Greece debt crisis: the role of credit rating agencies. Guardian. https://www.theguardian.com/business/2010/apr/28/greece-debt-crisis-standard-poor-credit-agencies. Accessed 29 November 2024

Wheatley J (2020) Emerging economies hold back on asking creditors for debt relief. Financial Times. https://www.ft.com/content/3b4a5684-81e5-4ed0-9a9a-660d85f024e9. Accessed 29 November 2024

Zhang K (2020) Not Equal: Toward an International Law of Finance. Picaset, Helsinki

Kangle Zhang is an Assistant Professor in Public International Law at Peking University Law School in Beijing, China. His research targets the linkages between international law and the economy, focusing on issuing ranging from economic inequality and financial market operations, corporations in international law, environmental protection in economic development, to sovereign debt restructuring. Prior to joining Peking University Law School in 2022, he completed his Ph.D. in international law at the University of Helsinki. Dr. Zhang is currently an affiliated research fellow at the Erik Castrén Institute of International Law and Human Rights, and has previously been a Visiting Scholar at the Georgetown Law Centre and the Manchester International Law Centre.

Chapter 32
How to Counter Attempts by Authoritarian States to Redefine the Concept of Human Rights: Russia's Use of Human Rights Justifications in Defense of its Invasion of Ukraine

Maria Grahn-Farley

Contents

Abstract Human rights justification refers to when States activate human rights to justify their decisions and actions. Normally, it is the individual who invokes a human right against the State but with human rights justifications, it is the State that invokes human rights for its own benefits and in so doing turns human rights from being a regime measuring State compliance into an instrument of State governance. Human rights justifications change the foundation of human rights from being the possession of the individual into an instrument controlled by the State. Human rights justifications are re-directed from being aimed at the violating State to instead serving the State. This chapter applies the author's legal theory of human rights justifications to the Russian full-scale invasion of Ukraine, demonstrating how Russia uses human rights as justification for an illegal war against Ukraine. The argument in the chapter is that when human rights are used against themselves in this way, the integrity of the human rights regime risks being weakened.

M. Grahn-Farley (✉)
University of Gothenburg, Gothenburg, Sweden
e-mail: maria.grahn-farley@law.gu.se

Institute for Advanced Legal Studies, London, UK

M. Klamberg et al. (eds.), *Reconstructing Power and Hegemony in Public International Law*, https://doi.org/10.1007/978-94-6265-743-4_32

Keywords Human rights justifications · HRJs · Instrument of governance · Regime measuring compliance · Illegal war · UN Committees · Multipolar world order · Russia · Ukraine

32.1 Introduction

This chapter analyses of how Russia uses human rights to justify its invasion of Ukraine. The study casts light on an under examined aspect of human rights law, namely when States become agents of human rights by proactively attempting to reshape the social and legal context upon which their compliance with human rights is to be evaluated. The purpose of this study is to examine how *human rights justifications* (HRJs) are used by Russia to defend its illegal war against Ukraine. The study demonstrates that States are not only reactive to their human rights obligations but also try to proactively reshape the context in which human rights are evaluated and addressed by redefining the purpose and function of human rights, from protecting the individual to instead protecting the State.

The thesis is that Russia's use of HRJs changes the context for the application of the UN treaty monitoring bodies, exemplified with the two Concluding Observations concerning Russia's implementation of the UN Convention on the Rights of the Child (CRC)[1] and of the International Convention on the Elimination of All Forms of Racial Discrimination (CERD), respectively.[2] By permitting Russia to use the UN Committees' monitoring system as a stage for HRJs, the Committees are at risk of aiding legitimization of the Russian use of HRJs in its war against Ukraine. How Russia uses the UN human rights monitoring regimes is on clear display from an analysis of the latest two Concluding Observations, issued after Russia's full-scale invasion of Ukraine in 2022.

The UN Committees, unlike the human right courts, do not have the authority to issue decisions that are legally binding for Member States. Instead, the UN Committees can use soft-law strategies such as "naming and shaming", for example through issuing Concluding Observations. These statements can only hold States morally accountable for their actions and decisions when it comes to the implementation of human rights treaties.

In the situation of the Russian invasion, efforts to change the context of the human rights application are not successful at the mainstream international legal level. The invasion is generally seen as a violation of both international law and human rights and has been condemned by several inter-State organizations such as the United

[1] Convention on the Rights of the Child, opened for signature 20 November 1989, 1577 UNTS 3 (entered into force 2 September 1990) (CRC).

[2] International Convention on the Elimination of All Forms of Racial Discrimination, opened for signature 21 March 1965, 660 UNTS 195 (entered into force 4 January 1969) (CERD).

Nations,[3] the Council of Europe,[4] the European Union,[5] and the North Atlantic Treaty Organization (NATO),[6] as well as through statements issued against the Russian invasion by international courts, for example from the International Criminal Court[7] and the International Court of Justice,[8] In this context, Russia's use of HRJs has not had the mainstream effect to turn a violation of human right into a justified legal action, but Russia's use of HRJs might still serve to defend the full-scale invasion internally within Russia. Further, HRJs can provide political cover for Russia's allies internationally. In plain litigation terminology, Russia muddies the water just enough to help legitimize support of the invasion, domestically and for its allies, even if use of HRJs will not be able to turn an illegal war into a just war based on a mainstream understanding of human rights.[9]

A compelling question is how to respond to the Russian use of HRJs: should it simply be ignored or should it be called out as misuse and violations of the human rights regimes? This chapter identifies a particular moment when Russia's use of HRJs matters, as they are connected to the UN Committee's Concluding Observations and therefore should not be ignored as something that concerns only Russia internally.

Basically, what Russia's use of HRJs does is to domestically create immunity against the international critique of Russia's invasion of Ukraine as a human rights violation. International human rights critique is described—by Russia—as a Western Russophobic-generated critique, and in line with this reasoning is not to be taken seriously. At the same time, HRJs allow Russia to harvest the human rights praise it receives through the Concluding Observations—and in contrast to the human rights critique, the human rights praise are to be taken seriously. In other words, the critique can be seen as false and the praise as true. This in turn risks the long-term preservation of the integrity of the human rights regime itself. If human rights can freely be used by States to defend themselves against human rights critiques when they are in fact violating human rights, human rights risk losing both moral and legal strength in protecting individual persons being abused by States.

---

[3] *See, for example*, UNGA 2022a, 2022b.

[4] Parliamentary Assembly 2023.

[5] *See, for example*, European Parliament 2023a; European Parliament 2023b.

[6] *See, for example*: Statement by NATO Heads of State and Government, Brussels 24 March 2022. https://www.nato.int/cps/en/natohq/official_texts_193719.htm?selectedLocale=en. Accessed 11 April 2025; Statement by the North Atlantic Council marking one year of Russia's war of aggression against Ukraine, 24 February 2023. https://www.nato.int/cps/en/natohq/official_texts_212268.htm. Accessed 11 April 2025.

[7] Situation referred to the ICC by 43 States Parties: March—April 2022, ICC-01/22, Suspects: Vladimir Vladimirovich Putin, Maria Alekseyevna Lvova-Belova, Sergei Ivanovich Kobylash, Viktor Nikolayevic Sokolov, Sergei Kuzhugetovich Shoigu, and Valery Vasilyevic Gerasimov.

[8] *See, for example*, pending cases: *Allegations of Genocide under the Convention on the Prevention and Punishment of the Crime of Genocide (Ukraine v. Russian Federation)*; *Application of the International Convention for the Suppression of the Financing of Terrorism and of the International Convention on the Elimination of All Forms of Racial Discrimination (Ukraine v. Russian Federation).*

[9] For a systemic outline of the Russian use of international law and narrative in defense of its invasion of Ukraine, *see* Värk 2022.

32.1.1 *Terminology, Method, and Scope*

The term "human rights justification" is developed by the author within the project HRJust, an EU-funded Horizon Consortium of which the author is the coordinator. Human rights justification (HRJ) refers to when States activates human rights with the purpose to defend their actions and decisions. By doing so, States turn human rights from a regime activated by the individual demanding that the State is in compliance with international human rights obligations, into a regime of governance activated by the State. Moving human rights from being the possession of the individual into an instrument controlled by the State. When human rights become an instrument of governance, they move from being a regime measuring State compliance and holding the State accountable for its international law human rights obligations, into an instrument lending legitimacy to acts and decisions of the State. This was not seen as a problem for democratic liberalism as long as it was the dominating narrative shaping a Global order. The dilemma from a liberal democratic position is that the post-Cold War dominance did not generate an awareness of possible backsliding, or that the same human rights regimes could be used to legitimize not only liberal democracy but also non-liberal democracies. This is the situation today, when this global narrative is contested by narratives that challenge the liberal democratic order, primarily by China and Russia but now also the United States, in demanding to take control over Greenland and expressing a wish that Canada become the 51st state of its territory. This chapter will focus on Russia only.

A mixed method between the legal method of black letter law and grounded theory will be applied in this text.[10] The approach of this chapter is interdisciplinary in the sense that the legal work is informed by grounded theory. The legal method is the dominant method, and grounded theory is subjugated to the requirements of the legal method.

The chapter limits its scope to documents from two time periods when human rights were referenced in public statements by Russia's Ministry of Foreign Affairs in defending its invasion of Ukraine. The first set stems from the months around the Russian invasion of Ukraine in 2022 and the focus is on the official Statements translated into English from Russian by the Russian Ministry of Foreign Affairs. The second set of documents are the English language press releases of the Russian Ministry of Foreign Affairs in March, April, and May 2024. This is an early study for the project HRJust; a HRJust legal theory is being applied as a pilot study on a concrete situation of the Russian defense of its full-scale invasion of Ukraine—an act that in accordance with all mainstream international law is a direct and serious violation of the prohibition of the use of force as a means of dispute resolutions between States. Further, the invasion is also a violation of the sovereign and territorial integrity of Ukraine. Russia is clearly not being deterred by international law. It is therefore interesting that Russia still tries to justify its invasion through human rights.

[10] Charmaz 2014.

32.2 The State as an Active Agent in the Reshaping of its Human Rights Context

There is significant research conducted on if and how States respond when being critiqued for human rights violations (to be addressed below). This chapter is different from that research in that we are not studying how a State responds when being critiqued for human rights violations but instead how a State is proactively—through HRJs—setting the stage for potential human rights critique in the future by using human rights as an instrument of the State.

Naming and shaming refers to when a State's human rights violations are called out and information thereon is disseminated to the public. A State not living up to its human rights obligations can be named and shamed out by States, intergovernmental organizations (IGOs), nongovernmental organizations (NGOs), or individual persons. Naming and shaming is frequently used to point out States' human rights violations in the hope of influencing them to adjust and realign their behavior to comply with their human rights obligations.

Quite a few studies have been done on the effectiveness of naming and shaming, with a variety of views in the literature on naming and shaming and its outcomes. In analyzing the Universal Periodic Review system, Yooneui Kim makes the argument that naming and shaming is misunderstood when studied as a State-to-State phenomenon—the better way to understand naming and shaming is suggested to be seeing it as a social phenomenon between States.[11] The argument is that States consider the cost of naming and shaming another state before doing so, and find comfort in acting as part of a collective of States, rather than as one State to another.[12] Kim finds naming and shaming effective because it is done by peers within the Universal Periodic Review system, and states that NGOs are able to provide valuable information underpinning the peer review leading to naming and shaming between States.[13] Rochelle Terman and Joshua Byun make similar arguments with more focus on politization. They find that States not only make deliberate political calculations when they name and shame other States but also take into political account what types of rights violations they will highlight in the naming and shaming.[14] Terman and Byun find that States usually chose less damaging human rights categories to complain about when their critique is directed at their friends compared with when it is aimed at States they are not friendly with.[15] Emilie Hafner-Burton has pointed out the complexities that come with naming and shaming.[16] Hafner-Burton identifies three categories of outcomes, the first being that naming and shaming works in generating new improved behavior, the second that change of State behavior depends

[11] Kim 2023 at 289.

[12] Ibid.

[13] Ibid.

[14] Terman and Byun 2022.

[15] Ibid.

[16] Hafner-Burton 2008.

on the rights themselves and how well-equipped a State is to feel the incentive of the naming and shaming—some rights are easier to comply with than others. The third and final category is when naming and shaming will worsen the behavior of a State. This is when the political gain for the State of not being seen as giving in to the pressure by internal (domestic) or external (international) actors—for example political oppositional parties or international adversaries. Hafner-Burton suggests that in such moments, naming and shaming can even lead to a worsening of human rights behavior by the State.[17] The commonality between these studies, though they arrive at different conclusions as regards the effectiveness of naming and shaming, is that they all see the State as reactive to this action.

This chapter, by analyzing the two Concluding Observations by the UN Committees on the Rights of the Child and on the Elimination of Racial Discrimination, finds that the Russian use of HRJs cannot be seen as an act in isolation as it also affects the way in which the UN human rights monitoring bodies are understood.

The chapter argues that the approaches used by Kim, Terman and Byun, and Hafner-Burton to study how States react to human rights critiques could be widened to also consider how States—through HRJs—are attempting to proactively reshape the human rights context in which they are to be evaluated. States are reactive not only to human rights as a form of compliance regimes where their behavior is measured and monitored by other States, NGOs, and IGOs. In fact, States are also proactive in relation to human rights and their own actions and decisions. In this example of Russia, it is taking proactive measures by using HRJs to reshape the context in which human rights are to be evaluated when it comes to its invasion of Ukraine. When Russia uses human rights to defend its actions and decisions, it turns human rights from a regime of compliance into an instrument of governance. Human rights help give legitimacy to the invasion of Ukraine. This shifts the balance of human rights from the individual possession of rights into something controlled by the State. The idea of the individual being in possession of her rights is the cornerstone of liberal rights ideology. This is a liberally anchored understanding of rights, as described for example by C.B. Macpherson in the 1960s; he refers to it as possessive individualism.[18] Once human rights have been transformed—from a regime where the individual possesses a right that can be used as a claim against the State, into an instrument of the State making it possible for the State to anchor the legitimacy of its actions in the source of human rights—the human rights regime moves from being firmly anchored within a liberal paradigm to being a functional tool for the interests of the State.

Human rights are normative, and they are ideological in the sense that they rely on a legal historical foundation of liberalism, even though they have in a post-Cold War era come to mean many more things. Climate justice as codified in the Paris Agreement is just one of the most recent frontiers of human rights expansion. The Paris Agreement is the only UN treaty making claims to fall within the umbrella

[17] Ibid.

[18] Macpherson 1962.

of human rights without including a discrimination prohibition.[19] Instead of having freedom and equality as its foundation, the Paris Agreement relies on vulnerability as a universal ground. This is a step away from a liberal foundation. The challenge is what to include under the umbrella of human rights when Russia uses words and arguments that look and sounds like human rights but clearly do not rest on a liberal foundation. Are these to be understood as human rights or as something else? For the purpose of this chapter, a human right is what the State defines as a human right when claiming it. In other words, falling back on basic treaty law, the meaning of a treaty and its obligations is that—absent a court—what is a human right is primarily to be interpreted by the State party in accordance with the ordinary meaning of the word. HRJs are usually in accordance with the ordinary meaning of the word.[20] It is possible to question if the interpretations made by Russia in defense of its invasion of Ukraine were made in good faith, which is a requirement in the Vienna Convention on the Law of Treaties (1969). However, this falls outside of the scope of this chapter, which studies the effects of the use of HRJs, not their legal validity before a court. The point of HRJs is that they occur in the place of soft law and outside the reach of courts. Such statements can seldom become the subject of a legal evaluation by a court.

32.3 The Russian Full-Scale Invasion of Ukraine

The full-scale invasion in 2022 was preceded by an almost ten-year escalation of tensions between Russia and Ukraine, centered on Ukraine's relationship to Europe and the EU. EU trade and association talks were suspended by the pro-Russian President of Ukraine, Yanukovych, on 21 November 2013. This led to large anti-government protests (the Maidan upraising) taking place in December 2013 and continuing into 2014. Twenty-six persons were killed on 18 February 2014, in the worst clash to that date between protesters and the government. An arrest warrant was issued for President Yanukovych by Ukraine on 24 February 2014. A new cabinet was announced by the acting Ukrainian president on 26 February—including representatives of the pro-democracy protest movement. The next day, the government building of Crimea was seized by pro-Russia gunmen and the Russian flag was raised on top of the building. Travel bans and asset freezes were imposed by the EU and the US on several Russian and Ukraine officials over the Crimea secession referendum held on 16 March 2014. The condemnation from the international community continued with a UN General Assembly vote, where 100–11 (58 abstentions) voted against recognizing the Crimea referendum result. The Federation Council of Russia voted

[19] On the connection between a prohibition of discrimination and liberalism, *see* Grahn-Farley 2022.

[20] That words should be understood in accordance with their ordinary meaning is stated in Vienna Convention on the Law of Treaties, opened for signature 23 May 1969, 1155 UNTS 331 (entered into force 27 January 1980), article 31.

to approve the Resolution authorizing the use of Armed Forces abroad, the day after the Russian recognition of Donetsk and Luhansk,[21] leading to the full-scale Russian invasion of Ukraine on 24 February 2022.

Russia has received consistent critique for its human rights violations in connection with its actions in the territory of Ukraine.[22] The UN Committee on the Rights of the Child urged Russia to investigate allegations of war crimes by the Presidential Commissioner for Children's Rights.[23] The list of alleged human rights violation is extensive. A few examples are presented below. However, this also raises the question of the role of HRJs and how UN human rights instruments and bodies are to relate to Russian participation within the UN human rights regime.

On 16 March 2022, as a direct consequence of the Russian invasion of Ukraine, the European Council in accordance with Article 8 of the Statute of the Council of Europe expelled Russia from the Council of Europe effective immediately, with Russia's response of withdrawal.[24] The Russian withdrawal was without legal effect as Russia was already expelled from the Council and consequently had lost all of its rights and was no longer obligated in accordance with European Convention on Human Rights.[25]

32.4 The International Community Reacts

Shortly after the Council of Europe's expulsion of Russia followed the UN Human Rights Council's suspension of Russia on 7 April 2022 (93 votes in favor, 24 against, and 58 abstentions).[26] Russia was found to be in violation of the prohibition of the use of force under the UN Charter article 2(4).[27] The General Assembly Resolution declaring the suspension of Russia followed a resolution adopted on 2 March 2022 where the demand for a Russian immediate, complete, and unconditional withdrawal of its military from the territory of Ukraine was presented.[28] In the same resolution, the "sovereignty, independence, unity and territorial integrity of Ukraine" were also emphasized.[29]

The International Criminal Court (ICC) issued an arrest warrant for President Vladimir Putin and Maria Lvova-Belova, the Commissioner for Children's Rights in the Office of the President of the Russian Federation, both allegedly responsible for

---

[21] Federation Council of the Russian Federation, Resolution authorizing the use of Armed Forces abroad, 22 Feb 2022. http://council.gov.ru/en/events/news/133443/#. Accessed 11 April 2025.

[22] *See, for example*: Committee of Ministers 2022a, 2022b, 2022c. *See also* UNGA 2022a, 2022c.

[23] UN CRC 2024, para 13.

[24] Committee of Ministers 2022a, 2022b, 2022c.

[25] *See* Committee of Ministers 2022c, paras 8–9.

[26] UNGA 2022c.

[27] UNGA 2022a, para 2.

[28] Ibid. para 4.

[29] Ibid. para 1.

war crimes that took place on 24 February 2022 when hundreds of Ukrainian children were unlawfully deported and transported from the occupied Ukrainian territories into Russia.[30]

Russia is no longer a party to the European Convention of Human Rights due to being expelled from the Council of Europe, but is still a party to the human rights treaties under the UN umbrella.[31] Since the invasion, Russia has submitted periodic reports to and received the Concluding Observations from the UN Committee on the Rights of the Child[32] and from the UN Committee on the Elimination of Racial Discrimination.[33]

Keeping Russia under the human rights umbrella of the UN is a mixed bag. The pro is that Russia is still bound by international human rights law, the con is that the Concluding Observations from the two committees give a false sense of normalcy: that the invasion of Ukraine and the war crimes of Russia can be bracketed within the regular reporting system.

Examples of the cloak of normalcy can be found in the UN Committee on the Rights of the Child's Concluding Observation. It writes:

> The Committee expresses its appreciation for the constructive dialogue held with the high-level and multisectoral delegations of the State party.[34]

This is of course a standard phrase of collegiality; it just sits oddly when in a section further down in the observations, the committee writes:

> The Committee urges the State party: to investigate allegations of war crimes perpetrated by the Presidential Commissioner for Children's Rights.[35]

The situation becomes even odder when the Committee praises Russia for its Government Order No. 122-r of 23 January 2021 declaring the Decade of Childhood.[36] It becomes even more bizarre when the Committee continues by encouraging Russia to make sure that the action plan of the Decade of Childhood should "[cover] all areas under the Convention and the Optional Protocols thereto and is supported by

---

[30] ICC, *Situation in Ukraine*, Presidency, Decision assigning the situation in Ukraine to Pre-Trial Chamber II, 2 March 2022, ICC-01/22-1.

[31] These treaties are: International Covenant on Civil and Political Rights, opened for signature 16 December 1966, 999 UNTS 171 (entered into force 23 March 1976); International Covenant on Economic, Social and Cultural Rights, opened for signature 19 December 1966, 999 UNTS 3 (entered into force 3 January 1976); CERD, above n. 2; Convention on the Elimination of All Forms of Discrimination against Women, opened for signature 1 March 1980, 1249 UNTS 13 (entered into force 3 September 1981); Convention against Torture and Other Cruel, Inhuman or Degrading Treatment or Punishment, opened for signature 10 December 1984, 1465 UNTS 85 (entered into force 26 June 1987); CRC, above n. 1; and Convention on the Rights of Persons with Disabilities, opened for signature 13 December 2006, 2515 UNTS 3 (entered into force 3 May 2008).

[32] UN CRC 2024.

[33] UN CERD 2023.

[34] UN CRC 2024, para 2.

[35] Ibid. para 13.

[36] Ibid. para 7.

sufficient human, technical and financial resources."[37] At the same time, the ICC has issued an arrest warrant for Maria Lvova-Belova, the Commissioner for Children's Rights in the Office of the President of the Russian Federation, for alleged war crimes against children.

The tone is different when it comes to the Concluding Observations issued by the Committee on the Elimination of Racial Discrimination.[38] Where the Committee on the Rights of the Child praises Russia for its collaboration with that Committee, the Committee on the Elimination of Racial Discrimination writes:

> However, the Committee regrets the refusal of the delegation to discuss and respond to questions posed by the Committee on issues related to the armed conflict and the situation in Crimea and the City of Sevastopol, which prevented the Committee from fully performing its function under article 9 of the Convention. The Committee highlights that the full engagement of States parties in the interactive dialogue with the human rights treaty bodies is a key component of the periodic review process, which provides a unique opportunity for the Committee and the State party to hold constructive and in-depth discussions in order to allow the Committee to assess the progress made and to indicate to the State party the areas where further efforts are needed.

Even if the Committee on the Elimination of Racial Discrimination is less focused on "business as usual" than the Committee on the Rights of the Child, it still provides praise for a variety of legislative initiatives: providing temporary identity documents to stateless persons, expanding social benefits to extended families of indigenous people, and instating a comprehensive plan of action for Roma people in Russia.[39]

The dilemma of if it is better to keep "bad actors" within the regulated human rights and treaty regimes as the UN is doing by maintaining Russia's obligations under treaty law, or if it is better to expel the State from the treaty body as the Council of Europe did, can be illustrated by the two Concluding Observations. They both point out the scope for improvement on Russia's part when it comes to the CRC and the CERD, but it also becomes painstakingly clear that these instruments are not suited to address serious war crimes: the Commissioner of Child Rights is accused of child mass kidnapping. It is horrifying to read—in the same document—the encouragement of proper funding for child rights initiatives, presumably to be led by the very same Commissioner of Child Rights accused by the ICC of war crimes against children. The argument can be made that access and the ability of holding Russia accountable make up for the disgrace to the UN Human Rights instruments themselves by making war crimes fit within the routines of periodic reports. This cannot be justified, as it is clear that Russia will not follow the two Committees' recommendations to end its human rights violations in Ukraine. To lend the legitimacy of the two Committees to Russia as a legitimate human rights actor can only be a win for Russia and a loss for the legitimacy of the UN human rights system.

This goes back to the dilemma often illustrated by the advisory opinion over the reservation made by Chile for the Genocide Convention (the Reservation Case). The

[37] Ibid. para 7.

[38] UN CERD 2023.

[39] Ibid. para 3.

Advisory Opinion finds that a reservation cannot go against the object and purpose of the treaty.[40] Compare the Reservation Case to later practice within the UN system of not expelling bad actors from the human rights regimes but instead keeping them engaged within the system where their human rights obligations can be brought forward to them, for example through the periodic review system. There must come a moment when this approach is no longer fit for purpose. That should have come with the Russian reporting to the Committees. To the credit of the Committee on the Elimination of Racial Discrimination, it makes full use of its opportunity to address Russia by holding Russia accountable for its human rights violations in the Russian illegal war against Ukraine.[41] However, this position is still problematic, as the procedures of the Committee and its soft-law use of naming and shaming are limited to recommendations of the following type:

> The Committee recommends that the State party:
>
> (a) Conduct effective, thorough and impartial investigations into allegations of violations and abuses of human rights committed during the ongoing armed conflict with Ukraine and other armed conflicts in which the State party is or has been involved, in particular against ethnic Ukrainians, and prosecute and punish perpetrators of violations with penalties commensurate to the offences.

It is doubtful if the Committee on the Elimination of Racial Discrimination's condemnation of Russia's human rights violations outweighs the legitimacy it gives Russia as being part of the international community of human rights actors, especially when it is obvious that its recommendations will not be adhered to by Russia.

32.5 Russia's Use of HRJs in the War against Ukraine

As demonstrated above, it matters how Russia is using human rights to justify its unlawful invasion of Ukraine because Russia is still a party and a member of the international human rights community and aspires to be one of the significant powers in a multipolar world order. This new multipolar world order would reshape the human rights regime itself, from what it is today—a liberal project based on freedom and equality with the function to check the State in its treatment of its inhabitants—into a State-centered regime where the ultimate limit of human rights would be the interest of the State in which they are to be applied. This way, human rights would change from a regime protecting the individual against the interest of the State into a regime limited by State interests.

Russia's justification of its invasion of Ukraine follows three core themes where HRJs are used as either direct justifications on their own or are insinuated within a supporting argument to help shape Russia's narrative of HRJs for the invasion.

[40] ICJ, Reservations to the Convention on Genocide, Advisory Opinion, 28 May 1951, 1951 ICJ Reports 15.

[41] *See, for example*, UN CERD 2023, para 4.

The three themes are the following. First, that the invasion was called upon because Russia is a protector of human rights. The second theme is that the international critique of the invasion is a result of a new multipolar world order that EU and the West cannot accept. The third theme is that the Ukrainian government is illegitimate.

32.5.1 Russia's Positivist HRJs

The invasion is justified by a general human rights critique against Ukraine, describing Ukraine as in a state of disarray and falling into human rights violations:

> We must note that the human rights situation has steadily deteriorated in that country over the past few years. We should have called this report not on the observance of human rights but on the failure to do this or even on the violation of human rights in Ukraine.[42]

One of the HRJs most emphasized by Russia is the protection of the Russian language and its culture.

> Immediately after this [the Maidan demonstrations], they embarked on a path of lawlessness and complete neglect for basic human rights and freedoms—the right to life, freedom of speech, access to information, freedom of expression, freedom of conscience and the use of a native tongue.[43]

Russia does not provide a clear explanation of in what way the Russian language is a human right, if it falls within the protection against discrimination or right to culture, for example. Language is the most common human rights violation described by Russia. The language issue is often raised in the context of attacks on Russians:

> In recent years, the Kiev regime has waged an all-out onslaught on the Russian language and infringed on the rights of the Russian and Russian-speaking people of Ukraine with impunity.[44]

The defense of the Russian language is at times tied to broader concerns of discrimination, for example against Indigenous people living in Ukraine.[45]

In the months following the Russian invasion, the Minister of Foreign Affairs issued a set of public statements translated into English by the Ministry of Foreign Affairs. The combination of human rights violations that Russia finds Ukraine to have committed in Ukraine was the reason for the invasion:

---

[42] Excerpts from the briefing by Foreign Ministry Spokeswoman Maria Zakharova, Moscow, May 23, 2024 (Another report on the human rights situation in Ukraine). https://mid.ru/en/foreign_policy/news/1952458/. Accessed 11 April 2025.

[43] Foreign Minister Sergey Lavrov's remarks at a meeting of the UN Security Council on Ukraine, New York, September 22, 2022. https://mid.ru/en/foreign_policy/news/1830851/. Accessed 11 April 2025.

[44] Ibid.

[45] Ibid.

> Everything I said goes to show once again that the decision to conduct a special military operation was unavoidable. We have said this more than once. We have presented volumes of factual evidence proving that Ukraine was preparing to play the role of the "anti-Russia" and was being used as a springboard for creating and implementing threats against Russia's security.[46]

Lavrov used a general HRJ, mentioning human rights as a general concept as seen in the quote below, but also listed specific rights—especially the one of the Russian language and culture often described in a context of Russophobia:

> Ukraine itself has in fact turned into an aggressive totalitarian state that approves discriminatory laws, carries out forced Ukrainisation, encourages Russophobia, and violates language, educational, cultural and other human rights on a large scale.[47]

Another justification for the Russian invasion was the protection of the people living in the regions of Donbass, Zaporizhzhia, and Kherson in Ukraine:

> Russia could not but come to the rescue of the long-suffering people of Donbass. Nor can it fail to defend the residents of the Zaporozhye and Kherson regions from this inhuman regime.[48]

This is not a direct HRJ but read in the context of the other direct HRJs it lends itself to be understood justifying the invasion to protect Russian language, ethics, and culture.

32.5.2 *Multipolar World Order*

One recurring theme is the security of Russia within a multipolar world order and how the West fails to accept the shift from a Western hegemonically led world into a multipolar world order where Russia has a given place. As described by Minister of Foreign Affairs Lavrov:

---

[46] Official Representative of the President and Foreign Minister Sergey Lavrov's remarks at a plenary meeting of the Federation Council of the Federal Assembly of the Russian Federation on the approval of the laws ratifying treaties between the Russian Federation and the Donetsk and Lugansk People's Republics and the Zaporozhye and Kherson regions and establishing new constituent entities of the Russian Federation, Moscow, October 4, 2022. https://mid.ru/en/foreign_policy/news/1832391/. Accessed 11 April 2025.

[47] Official Representative of the President and Foreign Minister Sergey Lavrov's remarks at a plenary meeting of the Federation Council of the Federal Assembly of the Russian Federation on the approval of the laws ratifying treaties between the Russian Federation and the Donetsk and Lugansk People's Republics and the Zaporozhye and Kherson regions and establishing new constituent entities of the Russian Federation, Moscow, October 4, 2022. https://mid.ru/en/foreign_policy/news/1832391/. Accessed 11 April 2025.

[48] Official Representative of the President and Foreign Minister Sergey Lavrov's remarks at a plenary meeting of the Federation Council of the Federal Assembly of the Russian Federation on the approval of the laws ratifying treaties between the Russian Federation and the Donetsk and Lugansk People's Republics and the Zaporozhye and Kherson regions and establishing new constituent entities of the Russian Federation, Moscow, October 4, 2022. https://mid.ru/en/foreign_policy/news/1832391/. Accessed 11 April 2025.

> Similar sentiments are echoed in other declarations, such as "we will lose our influence" and "Russia will reshape the world together with China, Iran, North Korea, Syria." These assertions do not denote self-doubt; rather, they indicate a realisation that there is, as they [EU and the West] openly acknowledge, a "battle" to maintain their hegemony, which essentially translates to the establishment of a new multipolar world order. While we may be getting tired of the term, we can reframe it as an equitable, just, and democratic international order where every nation adheres to the principle of the UN Charter—the sovereign equality of states.[49]

Russia interprets the human rights critique it has received from the EU and what it defines as the West to be made within the context of this struggle over the leadership within this new world order:

> In turn, Russia consistently counters attempt to manipulate the human rights narrative for the sake of political interests. This is why it regularly becomes the target of "punitive" measures from "collective" Brussels. The EU's policy of sanctions has nothing in common with concern for human rights and the real-life situation in our country.[50]

The multipolar world order encouraged by Russia was also a cause for a defense against the EU, often combined with the larger form of the West, as described by Lavrov:

> The 1999 Istanbul Charter for European Security had indivisibility of security enshrined at the top level. Countries are free to choose alliances, but they cannot do so if by strengthening their security they undermine the security of others.[51]

32.5.3 The EU and the West

Both the EU and the West are understood as threats to the interests of Russia, as described here:

> I would like to underscore an interesting point. Western countries are failing to understand that if we are put in a situation where someone seeks to defeat Russia, "strategically" eliminate it as a global player, we will not be intimidated.[52]

The critical position of the EU against Russia is understood as an expression of discriminatory feelings against Russians or Russophobia, as explained by the spokeswoman of the Foreign Ministry:

---

[49] Foreign Minister Sergey Lavrov's interview with the radio station Sputnik, Govorit Moskva, and Komsoloskaya Pravda, Moscow, April 19, 2024. https://www.mid.ru/en/foreign_policy/news/1945189/. Accessed 11 April 2025.

[50] Excerpts from the briefing by Foreign Ministry Spokeswoman Maria Zakharova, Moscow, May 23, 2024 (European Union hits Russia with new sanctions regime for alleged human rights violations, reprisals against civil society and the democratic opposition). https://mid.ru/en/foreign_policy/news/1952458/. Accessed 11 April 2025.

[51] Foreign Minister Sergey Lavrov's interview with the radio station Sputnik, Govorit Moskva, and Komsoloskaya Pravda, Moscow, April 19, 2024. https://www.mid.ru/en/foreign_policy/news/1945189/. Accessed 11 April 2025.

[52] Ibid.

> It is surprising that those living in the blooming EU garden (as Josep Borrell once put it) fail to notice obvious things: Such self-exposing Russophobic stunts merely serve to further consolidate our society that clearly sees the real goals of the European Union and the West with regard to Russia. All these escapades cannot influence our determination to act in accordance with our own national interests and to ensure the security of our citizens, as well as the real protection of their rights and freedoms.[53]

HRJs are used as a way of creating an alternative to the narrative of Russia committing human rights violations. Here is one of the clearest explanations for HRJs as an instrument for reshaping the narrative and context within which Russia is being evaluated for its human rights compliance:

> Russia consistently counters attempts to manipulate the human rights narrative for the sake of political interests. This is why it regularly becomes the target of "punitive" measures from "collective" Brussels. The EU's policy of sanctions has nothing in common with concern for human rights and the real-life situation in our country.[54]

Not only are the EU and the West accused of being supporters of neo-Nazis but also at times as being supporters of terrorists, as seen in the statement below:

> In the meantime, Western countries, apparently oblivious to the terrorist activities of their Ukrainian minions, are publicly encouraging them to strike at Russian regions.[55]

The Russian postcolonial critique of both Western power and the way in which the West has used human rights against the Global South is close to the critique of the EU and the West. This is how the postcolonial critique is expressed:

> We see these sanctions as a rude violation of international law, including the principle of non-interference in the domestic affairs of sovereign states. This is an open manifestation of neo-colonial approaches. When they use the concept of upholding human rights to accomplish their own narrow mercenary objectives, they turn it into a tool for dealing with undesirable countries.[56]

---

[53] Excerpts from the briefing by Foreign Ministry Spokeswoman Maria Zakharova, Moscow, May 23, 2024 (European Union hits Russia with new sanctions regime for alleged human rights violations, reprisals against civil society and the democratic opposition). https://mid.ru/en/foreign_policy/news/1952458/. Accessed 11 April 2025.

[54] Excerpts from the briefing by Foreign Ministry Spokeswoman Maria Zakharova, Moscow, May 30, 2024 (European Union hits Russia with new sanctions regime for alleged human rights violations reprisals against civil society and the democratic opposition). https://mid.ru/en/foreign_policy/news/1953753/. Accessed 11 April 2025.

[55] Excerpts from the briefing by Foreign Ministry Spokeswoman Maria Zakharova, Moscow, May 30, 2024 (Ukraine crisis update). https://mid.ru/en/foreign_policy/news/1953753/. Accessed 11 April 2025.

[56] Excerpts from the briefing by Foreign Ministry Spokeswoman Maria Zakharova, Moscow, May 30, 2024 (European Union hits Russia with new sanctions regime for alleged human rights violations reprisals against civil society and the democratic opposition). https://mid.ru/en/foreign_policy/news/1953753/. Accessed 11 April 2025.

32.5.4 *The Ukrainian Government as Illegitimate*

Another theme is the illegitimacy of the Ukrainian government. There is a variety of HRJs explaining why the government is illegitimate, with the Russian language almost always being mentioned, as seen in this statement:

> The radical nationalists who seized power in Ukraine following a government coup in February 2014 have conducted a policy of suppression with regard to Ukraine's Russians and Russian speakers throughout the subsequent period. They have branded as terrorists the residents of the Donetsk and Lugansk regions, who refused to recognise the criminal Maidan authorities.[57]

Russia repeatedly paints itself as fighting a Nazi regime in Ukraine. This is not a direct HRJs, but it provides a context to the Russian use of HRJs:

> We will not tolerate neo-Nazism on the territory of Ukraine. We are fighting neo-Nazis, rather than the people of Ukraine, and we have nothing against the latter.[58]

There are recurring historical references to World War II and the victory over Nazi Germany:

> This suggests a parallel with the attitude of Western countries to the Hitler regime on the eve of WWII. This policy received broad popularity under the name of "the policy of appeasement." It led to the bloodiest war in the history of humanity. Luckily for the current generations, this war ended in the victory of the anti-Hitler coalition with the USSR's decisive role. The idea of preventing such a calamity became a fundamental principle of the UN Charter.[59]

Russia describes itself has having an important historical legacy that obligates it to maintain its historical role in the fight against Nazis, justifying the invasion of Ukraine:

> The above facts once again confirm the timeliness of the objectives of the special military operation to denazify and demilitarize Ukraine and to eliminate threats originating from its territory.[60]

---

[57] Official Representative of the President and Foreign Minister Sergey Lavrov's remarks at a plenary meeting of the Federation Council of the Federal Assembly of the Russian Federation on the approval of the laws ratifying treaties between the Russian Federation and the Donetsk and Lugansk People's Republics and the Zaporozhye and Kherson regions and establishing new constituent entities of the Russian Federation, Moscow, October 4, 2022. https://mid.ru/en/foreign_policy/news/1832391/. Accessed 11 April 2025.

[58] Foreign Minister Sergey Lavrov's interview for the film, Nazism on Trial, Moscow, November 26, 2022. https://mid.ru/en/foreign_policy/news/1840230/. Accessed 11 April 2025.

[59] Excerpts from the briefing by Foreign Ministry Spokeswoman Maria Zakharova, Moscow, May 23, 2024 (Another report on the human rights situation in Ukraine). https://mid.ru/en/foreign_policy/news/1952458/. Accessed 11 April 2025.

[60] Excerpts from the briefing by Foreign Ministry Spokeswoman Maria Zakharova, Moscow, May 15, 2024 (Ukraine crisis update). https://mid.ru/en/press_service/spokesman/briefings/1950737/. Accessed 11 April 2025.

Pointing out the Ukrainian government as neo-Nazis is a consistent theme throughout all the messaging of the Ministry of Foreign Affairs. There is hardly a single press release that does not begin with describing Ukraine and its leadership as Nazi or at least mention this:

> The servile willingness of the current Ukrainian leadership to move the country along the path of self-destruction against the interests of its people, creating a Russophobic "anti-Russia" project out of it, is the reason why overseas handlers ignore the neo-Nazi nature of the Kiev regime.[61]

The labeling of the Ukrainian government as neo-Nazi is paired with accusations of it being a terrorist government in a terrorist State:

> The Kiev regime continues relentless terrorist attacks targeting Russia's civilian population and civilian infrastructure.[62]

Not as often, but at times, the President of Ukraine is mentioned by name and, if so, as a terrorist:

> Zelensky is destroying Ukraine in every conceivable way historically and by turning it into a terrorist cell.[63]

The HRJs for protecting Russians against discrimination for their language are sometimes combined with the Nazi accusations against the Ukrainian government:

> Kiev is making full use of its Nazi approaches as regards the Russian speakers of Ukraine. Everything Russian (language, culture, education, printed matter and the media) are prohibited. The process of de-Russification has reached its climax in education. Instruction in Russian and its study in schools are banned.[64]

32.6 Conclusion

Russia's use of HRJs is effective in that it shifts the terrain of the discussion away from its invasion of Ukraine to evaluating the validity or invalidity of its HRJs and accusations against Ukraine. For example, it raises the question if Russia is correct in that Ukraine is violating the freedom of information by banning information

---

[61] Excerpts from the briefing by Foreign Ministry Spokeswoman Maria Zakharova, Moscow, May 23, 2024 (Another report on the human rights situation in Ukraine). https://mid.ru/en/foreign_policy/news/1952458/. Accessed 11 April 2025.

[62] 18 of April 2024, Excerpts from the briefing by Foreign Ministry Spokeswoman Maria Zakharova, Moscow (Ukraine crisis update). https://mid.ru/en/foreign_policy/news/1952458/. Accessed 11 April 2025.

[63] Excerpts from the briefing by Foreign Ministry Spokeswoman Maria Zakharova, Moscow, May 15, 2024 (Ukraine crisis update). https://mid.ru/en/foreign_policy/news/1950737/. Accessed 11 April 2025.

[64] Excerpts from the briefing by Foreign Ministry Spacewoman Maria Zakharova, Moscow, May 23, 2024 (Another report on the human rights situation in Ukraine). https://mid.ru/en/foreign_policy/news/1952458/. Accessed 11 April 2025.

originating from Russia. This read on its own is a valid concern. However, it can be read as used by Russia to justify its human rights violations against Ukraine adults and children, and ultimately as an instrument through which it is defending an illegal war against Ukraine. The use of HRJs by Russia must be understood in its context, as an effort to justify an illegal war.

One should separate what Russia is doing by using human rights as an instrument of governance in applying HRJs to legitimize its full-scale invasion of Ukraine from reading the Russian use of human rights as a compliance regime. If one makes this kind of distinction, it provides an approach through which one can understand the Russian use of HRJs in defense of the invasion of Ukraine, without turning a blind eye to human rights concerns within Ukraine. A theory of HRJs provides a way out from a binary relationship to human rights, where a human rights statement automatically leads to a compliance assessment, even when it is used as a governance instrument in defense of the decisions and actions of the State. Russia uses human rights as an instrument of governance, justifying and legitimizing its invasion of Ukraine, while at the same time inviting the receiver of the justification to switch focus from the illegal war Russia is conducting against Ukraine to an assessment of Ukraine's human rights violations. This turns the Russian use of human rights as an instrument of governance into a compliance regime where Ukraine's human rights compliance is what is to be evaluated, not the Russian acts of unlawful full-scale invasion of another State.

It is important to understand that the Russian use of HRJs goes against the general understanding of Russia's actions in relation to human rights and human rights obligations under both the European and the UN frameworks.

The two different human rights approaches to the Russian invasion of Ukraine—the European approach of expelling Russia from the human rights regimes, and the UN approach that kept Russia within the human rights regime—significantly alter the broader effects of Russia's use of HRJs.

As long as Russia is treated as a legitimate human rights actor and full member of the UN human rights system, its use of HRJs will help legitimize its role as a global leader within both a multipolar world order and the international human rights community. Further, its HRJs become a part of how Russia maintains its role as a contender over the global narrative and can promote itself as a legitimate international actor.

This chapter focuses on how States are not only passive subjects, waiting for other States and institutions to make human rights compliance assessments, but also active entities, using human rights to actively reshape the ways in which human rights as a compliance regime is to be evaluated. Russia took a proactive role, using human rights not only as a regime of compliance but also as an instrument of governance, to defend and legitimize its invasion of Ukraine. This serves to shift the focus from evaluating Russia's invasion to what in a different context would be legitimate human rights concerns in Ukraine.

This chapter has demonstrated the importance of studying how a State can use human rights as an instrument of governance and how this is a way for the State to shift the narrative of human rights for its own application—and with that, the presumption of accountability.

The result of Russia's unlawful invasion of Ukraine led to two separate outcomes when it comes to its continued participation as a human rights actor in the international community. The Council of Europe reacted by expelling Russia from the Council and as a party to the European Convention of Human Rights, whereas the UN reacted by suspending Russia from the Human Rights Council but maintaining its status as a party to previously joined human rights treaties.

It is in this context that Russia's HRJs become relevant, as they still allow Russia access to an international human rights stage. The conclusion is that it serves Russia to be able to continue its human rights participation within the UN treaty bodies as usual. Even when it receives critique, it will also receive praise because of how the routine and procedures of the UN Human Rights Bodies are set up. Each report includes praise, as a part of its procedure, and as we can see with the CRC and the CERD Concluding Observations, this procedure will also be applied to Russia. Such praise, even when alternated with severe critique, is highly valuable to project an image of a Russian internal and international serious leader in a new multipolar world order. In this context, HRJs become another instrument of governance. It is also in this context that Russia's use of HRJs should be called out for what it is: a misuse of human rights that serves to undermine the legitimacy of the human rights regime itself, if the international community does not object to this.

References

Charmaz K (2014) Constructing Grounded Theory, 2nd edn. Sage Publications

Committee of Ministers, Council of Europe (2022a) Resolution CM/Res(2022)1 on legal and financial consequences of the suspension of the Russian Federation from its rights of representation in the Council of Europe, CM/Res(2022)1. https://rm.coe.int/2022-cm-resolution-1/1680a5b463. Accessed 15 March 2025

Committee of Ministers, Council of Europe (2022b) Resolution CM/Res(2022)2 on the cessation of the membership of the Russian Federation to the Council of Europe, CM/Res(2022)2. https://rm.coe.int/0900001680a5da51. Accessed 15 March 2025

Committee of Ministers, Council of Europe (2022c) Resolution CM/Res(2022)3 on legal and financial consequences of the cessation of membership of the Russian Federation in the Council of Europe, CM/Res(2022)3. https://rm.coe.int/resolution-cm-res-2022-3-legal-and-financial-conss-cessation-membershi/1680a5ee99. Accessed 15 March 2025

European Parliament (2023a) European Parliament resolution of 19 January 2023 on the establishment of a tribunal on the crime of aggression against Ukraine (2022/3017(RSP)), C 214/109. https://eur-lex.europa.eu/legal-content/EN/TXT/?uri=CELEX:52023IP0015. Accessed 15 March 2025

European Parliament (2023b) European Parliament resolution of 16 February 2023 on one year of Russia's invasion and war of aggression against Ukraine (2023/2558(RSP)), C 283/34. https://eur-lex.europa.eu/legal-content/EN/TXT/?uri=CELEX:52023IP0056. Accessed 15 March 2025

Grahn-Farley M (2022) The Human Rights Claim in Climate Justice: An Argument for Reintroducing the Principle of Anti-Discrimination and Strengthening the Anti-Domination Principle when Children Go to Court. Journal of Gender, Race and Justice 25

Hafner-Burton EM (2008) Sticks and Stones: Naming and Shaming the Human Rights Enforcement Problem. International Organization 62(4):689–716
Kim Y (2023) A network analysis of naming and shaming in the universal periodic review. International Interactions 49(3):287–314
MacPherson CB (1962) The Political Theory of Possessive Individualism: Hobbes to Locke. Oxford University Press
Parliamentary Assembly, Council of Europe (2023) Deportation and forcible transfers of Ukrainian children and other civilians to the Russian federation or to temporarily occupied Ukrainian territories: create conditions for their safe return, stop these crimes and punish the perpetrators, Resolution 2495. https://pace.coe.int/en/files/31776/html. Accessed 15 March 2025
Terman R, Byun J (2022) Punishment and Politicization in the International Human Rights Regime. American Political Science Review 116(2):385–402
UN Committee on the Elimination of Racial Discrimination (2023) Concluding observations on the combined twenty-fifth and twenty-sixth periodic reports of the Russian Federation, UN Doc. CERD/C/RUS/CO/25-26
UN Committee on the Rights of the Child (2024) Concluding observations on the combined sixth and seventh periodic reports of the Russian Federation, CRC/C/RUS/CO/6-7 https://docs.un.org/en/CRC/C/RUS/CO/6-7. Accessed 15 March 2025
UN General Assembly (2022a) Aggression against Ukraine, Resolution ES-11/1, UN Doc. A/RES/ES-11/1
UN General Assembly (2022b) Humanitarian consequences of the aggression against Ukraine, Resolution ES-11/2, UN Doc. A/RES/ES-11/2
UN General Assembly (2022c) Suspension of the rights of membership of the Russian Federation in the Human Rights Council, Resolution ES-11/3, UN Doc. A/RES/ES-11/3
Värk R (2022) Russia's Legal Arguments to Justify its Aggression Against Ukraine. International Centre for Defence and Security. https://icds.ee/wp-content/uploads/dlm_uploads/2022/11/ICDS_Analysis_Russias_Legal_Arguments_to_Justify_its_Aggression_Against_Ukraine_Rene_Vark_November_2022.pdf. Accessed 15 March 2025

Maria Grahn-Farley is visiting professor at the University of Gothenburg (with tenure), Sweden, and visiting research fellow at the Institute for Advanced Legal Studies, London, UK. The author is the coordinator of HRJust, an EU Commission-funded Horizon project, of which the chapter is a part. She earned her first law degree from University of Gothenburg, and her Masters of Law (L.L.M.) and her Doctorate of Juridical Science (S.J.D.) from Harvard Law School, USA. She wants to thank Professor Mark Klamberg for many insightful comments on earlier drafts of this text, Linnéa Holmen and Anas Qazi for the editing. She also wants to thank Dr. Wolfgang Bode as the Project Officer from REA at the EU Commission for his support throughout the coordination of HRJust. All mistakes are mine and mine alone.

Chapter 33
Contestation and Legitimacy in Global Governance

Jonas Tallberg

Contents

Abstract The past 75 years have seen the development of a rule-based system of global governance that plays a frontline role in fighting transboundary problems. The expectations on global governance to deliver have never been higher, but this system also appears more contested than ever before, potentially signaling a crisis of legitimacy. This chapter explores these dual features of contestation and legitimacy in global governance. It shows that contestation occurs through a variety of state and societal actors calling for reform, replacement, or rejection of international organizations. Yet a review of recent data on the popular legitimacy of international organizations shows little evidence of a broad-based legitimacy crisis. The chapter concludes that that contestation does not appear to be in opposition to legitimacy in global governance. Instead, contestation may be seen as a natural component of a dynamic political system of global governance, open to criticism and debate.

Keywords Contestation · Criticism · Legitimacy · Trust · Global governance · International organizations

Climate changes, health pandemics, financial crises, military conflicts, and refugee flows. All manifest the transboundary nature of contemporary societal problems and all underline the need for global cooperation. This insight has been a central driver in the growth of global governance during the post-World War II era. Building on the experiences of early internationalism, states have created a dense network of international organizations over the past 75 years. Examples include the United

J. Tallberg (✉)
Department of Political Science, Stockholm University, Stockholm, Sweden
e-mail: jonas.tallberg@statsvet.su.se

M. Klamberg et al. (eds.), *Reconstructing Power and Hegemony in Public International Law*, https://doi.org/10.1007/978-94-6265-743-4_33

Nations (UN), the World Health Organization (WHO), and the European Union (EU). In addition, recent decades have seen the development of newer forms of global governance, often with a prominent role for non-state actors, such as business, civil society, and science. The result is a rule-based system of global governance that has a frontline role in fighting transboundary problems.

The expectations on global governance to deliver have never been higher, but this system also appears more contested than ever before. Contestation refers to behavioral and discursive challenges against global governance, for instance in the shape of demands, protests, violations, and withdrawals. Rising powers, such as China, India, and Russia, are challenging the Western liberal order from the outside, contesting its legitimacy. Anti-globalist populists, such as Donald Trump, Marine Le Pen, and Nigel Farage, are mobilizing against multilateral cooperation from the inside, in the name of "regaining control". Another type of contestation comes from civil society actors, such as Fridays for Future, Global Justice Now, and Friends of the Earth, which demand a more ambitious and just system.

It is a common claim that such widespread contestation signals a legitimacy crisis for global governance. Legitimacy refers to the belief or perception that governing institutions exercise authority appropriately.[1] Legitimacy involves an underlying approval, confidence, faith, and trust in a governing institution, irrespective of the short-term benefits it generates. Legitimacy is of great importance to all governance institutions, but particularly to multilateral institutions, which do not have recourse to the same coercive power as national governments.[2] Legitimacy can make it easier for international organizations to secure mandates, obtain resources, attract participation, take decisions, and secure compliance. In addition, legitimacy is critical for the democratic quality of international organizations. If such organizations suffer from weak legitimacy among citizens, this shortfall contributes to a democratic deficit in global governance.

This chapter explores these dual features of contestation and legitimacy in global governance. It focuses specifically on classic international organizations, which remain core pillars of global governance and play frontline roles in combating transboundary problems. It begins by discussing core patterns in the contestation of international organizations. Who contests global governance and on what grounds? I show that contestation occurs through a variety of state and societal actors calling for reform, replacement, or rejection of international organizations. The chapter then turns to the issue of legitimacy. Do these multiple forms of contestation indicate a legitimacy crisis for global governance? Examining recent evidence on popular legitimacy beliefs toward international organizations in a broad range of countries, I show that such fears largely lack support in the data. I conclude that contestation does not appear to be in opposition to legitimacy in global governance. Instead, contestation may be seen as a natural component of a dynamic political system of global governance, open to criticism, debate, and reform.

---

[1] Tallberg and Zürn 2019.

[2] Hurd 2007.

33.1 How Is Global Governance Contested?

Contemporary global governance is contested in a variety of ways. In the following, I provide an overview of such practices by ordering contestation along two dimensions: the actors engaging in contestation and the demands expressed through contestation. In the first dimension, we may distinguish between two types of actors: state and societal actors. State actors include the political leaders and bureaucratic elites who represent the government of a state. Societal actors comprise a broad variety of organizations in society, from non-governmental organizations (NGOs) and social movements to private businesses and political parties, as well as ordinary citizens. In the second dimension, we may similarly distinguish between three types of demands: to reform, replace, or reject existing international organizations. Demands for reform focus on how prevailing institutions should be modified to meet concerns; demands for replacement on how existing organizations should be supplanted by new arrangements; and demands for rejection on how global governance as such should be surrendered.

State contestation of global governance is common and occurs through all three types of demands: calls for reform, replacement, and even rejection. A common theme in existing research is the grievances of certain groups of states, often regarded as disadvantaged by the prevailing institutions. Yet contemporary state contestation of global governance appears to be a more widespread phenomenon.

A first type of contestation consists of state demands for reform of existing organizations. Such contestation is particularly common among states that have historically been less well-positioned to influence these organizations, and tends to target either the institutional arrangements or the substantive policies of the organizations—or both.[3]

Extensive research has examined contestation of the liberal international order on the part of rising powers, such as Brazil, Russia, India, China, and South Africa (BRICS).[4] Such contestation targets decision-making structures and liberal policies that fit poorly with the political preferences of these states. Examples include demands for greater voice in decision-making in the International Monetary Fund (IMF), the World Bank (WB), the World Trade Organization (WTO), and the United Nations Security Council (UNSC), as well as demands for policy reforms in areas such as trade, security, human rights, and macroeconomic stabilization.

Scholarship has also explored contestation by the Global South, which partly overlaps with the rising powers but encompasses a more diverse set of countries in Africa, Asia, and Latin America.[5] In the context of the UN, the Global South advances its joint demands through the Group of 77 (G77), nowadays encompassing 135 developing countries. Demands include differentiated responsibility for combatting climate change and more impartial treatment of African leaders by the International

---

[3] Stephen and Zürn 2019.

[4] *See, e.g.*, Ikenberry 2010; Kruck and Zangl 2020.

[5] *See, e.g.*, Milner 2005; Zürn et al. 2019.

Criminal Court (ICC). Contemporary calls for reforms have an important historical precedent in the requests for a New International Economic Order in the 1970s.

However, demands for reform nowadays also come from established powers. In Europe, Britain waged a longstanding campaign against further deepening of EU cooperation, whereas other states have demanded reforms of bodies such as the UNSC, which has been criticized for its lack of democracy and effectiveness. In the US, reform demands have been particularly prominent during the presidencies of Donald Trump, but such criticism forms part of a broader pattern of US contestation of bodies such as the ICC, United Nations Framework Convention on Climate Change (UNFCCC), the United Nations Human Rights Council (UNHRC), and the WTO.

The second type of contestation consists of state demands to replace existing institutions with new arrangements. Such contestation moves beyond calls for reforms but falls short of shifts to unilateralism, by seeking to create new bodies that are more consistent with the preferences of dissatisfied states. Recent years have witnessed growing research on this type of contestation under the headings of "contested multilateralism"[6] and "counter-institutionalization".[7]

In several cases, rising powers' dissatisfaction with the liberal international order have led them to create competing bodies.[8] The formation of BRICS as an informal organization in 2009, and the decision to expand the grouping in 2023, is a key example. These competing institutions tend to be concentrated in the area of economic governance and include the establishment of the Asian Infrastructure Investment Bank (AIIB) and the New Development Bank (NDB) as alternatives to the Asian Development Bank (ADB) and the WB. Outside the economic sphere, the creation of the Shanghai Cooperation Organization (SCO) represents an effort to establish a parallel security structure among major authoritarian countries in Asia. More broadly, China and Russia have declared their joint ambition to promote a new global order based on multipolarity and state sovereignty. Part of this ambition is to create new, often less formal international organizations with limited membership.

Similarly, countries in the Global South have sought to promote alternatives to existing international organizations through new forms of south-south and north-south cooperation. One key strategy has been to initiate and deepen cooperation within regional organizations in Africa, Asia, and Latin America. Another strategy has been to call for new multilateral bodies with better representation of the Global South. The founding of the United Nations Conference on Trade and Development (UNCTAD) in the 1960s, as well as the more recent establishment of the Group of Twenty (G20), with its expansion to include the African Union (AU), answer such calls.

More paradoxically, demands to replace existing institutions have also been advanced by established powers in Europe and North America. Although these states have historically been favored by the liberal institutions they pioneered, they have increasingly explored alternatives to these organizations. For instance, coalitions of

[6] Morse and Keohane 2014.

[7] Zürn 2018.

[8] Stephen 2017; Zürn 2018, Ch. 7.

established powers have moved cooperation out of universal organizations and into exclusive bodies composed of like-minded countries. Dissatisfaction with existing multilateral institutions is also reflected in a shift toward minilateral and bilateral forms of cooperation, not least in the area of trade.[9]

A third type of contestation consists of state rejection of global governance. In its pure form, this type of contestation appears exceedingly rare. Research concludes that states dissatisfied with existing institutions often call for reforms and sometimes seek replacements, but seldom if ever abandon cooperation as such.[10] Yet, with a more expansive understanding, several state behaviors and discourses could qualify as rejection of global governance.

Some state actions involve retreats to unilateralism. A key example are withdrawals from international organizations and treaties.[11] Recent cases include the UK leaving the EU, the US leaving the Paris Agreement of the UNFCCC and the United Nations Scientific and Cultural Organization (UNESCO), and Burundi and the Philippines leaving the ICC. Similarly, states allowing international organizations to die or international treaties to expire could be seen as acts of rejection.[12] Most often, however, withdrawals, deaths, and expiries do not appear to represent shifts to principled unilateralism, as much as steps on the way toward cooperation in new constellations and arrangements.

Next to state contestation, *societal contestation* is a common feature of contemporary global governance. Like states, societal actors engage in all three types of demands: reform, replace, and reject. Whereas early scholarship primarily examined contestation on the part of NGOs, growing research explores contestation by other types of societal actors, such as political parties and ordinary citizens.

A first type consists of societal demands for reform in global governance. Much like state criticism of existing institutions, these societal calls for reform are typically directed at the institutional arrangements or the substantive policies of these organizations.[13] Demands for reform are particularly common among NGOs, but are also expressed by other societal actors.

NGO demands for reform of international organizations have attracted extensive attention.[14] Such demands were particularly intense in the late 1990s and early 2000s, when NGOs engaged in large-scale protests against multilateral economic institutions. In contemporary global governance, key areas of NGO contestation include climate change, development, finance, and trade. A central theme in these demands has been the need for reform of institutional arrangements in favor of greater democracy and justice, for instance through better representation of civil society, marginalized groups, and the Global South. But equally prominent are demands

---

9 Mladenov 2023.

10 E.g., Stephen 2017; Zürn et al. 2019.

11 Von Borzyskowski and Vabulas 2019.

12 Hulse 2012; Eilstrup-Sangiovanni 2020; Huikuri 2023.

13 Zürn et al. 2019.

14 E.g., Keck and Sikkink 1998; O'Brien et al. 2000; Eilstrup-Sangiovanni 2020.

with respect to substantive policies, which typically criticize the liberal orientation of many institutions and ask for greater attention to environmental and social concerns.

In addition, political parties have emerged as key actors in contestation due to growing domestic politicization of international cooperation, as discussed in greater detail below.[15] Parties in the political mainstream tend to be relatively supportive of international cooperation aimed at solving cross-border problems. In contrast, parties on the far right tend to criticize international organizations for their contribution to globalization, whereas parties on the far left tend to blame them for inadequate representation and insufficient redistribution. In recent years, contestation of international organizations has been a core component of the populist playbook used by politicians and parties such as Donald Trump, Marine Le Pen, Jair Bolsonaro, Hugo Chavez, the UK Independence Party, Alternative für Deutschland, Syriza, and Podemos.

When political parties contest global governance, it is typically with the aim of engaging another set of societal actors: ordinary citizens. Citizens may voice their discontent in several arenas, from public protests to social media and the voting booth. Research shows that citizens overall tend to be less supportive of international cooperation than political and societal elites.[16] The electoral gains of populist politicians in several countries suggest that these actors have been successful in exploiting and nurturing this discontent among citizens. In some countries—most famously the UK, but also Greece and Switzerland—such mobilization of popular dissatisfaction has contributed to voter-endorsed challenges of international organizations through national referenda.

Societal demands for existing international organizations to be replaced are not uncommon among NGOs, parties, and citizens, especially on the radical left. When the far left criticizes existing international organizations for poor inclusion, inadequate accountability, dysfunctional neoliberalism, and insufficient ambition, the demands for change often go beyond reform, to include replacement. Consistent with notions of leftist internationalism, the radical left tends to be supportive of cooperation as a means of tackling global problems and injustices, but skeptical of existing international organizations as vehicles.[17] This position leads actors on the far left to work for the replacement of prevailing institutions under banners such as "Another world is possible" and "Globalization from below". Examples of how these movements have sought to create institutional replacements themselves include the World Social Forum as an alternative to the World Economic Forum, and the Global Citizens' Assembly as a complement to the Conference of the Parties of the UNFCCC.

More broadly, societal actors have engineered moves away from classic interstate institutions and toward new modes of global governance involving greater reliance on private actors.[18] In this vein, NGOs and companies have set up entirely private governance instruments or endorsed public-private governance arrangements. One

[15] De Vries et al. 2021.

[16] Dellmuth et al. 2022.

[17] Hardt and Negri 2000.

[18] Barnett et al. 2022.

example is the establishment by NGOs of indices, ratings, and blacklists to name and shame states into compliance with international norms. Another illustration is the creation by firms and NGOs of private regulatory arrangements, such as certification schemes, as substitutes for classic interstate regulation. The ambitions of societal actors to develop alternatives to interstate cooperation are also reflected in their active support for hybrid governance, involving both public and private actors.

Lastly, some societal actors reject global governance as such. A key example is principled rejection of international cooperation among parties and citizens on the far right. Unlike the radical left, the far right not only contests the institutions and policies of global governance, but also cooperation itself.[19] This rejection is typically manifested in demands for governments to "take back control" by withdrawing from international agreements and institutions. Political entrepreneurs that fit this mold include Nigel Farage and the UK Independence Party, Marine le Pen and the National Rally, and Matteo Salvini and Lega Nord. When the far right gains control over government, such principled societal rejection may translate into actual state withdrawals from cooperation, as witnessed in Brazil and the US.

33.2 A Legitimacy Crisis in Global Governance?

Are these multiple forms of contestation in global governance indicative of a legitimacy crisis for international organizations? Although many voices have been raising the alarm about multilateralism in trouble, available evidence covering a broad range of prominent international organizations points to fairly solid levels of popular legitimacy. In the following, I substantiate this relatively optimistic assessment with reference to (a) recent survey results on public legitimacy beliefs toward six key international organizations; (b) trends over time in public legitimacy beliefs toward the UN and the EU; and (c) data on public criticism of 32 international organizations since 1985. Taken together, these data do not support a crisis narrative.

Regarding *recent survey evidence*, the latest edition of the World Values Survey (WVS), undertaken in 2017–2019, measured public confidence in six prominent global international organizations (the ICC, the IMF, the UN, the WB, the WHO, the WTO) in a large number of countries around the world. Here, we focus on a core sample of five countries—Brazil, the Philippines, Germany, Russia, and the United States—but aggregate numbers are broadly similar for a larger sample of 45 countries. Respondents in each country covered a representative distribution of citizens in terms of age, gender, geography, and level of education. Respondents indicated their level of confidence for the international organizations on a scale from 0 ("none at all") to 1 ("not very much"), 2 ("quite a lot"), and 3 ("a great deal").

Figure 33.1 suggests some interesting patterns. The aggregate average level of public confidence in the six international organizations taken jointly comes out between "not very much" and "quite a lot". Although this level is not high, and

[19] Hooghe et al. 2019.

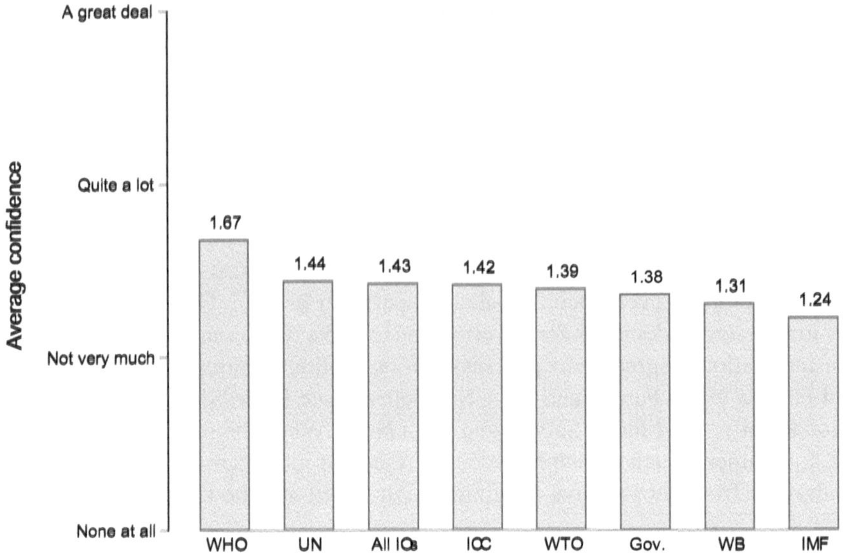

Fig. 33.1 Legitimacy beliefs toward international organizations. *Note* Post-stratification weights were used, and countries were weighted equally. Abbreviations: IO = international organization; Gov. = national governments. *Source* Dellmuth et al. 2022, 58

indeed suggests moderate skepticism, the score is also far from the low end that would suggest a legitimacy crisis. Instead, this evidence suggests that international organizations today have overall medium legitimacy among citizens across the world. Thus, although multilateral institutions may have vociferous critics in some quarters, these anti-globalists do not reflect average worldwide public opinion of international organizations.

Interestingly, these average levels of public confidence in international organizations are broadly similar to average levels of citizen confidence in national governments. In fact, the aggregate approval rating for national governments is somewhat lower than that for international organizations. This finding shows that citizens are not particularly "anti-globalist", in the sense of rejecting international organizations and instead embracing the nation-state. Rather, contemporary publics on average hold medium levels of legitimacy beliefs toward both international and national governance.

The absence of a general legitimacy crisis for international organizations is also evident when we examine *trends over time*. Existing longitudinal studies of public opinion toward international organizations do not show a consistent major decline in approval.[20] The widespread narrative that citizens at large are currently rejecting multilateral institutions appears to overstate the case. Although a minority of citizens are vocally critical of international organizations, this should not be mistaken for public opinion as a whole.

[20] Walter 2021; Dellmuth and Tallberg 2023.

Data on legitimacy beliefs vis-à-vis the UN and the EU provide an opportunity to examine such long-term trends in greater detail. These two bodies are arguably the most prominent international organizations at the global and regional levels, respectively. Data on the UN come from the WVS and the European Values Survey (EVS), whereas data on the EU come from Eurobarometer.

Regarding the UN, Figure 33.2 indicates that citizen confidence in this international organization across all countries surveyed worldwide underwent a gradual decline from 1994 to 2014 and then turned modestly upwards again in the late 2010s. The proportion of citizens who held "a great deal" or "quite a lot" of confidence in the UN dropped from 58% in 1994 to 46% in 2014, before rising to 48% in 2019. Although a 10-point decline is not insubstantial, positive ratings among half the population certainly do not suggest a collapse of legitimacy either. Overall, these figures point to fairly steady medium levels of legitimacy for the UN among citizens. Moreover, the upturn in public confidence toward the UN in the late 2010s runs counter to the supposed rise of populist anti-globalism at that time.

As for the EU, we see in Figure 33.3 that average public trust in this international organization across its member countries has fluctuated considerably over the period 2004–2021. In 2007, a peak of 53% of citizens tended to trust the EU. Thereafter, levels moved downwards to a low point of 31% in 2013, in the midst of the Eurocrisis, before rising again to 49% in 2020. Hence, after significant fluctuations, trust in the

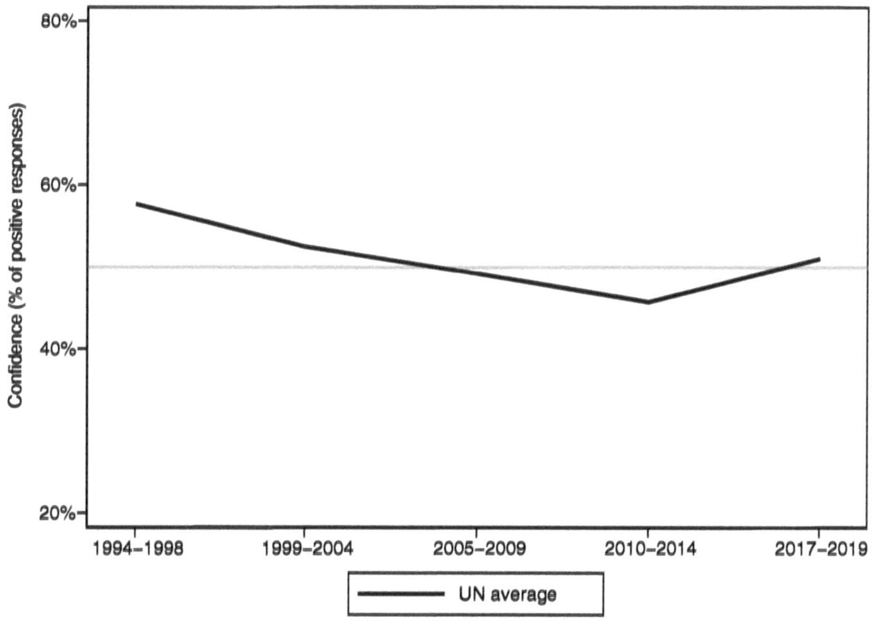

Fig. 33.2 Citizen confidence in the UN, 1994–2019. *Note* Positive responses refer to the percentage of respondents with "a great deal" or "quite a lot" of confidence in the UN. *Sources* Based on data from EVS 2021; Haerper et al. 2021

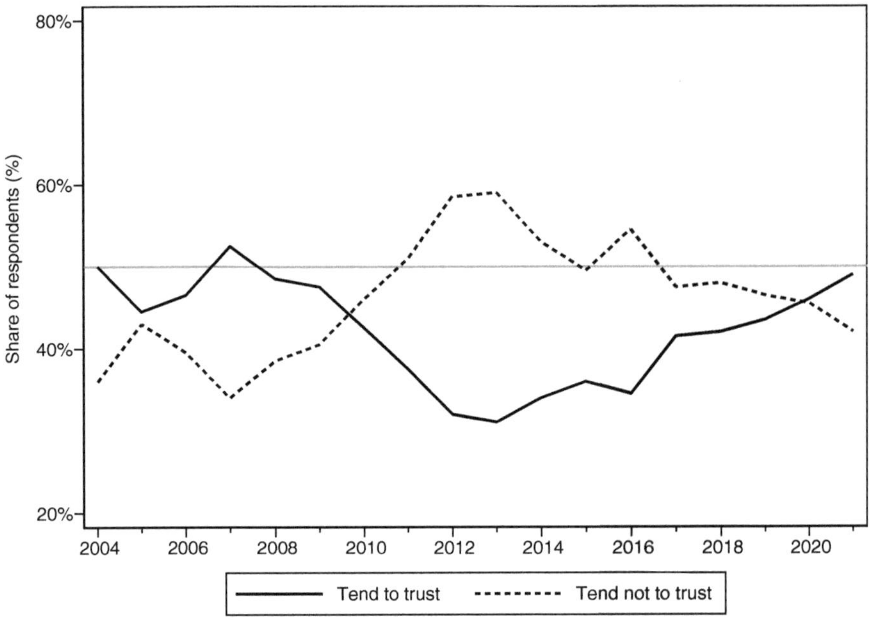

Fig. 33.3 Citizen trust in the EU, 2004–2021. *Source* Eurobarometer 2021

EU at the end of the observation period was back to where it started at the beginning. Overall, trust in the EU remains well within the medium range and clearly above a crisis level. If we look specifically at the most recent years, Brexit does not appear to have reflected a general legitimacy crisis; if anything, it seems to have solidified trust in the EU among the remaining member states. Moreover, the EU is not unique in a comparative regional perspective. Research indicates that public confidence in the AU has remained fairly steady over the past two decades, and that average citizen approval of Common Market of the South (MERCOSUR) has in fact risen significantly.[21]

A third way to interrogate the narrative of a legitimacy crisis around international organizations is to examine *public critique* of these institutions. For this purpose, I draw on Sommerer et al., who examine data on public critique of 32 prominent international organizations over the period 1985–2020, based on media coverage.[22] Peaks in media attention reflect moments when these international organizations are under more severe legitimacy pressure.

Figure 33.4 suggests that we cannot speak of a single comprehensive legitimacy crisis for international organizations at any time over the past 35 years. To be sure, certain moments have witnessed intense contestation of multiple organizations, notably the years around the millennium, when civil society organizations mobilized against multilateral economic institutions. However, the norm has been

[21] Dellmuth and Tallberg 2023, pp. 32–36.

[22] Sommerer et al. 2022.

3–4 international organizations facing intensive public opposition in any given year. Indeed, much of the period (especially before 1994 and in most of the 2010s) saw little or no noteworthy public criticism of international organizations. Public criticism rose briefly in 2016–2017 but then fell again.

That said, about two thirds of the international organizations examined in this study experienced at least one moment of substantial public challenge during the past 35 years. Moreover, the ten institutions that have escaped significant public protest—such as the Nordic Council (NC) and the Pacific Island Forum (PIF)—tend to have more limited power. Thus, more prominent international organizations would seem to come under substantial public pressure from time to time. Several organizations, including the EU, the IMF, the UN, and the WB, have faced intense public protest in 8–15 of the 35 years under study. Yet even for these more contested international organizations, the years of calm far outnumber the years of resistance.

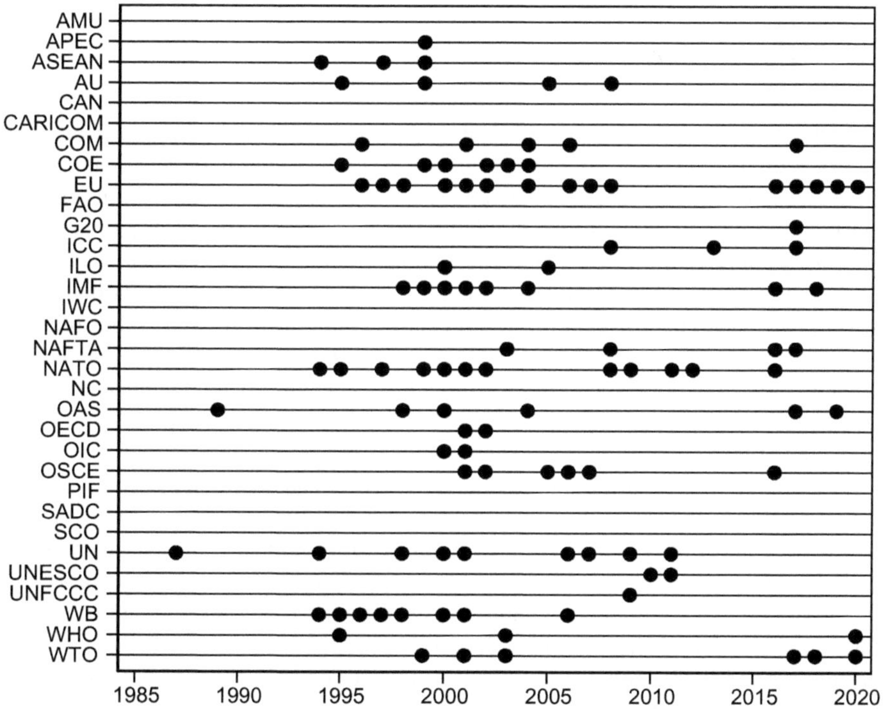

Fig. 33.4 Public criticism of international Organizations, 1985–2020. *Note* Abbreviations: AMU = Arab Maghreb Union; APEC = Asia-Pacific Economic Cooperation; CAN = Andean Community; CARICOM = Caribbean Community; COE = Council of Europe; COM = Commonwealth Secretariat; FAO = Food and Agriculture Organization; IWC = International Whaling Commission; NAFO = Northwest Atlantic Fishery Organization; NAFTA = North American Free Trade Agreement; OAS = Organization of American States; OECD = Organisation for Economic Co-operation and Development; OIC = Organisation of Islamic Cooperation; SADC = Southern African Development Community. *Source* Sommerer et al. 2022

Indeed, over half of the institutions have faced no significant public opposition since 2010.

Moreover, public discontent has usually been directed at a particular international organization in a particular context, rather than reflecting general disapproval of multilateral institutions as such. For instance, the Association of Southeast Asian Nations (ASEAN) and the IMF faced their greatest critique in the late 1990s, whereas the Organization for Security and Co-operation in Europe (OSCE) met larger critique in the early 2000s. The EU has alternated between periods of public calm (1985–1995 and 2009–2015) and periods of notable opposition (1996–2008 and 2016–2020). The G20 experienced major street protests in connection with its Hamburg summit in 2017, whereas the WHO faced heightened public disquiet in 2020 with its response to the COVID-19 epidemic, but otherwise these two institutions have operated without significant public pressure.

33.3 Conclusion

This chapter has explored the dual features of contestation and legitimacy in contemporary global governance. It shows that contestation of international organizations emanates from a broad range of state and societal actors. State contestation is particularly common among countries that have less voice in existing international institutions, notably rising powers and the Global South. However, recent years also provide examples of how established powers, such as the US, are contesting global governance. Societal contestation is especially common from NGOs, but recently also from political parties and ordinary citizens, as global governance has gained greater salience in domestic politics. Frequently, state and societal contestation feed into each other, as state actors respond to societal pressures, or societal actors join states in expressing particular grievances.

Although observers often submit that such widespread expressions of contestation signal a legitimacy crisis for global governance, existing empirical studies do not appear to confirm this claim. The latest public opinion data from the WVS reveal overall medium levels of confidence in international organizations, which often equal or surpass citizen confidence in national governments. Long-term studies of public faith in the UN and the EU show largely persistent medium levels of approval, despite a rise in anti-globalist populism in recent years. Data on public opposition to international organizations indicate no general legitimacy crisis over the past 35 years and, if anything, reductions in discontent in recent years.

This co-occurrence of widespread contestation and stable legitimacy suggests that we should not interpret criticism primarily as a rejection of global governance per se, but as the expression of political preferences with regard to how global governance should best be structured and developed. Contestation, in this sense, is a natural feature of any political system. It is noteworthy that the most radical forms of contestation are also the least common, whereas contestation aimed at reforming policies and institutions are more frequent. Although anti-globalist populists have been successful in mobilizing vocal pockets of populations, a large majority of citizenries worldwide remain supportive of joint efforts to combat transboundary problems.

References

Barnett MN et al (eds) (2022) Global Governance in a World of Change. Cambridge University Press, Cambridge

Börzel TA, Risse T (2016) The Oxford Handbook of Comparative Regionalism. Oxford University Press, Oxford

Börzel TA, Zürn M (2021) Contestations of the Liberal International Order: From Liberal Multilateralism to Postnational Liberalism. International Organization 75(2):282–305

de Vries C et al (2021) Politicizing International Cooperation: The Mass Public, Political Entrepreneurs and Political Opportunity Structures. International Organization 75(2):306–332

Dellmuth L, Tallberg, J (2023) Legitimacy Politics: Elite Communication and Public Opinion in Global Governance. Cambridge University Press, Cambridge

Dellmuth L et al (2022) Citizens, Elites, and the Legitimacy of Global Governance. Oxford University Press, Oxford

Eilstrup-Sangiovanni M (2020) Death of International Organizations. The Organizational Ecology of Intergovernmental Organizations, 1815–2015. Review of International Organizations 15:339–370. https://doi.org/10.1007/s11558-018-9340-5

Eurobarometer (2021) Standard Eurobarometer 95, Spring 2021. European Commission, Brussels. https://europa.eu/eurobarometer/surveys/detail/2532. Accessed 15 February 2025

EVS (2021) EVS Trend File, 1981–2017. GESIS Data Archive, Cologne. ZA7503 Data file Version 2.0.0. https://doi.org/10.4232/1.13736

Haerper C, Inglehart R, Moreno A, et al., eds (2021) World Values Survey Time-Series (1981–2020) Cross-national Dataset. Madrid, Spain & Vienna, Austria: JD Systems Institute & WVSA Secretariat. Data File Version 2.0.0. https://doi.org/10.14281/18241.15

Hardt M, Negri A (2000) Empire. Harvard University Press, Cambridge, MA

Hooghe L et al (2019) Contested World Order: The Delegitimation of International Governance. Review of International Organizations 14(4):731–743

Huikuri TA (2023) Constraints and Incentives in the Investment Regime: How Bargaining Power Shapes BIT Reform. Review of International Organizations 18(2):361–391

Hulse M (2012) Silencing a Supranational Court: The Rise and Fall of the SADC Tribunal. E-International Relations. https://www.e-ir.info/2012/10/25/silencing-a-supranational-court-the-rise-and-fall-of-the-sadc-tribunal/. Accessed 18 November 2024

Hurd I (2007) After Anarchy: Legitimacy and Power in the United Nations Security Council. Princeton University Press, Princeton, NJ

Ikenberry GJ (2010) The Liberal International Order and Its Discontents. Millennium: Journal of International Studies 38(3):509–521

Keck M, Sikkink K (1998) Activists Beyond Borders: Advocacy Networks in International Politics. Cornell University Press, Ithaca, NY

Kruck A, Zangl B (2020) The Adjustment of International Institutions to Global Power Shifts: A Framework for Analysis. Global Policy 11(S3):5–16

Milner HV (2005) Globalization, Development, and International Institutions: Normative and Positive Perspectives. Perspectives on Politics 3(4):833–854

Mladenov N (2023) Minilateralism: A Concept that is Changing the World Order. The Washington Institute for Near East Policy. https://www.washingtoninstitute.org/policy-analysis/minilateralism-concept-changing-world-order. Accessed 18 November 2024

Morse JC, Keohane RO (2014). Contested Multilateralism. Review of International Organizations 9(4):385–412

O'Brien R et al (2000) Contesting Global Governance: Multilateral Economic Institutions and Global Social Movements. Cambridge University Press, Cambridge

Sommerer T et al (2022) Global Legitimacy Crises: Decline and Revival in Multilateral Governance. Oxford University Press, Oxford

Stephen MD (2014) Rising Powers, Global Capitalism, and Liberal Global Governance: A Historical Materialist Account of the BRICS Challenge. European Journal of International Relations 20(4):912–938

Stephen MD (2017) Emerging Powers and Emerging Trends in Global Governance. Global Governance 23:483–502

Stephen MD, Zürn M (2019) Contested World Orders: Rising Powers, Non-Governmental Organizations, and the Politics of Authority Beyond the Nation-State. Oxford University Press, Oxford

Tallberg J, Zürn M (2019) The Legitimacy and Legitimation of International Organizations: Introduction and Framework. The Review of International Organizations 14:581–606

Tallberg J et al (2013) The Opening Up of International Organizations: Transnational Access in Global Governance. Cambridge University Press, Cambridge

von Borzyskowski I, Vabulas F (2019) Hello, Goodbye: When Do States Withdraw from International Organizations? The Review of International Organizations 14(2):335–366

Walter S (2021) The Backlash against Globalization. Annual Review of Political Science 24:421–442

Zürn M (2018) A Theory of Global Governance: Authority, Legitimacy, and Contestation. Oxford University Press, Oxford

Zürn M et al (2019) Conclusion: Contested World Orders—Continuity or Change? In: Stephen MD, Zürn M (eds) Contested World Orders: Rising Powers, Non-Governmental Organizations, and the Politics of Authority Beyond the Nation-State. Oxford University Press, Oxford

Jonas Tallberg is Professor of Political Science at Stockholm University and co-director of the Stockholm Center on Global Governance - a center of excellence funded by the Swedish Research Council. His primary research interests are global governance and European Union politics. Tallberg currently directly the ERC Advanced Grant project "Democracy, Autocracy, and International Cooperation" (DEMCOOP). From 2016 to 2021, he directed the collaborative research program "Legitimacy in Global Governance" (LegGov), funded by Riksbankens Jubileumsfond. Tallberg has been a visiting scholar at Harvard University, Stanford University, McGill University, and WZB Social Science Center Berlin. In 2019, he was elected to the Royal Swedish Academy of Letters.

MIX
Papier aus verantwortungsvollen Quellen
Paper from responsible sources
FSC® C105338

If you have any concerns about our products,
you can contact us on
ProductSafety@springernature.com

In case Publisher is established outside the EU,
the EU authorized representative is:
Springer Nature Customer Service Center GmbH
Europaplatz 3, 69115 Heidelberg, Germany

Printed by Libri Plureos GmbH
in Hamburg, Germany